D1168324

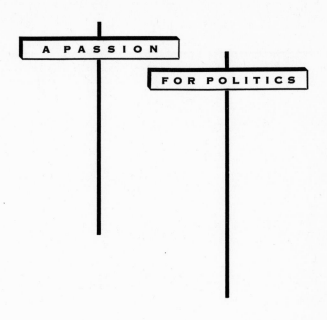

A PASSION

FOR POLITICS

Louis Brownlow
January 1909

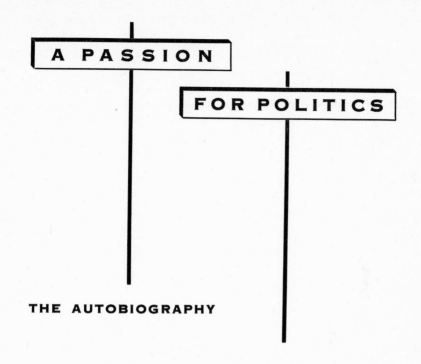

A PASSION

FOR POLITICS

THE AUTOBIOGRAPHY

OF LOUIS BROWNLOW

FIRST HALF

THE UNIVERSITY OF CHICAGO PRESS

92
B885t
v. 1

Library of Congress Catalog Number: 55-5114

THE UNIVERSITY OF CHICAGO PRESS • CHICAGO 37
Cambridge University Press, London, N.W. 1, England
The University of Toronto Press, Toronto 5, Canada

*Copyright 1955 by The University of Chicago. All rights re-
served. Copyright 1955 under the International Copyright Union
Published 1955. Composed and printed by* THE UNIVERSITY OF
CHICAGO PRESS, *Chicago, Illinois, U.S.A.*

TO

BESS

CARNEGIE INSTITUTE
OF TECHNOLOGY LIBRARY

PREFACE

My memory extends over a little more than threescore years and ten. It is difficult to be exact about it, since memory begins in fits and starts in the very young just as it moves less securely and less evenly as one grows old. But it is the primary source on which I depend.

I have frequently checked myself against letters and newspaper files but rarely against the memory of others; and I have attempted to avoid the obvious safety of hindsight interpretation. To the end that I might be able to confine my comments on events to what I thought at the time, I have made rather free use of extracts from the things that I wrote.

All of this I have done quite deliberately, since I believe that what a man actually remembers, even if sometimes inaccurately, has a greater effect on him than what others might feel that he should have remembered.

The present volume, as I wrote it, contained much more diversionary matter and the accounts of many episodes that seemed to me to be worth recording but which of necessity had to be cut out. To the anonymous editors of the University of Chicago Press I am indebted for most skilful word surgery. When some five hundred pages of the original typescript had been eliminated, I expressed my appreciation in a letter in which I said:

"Your amputations, excisions, and -ectomies are skilfully done. I have no kick, but nevertheless they remind me of the story of the Confederate veteran who left his home in Mississippi bound for the World's Fair in Chicago in 1893. He left the Illinois Central train in the station at Twelfth Street and Michigan Avenue in Chicago. He wore the Gray—a handsome Confederate gray frock-coated suit and a broad-brimmed Confederate gray hat. Just outside the station he saw seated on the sidewalk a man in a blue uniform and a wide-brimmed hat adorned with the gold cord and acorn of the Grand Army of the Republic. The man in blue had no legs, only one arm, was minus an ear and minus an eye. In his remaining hand he had a tin cup.

Preface

"The old Rebel stopped, looked at the man in blue, plunged his hand in his pocket, came up with a twenty-dollar gold piece, and dropped it in the cup.

"The old boy in blue looked up and said, 'You're a Johnny Reb. Why do you give me this much money?'

" 'Because,' said Graycoat, 'you're the first damyankee I have ever seen trimmed to suit my taste.' "

This book is the first volume of my autobiography. In it I record my memories of my childhood in a small town in the Missouri Ozarks, something of my work as a newspaper reporter in Nashville and Louisville, some of my observations as a Washington correspondent, and more perhaps of what I saw and heard in my travels abroad as a correspondent for the Haskin Syndicate.

I have ended this part of my story on January 26, 1915, when I took the oath of office as a commissioner of the District of Columbia and by that act, although unwittingly, forsook forever what had been my chosen profession of journalism and determined that ever thereafter my principal concern would be in the field of public administration.

The first volume accounts for my formation and education. The second is perhaps another tale—what I tried to make of it all. The second volume will tell of some of the things I tried to do, as well as many of the things I failed to do, in the years from 1915 to 1930 as a commissioner of the District of Columbia, as city manager of Petersburg, Virginia, and of Knoxville, Tennessee, and as municipal consultant in the building of Radburn, an experiment in limited dividend housing, in Bergen County, New Jersey.

In 1930 I became director of the Public Administration Clearing House and participated actively in the programs and affairs of many organizations of public administrators, some of them centered in Chicago adjacent to the University of Chicago, some of them elsewhere in the United States, some of them in other countries. Through them I came into contact with administrators of all levels of government, local, state, national, and international. I also served as a member of the Commission of Inquiry on Public Service Personnel, as chairman of the Public Administration Committee of the Social Science Research Council, and as chairman of the President's Committee on Administrative Management.

In all these activities I was attracted by the same thing that had been

Preface

my primary interest since earliest childhood—politics. Whether it was the politics of a backwoods Missouri town, the politics of a state or local government or of a presidential campaign, the politics of important administrative decisions, or the politics of people working together anywhere and everywhere—it is all the same. And it is only against this background that I have set down my personal experience in contact with the march of history through nearly three-quarters of a century.

Louis Brownlow

ACKNOWLEDGMENTS

The generous concern and sustained interest of Herbert Emmerich, director of the Public Administration Clearing House, and of my fellow-trustees of that institution have encouraged me to write this autobiography. To them, to the late Charles E. Merriam, to other associates in the University of Chicago, and, above all, to my colleagues in the field of public administration, I acknowledge my debt and at the same time acquit them all severally and collectively of any responsibility for anything in this book.

Acknowledgment should also be made to the Massachusetts Historical Society for permission to reprint a passage from *The Education of Henry Adams.*

In the preparation of the manuscript for this, the first volume of my autobiography, I have had the assistance of several competent secretaries. My debt is especially great to Mrs. Eleanor Limbach Gozinsky, Miss Louise Eaton, and Mrs. Nita Gavaris Kraft.

The entire manuscript was retyped and prepared for transmission to the publisher by my present secretary, Mrs. Grace Geer Brown, who served for many years on the staff of the International City Managers' Association and with whom I have been associated directly or indirectly for nearly a quarter of a century.

To all of them and to those who in their turn have helped them, I am deeply grateful.

L. B.

TABLE OF CONTENTS

Table of Contents

INDEX

PART I

BUFFALO, MISSOURI

I WAS BORN IN MISSOURI

I was born in Buffalo, the county seat of Dallas County, in the Ozark Mountains of southwestern Missouri, on the twenty-ninth of August, 1879. My father was postmaster at the time, and the post office was in the front room of the family house; so that in a sense it may be said that I was born directly into politics, government, and public administration. At any rate, it is certain that these matters did become for me things of absorbing interest by the time observation and verbalization had produced memory.

A few days after my advent the *Buffalo Register* in its weekly issue of September 4, 1879, published this item:

> Postmaster Brownlow has a well executed stamp of small denomination received last Thursday that instead of sticking with a lick will no doubt require him on some future occasion to lick with a stick. It is a boy and a ten-pounder.

Mr. Joseph P. Dumars, the editor of the *Register,* thus dedicated me to philately; but the circumstances which molded me or the choices which I made resulted in my absorption in the politics for which a post office was then the chief sign and symbol, rather than in the gummed bits of paper that are the currency of the postal business. I never had a stamp collection in my life.

That my father was postmaster in that particular place at that particular time was a political fact of significance. He had been born in Tennessee in 1844. When he was sixteen, he was a soldier in the army of the state of Tennessee; and by the time he was seventeen he had been mustered into the service of the Confederate States of America. At twenty, when the war ended, he was in a military prison in the Arkansas state penitentiary. By the time he had reached the war's end at Little Rock, he had been severely wounded four times; and he carried in his body a Minié ball that many years later was to end his life.

Dallas County in the Ozark Hills had been loyal to the Union during the Civil War that disrupted Missouri as well as the whole of the Union; its politics was overwhelmingly Republican; it had but few Confederate veterans; and, although there were some third-party dissidents (then known as "Greenbackers"), there were few Democrats. In fact, one of the earliest things I can remember about Democrats is the local saying, "We hunt them with dogs!"

Why, then, in 1879, only fourteen years after Appomattox, when there was a Republican President in Washington and many really believed that a Democrat never again would enter the White House, and in a day when civil service and the merit system had hardly been heard of, was a Rebel soldier postmaster in the county seat of a Republican county in the Ozarks?

The answer to that question is, indeed, important. It was a sign that the war was over. It was a symbol of the dawn of peace. It made manifest at the very grass roots the new and stronger union of the states in a nation reborn and in a union thereafter to be universally accepted.

The story as I heard it in part in my childhood and later in part from some of the active participants is this:

The famed disputed election of 1876 provided a new threat to the nation still but beginning to recover from the ravages of its Civil War. The question was whether Rutherford B. Hayes or Samuel J. Tilden would hold the office of President of the United States; and the dispute raged furiously until the eve of the inauguration itself. Historians still debate the details of that fight, and it is unlikely that a precise account of the dickering ever will be known.

Years later I heard parts of the story from three men who became my good friends: Richard P. Bland, Joseph C. S. Blackburn, and Henry Watterson, all three of whom, in the early months of 1877, were members of the House of Representatives. Blackburn and Bland were holding out with every possible scheme for delay—they wanted one thing. That one thing was a promise that Hayes would withdraw the Federal troops from the South. Mr. Watterson was their go-between. At about half-past three on the morning of March 2, 1877, with the debate in the House centering now on the qualifications of one of the Wisconsin electors, Mr. Watterson stepped up behind Mr. Blackburn, who at the moment was on his feet directing a filibuster.

"All right, Joe," he whispered. "Hayes has agreed."

Mr. Blackburn withdrew his demand for a roll call on the pending question; and at ten minutes after four, when General Grant's term had but two more days to run, the two houses of Congress formally completed the canvass of the votes of the members of the Electoral College and declared that Rutherford Birchard Hayes had been duly elected President of the United States. Whatever the dicker and to whatever it was that Hayes agreed, it is known to all the world that, very soon after he went into the White House, the Federal soldiers who were still occupying parts of the conquered South were withdrawn; and the military phase of the War of the Rebellion was ended.

Dallas County, Missouri, although it was overwhelmingly Republican, was, by virtue of a careful gerrymander on the part of the Democratic Missouri legislature, a part of a congressional district which elected a Democrat to Congress. That Democrat was already a national leader of one wing of his party; and he was twenty years later to come very near to being its nominee for the presidency. He was Richard Parks Bland, the free-silver leader to his followers, the unsound money man to his detractors, and the father of the "Bland Dollar." This was the silver dollar which the mints had resumed coining in 1878 as the result of Mr. Bland's partial and imperfect effort to remonetize silver after "the crime of '73" which had put us on the gold standard. Whether or not Mr. Bland had anything to do with the trading during the first three days of March, 1877, I do not know; but he knew all about it, and he certainly became a close personal friend of President Hayes.

In those days there were about forty-three thousand post offices in the United States. All but a minute minority of the citizens saw the federal government, now that the army had been demobilized, only in and through the post office. No other federal activity was known, except to those few who paid customs duties on imports or excise taxes for the manufacture of whiskey, tobacco, and matches or bought revenue stamps to validate their bank checks.

The appointment of a postmaster was partisan political patronage and nothing else, and it was deemed so important that, although there was a postmaster-general to make recommendations, the final choice continued to be made by the President in person. This was the more necessary at this particular time because post offices were the most important prizes of political party patronage, and the Republicans were not entirely sure that Mr. Hayes had done right by them in his choice of a postmaster-general. He named to that post, and stood by the nomination in a long fight for confirmation, an ex-Rebel colonel who also was an ex-senator and a Democrat—David McK. Key of Tennessee.

Now here is where my father came in: Postmaster-General Key had reported to the President that two factions of the Republican party in Buffalo, Missouri, were unable to agree on a candidate for postmaster to succeed J. Walter Coon, who had resigned early in 1878. Thereupon Mr. Bland, the Democratic congressman, was summoned to the White House. The President told him that the quarrelsome Republicans in Dallas County could not make up their minds and asked, "Haven't you got a good Rebel over there that I could appoint?" Mr. Bland thought he had.

"Silver Dick" Bland himself was not without some skill as a politician. When the President had asked him for the name of a Rebel to appoint postmaster, Mr. Bland protected his rear by ignoring all the ex-Confederate soldiers in Dallas County who were Democrats; and they were all Democrats but one. This made his choice of Robert S. Brownlow quite simple and perhaps more gratefully received by President Hayes and Mr. Key.

But let no one think that my father was a Republican. Far, far from that. He was then a Greenbacker, as he had been theretofore a member of the Anti-Monopoly party and was thereafter to join the Union Labor party, then the Farmer's Alliance, and then the People's party, to remain a Populist until the Populists under Bryan, by boring from within, captured the democracy itself. In other words, and in the modern idiom, he was addicted to "left-wingism" and dissident political activity.

So that was why my father was the postmaster, that was why I was born in a post office, and that was the way the Civil War came to an end; and people began to remember it not as a war that was on but as a war that had been. Both my parents told me from the first and told me over and over again that the war (it was always "the war" or sometimes "the Civil War," but never the pretentious "War between the States," and, of course, never the odious "War of the Rebellion") was a mistake; that the fault was mostly on the side of the South; that slavery was not only indefensible but utterly wrong; that the war had ended in the right way; and that the reconstruction was a crime. Here they diverged, Mother holding much more firmly to the doctrine of states' rights than did Father with his Whiggish ancestry. Nevertheless, despite this conscious acceptance of the great central fact of the unity of the nation, they did transmit to me a sentimental and emotional attachment to the South and its Lost Cause; and my Valhalla early filled with heroes clad in Confederate gray. However, when I was six, I demanded for a Christmas present something wonderful that I'd seen in Frank Furth's Famous Cash House store—a little Yankee captain's uniform complete with saber and rakish kepi. My elder brother, Joe, derided me because the uniform was blue. I hotly defended my status as a citizen of the United States and loudly called the uniform not Yankee, but American. This was very soon after I had set General Grant among my heroes ever so little below General Lee. I got the uniform, and I waved the sword, shouting "the sword of Lee." The blue coat didn't seem to mind.

It was my parents' philosophy that the South was conquered and knew it, that it had been pretty roughly handled, but that in the long run the event would prove to be for the good of all—a philosophy that did not deny but in fact depended upon a pride in the past.

The Civil War actually ended when the Federal troops marched out of New Orleans on April 20, 1877, but I carried it on personally for a little longer. On July 23, 1885, General U. S. Grant died. A few days later a memorial service was held in the courthouse, and during those intervening days the whole town was alive with preparations for it. Miss Emma Morrow's piano was taken up into the courtroom—no mean feat considering that it was a block-and-tackle job and that Miss Morrow was a Democrat. Choirs practiced, the soprano and the baritone solos were sung over and over again, and the courtroom was decorated.

One morning the ladies of the committee decided to hang high over the judge's bench three huge letters to be cut out of pasteboard and covered with twigs of cedar. The three letters were G.A.R. They turned to a man standing by who, as everyone knew, had cedar trees in his yard, and they asked him to go and bring enough twigs to cover the pasteboard letters. I was there, too; and Sam Pittman, who not only was a Democrat and the keeper of a magnificent livery stable but had been a Rebel soldier himself, took me by the hand and asked me to go and help him. I helped pluck the twigs and carried some of them back and saw them sewed on the letters. From that moment General Grant was hero to me just as was General Lee—and for me the war was over. The letters hung there for more than a dozen years, their green turning to dusty, dirty brown; but their meaning for me never faded.

II

Just when or where Pa met Ma I do not know, if I ever was told; but I do know that it was after the close of the war. Their part in that war not only determined their future lives but also profoundly affected mine and gave me almost from babyhood the conviction that politics was the most important force in the world, that political events were not foreordained by fate but might be molded by the action of men, and that it was worth while to explore the frustrated "ifs" and the bungled "but onlys" of the past in order that we might at least try to avoid making the same mistakes over again.

It was not from anything I ever heard from either Father or Mother (perhaps it came from some of her kinsfolk) that I early got the idea that, so far as family went, my mother was a cut above my father. Afterward I came to the conclusion that this was not, even according to the rigorous standards of middle Tennessee with their infinitesimal gradations of caste, so much a distinction of ancestry as it was of personal circumstances.

When I came along, my mother was thirty-six years old and my father a year her junior; so that they both were in their forties when my memory of them becomes quite clear. I can remember that I then thought that she was beautiful and he very handsome, an impression that I never was to lose and which, indeed, was heightened as I became acquainted with photographs taken when they were much younger.

Father was tall, a little more than six feet, his brown hair and long brown beard were curly, and his large blue eyes nearly always twinkled with fun. Mother had black eyes and raven's-wing black hair, luxuriant and always so long that she could sit on it. Her name had been Ruth Adelia Amis. My father called her "Delia," and to a very few intimate friends, cousins by marriage and of Tennessee connection, she was, in the Ozark dialect, "Delie." To others of the Missourians, no matter how close the friendship or of what age the friend, she was always "Mrs. Brownlow." That is, with the exception of the preachers, and to them she was, of course, "Sister Brownlow."

Mother never spoke of or to Father except as "Mr. Brownlow." I am sure that she never even thought of him as "Robert," much less as "Bob," as all others in Dallas County called him. That convention by which a wife was expected to call her husband "Mister" was a Tennessee custom which appertained in Buffalo to a certain consciously distinguished stratum of society. It was not shared by others in the Buffalo community unless they also came from Tennessee or Kentucky or Georgia or southern Indiana, where the same rule held.

The other members of my family were two brothers: Joe, ten years older, and Walter, two years younger than I. Another boy and a girl, who came between Joe and me, died before I was born. Joe was working in a store by the time he was thirteen, and the custom then was that the youngest clerk slept in the store at night. I cannot remember when he slept at home. Of course he ate his meals with the family, and he was a lively, not to say contentious, participant in the arguments about politics which seemed to be as important and certainly were much more abundant than the food. Even so, he disappeared quite early from our intimate family circle because he followed the custom of the country and married young, at nineteen, and set up a household of his own. So, for the most part of my growing up, my family was Father and Mother and my younger brother, Walter. Or rather, as both Walter and I would have said, "Pa and Ma and us."

My father as an orphan early knew the poverty which he never was to overcome. His father, a country storekeeper and a Baptist preacher, lived in Giles County, Tennessee, somewhat cut off by intense religious rivalry from his Methodist brothers and sisters at Huntsville, Alabama. Grandfather Brownlow had married, shortly after the War of 1812, the daughter of Paris Sims. They both were born west of the mountains but of Virginia parentage—Paris Sims's uncle was Colonel Charles Simms of General Washington's staff, whose body lies in Christ Churchyard in Alexandria. (The younger Sims dropped an *m* and thus changed the spelling of the patronymic.) Grandfather Brownlow's grandfather and grandmother, when they came from Ireland, had settled first in Georgetown, Maryland, and had set up a Latin academy on or near the site of what is now Georgetown University in the District of Columbia. Later they were to go to Lexington, Virginia, and there set up a Latin academy which in turn, although not by direct descent, was a forerunner of the Columbia Academy, King and Queen College, Washington College, and then Washington and Lee University.

My father was more unfortunate than most. When he was about six years old, he was riding behind his mother on a horse when the horse ran away, threw them both, killed my grandmother, and broke my father's arm. Only three years later he was riding in a wagon with my grandfather when the team ran away, and in the resulting crash my grandfather was killed, and my father suffered a broken leg. Hearing when I was but a child these tales of how my father was orphaned, I conceived a fear of horses which I have never been able to conquer—a fear that amounts to dislike, so that I was glad when the automobile took the horse out of the shafts of the buggy. I was glad too when fate lifted me out of the harness-and-saddle factory, which was my only industrial job; and my wife has never forgiven me for nudging her in the side, when the horses at Hialeah were thundering into the home stretch, to ask her to look at the flamingos parading in pink and black in the center of the track.

Left thus an early orphan, Father was brought up by his eldest sister, twenty-two years older than he. Aunt Martha was married to Thomas English, a farmer, a politician, a sheriff of the county, who, though not too prosperous, managed to bring up a huge family and, until his dying day, to defy the rest of the world. When the Yankees overran middle Tennessee, Uncle Tom, too old and infirm for the army, prepared himself for the inevitable arrest by copious drafts of what was euphemistically known as "spiritus frumenti." Thus fortified, he faced his captors as they demanded to know the whereabouts of his sons. They knew and called the names of the boys, one after another, and for each of them, until the youngest and the last, Uncle Tom proudly confessed that the boy was in the Confederate Army. When it came to his youngest son, he told the truth and said that the boy was away from home but that he did not know whether he had got to the army or not. Then to the threatening bluecoats he drew himself up and said, "But I know this, that if he were thrown in the middle of the Ohio River and I was on the south bank with a rifle, and he started to swim north, by God, he'd never reach the bank." It was along with his cousins, the sons of this fire-eating father, that my father enlisted in the rebel army in 1861.

Father almost died that autumn of typhoid fever, and the following winter of measles. He was wounded at Fort Donelson in February, 1862, and imprisoned and wounded again in Chicago in March of the same year. He was exchanged and rejoined his regiment before Vicksburg; and he was the only survivor of six volunteers who swam down the Mississippi with oil-silk belts containing percussion caps to aid the besieged Pemberton, and inside the fortifications shared the starvation that ended only with the surrender on July 3, 1863. He managed to escape then and rejoin his company and regiment, which had not been included in the surrender. He was wounded at Chickamauga, and he was hurt again in a snowball battle at Dalton in the winter camp of Joe Johnston's army; but he was back in the ranks at the Battle of Peach Tree Creek in Atlanta. There, just as he was saying wistfully to his captain close by, "I wish one of those furloughs would hit me," a Minié ball crashed into his side.

He was laid in a trench with the dead, but Sherman's men came so fast that the burial squad fled before the trench had been back-filled. A Negro passing by saw a boot move, and he took Father out of the grave. The Negro and his wife nursed the ragged Rebel boy through his partial recovery from the wound.

Again Father joined his regiment, this time under Hood on the foolhardy march to Nashville and the north. On the retreat from Nashville he fell out with a half-dozen others who, correctly believing that the army was forever whipped, decided to make their way to Mexico. They were caught swimming the Mississippi, and, when Appomattox came, Father was in prison in the state penitentiary in Little Rock.

A few days later when Lincoln was assassinated, the commandant lined up his prisoners and counted them off by tens, each tenth man to be shot. My father was one of the "tens" and stood before his coffin and open grave when rescued by the commanding officer of the Union troops who had heard of the foolish act of reprisal and arrived on the scene before the firing squad had been given its final, fatal order.

With other prisoners he was put on a steamboat at Memphis to go up the Mississippi, the Ohio, and the Cumberland, to Nashville, to be paroled and to walk the seventy-five miles back to his sister's house. The compassionate commandant of the escort gave each of the prisoners a few dollars in United States greenbacks—five, I think it was—and on that boat Father contrived to buy a pair of overalls and a shirt from a Negro deckhand. Donning them, he wrapped the remaining rags of his Confederate uniform with all its buttons and with everything that had any identification with the war or with the habiliments of a soldier into a bundle and threw it in the river. He got home in that early summer of 1865 still slightly limping from the Minié ball in his hip, weakened by disease, wracked by wounds, and already tubercular. He was twenty.

Mother was born in 1843 in Culleoka, near Columbia, in Maury County, Tennessee. Her father (who died before I was born) was a prosperous but not really wealthy farmer and stock-raiser and something of a politician and community leader in his rich county where there were many wealthy families and relatively few who were landless or quite poor. He had kept the family name of Amis in direct descent from the time Louis Amis came to Manakintown, Virginia, with the Huguenot refugees from France, after the revocation of the Edict of Nantes in 1688. In the course of time the "Louis" became anglicized to "Lewis." My own affectation of the return to "Louis" was because Mother was a sentimental Francophile (as I, too, was to become in my earliest boyhood), and I never have been forgiven by others of the Amis clan for that affectation.

Maury County knew little of the luxurious plantation life of the cotton country fifty or seventy-five miles to the south in Alabama. It did not experience the plantation economy prevailing under the reign of King Cotton. Its slaves were relatively few in number, and often their masters worked with them in the fields, barns, and pastures, raising a little cotton perhaps, but mainly wheat and corn, cattle and pigs, and, above and beyond all, horses and mules.

Much of the land in the county itself had been a part of the Revolutionary War bounty granted by the Congress to General Nathanael Greene and sold by his heirs in huge tracts to Carolinians and Georgians not of the hardy pioneer type but the wealthier and more stable people who wanted to make familial and even clan settlements in the rich new country west of the mountains. One such clan was Carolinian, Presbyterian, and aristocratic; another was Carolinian, Episcopalian, and aristocratic; while another was Georgian, Methodist, and aristocratic.

During the four decades from the time of the settlement until one of the citizens of Columbia, James K. Polk, went to the White House, the county had bloomed and become fruitful. It had built a beautiful town on a plan made by a Scotch architect; its town houses were like those of Savannah and Norfolk, and the country houses, eschewing the pretension of the pillars and porticoes of Alabama and Mississippi, were good red-brick Georgian. A few families, richer than the others and mostly of the Episcopalian group, built great country houses, devoted their sons, and daughters as well, to travel and the liberal arts, or to the church or to arms, and overshadowed all the rest with the great clan names of "Polk" and "Pillow" and "Gray," while their Presbyterian and Methodist neighbors vied with them in their ardor for the pursuit of learning.

In the earliest days both their sons and their daughters were sent back to Asheville to the University of North Carolina, coeducational until the 1820's. When that university closed its doors to women, a problem was posed which had to be solved. The sons continued to be sent back to the University of North Carolina, to the University of Virginia, to Princeton, and even to Oxford and Cambridge. For the girls, Columbia set up the first women's college in the South and one of the earliest in the country, but they could not quite bring themselves to call it a college. So with the blessing of Bishop Otey, the first Episcopal bishop of Tennessee, the Pillows and the Polks and the others set up the Columbia Female Institute.

When, long years afterward, Mark Twain was to describe and appraise the aristocratic influence in the Mid-South, he used this Institute to illustrate his meaning. In the first edition of *Life on the Mississippi* an engraving of its turreted and castellated building was used to show how an American rural aristocracy, through the Episcopalian preference for the Gothic in ecclesiastical architecture and devotion to medieval chivalry as interpreted by Sir Walter Scott, had created its own fantastic and unreal world.

Mother was one of thirteen children. Her father had been to

CARNEGIE INSTITUTE
OF TECHNOLOGY LIBRARY

Chapel Hill. As a matter of fact, my mother's older sisters went to the Institute; and one of them, the eldest, was considered "accomplished" with her poetry, her fluent French, and her somewhat startling proficiency in mathematics. Mother was graduated from the Institute in 1859, which, among other things, may be taken to show that the Institute, with its then collegiate rank, was roughly the equivalent of a mid-twentieth-century high school, with perhaps a good deal more emphasis on Latin and Greek.

Mother's earliest memories, so she told me, were much of the war with Mexico and its immediately following events. Her Uncle William was killed in Mexico. She knew many soldiers and officers who fought in that war, and, of course, President Polk was a neighbor and Mrs. Polk a good friend of her mother's. So she, too, from babyhood, was dominated by a ruling passion for politics and public affairs which continued until her very last day. She was, of course, a Democrat but, like many Tennesseans, pro-union and anti-secession, hoping until the last that Tennessee could stay neutral, since it was unthinkable that it should fight to coerce the South. But, of course, she was swept along with all her family and that whole part of the state when Lincoln's requisition for troops made it impossible to affect a neutrality that could not exist.

Maury County during the greater part of the war was occupied by the Federal troops, and during all that occupation a guard post was set in the great lawn in front of Grandma Johnson's house, where Mother lived, convenient for the watch and ward that was necessary to be kept on the wooden railroad trestle that carried the Nashville and Decatur Railroad high over Fountain Creek.

To a girl of her age, her spirit, and her horsemanship, there was the inevitable challenge of maintaining communication with the Confederates beyond the zone of occupation and on occasion, when the Confederates came back into the territory, of continuing that work. In plain words, she was a spy in the Confederate service. She knew how to smuggle quinine across the lines; she learned how to keep in touch with the infiltrating agents of the Confederacy; and, though she could not ride with Forrest as did her younger brother, she did ride *for* Forrest. She went time and again, usually with her eight- or nine-year-old brother for escort and chaperon, into the Union lines to glean straws of information to be taken back and relayed to Forrest's scouts; and on at least one occasion she reported to the great Forrest himself.

Mother saw even more of the war in that bitter winter of 1864 when Hood marched north, only to have his army decimated on the bloody field of Franklin and defeated at Nashville. She saw the retreat which passed by her aunt's home, where she was staying at the time, and saw, too, the pursuit—six or seven days of the marching of ragged, shoeless, almost starving men, followed by two or three weeks of marching well-clad, well-shod, well-fed, well-equipped soldiers. She knew that the Cause was lost. The day after Franklin she had sung the funeral hymns at Ashland Church when thirteen general officers were buried, and she knew that her own fiancé had been killed in that same fight.

The next spring came Appomattox, and for her the war was over and a life of poverty had begun. She was twenty-one. At the end of the war in 1865, my grandfather had, of course, lost his few slaves and all his livestock and equipment. His barns had been burned, and he had nothing but the bare land on which to begin all over again.

But, no, he had one other thing. He had one twenty-dollar gold piece. He had had it long before the war, and, because it was minted in Charlotte of the pale-yellow North Carolinian gold of his native state, he had kept it for a pocket piece. In that dreadful summer of 1866 a ragged ex-Confederate soldier came to Culleoka. He had nothing in the world but his Latin and his Greek and a burning desire to teach. Grandfather's twenty-dollar gold piece was his capital, and, with it and my grandfather's promised patronage, W. R. Webb, very soon to become known as "Old Sawney," set up Webb's School at Culleoka.

In 1868, Mother, who lived at Culleoka in Maury County, married Father, who lived at Campbellsville in Giles County, perhaps ten miles away. At Campbellsville they set up housekeeping while Father ran a small store and taught a school. My elder brother was born there. Then Father was ill. When he recovered, they attempted to start up life again at Kenton in Obion County in western Tennessee, where one of Father's elder brothers was a merchant; but again he fell ill. The doctors all thought it was consumption, and at that time the tubercular were accustomed to be sent to the Ozark Mountains, where it was believed the climate would restore them to health.

Long before the war there had been an immigration from Giles County in Tennessee to Dallas County in Missouri, headed by John Walker Alexander. Mr. Alexander had fought in the Union army and had established himself on a fertile farm on Buffalo Head Prairie. After the war my father's cousin, J. P. Brownlow, who had been a trooper with Forrest, went to Dallas County. His wife was a sister of Mrs. Alexander. Then there followed another brother-in-law, Major Joseph P. Howard, who had been a gallant officer in the Confederacy and in my father's regiment; and following him went Joseph P. Locke, who at the end of the war was the captain of my father's company in the Confederate army. All these then were settled in Dallas County, and it was natural that, in his search for health in the Ozarks, Father, too, with my mother and their then infant sons, should have gone there.

Father's health did improve, and the family settled on a farm near Reynolds Chapel. The farm was not a success. I doubt that Father was ever up to it, either physically or in any other way; but, at any rate, before I was born the family had moved into town, my father had set up a grocery store, and then had become postmaster.

Such was the place in which I was born, such the family into which I came, and such the setting for my own education. But it was an education born of disputes which had divided the nation in war and would continue to rage in the comparative peace of politics throughout my life. Political argument was, as I have said, an important part of family life; and I learned early the need for making judgments and taking sides.

My father's nonconformity with what was then usually considered normal conduct for an ex-Confederate soldier, as witness the scorn heaped on such renegades to Republicanism as General Longstreet and Colonel Mosby, had its roots far in the past. In his teens he had been "anti-secesh" and pro-union in the Tennessee elections held to decide whether or not the state would withdraw from the Union, but he "went with his state," as the saying was, eventually. He disowned his distinguished cousin, Parson William G. Brownlow, who was soon to make an uneasy peace with his hated Democratic rival in Tennessee, Andrew Johnson, only because both were devoted to the Union. It may seem now that it wouldn't make very much difference for a sixteen-year-old boy to disown a famous cousin whom he had never seen, but it really meant something at the time.

When my father was wounded and captured at Fort Donelson, he was taken to a prison in Chicago. While he was there in a hospital, Parson Brownlow, who had somehow heard that a young Rebel cousin of his was in the prison hospital, went down the wards asking each soldier if his name was Brownlow. When he got to my father's side, my father looked at him, solemnly averred that his name was Robert Sims, and he never again saw the parson, who was later to be governor and senator. At that moment he undoubtedly lost a chance to get out of prison.

It was doubly unlucky for him that he didn't get out of prison, because just a few weeks later, when he was convalescing, he was sitting outside the hospital on a spring morning with other Rebel wounded when a boy, thirteen or fourteen years old, came up to the guard who was pacing the runway on the outside of the prison stockade and said, "Lend me your gun. I want to kill a Rebel!"

The invalid Confederates, with that scorn which all front-line soldiers bear for prison guards, home guards, and other like cattle, cried out: "Go on, give him your gun. That's the nearest you'll ever get to have a shot at one of us!"

The misguided, probably rattled, and maybe half-witted soldier turned his musket over to the boy; the boy instantly brought it down, fired, and hit my father's right leg just below the knee, breaking the bone to bits. It probably was pretty bad at the time, but my father got a lot of satisfaction out of it later by being able to claim that he was shot farther north than any other Rebel.

Even during the war and as early as when he was only seventeen years old, he manifested his nonconformity when he and another soldier of his company, marked out from the herd by being an Irishman and a Catholic, wrote new words for the Confederate battle song and persuaded their company to go through the war singing it, not as it should be:

> We are a band of brothers
> All native to the soil,
> A-fighting for the property
> We won by honest toil.

But rather, before bursting into the chorus of the "Bonnie Blue Flag," I Company, Third Tennessee Infantry, C.S.A., sang:

> We are a band of brothers
> All native to the soil,
> A-fighting for the property
> We never owned a'tall.

Quite early I decided to follow my father in this tortuous and uncomfortable path. Perhaps I would have persisted in that line had it not been for the more conservative influence of my mother, who always had been and was and always remained what we used to know as a "red-hot" Democrat. She knew that there was nothing to be gained by following little bands of earnest thinkers, chasing after will-o'-the-wisp utopias, and that in the long run one got further by staying in the party and fighting as best he might for what he thought should be. By the time the presidential election of 1884 rolled around, the first that I can remember, my mother's influence had predominated and I had become a Democrat.

I think it must have been pretty hard for even my father to stay out of the ranks that year, for the third party for that day, and that day only, known as the Anti-Monopoly party, had nominated for President Benjamin F. Butler of Massachusetts ("Beast Butler" to my mother), a man whose very name was anathema to every southerner. In fact it was many years before my father actually confessed to her that he had voted for Butler. Even then, although Bryan was the nominee of both the Democratic and the Populist parties and they had made up their political differences, what a storm that confession did raise!

I was five at the time of the election of 1884, and many of the things about it are my own memories, but supplemented by hearsay. One was my first torchlight procession, the thrill of the swinging coal-oil lamps over the shoulders of the marching G.A.R. being dampened somewhat by the steadiness of the marchers' chant, "Blaine, Blaine, James G. Blaine."

I remember, too, when the dentist, Dr. John George, got from St. Louis his white stovepipe hat and wore it all the time—the Cleveland hat of the campaign—a circumstance which led naturally to Dr. George's being appointed postmaster as soon as Cleveland was elected President.

I remember, too, reading—for I had already learned to read—the headlines and even some of the political news or views in the great political dailies of the state, the *Missouri Republican* being the Democratic organ, and the *St. Louis Globe-Democrat,* the Republican "bible." I can see now before my mind's eye in old-style type face the heading, "Missouri Republican," which so soon thereafter was partially to destroy this interesting political anomaly by changing its name to the "St. Louis Republic" and by changing its type dress at the same time. By that time I was a regular reader also of the two great comic weeklies, *Puck* and *Judge,* which gave the cartoonists their chance to support respectively the fortunes of the Democratic and Republican parties. Of the campaign of 1884, this one thing I remember most distinctly. Just after the election one of these weeklies had a two-page cartoon about the untoward fate of the third parties. There was more than one of them that year, and, as all the world knew, there were enough votes in New York State for these rag, tag, and bobtail outfits, and especially after Dr. Birchard's rum-Romanism-and-rebellion speech, for the Prohibitionist party vote to throw that state from Blaine to Cleveland and give the presidency to the Democrats for the first time since the Civil War.

As I remember, the cartoon was entitled "The Busted Side-show," and it was a picture of a group of side-show performers walking the railroad tracks back home. Now a railroad track at that time was something beyond my own personal experience; but somebody, probably Mother, explained to me what walking the tracks back home must have meant. I can still see in that picture General Butler with his drooping eye, General St. John, and Mr. Fisk, the Prohibition candidates, and the great Belva A. Lockwood, far, far, ahead of her time, the first and only woman who ever ran for President of the United States. Whether that cartoon had anything to do with it or not, I thenceforward was definitely on Mother's side with Cleveland and the Democrats in every political argument.

These political arguments in our house were three a day at a minimum—breakfast, dinner, and supper. I know that there never was a meal at which politics or public affairs or the news of the day were not discussed, greatly to the delight of my contentious elder brother and greatly to the disgust of my younger brother, who hated it all. But all these discussions (we always called them "arguments") were concerned with the present and with the future; there was no repining for the past. "Before the war" was a definite part of the family background, but it was quite definitely past, and one with Nineveh and Tyre.

III

Through the years when I have thought in my dreams, sleeping or waking, of my home town, it nearly always has been the fall of the year. On the margin of the roads and in the fence rows there is a blaze of prairie flowers, red, white, purple, and orange, of every hue and color; the sides of the streets in the town are knee-deep in spicy dog fennel, all white and yellow; and a hot blue haze hangs over the fields and the apple orchards all the way to the distant Blue Mounds. Buffalo and Dallas County were, quite properly and naturally, the center of my universe.

Having no railroad, no telegraph, and, until the turn of the century, no telephone, Buffalo's lines of communication and transportation were by horse. The livery stables kept the rigs which people hired to make trips to the railroad, twenty-eight miles east to Lebanon, or twenty-two miles southeast to Conway, or twenty miles west to Bolivar. They also kept the side-bar buggies and cutters, so useful for summer and winter courting purposes. I can well remember when the huge hacks with their tops lined with red-checked tablecloth material gave way to the surrey with the yellow wheels and, veritably, "with the fringe on top."

Having but little, it was up to our people to make the most of that little, and that they did. The prairie land was fertile, and, of course, everything came from the land; but so much of the land was not prairie and was not rich. We grew clover seed and, for the St. Louis pharmaceutical houses, even sage, lobelia, and other herbs. Coal oil (I never heard it called "kerosene") came in from oil companies for our lamps, but the buggies and surreys of that time were lubricated not by petroleum products but by castor oil; and in Dallas County we grew castor beans by the acre.

Salaries and wages were as low as they were rare. Most of the farmers traded chickens, eggs, wool, and other produce directly for sugar, coffee, and cloth; and money transactions were relatively few. The professional men—the clergy, the lawyers, and the physicians—

often took their fees, too, in kind; while the editors were always glad to exchange subscriptions against cordwood for the winter or split stovewood for the cook stove at any time of the year. A top salary was forty dollars a month for a clerk or a schoolteacher—few, a very few, exceeded and not many reached that figure. But, then, eggs were ten cents a dozen, chickens ten cents apiece, and beef, on the rare occasions when somebody slaughtered a cow, ten cents a pound; while a house on occasion could be rented with all of its three rooms for five dollars a month.

When I was about eight years old, the prosperity that flooded the nation and for which we in our family gave thanks to Cleveland and the first Democratic administration after the war seemed to fore-shadow none of the dreadful things that were to come in '93 with Mr. Cleveland's second term. In Buffalo the prosperity of the eighties brought a virtual rebuilding of the town. Whole families of brick-layers and of carpenters came in from Illinois and Indiana and other far places. Whole blocks of brick store-houses replaced wooden ones on three sides of the public square, and the wooden village with a scarce three or four brick buildings became a red-brick town with only three or four wooden houses around its square.

When the terrible hard times of the early nineties closed in and the prices of produce fell so that it was not worth shipping to St. Louis or Kansas City, and the stores dismissed their clerks and the artisans had no jobs, the county and its people fell back on the United States Treasury for support. There were many Union soldiers in the county, most of them home guards who were put to it to prove their ninety days' service, and many of whom had never slept away from home. But all, under the liberalized pension laws of the early years of the Harrison administration, were entitled, as the phrase went, "to draw" a pension.

There was always the pale flush of a faint hope that some time somebody might find a source of wealth in the underground resources of the county, and, indeed, at one time a lead mine had been opened long enough to give its name to a post office and a tiny hamlet. Al-though we boys were always cracking open rocks to find little bits of crystalline lead, there was never enough of it. We were but a short distance from real lead mines and not far from coal mines and the great zinc deposits around Joplin. But there never was a piece of coal in

Dallas County that had not been brought in at a charge of forty cents a hundred pounds for the use of one of the two or three blacksmith shops of the town. Forty cents a hundred was the tariff the wagoneer freighters charged for coal or coal oil; salt or sugar; molasses or vinegar; denim or velvet; quinine or morphine or attar of roses.

Perhaps it was not too much unlike any other midwestern county seat town at that time, except that it did not have a railroad; and therefore it was more isolated from the outside world than was common. We were inlanders and cut off from the outlanders. As children we prayed for the railroad to come. As adult citizens we strove for it and hoped against hope, never dreaming that the motorcar and the motor truck would relieve us and that, thanks to the federal aid to good roads, the need for the railroad would vanish.

Buffalo had in 1880, according to the excellent United States Census of that year, a population of 797, that had grown to 989 when I left it for good in 1900, and to 1,213 in 1950; while the county, which had 9,263 in 1880, rose to its peak of 13,903 in 1900, to decline to 10,392 in 1950.

Several years ago, just before an election in which the few surviving Democrats did not even put up a ticket, I asked Charlie Smithpeter, who was about to be elected to the legislature, where all the people had gone. His answer was concise, positive, and final—"To California!"

CHAPTER II

LEARNING BY DOING

The earliest event that I remember and to which I can fix a day is marked by my shameful memory of my failure to meet adequately the conventional demand of a great occasion in the public life of my community. During my whole life, from time to time, I have awakened from reliving that moment in my dreams and always suffused with shame.

My shame was this: Two famous men were coming to Buffalo. Both had been members of Congress, both had been governors of Missouri, and I am sure that I must have been much excited by what I had heard of them. I went with my father to the public square and climbed the few steps to the elevated platform in front of Mr. Roll's store, a high platform that interrupted the level of the sidewalk but was adjusted to the convenient and direct loading of wagons. I knew that something was expected of me and that I should say something polite, but in my embarrassed fright I forgot what I had been taught to say on such an occasion. With grim determination not to be entirely dumb, I fetched forth a polite expression that I had been taught to use in quite another connection. I exclaimed: "You're welcome!"

Mr. Roll laughed; Governor Phelps laughed; Governor McClurg laughed—and I was to be ashamed for better than seventy years. This happened on July 4, 1881, and I had not been full two years old until the twenty-ninth of August to come. Of the other tremendous things that must have been already known that day (for the telegraph was only twenty miles away), of the shooting of President Garfield and its attendant sensation, I remember nothing at all.

In 1884, when I was five years old, Mother took Walter and me with her for a visit to Tennessee. Oddly enough, since my whole childhood was preoccupied by praying for a railroad, I can remember nothing whatever of that journey on the railroad or of my trip in what then still were known as "the cars." Of that journey my memory has kept a few vignettes: seeing my cousin Walter Nance at work in the carpenter shop (he was just a boy then, and, when next I was to see him, it would be in Soochow, China, and he would be a professor in Soochow University); the little Negro boy sitting on the porch outside the dining-room, pulling the ropes to the punkah in what had been Mother's home but was now the home of Cousin Charlie and Cousin Zora Williamson.

These too: wading in the cold spring branch just below the spring-house, where Aunt Martha English (who reared my father) was set-ting huge crocks of milk; the teasing English boys and girls, Aunt Martha's grandchildren, I suppose, terrifying me by alternate threats to shoot me for a Yankee or hang me for being one of the James boys.

I also remember the deep impression that was made upon me when we visited the homes of Mother's more well-to-do and even wealthy cousins in Columbia and Nashville, the particular things that I re-member being the silver, the napery, and the candles. That I was acutely aware of the different manner in which the poor and the rich lived is proved not by what I can remember but by what my mother so often teased me about—that at that time I both spoke of and to my more highly placed relatives as the "big 'uns," something that I dis-covered long years afterward had been remembered by the "big 'uns" as well as by my mother, and that naturally I called the rest of us "the little 'uns."

The highlight of that visit to Tennessee was, and for me it was a matter of course, the great joy of that November night in 1884 when it seemed so certain that Grover Cleveland had been elected President of the United States. I remember the bonfire and the excitement and especially the elation of Mother's uncle, Judge William F. Flemming, chancellor and a leader of the Maury County bar. It was the climax of the campaign that even in Buffalo earlier in the year had given me my first torchlight procession and first political posters—I can see them now, so plainly: "Cleveland and Hendricks"; "Blaine and Freling-huysen."

I had learned to read before all that, but precisely when I don't know, and just how I know only what was told me. We were too poor very often to afford the luxury of a "hired girl," but we did have one for a time when my baby brother was born and maybe for a year thereafter. Her principal task was to take care of me. She was what we called a "country girl" and had had no schooling. This horrified my mother, who promptly began to teach her to read in the old-fashioned way, with ABC's and then a primer with "Ann can catch Rab" and all the rest of it.

The girl soon found that the best way to keep me quiet was to have me stand at her knees while she read her book. She read, of course, slowly, and she pointed her finger to each word. That was a process that apparently enraptured me.

One day I came running into the house with a newspaper that had been thrown into the yard and cried out to my mother some piece of news contained in the headlines.

"Who told you?" she asked.

"Nobody told me," I replied. "I read it in the paper."

"You can't read!"

"Yes, I can, too, read," and I read her the headline—but, of course, I read it upside down.

So I came to read without bothering with the alphabet, being taught by what the pedagogues later were to call the "word method." My mother had a hard time turning me around so that I would, of my own choice, read right side up. Later, of course, in newspaper work the mirrorwise reading upside down of type was to become perfectly natural to me; and, until this day, the only difference I make in reading a printed page is that upside down I take it a word at a time and right side up, if the column is not too wide, I take it a line at a time.

In the spring of 1885, when I was six, came the illness which was to determine the course and manner of my education, to keep me out of the schoolhouse, and to give me what I soon was to recognize and claim as a right, the high privilege of an invalid child who, by common consent of the community, has little or no life-expectancy. I was very ill, and from all I can now determine the illness now would be diagnosed by the best of modern physicians precisely as it was at that time by Dr. Van Burke Gatewood. He called it rheumatic fever. He may or may not have known of its portent for the heart, but I distinctly remember the fury with which I protested his injunction that I be kept in bed for, as it seemed to me, always and always. How long I don't know, but Dr. Gatewood used to come in the evenings and sit and talk with Father and Mother in his gay and witty fashion, his slightly malicious wit being sharpened by his peculiar enunciation. It was a lisp, but it wasn't quite a lisp. It was a stutter, but it wasn't quite a stutter. It was like nothing ever heard before or since. It was the result of a Rebel bullet that had clipped off the end of his tongue when he was a young surgeon in the Union army. He was from West Virginia and a Democrat. He had married a lady from New Orleans, and it was hard for me then, as it is now, actually to put him in the Grand Army of the Republic when he seemed to us to be so fully qualified by every other test than his military service for the United Confederate Veterans.

I got up from the illness, and Dr. Gatewood and my parents tried their best to keep me quiet, and so I was told not to run with the boys, not to play games, not to try to swim, not to swing high. Furthermore, enkindling the resentment of my younger brother, an anger the traces of which lingered for many years, I was excused from carrying wood or splitting stovewood or hoeing in the garden and all the other chores. These exemptions I soon discovered gave me certain advantages among my coevals. What is more, I could not help but hear the *sotto voce* remarks of kind persons, talking about me to my mother as they did, shaking their heads and saying, "I hope you'll be able to raise him." I soon found out that that, while it might mean a sentence of death, which I didn't take seriously, certainly did give me a position which I was not at all slow to exploit.

All this was heightened a half-dozen years later by the consequent chorea, or St. Vitus Dance. My uncontrollable flailing right arm was a visible symbol of my peculiar and separate status, plainly to be seen by young and old alike, and by both to be recognized as something or other—just what they might not know, but certainly it was different. Then also there was trouble with my eyes.

So I didn't go to school. That is, I didn't go to school as did the other children, regularly and under discipline. I went to school whenever I liked, for as long as I liked, and to whatever "room," as the grades were called, pleased my fancy, to listen in on whatever teacher might at the moment seem most interesting. But there wasn't much even of that. I found other and much more entrancing things to do.

My privileged position was not all to the merry, since it made me an enforced spectator of most of the games and did not permit me to participate in much of the fun. However, it was a long time—not until

Learning by Doing

I was fourteen or fifteen—before I began to experience and recognize the bitter scorn of those who despised anyone who refused to compete in contests of athletic prowess. I buttered up my physical inferiority with a lively and no doubt grossly exaggerated self-appreciation of my self-recognized intellectual superiority. There was some unhappiness in all this business. I even tried sometimes to do things about it—to compete at target-shooting with a .22-caliber rifle, for instance. But it was no go. Even then bad vision defeated me. I fell back on myself.

Nevertheless, I was a social being, gregarious by nature and never content to be alone with myself. If, in those early years, it wasn't a book, it had to be the boys. Then, if the boys were busy at school or with their games, I soon discovered that old people were people too. That, of course, was a startling discovery, rarely made by the very young, and I fairly reveled in it.

I remember that I was sitting in Mr. William L. Morrow's lap, listening to a tale of the pioneer days, just within the door of his store, he having pushed his chair into the shade from the westering July sun, when Ernie Lovan, who carried the papers then, came up with the *St. Louis Post-Dispatch* to tell us that General Grant was dead. I was just getting over my illness then.

I inherited the job of carrying the papers just before I became ten years old. It meant this: When the mail came in from Lebanon about three o'clock in the afternoon, three packages of newspapers, a big one of twelve or fifteen copies of the *Post-Dispatch* and two small ones each with five or six copies of the *St. Louis Globe-Democrat* and the *Missouri Republican*, would be snatched out of the mailbag by the postmaster and tossed through the door which separated the inner from the outer precincts of the post office. I seized these packages, ripped them open, and raced madly around the square delivering the papers and shouting the news. For there were always two or three extra copies of the *Post-Dispatch* which a boy could sell to a chance stranger.

My main interest centered in either politics or murders; but I soon learned that at the hotel, where the mule-buyers and "horse jockeys" (as we called them) were wont to assemble, there was an interest in the financial news. The *Globe-Democrat* every day carried a one-column cartoon representation of a bull and a bear engaged in a never ending battle, and I soon learned to tell from that cartoon whether the market was up or down and accordingly varied my street cries for the edification of those gentry who sat at the hotel, on the sidewalk tilted back against the wall in the summer, around the stove on the inside in the winter, conveniently placed with respect to the circle of cuspidors arranged in defensive fashion about the wood-burning heater.

It didn't take long to deliver the papers, and I was always back to plunge into the milling crowd in the outer room of the post office long before the shutter was taken down from the window and the mail was "opened." There, every day, rain or shine, but of course not on Sundays, I saw Mrs. Roll. The first thing I did when I opened the papers was to give her her *Globe-Democrat,* for she was a good Republican, and she read every word of that paper every day. When I came back, she would have seen enough of the new paper to give me a good tittering and giggling going-over for some Democratic shortcoming or deficiency. This was a great game, because I had not had time to read the latest news, of course, and so had to fall back on "general principles" in my reply; but the argument went on day after day, and we never lacked auditors. Indeed, when she pressed me too closely, Dr. George, the leading Democrat, or Mr. Greever, the patriarch of the Greenbackers, would come to my aid; and I remember once that I had her so far at a disadvantage that George O'Bannon, her son-in-law and the Republican boss whom she could not abide, grumblingly chipped in on her side.

Thus, by 1888, I felt myself fully able to take a major part in any political argument that was going on anywhere about the town. One very exciting thing happened during the campaign of that year. Mother, of course, was for Cleveland and Thurman, but Father thought that Cleveland was too much of a New Yorker, too much devoted to the gold standard, and not sufficiently interested in the farmer or the laborer, so he was all for the Union-Labor candidates, Andrew Jackson Streator of Illinois for President and C. E. Cunningham of Arkansas for Vice-President. A truly wonderful thing happened in Buffalo. One of the national candidates in a national campaign came there! That such a thing could happen to us in Buffalo was to me undreamed of, an event of an importance beyond the power of imagination to conceive; and not only did he come to Buffalo and make a speech in the courthouse, but he actually stayed all night at our house! And, furthermore, when he went away the next day, he left behind a cake of Pear's soap, the first I had even seen in being, although "Bubbles," which a member of the Royal Academy had stooped to paint for sweet advertising's sake, was a cherished picture on the wall of my attic den.

The great man was C. E. Cunningham of Arkansas, the Union-Labor candidate for Vice-President of the United States.

We didn't often see great and famous men from the outside world, a circumstance which I, at any rate, attributed not to our backwoodsiness but to the fact that the devil himself had kept us from getting a railroad. Therefore, when one did come, his visit was exciting; and I followed him around the town like a dog, yapping questions at his heels in an attempt to satisfy my insatiable curiosity. I had no shrinking fear of grownups, and I suppose that, short of a box on the ears, none of them could have done anything to get rid of me. One of them, I remember, stayed all night at our house, as had the vice-presidential candidate, Mr. Cunningham. He also was a campaigner, but not in the interest of a party. He was a crusader for better farming, and he came to speak to the Teachers Institute, to try to get the teachers interested in spreading the gospel of how to get more and better crops, more and better farm animals. That was long before the day of the county agent and the 4-H Clubs, but he, Norman J. Colman, who was to be the first Secretary of Agriculture, already had glimpsed the mighty things to be under the encouragement of the great Department of Agriculture.

Another who visited in our home had a great many good stories to tell (I now suspect that I was one of his most faithful auditors). He had long, long tales of the strange lands in which he had traveled; and, while I really understood very little of what he told me, he enkindled my determination that somehow or some way I certainly would go to India and to Siam. He was Ernest Baldwin, who had been a vice-consul in Calcutta and in Bangkok, and, not only that, he had spent years in the even more fascinating city of Washington. And Washington, of course, was my destination, as much as was ever Heaven that of Tittlebat Titmouse.

This was the most adventurous period of my life, from 1888, when I began to carry the papers, until 1893, when, at fourteen, I began to work at a regular full-time job. It was a period of daring quests and amazing discoveries, every day packed full with excitement. My parents were distracted because of my activities and tried their best to keep me quiet and to that end invoked the aid of everybody in the town, little reckoning that the help so freely given them was only to add fuel to the fire. The theory was that I was "such a nervous child," accompanied by the generally accepted notion that I might at any time suddenly expire, so that everybody did everything possible to keep me quiet. As a consequence, everyone humored my presence and would let me do almost anything that would stop my questioning tongue or bring about a period of peace.

For my part, I pounced on the perquisites of my privileged position and proceeded to do that one thing that interested me more than anything else—to find out everything that was going on and how it went. John Dewey, the philosopher, was but a stripling then, and educators like Miss Patty Hill and Colonel Francis Parker were yet to be heard of. It is true that I had a little encouragement from my father, who in his schoolteaching introduced some little measure of pupil participation; but for the most part I was on my own. Under compulsion of curiosity, I made for myself my own system of progressive education, using the Dewey methods, perhaps, but naturally ignoring the Dewey concepts of teacher guidance, and marked out my own projects and carried them through in my own way—a way often devious, frequently surreptitious, and of necessity to be kept a profound secret from prying elders.

Some of my projects, however, were carried on quite openly. When Topsy, my black cat, died, she was given no ordinary funeral. I made a box for her coffin and lined it with white cloth padded with excelsior and nailed down with little tacks. The cloth, the nails, the little embroidery finishing ribbon which ran around the top, and the very special tack hammer with its magnetized end that would so properly pick up the tacks by their tops, I had borrowed from Mr. Jack O'Bannon. Mr. O'Bannon ran the furniture store, and in the rear of it there were coffins, for he was also the undertaker. I had helped him line coffins for human beings, so that I knew just how it should be done for Topsy. The funeral was attended by all the small fry (boys, of course, because that was a pre-girl world), and I, who couldn't carry a tune, persuaded Ralph O'Bannon to sing a solo. I could not abide that Topsy should lie in an unmarked grave, so I went to Mr. Rinear, who ran the monument works, and asked him to carve her a tombstone. He would have none of it. He swore that cats were unlucky—unlucky when alive and most gosh-awful unlucky when dead. So he took a piece of broken marble and gave it to me. He showed me how, with rough chisel, to shape it, and then he let me use the water and the sand and the pumice stone to polish it. After that, with many false starts on badly broken bits of stone, he showed me how to incise the letters. After days and days of the hardest sort of work—once Mr. Rinear had to polish a new plane on my piece of stone that I had ruined so that Topsy's final headpiece was only half as thick as it was when I began—finally there was her name, TOPSY, cut in enduring marble.

My education developed freely and in whatever direction seemed convenient and profitable at the moment. There was the chemistry textbook which Mother had used in school. To me it was an absorbing book, and I think that at that time I knew it almost by rote. I don't know how many fewer than ninety-two elements were then set down, and, indeed, I remember little or nothing about the book except some things that I should have forgotten—for me, for instance, common salt still is muriate of soda and not sodium chloride. When I first found the book, Mother said that her chemistry teacher had said that she would probably live to see the time when one wishing to kindle a fire would bring in a bucket of water and that there would be some simple way to separate it into oxygen and hydrogen and then start the fire. Little did she think that this joking remark, jokingly repeated, was to set me off on a career as a chemist, with special devotion to explosives.

Mr. Weatherby and Mr. Gleason ran the drugstore—I mean the *drug*store, the one devoted to drugs and not to drinks—and both of them were kindly men and might have tolerated me even had not Dr. Gatewood practically imposed me upon them by emphasizing my precarious health and my need for special consideration. Here was my most available approach to my career as chemist.

The drugstore was in one of the new brick buildings on the west of the square, a wide, deep, high-ceilinged room. Down each side of the room ran counters topped with showcases of plate glass and German silver mountings, except at the very back, where a little space on the counter on each side without a showcase was devoted to wrapping parcels and the like. The rows of counters were interrupted twice by openings to give access to the regions behind the counters. In each of these two openings on either side were set tall mirrors that went from the floor to the ceiling, and, when I looked in one of them, I could see myself over and over and over again until I disappeared as a tiny midget in the distance. The two counters at the back were joined by a work of carved oak and colored glass, the prescription screen, behind which were carried on all the secret and mysterious things that are done in pharmacies.

On the left side as one entered the store from the square were whole rows of shelves filled with bottles of drugs, bottles of varying size but of uniform design, and all with beautiful labels bearing gilt letters under glass. Some of them were partly filled with liquids, some with powders or crystals, and all of them were to be used in filling prescriptions. It was a beautiful sight to see. On the other side the shelves were filled with patent medicines, all the great array made familiar by the almanacs and the advertisements in the newspapers as well as by the signs on the country barns and fences.

The contents of the showcases, too, were wonderful. The first one on the right was filled with books, for this was the only bookstore in town. There were bound books, novels in the "Caxton" series—seventy-five-cent reprints of popular novels, sets of standard authors, volumes of poetry. There were also two or three rows of paper-backed books— the "Seaside Library" series, which made available for all of us at twenty-five cents per volume the accepted and classic literature of the English-speaking peoples and translations from the rest of the world. These cheap books were to disappear in the United States with the cancellation of their cheap second-class postal privileges and the tightening of the copyright laws, not to come in again for nearly a half-century. On the shelf behind the counter, half-covered up most of the time in deference to certain prejudices entertained by some of the best church people, were "Beadle's Dime Novels," and, a little later, such things as *Deadwood Dick, Nick Carter,* and *Frank Merriwell,* the ten-cent fiction that was making its mark on its time.

The next showcase on that side was full of candy, chocolate drops, and pieces of cocoanut candy made to simulate strips of bacon, burnt almonds and Jordan almonds, rock candy and caramels, all displayed in glass trays, as were also the stick candies, the red-striped peppermint, the translucent lemon, and the dark and luscious horehound. In the showcase on the other side in the front there were combs and brushes and sets of toilet articles to be disposed on dresser tops, perfumes, Eau de Cologne, and so on; and in the remaining showcase other brushes, tooth soap (I was condemned to arnica tooth soap that came in a hinged metal box), and such things as fancy soaps and face powders.

Besides Mr. Weatherby and Mr. Gleason there was Virgil Greever, a clerk, my elder brother's best friend, and for one reason and another a hero to me. Mr. Weatherby and Mr. Gleason indulged me; Virgil petted me. So I began to help in the drugstore. When all the mess of ground powders were mixed together to make that awful concoction known as "AB Physic," I would turn and mix and cut with a spatula, crush the lumps, and finally receive the accolade of Virgil's thanks when I had done for him a most unpleasantly pungent chore. I soon was twirling filter papers into cones and carefully decanting fluid extracts into glass graduates in the process of making the tinctures, and I remember how happy I was on the day when Mr. Weatherby himself let me take two drops of the mysterious and priceless attar of roses and myself put it on the cotton in the filter and myself turn in the distilled water to make a whole gallon of the rose water so much required for lotions.

Early in the morning when Virgil opened the store, he filled a huge sprinkling can from the pump in the courthouse yard and with that sprinkled the floor of the store preparatory to sweeping all the dust and litter, plus a moiety of splinters from the soft pine floor, out across the sidewalk and into the square. Then every morning came the process of polishing the German silver mountings of all the showcases and cleaning the four tall mirrors. This rite was performed with the aid of a mixture of prepared chalk and ammonia applied with a cloth, permitted to dry, and then polished off with a chamois skin so that every bit of metal and glass fairly shone. To help with this daily task of polishing was a tremendous joy to me.

In a short time another drugstore was opened with Virgil and Billy O'Bannon, who had a crippled leg and walked on a crutch, as proprietors, and they had a similar problem of polishing. I was more than delighted to do a part of the work, especially since Billy was generous with both the candy jar and an occasional nickel or a dime.

Once upon a time a man came through with a wonderful new contraption in a spring wagon. It was put up in Billy O'Bannon's store, and there its master and exhibitor invited all and sundry to acquaint themselves with its magic at a price of a nickel a head. The thing had a half-dozen rubber tubes dangling from it, and the end of each was bifurcated, ending in two little hard-rubber bits that were to be placed in the ears. As soon as the showman could get six persons attached, he wound a piece of clocklike machinery, set the thing off, and we heard, "As played by the Columbia Phonograph Company of New York and Paris," and so on into the song or the march. I remember standing by this thing, penniless, fairly bursting with curiosity and eagerness, so much so that Billy O'Bannon looked at me and without a word handed me a nickel. I handed it to the man and got my earpieces. From then on, as long as the repertoire lasted, Billy would hand me a nickel, I would hand it to the showman, and so I stayed for the whole performance. And among the things I heard with the greatest joy was John Philip Sousa and the United States Marine Band playing "The Washington Post" and the "High School Cadets" marches.

It was not too difficult to borrow from the drugstore small quantities of sulfur and saltpeter to be twisted with sugar and charcoal in cigarette papers to make little torpedoes that sounded just as loud as boughten firecrackers and were much more astonishing to the boys of my gang.

But the drugstore wasn't the only place in town where folks fooled about with chemicals. There was also the photograph gallery. Mr. John James, the photographer, was a stoop-shouldered man with a flowing red mustache, whose English accent and dark-brown-stained fingers both intrigued me. He was born in England and in London, and I am quite sure within the sound of Bow bells. He had brought his photographic establishment, which he had taken about the country from village to village in a covered wagon, to its resting place in Buffalo; and he lived not far from us with his wife and his two boys. It was a little harder to get in with him than it was with some of my other older friends, and, indeed, he never did permit me to go into the darkroom or to mess around with his "hypos" and such. But he did let me use his hard pencils, sharpened to a long, long point, in retouching spoiled negatives, with my head under a black cloth hood and the negative against the light, just as he retouched those which were rated as unspoiled from which prints were to be made for his customers. He did let me help make the prints, putting the papers against the negatives and exposing them in their frames in which they were fastened with brass springs to the center; and he did permit me to help paste and polish, in a machine that looked like a clothes wringer, the photographs as they were being finished. Therefore it was no trick at all for me to borrow a printing frame and some clear glasses from which the sensitizing solution had been washed. This particular borrowing was in pursuit of my preparing to repeat the experiments that had led to the discovery of photography, and I intended to do that by making blueprints. So I borrowed.

I wonder what the commotion would have been if anybody had found it out. A little citrate of iron and ammonia—slimy little garnet-colored flakes that half-melted on exposure to air—and some chunks of prussiate of potash—greenish-yellow lumps. Prussiate of potash now is best known to the English reading world, or at least to that part of it which reads murder mysteries, as cyanide of potassium. I knew that the stuff was very poisonous, but I hadn't expected it to be so refractory, and I had a hard time melting it in water, crushing it in a mortar, and in bringing it to any sort of shape so that I could combine it with the citrate of iron and ammonia to make the sensitizing solution which I was going to spread on paper; but at last it was done. Then I passed sheets of writing paper through the solution, put them in my printing frame against fronds of ferns, maple leaves, or pansy blossoms, exposed them to the sun, ran them through a fixing bath, and had the priceless reward of my own blueprints, of my own botanical specimens selected from my own beloved garden.

That was not enough. In each November there came in the mail a marvelous treasury of wonders, the annual premium list of the *Youth's Companion*. In it one could see the marvels that might be had if one would only send in two or four or five or seven new subscriptions to the *Youth's Companion* at $1.75 each. I worried and nagged one year until I got enough to enable me to send for a chemical set. I had a spirit lamp and some test tubes, some pipettes and a little retort, some boxes of powders and some bottles of liquids. Also, of course, there were a book of instructions and, very much more interesting, a sheet of warnings. The warnings interested me more than the instructions, and, although I have now forgotten exactly what happened, I do know that that particular series of experiments ended in an explosion, with my eyebrows singed off and a general retreat (so far as the family and the public were concerned) from further adventures in that line.

But there were other lines. I thought it would be a good idea to make a steam engine that would make an interesting and acceptable noise by drilling a hole in the side of an earthenware bottle and tying over that little hole a penny whistle. The bottle I half-filled with water, corked it tightly, placed it in a length of stovepipe, with the whistle up, and laid the length of stovepipe on a "furnace" which was made of a few flat stones with a roaring fire between. The bottle began to roll around, and all of us, for this was a communal experiment, took turns looking at it. Derby Stanley was "next," and, when he leaned down to take a look, the whole thing exploded. Now that bottle had contained ink, Arnold's writing fluid, and there was enough left in it so that Derby's face not only was scalded with boiling water but was painted a green-black, which made him such a terrifying figure that everybody but me ran. The reason I didn't run was that I was paralyzed with fright.

Of course, Buffalo had no electricity, except perhaps the magnetized tack hammer that Jack O'Bannon used in his capacity as undertaker. I set out to fill this lack by attempting all sorts of things with drug-store bottles and tin foil to make Leyden jars, making pith balls from the elderberry bushes, and wet batteries rigged up with all sorts of odds and ends, never resting until I found a way of dissolving copper and depositing it as copper plate on odds and ends of metal. At last, and a kindly God has rubbed out the memory of exactly how I brought it about, there was an explosion big enough not only to singe my eyebrows and my hair but to set fire to the attic den where I carried on my secret and mysterious alchemy. I managed to put the fire out without anybody else being the wiser, and then and there wrote "finis" to my career as chemist, physicist, and electrician.

Harness-making and tinsmithing came to me bracketed by reason of the fact that my brother was the junior partner of his foster father-in-law in the firm of Lovan & Brownlow, which dealt in saddlery and harness and also in hardware. My brother Joe was a harness-maker and saddler (a business which he carried on throughout his life), and Mr. Lovan was a tinsmith, so I was permitted to mount the wooden horses, clamp bits of leather in their teeth, make the wax end threads, and stitch pieces of leather together in the way that my brother was doing for really truly. Mr. Lovan was a very careful person, and he was afraid that I would get burned; but I soon discovered how to get on his soft side so that he not only would permit me to use the snips to cut pieces of tin and sheet iron but actually would let me use the soldering iron and solder together pieces as well as crimp them, roll them, and the like. His soft side, for purposes of such an approach, was through his interest in theology. He was a faithful Baptist and a regular subscriber to the *Homiletic Review,* a serious journal and the first of the quarterly-review type that I had ever seen. I didn't know what it was all about, but I would read anything; and, when Mr. Lovan would see me read through one of the articles or sermons in that *Review,* his hopes of converting me to be a Baptist ran so high that he would let me play with the soldering pot.

Leather smelled good, and I could actually make things that I imagined to be of some use, so that the harness shop could not confine me. I liked even better Taylor Booher and his shoemaking establishment. A part of the time his assistant, Mr. Barton, was not there, and that left the other cobbler's stool free. That was a perch for me, and the kindly Mr. Booher, who smiled much but spoke little, played up to the general community purpose of keeping me quiet by letting me handle awl and hammer and pegs, by letting me roll bristles into wax ends, and so on. There was no machinery in Taylor Booher's shop, and shoe-repairing was altogether a matter of handicraft but, from my point of view, was too often practiced in the silence which was Mr. Booher's outstanding characteristic.

Therefore it was a matter of great joy to me when Mr. Booher was called upon in his other capacity as justice of the peace to conduct a trial of some suit at law. This he did from his cobbler's seat, never ceasing to cobble, while I, Mr. Barton being absent, sat in the other cobbler's seat and listened. Mr. Justice Booher in his judicial capacity was attended by Mr. James Sharp, constable, and here were heard the causes of the people. Sometimes there were criminal cases of such a nature that I was shooed and shushed out of the shop, but often they were civil actions, suits to collect debts, actions in replevin, and the like. It would have been impossible for anyone in the time and the place to have listened to the clever and sometimes the eloquent presentation of their clients' cases by such great lawyers as Mr. Haymes and Mr. Scott, such eloquent advocates as Mr. Stanley and Mr. Robertson, without being compelled perforce to decide once and for all to study law and become an ornament of the bar. I decided to be a lawyer. The law was more than just a childish fascination for me, particularly in view of its inextricable relation to politics. Within our community the courthouse stood as a symbol of that relationship. It towered over the town corporally as well as politically.

The circuit court sat for a week in the spring and a week in the fall, although occasionally there would be enough business to carry over into a second week. During the early days of my faithful attendance upon the court the judge was Washington Irving Wallace of Lebanon, the county seat of Laclede County, twenty-eight miles to the east. Judge Wallace was short, fat, round, and very nearsighted. He peered out at the world through thick-lensed spectacles and seemed always to be on the very verge of a chuckle, which, when it did come, exploded into a laugh to be heard all around the square. His geniality, no doubt, helped promote his political career and get him votes at the elections; but it was also a delusion and a snare for any who expected it to betoken leniency for the evildoer or any whose erroneous judgment led him to believe that the Wallace Scotch blood had been in any degree diluted through generations in New England and Ohio and who improvidently and with futility asked him for the loan of a half-dollar.

The time came when the great Judge Wallace decided not to run for re-election. The Republican judicial convention which was to nominate his successor was held in Buffalo. It was my first and one of my most exciting political conventions. It met in the biggest hall in town, the O'Bannon Opera House, and its permanent chairman was George O'Bannon himself. Dallas County had its own candidate, O. H. Scott, a good but not a particularly successful lawyer, being a little too much on the intellectual side for the good of his own pocketbook and a little too much on the independent side to engage for him quite the hearty support that the O'Bannon machine might have produced for a more malleable member of the bar. Nevertheless, Dallas County was for Scott; Polk County was for Skinker, despite the damning fact that he was a renegade Democrat; Webster and Laclede each had its favorite candidate; but Wright County was for Argus Cox. On and on the convention went, roll call after roll call; and, at the end of each, George O'Bannon in his deep bass would announce the result and declare, "No candidate having received the majority of votes cast, there is no nomination, and the clerk will call the roll." At the end of the roll was Wright County, and through the two whole days and nights, a tall man with a long beard would rise and, in a most sepulchral voice, intone: "Wright County casts its six votes for Argus Cox."

Mr. Scott was too much the lawyer and too little the politician to make some of the compromises suggested; Mr. Skinker was too much the ex-Democrat to be much respected with regard to party fealty; and in the end sheer pertinacity won. Argus Cox was nominated, and so Argus Cox became for me and for all of us the embodiment of what a judge should be and should look like. He was bald, he was bearded, he had a high sharp voice, and the rigidity of his upright shoulders reflected his impeccable judicial bearing. There were sometimes murder trials, juries were locked up, sometimes juries were hung, and all about the place in the spring and fall there was the great excitement of court week.

This, of course, was an experience common to all country towns that were county seats, but our particular courthouse had a particular excitement that was shared by but few indeed, and that was the annual spring meeting of the county court when it was by law required to fix the county tax levy for the ensuing year.

The county court in Missouri is an administrative, not a judicial, body. It is what in most states is known as a board of county supervisors or county commissioners. It levied the taxes and made the appropriations for the county business and generally was responsible for what management the county's affairs were to have. The county court consisted of a presiding judge elected from the county at large and two district judges, one from the northern end and one from the southern end of the county. The county had long since declined to pay any of the interest, let alone the principal, of the bonds that it had issued for the railroad that never came. The first efforts to compromise the issue with the owners of the defaulted securities were made under the authority of a popular election authorizing a compromise offer of part payment in full liquidation of the debt, as early as 1879, the year I was born.

Mr. John B. Henderson, who had been a Republican senator from the state of Missouri and who had distinguished himself by voting "No" and thus preventing the conviction of President Andrew Johnson when on impeachment trial, owned many of these Dallas County bonds. Efforts to enforce payment in the state courts having availed him nothing, Mr. Henderson and his lawyers went to the federal courts. The federal court issued a writ of mandamus against the county court of Dallas County requiring it to levy sufficient taxes to pay the defaulted interest on the railroad bonds.

Ever thereafter the rivalry of the three parties, Republican, Populist, and Democratic, was softened in Dallas County with respect to county judges. In fact, county judges were selected not because they belonged to a political party or were the supporters of a particular faction or boss; they were selected solely on merit—merit determined by the special abilities and skills required for the job. He who could convince the voters that he was best able to hide out in the bushes and escape the service of a summons by a United States marshal was sure to be elected.

So the county court did most of its business at odd places around the county and at night in the homes of tried, true, and trusted natives. However, one act was required by law to be done in the courthouse, and that was the annual act of levying the tax for the coming year. For weeks before the spring session of the court, every stranger who came to town, even be his business so innocent as that of selling sugar, coffee, and other groceries, was suspect. He might be a United States marshal in disguise, and every boy over the age of six or seven, at any rate, constituted himself chief of the detective force that was to spy out the invading minion of the federal court and warn our noble judges of their danger.

On the eve of the day when the court had to meet, we all stayed up until after midnight; we hid in the trees and behind shrubs, in doorways and up stairways, and in all the nooks and crannies around the dark and quiet square, watching for the federal monster and bursting with the final thrill when, one minute after midnight, all three judges would hurriedly sign their names by the light of a single match to the ordinance already prepared and waiting in the office of the county clerk. Then the darkness, the silence burst by the yells of the triumphant watchers, and the retreat of Their Honors back to the obscurity of the woods.

Once in a while, of course, we did get us a judge who was not qualified for his position, a fact amply demonstrated when he was unwary enough to permit himself to fall into the clutches of a United States marshal. Then off to Kansas City our judge would be taken to languish in the jailhouse. It had been decreed that, as long as a judge was in jail for his contumacy in refusing to vote for the tax levy, he was thus in attendance at a session of his court. The county judges were paid a per diem for attendance on their court. So when a judge got himself in jail, he drew five dollars a day from the country treasury as long as he was locked up. But, as all he had to do to get out was write a letter of resignation and send it to the governor, sometimes one stayed in jail just to "draw" his per diem. So it is not to be wondered that occasionally we elected ourselves a judge who was suspected of conniving with a United States marshal to get himself put in jail. But such a one, once he was out of jail when his term expired and the United States no longer could hold him, never came back to Dallas County. Of that you may be quite sure.

So my education continued on its merry if somewhat erratic way, in and out of the shops of the town. The carpenter shop, for example, with its joint appeal to the senses of sight and of smell, was deemed not a place for small boys who might so easily get hurt. At last Mr. Bill Hunt, who was six feet five and a most genial person, let me in. I cleaned out the shavings from where he had been using the plane and did other little odd jobs for which in return he showed me how to use the vise, how to use the jack plane, and then at last the miter saw and the miter box. With this and odd bits of quarter-round and other molding I made picture frames. I was particularly in need of picture frames, because I had then embarked on my career as an artist, and it was necessary to have frames both for my pen-and-ink drawings and for my oil paintings.

Once made, the picture frames themselves needed paint or something. I persuaded the painters to induct me into the beginnings of their entrancing mysteries, with the result that I myself gilded the frames that I had made in Mr. Hunt's carpenter shop. I even borrowed enough varnish to varnish one of my oil paintings, as I had read was the proper thing to do, but unfortunately the opaque varnish on hand at the moment blotted forever from human eyes that particular masterpiece.

Mr. Tuckness and Mr. McPheeters, the painters, were paper-hangers too, and they let me turn the roller of the machine that cut off the unnecessary selvages from the rolls of paper. They even let me help mix paste, and sometimes in places where it wouldn't be noticed too much they let me do a little bit of paper-hanging, just as they also permitted me to swing a brush on a fence or a barn or some other place where it wouldn't hurt too much. I remember paying Mr. Tuckness for the high privilege of painting a picket fence by reading to him aloud at the rest period how Tom Sawyer managed to get a fence whitewashed without doing any of the work himself. It was years before that practical joke at my expense became evident to me.

On Saturdays, busy trading days, I usually attached myself to some one or other of the mercantile establishments about town just for the fun of mixing in with the excitement and of "helping out." I counted eggs from the baskets of the farmers' wives who brought them in to barter; I weighed out sugar and coffee and sometimes even was permitted to measure out calico or shirting with a brass-ferruled yardstick. These chores were rewarding in themselves, but I did not despise as an additional reward a lump of sugar from the brown-sugar barrel or, once in a while, a dime.

A favorite store for helping out was that of Frank Furth—the Famous Cash House—where I had two other juvenile colleagues, Bob Furth, a year or two older, and Ernie Furth, a year or two younger than I. We three were together at play most of the week anyhow, when the Furth boys were not in school, and so the Saturday work was a wonderful thing to do.

So, too, I hung around the Morrow store, but I carefully stayed away from the other big establishment, George O'Bannon's, because I was afraid of Mr. O'Bannon. He was, at that time, relinquishing his post as the Republican boss to his younger brother, Jim; and it was several years before I discovered that his growling gruffness to me was a game that he was carrying on, much to his own amusement and that of the rest of the town, because, when I had had the temerity to back him up a tree on a tariff argument, he grunted and growled, and I retreated in terror. Later, when I discovered his secret, he became my favorite confidant; but that belongs to a different era.

This business of counting; weighing; measuring; selling goods for barter or for cash; making up lists of things sold, later to be charged on the ledgers—these things all involved arithmetic, and so, perforce, I had to learn some arithmetic. Most of that I got from my father's love for mental arithmetic, and he had had me doing all sorts of problems, up to the rule of three, in my head before I learned how to put any of them down with pencil and paper or, rather, on a slate with a slate pencil, which was much more satisfactory for purposes of quick erasure.

The problems of mental arithmetic, Mother told me, were easier to do if one used algebra, and so, under her guidance, soon I was letting x equal the unknown quantity, and that, of course, also all in my head. My mathematics never got much further, because, not being regularly required to go to school, it didn't seem to me to be necessary to pursue too far such a painful process. I did dip into the first books of Euclid in the textbooks that my mother had had before the Civil War, and, while I got a glimpse of the pure beauty of the demonstrations of the simpler theorems, I stopped there. The lack of mathematical training has undoubtedly been a handicap to me all my life, and I still keep books in the only way I ever learned to keep them—in my head.

Most of these activities in the stores and the shops, except possibly for busy Saturdays, were mine and mine alone so far as boyhood was concerned, since the other boys were not interested and also because, if they were not busy with their own affairs, there were two other establishments which claimed for them a greater interest—the livery stables and the blacksmith shops. Now these I did not care for. I was greatly tempted by the forge, the anvil, the hand-drill press, and such things at the blacksmith shop, and on occasion I would stand and stare and ask questions. However, there was one thing that blacksmith shops and livery stables had in common that I not only didn't like but that I greatly feared. That was horses. To me horses were not only things to be afraid of but things to be avoided if possible and certainly of no use whatever unless hitched to some sort of a rig and tolerated as a necessary if evil price of getting somewhere.

There were several places "out in the country" to which I sometimes went and to which I always was begging to be permitted to go. One was the Alexander farm. Uncle John and Aunt Becky were not only old settlers in Dallas County but they had been married in Giles County, Tennessee, and had migrated to Missouri before the war. Uncle John was kindly and extraordinarily slow-spoken. Aunt Becky was kindly and spoke with a rapidity that was a marvel to hear, and she also had a fund of funny stories that she wasn't above sharing with small fry. Also, and this was not to be despised, under any and all circumstances Aunt Becky had more different kinds of jams, jellies, and preserves than any other person ever would have. If from any other corner of the county came some rumor of a threat to her supremacy in this particular, she would invent on the instant at least half-a-dozen new kinds for the table. I gloried in Aunt Becky. She had a spinning wheel and a loom, and Uncle John raised plenty of sheep. I helped her and so learned how, myself, to wash the wool and card it and to spin it. She taught me how to harness the loom and, with yarn dyed black in logwood for the warp and brown in butternut for the woof, to weave heavy jeans.

But delight of delights when I could get to the country was when I could go to Cousin Mark Reynolds, who lived at the nursery. For me, the best thing at Cousin Mark's (other than Cousin Sally's pies) was the greenhouse. Here I was permitted to help. I cut slips of geraniums to be set out in tiny little pots, such gorgeous ones as my favorite pink one with black penciling on the petals, the Souvenir de Mirande. Here I sat up one night until after midnight to see the night-blooming cereus. The most fun of all was the grafting and budding. To see that the field-grown La France and General Jacque-minots were grafted on the wild rose stock and to lay the plans for a tree that would bear both apricots and peaches—all this was en-trancing. The twine and beeswax, the sharp knives—they were fun to play with, and, above everything, there was the rich reward of the heavy, steamy, scented air that one breathed inside that glass-roofed haven of delight.

These things led to two other enthusiasms. One was the flowers at home, which I helped my mother tend, the flowerbeds and the rock garden in the yard, and the potted plants to be kept at the south window all through the winter; and the other was the attempt to identify and classify every plant, weed, or tree that I found in the fields, on the prairies, or in the woods.

There was another clan out in the country, the Tinsleys and the Fowlers, who were deemed to be almost as close as kin because they, too, were from Tennessee; but, having come from the upper reaches of the Cumberland River (Cordell Hull country), they were not close enough to be "cousined," but they were nonetheless esteemed.

The Tinsleys were always searching for knowledge. Ardently re-ligious, they seemed to believe that salvation, while it was to be achieved through the Campbellite way of life, was not to be entered into and enjoyed except through education. There were ten sons and daughters in the Thad Tinsley household, and, with the possible exception of the three eldest, they all were destined to go to college, to become preachers or teachers, and so were their children and grandchildren to the third and fourth generation. This was remarkable, because very few in our part of the world ever dreamed of going to college. So also the Fowlers, and, although there were but a few acres of not the very richest land to support them, by dint of hard work and thrift they made their way. That could have been done only because there was in that day and time, especially for those who belonged to the Church of the Disciples, that remarkable institution, Valparaiso College at Valparaiso, Indiana. There a student could get room and board for a dollar and a half a week.

Even then, at nine years old, I had made up my mind very definitely about one thing. Although I greatly enjoyed my visits to the country, I wanted no part of country life in mine. I was all for the urban way of living. Now "town" to me was only Buffalo and its eight hundred people; only Buffalo, cut off, it seemed, by a special curse from the world of railroads; only Buffalo, without water or sewer, without paving or lights, only a tiny village so small that even the most indulgent statistician in the census must needs classify it as rural—yet to me it was town, and it wasn't country, while the farm was country and nothing else. Out on the farm it was lonesome at night, and one couldn't run out to a neighbor's. The lonesome sounds made it too noisy to sleep of nights. The moon shadows were too dark, and, when there was no moon, the fireflies in the great caverns under the trees could not drive away the dread of that deep darkness. In short, I liked people in large numbers; there were never enough of them on a farm, even where there were twelve in a family. The twig of my gregariousness then was bent, and thus the tree of my devotion to urban life inclined. To this day, while I may enjoy a day in the country, I'd rather not stay overnight.

II

When I can first remember, the public school system in Buffalo had not yet completely conquered its rival institution, the private subscription or so-called "old-field" school, which specialized in grammar, penmanship, and mental arithmetic. The Civil War had interrupted all schooling, and, after it was over, the schools were slowly re-established, but of course much more rapidly in Missouri than in Tennessee. Indeed, about the time I arrived on the scene, Missouri was beginning to boast of its liberal support of its public school system, of its normal or teacher-training schools, and of the expanding state university at Columbia. Still there were those, fewer in Missouri than in Tennessee, who could and would use, in ordinary conversation, deprecatory locutions concerning public schools such as, for instance, "as ragged as a free-school scholar."

The public schoolhouse in Buffalo then was a brick structure containing four schoolrooms. It already was overcrowded, and after the collapse of the "subscription school" one class was maintained in a rented room upstairs over one of the stores, while the agitation went on for a newer and bigger schoolhouse. Mother sometimes was a teacher of what might, in terms later to be used, be called the second and the third grades, but usually she had the beginners, while Father taught the older boys and girls in the outside rented room. Neither of them taught every year, as it was the accepted custom of the community as reflected by the school board to pass the jobs around; and there were always more teachers than jobs. However, Mother in these early days was more continuously employed than was Father, who stepped out from time to time on one or another of his varied ventures.

Then, probably in accordance with rising state standards, a principal was employed. He was dignified by the title of "professor," was required to be a graduate of a state normal school, and was given responsibility for the entire school and the enormous salary of fifty dollars a month. The first of these superintendents, I think, was C. A. Jamison, who lived next door to us and who, when he was not in a schoolroom, could hardly escape me and my pestering questions. He made the mistake of showing me a set of blocks that were supposed to visualize and typify the arithmetical process of the extraction of the square root and the cube root of numbers. I never rested until I had that matter in hand.

Every spring a special election was held in the school district to vote the extra levy which alone would furnish enough tax revenue to enable Buffalo to continue its special schools. At that time the villages of Urbana and Louisburg had two- or three-room schools. But in all the rest of the county each district had its one-room school and one teacher who taught everything and everybody from the *Primer* right straight through to *McGuffey's Sixth Reader* and *Ray's Third Part Arithmetic,* which together formed the roof of the curriculum. Sometimes Father taught in these country schools, and on occasion it was a great joy for me to visit him and the school, which I frequently did, especially when he was teaching at Reynolds or at Benton Branch.

Buffalo was not content with what it had and in 1889 made the decision to build a bigger and better school. There were, of course, difficulties about the site and so on; but at last a big piece of property, two or three acres, was purchased, and the new schoolhouse built with six schoolrooms and an assembly hall. In that new building in 1892 the school was fully graded for the first time, from Grades I to XII, although, of course, some teachers would have two or three grades in a room. Mother had the first and second grades. The whole thing was conducted under the vigorous leadership of the new superintendent, Professor I. W. Wingo, who himself taught the four grades of the high school—all in one room.

There I exercised my privilege of attending as an auditor to a greater degree than ever before. I went so often, and sometimes for nearly a whole day at a time, that Mr. Wingo gave me a regular seat just as though I had been a regularly enrolled pupil. What got me so interested there was a particular class which was going through a particular textbook, Barnes's *Thirteen Weeks in Zoölogy.* There was no laboratory. Nobody even dissected a frog. But I, at any rate, had a lot of fun with the book, which I memorized word for word in order to be able to display at the slightest provocation—or without any—my ability to rattle off the whole pedigree, or whatever one might call it, of some animal, from his kingdom down to his family, genus, and species. It was really a dreadful thing and a dreadful time, for I would not address my cat as other than *"Felis domestica,"* and I actually hung around the back end of the produce store so as to be present when somebody brought in a dried skunkskin in order to display my learning, as I would quite uselessly descant on the peculiar defense mechanism with which Dame Nature had endowed *Mephis mephitica.* That was the nearest I ever came to "going to school," but I was free to go as well as to come, and my attendance was not regular. Perhaps some would say that it was characteristic, but, be that as it may, I was never there for a test or an examination. In fact, I have taken only one written examination in my entire life. I am glad to say that I passed that one. It got me a driver's license in New Jersey in 1928.

Mr. Wingo, tall and straight with a bald head and a flowing mustache, seemed to me to embody the whole of learning. I soon found that he would do more for me at home after school than at school, because he was generous with his books and let me have them so that I could absorb a book a day rather than a page or two at a time, as was done in the class. This gave me full sway with his textbooks in history and English literature and rhetoric and the like, but of course it was not so good for mathematics, which I never pursued further.

The house in which we lived my father built in 1886. One entered from a front porch into a small hall from which doors on either side opened into large high-ceilinged rooms. Between these two rooms, behind the hall, was a large linen and clothes closet, nearly as big as a small room. Both of these rooms opened in the rear into a long transverse hall which led from a rear porch on the south all the way through to a side hall at the north. On the ground floor there was, at the north, a small bedroom. Then there was a large combined dining-room and kitchen, although in the summertime the porch, screened with mosquito bar, served as the dining-room. From the back hall a stairway led up to a single upstairs room which was as big as the dining-room and bedroom together but whose sloping roof degraded it to the status of an attic. After a time the small bedroom downstairs was sacrificed and turned into a kitchen, and thereafter the big room was a dining-room all by itself.

The attic room was part of the time my bedroom but all of the time my special retreat, even when the summer sun on the sloping roof made it almost unbearably hot, or when freezing weather in the winter demonstrated the inadequacy of its heating arrangement—a drum affixed to the stovepipe from the kitchen stove beneath. This attic room was my laboratory, my library, my atelier, and my oratory. There I could read forbidden books, there I could pray without the consciousness and embarrassment imposed by cupped ears or prying eyes, and there I could indulge my flights of fancy as one after another I achieved brilliant careers in nearly every one of the arts and professions.

The protective coloration afforded me by my physical disabilities enabled me to roam a much wider range than would be possible for a boy who, lacking special privilege, is compelled to conform to the conventions and standards of his playmates. I am sure that any other one of the boys who left the gang to go and hang around old people would have been driven into the desert as a pariah. But I was sick and therefore by boy law entitled to be odd. The dispensation permitted me to indulge myself in all sorts of stimulating company, even aside from those whom I flattered by endeavoring to learn their several handicrafts.

Thus I could spend long hours with Mr. William L. Morrow in his store to hear his tales about the early settlement of the county and also about the great struggle of 1860 and 1861 as to whether Missouri would stay in the Union or go with the Confederacy. Mr. Morrow was elected to the state senate in 1860. At that time he was a Douglas Democrat and a slaveowner, but he was first of all a Union man and, after the war, always a loyal Republican.

Mr. James Southard, who was elected to the House of Representatives in 1860 as a Republican, the first, I believe, so to be elected in Dallas County, in my time was probate judge. He also found in me an eager listener to the tales of those stirring times that he had told so often that most older people had begun to run out on him. But not I. Thus, to me, the struggles between the Union men and the Secessionists, between Frank Blair and Claiborne Jackson and between Nathaniel Lyon and Sterling Price, remain today almost as though I had been a participant.

Certainly the bits and parts of history that came to me in this fashion before I was ten years old have a rare and special quality that endures for me until today. My father seems to have caused all this, because he encouraged me in my talks with these older people and often would sit with me while I plied them with questions. One day he came home and said to Mother, "Delia, I am going to take the two boys out in the country this afternoon to see Mr. Maloney. I hear Mr. Maloney is about to die, and I want the boys to see him. Walter will probably be too young to remember, but Louis is old enough, and I would like him all of his life to be able to say that he talked with a man who fought in the Battle of Waterloo."

So that afternoon my father took Walter and me in a buggy, hired from the livery stable, and drove out five miles to the Fraker neighborhood, where we went in to see Mr. Patrick Maloney. Mr. Maloney had been born in Ireland in 1798 (as I afterward took the trouble to ascertain), and he was a trooper under the Duke of Wellington in that great battle at the end of which Napoleon's star of destiny forever set. When we went in, Mr. Maloney was propped up in bed. His daughter-in-law said that he was much better than he had been and was glad to see company. Father told him why he had brought us boys to see him. Father then told me to ask the questions that he had so carefully drilled into me on the trip out from town.

"Please tell me, Mr. Maloney," I asked, "just what did you see of the Battle of Waterloo?"

I didn't know that that request was so carefully phrased as to bring forth what Mr. Maloney had for years been wont to reply to such interrogations, but I can never forget what happened. He straightened himself in the bed, seized his long beard with his right hand, ran his left hand through his long hair and thundered, "I saw all there was of the Battle of Waterloo, as much as Napoleon or the Duke himself —a lot of smoke, a lot of noise, and a hell of a stink!"

Associates among the elders I selected largely because of their story-telling skills. If the oldster could tell a tale, I went again and again; if he could not, never again. Mrs. Irene Stanley Slavens, wife of Dr. Zenas R. Slavens, had a wonderful store of knowledge of Greek and Roman mythology which she didn't mind going over for me as often as I liked. And then there were tales of England to be heard, especially from Mrs. William Harris, who was the wife of one of the three brothers Harris who had emigrated from England, one a saddler, one a baker, and one (her husband) a gardener. Mrs. Harris in her youth had been a governess in a county family in Hants, and she helped me to resolve many puzzlements encountered in my endeavor to create reality out of the pictures which I found in my English novels. Indeed, she was a living annotation to Washington Irving and *Brace-bridge Hall;* the key that enabled me to construe Tom Brown through Rugby and Oxford.

About that time (I was nine) Thomas H. Slavens, the doctor's son, came home from West Point for a whole summer on his two-year furlough. His tall and handsome figure in its gray uniform set the girls of the town in a flutter, while for me, every time he walked forth was the occasion for alarums and excursions. I followed like a dog at his heels until sometimes he had to threaten me with physical harm if I didn't vamoose. I decided to go for a soldier. I made up my mind then and there that the congressman from our district had to give me an appointment to West Point, and I began preparation in what I suppose was an entirely acceptable classic manner. I read Caesar, in translation, of course, for Mrs. Slavens hadn't been able to persuade me to stick to my Latin. I read a life of Napoleon that I found somewhere, by whom I don't know, but it was uncritical and laudatory and caused me, when nobody was looking, to pull down a forelock and thrust my right hand into my buttoned jacket. Furthermore, I began then and there to read every available scrap about the Civil War.

Something was always interfering with my plans, however, and I would no sooner get firmly set on a career as a swashbuckling free-lance man-at-arms than somebody, such as Peter Humphrey, would set me off on another tack. Peter Humphrey was an old, old man who had the reputation of saying very little. Very few were keen enough to observe that he had had very little chance. His mother talked most of the time, his sister Louisa Gammons talked all the rest of the time, and beyond that there were several interferences by his own garrulous wife and daughters. His brother Henry had a blacksmith shop, and he talked all the time. The youngest of the Humphrey brood, Lafayette, was never known by any name other than "Boss." He never married, rarely spoke, and lived with his mother until she reached almost the century mark, she doing not only the spinning for Eve's part but the delving for Adam's as well. She hoed in the garden in her nineties while Boss sat around listening. Mrs. Humphrey lived only two doors away from us and affected the idiosyncracy of keeping a dinner bell on the house just as though she were still living on the farm and not in town. Three times a day that bell spoke out to summon Boss home to eat. All of us knew exactly what it said. It had been taught by Mrs. Humphrey herself. Its song was staccato, allegro:

> Run, Boss, run,
> The pig tail's done;
> If you don't run,
> You won't get none.

It was for me to discover, however, that Pete would talk if none of his family was around. He liked to go fishing, and I now suppose that everybody thought that that too was part of his search for silent solitude; but I went fishing with him and found that he could talk, talk, talk, just as much as any other Humphrey. Pete Humphrey was a realist, and his tales of his life as a soldier and his being shot while storming the castle of Chapultepec in the Mexican War gave me to think that perhaps, after all, it wasn't absolutely necessary for me to take up the profession of arms. I listened to Pete and decided to be an explorer. Pete Humphrey went to California in '49, across the plains, and was a survivor of a party more than half the members of which perished on the journey. He came back by ship and by the Isthmus of Panama and had survived not only the dangers of the deep but the pestilences of the jungle. Then he had gone again across the plains, not horseback this time but in a wagon train, and back by ship that went round the Horn. He had seen many things, even some of the gold of which he had got for himself so very little that there was none to bring home. He had fought in the wars again, in the Federal army in the Civil War. He not only told me his tales but he told me also that he didn't like being a soldier but that he did like going places. The last time I saw him, many, many years after our fishing expeditions along Greasy Creek were over, he told me the most marvelous tale of all, of how at eighty-eight he had driven to California and back in a Model-T Ford. It is a pity that he never did it by Pullman, and more's the pity that he did not live to do it by airplane.

As I live over those days in memory, one odd thing strikes me. I would be a soldier, an officer, of course, and preferably a general; I would be an explorer and go to far places, preferably to Africa and Asia; but I never was an Indian fighter. I don't know why unless it was that Sitting Bull had just come to the end of the chapter at the Battle of Wounded Knee and that that was a part of my own newspaper-gained knowledge. The West at that time was a land of romance for me, what with the visual aid of Frederick Remington's illustrations and Peter Humphrey's tales, but I never wanted to fight Indians, and I didn't particularly want to go to California, which was where every other one of my contemporaries firmly intended to go. As a matter of fact, most of them did.

I didn't. I wanted to go east. I wanted to go to Washington, to New York, to London, to Paris.

CHAPTER III

...AND FROM BOOKS, TOO

To read was my passion—overwhelming, compelling, ruling. Of the very earliest things I read, I remember nothing but the news—the news of the presidential campaign of 1884. I suppose, of course, that there must have been some books, if only a child's picture-and-story book, but of such my memory retains no trace.

Then came my illness. I remember, still with a tinge of bitterness, that I was not permitted to read during those long weeks in bed, as I also recall with gratitude that the first thing they let me do when I began to sit up was to read and not only that but to read books.

The first books that came to me as a reward when I began to get over rheumatic fever were four from a uniform series, printed in large type and profusely illustrated. They had in common the characteristic subtitle, "In Words of One Syllable." They had been written down for children, and while, of course, they actually contained some words of more than one syllable, they were much oversimplified. They were *A History of the United States, A History of France, Pilgrim's Progress,* and *Robinson Crusoe.* I swallowed them whole. The history of the United States wasn't so good, because, of course, when it came to the Civil War, I already knew a lot more than the history book; but the others I accepted at full value. It was too bad, because it meant that to this day I have not read through from beginning to end either of the great classics *Pilgrim's Progress* or *Robinson Crusoe.*

In our town *The Chatterbox* was a standard Christmas present for any child who liked to read or whose parents were trying to persuade him to do so. It consisted of fifty-two weekly numbers of an English child's magazine, bound together as an annual for sale in the United States. It was fun to chase the continued stories helter-skelter through the book, but here again most of the details have left me except those

[53]

that had to do with history or politics. For instance, there was a series, which ran nearly throughout a year, of illustrated articles on the story of the French Revolution—articles that caused me to weep with sympathy for Marie Antoinette, to recoil with horror from the excesses of the Terror, and even at the end to bear a lingering hope that some day a son of St. Louis would ascend, not to Heaven, but to the throne of France. I have not seen it since, but I well remember a full-page picture of the aged and decrepit Charles X sitting in a chair with blankets and shawls about him, with his hand on the head of a kneeling little boy, the Comte de Chambord, while the King looked up toward the martial assembly of his generals as he said, "Keep the crown safe for Henri V." But it wasn't long until I was all wrought up over the threat to my new love, Republican France, from the "Man on Horseback," General Boulanger, news of whose doings was in the newspapers every day as I approached the age of ten.

After the children's books, I began by devouring the books we had at home. Among these were several sets of books: the works of Irving, Cooper, and Scott, with an odd assortment of novels, volumes of poems, old textbooks, and the like. In popular terms, the classes in school were denominated by *McGuffey's Readers,* so that a child, instead of saying that he was in such-and-such a grade, if asked where he stood in school, would reply, "I am in the Third Reader" or "in the Fifth Reader." I went through all six of the *McGuffey's Readers,* when by rights I should have been devoted to the Second or Third Reader alone. And of course there were the newspapers and the magazines which had first claim, especially after I began "carrying the papers."

Every Sunday came the *Sunday School Visitor,* and in our family, with Father a Disciple and Mother a Methodist, both the *Christian Evangelist* and the *Christian Advocate,* each of which ran an excellent comic column. A whole world opened up for me when at seven or eight I found Charles Dickens' *Child's History of England,* and from that time on, if a book had the word "history" in the title, I was sure to prefer it to all others. Then I found out to my huge delight that some novels were historical, too, and I plunged into Scott, at least through *The Talisman* and *Ivanhoe* and *Quentin Durward.* Why in the world it should have been so I cannot in retrospect imagine, but I did take up Washington Irving's *Sketchbook* before I tackled Cooper or Scott except for the two novels about Richard the Lionhearted and the one about Louis XI.

I knew my kings and queens of England from Egbert to Victoria as well as my Presidents from Washington to Cleveland, but I didn't neglect the juvenile books at all. I am sure, too, that my delight in Frances Hodgson Burnett's *Little Lord Fauntleroy* or Thomas Nelson Page's *Two Little Confederates* was no whit diminished because they came to me years after, when I gulped each of them in half a day in betwixt all sorts of grown-up matter.

The trouble was that I read too much. Or at least that was what all the grownups decided when my "nervousness" seemed to be getting worse instead of better. An oculist came from Springfield, and, while he put glasses on my farsighted younger brother, he didn't seem to think that my astigmatic eyes required any aid. I went on reading.

Then Dr. Gatewood put his foot down and said that I was ill because I was reading too much and that I must not read. There was, of course, the compromise that permitted me to look through the newspapers every day, but books were forbidden, and I was ordered to play with the boys. I did go to play with the boys. In fact, I never had entirely stopped it even for my books, and with them I found that my reading had done me no harm. Out of *Ivanhoe* and *The Talisman* I reconstructed the pomp and circumstance of the chivalric field of honor. I organized the boys into Crusaders and Saracens and managed somehow or other myself to control just who on a particular day would be Richard Cœur de Lion and who Saladin. I did not in the least regret the absence of horses, and the other boys did not miss them, since all our knights were well provided with lances—the long, straight, tough stems of Indian hemp. A tilt with these was adventurous and sometimes resulted in scratches and bruises, but it was always huge fun.

(How in the world was it that, while we smoked corn silk, grape-vine stalks, and even the leaves of lobelia—which we called "Indian tobacco" —we never once tried to smoke the leaves of Indian hemp which we stripped in such great quantities for our lances? Hemp was only a weed left over from an earlier day when it had been grown in Dallas County for its fiber by immigrants from Kentucky. Even then I knew that it was the very plant, *Cannabis indica,* from which the oriental hashish was made, but I am sure that I must have supposed that it had to go through some difficult process of distillation. At any rate, it never was turned into "reefers." What that abundant supply of marihuana would have done to us, I tremble to think!)

Everybody in town was told of Dr. Gatewood's edict that I should read no more books. Everybody promised not to lend me any books. But the prohibition was not to be borne. I had to read. I went underground.

Nobody in the town had a collection of books large enough to be dignified by the word "library," but in many of the houses there was a bookcase or a bookcase-secretary full of books, and these, at Mother's request, were locked up to keep me out of them. That seriously curtailed my supply.

There was always available the Holy Bible, which they didn't suspect would tempt me too much and which, of course, could not be forbidden. I had had a good deal of the carefully selected extracts of the Bible that came in Sunday-school lessons, but now I retreated to the attic with the Holy Book, and I read it all the way through—something that I was to repeat more than once.

I discovered other treasures in Mrs. Tom Brown's attic, to which I had access from the back yard without her knowledge. There were the back numbers of *Century* magazine through the late seventies and eighties and in them, of course, in the separate articles by the great generals of the two armies, North and South, the history of the Civil War. That was my meat.

There was another whole category of books scattered about the town that nobody suspected that I would care to read and which the owners so rarely looked at that they never missed a volume that I had sneaked out. Dr. Gatewood's office was in a one-room building detached from all others, the door always open and the doctor rarely in. His medical library was not large, but, as I purloined a volume at a time and made away with it to my hideout, I discovered that medical books and their illustrations could be extremely interesting indeed. I decided to be a doctor.

Likewise the lawyers' offices were always unlocked and the lawyers rarely in, so that I began to read law. A measure of what I read for the mere sake of reading may be taken from the fact that, laboring under my compulsion, I doggedly and determinedly read most of Blackstone without, I am sure, understanding a sentence or a paragraph. This discouraged me, but I found the *Revised Statutes of the United States* a little easier going, and, although I had wavered, I again decided to be a lawyer.

Among the boys of my own age was Albert Hopwood, whose father was the pastor of the Christian church. Elder Hopwood had a great many books, and, until the edict was issued, he had been most generous in lending them to me and in helping me understand and comprehend some of them. He was soft-spoken and in his slow, drawling voice helped me through many of my literary problems and vexations. But, of course, when Mother asked him to shut off the source of supply, he complied instantly. In fact, he, too, locked the doors of his secretary-bookcase. There were, though, some big volumes bound in calfskin that were on the lower shelf which had no doors. I succeeded in corrupting my friend Albert and not only him but his sisters, Cordie and Carrie, just older and just younger than he, to the extent that one of the girls would take out a book, leave it where Albert could get it, and Albert would bring it to me. In that way I acquired and read Josephus' *Antiquities of the Jews* and, most wonderful of all, Gibbon's *Decline and Fall of the Roman Empire.* Since the Hopwood family moved away from Buffalo early in 1889, I could not have been over nine at the time I read these things.

So also belonged to this period my reading of other books that, under any circumstances, would have been forbidden—the blood-and-thunder dime novels. These too I read when I couldn't get anything else to read, although I never liked them very much. Their staccato sentences bored me, and their clichés enraged me, as their bad Indians always became good Indians by the same process of "biting the dust." It was simply that I had to read and that I didn't intend to let anybody tell me that I mustn't read. Incidentally, of course, the dime novels didn't have any special charm as forbidden fruit, since all other books were equally touched by that magic.

There was, however, the "Seaside Library." The "Seaside Library" was published periodically so as to take advantage of the second-class postal rates. Of course, the cheap paperbound book always had been available in Europe, but it was also available in the United States when I came along. The "Seaside Library" was subscribed to by the drugstores as well as by several individuals in the town. The drugstores sold the volumes for twenty-five cents. The individuals who took the whole series read some of them, gave some away, and just let the others lie around. No such care was taken of them as was taken of the bound books, and so it was easy for me to get my itching fingers on them. Within these paperbound books I found Dumas and lived vicariously the adventurous life of Edmond Dantes and shared the dangerous days of D'Artagnan, Porthos, Athos, and Aramis. Here I breasted the ice of arctic seas and the hot sun of African deserts with McClintock and Stanley, to say nothing of both Algeria and the mystic beyond with Marie Corelli.

And all the time I read poetry. In many homes a bound volume of poems, sometimes in a very ornate leather binding, was used as an ornament of a parlor table—but rarely for reading. My selection thus being determined largely by availability, I read the collected poems of Mrs. Hemans and Mrs. Sigourney, as well as those of Moore and Burns, Byron and Tennyson, and both the Brownings. I read Longfellow and Lowell and Poe and Pope's *Essay on Man*. I read Milton and, in translation, of course, Dante and Tasso. I even read Ossian.

Of Shakespeare's works, scattered everywhere about and always available, I read little. I don't know what then was in my mind as I rejected the works of the greatest of the poets. However, the fact that I did read the sonnets, "Venus and Adonis," and "The Rape of Lucrece," leads me to believe that I simply couldn't make out what the dramatic poems were about. I had never seen a play, I had no one to help me in my forbidden pursuit, and I suppose that I simply gave up because I couldn't understand what it all meant. Of course, I got little out of all this poetry. I was a child and I couldn't understand it, but what I did like was the flow of words, the rhymes and the cadences, and, of course, under my compulsion, the sheer reading of it. Perhaps it was because even from babyhood I had been taught to recite poetry that it was the poems alone that I read slowly enough to read aloud, and in that way I must have savored something of the artistry of poesy even if its purpose, portent, and philosophy were beyond me. Most of these poets I have never since looked into, and therefore my knowledge of them is a knowledge rather of form than of substance. What came to me afterward from the poets is a part of a later phase.

Of course Dr. Gatewood and the family were all wrong about the reading. Whatever it was, it wasn't the reading that made me worse. But when I got better, as I did when I got to be about ten years old, they thought and continued to think that it was because they had

stopped my reading. As a matter of fact, at about that time my whole
range of interests widened considerably. There had to be more time for
play with the boys—and with the girls, too. There had to be more time
for the drugstore, the cobbler shop, the marble shop, the carpenter, the
painter, and all that.

The year 1889, when I was ten, was thick-studded with mileposts for
me. In that year my elder brother was married. My health improved,
and the prohibition of books was repealed. If now in my seventies
someone should ask me suddenly, "What most distinguished the year
1889?" I would answer instantly, I am quite sure, that Benjamin Harrison succeeded Grover Cleveland as President of the United States.
That would be, however, only because of a lifelong habit of associating
particular years (or even particular telephone numbers) with particular political events.

I would have said also that it meant the year when four new stars
shone in the flag—Washington, Montana, and the two Dakotas, the
latter seeming strange and odd to me, for two states spelled "Dakota"
to take the place of one great big territory spelled "Dacotah."

I would also be reminded of that early morning of May 31, 1889,
when Mother dressed my younger brother and me carefully and im-
maculately in new, white summer suits, and we set out with her and
Father to walk to the house where my elder brother, Joe, was to be
married. The day before had been Decoration Day, and I had followed the blue-clad Grand Army of the Republic march through
the square to the cemetery, later to trudge the long way back home,
wet with sweat and all but exhausted by the trying heat of a day
worthy of mid-August. It was cooler that morning of the wedding.
It was cooler as we walked through the town toward the house, and
it was cold when we got there, perhaps a half-hour before the ceremony. It got colder and colder. I shivered, and my teeth chattered,
and somehow I found my way into the kitchen, where Uncle Henry
Lovan, always thin and always cold, was warming himself by the
kitchen stove. After the ceremony the bride and the bridegroom
climbed into the surrey that was to take them the long twenty miles
to the railroad for their honeymoon trip, and Aunt Mary Lovan
wrapped me in a blanket so that I could get home without freezing.

That hot May 30 and that cold May 31 in my Ozark village were
parts of the great storm that swept the country and which found its

tragic and imperishable monument in the great Pennsylvania disaster of the Johnstown Flood.

When Joe and Bertha came back and set up housekeeping in the house next door to us, a new day dawned for me. Joe had never had any patience with Dr. Gatewood and the others for keeping me away from books, and, when he set up his own establishment, there was not only Bertha, kindly, sweet, and tolerant toward all children and especially toward me, but something else. The first thing Joe did for his new home was to buy a set of the Ninth Edition of the *Encyclopaedia Britannica,* and around it he brought in the books that he had bought and lent out to Tom, Dick, and Harry all over the town and the county, together with a bushel basket of paperbound books out of the "Seaside Library," to which he was a direct subscriber. I moved in.

Thus in the summer of 1889 I achieved freedom to read. That newfound freedom brought with it freedom to talk about what I was reading with anybody who could be persuaded to listen. Consequently, I began to ask questions, to enter into discussions, and to find out how many things I knew that weren't so. For instance, in the matter of the pronunciation of words, many of which I had never heard, I had ascribed to their printed symbols sounds that never before had been uttered in the English tongue. When I used such words, I was to be laughed at and humiliated as well as corrected and reproved. More than a half-century later, every little while, I still bring into my talk some word which I will endow with my own peculiar infantile pronunciation, to be greeted with a lifted eyebrow or sometimes an astonished but superior chuckle.

Of even greater importance, as I see it now, was the fact that, when the necessity for surreptitious reading came to an end, I was in part relieved of the compulsion to read. No longer was it necessary for me to read practically all the time; no longer was I to count an hour lost from reading as something that had to be caught up. With the relief from this compulsion, for the first time I began to be interested in the subject matter of what I read, in the communication of fact and idea rather than primarily in the number of books I could get through.

While I was thus early relieved of a compelling necessity that seems now to me to have been almost pathological, I was never to recover from it completely. The experience left traces of a compulsive pattern which has manifested itself in at least two ways throughout my life. One is that I have never been able to skip about through a book, whether guided by fingers and eyes, as I see some casual readers do, or whether instructed by inspection of tables of contents and outlines of chapters, as I see other careful students do. If I read a book at all, I am compelled to start at the first page and read straight through to the last word on the last page.

The need to read a book all the way through fortunately was counterbalanced by the early acquisition of the trick of reading with extreme rapidity. Then, in turn, rapid reading by very necessity drove me away from the books and articles in which the sequence of word symbols is interrupted by symbols which by their essential nature require a longer time to take in. This had a determining influence upon the things that I would read and would learn. It perhaps can best be illustrated by what the *Encyclopaedia Britannica* has meant to me.

When my brother Joe first bought it, I conceived the project of reading it through from beginning to end. I am sorry I do not remember precisely where I met with my comeuppance, but I am sure in my own mind that it was some article on mathematics, probably algebra. Nonetheless, it was all an exciting experience.

The Ninth Edition of the *Britannica*—as needs must with the knowledge of the world caught and fixed, as it were, in an instant by the printing press of 1870—revealed a world of history and literature and art, of religions, politics, and war; but for all that a world admittedly limited even in the knowledge of its own geography by the great blank spaces of the unexplored regions on the globe.

The outward boundaries of my curiosity led me to attempt to relate with experimental eye some of the wonders of astronomy that I found in the *Encyclopaedia*. But the identification of the constellations of the heavens by name was enough, and I lacked the drive to pursue through the mathematical articles which simply could not be read a line at a time even though they might have made the story of the stars more meaningful to me.

The inward boundaries were determined by the inadequacy of my experimental laboratory equipment that I got as a premium for getting subscribers to the *Youth's Companion,* and there would have been nobody to tell me how to use it had it been better. My test-tube adventures seemed always to be in search of explosives, searches too suddenly and too successfully rewarded. The *Encyclopaedia* articles on chemistry in the Ninth Edition were, of course, nothing like so cluttered up with symbols as they are today; but here again mere words were not enough, and I had no instructor, no laboratory except of my own contriving. While curiosity of a sort endured, attempts personally to satisfy it soon perished.

After all, that edition of the *Encyclopaedia* didn't know what Pasteur was to find out about the effect upon the bodies of the Lords of Creation of the very little plants and animals; it didn't know that Bell and Hertz and Marconi were so to extend the range of the human voice as to make it possible for one man to speak instantaneously to many other men; it didn't know even that Lord Kelvin and the Curies were then beginning to develop those formulas that were to eventuate in the fission of the atom and the mastery of the terrestrial by the infinitesimal, even before my days of searching the *Encyclopaedia* were to end.

Two other "works" in addition to the *Britannica* tempted me to skip about and read not what I opened them to find but what I might find after they were opened. One was Webster's *Unabridged Dictionary* and the other was *The Compendium of the Census of 1880*. Exceptions, perforce, to my habit of reading through from beginning to end, they yet tempted me to browse far afield from any purposeful resort to reference. There were several big dictionaries in the town, although none at our house. Only one of them, however, was set on its own stand, a metal contrivance that held it ready to be opened and hospitably inclined at an angle inviting to the eye. This marvel was a part of the office equipment of George Edmisson, a huge man whose good humor was deemed to be a trifle the better part of his professional stock in trade than was his profundity in the law. He had also a son, Felix, a little my senior and a fellow of great heart whose kindness to me was as genuine as it was blustery. It was he who gave me the run of the office and the use of that magnificent new dictionary.

George Edmisson had another piece of office equipment. It was a Smith-Premier typewriter. It was the only typewriter in Buffalo. Felix taught me to use it and gave me free rein to practice, in return for which I volunteered occasional copying jobs to help him with his study of the law. And then he in turn helped me in my study of the law. For then I had decided to be a lawyer. Of that smattering of looking to lawbooks but few traces remain. There is the name "Greenleaf" forever associated with Evidence; a dim recollection of an unsuccessful bout with the Rule in Skelly's Case and a much clearer memory (because refreshed in later years) of my first dip into Robert's *Rules of Order*. That Colonel Robert wrote his manual to help the struggling beginnings of the Citizens' Associations in the District of Columbia, I had, of course, no notion. That I should become in time, as Colonel Robert had been, a Commissioner of the District of Columbia and deal with those same Citizens' Associations, I could not possibly have imagined.

But the dictionary was my meat. I sought it to find the meanings of strange new words; I looked to it once in a while as a crutch to my crippled spelling, even now and then for help in pronunciation. But most of all it was to find new words, old words that had for me secret and mystical meanings hidden behind such symbols as "(obs.)" and "(archaic)"—words that I thought might be known only to me that I might spill to the discomfiture of my opponents in a chance argument, or startling words to be sprinkled like pepper and salt to enhance the flavor of the letters that I was ever writing. All this served me well in widening the range of my vocabulary and in giving me a feeling for words, but it came too soon to be retained as a habit of maturity, and I later lacked the self-discipline to keep it up that a good teacher might have instilled in me.

I adore words, but I have not wooed them with that ardent assiduity which alone can induce them to requite the passion. Thus I now fumble for the right one when I might have had it leaping instant to my tongue's end had I but been taught aright. This is one of the major lets and lacks in my education.

The *Census* was in some twenty or twenty-five fat, black-bound books that collectively filled two whole big mailbags when they came to my father under the frank of his old friend, Congressman Bland. A shelf was built for them in the back hall, and I began at once to steep myself in statistics. Eager to discover what were the figures, I made Dallas County the center and Missouri the epicenter of the nation, and I learned by rote what still stays with me, the alphabetical disposition of states and counties as well as their arbitrary spacing in the listing by which the eye was enabled the easier to track down its quarry.

What contribution to my education was made by the specific statistical information I gleaned from this search of the *Census of 1880* I do not know, but I am sure that the habit it induced has had a marked and permanent effect. It has kept me curious through more than sixty years to see what any statistical table may contain and has contributed to a certain trick of memory which has enabled me to retain a visual picture of a table of figures in my mind, from which by conscious effort I can educe particular figures. It has been a useful habit in that it has given me a storage bin full of all sorts and conditions of statistical oddments which come to my aid in checking the significance of newly found facts of the same general type.

The same habit has enabled me to "keep books in my head," as so many of my accounting and budgetary aides have called it in later years. The way the trick works is this: If there is a need to recall what was spent for a certain purpose in a certain year, and if I cannot at once remember the figure, I reconstruct the budget summary for that year. First I bring back by conscious effort the net balancing figure, black or red. From it I build up the principal summary items on both sides, income and expenditure, and, from that table which I can see and read in my mind's eye, I frequently can find the figure that it was needed to recall. Of course this is not an infallible process, and I never relied upon it for final action without checking with the books. Nevertheless, it has been one of the most useful tricks of the trade to me as an administrator, enabling me to check the oral reports of subordinates as they are made without dragging in the bookkeepers. It is also a habit that, I suspect, must be acquired when one is about ten or eleven years old. It has its amusing side in the startled facial expression of an accountant, who already knows that I can't add a column of figures given pad and pencil, when I bring up from the past some set of figures that he has correctly computed but has forgotten in the process.

During the time when books were forbidden me, I found another secret treasure-house. That was the little bedroom Jim Morrow contrived to set up on the upper floor of the William L. Morrow store. Jim had come back from many voyages into the outer world. He was on the very best of terms with his mother, Mrs. Minerva Morrow, who lived just across the street, but he shared with her one idiosyncrasy. Neither Jim nor his mother liked to be regular at meals, nor for that matter did they have any particular desire to adhere to any fixed schedule as to their goings to bed and their gettings up in the mornings. In this, of course, they were individualistic in pursuing quite shocking ways contrary to the mores of the community. Since Mrs. Morrow had no particular meal hours, Jim gradually found his way to eating out in restaurants or hotels and, later on, discovered that it might be better for him if he didn't even sleep at home. So he rigged up, with a wooden partition, a room in the upstairs floor of the Morrow Block, as the two-story building in which his uncle's store was situated was called.

In this room was a bed, a table, and two or three shelves that served as a bookcase. And on these shelves were disposed Jim Morrow's library, several volumes—a dozen or more. Since he was never there in the daytime and since I could reach the unlocked and open door by a broad stairway which left visits unnoticed, I discovered those books.

There I found two great novels, two of the greatest, *Don Quixote* and *Les Misérables*. Still at that time under compulsion, I read each from the beginning to the end. I must confess that the great Spanish classic sometimes bored me. I liked the beginning. I liked the fun. I could grasp the ridiculous qualities of the great knight's identification of the sheep and the windmills with giants and with armies in full panoply, but I am a little bit afraid that even the repetitious dialogues of conflict between the noble Don and his faithful Sancho bored me. And I am quite certain that there was entirely too much about Dulcinea del Toboso.

But with the other novel, *Les Misérables,* it was entirely different. That tale entranced me from the beginning. The Bishop and his candlesticks made a good story as well as a most moving one—but all the rest of it was also a good story. Some persons, I have discovered, in talking about Victor Hugo's greatest work, turn to his description of the Battle of Waterloo as though it were almost the only thing in the book, just as I myself sometimes have turned to the Battle of Borodino as though it were the whole instead of merely an integral part of Tolstoy's great novel, *War and Peace*.

But to me, *Les Misérables* was much more than that battle. It engaged and held my boyish attention from beginning to end. The romantic mood which then was so engaging to me in Sir Walter Scott, which then was represented in my diffidence with respect to girls, was already in full flower so far as girls in books were concerned. While everybody in the town knew I was inordinately fond of flowers, I am quite sure that no one suspected why for nearly the whole of one summer I carried a rose in my mouth. It was not because I particularly liked the taste of the rose stems, not because I favored the fragrance of rose petals over that of many another flower, but because I was imitating Marius, the lover of Cosette. While I have reread a part of the book—the section concerning the Battle of Waterloo at least twice—I am sure that I never yet have gone through it all. And so, out of my early boyhood, I discover myself remembering my identification with Marius and suffering with him that dreadful experience in the sewers of Paris when the novelist sums up the character of his young hero in a line—I cannot quote it exactly—which after sixty years I remember as this: "The water came in through the soles of his shoes, but the stars shone through his soul."

There were four other books in Jim Morrow's forbidden library, which was no more out of bounds to me than was any other library in the town. One was an abridgment of Bullfinch's *Mythology*. I devoured it. The other two were translations of collections of tales which certainly would have been forbidden to me had not all other books been under a similar interdict. One was the *Heptameron of the Queen of Navarre,* and the other *The Decameron of Boccaccio.* Thus Jim Morrow contributed to my education by unknowingly permitting me access to his choice little library.

My friends the books, found here and there, sometimes in strange company, were indeed my close friends during those four years from the time I was ten until a sharp change was to come when I went to work at fourteen. Thus my friends the books were my counselors, my guides, my molds, when, with Tennyson,

> . . . I dipt into the future, far as human eye could see,
> Saw the Vision of the world, and all the wonder that would be.

The experience of sharing with others by questions and discussion the things that I read was definitely made important to me by another event in that same year of 1889. My mother became a member of the local chapter of the Chautauqua Literary and Scientific Circle.

... And from Books, Too

At that time the word "Chautauqua" was the shibboleth of middle-class small city and rural culture in the United States. There was not only the great Chautauqua Assembly itself at Lake Chautauqua in New York, but there were the other assemblies at lake and mountain resorts throughout the country where people were invited at one and the same time to restore their bodies and improve their minds. There were also the Chautauqua lecture platforms that sprang up all over the country to bring entertainment and knowledge to the populace under the big tent top—the Chautauqua circuit that was to rise to its zenith at the turn of the century, with the Swiss bell-ringers and Mr. William Jennings Bryan as its chief attractions.

There were also the local chapters of the Circle. These were created by the organizing genius of Bishop John H. Vincent, the chancellor, and they were to be found all over the country in big towns and little. In Buffalo the initiative was taken by a lawyer, Mr. O. H. Scott, and the Circle had five or six members. Each member became a subscriber to the monthly magazine, the *Chautauquan,* and each purchased the books that were to be used as texts for home study and for the discussions in the local Circle. These discussions were sharpened up by a series of questions based upon the text of the outline of study, questions which were printed in each monthly number of the *Chautauquan,* the definitive answers to which would follow in the next monthly issue.

The meetings of our Buffalo Circle were held in the homes of the various members but most frequently at Mr. Scott's house, and, as nothing in the world could have prevented my reading my mother's textbooks and the *Chautauquan,* so nothing short of actual physical control could have prevented my attending all the meetings of the Circle. Once there, nothing could have stopped my talking, nor, I must say in grateful remembrance, did Mr. Scott try to keep me quiet. On the other hand, he and Mrs. Billy Morrow and Mrs. Billy O'Bannon and Mrs. Jim Ballard and the others actually encouraged me. During the two or three years that this Circle continued its life and I attended its weekly meetings, we read the texts of several books, and of course I read every word of them as well as every word of the monthly *Chautauquan* as it came out.

We read the concluding chapters of *The American Commonwealth* by James Bryce published especially for the *Chautauquan* under the title, "Social Institutions of the United States." We read *Political Economy* by Richard T. Ely, also in a special edition prepared for the *Chautauquan,* one of the earlier of his many revisions, made just after he had left Johns Hopkins and at a time when some timid souls were wont to shy away from "Ely the radical." Thirty years later I provoked him to the verge of apoplexy by proclaiming one night in the Cosmos Club in Washington, D.C., some sound principles of economics that I had thought derived directly from his work. Still later, when he was in his eighties and I saw more of him, he seemed to enjoy my twitting him about what an evil influence he had had upon me in my young boyhood. Dr. Ely, the octogenarian, pushing his newly born son in the baby buggy about the walks of Radburn, our town for the motor age, seemed sufficiently satisfied with himself and his works not to mind my joking him on the robust youngster that I called his eighty-second edition.

We also read and discussed three outline histories, one of Rome, one of England, and one of the United States, collections of outline material by various authors, edited by Bishop Vincent and members of his Chautauqua staff. I remembered the substance without remembering the names of the authors, so, as I had got my first glimpses of Malthus and Adam Smith from Mr. Ely and knew it, I find on recent inquiry that I got my first picture of the English constitution from Woodrow Wilson and had forgot it, just as I got my Rome from President Adams of Cornell and my America from many contemporary scholars and historians whose names have not come down with me through the years. Nothing was so provoking and intriguing as the America that I found all around me, through the eyes of James Bryce or the "very present help in time of trouble" that Ely gave me in my arguments with the Republicans about the protective tariff.

The help of Ely in the matter of political arguments was an advantage which I did not hesitate to press in street-corner and sidewalk debates with my elders as well as with a few choice spirits among the young who also were inflamed by the political campaign of 1892. Indeed, Mr. Scott, who was the leader of the Chautauqua Circle, thought I had got entirely too much Free Trade indoctrination out of Ely, for he was a Republican, albeit a mild and gentle controversialist; so he sought to correct my views and induce me toward Protectionism by giving me *The History of Protective Tariff Laws* by R. W. Thompson. Rightly or wrongly, I read Thompson with a jaundiced eye, believing him to be little if anything better than a Republican propagandist. My mentor's well-meaning efforts had but little effect upon me.

But the most permanent and enduring influence of the Chautauquan reading in my life and thought was Bryce. The history that had so absorbed my imagination had been that history in which my immature and boyish imagination was captured by the heroes who were the protagonists of the struggle for power. These heroes in the main, of course, were soldiers, kings and captains, generals and admirals who at one time or another had led the hosts in the struggle between nations or in revolutions against tyrants. My concept of a nation was naturally naïve. To me republican and imperial Rome as well as medieval England and France were nations in the modern sense such as my own United States. This made *Quentin Durward* hard to understand, and it was long, long before I corrected for myself Sir Walter Scott's romantic bias against Louis XI and his drive to destroy the counties, the feudal baronies and duchies, in order to create a nation in France.

Lacking the tutelage of a proper pedagogue, I owe a great deal indeed to Bryce. Reading his book as closely as I did and discussing it in the Circle as we did, I got for the first time a sense of the impact of history and politics on social institutions and the relation of these social institutions to the way in which men and women and children lived their everyday lives at home, even in such a backwoods home as we had in the Ozarks. The experience of that book taken together with some things that were happening to me at the same time with respect to my religious beliefs caused me ever thereafter, for good or for ill, for right or for wrong, to apply to every event that transpired a test of social utility: Did it help the ordinary man to climb upward to better things, or did it throw further obstacles in his path?

After that book, for me no more Napoleonic nonsense—already I had had enough of that to cause me later to suffer a tug at the heart in reading *Les Misérables* and even, I fear I must confess, many, many, years later in reading *War and Peace*. Not even Carlyle, whose *Heroes and Hero Worship* I read at almost the same time, could overcome the influence of the great English observer who was earlier than any American to appraise the accomplishment of the American man in the American continent and to point out his almost limitless possibilities. I was not to read De Tocqueville for decades thereafter, nor would the great Frenchman have made such an impression upon me, for I could see Bryce and his work all around me as well as in the newspapers that I read and in the awakening awareness of people and things that came to me in the ordinary process of growing up.

In those same years of 1889 to 1893, from the time I began to pay attention to what I was reading until I went to work, there were four periodicals other than the *Chautauquan* which I read from "kiver to kiver" and missed nary a word. One was a weekly, the *Youth's Companion,* and that of course was mainly fiction, inspirational and improving articles for the young, and odd bits of unsorted information. I regarded it as entertainment pure and simple. Two were monthlies —the *Century* magazine and the *Art Amateur.* One was a quarterly —the *Homiletic Review.*

The *Century* was a marvelous magazine. Old numbers ranging back into the seventies I had devoured during the period of my surreptitious reading, but, except for some of the articles about the Civil War, they left little in my memory. But, when Joe married and became a subscriber to the *Century,* I came for three or four years to share in the wide-ranging, deep, and lofty interests of that greatest of American editors, Richard Watson Gilder. Of the things that through all the years I have remembered and identified with the *Century* were Nicolay and Hay's "Life of Lincoln," the exposure of the horrors of Siberia by George Kennan, and the opening of the windows of the world on Tibet by W. W. Rockhill. The Lincoln, coming to me early, was perhaps a necessary antidote to my word-of-mouth history of the Civil War which I could not help absorbing from my parents and their tragic experiences in the South. At any rate, it made Lincoln one of my principal heroes and that without invalidating my emotional devotion to Lee—a process infinitely easier now than it could have been then, not a quarter of a century after Appomattox.

Kennan was doubly significant in that he was helping to explore the unknown, blank places on the map and at the same time was painstaking in his revelation of the horrors of the czarist regime as they bore down upon the little peoples of all the Russias. Rockhill's travels in Tibet and Mongolia were a sheer delight in exploration, not the least because they were accompanied by such marvelous illustrations.

At that time I decided to be an explorer. As a matter of fact, I was a little closer to the terra incognita than one finds it easy in the mid-twentieth century to imagine. Only a little more than one hundred miles away lay the Indian Territory. And in 1889 in the very middle of the Indian Territory there was opened for settlement a tract of land known as Oklahoma. For a while it had almost no government worthy of the name. It was wild and untamed; it was open, and the land was free; and, even when the territory of Oklahoma was established by the Congress in 1890, no man could be quite sure whether to put his ultimate dependence in the writ of the United States marshal or in the resources of his own hip pocket. One thing was sure, and that was that there was not enough land; and the deepening depression that led to the panic of 1893 was measured step by step and march by march by the opening to the whites of more land in the Indian Territory until the climactic rush of 1893, when the opening of the Cherokee Strip ended the epoch.

But back to my reading. It was only of Lincoln, of Siberia, and of Tibet that I remembered throughout all the years my debt to the *Century* magazine. However, as I have been writing these memoirs, I have again glanced through the volumes for those years. I find so many things that were part of memory, but I had forgot whence they came. Among such priceless treasures were Joseph Pennell's travels with pencil and with sketchbook among the cathedrals of England and the châteaux of France; one of my earliest puzzled adventures with the subtleties of the psychological novel with Henry James in *The Anglomaniacs,* illustrated more understandingly (to me) by a pre-Gibson-Girl Charles Dana Gibson; the delightful stories of Harry Stillwell Edwards and Young E. Allison, both of whom were later to be numbered among my good friends; and the joint creation of "Uncle Remus" by Joel Chandler Harris and E. W. Kemble.

The *Art Amateur* came into my ken through my new sister-in-law, Bertha, and for three years I devoured its every word and absorbed in one way or another almost every picture. The *Art Amateur* was consciously devoted to the cultivation of art in the household, and what Bertha particularly wanted of it had to do with china painting and with embroidery. Of these topics every month there were not only articles of instruction but designs and patterns actually to be employed.

But the scope of this monthly magazine was by no means limited to such helpful hints. Each month the magazine brought with it at least one large reproduction in color of a painting. Most of those found their way into frames and onto the walls of some house in the town, while others were models for copying.

One of the things I did was to attempt slavish copies of the colored supplements that came with the *Art Amateur* or pictures of the kind that I would pick up anywhere. So far as I know, there is but one surviving example of my painting in oils. It is, I fondly believe—and a recent look at it has done nothing to shake my faith—a rather good picture of a white cow wading in a brook in the foreground, while a luscious green pasture stretches away to the background. Others who see it now say that the cow is not white but green; that the brook seems to be filled with concrete, not water; and that the pasture, instead of being covered with green grass, seems to be the sear and yellow aftermath of a prairie fire. Nevertheless, I thought it good then, and I still think it good.

I was determined not only to paint but also to draw with pen and ink. My monthly mentor overflowed with samples of the pen-and-ink drawings that were just beginning to be reproduced by photoengraving and thus to reflect that great liberty of line that was impossible when reproduction depended upon engraving on wood or steel, and which likewise gave a new freedom in choice of subject not known to the etchers or the lithographers. So with India ink and crow-quill pens and Bristol board I set about to capture this skill, but again I was to be defeated not only by a lack of inspiration but by the dogged habit of slavish copying.

My absorption in the *Art Amateur* taught me just as I was coming into my teens to recognize instantly the style of many of the masters, old and new, and to put on an equal footing for my own enjoyment mastery of line and form and color, whether in painting or sculpture or tapestry, whether of a building or its façade or its furniture.

One of the books that we had in the Chautauqua Circle was called *How To Judge a Picture* by Henry Van Dyke. Most of the pictures that I had any chance to judge were those that came in or with the *Art Amateur,* but I did not permit the lack of gallery to diminish my interest, much of which of necessity I pursued in secret. In fact, it was not until after I had moved the easel from the place where it was publicly set up in my brother's home to my attic atelier that I attempted to copy a Rembrandt head—and I blush as I write the words.

One thing more all this did for me. The *Art Amateur* and Henry Van Dyke sent me to Ruskin to read about art, and I remained with Ruskin to learn about politics.

Nevertheless, as times got harder and harder, and we became poorer and poorer during that quadrennium of the Harrison administration from 1889 to 1893, I cannot now remember that the suffering or the deprivations, real as they were, ever burned into me as did the anguish of the fact that in 1893 my family was so poor that no one could even think of my going to Chicago to see the great World's Fair. It is easy to rekindle the fury of frustration with which I greeted those friends, who were richer and who could and did go to Chicago, when they came back. I asked them about the pictures in the Fine Arts Building, and they told me about the Ferris wheel on the Midway. I asked them about the buildings and the lagoons and the lights, and they sang to me Charles K. Harris' "After the Ball Is Over."

It must not be thought, because I have written so much about particular periodicals, that during this time I neglected either my newspapers or my books. These were just the right years, when I was eleven and twelve, for Dickens and Scott, just as the years of thirteen and fourteen were just right for Thackeray and Elliot, and I read them all or rather I seemed to live them all.

But I did not despise the literature of the moment. At that time even many of the good, solid, country Protestant people who still looked askance at novel-reading made exceptions in the case of the works of the Reverend E. P. Roe, and I followed him through the Chicago Fire, the Charleston earthquake, and mild love affairs in *Barriers Burned Away, The Earth Trembled,* and *He Fell in Love with His Wife.* More exciting, perhaps, because it was a foretaste of the regional novel yet to come and struck close to the Ozarks, was Opie Read with *Emmett Bonlore, The Arkansas Judge,* and *The Jucklins.*

My parents were not so entirely neglectful of my reading as might be supposed from what I have said about my own selections. Father had certain notions about what were good books to read as well as what were profitable, and he encouraged me to read the things that had to do with geography—the tales of the explorers and the like—as well as those that had to do with politics. He also tried to guide me to his favorite poets, and, when I would be talking excitedly about something in one of the Waverly novels, he would make me promise to read *Marmion* or *The Lady of the Lake;* and of course I liked the lilt of Scott and delighted to declaim "Young Lochinvar" and "Lord Ullin's Daughter."

To explore the earth and the wonders thereof in books was not, however, necessarily for me to travel into the unknown, for not only were the blank places on the map to be seen but the oldest of all the parts of the map were to be revisited. Those I had explored were west with Washington Irving in *Astoria* and *The Adventures of Captain Bonneville,* and with the same author I had stood beside Columbus and discovered our new world with the "Santa Maria," the "Niña," and the "Pinta," all in the quest of the unknown. It was also Washington Irving who taught me to go back to the old places of the earth to see what there might be seen, to old New York and to Sleepy Hollow, to old England, and in *The Alhambra* to keep trysts in the Court of Lions with not only Catholic Spain but Moslem Spain and Roman Spain as well.

Father liked to recite, too, and I learned from his lips rather than from reading not only "Oft in the Stilly Night" but many others of Moore's lyrics and Burns's songs. I also learned from him to say by rote a whole series of verses that in his mind were tied up with his own personal tragedy as a wounded and broken Rebel soldier—the verses of Thomas Buchanan Read, Fitzgreen Halleck, and Thomas Dunn English, as well as those of Father Ryan.

There were two reasons why both Father and Mother, who most of the time were entirely too busy to supervise my reading, even if I had been willing to give them a chance, took this trouble to teach me to declaim these pieces of poetry. One was the absolutely sufficient one that I couldn't sing and the other was, I am inclined to believe, that the extreme rapidity with which I read left them skeptical about how much of it I could possibly understand.

As pedagogues, both my parents thought that to teach me to recite the poems would have the effect of slowing me up, of making me remember, and of substituting something for the impatience with which they regarded my inability to carry a tune. This disability, which may possibly have been regretted in the family, was recognized by the general run of the community as represented in Sunday school and church, the community's decision that I be forever silenced being unanimous, instant, and unequivocal. The boys, when I was very little, used to try to encourage me to attempt to sing so that they could hoot at me with derision. There was one particular thing that I wanted so very much to sing, and I would try so hard and the boys would make so much fun of me that the song has a special place in my more poignant memories; it was "Ta Ra Ra Boom De Ay."

Mother too had her favorites among the poets. One of them, whose verses she taught me to recite and which still have for me a special quality, since their own haunting tunefulness is freighted with my memory of her contralto voice and her soft slow speech, was Poe. Father, with quite impartial ambivalence, alternated between a radical political creed of progress and a fatalistic philosophy of pessimism. In the latter mood he liked to stop me in my enthusiasms, or perhaps he thought it was his duty to check my runaway daydreaming, by quoting over and over, often and often:

Ye who listen, with credulity, to the whispers of fancy, and pursue, with eagerness, the phantoms of hope; who expect, that age will perform the promises of youth, and that the deficiencies of the present day will be supplied by the morrow, attend to the history of Rasselas, prince of Abissinia.

Father had a well-worn copy of *Rasselas,* and at his prompting I not only read but reread it and believed the tale about how Johnson had written it in one night to pay for the funeral expenses of his mother. But I was very young; I was the more thrilled by the illustrations in that particular copy—steel engravings, one of which portrayed under the stars the prince, led by his mentor, to the foot of the Pyramids. I was too young, too credulous, and entirely too hopeful to yield to pessimism, even when so cogently presented by the great Tory doctor.

I didn't pick up the book again for decades and did so then only because of the circumstance that I had caught with my mind's eye in the news of the day the fact that the Emperor Haile Selassie, when he was but a prince, had had the title of Ras and that his name was Selas, the same that the good doctor of Litchfield had writ, title and name together, in one word, "Rasselas." It was at this later time when the Emperor of Abyssinia was not yielding to pessimism but was pleading his case at Geneva before the League of Nations that in my last reading of the book I was caught up by the dissertation on the art of flying and its prediction that even captives of the happy valley of Amharie, Abyssinia, might one day be swarmed upon by a flight of northern savages lighting upon it with irresistible violence. And at the same time I found, too, that even the Johnsonian pessimism was lightened by the hope of learning.

CHAPTER IV

... BUT ALSO FROM PEOPLE

As I grew a little older, I found myself less preoccupied with my friends the books and more inclined to cultivate my friends the people of the town. There were social values to learn, manners and customs which were an important part of my young life.

We talked a lot and perhaps we gossiped a bit; but for the most part I listened to and learned from people like Mrs. Harriet Morrow Sturgeon. She was the daughter of William L. Morrow, the Pioneer. She was a divorced woman, and there were not many such in Buffalo. Her husband, still living, was a hazy figure, occasionally heard of from someone who had happened to meet him on the street in St. Louis.

Mrs. Sturgeon was, according to the standards of the time and place, well to do. She had an income that enabled her to live without work. But she also was a person who liked to mingle with the life of the place, and therefore she always kept a store. In the long, hot summer afternoons when most of the grave and reverend seigniors of the town were occupied under the protection of the slanting shadows of the buildings on the west side of the square playing marbles at taw, the westering sun heated the front part of Mrs. Sturgeon's store almost to incandescence. Customers were few, except perhaps on Saturday, which was market day. So Mrs. Sturgeon and her son Willie retreated of afternoons (we said "of evenings") to the rear of the store where an office was set aside behind a great balustrade—an office dominated by a big burglarproof iron safe, flanked on one side by an old-fashioned high desk upon which Willie was forever keeping books. Mrs. Sturgeon sat at her father's old desk in her father's old armchair and presided over the company. On such an afternoon there was always company.

In the embrasure of the window, set in the thick brick wall looking toward the north, there would be set up a huge crockery jar. Then, after the allocation of the financial responsibility, into that jar went the ice, the lemons, the sugar, and the water from the pump in the courthouse yard, to compound the afternoon's lemonade. It was an afternoon fiesta to which the cognoscenti came because they knew that not only would there be a cool refreshing drink but there would be talk and gossip and gaiety and laughter. On these afternoon lemonade parties the topics that were discussed were the love affairs of the boys and girls about the town, the goings-on in the society of the town and the surrounding country, and whatever else was up for talk.

Much more important to me, however, was Mrs. Sturgeon's sister, Julia Morrow Pittman. Mrs. Pittman, for reasons of her own, held her court at home. She presided over morning and afternoon sessions of people who just dropped in to call on her in the great front room of her house where she was always ready to receive them. She was an exciting individual, a woman of great native intelligence, who gave scant attention to books and little to current affairs as represented in politics and economics but devoted her attention to character analysis. She knew everybody in the county, their faults and their virtues. She had a few immutable prejudices, but, since most of them were directed toward persons who were far away and unknown to us, they certainly had little harmful effect upon us. She did not like the Roman Catholic church, but there were no Catholics in our town or county, so her prejudice was unpersonalized and hence not within the orbit of her effect on her familiars.

She adored her daughters. Nell, the eldest, was a beauty—the reigning beauty and the acknowledged belle of the town. Her sister, Fannie, a little younger than she, just a little older than I, was, among all the people of my age, the intellectual of the town. She was an inveterate reader of books, a possessor of a tenacious memory for verse, and a limitless curiosity—almost matching my own. Younger than she was Jennie, in grace and beauty of her brown hair and eyes the very prototype of Stephen Collins Foster's "Jeannie with the Light Brown Hair." The circle was completed by the youngest, in my day a very lively little girl, Alice, whose fate it was to run errands. In the capacious cellar of that great house, which as a matter of fact had been built for a hotel, there always were apples. When the gossip got around, as it occasionally did, to a point that Mrs. Pittman did not care to discuss or to have discussed in Alice's presence, Alice was sent to the cellar for a basket of apples. And so it came about that we alternately munched apples and mouthed gossip and had a generalized good time.

It must not be taken to mean that the good talks and gossip in Mrs. Pittman's living-room ever verged on scandal. If she suppressed anything because of her youngest daughter's presence, it was not on account of any supposed salacity. In fact, gossip of the kind that then so intrigued me was strictly of the tea-table sort—more fitted to the tastes of a reader of Jane Austen than to that of a devotee of John O'Hara—a lot of tittle-tattle about personalities, sometimes faintly tinged with malice, but hardly what nowadays, a half-century later, would be glorified as being called gossip at all.

While, as I have said, Mrs. Pittman paid scant attention to political and economic affairs of the nation and the world at large, she knew all there was to know and was perfectly willing to talk about the personal characteristics of the local persons who held office, or ran for office, or hoped to run for office. She was a Republican; her father had been a slaveholder and a Union man, but she had married a veteran of the Confederate army, a Democrat. Consequently she had a greater tolerance, perhaps, for the Democratic minority than did many other Buffalo women of her age and circumstance.

There were other houses to which I repaired of mornings or afternoons to talk with older people and sometimes with others who were not so greatly my seniors. One such home in particular was that of Mrs. George W. O'Bannon. She was the second wife of one of the leading merchants who earlier had been the political boss of the Republican party but had turned that sector of influence over to his younger brother, James. There would also be her mother, Mrs. Roll, who kept up with the world through the *Globe-Democrat,* and her lovely step-daughters, Claudia, Daisy, and Myrtle.

But it was Mrs. O'Bannon (Fannie was her first name) who ruled the establishment. Her conversation was witty, lively, interlarded with anecdotes, and her sharp characterization of people and events made a lasting impression on me. She could be caustic, but she never was cynical. She could be condemnatory, but she was always willing to search out something good even in the life and conduct of the persons she condemned.

My frequent and close association with Mrs. Pittman, Mrs. Sturgeon, and Mrs. O'Bannon, as well as with others of my elders—men as well as women—stemmed in part from the fact that I was a nonconformist in respect to the habitual attitudes of my age group. Although I managed to keep somewhat in touch with the boys of my age, those a little older and a little younger, on such things as swimming and fishing, I could not see well enough and I could not control the muscles of my right arm sufficiently well to play baseball or any of the other games. This left me free not only to read but to associate with my elders in a manner that other children of my age group disdained.

Most of the time my irregularities were forgiven by even the boys and girls of my own age, so that I could go where I pleased, with whom I pleased, provided always that I was personally acceptable. There were among us some who did not accept me at all. I rejected for my own part some of the strictly construed customs of my adolescent coevals; and, on the other hand, it is equally true that my coevals rejected me.

II

In 1892 I was thirteen years old. Time was no longer so free for reading, and no longer could I spend so much of it in the secret and solitary world of my attic. First and foremost, there was the presidential campaign, and I needs must spend most of my days around the courthouse and the stores on the square, listening to and breaking in on the political debates.

It began to dawn upon me that girls were not altogether unmitigated nuisances, and I began, albeit in my own particular fashion, to go to parties and picnics and the like. And then in the spring of 1893 I went to work, and from that day forward I had to snatch bits of time out of work in which to read rather than to give all my time to reading except those bits which were snatched out for chores.

Most of what my parents taught me came under the general vinculum of public affairs, those of either church or state, and their pedagogical methodology was confined to the family conversation. But there were a few things that required more direct action on their part. One, of course, was discipline. I don't remember too much about what happened in my babyhood years, and by the time I was about six my illness furnished me an automatic defense against what was euphemistically known as corporal punishment. Nevertheless, I did not fully escape, and in the years when I was around eight or ten I frequently was paddled or sometimes boxed on the ears and more than once deprived of my supper. But nearly all these punishments that I can remember were for the one single and heinous crime of lying. The lies I told were mainly about adventures in the woods with lions, tigers, and elephants and would have been passed over as harmless except that I tried to make my tales more realistic by involving stories about perfectly terrible things which some of our neighbors had done. Something had to be done to stop my spreading scandals.

But perhaps the most important of all the deliberate and solemn teaching that came to me from my parents was in the matter of tolerance.

Such a rural Protestant community as ours was apt to be shaken from time to time with anti-Catholic agitation; indeed, in the time of my teens the Know-Nothingism of the 1850's was revived by the American Protective Association in what was known as the APA-ism of the 1890's. After the Flinn and Corkery families had moved away in the eighties, there were no Roman Catholics in the Dallas County of my time (the first Catholic church in Buffalo was dedicated in the summer of 1945), and what we heard about the Pope and the papacy was hearsay—uncorrected by any acquaintance with any communicant of the church. I must have picked up something from the APA agitation and said something about it at home, for I remember how solemn and stern Father was when he reproved me. He told me that he would not have survived his wounds of the Civil War had it not been for the Sisters of Charity and members of other nursing orders who nursed him in the hospitals of the South and in the prison at Chicago; he appealed to my own admiration of Father Ryan, the poet laureate of the Confederacy; and he told me that I never, never was to hold it against any person that he held a different religious belief from mine. This solemn admonition was strengthened day to day by the circumstance that Mother and Father belonged to different churches and by the amusement with which both of them frankly ridiculed people, either preachers or laymen, who were too intense about their particular sectarian doctrines.

Mother in quite another way played a most important part in giving me a tolerant outlook, at the very least, with respect to race. When I can first remember, there were a half-dozen or more Negro families in Buffalo, and there were a sufficient number of children to enable them to have a separate Negro school, for of course the mores of the time and place demanded segregation. I remember seeing that little school often; and, indeed, I went to visit it because I greatly admired the crippled schoolteacher, Mr. Simpson, who was compelled to swing himself along on two crutches, a performance which engaged my utter interest. I followed him about to see the way he walked, and of course I had to talk with him to keep him from knowing why I was following him. So we became good friends. But most of the Negro families moved away, or those who were left for a time, such as Tony Watts, the barber, and the Tucks, father and son, had no children, so there weren't enough Negro children for the separate school, and it closed. That left Mary Morrow with her two and the Waldo Prestons with their one boy and the Bonds with their boy and girl and no school to go to. Mother thought it was wrong that these children should grow up in ignorance, so she had them come to our house, all five of them, Romie and Charlie Morrow and Frederick Douglass Preston, and the little Bond boy and girl. They were about my age, although I believe Frederick was a little younger. Mother taught them to read and to write; and I had such a lively interest in this performance that I attempted to substitute myself as a teacher, but Mother didn't trust me to do that, although she did let me teach them their Sunday-school lessons.

The children were not nearly so enthusiastic about getting an education as Mother was about helping them to get it. Their parents were not too enthusiastic either, so the arrangement didn't last long. But I do think that all of them did learn to read and to write and maybe to cipher just a little.

The lasting effect on me was that we, a southern, Confederate, Democratic family stood up in a solid Union, Republican community for the right of the Negro children to a primary education when the ordinary machinery had failed. I hope that I was not too superior about it at the time, and, indeed, I cannot even pretend that I then escaped the heritage of race prejudice against the Negro that was a part and parcel of my time and place. It did, however, give me a tolerant outlook and was greatly to affect my future life, my relations with Negroes, and, much more importantly, to manifest itself in my efforts to insist upon more equitable treatment when long years afterward I came to be a municipal administrator.

But so far as Dallas County was concerned, the race question was soon solved. Tony Watts, the barber, went away; Mary Morrow and her brood left; Henry Tuck, gray, grave, and dignified, died; the Bonds also left; and Waldo Preston and his family disappeared about the time, as I recall it, that the old jail was torn down and a new jail built. The old jail had a barred window looking on the street just a short block off the public square, a window that was large and low and convenient, and on the inside Waldo could sit in comfort to watch the passing scene. Indeed, if he grew lonesome, he had but to take up his banjo and begin "Chicken in the Bread Tray," and pretty soon he would have plenty of company, albeit his gossips might be on the outside looking in. The new jail had its barred "winders," mere narrow slits, eight feet from the floor. Waldo said without any reluctance in the hearing of all and sundry that the new jailhouse "wasn't fittin' for man or beast." He and his family disappeared.

That left only one Negro in the town. He was Ned Tuck, son of Henry, a person possessing courtesy of manner, a man of innate charm, embracing geniality, and the ability to laugh at any funny story told him by anyone and to laugh so loudly that anybody on any part of the square could always tell when somebody had told Ned a new one. He toiled not, neither did he spin, but there were evidences that sometimes grumblingly he swept out a drugstore, one of the "blind-tiger" variety, and there was nearly every day evidence that he had been recompensed for his task, whether performed or not, in kind. Twice a year perhaps, when a fishing expedition went away for a week's, ten days', or two weeks' stay, Ned was forced to accept work. He accompanied the covered wagon that contained the commissary and was by title and un-der protocol the cook for the camping trip. Once actually in camp, of course, he was either too gay or too tired to do any of the cooking, but nevertheless his position was respected, no one dared to derogate his dignity, and indeed his company was esteemed as priceless. When not laughing uproariously, he was either grumbling audibly or humming some popular air under his breath. Just in the nick of time a popular ditty that seemed to have been written especially for him reached Buf-falo, and toward the end he could be seen shuffling slowly down the slight hill on the north side of the square singing softly, *con amore:*

> And when I die, don't bury me a-tall,
> Just pickle my bones in alcohol.

Then there was left of all the Negro population in Dallas County only Henry Roper, his half-breed Indian wife, Mandy, and their handsome son, Tom. The Ropers owned a good farm three or four miles west of Buffalo and were generally esteemed as responsible citizens, while Mandy was feared and admired for the looseness of her tongue as she walked from store to store, discussing in the loudest of tones all the news of the day and not by any chance omitting any item that verged on the intimate or contained the hopeful hint of a juicy scandal. She reaped her reward in suppressed giggling and furious blushes, and she always gathered a bumper crop.

Long after, when Henry and Mandy both had died and Tom, somewhat late in years, had married and had children, he reluctantly was forced to sell his good rich farm and move away because in Dallas County his children could not be admitted to the schools, and there was no way in which he could stay in his ancestral home and educate his children.

Most of the people in our county were native-born Americans. There were a few English-born, the Harris families and John James, the photographer; there were a half-dozen or so immigrants from Germany: Englekings, Kellers, and Duffners; but there was only one Jewish family in the county, the Furths.

Frank Furth was the proprietor of the Famous Cash House, a general store that together with its rival establishment owned by George O'Bannon, in my earliest childhood, challenged and overcame the supremacy of Morrow Brothers, the pioneer merchants who had set the pace in trade from the 1850's through the 1870's. Mr. Furth's family was made up of his wife and six children. There was also his bachelor brother, Harry Furth, who lived upstairs over the store, kept and trained mocking birds in huge cages, and was a milliner.

Frank and Harry Furth were by long odds the best-educated men in our town because they had acquired in this country the learning that was common to our most cultured native groups—the physicians, the lawyers, the teachers, and the preachers—and in addition they had brought with them from their native Bohemia a knowledge of German, a taste for music, literature, and the arts. The two brothers gave expression to their cultural heritage in quite different ways.

In a town where everybody, man to man, was George or Jim or Tom, and "Misters" were common currency only in the mouths of women and children, rarely to be used by grown-up males except to strangers or in the politeness of studied insult and hostility, Frank Furth was never called Frank; he was "Mr. Furth" to everybody, and certainly nobody wanted to be cold to him or to insult him. If his first name was used at all, both names were used, and he was called "Frank Furth." It was an unconscious tribute to his dignity and reserve, and yet he was as cordial and as genial as any merchant selling a bill of goods could possibly be. Mr. Furth spent a great deal of time at home, much more than did our native merchants, who stayed in the store all the time, the store being opened at six in the morning and kept open until ten at night, the merchant and his clerks going back home for breakfast, dinner, and supper. Mr. Furth, instead of going back to the store after supper to loaf and talk, stayed at home and read.

As soon as his children were old enough, off they went to St. Louis to high school and on to normal school and so on to become teachers; and Buffalo saw them no more except in the summer vacations, when they would come and bring with them their schoolmates and fellow-teachers, gay and sparkling Jewish girls from St. Louis, seeing the backwoods and the hillbillies for the first time. By accident I discovered that these city girls were "wild about flowers," and so I, from the resources of my mother's flowerbeds and those of the neighbors, went every morning to see them with fresh bouquets, vases, and trays of flowers arranged with an art I had tried to learn from Mr. William Harris, the English gardener. Their squeals of delight were recompense enough, perhaps; but, in addition, they tolerated me (I was around ten or eleven) and told me stories of the life in the city, that St. Louis which at that time, as a loyal Missourian, no less than any member of its Mercantile Club, no less than the most optimistic of its Veiled Prophets, I was certain sure would outdistance Chicago in the race for business and would become not only the biggest city in America but the future capital of the United States. (I think it was Mr. Pulitzer in the *Post-Dispatch* who was then advocating moving the capital from Washington to St. Louis to get it closer to the people.) Furthermore, these girls were always telling me that when I came to St. Louis I could visit with their families, and the one thing above all things in the world I wanted to do was to go to St. Louis.

Mr. Furth read Goethe and Schiller as well as Dickens and Mark Twain, and he liked to talk about what he read. His difficulty was that it was hard to find an audience. Mrs. Furth was far too busy and far too impatient; his bother Harry would have no truck with his notions and ideas; and among his children only Bob (who was just a little older than I) seemed to care much about books. So it came about that Bob and I listened to him tell about the wonders that he had read, but much of the time Bob had other fish to fry, and I was left alone to listen.

Mr. Furth took his full part in the "arguments" that went on around the square and in the stores, but he was a little too shy, a little too conscious of his slight German accent, really to let himself go. When he found out that I was willing to sit at his feet, he gave me an attention beyond my deserts in either years or understanding. He even proposed to teach me German, but both his method and his pupil were refractory; at any rate, the strangeness of the Gothic alphabet and what was to me the meaningless mystery of the gender of German nouns soon ended that. He would translate for me, of course, not in verse but in running prose from the songs of Schiller, and he did interest me in Goethe. As far as I remember, he had no Heine. But his passion was democracy, and he found more to read and more to talk about in English than in his native German. His prophets were Dickens and Mark Twain. He laughed and cried with them and indoctrinated me with his belief that these two writers concerned mostly with the plain people (he would quote Lincoln to justify his adjective) were writers who, if they had known us, would have sympathized personally with him and with me.

Three of the Furth children were in my general age group: Bob, just a little older and for much of the time my closest chum; Ernie, just a little younger and much of the time the playmate of my brother Walter; and the youngest, redheaded, green-eyed Lily, who kept things lively and had a devilish genius for infuriating her mother into all sorts of violent outbursts which all of us children admired extravagantly. Mrs. Furth was voluble, excitable, not too much pleased with being kept away from her kith and kin in the city, but she was also kindly and generous and a very close friend of my mother. She had, I am sure, long before my time abandoned hope of holding her family flock to more than an extremely tenuous devotion to the ritual of her faith. She even had abandoned much of the dietary laws, but she did cook with goose grease instead of lard and wouldn't have bacon or ham in the house, although she knew perfectly well that Bob and Ernie liked to eat at our house for the very reason that they did like ham.

At the Passover she always brought all the leavening in her house to Mother to keep for her through the holidays. But beyond that, in this world of the goyim, she joined her husband in attempting little more than to instruct her children both by precept and by example in a code of high ethics.

[86]

That instruction embraced me also as being always about the house, and it seemed to me to be just a part of the same thing that I was learning in the church and the Sunday schools and from our Christian code. That I have ever held them in such high regard and deep affection is my tribute to these two who seem to me to be my father and mother in Israel.

Mr. Furth was a Democrat. He never hesitated to sponsor me as his deputy in political arguments, and, on the occasion when he would be chairman of the Democratic county committee, he would always give me an appointment, the first of which was as a member of the county committee itself for the campaign of 1892. Harry Furth was a Republican. The current talk was that this division was based on a purely economic notion that the Furth brothers intended to "catch 'em a-comin' and a-gwine." Indeed, in that overwhelmingly Republican community perhaps Mr. Furth did need some help from the other side of the fence politically, but I am quite sure that the division was not deliberate, nor was its purpose commercial. It was simply that Harry automatically took t'other side from anything that Mr. Furth did or said; that he didn't like arguments or long talks and that this attitude forced him not only into opposition to his brother but to a retreat in silence on all controversial topics. His politics consisted simply in saying, "I am a Republican," and he didn't think it necessary to say why.

Harry was, and his business kept him, interested in women's clothes. Women's dresses then were made at home or by local dressmakers—the only things that were imported from the city already made up were cloaks and suits, a circumstance that has carried into the trade for more than half a century such phrases as "cloak and suiters" despite the fact that few of them now make either.

While Harry did go to St. Louis to buy cloaks and did sell them to his women customers, while he did buy and sell piece goods and patterns and advise all and sundry with respect to the styles, his ruling passion was millinery. With the shapes that came from St. Louis, with those his own deft fingers fashioned from scrim and crinoline and straw braid, with feathers, with ribbons, with artificial flowers, and with the aid of loops of wire, rhinestone buckles, and jeweled hatpin ends, he made fabulously beautiful creations. He shaped them on the heads of his customers; he tied bows and held them this way and that, in this shadow and in that highlight, designing within the current mode his own interpretations of what would crown the beauty and glamour of his customers. Whatever the limits of his medium, whether freely chosen or forced upon him, he was a true creative artist.

Harry had a great effect upon me but an even greater and what turned out to be a determinative effect upon my brother Walter. What was to last me through life as an extraordinary interest in women's clothes and hats became Walter's obsessing interest, trade, profession, and lifework. My conscious and remembered interest in women's clothes began in 1885, when I was six, at the wedding of Jenny Reynolds to George Tippin in the old brick Reynolds homestead (long since destroyed) that stood between Reynolds Chapel and the Reynolds Nursery. The bride wore a white-satin dress with a long train and a veil that swept the floor all about her. She had a wreath of orange blossoms in her hair, and that satin gown itself was sculptured over an enormous bustle, a tightly laced wasp-waist corset, and ornamented with elaborately and intricately draped overskirt and polonaise. The other women present affected the tight basques made of velvets in rich dark colors—purples, burgundies, and hunter's green—blazing down the front with gold or silver or crystal buttons, often with gay plaid polonaise draped over plain black-stuff skirts supported from within by hoops. It was near the end of the day of the hoop skirt—they were not outrageously wide—but they still were well within the scope of my ken. I see once in a while now a photograph of a dozen Buffalo girls, all of them eight or ten years older than I, taken when they all wore the tight basques and the high upswept hairdos of the period; and it still seems to me as though almost any one of them might well be the challenger at Atlantic City for the title of Miss America.

The next year after this wedding there was another wedding which I did not see but which produced a greater output of pictures and more talk about dresses and styles and fashion than ever before had been known in the whole history of the United States. Miss Frances Folsom was to marry Grover Cleveland, the President of the United States, in the White House; and women's fashions, which up until that time had been a thing apart, became a chief concern of publicists and public alike.

III

Most of the inhabitants of the town lived below a level which in the beginning of the twentieth century would have been considered a decent standard for the maintenance of physical, mental, or moral health. But there were gradations, of course. There were those who relatively were rich, those who were well to do, those who were on the border line, and those who had been precipitated into the abyss of direst poverty and who lived on the scant charity of the churches and their neighbors; and there were even a few who were below that, who were classified as paupers to be sold at auction for their maintenance or else immured in the incredibly shabby establishment known as the county poorhouse.

Not only was there poverty, but there was vice. And not only vice, but crime. Indeed, I think that by the time I made ready to leave Buffalo for good, at the age of eighteen, I had some knowledge of almost every form of crime and vice that I have ever heard about, right in my own community. There were rural gangsters. One organized group of train robbers and bank robbers who were natives of the county maintained headquarters only a few miles south of the courthouse. There were native-born burglars, counterfeiters, embezzlers, sneak thieves, and indeed every sort of robber with the possible exception of a pickpocket. I do not remember any such case. Occasionally there was a murder. Sometimes the motive of the murder was robbery. Sometimes it was revenge. And occasionally it was the result of the eternal triangle.

I myself set the type for briefs on an appeal from our Dallas County Circuit Court to the court of appeals or perhaps to the supreme court of the state in a case of a man convicted of incest. I remember reading in the Missouri reports what I believe was the first reported decision on an appeal from Dallas County. It was a case involving conviction for sodomy.

Prostitution was by no means unknown, and, while its practitioners were nearly always confined to the lowest of economic groups, those most direly steeped in poverty, in alcohol, and in narcotic addiction, that was not always the case. There were rural traveling prostitutes who made their way from town to town, sometimes staying in the little hotels, sometimes camping out in tents pitched in woods or fields near the village. Then there were some complacent ladies of a higher economic class who were cut off severely from all social contact with young people of their own age yet managed always to be seen in church on Sunday and at prayer meetings on Wednesday nights, and whose habit it was to parade past the two hotels to catch the unwary eye of the drummer or other traveling man—although of course they did not disdain a date with one of the local gentry.

The places where the gossip about all such carryings-on was centered, and around which scandals were communicated by means of word of mouth, insinuation, and guffaw, were principally the barber shops. Each barber shop was ruled by a strict code that enabled it to switch, on the instant, the type of its prevailing conversation in accordance with the personality and known prejudices of the next person to come in the door. The entrance of a preacher or one of the leaders of the church would be the index for such a sudden switchover that an auditor barely out of earshot could not have detected that there had ever been any change in the direction of the conversation. In the barber-shop scandals originated the more sordid tales that found themselves set up in type and printed in the *Kansas City Sunday Sun,* a blackmail sheet that during its life had a great prosperity in all the rural towns and villages of Missouri and Kansas as well as in the greater centers of population— a scandal sheet that exceeded in license anything of the sort that I have since seen.

The barber shop, too, was the center in which juicy bits of scandalous gossip about the more respectable people of the community were carefully nurtured and disseminated. It was there that one heard earliest of the pregnancy of an unmarried girl, and it was there that the putative fatherhood of the occasional illegitimate child was determined (whether truthfully or not) by action, more generally accepted than the verdict of any modern court of domestic relations. The tongues of scandal and of slander indeed reached upward into the very highest ranks of the community. There was "talk about" some of the very leaders of the church and the community. Some of this was slander pure and simple, unsubstantiated and, indeed, hardly spoken but conveyed with giggle and wink—the process by which the most innocent and casual accidental meeting might be turned into an incipient scandal.

It is perhaps unfair to say that the barber shops were the only centers of such corrupt communications. The livery stables had their share. Sometimes there were gatherings of the sort in one of the offices of the county officials in the courthouse. It wasn't at all the fact that the barbers themselves were conductors of schools for scandal that made their shops such centers. It was merely the fact that it was in the barber shops that the male inhabitants of the town found it easy to get together, found the accommodations for loafing and talking superior, and found also release from the compulsions of time.

Yet the important fact seems to me to be that the generally high code of morals by which the community regulated itself and by which its people ultimately were judged was so high that it was easy for a young person to brush all the sordidness of the seamy side of life to one side and to think then, as he thinks now a half-century later, only of the better things that characterized the neighborhood that shaped him.

My friend, the late Charles E. Merriam, who grew up in a small town in Iowa, had similar experiences in his youth. They led him, years and years after he had become a professor of political science and had had a career on the Board of Aldermen in Chicago, to describe the boundary between vice and crime as a "meandering line."

Of crime as I knew it in my backwoods home county, there was little doubt. The standards by which vice was described were flexible indeed. There was of course no question about violations of the code of sexual conduct. They were put down as vicious and sinful. There was not so much certainty about some others. Addiction to morphine or opium was almost always considered not as a vice but as an affliction. Usually its origin was imputed to a battlefield amputation or some extremely painful disease which had resulted in the entrapment of the victim in an inescapable habituation from which he could be extricated neither by his own efforts nor by the help that might be given him by others. The crime of illicit dealing in narcotics, of course, was non-existent, since there was no prohibition, and anybody could purchase morphine, opium, or chloral hydrate at any drugstore without a prescription or any formality.

The local code proscribed certain other minor vices that in the present day would not be considered as vices at all, even in that same community. Most of them are by this time no longer regarded even as venial sins. Such were the things that fell under the condemnation of a Puritan code of conduct already beginning to be ameliorated in its severity by the time I left Buffalo. First to go, perhaps, was what was regarded as the sin of reading novels. That was transferred at first from the reading of any novel to the reading of the so-called dime novels—the blood-and-thunder Indian fighting, western adventures, and detective novels—which were supposed to be so bad for the young. Then there was the sin of playing cards. A deck of playing cards was considered to be no less than fifty-two separate arms of a personalized, octopal devil. There were the invented card games—flinch, for instance —that still flourish in many parts of the rural United States, especially in the Midwest. Nice people, churchgoing people, Christian people, simply did not play cards. This does not mean that there was not card-playing. The ungodly and the unchurched played seven-up, high five, casino, and such games in retreats screened from the eyes of the elders; but, even in most of such clandestine games, there was little or no gambling.

Another practice which was put down as sinful was that of dancing. The town people and the country people were differentiated in the rationalization of the desire to dance and the desire to conform to this code. In the form of games, the younger townspeople found an outlet for their energies in imitations of square dances, whereas the country people frankly and openly danced to the tune of a fiddler. The waltz and the other round dances which came later were at first much frowned upon, but gradually the high-school pupils, generation after generation, succeeded in breaking down the interdiction.

Among the small fry there was a constant bickering warfare carried on between those who, obeying strictly their parents' injunctions and admonitions and that of their Sunday-school teachers, refused to play marbles "for keeps" and those who felt themselves not bound by such preachments. This differentiation ascended with age so that, even among the adolescents and young adults, there was one group that would toss pennies at a line in a game of crackaloo for keeps, and others, obeying the code, would refuse.

Yet there was one insidious type of gambling that did exist and did manage to attract the patronage of some of those even among the high-ly churched. It was the lottery. The Louisiana State Lottery still flour-ished. Tickets in all sorts of fractional multiples were purchasable. One of the troubles was that, when the "drawing" was made in New Orleans under the superintendence of the ex-Confederate General Pierre T. G. Beauregard, the people who lived along the railroad and the telegraph lines got the news considerably earlier than could we who were twenty-two miles away from the telegraph office and, in those days, had no telephone.

On one occasion a patron of the lottery was made the victim of that sort of practical joke which so delighted our people. He was Peter

Keller, a pillar of the Southern Methodist church, a budding merchant at that time employed as a clerk in Furth's Famous Cash House, the son of a German immigrant who lived ten or a dozen miles northeast of the town, and a person wholeheartedly addicted to catalogues, mail orders, puzzle contests, and all that sort of near-gambling which flourished in the journals of the time, daily as well as weekly and monthly.

On this occasion Peter had a fractional part of a ticket in the lottery. For some reason or other, he deemed it to be particularly lucky because of its combination of numbers in which "13" appeared three times—132639. On the day of the drawing for that particular prize, it was raining, the roads were muddy, the creeks and rivers were up, and there appeared to be no possibility that the mail hack would be able to ford Niangua River or even Greasy Creek and get through from the railroad. There appeared to be no likelihood that the news from New Orleans could come that day.

Yet around noontime a solitary stranger, much mud besplattered, came in from the east, went round the square, and put his horse up in the most distant livery stable. When asked if he had come from the railroad, he was evasive but finally said "No," that he had been caught between the two swollen streams and could make his way neither back to the railroad nor on to his place of destination and therefore had come to Buffalo to find lodging and food until the floods should subside.

A little while later, Harvey Morrow, a fellow pillar of the Southern Methodist church, came in and after a long aimless talk wanted to know what Peter would take for his ticket. Peter, of course, declined to sell.

Then, thereafter, at intervals of fifteen or twenty minutes, other individuals, and among them the leading citizens of the town, came in and offered to buy Peter's ticket. The offers went up from fifty dollars to a hundred dollars, to a hundred and fifty dollars, to two hundred dollars, to three hundred; and, of course, Peter, looking out of the store windows, could see knots of conspirators in close conversation. Then, one after another, an emissary from some such group would come in and offer him more money.

By hint, by insinuation, by innuendo, Peter became firmly convinced that the mysterious stranger had come from the telegraph office and had discovered that Peter was the owner of the lucky ticket that would draw its aliquot part of the grand prize of one hundred thousand dollars. Peter held on and finally refused to sell to a syndicate of local bigwigs for the enormous sum of five thousand dollars.

The next day the mails came, and, of course, Peter's ticket had drawn no prize. The mysterious stranger was one of the home-town boys in disguise, and his mad gallop through the mud had been no longer than half a mile.

So it was in those days. But let it not be thought that even in our innocence there was not even then a connection between government and vice—a direct relation between law-enforcement officers and the habits of the people who desired for one reason or another to evade the law. This was in our time most evident with respect to alcohol. When I could first remember, there were one or two licensed saloons in Buffalo; but, for the most of the time of my growing up, liquor was dispensed through "blind-tiger" drugstores. Their unimpeded and profitable operation depended somewhat upon the co-operation of the local law-enforcement officers—the sheriff and the prosecuting attorney. In every election—and that means not only the general elections where the sheriff and prosecuting attorney were formally elected but in the primary elections, or, in an earlier day, the conventions, in which the parties nominated their candidates—almost the sole interest, aside from the merely personal one of helping somebody get a job because he needed a job or was a popular member of the community, was the question of whether or not the antiliquor laws would be strictly enforced or whether there would be a tolerant and wide-open policy. Sometimes one side won, sometimes the other. If the antiliquor forces won, that meant that the blind-tiger drugstores woud have to be very much more careful in their operation. And during the year, if the prosecuting attorney could persuade successive grand juries to act upon his request for indictments, they would pay a greater number of fines, and the fines themselves might be greater in amount. If, on the other hand, the liberal element won, then the fines assessed against each of the offending druggists would be small and infrequent. And, occasionally, no matter which crowd was in, there would be whispers of favors given, even of favors asked—whispers of corrupt communication between the enforcers of the law and the violators of the law—a pattern which differed in degree rather than in kind from that which has plagued the local governmental institutions of this country ever since.

CHAPTER V

"A CHARGE TO KEEP"

In such a family as mine and in such a place as Buffalo it was natural that from infancy I would find myself in Sunday school, in church, and breathing an air that admitted of no other thought than that the church was the center of the true and everlasting life. The fact that Mother was a Methodist, and Father a member of the Disciples, called in everyday speech the Christian church, kept me from being as deeply sectarian as otherwise I might well have become. Furthermore, it operated to keep open the door to theological and religious matters when my curiosity was engaged, in a manner that might have seemed impious or even sinful, had I been drilled in any one faith as the one true faith.

When I was twelve years old, acceptance of the church as part of the environment in which I lived changed utterly. What had been a social custom now became a matter of the most intensely individual importance. I found myself with a personal charge that I could neither evade nor ignore; it was a responsibility inextricably bound up with a duty—in short, I found that, in the words of Charles Wesley's hymn,

> A charge to keep I have,
> A God to glorify,
> A never dying soul to save
> And fit it for the sky.
>
> To serve the present age,
> My calling to fulfill
> O may it all my powers engage
> To do my Master's will.

My life, as I heard all about me, was destined to be very short. ("You'll never raise him!" I heard the women whisper to my mother.)

It all required an awesome choice, and for the choosing I sought guidance. I went to the Throne of Grace in prayer; I went to the Bible; I turned to the priests and the prophets who had expounded the Gospel in the written and the printed word; I listened to the preachers and the elders. And, while thus pursuing my search, I found along the way scores of things to titillate my curiosity, dozens of things for me to do.

There were then ("then" being a variable but of fairly constant status for the years between my thirteenth and eighteenth birthdays) five churches in Buffalo: Presbyterian, Baptist, Christian, and two Methodist —one North and one South, although the former did not avow the sectional adjective. The Presbyterian was "northern" and the Baptist church "southern," but, as there were no local rivals, these affiliations meant little for us. Outside Buffalo, in the county, there were many other Baptist, Christian, and Methodist congregations. There were also Freewill Baptists and one congregation of Primitive or Hard-Shell Baptists as distinguished from the Missionary Baptists in the town and all over the rest of the county.

Avid as I was for controversy in politics, the fact that for a long time my parents belonged to different churches made me shy away from religious arguments. I was not sure which of the churches was right, if any, and I early found the supreme solace of conscious superiority when I disdained to join in the doctrinal disputes that raged all about me. My silence was accepted, as tolerance is usually accepted, as agreement; and thus I was free to do many things that I could not have done had I been enrolled in anybody's particularistic list of goats (or sheep, either, for that matter).

When I was small, I went to the Presbyterian Sunday school in the afternoon, after having been to the Christian Sunday school in the morning, and to the Methodist church, one or the other of them, for the preaching. But Mr. Gotsel (a Welsh Calvinist Methodist) gave up the afternoon work in the Presbyterian church, and then the Southern Methodist church changed its Sunday school from the morning to the afternoon. At about that same time the Christian church organized a Christian Endeavor Society for its young people, which met Sunday evening just before the regular church services.

This arrangement went well for me. I went to the Northern Methodist Sunday school in the morning and sat in the Bible class under Dr. Slavens, although all its other members were adult. I taught a class of

younger boys at the Southern Methodist Sunday school in the afternoon. And in the evening I presided over the Christian Endeavor Society at the Christian church. When I was thirteen, Dr. Slavens became
ill, and I took his place—the boy teacher of the grown-ups' Bible class
in what was then the biggest Sunday school in town. This led me to
abandon the boys' class in the afternoon that I might sit in the adult
Bible class at that church under Mr. O. H. Scott, who, though no
Methodist (some even whispered that he was an agnostic), was a good
lawyer and a good teacher. He had been persuaded by my brother Joe
(the superintendent of the Southern Methodist school) to take this class
in order to bring in the not inconsiderable group of the intellectually
curious of the town who belonged to no church. I was of that group.

I had been baptized when a baby by my uncle, a young Methodist
parson, when I was in Tennessee on a visit with my mother. But, if I
had ever been told of it, I had forgotten it, and it would have meant
nothing to my father, who, as a Disciple, was dead set against the pedo-
baptists anyhow. I did not learn of my baptism until after I left Missouri and went to Tennessee.

Furthermore, I had made no public profession of faith, or religion,
according to the mode of those who were baptized by immersion into
the Christian church; nor had I been converted at the mourners' bench
and been received into the Methodist church; nor had I been elected
and then baptized by immersion into the close communion of the
Baptists.

Living thus without the church but being preternaturally active in
its work, I held for myself (and, of course, to myself) a position of high
privilege. I quite literally made my own laws to govern my own conduct and found that, so long as I adhered to that code, almost no one
would challenge me—at least I was challenged seriously but once.

That was by Mr. McMasters, the pastor of the Northern Methodist
church. It was at the very beginning of my urge to activity in church
matters, just about the time I had succeeded in mastering my compulsion to constant reading. It was also about the time that I had begun to
be a politician and a journalist, but about those careers I had no such
inner anxiety as beset me with respect to religion.

The Christian Endeavor Society had been set up as a nonsectarian
organization of young people in the church and as yet had not been
followed by or imitated by the denomination organizations such as the

Epworth League for the Methodists, the Baptist Young People's Union for the Baptists, and so on. I got the literature and the manual of instructions for organization from the Christian Endeavor Society's national headquarters and resolved to set up C.E. in Buffalo. I went to Mr. McMasters. He was my very good friend; it was at his suggestion that I had first gone into the adult Bible class under Dr. Slavens. It was with him I discussed the many things I was reading in the religious press. He was sympathetic and understanding and came as near to being a true father-confessor as I ever had. I have forgotten the precise words of the membership pledge of the Christian Endeavor Society, but they included an affirmation of a willingness to obey the commands of Christ. That, Mr. McMasters thought, would include what he construed as a command to join the church. I went away sorrowing.

Just a little earlier I had been a devoted follower of a pastor of the Christian church, Mr. J. W. Hopwood. Mr. Hopwood was a person of saintly countenance; his long beard did not conceal a smile that was the very essence of kindness; his heavy-lidded eyes looked out on the world with compassion but without anxiety or accusation. He, too, had helped me with my reading and had instilled in me the beginnings of a tolerance in things theological that might have startled even his own secretaries had they known of it.

Mr. Hopwood had gone. There was a succession of other pastors at the Christian church. Mr. McMasters having rejected me, I went to the Christian church and there set up the Christian Endeavor Society of which I was an officer and frequently the leader of its evening service. A few years later another pastor, Mr. Gideon, came to the Northern Methodist church. Elder Joe Babb at the Christian church had decided, as had Mr. McMasters long before, that only church members should be officers of the C.E. Society. Thereupon I went to Mr. Gideon and gained his permission to organize an Epworth League at the Northern Methodist church, of which I promptly became president for a time and a leader as long as I stayed in Buffalo.

All this came about because I would not join the church. I could not for two reasons. One was that I had experienced no miraculous conversion. The other was that Mother and Father were of divided sectarian loyalties. Not much was said by them to me, but Mother herself went so far as to join the Christian church, accepting rebaptism by immersion in order to "be with Mr. Brownlow." But yet I could not.

My participation in these activities—teaching two Sunday-school classes and running a young people's meeting (three appearances at three different churches every Sunday)—gained for me a reputation as a "good boy," which together with my "knowledge of the Bible" kept me free from the pressure to "join the church" to which all my coevals were subjected. During the seasons of the revivals or protracted meetings this pressure was great, public, and highly emotional.

When some evangelist had besought sinners to come forward, to confess, to be saved, when the leaders in the church went into the congregation and whispered pleading admonitions in the ears of the sinners, when the outward and visible distinction between the sinners and the saved was church membership (even if there were slight differences about how this salvation was to be seized upon)—during such a time I remained by definition a sinner. But I was free from the pleadings, and my shoulders were dry of the tears of the saints.

Of course this would not have been so had I not adhered strictly to the current code of manners and of conduct that was acceptable. But even being "good" would not have given me that quiet immunity had I not at the same time pushed my pretensions to scholarship.

I read widely if not deeply. And because I was not sure—as I was about things political—I discussed what I read quietly and nondisputatiously with the few persons who seemed to me to be safe to talk with. They were some of the preachers—Mr. Hopwood and Mr. McMasters, Mr. Strong and Mr. Dowdy of the Southern Methodist church—some of the young theological students who came in the summer to minister to the tiny Presbyterian flock, the town's two agnostics, and its inevitable atheist. And, upon rare occasions, I talked about these matters with Mr. Furth, the Jew. There was no Catholic or any representative of Catholic thought; there was no representative of those who might set out either the aesthetic or the intrinsic values of liturgical worship. There was one other—Uncle C'lum Wisdom of the Hard-Shell Baptists.

In the family, at our house and that of my brother, came three weekly religious papers—the *Christian Advocate* of Nashville and the *St. Louis Advocate,* both Methodist, and the *Christian Evangelist* of St. Louis, the Christian church publication. There also were the Sunday-school quarterlies and monthlies devoted to the texts and expositions of the standard Sunday-school lessons as agreed upon by the nonsectarian Protestant church authorities. The weeklies for the Sunday-school children I ignored except as I used them for my classes.

I had as a help for my reading of the Bible Cruden's *Concordance* and a big thick volume called *The Bible Cyclopedia*. I had also for my aid the *Britannica*. Of course I knew no Greek and no Hebrew, but I was conscious of the fact that my Bible was a translation. When Mr. Furth in blessed innocence brought me as a present from St. Louis a new Bible, he had no notion that it was the Douay edition. Then my brother bought the new Revised edition, and I had three texts, three translations, three different Holy Books to consult. I am afraid I was disappointed, so far as my curiosity went, that there were so few differences among them. Our people, for the most part, believed that Catholics were not permitted to have Bibles (else how on earth could they not know, etc.) or at least that they were not permitted to read it and that their priests read it only in Latin. But I used the King James and the Revised versions in my classes and the Douay only for special conversational purposes.

What troubled me (I can see it now, but I could not see it then) was that the Bible was accepted by all about me as universal authority on all subjects. If it were an absolute authority, I expected from it consistency and clarity. Those qualities it could not possess, else there would be no disputes as to its meaning. To ease that trouble, I read more. The more I read, the greater the trouble grew.

Consider the time. It was the last decade of the nineteenth century. The scientists, typified by Darwin, painstakingly and without reference to authority, had told a new story of the world, had painted a new picture of its relation to the sun and stars of heaven and to its own men and beasts.

Consider the place. A backwoods village remote from a railroad, having no telegraph or telephone, having but few contacts with the outside world except by way of the printed word.

The great stir in the world, the great effort to reconcile the dogmas of religion with the discoveries of science, nevertheless reached into this remote recess and affected all of us there, but me—a boy—more consciously and directly, perhaps, than it did many of my fellows and local contemporaries.

Mr. Henry G. Lovan was a subscriber to the *Homiletic Review,* a scholarly journal edited by and for preachers, as its name indicates, and published monthly for the preaching profession. I read the *Review* with intense application. Its exegetical articles were beyond me, as they were beyond most of the preachers in our neck of the woods, since they quoted directly from the Hebrew and the Greek and disdained parenthetical translations as if they had been slurs on the scholarship of their readers. Indeed, I do not remember that anybody but Mr. Lovan and I read the *Review*.

It had many articles, however, that were in straight English. And in those years a great many of them were devoted to the storm that was raging. The "higher criticism" which applied to the Bible the tests that might be applied to any other ancient text available only in its variable translations was discussed in the *Review*. It is true that nearly all the discussion was in refutation of the writings of the German scholars and their fellows. I have no doubt that exegetical discussions were also in that manner. But in this indirect way I heard whispers of what was going on in the scholarly world that was no longer willing to accept the Book as being the literally inspired revelation of the Word of God. It was enough to make me curious about Mommsen and von Harnack; more than enough to whet my appetite for more.

I had found out for myself that there were two stories of the Creation in the first two chapters of Genesis, even that the division of the chapters ignored the transition from one to the other. My own reference books had taught me that one story was of El—of Elohim—and the other of Jehovah. The literal belief in the creation of the universe in six days was demanded as a condition of faith by many about me. But there were others who said that the story was allegorical and that what was meant was six geological ages, and there were books available to the pastors to prove it. These books fitted neatly a day to an age, and there were geologists to witness the truth of the neatly fitted pattern.

Then, when I was about fifteen, I began to do some exploration outside the Bible. Miss Bernice Marshall was a printer, and she came to work in the office of the *Record* as a typesetter. She was an object of great interest to me, for it was well known that her father was a Mormon. Edging around with great care to the subject, I found that she was a Mormon, too. Also that she had never read the Book of Mormon but that she had one. The next day I plunged into that. I never finished it, I must admit; but I did go through it with a hop, skip, and jump and was much puzzled.

At just the same time, in answer to one of my letters pleading for "exchanges," there came from faraway Madras a copy of the monthly magazine, the *Theosophist*. What caused me to write for it I cannot remember. But it came every month, and it excited me to increasing curiosity and wonder. Its Urdu and Pali were as impossible of course as the Hebrew and Greek of the *Homiletic Review,* but its English text was within my range. Its mixture of Buddhism and philosophy, its tales of the wonders of mesmerism and hypnotism, its bland faith in miracles, and, more than all, its interesting biographical material about Mme Blavatsky, Mrs. Besant, and Colonel Olcott absorbed me.

This comparison of religions (such as it was) naturally had to be pursued in secret. It was a matter not to be shared with people of my own age who might have poked fun at me; it was something I was afraid Mother and Father would not approve; I knew it was not to be talked of with the preachers or the faithful. Except for two middle-aged men who were suspected of being agnostics, or even, people whispered, infidels, I could talk to nobody.

Of these two I had no fear. They would not betray me, I knew. Neither of them was interested in Mormonism. One liked to talk to me about the "higher criticism" and the reconciliation of the Bible with science. (He, too, taught a Bible class.) He shied away from the *Theosophist*. The other, a somewhat older man, a veteran of the Union Army and a Democrat, took to Buddhism. With these two men I shared one of my many secret lives. It seemed to me that I learned then that one of the principal reasons we are able to live with each other in any sort of tolerant and tolerable peace is that each of us finds some comfort in these strange secrecies. It is by this tacit conspiracy of silence and secrecy that minorities meet majorities; that weakness meets might; that impotence meets power, as we see in the case of children and grownups. It is when someone breaks the silence, as in all conscience sometimes he must, that conflict results.

The last thing that I would have thought of was that I was playing with dangerous things. They seemed not dangerous to me, for in some manner I kept them all apart from the world of real things, in a sort of separate intellectual jackstraw game that could not conceivably affect my conduct or the conduct of anybody else.

The *Theosophist* continued to come every month. I shared it and discussed it with my friend, the Buddhist. As time went on, he began to talk too much about it, especially as he began to apply to our Western world and our own Missouri scene his own imagination about transmigration of the soul.

One Sunday morning he was missing. The whole town was alarmed, and a search was organized. He had said strange things to his wife and to his brother. Men and boys swept through the surrounding woods, and there in a hazel thicket he was found asleep. A partly emptied bottle of morphine was by his side.

A big table was set in the courthouse yard. Men worked with him, and, at last, when he was partly awakened, they made him walk. Walk, walk, walk. Wake! Wake! Wake! He pleaded and he pleaded for rest—but there was no rest to be allotted to him. More black coffee. More walk—walk—walk.

And there was I. My own agony was almost as great as his. It was of course all my fault. I had led him astray. I had led him into the high places of the false gods. I had destroyed him, and for Eternity.

At last he waked. The doctors let him rest. He was taken home. They said he would live. Never did a blacker sinner plead for mercy, never did a blacker sinner send up thanks, as did I in my attic oratory that night.

The next day I went to see him. Everybody else went out of the room for some reason or other. I began: "Oh, Mister—" when he stopped me.

"You are not to blame. You have kept me from it for two or three years with your theosophy." Someone came in before I could say anything.

"If I could sneeze," he said; "if I could only sneeze I would feel better—help me to the window so that I can look at the sun—it might make me sneeze!" He looked at the sun. He tried to sneeze. But his lungs were filling up; it was pneumonia. In a few hours he was gone.

My grief and my doubt were a double agony. My suffering was all the more terrible in that it had to be secret from all humankind. I could but pray.

In my old age I wonder what would have happened to me then if he had not revived long enough to give me that ray of hope that it was not I who was to blame. I even now have a twinge of doubt of whether I should even now—for the first time—tell the secret. Is it mine? Or his?

It is, of course, impossible for me to remember the chronological order in which these spiritual and intellectual experiences came to me, but the memory of them as separate but related incidents is sharp and clear. At the first, there was only the most naïve and simple acceptance of an anthropomorphic God sitting on a throne in the clouds, above the clouds, even high above the vaulted blue of the cloudless sky, and from there, in the company of His angels, looking downward upon a world of sinners for whose salvation His only begotten Son had been crucified. My imagination required these pictures, perhaps, but it certainly was aided by the pictures that I pored over in the books. These included few if any examples of medieval art, no Italian Primitives, no sacred pictures by the old masters, since we were quite cut off from the Catholic church and Catholic publications, and since there was of course no art gallery in the Ozark Hills. My pictures were engraved for me, for the most part, by Gustave Doré. There was a Doré Bible; not only that, but there was also in the town a Dante's *Inferno* with the Doré pictures. So it was Doré who gave me the images around which I arranged the story of the Bible; it was Doré who gave me my visual pattern of Heaven and of Hell.

To this day the Deluge in my mind's eye is the mother tiger with her kitten in her teeth, the human mother with her baby in her arms, clinging to the last pinnacle of solid earth not yet engulfed by the overwhelming waters. To this day the light that never was on land or sea strikes to my eyes from the wall of Belshazzar's palace, shining in intensity from the fateful "Mene, Mene, Tekel, Upharsin." To this day I see Jacob wrestling through the night with the winged angel until the overcoming of the dawn, the dedication of Israel, and the naming of the place of God—Beth-El.

And, by some odd quirk, when I think of Hell, what I first see are the feet and lower legs of those plunged head downward into the eternal pit for the sin of simony. (How this should be I cannot explain, for, whatever may have been the faults of the church and the churchman, certainly simony was nothing to worry about in the Ozark Mountains in Missouri in the 1890's.) There were pictures other than Doré's. Some of them, and in particular the ones that permanently affected me, were illustrations of the weekly Sunday-school lessons.

There were a few other pictures, too; not many, but one I must have seen quite early. It was Michelangelo's "Jeremiah," but I thought it was a picture of Jehovah, and in that image I created my God.

Doctrinal arguments were part of the internecine strife of Protestant-ism. The church was not conceived as having authority in its own right, so that every preacher, every advocate, every partisan, turned directly to the Bible as the final and only authority, and thus we were compelled to search the Scriptures. If in our search we found different things, varying values, not for one moment were we disturbed in our confident possession of the absolute truth.

Theologically we were divided, of course, into two camps: the Calvin-ists and the Arminians. Denominationally we were split up into a half-dozen sects, and within each denomination there were varying schools of thought. Furthermore, the denominational lines were in part de-termined not by theological doctrine but by different practices with respect to the sacraments, church government, and the like. This di-chotomy was carried over into ordinary speech when a Baptist would speak of the faith and order of his church, a Methodist of the doc-trines and polity of his church, and a Disciple of the faith and prac-tices of his.

The Calvinists were represented by the Presbyterians and the Bap-tists. The Arminians were the Methodist churches, while the Christian church represented a turning-away from Calvinism and, therefore, found within its membership some who thought of themselves as still being Calvinists and others who considered themselves all the way over to Arminianism.

The Presbyterian church, small and weak as it was, was loyal to Calvin and to Knox, wavered not from its firm foundation on the Westminster Confession, and likewise was quite sure that its presby-terian form of government was that ordained by the Bible. Its prin-cipal lay leader, after whose disappearance the congregation went to pieces, was not a Presbyterian at all. Mr. Herbert Gotsel was a Welsh Calvinistic Methodist, and for his high Calvinism he could not go elsewhere than to the Presbyterians, for the Primitive Baptists would not tolerate his evangelistic zeal; and the other Baptists, he thought, tended to compromise their strict predestinarianism.

Because in my family we were either Methodists or Disciples and because I heard at home and in most of my relationships with the preachers but little if any Calvinism, I was by the time I was thirteen firmly fixed in Arminianism.

The greater number of the Calvinists were Baptists. There was the

Primitive Baptist church, the Hard-Shell Baptist church, the citadel of high-and-hard Calvinism. Then there was the Missionary Baptist church, whose adherents were more numerous than those of any other denomination in the county, who were of course true Calvinists but whose degrees of hardness and highness varied. And then also there were the Freewill Baptists, who themselves had deserted Calvin for Arminius.

Now we didn't go around every day calling ourselves Calvinists or Arminians. In fact, most of us who were Arminians hardly knew the word. Brother Proctor, a superannuated Southern Methodist preacher, let me range through his three-foot shelf of theological books, and I knew about the Arminian revolt against Calvinism in the Netherlands and why we thought we were Arminians. But most other Methodists knew little and cared less about that, just as most of the Baptists knew nothing about John Calvin and his theological system.

For the ordinary purposes of daily warfare we went straight back to the Bible and based every one of our arguments on the texts we could find there. What we disputed about were such questions as original sin, total depravity, infant damnation, infant baptism, baptism by sprinkling or by immersion, falling from grace, the perseverance of the saints, and the like. We disputed with each other about the sacrament of baptism itself and its meaning and about the sacrament of the Lord's Supper and as to when and how it should be celebrated and as to who might partake of it—whether in open communion or closed communion.

Then among the Disciples or Christians there was the cleavage between the more progressive and liberal groups, on the one hand, and the more conservative and traditional, on the other, which divided the Disciples into two camps. The Disciples, representing a great and indigenous American religious movement, substantially agreed that the Disciples of Christ might find their whole body of faith and practice in the New Testament, and thus under the New Dispensation. Thus, if one had an argument with a Disciple who held that it was a sin to have instrumental music in church, it was of no use whatsoever to quote to him the One Hundred and Fiftieth Psalm, because that was to be found in the Old Testament, and its application was restricted solely to the Old Dispensation, which had passed away with the coming of Christ. The word "organ" was not to be found in the New Testament.

The Christian church in Buffalo was pro-organist from its beginning. In its very early days there was a meeting of the congregation to discuss the calling of a new pastor. It was decided to call Mr. J. W. Hopwood, a learned man who had been to college, and for him it was necessary to raise a salary of six hundred dollars a year. One of the members, who came in from the country as the result of a special appeal from some of his brethren who had confidence in his solvency, was much impressed with the merits of Mr. Hopwood. He rose and stood with his hand on the organ (a cottage type) and subscribed fifty dollars for the new preacher's salary. The money was raised; the call was made; Mr. Hopwood came. But this brother never paid his fifty dollars. He had been tricked, he had been tricked, he said, and he had had his hand on the Ark of the Devil when he pledged the money, and therefore he was absolved of obligation to pay it. What we tittered about was that he didn't know it was an instrument of the Devil, because he had never seen an organ, having theretofore refused to go even into a private house where one of the pesky things was tolerated.

The Primitive Baptist church was the citadel of the predestinarians. It was established at Louisburg, Missouri, fourteen miles north of Buffalo. Its sparse and shrinking membership was spread over two or three counties and a radius of fifty miles, and its unpaid pastor, Elder Columbus Wisdom, was to me a most intriguing character. I don't suppose many people went to his church except to May meeting, when they came in buggies and in wagons and on horseback from fifty miles around for the annual foot-washing; and, while the faithful may have been few, the spectators and the curious, the sparking couples and the hell-raising youth, were numerous indeed.

The Primitive Baptists, as they called themselves, were called "Hard-Shells" by everybody else. They were not only high-and-hard Calvinists, they were not only strict predestinarians; but they were violently and vociferously opposed to what they called "effort." Therefore Sunday schools and temperance societies were institutions founded by the Devil himself. A Sunday school was an effort to teach the young and therefore sinful. A missionary was an effort to bring people into the church and therefore sinful. All these things had been predestined and foreordained, and there was nothing man could do about it, and nothing man ought to try to do about it.

Mr. Wisdom was ordinarily known as "Uncle C'lumb." He lived off the proceeds of his farm and accepted no money for his churchly ministrations. But he did mightily like some of the good things of this earth and so was in the habit of visiting in the homes of the members of his flock, especially in those homes where it was believed that the man was a good provider, that the woman set a good table, and that somebody, maybe the oldest boy, would frequently be in possession, if not of a jug, at least of a vial of good corn liquor.

These visitations Uncle C'lumb made on horseback, and with him in his saddlebags he carried his complete library. It consisted of three books, one of which I had already read and the other two I mightily wanted to read. Now, these were religious books, and so I couldn't ask Uncle C'lumb to let me read them or to lend them to me, because for him to have done so might have been construed as "effort," which would have been almost as sinful as if he had set up a regular Sunday school. Therefore it was necessary for me, when I encountered him at Uncle John Alexander's or at Green Marsh's house, to take certain steps on my own initiative. These steps were, first, to find out where he parked the saddlebags in the stable; next, to steal the books; and then to get them back surreptitiously before he discovered that they were gone. It was thus by stealth that I got hold of two of the three books in Uncle C'lumb's library. (To the Holy Bible I had access, and therefore I did not steal it.) The other two that I absorbed so eagerly were the *Confessions of St. Augustine* and *The City of God*. Thus in the stable at Uncle John Alexander's place out on the prairie nearly halfway to the Blue Mounds, when I was about thirteen years old, I made the acquaintance of the great African saint and doctor.

Under the circumstances I may be forgiven if I did not in that first hurried reading get too much grounding in Augustinian philosophy. Indeed, I did not at the time recognize that I was in the presence of one of the great intellectual achievements of all time, when the City of God was erected to take the place of the falling city of Rome. And yet even then to me, unlettered, unlearned, and but a child, the great book was truly a great book, as years afterward I was to agree with what somebody once wrote of it: "Never was thought so abstract expressed in language so popular."

The *Confessions* was a different matter. I was thoroughly accustomed, of course, to the Old Testament, and I knew that some of the good and great sometimes deviated from the strict path of virtue as set up to guide us in what I thought of as the New Dispensation under the New Testament. But I was not prepared for such carryings-on by a Christian saint. That he did win through in his battles against the flesh I recognized, as I did that I was again reading a great book.

I but dimly perceived that the reason why Uncle C'lumb had these books was that in some measure they supported him in his supralapsarianism. Not all even of the Hard-Shell Baptists were supralapsarians; some indeed were infralapsarians and believed that the division of the goats and the sheep took place after the fall of Adam, whereas Uncle C'lumb believed the foreordination was one with foreknowledge and predestination and antedated the Creation. What comfort he got from St. Augustine for this straitness might have crumbled had he read all of Augustine, so theologians have assured me in my later years; but Uncle C'lumb was not one for borrowing trouble. He had his authorities, and he carried them in his saddlebags, and, deriving from those authorities, he preached the Gospel.

However, he didn't preach like the other preachers. His was not the art of exposition, his not the skill of the logician, his not the fervor of the exhorter. His was the high whining intonation that in some mystical manner for him and his supplied the lack of liturgy. We boys and girls used to imitate him and endeavor to pitch our singsong high as we mourned the departure of the faithful into Limbo:

> Gone where woodbine twineth—oh!—ah!—ah!
> And the whangdoodle mourneth for its first-born—oh!—ah!—ah!

Aside from these two books by St. Augustine, all I knew about the early Fathers and the great Doctors of the church came from a curious source. There was somewhere about the town a beautifully bound book, brown leather stamped in gold, called *History of the Church*. I can't remember who owned it, but it was a newly published book when I got hold of it when I was about fifteen or sixteen years old.

It purported to be the History of the Church of God from the Creation in 4004 B.C. to A.D. 1885—from Adam to Grover Cleveland. It was a fat volume printed in fine type. Its purpose was to prove that the Primitive Baptist church was the first church, that Jesus Christ was a Primitive Baptist, that the Primitive Baptist church had existed continuously throughout all the years since the Ascension of Our Lord, and that the popular notion that for a time the Roman Catholic church was universal in the Western world was an error. St. Augustine it claimed as a Primitive Baptist or "Old Catholic," but never, never, according to it, was the Bishop of Hippo a *Roman* Catholic.

Little of it sticks in my memory except the curious circumstance that the Lollards of England refused to take oaths by any created thing— they would not swear on the Book—and that a few of our own Primitive Baptists refused to swear at all but in lawsuits would only "affirm." Yet out of it I did get something of the sense of the great history of the church, which served me in good stead later when I came to extend my reading.

These doctrinal disputes which went to the matter of faith were paralleled by other arguments about the conduct of public worship and the government of the church which went to the matter of order, polity, and practice. While none of these was so violent and long continued within any particular denomination as was the struggle between the organists and the anti-organists in the Christian church, still the interdenominational differences gave rise to plenty of controversy, most of which was thoroughly enjoyed by all the participants.

In the first place, there was the matter of nomenclature affecting the preachers themselves. All the churches consented in an informal way to the title "Pastor," but the word "Reverend" was enough to stir up a ruckus. The Presbyterian pastor, when there was one, naturally expected himself to be called "Reverend." I am afraid that the usual practice was to use the abbreviation "Rev." before a man's surname, so that we would speak of "Rev. Jones" or "Rev. Smith." It was the Reverend Mr. William Mooney who explained to me in my salad days, and to me the explanation meant much because I was an editor and a printer, that the title "Reverend" always should be preceded by the definite article and always followed by the courtesy or honorific title of "Mr." or "Dr." and was always to be prefixed to a man's full name and not merely his surname.

Mr. Mooney was a learned man, an elderly man, an alumnus of Princeton, which latter fact in my mind was sufficient to put a glowing halo over his white and balding head and seemed to make his long gray beard an appurtenance of a true prophet. He was a retired minister who was sent out to our struggling Presbyterian congregation to try to bring new life into it.

Unfortunately, Mr. Mooney was an Old School Presbyterian minister who believed that a sermon should be a scholarly written document, to be read to those who sat under him from firstly to sixthly in a march as inexorable as the progress of the logical argument it set forth. Our people didn't believe in written sermons. To the Hard-Shell Baptists they were sinful; to most of the others they were boresome. And so Mr. Mooney and his scholarly sermons, written in a handwriting that was almost illegible even to Mr. Mooney, failed to fan into a blaze the tiny spark of life that still remained in the Presbyterian fold.

The Methodist preacher was, as a matter of course, "Reverend." He was not freely chosen by his congregation but had to be appointed by his bishop to the charge of the church. He knew (at least in those days) that under no circumstances could he remain with one church for longer than four years, and there was always the annual conference to be held in the autumn at which the bishop might uproot him and his family and send him to a far-distant place. The Baptists and the Christians with their congregational autonomy chose their own pastors, but in my time none was permitted to assume the title "Reverend," although occasionally a Baptist who had come in from some far-distant and more urban community did not disdain the title. The others always were called formally "Elder" and informally "Brother." The Presbyterian congregations of course elected their deacons and their ruling elders, but their teaching elders had to come with the sanction of the Presbytery, and that sanction had to be obtained after an examination into the educational and other qualifications of the would-be teaching elder under rules and regulations set up by the Synod, and even by the General Assembly. The Baptist congregation sent messengers to the County Association, and through that held to some tenuous lines of loyalty to the great Southern Baptist Convention, but there was no authority that could coerce a congregation. It elected its own elders and its deacons, but it was by custom restricted in the employment of a pastor to a teaching elder who had been licensed to preach by a county association. In the Christian church the congregation elected its deacons and elders, and there was no division among the elders. In fact, many adherents of this denomination were so intent upon their belief that the church should be governed always by a plurality of elders that they were hesitant to give the one elder who was the preacher either any title or any authority; and certainly any elder had as much right to preach, to teach, and to administer the sacraments as did any other. In the Methodist church the orders of deacon and elder were reserved to the ministry; and, as there was never but one minister and he was never given a pastorate until after he had been ordained first a deacon and then an elder, the use of the word "elder" as a title was unknown.

In all these churches the word "elder" was quite simply and naturally equated with the word "presbyter," but no one, not even the Methodists, would have admitted that "presbyter" might also be equated with "priest." None of the churches was ritualistic or liturgical, but there remained in the Methodist church a little more of the ancient forms than were to be found elsewhere.

Holy Communion was celebrated among the Methodists quarterly, usually on the occasion of the visit of the presiding elder of the district, that might comprise a dozen or more congregations. The Communion service, as fixed in the Discipline, was read responsively by the minister and the congregation and, with some omissions and elisions, followed the form of the Book of Common Prayer of the Church of England. The communicants were asked to come to the chancel rail and kneel for the partaking, and only an ordained clerical elder or deacon might serve or assist in the serving. In the course of the celebration the congregation, standing, recited the Apostles' Creed, there were always a few who bowed their heads as they said the Holy Names, and there were many who knelt in silent prayer in their pews after they had returned from the Communion table.

It was this business of saying the Creed that excited the intense opposition of the party at the other extreme—the Disciples. They made it an especial point that they rejected all man-made creeds and they based their faith and practice directly on the Bible, and in the Bible on the New Testament. They admitted nothing approaching a priesthood; they gave no exclusive franchise of any biblical order to the ministers.

In the Christian church Holy Communion was celebrated every Sunday, the communicants remaining in their seats to be served by the lay elders in a service which consisted entirely of quotations from the Bible. However, Methodists and Christians agreed in offering the Communion to any who, guided by his own conscience, desired to partake, while the Baptists and the Presbyterians (at that time and in that place) accepted for Communion only those who were members of their own denominations.

Thus the creed-reciting Methodists and the creed-rejecting Christians were on the side of open Communion, while the Baptists were the uncompromising advocates of closed Communion.

The Methodists and the Presbyterians felt themselves to be a part of the "Holy Catholic Church" and found in the Apostles' Creed no rock of offense; but here Baptists and Christians were united against the Creed. Methodists and Presbyterians alike baptized by sprinkling, although the Methodist pastor would always baptize by immersion if he was asked to do so; and both baptized infants, while Baptists and Christians united in denying that baptism was indeed baptism if administered to an infant or if administered in any other manner than by immersion. But here the Baptists and the Christians parted in their theological interpretation of the effect of the rite of baptism, which with the Baptists always must be preceded by election and with the Christians only by the act of confession of faith.

All these matters were of great concern to me. They affected me profoundly and radically because, since I was not a partisan of any one of the schools and therefore tended to listen with tolerance to all of them, I was molded in my thinking toward the conclusion that none of these narrow questions of doctrine and of practice made any real difference. All this helped to turn me into a liberal.

Here, of course, I must account something to my family, or perhaps even to a predestined faith. It may be that in this matter all of us find ourselves more determined than determining.

It was about this time that I had been inclined to accept some degree of determinism in the field of politics by Mr. W. S. Gilbert and his immortal declaration in *Iolanthe:*

> Every little boy or gal that's born into this world alive
> Is either a little Liberal or else a little Conservative.

In another respect I was brought into even closer communication with some Baptist preachers than with any others. While the Baptists didn't read their sermons to the congregation, they had no objection to writing them and reading them to each other. Indeed, it had become a custom for the moderator of the County Association not only

CARNEGIE INSTITUTE OF TECHNOLOGY LIBRARY

to write his annual sermon but to have it printed; and I as a printer read these sermons, set the type, corrected the proofs, and entered into long discussions with their authors. Elder Daniel Hitson, Elder John H. Stinecipher, and Elder Daniel P. Brockus were three of the Baptist preachers whose sermons I thus came to know so well, and with whom I therefore was entitled to carry on discussions—exegetical, theological, and philosophical. All of them informed and enlightened me, but I was not convinced even to their mild Calvinism, nor was I persuaded of the final validity of the proof texts which were the objects of their exegetical ingenuity. And certainly on one occasion, when I attempted to quote a variant text from the Douay Version, Elder Hitson not only was completely unconvinced by me but was horrified by my daring.

In the Christian church the very lack of a creed became in itself almost as much of a stumbling block as any interpretation of any phrase of any formulated creed might have been. But, on the other hand, in the Christian church and in the conventions of its preachers there was such wide freedom of discussion and there were represented such differences in background among the participants, who in this new and completely American church had come from family backgrounds Presbyterian, Baptist, Methodist, even Episcopalian, Universalist, and Unitarian, that genuine free discussion was engendered.

Here already in my day, through the journalistic agency of the *Christian Evangelist,* a liberalizing tendency was to be observed, a readier willingness on the part of some preachers to accept the newer learning developing out of the scientific method, a more truly catholic spirit, although but few of them in that day would have openly avowed that adjective. Of course this liberal tendency among those who later were frequently called "progressives" ended at last in the division in which the conservative group went off to form the Church of Christ. This division also affected all other Protestant churches, but at the time of which I write and at the time when these things were shaping my thought and contributing to my education, we had not yet heard the word "fundamentalist," which later was to define the cleavage among American Protestants. At that time, however, we were aware of the great stirring within all the churches. We followed the case of the Reverend Dr. Charles A. Briggs of the Union Theological Seminary of New York, who was being tried for heresy. We resisted the higher criticism. And yet most of us felt that in some manner our differences would be composed, our questions resolved, and our hot and violent disputes relegated to dark corners of old men's memories, finally to be consigned to the limbo of dust-gathering books no longer read by any but antiquarians.

What we called "doctrinal arguments," while carried on with stubborn insistence, rarely led to any personal quarrels or to the proscription that might have been assumed to result from such deep differences on matters of such high concern and eternal meaning. As a matter of fact, the preachers and the active laymen in the several churches were accustomed to put aside their theological differences and band together in action against what they considered to be the common enemy.

The ever present enemy was, of course, the Devil, and the Devil was represented in our community by those who had been deceived by him into yielding to temptations. These temptations mainly were temporal, and the measure of the Devil's triumph was to be found in the conduct of those he had lead astray. All churches were in substantial agreement as to what conduct should be.

In the Methodist churches, of course, Mr. Wesley's general rules were read once a year, and all Methodists were supposed to conform to them. When John Wesley drew up his general rules for his Society of Methodists, he had no notion, of course, that he was founding a new church or setting up a new denomination or separating a sect. His purpose was to reform the Church of England and to invite to help him those who had "a desire to flee from the wrath to come and to be saved from their sins." Mr. Wesley believed that that desire would be evidenced in three ways: first, by doing no harm; second, by doing good; and, third, by attending upon the ordinances of God; and he drafted his rules of conduct in accordance with these three categories.

Actually, in Methodist theory and, in my childhood, in practice as well, emphasis was laid on the things forbidden, and they were chiefly profanity, Sabbath-breaking, drunkenness, brawling, wearing gold and costly apparel, taking diversions, singing songs, or reading books that could not be used in the name of Jesus. Not much emphasis was placed on some of the other things forbidden, such as smuggling (which was utterly unknown to us), usury, or speaking evil of magistrates and ministers. Of course the interdictions of the Ten Commandments were taken for granted.

[115]

The strait and strict among us seemed to pay most attention to the forbidden diversions. There was no quarrel about drunkenness and brawling, of course, and church members were expected to be both total abstainers and prohibitionists; and usually they were. Church members might not go to the theater—there was very rarely any theater to go to—but woe betide the church member who danced or played cards. By my time the prohibition against jewelry had been abated, and most of the godly dressed as well as they could; but general economic conditions took care that there was little violation of this particular Wesleyan interdict. Singing of songs that were not actually bawdy but could by no stretch of imagination be called sacred had come to be permitted. However, in my time a few of the most faithful still held that to read a novel was a sin. As I made it a practice to read a novel a day if I could get the novel (and I usually could), this was one rule of conduct that left me clearly and cleanly on the Devil's side. Sometimes I was upbraided for it, but for the most part my conduct—I didn't dance and I didn't play cards and naturally at that age had none of the grosser vices—seemed acceptable.

The Christian church and the Baptists (except for the Hard-Shells) held generally to the same rigorous code, with the exception that the Presbyterians put much more emphasis on keeping the Sabbath. When I was very, very young, around five or six, the family which lived next door was Presbyterian. There was a little boy of my own age, and on Sundays he was not permitted to play. His mother thought it was so wonderful that five or six other little boys in the neighborhood were willing to come every Sunday afternoon and sit with Lee in the semi-darkened parlor, not only keeping him company but thus themselves abstaining from wicked play and the profanation of the Sabbath. What she did not know was that we were fascinated by Lee. The real business was that Lee was holding a neighborhood seminar in cussing and dirty talk, in which he excelled and in which he went to lengths that none of the others of us would have dared for fear of being struck dead on the spot. To keep from being lonely, he invented new things from week to week and was always sure of company. The family moved away from the town, and I have never seen him since, but I have often wondered how far he carried his vocabularian protest against the unco guid.

Of course there were always church members who looked on the wine when it was red, and there was always discussion about whether or not they should be thrown out of the church; and among the ungodly there were ribald references to some of the church leaders who were not averse to a sly snort out of the jug or even a snifter in good company behind the prescription counter in the drugstore. And sometimes even among the well-churched there was gossip touching on the Seventh Commandment.

All these things, which sometimes are called "puritanical" and sometimes "Wesleyan" and sometimes by other names, underwent a great change during my boyhood. When I was twelve, the rules of conduct were strict, and persons disobeying them were punished from time to time by actual expulsion from the church. By the time I was eighteen no one any longer objected to reading novels or singing profane songs. By the time I was twenty and had left Buffalo for good, round dancing had come in; and the only one of the sinful diversions still strictly under the ban was card-playing, an evil practice indulged in by boys and men on the sly, but by very few indeed of even the bolder women.

In another field the churches, and particularly the preachers, forgot their denominational differences to fight the common enemy, the Devil, and that was when he had deceived persons into yielding to the temptation of unbelief. This went on at the same time with the doctrinal arguments about particular beliefs, but there was certainly a united front against the infidel. There was enough of this so that I read eagerly all the infidel books I could get hold of, chiefly Colonel Ingersoll and a little later Brann's *Iconoclast* and the atheistic *Appeal to Reason*. Oddly enough, Colonel Ingersoll's eloquent and resounding periods failed to impress me, not so much because I was intrenched in the faith, but because of his habit of proving his point by appeal to authorities in the very way that the orthodox theologians proved theirs. He, too, would turn to the Bible but find his authority there rather in contrasting inconsistencies than in a quotation to support his thesis. The very indoctrination that I was getting in the "higher criticism," which tended to invalidate literal acceptance of the Holy Scriptures, also inclined me to reject the Colonel and his *Some Mistakes of Moses*.

Not that I was not also a literalist in a fashion and an inveterate quoter, although I was quick on occasion to recall the saying that the Devil may quote the Scripture for his purpose. It was probably because I was a Bible reader, that I was known to be familiar with Cruden's *Concordance,* and had a Clark's *Commentary* and a *Bible Cyclopedia,* that sometimes I was let into the disputations that went on among the preachers themselves. Most of the preachers in the county had had very little schooling. But the younger ones who were growing up, young men just a few years older than I, were trying desperately to get a few months somewhere at college, were doing their level best by the very hardest work to repair their lack of education.

There were a great many young men who were called to the ministry, most of them Baptists and Christians. In fact, we had so many of the latter that Dr. Gatewood always had a ready response to those who falsely asserted that our county was the poorest county in the state. While the rest of us could think of nothing better to say in such circumstances than baldly to assert that Camden County at least was poorer than Dallas, Dr. Gatewood was wont to reply in indignant tones: "Hell, Dallas County is the richest county in the state and grows the biggest crops. What other county raises as much hell and as many Campbellite preachers?" Now, fifty or sixty years after the times of which I write, that county is still contributing a steady quota to the men who have made the Christian church strong, and for the last twenty or thirty years every autumn some thirty or forty ministers of the Disciples repair to the Christian church in Buffalo, in their native Dallas County, for a week's retreat.

The Baptists were almost if not quite as prolific, and the meetings of the County Baptist Association at which aspiring candidates for licenses to preach were expected to deliver their maiden sermons were great occasions for me. While I inclined doctrinally toward the Christian church, I was quite impartial with respect to my personal interest in the Baptists; and I liked to hear the young men, the frightened but determined young men, who were endeavoring to answer their call.

I remember one occasion on which I undertook to help one of these young men out of my brash knowledge. I had heard him at a prayer meeting make a little talk from a text, and I was sure that he was practicing for his sermon. The next day I found him and asked him if that was to be his sermon. When he said it was, I undertook to turn him completely around. His text was from Eccles. 12:13: "Let us hear the conclusion of the whole matter: Fear God and keep his commandments, for this is the whole duty of man."

Now, the word "duty" in the King James Version, which was the only one he knew, was printed in italics, and he had based his talk on

the emphasis thus given in the Holy Writ to that word. Very bump-
tiously I showed him that the word italicized in the King James Version
meant that it did not appear in the original language itself but had been
inserted by the translators in an effort to perfect the sense. I am sure that
he would have been forgiven both here and hereafter if he had knocked
me down for my presumption, but he did nothing of the kind. He
thanked me and got me to help prepare his sermon. When he went
before his elders, he used the same text, omitting the word "duty," and
so impressed the company with his erudition that he was given a license
to preach after the first trial sermon, something that most of the young
men didn't get until after the second or third start. I was then uncertain
whether or not to be sorry that I had not shown him my Douay Version, but that would have surely been too great a shock. It reads: "Let
us all hear together the conclusion of the discourse. Fear God and keep
his commandments: for this is all man."

In our doctrinal disputes about salvation by grace, justification by
works, in the whole complex of differences growing out of the various
shades of Calvinist and Arminian opinion, we were all unwittingly
being affected by the deep stirrings that were going on throughout
Christendom as the result of the spread of the scientific method and
the technical changes that were shaking the foundations of the world.
Our church papers and magazines brought us the news. We knew how
valiantly Mr. Gladstone was defending the faith of the fathers. But we
learned in the same journals, even if we read only protest and refutation, what Darwin was doing to the processes of men's thinking and
how damaging was Spencer's materialism to our old modes of thought.
Many of us rigidly stuck to it with Bishop Ussher that the world was
created exactly 4,004 years before Christ, but most of us were not so
sure; and for a few of us von Harnack and his higher criticism were
shaking our confidence in the final authority of even the scriptural text.
We were beginning, not indeed to reject utterly the fact of revelation,
but to adjust the meaning of that word to fit new knowledge.

For the most part these matters, so far as I was concerned, were kept
quiet; but on one occasion the whole thing blew up in such a way as to
involve everybody in the town in a whirling quarrel. Mrs. Addie
Cherry Morrow, who read the *Century* and *Harper's* and *Scribner's*,
had read about a new novel that had shaken England and was about
to cause America to tremble. She sent for it and read it. That fact, even

if it had become generally known, might have been forgiven her be-cause of her high standing in the church and the community, but it didn't stop there. She lent the book to me, and that fact got out; and that a woman grown and a member of the church should give a young boy of fourteen such a book, which undoubtedly would tend to under-mine his faith and which in the view of the still strict minority had been inspired directly by the Devil himself, was a scandal. The town rocked with it. Some elderly people wanted to revive the interdict against all novel-reading. Others thought that Mrs. Morrow should be publicly reprimanded. Of course nothing happened to her and nothing happened to me. What did happen was that the novel went quickly from hand to hand and was read by more people in a short period of time than any other novel that had hit Buffalo since *Huckleberry Finn.*

The book was *Robert Elsmere* by Mrs. Humphry Ward. Few now recall what a sensational stir Mrs. Ward made in this great essay, the design of which was to reconcile religion and science with a social gospel.

It was at this same time, from my fifteenth to my eighteenth years, that I got from the *Homiletic Review* my introduction to sociology. Every month this preachers' trade journal carried a department under the heading of "The Social Problem." That phrase had nothing to do with what it later came to mean in a very narrow and special sense. In fact, the words were used in their broadest possible meanings and with the general intent and purpose that true Christianity was identified with social democracy. If I had read, as of course I had in most of the news-papers of the day, that Mr. Eugene V. Debs in the railroad strike of 1894 had struck a blow at the foundation of home and church, I could also, as I did, read in the social section of the *Homiletic Review* how right Mr. Debs had been in many of the causes for which he fought. Here in this religious magazine I found support for my political beliefs, and here I found a great deal of what I put into my teaching in my Sunday-school classes. Sometimes I tremble to think what political heresies I must have introduced into that Northern Methodist Sunday school, all but solidly Republican, with my Democratic, Populist, and even socialist notions!

This section of the magazine, "The Social Problem," was the work of Dr. J. H. W. Stuckenberg. He, a Luthern clergyman who had studied and worked in Berlin, had been affected powerfully by the Christian

Socialist movement in Germany. He, so I read many, many years later, was one of the great pioneers in the field of sociology in the United States. Certainly it is to him and his monthly lessons that I owe my introduction to sociology. Perhaps it is even to him that I owe a certain impatience with, or even what some might call "prejudice" against, the sociologists of the school of Ward and Small who would have us observe the things that are happening in order that we may measure trends but seem somehow to tell us that as true scientists we should not endeavor to affect those trends. Stuckenberg was a tendentious sociologist, and he was mightily moved by his desire to affect the shape of things to come; but nonetheless he dared to look his facts in the face. If I am wrong, then I must admit that I am stubborn in my wrongness, for I am glad that I found Dr. Stuckenberg and that I found him when I was young and that he was one of the great teachers whose written word helped me to set up a scale of values by which I have tried to measure my life.

But before I leave Buffalo—the country, the backwoods, and the topic —I am impelled to say that it was none of these things—not the church, not the religious journals, not the theological disputes, not the little dip into the study of comparative religion—that molded my lifelong attitudes.

It was in another place that I found what to me became the most meaningful words with which to reward my searching for the truth. That other place was in the nineteenth-century poets, American and English, as perhaps best typified and epitomized by Tennyson. In "Locksley Hall" God and man work together for

> ... the Parliament of Man, the Federation of the world.
> And the common sense of most shall hold a fretful realm in awe,
> And the kindly earth shall slumber, wrapp'd in universal law.

And in another poem, "In Memoriam," I found the basis for my belief in

> That God, which ever lives and loves,
> One God, one law, one element,
> And one far-off divine event,
> To which the whole creation moves.

These are brave beliefs for these dark days. But this was the faith I sought, this the faith I found, and this the faith I hold.

CHAPTER VI

"FOUR YEARS MORE OF GROVER"

The year 1892 was marked by events that transformed my life and brought me out of my three years' devotion to literature and the arts. Grover Cleveland was running for President again after four years of Harrison in the White House; hard times were beginning; religion began to be a personal problem; girls miraculously were transmuted into glamorous mysteries; the center of my somewhat diminishing literary interest shifted from history and adventure to romance and religion or to current affairs; I put on long pants; I became thirteen years old.

What seemed to me to be but a natural interest in affairs but what may have been regarded by grownups as a precocious propensity to butt into their arguments on public affairs brought me into personal participation in organized politics when Frank Furth in the summer of 1892 made me a member of the Democratic county committee, of which he was chairman and my brother Joe was secretary. To others it may have been a joke, but I was thirteen years old, and I took upon my own shoulders the full responsibility of getting for the country the "four years more of Grover" ("and we'll all be in clover") that I thought it needed.

It is true that there were no duties attached to my exalted position; it was equally true that the Democrats were a weak third party in the county—weaker, in fact, in that election than usual because the People's party was in the full tide of the midwestern movement to effectuate the Ocala Platform and was running General James B. Weaver of Iowa for the presidency. But these considerations did not prevent me from reading the newspapers, clipping many articles from them for Mr. Furth to read, and, in general, giving an "official" air to my arguments. These

[122]

were mainly about the tariff, for the silver question went underground in our country in 1892. Everybody was for free silver, the Republicans as well as the Populists and the Democrats. Only Weaver among the three candidates was candid on the "money question." Neither President Harrison nor Mr. Cleveland seemed to want to stir up that mess.

November came and with it victory. The teen-age Democratic contingent—Dean and Derby Stanley, Bob and Ernie Furth, and I—strove mightily with a few of our elders to bring broken boxes and such like to the front of Furth's store for the bonfire—the last that was to be lighted by Democrats for a national Democratic victory for twenty years. But we did not know that, and we whooped it up.

Yet even in that year I was troubled. The very day after we knew the results of the election, Mr. John Greever, Sr., in the post-office lobby, paying no attention to the glum Republicans all about him, was heard to declare that the Populists had elected Cleveland (Mr. Greever was a Populist), that only the fact that Weaver had won twenty-two electoral votes had made Harrison's defeat possible, and that a "part of the deal" was that Cleveland had committed himself to free silver. I doubted it. Mr. John S. Haymes, the best lawyer in the county and the best Democrat too, had doubted it all through the campaign; and from him I had absorbed a disturbing skepticism.

The scene has come back to me time and time again when the struggle between the two wings of the Democratic party has resulted for the time being in the dominance of the conservatives; and I have found myself volubly expatiating on the fact that the candidate has been "committed" to the liberal program and is therefore better to be trusted than his Republican opponent. So it was with me even in 1904, when Judge Parker was set up against Theodore Roosevelt, and that despite the fact that the learned jurist from his home in Esopus literally plunged the national convention in St. Louis into chaos by his telegram explicitly repudiating the monetary plank of the platform which had sought to "commit" him to "silver" as against his known and avowed "gold" predilections. Thus it was also in 1924, when John W. Davis was nominated, and in 1928, when Al Smith made Raskob chairman of the national committee.

By the time I was thirteen I had developed a party loyalty that was engaged by the symbol of the name "Democrat." But by that same age I also had developed a loyalty to those elements in the party that held

fast to the faith symbolized by the same word without its capital letter
—I was a "little 'd' democrat," too.

We had names for our faction, even then. We were "unterrified
Democrats," "Jackson Democrats" (perhaps that was the best of all the
names), or sometimes, even then, merely "liberals." We were also "red-
hot Democrats" or "unreconstructed," but these two names might include also the conservatives of the party as well. Our campaign badges
were red; those of the Republicans always were blue. They called themselves "true blue," and we called them "black" Republicans—they not
infrequently called us "rebels." The Civil War was not yet over, and the
"bloody shirt" still was waved in political campaigns for the purpose,
so it seemed to us, of keeping the "liberal" Republicans at home in the
wrong camp when they really belonged with us.

The lines were laid out. They were to lead me through Bryanism to
Wilson and the New Freedom, to Roosevelt and the New Deal, to
what we were later to call "liberal" and our detractors to call "left
wing," to that position in the Democratic party in the United States that
seems to me now to be the middle ground (perhaps a trifle to the left
of center) between the extreme right and the extreme left. It seemed to
me then to be the golden mean between the reactionary Republicans
and the socialistic Populists.

The boom of the late eighties pervaded even the backwoods of the
Ozarks, and Buffalo had enjoyed it along with the rest of the country.
The town was half-rebuilt in brick instead of wood. Land speculation
seemed to promise riches for everybody. We heard the tall tales of the
millions being made in Wichita and other Kansas towns. Some of our
own folks were to lose their money in Eureka Springs, which seemed
destined to be the Arkansas super-spa; and the big mortgage companies
were ever ready with credit. The western land boom began to crumble
in 1888 and had collapsed by 1890. We knew when Baring Brothers
failed in 1891 that the crown of thorns was being pressed down.

The Farmers' Alliance rose to demand relief. In my own county and
in my own time I had known a little of its background. The Granger
movement had of course touched the community, but our county was
hardly prosperous enough to carry on a Grange organization as that
later developed. My memory of it is only the reading and rereading of
the secret ritual of the Patrons of Husbandry in which my father was a
leader and in which my mother served in the offices of Ceres, Pomona,
and Flora. The little book was among her things—she never knew I

stole it out—and it was the only piece of "secret" lodge literature I ever read.

Then followed "The Wheel," an organization of farmers and political Greenbackers who listened to Ignatius Donnelly, who from his editorial tripod of the *Economist* in Minneapolis preached fiat money and the Baconian theory of the authorship of Shakespeare's plays. "The Wheel" attempted in our part of the country to set up limited-profit stores and produce-trading establishments, not as true co-operatives but as farmer-owned enterprises. The ceiling of 10 per cent retail markup as well as ineptitude for management led to their early death; but I remember going out in the country to the "Wheel" stores (they avoided the towns), and I knew what men in the county were "Wheelers" just as I knew that the same men therefore had been Greenbackers and Grangers.

Then came the Farmers' Alliance. It didn't get going in our county until after the elections of 1890, when it had won the Democratic machinery and had elected the governors and congressional delegations from most of the southern states and when, as a sort of a new third party, it was sweeping Kansas, Nebraska, and the Midwest.

The reason why I can remember so plainly the Alliance and its feat of winning so many governorships in 1890 is that I knew all the governors by sight—that is, I knew their pictures. *The Courier-Journal* of Louisville at that time published biennially a big two-year wall calendar. This carried the pictures of the President, the Vice-President, the Speaker of the House of Representatives, and the members of the Cabinet, as well as the names and political affiliations of the members of the two houses of Congress. Also, as befitted a states' rights Democratic newspaper, it displayed a separate portrait of each of the governors. In that fateful year there came on that big sheet the pictures of Buchanan of Tennessee, Northen of Georgia, Hogg of Texas, and, more exciting even, that of "Pitchfork Ben" Tillman, the one-eyed tornado of South Carolina. My father's bragging was enough to fix the event as well as the pictures of those men in my mind forever. In the calendar just before—with Marks for Tennessee and my hero, Simon Bolivar Buckner, for Kentucky—there had been but thirty-eight governors. In this one of 1891 there were forty-four.

Then about a year before the election of 1892 came the Ocala Platform. There had been a meeting in Ocala, Florida, and there a set of "demands" was adopted upon which the Farmers' Alliance was to base its fight. In the South, where the Alliance had already captured the Democratic organization in nearly all the states, it was the basis of an intraparty fight. In the West it was the basis of a new third-party movement. In my family the Ocala Platform was the basis of furious mealtime argument.

Father, the faithful dissident, orthodox in his nonconformance, hailed the Ocala demands as the new Gospel. Mother and Joe and I hooted at them. The Ocala Platform declared for lower tariffs, for free silver, and for stricter regulation of the railroads, failing which there must be government ownership. These were good enough Democratic doctrines for our part of the country.

It was not too difficult for us Democrats also to go along with Ocala in demanding a graduated income tax, although our two lawyers, Mr. Haymes and Mr. Stanley, said that to do this would require an amendment to the Constitution. But when it came to demanding that senators be elected by the direct vote of the people, Messrs. Haymes and Stanley agreed that that would upset the very basis of our constitutional scheme.

These things were not, however, the rock upon which our family split. The Ocala Platform demanded the abolition of national banks (which left us cold) and in their stead the establishment of a subtreasury system. These subtreasuries were to be set up in every state. And what were they to do? Why, they were to lend money at low rates of interest, not to exceed 2 per cent per annum, on farm produce and on land!

Father was for it. Why, we said, it is ridiculous. It will bust the Treasury. He said it was meant only for nonperishable farm produce. We said that the potatoes would rot, that the wheat would get weevily, and that it was altogether a crazy scheme. And, furthermore, Cleveland and the Democrats would get back in—the off-year election of 1890 had looked good to us—and the tariff would be lowered and the monopolies broken up, and then everything would right itself without these new-fangled and dangerous socialistic schemes.

I know now that the Ocala Platform was but one of the declarations that led to the creation of the People's party and to the entrance of the Populists into the campaign of 1892. But it is the only one I remember to have heard about or talked about at that time, and that memory is as vivid as though the event were one of yesterday.

The Populist party was organized, of course. Its nomination of General James B. Weaver of Iowa for President was a bitter pill for Father,

General Weaver not only was a Yankee general but had been in command just after the war in Pulaski, Tennessee, my father's home town, at about the very time Father was the first person initiated into the Ku Klux Klan, then a local organization. General Weaver had not been too tender with the susceptibilities of the people of Giles County.

Mother derided Father for even thinking that he could vote for Weaver. But the Greenbacker who had swallowed "Beast" Butler in 1884 would not retreat. Had not the Populists also nominated General Field, a one-legged Rebel brigadier, for Vice-President? Wasn't the war over? Weren't we all Yankees now? Father didn't waver. Neither did we.

But a few weeks later we did waver a little—at least I did. All over the Midwest the question of fusion was the main topic of political discussion. But the Democrats were not ready for that—save for county tickets here and there. So in Missouri the People's party held its state convention at Sedalia and put up its own state ticket. Dallas County sent seven or eight delegates. Among them was Mathias Wilkinson.

One night about nine o'clock just as I was getting ready for bed "Thi" Wilkinson came to the front door. Father met him on the porch. "Thi" was just back from Sedalia.

"Well, Bob," he said to Father, "we done it."

"What did you do?"

"We nominated you!"

"For what?"

"For state superintendent of schools! That's what!" shouted "Thi."

To have one's own father a candidate for a state office even on a third-party ticket was something! I almost became a Populist. But not quite. Neither did Mother or Joe. But, years after that, I got a lot of satisfaction in running down the old election returns and seeing that Father got more votes than any other Populist on the state ticket—over twenty-five thousand. The fact that he was the tail of the ticket and that the people did not care to "throw away a vote" on the more important positions may have contributed to his greater total, but that circumstance did not diminish my pride.

There were other troubles that summer. Mr. Haymes was afraid of Cleveland. I was not, of course. But Mr. Haymes communicated some of his doubt to me, and for a time, I can remember, before the convention met, I thought of myself as being for Hill for President. The cartoons of Governor David Bennett Hill of New York in *Judge*, with the feather in his hat emblazoned "I am a Democrat," may have helped me.

Certainly I was against Harrison, and particularly was I against his vice-presidential running mate, Whitelaw Reid. Mr. Reid was known to us as the owner of the *New York Tribune,* as a "gold bug," and as the proprietor of a country place called "Ophir Farm." This last circumstance tempted some of our Missouri Republicans to trot Mr. Reid out as a farmer. I remember the devastating series of cartoons in *Puck* which exploded this dirt-farmer myth. One (as I remember it—I have never seen it since) had a picture of Mr. Reid in overalls seated at the richly garnished table in his palatial dining-room eating peas off a knife, his pitchfork leaning handy-like on the edge of the table.

But when the nominations were made, and when Mr. Furth named me to the county committee, I was to put in my cap the feather with the same device that Dave Hill wore.

However, the Ocala demands have pursued me throughout my life. They are all but forgotten by most other people, even of my own age, being absorbed into their proper place as only one of the expressions of agrarian discontent that marked the closing decade of the last century.

There *is* now a graduated tax on income. Senators *are* now elected by the direct vote of the people. The two demands of Ocala were met by constitutional amendment. The national banks as they were then constituted *were* abolished and absorbed into the Federal Reserve System. The currency *has* been expanded so that it is "not less than fifty dollars per capita." The railroads *are* under closer government supervision. And of a surety the government *has* lent money to farmers at a low rate of interest on farm produce as security, and it *has* lent money on land—rural and urban.

Of all the major Ocala demands that I can remember, but two remain unsatisfied. We haven't got free silver. Neither have we free gold. Nevertheless, we have found a way to expand the circulating medium. And we haven't got a low tariff.

The forgotten men of Ocala have won.

But back to 1892. We won. There was trouble ahead, of course, but I was personally too happy to worry about economic storm clouds.

II

In the year 1893 I got a job, I became fourteen, and I began to shave. The job was in the field of public administration. It was that of clerk in the post office. It was political, and it was patronage; but perhaps I may be permitted to cling to the notion that it was held for a time on the basis of merit.

Mr. Cleveland came back to the White House on March 4, and the pie-hungry Democrats of the country were not too much impressed with his professed purpose to extend the civil service or, a little later, with his continuance of Theodore Roosevelt as a civil service commissioner. But that didn't bother us much in Buffalo, for neither the President nor Theodore Roosevelt had so much as dreamed of taking post offices out of the apple-dumpling category—something to be passed around with every change of party administration.

Democrats in our neck of the woods were few and far between, but such as had eluded the bloodhounds of the local majority were nonetheless avid for the loaves and fishes. The "organization," that is, the county committee, was sore beset by two prominent aspirants; and Mr. Bland, the member of Congress, as well as both the senators, Mr. Vest and Mr. Cockerill, had put the responsibility for a choice on the "organization." Dr. John George, a Confederate veteran, who had been the postmaster in Cleveland's first term, naturally assumed that he, too, had been re-elected. Mr. Theodore G. Weatherby, a Union veteran who had proved his party standing by casting in the field the only vote in his Ohio regiment for McClellan against Lincoln in 1864—a viva voce vote at that—thought that he was deserving. What was more, from my point of view, was that Mr. Weatherby promised if elected to recognize the third-party allies by making my father deputy postmaster. There were a half-dozen other aspirants including one whose claim was based on the fact that he was from Sullivan County, Indiana, where Democrats were just naturally more partisanly Democratic than they grew anywhere else.

To settle the matter our particular member of Congress (already an active candidate for the presidency) appealed to a new-fangled device that already was beginning to undermine the strength of the county convention and destroy the power of the party boss—the direct primary. The whole thing was to be left to the rank and file of the Democrats of the town. There weren't many of them, so they were assembled one day in the courthouse, and there they beheld a ballot box. Gone the trappings of the convention; gone the nominating speeches; gone the intrigue and the trade. Every man who could convince the secretary of the county committee, who was my brother Joe, that he was a Democrat—and in that community a seal was set on the forehead of every man that certified his politics—put his secret ballot in the box. The votes were counted. The gray veteran, John George, was third. The blue veteran, Weatherby, was second. Jim Ballard, late of Indiana, who had been deemed by the wise ones as the darkest of dark horses, led the poll.

So James E. Ballard in due time—and in a short time at that—was postmaster.

And I became a clerk in the post office. It was party patronage. It was recognition of my own precocious zeal. It was recognition of my brother's official position as secretary of the county committee. It was recognition, of a sort, of my father's third-party alliance against the Republicans. I never doubted that I had earned the post or that public positions ever could be disposed of in any other fashion. But at the same time I put into the job a furious devotion, for I was conscious of the fact that only the greatest of industry could possibly justify such an enormous salary—twenty-five dollars a month! Mrs. Ballard was her husband's deputy; his stepdaughter, Lily Bennett, was the other clerk; and their pay had to come out of the postmaster's own compensation, which was determined by the value of the postage stamps canceled in the office. The clerkship I held had a salary fixed by Washington and was an allowance in addition to the stamp-cancellation calculation on which the pay of a fourth-class postmaster was based. It didn't occur to me that there was anything wrong about all that, but by the community in general—and my fellow-Democrats in particular—it was not deemed fitting that a mere child should "hold an office" and "draw" a grown man's pay. Even for me it was plain and palpable that such a plum should be a prize awarded in rotation to the faithful. So when Jim Morrow—as good a Democrat as there was on earth—came back home (he had the added merit of once having been a railway post-office clerk), I thought it but just that Mr. Ballard let me out to give Jim Morrow the job.

Nevertheless, I had had some six months of work, and I liked it. The post office was maintained at the personal expense of the postmaster, and Mr. Ballard had found a tiny little box of a one-story building on the south side of the square. He purchased the furniture, including the screen of boxes, call and lock, from the outgoing Republican,

James S. Hazlett, and moved the fixtures into the much smaller place he had rented. There was hardly room outside the grill of boxes for the crowd that packed the place every day when the mail came in—an event that was the high side of town interest and excitement.

This event was due to happen at eleven o'clock in the morning, when the star-route subcontractor, with what flourish his tired horses could manage, swung into the square from the east and clattered up to the post-office door to throw out the locked, leather letter pouch and the canvas bags that held the lesser sort of mail. He had come through the dust or the mud of the twenty-two miles from the railroad at Conway. Time was fixed for all by his coming. Once in a blue moon and in the summertime he might be five or even ten minutes early. That caught the town off base, and many felt cheated that they had not been there at the very first of the "distribution" behind the closed shutters of the two wicket windows. More often the mail-carrier was late. The roads were rough and deep, and when that depth was mud or snow, or when either Niangua River or Greasy Creek was "up," he would be very late. If there was a flood, and there often was, the streams were unfordable, and the mail didn't come at all.

Once the mail was in, the work came on to be furious behind the screen. Mr. Ballard would open the locked pouch, segregate and open the packages of letters whose face-slips showed they were for Buffalo, stamp each letter on the back with the official date of receipt, and hand them to me or Mrs. Ballard or Lily. We threw them into the boxes with lightning speed. Then the heavy canvas bags were dumped. One of us would take the papers and the bundles and throw the Buffalo ones to the others to be "distributed" and the ones bound for the little post offices around us into the bags whose stretched-open mouths yawned for them. Once in a while there would be a special-delivery letter, and then the routine was upset while the postmaster in person entered the letter in a book, "claimed" the eight-cent fee, and himself opened the door of the screen and pushed his way through the crowd to carry the letter to the marked and distinguished recipient whose name was already known to the mass in the lobby.

While this was going on, the lordly tenants of lock-boxes from time to time extracted from their "get-at-able" repositories their letters and papers; but none ever thought of leaving until the "mail was open." That time came, the wicket windows opened, one of us waited on the call-box window to deliver to those who had already craned their necks to see their prizes through the glass windows of their boxes, and another of us "waited" on the general-delivery window, where, of course, the answer to the great question, "Anything for me?" was still a dark mystery.

The mail was open, and in a few minutes the crowd had left. There was a secondary seance at night, about six or seven o'clock, when the mail came in from Bolivar, twenty miles to the west; but that brought fewer people, although it was one of the best possible reasons for not staying at home after supper. There were other mails, daily from Urbana and Louisburg to the north and twice or three times a week from other star routes that spread over the county, but these excited little public interest.

Inside, we also had to "make up the mail." That was even more exciting. I learned the various railway post offices and liked to think that I was most expert in tying packages of letters and putting on the right face-slips—those for St. Louis or Kansas City were easy, but I knew all the mysteries of how to tie the letters that were to go down the Frisco to the Indian Territory and Texas, and those that should go toward St. Louis to be tied out on the railway for places east of St. Louis, and whether these went directly toward New York or toward Chicago. It was great fun.

At other times there was little to do. An occasional money order to make out or a letter to register, someone who hadn't got there when the mail was opened coming in for his mail—these mostly country people.

So there was time for talk. Long talks with Mrs. Ballard, who liked to read and was regarded as definitely "literary" in her tastes and accomplishments. Long talks with Lily, who was just a year younger than I, about the goings-on in society. And time, too, for writing letters.

III

I began to write letters when I was about nine years old—just at the time when reading was no longer merely compulsive, and I had a greater choice of things to do. At first my letters were to total strangers. We subscribed to two weekly newspapers, or rather to the weekly editions of two great daily newspapers—*The Courier-Journal* of Louisville and the *Detroit Free Press*. The dailies then had a custom of boiling down their material into a weekly for rural circulation and also to attract

THE BROWNLOWS, 1883
Joseph W.
Robert S.   Ruth Adelia
        Louis   Walter

THE BROWNLOW BOYS IN 1885

Joe, age sixteen   Louis, age six

Walter, age four

THE DALLAS COUNTY RECORD

THURSDAY, JULY 4, 1895

VOL. I   —   NO. 52

B. S. BROWNLOW, } Editors and Publishers
LOUIS BROWNLOW, }

PROFESSIONAL AND BUSINESS CARDS.

Henry Humphrey,

BLACKSMITHING AND WAGON WORK at bed rock prices. Give him a call. East side the square on Lebanon street.

Levi Engle.

ATTORNEY AT LAW, NOTARY PUB-LIC and Conveyancer. Does a General Law and Collection Business. Practices before the pension and other departments at Washington D. C. Writes and takes acknowledgments to all kinds of deeds, conveyances, &c., takes affidavits of all kinds. Office bank building southwest corner public square, Buffalo. MO.

Fred Pittman,

LIVERY AND FEED STABLE! north west corner of the square. The best rigs, the best attention to stock and the best feed and the best water in t t city. Call and you will be well treated

THE "BUSTED" SIDE-SHOW.

"The country is full of wrecked theatrical troupes walking home."—*Daily Paper.*

AN EARLY RECOLLECTION

(from *Puck*)

readers far beyond the ordinary boundaries of their daily circulation territory. We took *The Courier-Journal* because Mother wanted to read Marse Henry Watterson's editorials; the *Free Press,* because Father wanted to keep up with the humorous contributions made anonymously to that journal under the pseudonym of "M. Quad."

Both weeklies had a young people's section. In one or the other it was called "Y.F.D."—young folks' department—and these printed letters from children. I know how it puzzled me that my letters to the "Y.F.D.," instead of being sent to Louisville or Detroit, had to go to some lady in Bayonne, New Jersey. She evidently was a pioneer woman syndicater, but I didn't know that then. Some of the children's letters suggested that letters from other contributors to the department would be welcome.

My first written contribution to be published appeared in *The Courier-Journal,* and it made, in print, seven or eight lines. In these I managed to say I was interested in politics, and I would like to get letters.

Pretty soon two letters came, one from a boy in Victor, Colorado, and the other from a boy in Plaquemines Parish, Louisiana. The Colorado boy was ten or eleven years old. I remember he said he was older than I. He also shared my interest in politics. He said he thought that everybody ought to vote for Harrison and turn old Grover out to grass. I was furious and wrote him to tell him how wrong he was. There were two or three exchanges of abuse. He caught me with a word spelled wrong and imputed it to my Democratic ignorance. I countered with *two* words misspelled in his letter and imputed his profane use of the word "hell," which I said was "agin the law," to all Republican unrighteousness. Thus ended that correspondence.

The Louisiana boy also was interested in politics. We wrote to each other for several years and finally broke up in a quarrel about prohibition. He was "agin" it, and I was for it. I was sorry when it ended because the boy had a French name—I have forgotten the surname, but the first was "Achille"—and that appealed to my ancestral and cultivated Francophilism.

There were others, but for several years they were all boys. Of course my letters to *The Courier-Journal* and the *Free Press* were more frequent and tended to grow in length, and I also branched out to write to similar children's pages in the *Sunday School Visitor.*

This kept up for a long time and didn't come to an end until I was about twelve. One week in the *Free Press* I had a letter in which I managed to suggest that I would like to correspond with a girl! And in the same issue there was a letter from Evelyn McCann of 333 Besserer Street, Ottawa, Canada, which managed to hint that letters from boys as well as girls might not be unwelcome.

I wrote to her. She wrote to me. Our letters crossed. I answered hers. She answered mine. And thus we had two letters going all the time. After a while it settled down to a unitary exchange, but then it became more exciting as the letters themselves changed in tone, from casual prattle to personal confessions of likes and dislikes, from the discovery of common interests and common aversions, into a series of love letters that were on my side as passionate as I could make them with all the literature of love to draw upon for models. When we got to be about eighteen—she was only six months younger than I—the affair cooled off; but still there was an occasional exchange, and she remembered to write to me to tell me when she was about to be married.

Years afterward when I was past thirty and also was married I found myself in Ottawa. I went to the well-remembered 333 Besserer Street. There I found her mother, who seemed more than delighted to see me and who with Irish roguishness made me blush by quoting from some of my letters. I found then that Evelyn had showed them to everyone she knew in Ottawa, just as I had showed *hers* to everybody I knew in Buffalo. Evelyn was living in Hamilton, and two weeks later, when I invented an excuse to go to Hamilton to see how the political campaign was going there (it was the great Laurier-Borden campaign of 1910 on the issue of reciprocity with the United States), I found to my dismay that Evelyn had gone to visit her mother in Ottawa. So I never saw her. But I spent a delightful hour or two with her husband. He had sacrificed a career in the church and left his theological seminary to marry her; and he, too, from his boyhood days had read my letters to her whom I fondly knew and now fondly recall as "my Canadian girl."

Somehow or other all these correspondences, and there were dozens of them, came before too long to be with girls and only girls. And to the strangers I began to add one or two that I knew.

One of the lively members of the Morrow tribe had married Harry Mitchell, who ran a newspaper at Clinton. His daughters (and sons, too, for that matter, but they didn't count much with me) were at least as

lively as their mother, and, when in the summertime they came to
Buffalo to visit their Grandmother Morrow, I delighted in them. They
often would also visit their cousin in Humansville in Polk County,
which adjoined Dallas County on the west. Three of the Mitchell sisters
were subjected to what at that time, I am very much ashamed to admit,
I probably would have termed "my epistolary attentions." They were
Maude and Bess and Hattie. But for some reason the fire kept up
longer with Maude. She was Republican and of the deepest dye. (I
would have called the color black but she thought it was merely deep,
true blue.) Maude kept it up and wrote editorials for her husband's
newspaper in Colorado Springs until his death and after; and, from a
single exchange of letters in the 1930's, I know she is still Republican.
I discovered in 1952 that things still hadn't changed. Her cousin, Meta
Mitchell, whose husband, Cleveland Newton, was a Republican member of Congress and a secretary of President Hoover, teased me at a
cocktail party in Washington in 1946 about those letters to Maude. She
seemed to remember in them a strain not altogether political.

I dare say she was right, because for a time I literally counted that
day lost when I did not write at least three or four love letters—and get
as many in my mail, too. In fact, there was a period when I deemed it
impolite, not to say boorish, to write to a girl unless I made it a love
letter. A sheaf of these came back to me in the autumn of 1945. They
were written to a girl a year or two older than I, and, when she died in
1945, her sister found them and sent them to me. Maybe at past seventy-
five, I may be pardoned the hope that no more will show up.

But I didn't do all this love-letter-writing on my own hook. I built up
a little local fame in that line, and my aid was sought by some who had
less faith in their powers than I had in mine. For Vic Proctor and Wilbur McPheeters and Charlie Lindsey I wrote letters to their girls, which
they copied out in their own handwriting to send. I was not partial to
the boys. I did the same for three or four girls. In fact, in Vic Proctor's
case I accommodated his sweetheart as well as him and so had the fun
of writing the letters on both sides—of course a priceless secret which
they never suspected.

I don't know whether Clayton Meeks was really shy and timid, or
whether I invested him with those characteristics. At any rate, he rarely
went to parties or out with girls. And when he moved away to Humansville—perhaps twenty miles distant—I told him he ought to write

to Lizzie Edmisson, who, I told him, was really in love with him. She wasn't, but she was a tease and didn't mind my mixing him up. So every day for more than a year I wrote a letter to Clayton telling him about Lizzie, and every day for more than a year Clayton wrote to me, not telling me about Lizzie. These letters also took on a literary quality, for in them we criticized, each for the other and for Lizzie, the books Clayton and I were reading but which Lizzie was not reading.

Clayton was an agnostic, I was a Christian, and we attacked the books we read from the point of view of that dispute between us. So these letters were not to be shown around, except to Lizzie, who swore discretion, because it would not have been fair to Clayton, who might some time come back to Buffalo, to give him the name of "infidel." He was a marble-cutter and made tombstones for a living. It would have hurt his business.

My greatest success as a writer of love letters was achieved when I was fourteen years old. The date is quite fixed in my memory, because it was during the time I worked in the post office in 1893.

The postmaster's stepdaughter, Lily Bennett Ballard, was gay and a bit on the daredevil side, and, although she was a year younger than I, she felt quite superior to me, as was quite natural for a girl to feel about any boy at that age. Lily had a beau—Howard O'Bannon. I didn't have a girl—although I had confessed to Lily that I worshiped the ground upon which her chum, Alice Weatherby, deigned to walk. I was too shy to say anything to Alice. (There did come a time, a little later, under a full moon, that I overcame that shyness and had something to say to Alice—to no avail.) So naturally Lily felt older and wiser and altogether above me. But there was one thing that troubled her. Of course she read all the love letters I wrote and received, and certainly neither she nor Howard did anything like *that*.

One day we were sorting out old papers uncalled for in the general delivery and ran across one which was broadcast far and wide for the sake of its "lonely hearts" column. Lily suggested that I write to one of the advertisers, a boy, and then she would copy the letter in her handwriting, and we could both have some fun. That was grist for my mill.

We selected one Lucius Claudius Robinson of Galesburg, Illinois. I liked his name because it reminded me of Lord Macaulay and his *Lays of Ancient Rome*. Lily liked his letter because it said he was a blond.

I wrote the letter. Lily copied it. I made her kiss it just as she handed it to me to cancel the stamp. Just for luck, I said.

"Four Years More of Grover"

A week later I was at home raking leaves in the front yard. Why I hadn't been able to palm off that chore on my brother Walter I cannot for the life of me remember, but there I was almost knee-deep in autumn leaves. Along the wooden sidewalk, always rickety, came Lily and with her my adored Alice. Lily was waving a letter.

"He answered it!" she called out, as she came within hearing distance. "He's an artist!"

"What kind of an artist?" I asked.

She looked into the letter as the two girls stopped opposite me.

" 'Tonsorial,' it says here," she replied.

I rolled over and over in the leaves with my laughter and at last came up breathless to tell the girls what kind of an artist that was.

I did my very best in reply to Lucius Claudius. It kept up for a year, after I had gone from the post office and was working in the newspaper office. I wrote the letters, she copied them, the gentleman from Galesburg kept up, and right merrily and well did he keep up, indeed.

Then one day came a letter that left Lily and me both speechless. We had been teasing him to come to Buffalo, never dreaming that he would do it. Then this letter. He was on his way. He would be there on the mail hack from Conway the next day but one!

Then the busy twenty-four hours of begging everybody who knew to keep the secret; of calming Mrs. Ballard, Lily's mother, who had read all the letters after the first few and even made suggestions about what we were to write; of Lily's and my endless discussions of what I was to do and to say and to know and not to know.

Lucius Claudius came. He was a nice fellow, and in a day or two everybody in town called him Claude.

A quarter of a century later I was in Kansas City to make a speech to the Citizen's Union about the city-manager form of government. Lily came to hear me, waited for me, and insisted that I come the next night to dinner at their house. She wanted me to tell her daughter and son-in-law, who wouldn't believe it at all, the tale of their courtship. There was never a gayer supper than that. Claude was still a tonsorial artist, then. They had a happy life and a happy family all together until his death in 1951.

I have always accounted that my most successful love-letter affair. Of course I wrote others, and to me much more important love letters, later; but these were supplemented with the spoken word, or I doubt that they would have been so successful. *That* series still goes on.

All this business made a heavy draft on my accumulated store of poetry, and I became a sort of walking Bartlett's with respect to what I very much fear I used to call "the tender passion." I drew on my Burns and my Moore and the other lyricists; on the Brownings and on Tennyson for some passages of sorts; took heroics from Sir Walter and mysterious allusions from the somberest parts of Poe; made use of my little Shakespeare and my even smaller store of the ancients. But, when I wasn't being too subtle, my main dependence was Ella Wheeler Wilcox. Her little volume of *Poems of Passion* was an ever ready help in this particular enterprise of mine. What better way to end one of them than

> If I by the Throne should behold you,
> Looking up with those eyes loved so well,
> Close, close in my arms I would fold you,
> And drop with you down to sweet Hell.

In writing letters to city girls, I had another line. I wanted to get out of the country, but soon—as modern slang would have it. For the city girls I had Nathaniel Parker Willis, the New Yorker poet laureate of the 1830's. I had for them "The White Chip Hat," "The Lady in the White Dress I Helped into the Omnibus," "The Lady in the Chemisette with the Black Buttons," and most especially and particularly:

LOVE IN A COTTAGE

> They may talk of love in a cottage,
>   And bowers of trellised vine—
>
> But give me a sly flirtation
>   By the light of a chandelier—
> With music to play in the pauses,
>   And nobody very near;
>
> True love is at home on a carpet,
>   And mightily likes his ease—
> And true love has an eye for a dinner,
>   And starves beneath shady trees.
> His wing is the fan of a lady,
>   His foot's an invisible thing,
> And his arrow is tip'd with a jewel,
>   And shot from a silver string.

That I liked, whether the city girls did so or not. For those for whom Ella Wheeler was too much and for whom Nathaniel Parker Willis was too little, I could always fall back on Ben Jonson or Tom Moore and with my "rosy wreaths" be wistful for some never-never land such as, say, Venice—

> Row gently here, my gondolier,
> So softly wake the tide
> That not an ear on earth may hear
> Save hers to whom we glide.

With so many affairs in the air at once I had to do my homework with the lyricists, but it wasn't too hard.

Why in my adult life, at least since my mother died—for to her I always did write long letters—I lost utterly the urge and skill to write letters, I do not know unless it be that I wrote myself out, so far as letters were concerned, in my boyhood. At any rate, it is true that I am dilatory and put off as long as possible writing letters that must be written; that I have found that some letters neglected seem to answer themselves in time; that, when I am dictating, I manage to postpone all but the very easiest letters until the next time; and that I make every possible excuse to telephone instead of to write.

Then in my life as an administrator I developed a maxim to which I firmly hold: Never in the course of a negotiation write a letter that says more than "I will see you at lunch next Wednesday" or "Meet me in my office this afternoon." When the negotiation is completed, then write a letter confirming the understanding arrived at. This course avoids misunderstandings. It keeps down friction. It saves wear and tear on typewriter ribbons. I sometimes think it is a Rule Number One for the administrator.

CHAPTER VII

PRINTERS AND POPULISTS

At some time or other, when I was about nine years old, I learned to set type. Miss India Richardson was the foreman, for most of the time the entire typographical staff, of the composing-room of the *Buffalo Reflex*. The *Reflex* was the solid Republican paper that enjoyed the county printing; it had been established in 1869, and it had outlived many competitors and rivals; just as in 1955 it still comes out every week, and it still calls itself what it called itself toward the end of the nineteenth century—"The Old Reliable."

Miss India indulged my curiosity and gave me a broken-backed chair to stand on. (the footstools provided for short-statured printers were not high enough); she gave me a composing stick, a composing rule, and an unlimited amount of kindly advice and taught me to set type. I wasn't tall enough to kick the old Gordon job press, much less big or strong enough to do anything with the Washington hand press on which the *Reflex* was printed; and therefore I didn't hang about that printshop too long. But it was long enough to have "learned the boxes" (as we called memorizing the divisions of the type cases in which were to be found the particular type letters, lower case and upper case) and to be able, by scrambling hard and high for the capital letters, to set sometimes as much as three or four lines of pica type at a time. Miss India calculated that pica was as small as I could manage.

This was the first and only one of the trade skills that I had dabbled in that I afterward put to use. It came about in this fashion, and, as it set the lines within which I have lived my whole life, I will try to tell the story whole.

During the campaign of 1892 the third-party people of the county, invigorated by the new name of the People's party and its seemingly bright prospects, decided to start a newspaper. There had been a Democratic paper in the late seventies and early eighties which, subsidized by the state committee, had lingered for a little and then languished into decline and death. The equipment, presses, type, and so on, had been gathering dust in the upstairs part of Sam Pittman's livery stable for years and years. Mr. Pittman had died, and no one knew very clearly in whom the title of the outfit was vested; but the chairman of the Democratic county committee, Frank Furth, hoping for aid in his war with the Republicans, gave consent for the Populists to take it over.

A newcomer, Dr. Daily, was to be editor and publisher. What sort of a "doctor" he was I have forgotten, but politically he was a mighty man whose vigor had been tested as a Greenbacker, a Granger, a Wheeler, and a Farmers' Alliance man. He had a long beard and long hair, both of which were dyed black, and his age was a complete mystery. One of the Populists who helped finance the moving of the plant to the upstairs rooms of the Hardy Brick, get it cleaned up, and obtain the requisite credit from the Western Newspaper Union in St. Louis, which would furnish the necessary patent insides for the new journal, was Jack Kirby. ("Patent insides" was the common name for the paper on which the newspaper was to be printed and which came once a week from St. Louis by express to the railway station at Conway and thence via the mail hack to Buffalo. One side of the double sheet was already printed, filled with general news, with miscellany, with some national editorials—Populist in tone, of course—and with some national advertising. The two pages on the other side of the double sheet were then printed and so made up the four pages of the paper.)

Mr. Jack Kirby was an Englishman, a brawny Yorkshireman, and a radical. He was a good friend of mine, for I tried to understand his speech—a difficult thing to do if he were excited and talking rapidly, and most of the time he was excited. He indulged my curiosity, however, and even read to me, when I took him the book, Tennyson's *Northern Farmer, Old Style and New Style* in the north-country dialect as they should have been read.

Along in the late summer of 1893, when the panic that gripped the whole nation had reached into the nooks and crannies of the backwoods and had paralyzed even the little business there was in Buffalo, Dr. Daily gave up the struggle and turned the future of "The People's Paper" back to the Populist committee. Always hard up and now hard hit indeed, with no teaching job at the time, Father "bought" "The

People's Paper." When Jack Kirby and some of the others promised to do all they could to help him, he shouldered Dr. Daily's accumulated debts to the patent insides concern and took over.

As I have said, my post-office job, as seemed proper, had been taken over by rotation by Jim Morrow; I was fourteen years old; I could set type; and now I was tall enough to pull the Washington hand press and kick the Gordon job press. I was to work with Father. The wages were of course not nearly up to the princely salary of twenty-five dollars a month that I had drawn in the post office, but three dollars a week was standard wages for a printer in that town and time, and I could do no better.

As a matter of fact, I was more than delighted; but I hadn't liked Dr. Daily, and I wasn't myself a Populist. So I made a deal with Father. I represented that the name of the paper was no good for any but dyed-in-the-wool "Pops," that there were many others in the county who didn't like the *Reflex*—even some of the Republicans—and that we ought to try to get their patronage as well as that of the third-party men.

Father agreed, and together, with the assent of Mr. Kirby and others, we changed the name to the *Dallas County Record*. After a few weeks we got the patent insides corrected, and I myself set up the new title for the front page.

The editorial masthead was on the inside—printed in St. Louis. It took two or three weeks to get changed from "The People's Paper" and "Dr. Daily, *Editor*" to the new masthead:

THE DALLAS COUNTY RECORD
R. S. AND L. R. BROWNLOW
Editors and Publishers

Thus at fourteen I broke into print with my name. The "R. S." was for Robert Sims, and the "L. R." was for Louis Richmond; and the use of the initials was merely a decree, deliberate or accidental, of the Western Newspaper Union, which printed the insides and obtained for us the "canned" but adequately Populistic editorials.

There were two rooms upstairs in the Hardy Brick, which had been built by my sister-in-law's father. It was on the wrong end of the wrong side of the square, and no business it ever housed had flourished. The upper story, which was vacant, was reached by a flight of wooden steps that ran up in the open on the outside of the building to a door cut into the west wall. These steps were always rickety, and for sixty years I have perished on them as I still continue to perish in occasional nightmares when the steps collapse as I am halfway up them.

The outer door entered the larger of the two rooms, and access to the smaller was through it. The smaller room at the back was the "office" and had a high desk and a high stool and a bookcase of sorts. The big room had a window to the south and three big windows to the west looking out over the square and the courthouse.

In this room were set up the big Washington hand press, the little Gordon job press, the cases for type and the printing furniture, a small paper-cutter, and a cabinet for paper stock of different colors and sizes. In the very middle were the two great imposing stones set in their heavy wooden turtles, each big enough to accommodate two full chases of nine 13-em columns. We were using only seven columns, so were forced to handle equipment and a press too big for our purposes, a circumstance that I recall vividly because of the catastrophes and disasters of pied forms and warped furniture which resulted.

Of course the little that I had learned as a child from Miss India— merely to set type—was not enough. But I had a wonderful teacher. Just as we were taking over the paper, one of Buffalo's wandering sons returned. He was a gentleman, a scholar, and an artist; he was well read and well schooled in grammar and in style; he was a master journeyman printer.

He was Francis Marion Wilkinson, the son of Uncle Dick Wilkinson, who was in turn the son of Richard Wilkinson, the settler and surveyor, who laid out the town of Buffalo in the 1840's. Marion Wilkinson was a little bit of a dandy—almost a "dude," in fact—but he was also a little odd in that he was sticking faithfully to the extremely tight trousers, the high-cut lapels, and the hard-boiled hats of an earlier era. His huge mustachios were curled and waxed at the ends, and he stood very straight to compensate for his small stature.

Marion had traveled much. He had learned much on his travels. He was also "close-mouthed," as we said. He would not talk about his travels except to one certain category of companions. If the would-be listener were a printer, Marion would talk and talk, long and volubly. If he were not printer, Marion had nothing to say to him.

Marion taught me to be a printer, and, as I progressed in my mastery of his mystery, he talked to me, more and more and more. Proud of his trade, he would take from his coat pocket his own personal composing stick and from his vest pocket his own personal thin, worn composing rule and with all solemnity instruct me not only in what we now call the "know-how" of being a printer but in the essential philosophy that made a printer a better sort of man, set apart from his fellows by the very nature of his high calling. A printer, he said, was an artist. He was a practitioner of the highest of the arts, "the art preservative of all arts," without which learning and culture would perish from the face of the earth. Then, with a bitterness that veritably curdled my insides, he would curse the demons that had permitted the invention of the typesetting machine and were about to plunge the world into that black chaos that was bound to come when there were no more journeymen printers to save it with hand-set type.

He told me tall tales of his travels; of St. Louis and Chicago; of Washington and Philadelphia and New York; of Boston, even, and the composing-room of the *Transcript*. He had seen Dana in the composing-room of the *Sun,* and he had seen Mr. Watterson in the flesh, bending over the imposing stone in *The Courier-Journal* shop, making up the Great Page.

He had drunk deep of the Pierian spring and also, as it fell out, at other fountains. In short, Marion was a tramp printer.

Being what he was, Marion of course didn't stay long, but he was there long enough to make me quite confident that I had a right to a card in the Typographical Union as well as to membership in the United Typothetae of America. I was both a printer and an employer of printers. I affected the practice of carrying my stick and rule with me all the time, and I addressed letters to great folk in Chicago and New York on letterheads that proclaimed me as publisher. I was not insensible to the fact that I also was reporter, commentator (that word we didn't know, of course), and editor. I had other letterheads for other purposes on which it was simply "Editor." The mate of the Captain's gig had nothing on me. Of the editorial part of my job—well, as a young British-Indian writer was just then beginning to teach us to say—that is another story.

The types were at once my joy and my despair. There were six stands of type, each with its top two trays set at their appropriately different angles, and underneath filled from the top to within four inches of the floor with other trays of other kinds of type, from those reserved for the general letter press throughout all the different sizes of display type that might be used for headlines or for job printing, all the way from gothic nonpareil up to the mammoth 144-point wooden type that we called "stud horse" because of the use to which it usually was put when we got a job of poster printing.

Types had been but recently standardized on the basis of 72 points to the inch. Under Marion's tutelage I preferred the old names, "nonpareil," "minion," "brevier," "long primer," and "pica," to 6-, 7-, 8-, 10-, and 12-point. I think I even said "double-pica" for 24-point, but beyond that I was new-fangled for 36-, 48-, and 72-point; if they had old names, I have forgotten them.

The trouble in our shop was that we did have some minion that wasn't precisely 7-point. That didn't bother us so much, however, as the brevier that wasn't exactly 8-point. We rarely used the minion, but, if we did, it was sufficiently differentiated to cause but little confusion, for we had no 7-point. The brevier was the trouble. We had fonts of old brevier and fonts of new 8-point. The difference was hardly visible to the naked eye, and the faces of the types were the same. When *those* fonts got mixed up, *then* there *was* trouble! Pi. Right out of the ever so carefully locked-up chase, as it was being lifted from imposing stone to press bed, would drop whole handfuls, and the whole business was to be set over again. And, oh, the painfulness of distributing pi, without the words to guide one's eyes and fingers, and the necessity of trying to decide for each individual type what was standard 8-point and what was bastard brevier!

I liked the brevier better for its face, for its old style, and I liked the way the figure *1*'s were squared off top and bottom. I liked the figure *5*'s with their drooping curved tails. I liked the upswept stems of the *6*'s and the downswept stems of the *9*'s.

Our long primer, or 10-point, was new; it was standard; we had nothing to get it mixed up with, and of course it was easier to set. It was new-style face. I didn't like its even rows of *1*'s, *5*'s, *6*'s, and *9*'s, and the like; but I gave up, and most of the time we set the paper in long primer. That is, unless we got a legal advertisement that had to be set in nonpareil. Most of these went to the *Reflex,* but the eastern mortgage companies were foreclosing, and, when a Populist or a Democratic lawyer could wangle it, we would get the sales advertisement. Sometimes even a Republican who was not too well pleased with the dominant O'Bannon machine would throw us something. And the land office was Democratic, so we got the homesteading ads of those who were "proving up" their titles to the miserably poor public lands that still were open to settlement in our county.

These legal ads were set in nonpareil, and the tiny 6-point types were hard to handle—hard to set, hard to impose, hard to distribute. I did it when I had to. But most of the time I would put that off on the girl typesetter and devote my precious time to setting ads and job work.

After Marion resumed his travels, we always had a girl typesetter. I think the wage was three dollars a week, but sometimes seniority may have upped it just a trifle. The first girl was Ida Welch. She was swift, accurate, and easy to get along with; but she was mostly silent, and I would have preferred a chatterbox.

What I liked least was that most of our display type was hopelessly old-fashioned. It had all sorts of curlicues and fancy faces and dated us as of the seventies. The beautiful catalogues of the type founders came to us, and I pored over the wonderful new faces, admired the new and simpler fashions, and begged first Father and later the other owners to order new types. I read every month the *Inland Printer* and kept up with what was going on in the graphic arts. I knew by heart my Barnhart Brothers & Spindler catalogue. One year it repeated in every size and style of type as much as could be set in each size of Longfellow's "Excelsior," and I followed the upward struggles of the youth "bearing the banner with a strange device" through hundreds and hundreds of pages.

The great Theodore De Vinne of the De Vinne Press was attempting to reform the typography of the nation. In the first few months of Father's regime we bought the new face, De Vinne, in several sizes and also a new Old English type, Tudor, in several sizes and in both extended and condensed forms. With these I revolutionized the standard letterhead designs of the town and county and even attracted some business away from the staid old *Reflex,* where Miss India still set every letterhead in exactly the same fashion with exactly the same old "shaded" type face.

For sixty years I have reaped a rich reward from all this part of my education. Actually I have not touched a type (except maybe to see if I still knew the boxes) since the very turn of the century when Aubrey Beardsley and the Bradleys set their seal on new styles—new styles that Elbert Hubbard at East Aurora was to make so much to-do about in this country. Yet during all that time I have thrilled to the message of a clean-cut, new type face; all that time printing has been to me an art, not merely preservative to the other arts, but an art in and of and for itself in which my soul delights.

Perhaps it is just here that I would like to make a note of what I deem to be an almost permanent curse of the typesetting machine, although there are now some signs that printing may yet recover its lost ground. In the hand-set days we knew the value of emphasis in the printed as well as in the spoken word. We put in *italics,* or SMALL CAPITALS, or CAPITALS whenever or wherever they were indicated by the author, by the editor perhaps, or by style—such as the style that the name of one's own paper was always set in small caps, the name of another newspaper always in italics. And we could and would and actually did use italics for emphasis.

The early Mergenthalers with their single magazines couldn't do italics, and italics went out of fashion, just as the more beautiful "old-style" letterpress had gone out. With the disappearance of italicization went out also the point to the American anecdote. The anecdote still could be told, but it couldn't be printed, because you no longer could italicize the punch words and the punch lines. For an example, many of Mark Twain's funniest incidental tales were really funny when he could indicate in type that drawling underscoring of a pronoun— "That's what *she* said"—that he used on the platform. Read his earlier editions, and the point is still there, properly set up with italics. Read his later editions, and not only the point is not there, but there is no point to printing the thing at all.

Even when the multiple-magazine Mergenthalers came in—many years ago—the style had changed. Copy was typewritten, and the writers didn't underscore. The italics dropped out. Now at last italics are coming back, and I greet the italicized words with nostalgic paeans of joy, for that which was so good in the good old days is still good even to one who thinks he faces the future without fear and is inclined to hope that the future will bring us New Deals the startlingness of which we cannot even yet imagine.

This was the very time of two revolutionary events in printing—the substitution of machine composition for hand composition in all the larger newspapers and book-publishing houses and the simultaneous change in taste with respect to typography that we then were perhaps too apt to associate with the handy handle of *"fin de siècle."* The machines affected me and my own printshop but indirectly. We had no power for our presses but that of foot and hand, and we had no way of setting type but the old way. The indirect effect was in the increase in the numbers and range of tramp printers. These journeymen, finding their day's work and their numbers cut by the machine, took literally to journeying about the country—and deep into the country, at that—to escape the destruction of the machine. That was why Marion Wilkinson came back to Buffalo just in time to be my first teacher. And he was followed by others, for whom sometimes, when we had a lawyer's brief or some such book job on hand, we would find work for a week or two.

One of these was Ward. I have forgotten his first name, but I have not forgotten Ward. He was a dark, slight man of about thirty, addicted to poetry, belles-lettres, art, and liquor. The poetry he recited endlessly and to my great delight. (I think he had been stage-struck, too, for he had a way of manipulating a falling lock of long black hair over his forehead when he declaimed his *Hamlet* and his *Othello*.) His belles-lettres he cited to me for my future education, advising Milton for grandeur, Addison for style, and Swift for satire, being at the same time indulgent to my own more utilitarian Ruskinism. His art found a medium of expression in wood engraving and in typography, and he undertook to teach me both.

About the shop from the days of the seventies, when the equipment had first come from St. Louis, there were two unused hinged boxes. The smaller contained a brand-new set of graver's tools. The larger had a store of virgin boxwood blocks, type-high and accurately joined in squares, some 13-ems pica and some 26½-ems pica—in other words, all ready for one- or two-column wood engravings. Ward cut some fairly good ones, and he faithfully attempted to teach me the rudiments of the art. I can remember little but the feel of the heel of the burin in the palm of my hand and the dig of the graver in the dense, close grain of the boxwood. I achieved but one thing "fit to print." It was a crowing rooster to be used to celebrate election victories.

His other addiction, the liquor, led Ward to his poetry, and thus the compass round was fetched from the week end to the week end. He disappeared one Saturday with all of his five dollars, and we saw him no more.

But before he went he had made me uneasy about my typesetting. For display advertisements and for job work—posters, letterheads, and so on—I had followed the prevailing style that permitted a printer, aye, even encouraged him, to use as many different type faces as it was possible to arrange within the limits of his copy—almost never two lines together of the same type face. This hodgepodge was further messed up with cast "ornaments" and even with curlicues home-made out of bent brass rule. Often these jobs were impossible to justify line by line with the proper use of quads and spaces, and we had to set them in the form with plaster of Paris so that they might be lifted, without pi, to the press bed.

Ward said that was all wrong. He had two or three books with him. One was a pamphlet by William Morris, protesting the hideousness of the current type styles. Another was a copy of the *Yellow Book*, with illustrations by Aubrey Beardsley. Then there was the *Inland Printer*, with its new fashion being expressed by Will Bradley. After a time, I engineered the purchase of some fonts of the new Jenson old style and reveled in setting ads and jobs in the new way—all in one type face, mostly in one-size body, using ornaments and initials to try to make it all look like an illuminated manuscript. We also got some fonts of Bradley—a condensed Old English letter named for my far-distant idol, Will Bradley. It took some doing to get this Jenson and Bradley, incidentally, for it meant deserting Barnhart Brothers & Spindler, who advertised themselves as the antitrust type founders, to patronize the American Type Founders, who were the trust. That was hard for a Populist paper, but art won over politics in that contest.

Elbert Hubbard and the Roycrofters soon made these new styles familiar everywhere, but I think it was the machine, the Mergenthaler Linotype so soon followed by the Lanston Monotype, that cut down the number of type faces in use and introduced for their long sway the simple fashions in printing that have been universal since the first decade of the twentieth century. Only the curious searching in old libraries now may discover what heterogeneous atrocities the old hand-set typographers could turn out.

Never for one moment did my preoccupation with the printing craft obscure my determination that one day I would be a newspaperman and a city newspaperman at that; never for one moment did I think of all that manual skill as being other than contributory to the higher calling of "editor." The facts were, though, that there wasn't a great deal of range for reportorial or editorial experiment on the *Record*. The news we printed in our two pages of seven columns each, diminished as much as possible of course by display advertisements, was nothing much but "personals"—little items of from three to six lines, and a part of them was contributed by the "country" correspondents from the outlying communities in the county.

However, the *Record,* in addition to its canned editorials that came printed on the patent insides, did print for itself a column or a column and a half of local editorials, nearly always of a political nature; it published obituaries and, in season, longer accounts of revival meetings and other church activities. These were my meat.

Quite early I learned the trick of evading the blue pencil of the editor—either my father or his successors—as well as that of making it difficult for the censor—any elder in a position of authority. I managed this quite simply by refusing to write my stuff. I simply set it up out of my head into the composing stick. Of course, there was a chance that the elders would see it in the galley proofs, but they were often content to leave proofreading to me, so that the elders were as much surprised as was the general public with what I had to say.

The Republican boss of the county, Jim O'Bannon, was a mountain of a man who never made a speech and used words but frugally for any purpose. His chief lieutenant was Frank Wilson, who didn't make public speeches but knew how to use all the words—in and out of the polite dictionaries—in issuing the orders that made the machine work. To me, so deep always in my Bible, what easier than to make Mr. O'Bannon into Moses and Mr. Wilson into Aaron?

And so, week after week, my editorial came out: "And Moses said unto Aaron, go forth and tell my people . . ." or "In those days it came to pass that Aaron went into the land of Louisburg," and so on. The most successful was one that had to do with the importation into Buffalo of a very clever Republican politician from Urbana, eighteen miles to the north in our county. He was to be an aid to Aaron; his name was Coon. I had almost a column of biblical imitation concerning the woes of Moses and Aaron and their decision to send for help. Then, breaking into the refrain of a current popular song, I concluded: ". . . and it came to pass that Aaron lifted up his voice and cried, 'Oh, Moses, behold there is a new Coon in town.'"

All this was irreverent. It was mostly irrelevant and immaterial, too, but it was principally irreverent, both in that one of my age should be so free with his elders and that it was written in the style of the Book. Everybody threatened to stop me. Nobody even tried. I had fun.

Most of my editorials were political, but not all of them were partisan. I was, for instance, an enthusiastic advocate of woman's suffrage and, as a matter of course, of prohibition. Perhaps one sample of the sort of editorials I wrote or rather the sort that I composed directly in type without the intervention of manuscript may be endured. It appeared in the *Dallas County Record* on July 25, 1895:

Mrs. Lewis of the W.C.T.U. lectured to a large audience at the M.E. Church last Sunday night. She is an eloquent speaker, and made an earnest appeal to the people in behalf of the cause which she advocates. She is enthusiastic on the subject of Women's Suffrage and thinks it the only way to get prohibition. She made the best speech and more to the point than has been made in Buffalo for more than a century, and should Mrs. Lewis and I arrive at the ballot box at the same time, I would (adhering to that inborn chivalric spirit) gently lift my hat and allow her to vote first, knowing that she would vote for the good of all, while I might be biased just a little bit by what is usually known as party prejudice. Down with the foolish idea that it would degrade women to allow them to vote. The man who opposes it will sit complacently on a goods box all day long and argue politics, then go home at night and "fuss" at his wife because supper is not ready—remembering at the same time, that he had neglected to provide stovewood. Yes, your wife has sense enough to cook, wash, chop wood, and do all the menial labor belonging to the household, while you do the voting. Isn't this nice? I have heard men even in the town of Buffalo animadverting on the degradation to which women would be brought were they allowed to become citizens, and at the same time I knew that those same men's wives were supporting the family, by washing the dirty linen of the parties with whom they were arguing. "Consistency, thou art a jewel."

CHAPTER VIII

...AND POLITICS, 1896

In my memory little remains of my editorial activities on the *Record* other than those inextricably bound up with the political campaigns of the time. Of those, I retain something of the squabbles for the loaves and fishes of the local offices and that sort of thing; but mostly I remember the things that then seemed to me the matter of supreme and eternal importance—national politics. Times were hard—very hard. There was to come the campaign of 1896. The crown of thorns pressed deep into bloody brows.

Not only were the times hard in general but the *Dallas County Record* simply couldn't make the grade. The Populists who had supported it could do so no more. My father couldn't make ends meet, and so in the spring of 1896 the paper was turned over—I suppose at the time we euphemistically said that it was "sold"—to John W. Miller. Mr. Miller was a lawyer, a Populist, and he had had sufficient political strength once, when the Republicans were split, to be elected prosecuting attorney. I don't think all of us quite realized at the time the transfer was made that he had an assurance of the necessary financial support to meet the deficit from his brother-in-law, Israel Shantz. Mr. Shantz was a Republican, but he was frequently accused of making offside plays in the furtherance of his ambition to supplant Jim O'Bannon as the Republican boss of the county.

At the very beginning Mr. Miller himself wrote vigorous editorials on the Populist side and permitted me to do likewise. I had been sold with the paper and stayed on at three dollars a week, but of course my name came down from the masthead, and I no longer was an editor. I was just a hired man. We also continued to get the patent insides from St. Louis, and this proved to be our undoing. A Populist editorial in the patent insides was so offensive to the Republicans that

Mr. Miller, prodded no doubt by Mr. Shantz, dropped the patent insides altogether, and we began to print the whole four pages of the paper at home. That made a lot more work, greatly increased the opportunity for my editorial indulgences, and was hailed by all and sundry as great progress, which it was.

But at the same time we were undone politically because the paper became independent. A little later, as we went into the campaign, its editorial columns were neutrally silent with respect to the most exciting campaign in history.

What Mr. Miller did was to turn over a column each week to each of the three county chairmen of the three political parties, Mr. O'Bannon for the Republicans, Mr. R. A. Morrow for the Populists, and my brother Joseph W. Brownlow, for the Democrats. Since Mr. O'Bannon had his own newspaper, the *Buffalo Reflex,* and, it must be admitted, for other good and sufficient reasons, he permitted his column to be ghosted by John S. Lindsey. Mr. Morrow, whom we called "Doc," wrote his own. Joe, my brother, in the interest of getting votes, temporarily abandoned the ancient and honorable name of his party and headed his weekly contribution "The Silver Party," and I ghosted it for him.

The first shock of my disillusion came earlier, however, in June, just before the paper was turned over to Mr. Miller, and the Republican National Convention met in St. Louis. Mr. McKinley was nominated, but Senator Platt of New York was there as well as Mark Hanna, and the "gold plank" went in the platform. Senator Henry M. Teller of Colorado led the bolt from the convention, but only too few Silver Republicans followed him, and they only from the silver-mining states.

Worse than that was what happened at home. Party loyalty triumphed over all things else, and Jim O'Bannon led his party followers over to gold, over to the very thing that they had hated Cleveland for. To me at seventeen, it was all but incomprehensible. I had deserted my Democratic President; I thought the Republicans ought to desert their candidate, who himself had deserted his own principles. As a matter of fact, Major McKinley had never been an out-and-out free silverite, but he had squinted in that direction once upon a time with talk of bimetallism; and we were inclined to hold him to his squint.

Years afterward, when I went to Washington just a few days before Mr. Hanna died, I heard from the lips of one of his closest friends a story that Senator Hanna was wont to say was the best political story of his career. Mr. John W. Yerkes, the commissioner of internal revenue, who had been, according to Republican belief, "counted out" when he was the Republican nominee for governor of Kentucky, told me the story because Mr. Hanna was at death's door and because of my name. As Mr. Yerkes told it, the tale ran thus:

"In '96 I went to St. Louis with just one thing in mind," said Mr. Hanna. "It was to nominate McKinley. I wasn't afraid of the silverites because I thought they would peter out, but I didn't want to stir them up. Platt went there to get a gold plank. We both won. I got McKinley. Platt got his gold plank.

"Well, it seems that there was a terrible ruckus in the Tennessee delegation at St. Louis. They were not fighting about silver or gold but about who was to be national committeeman. In the end Walter Brownlow won over Henry Clay Evans by a whisker, and Brownlow went on the national committee.

"McKinley was nominated, and I was made chairman of the national committee," continued Mr. Hanna, "and I went on back to Cleveland to get ready for the campaign. I had hardly got home when I began to get letters from every crossroads in Tennessee—all from Evans men, of course—saying that something would have to be done to put Walter Brownlow off the national committee. They said he was a silverite who had got his nomination for Congress that very year by campaigning for the free and unlimited coinage of silver at the ratio of sixteen to one.

"It bothered me so much," Mr. Hanna continued, "that I finally wrote to Brownlow and asked him what about it. I shall never forget his reply. It was couched in the East Tennessee vernacular, but I was able to understand it. He wrote:

"'Dear Mr. Hanna: I done got your letter. It is so that I made some speeches arly this here past spring when I was a-runnin' for the Republican nomination for Congress. I hadn't never run for no office before, and I hadn't never made no speech. I knowed I didn't have sense enough to git me up a speech so I jist thought I'd git a speech some other feller had made and git it by heart and jist say it. I happened to pick a speech made by a feller by the name of McKinley to the Stark County, Ohio, Farmers' Alliance a couple years or so back. I aim to be mighty busy in this here campaign, but if Mc flops agin, jist wire me. Yours truly, Walter Preston Brownlow.' "

But to get back to Dallas County. Not all the Republicans were so ready to climb on the band wagon. But the trend was that way, and we saw we were going to have a hard fight. The little space of time after the St. Louis convention shut many a hitherto ready Republican mouth.

For the first time we really had to fight for silver. Coin's *Financial School* and Mr. Bland's speeches came into more frequent requisition. Even the speeches of an obscure young congressman from Nebraska were found useful, a fact that was to be indelibly impressed on my memory by the tragic events being unveiled at the very time in Chicago.

There was no telephone in Buffalo. We heard the news the next day when the mail hack came. We had thought that there would be a few ballots, perhaps, to give the favorite sons a ride. We had thought that even the easterners, who were voting for David Bennett Hill, would come over at the end and make it unanimous for Bland.

Even when the papers came, and we were thrilled to the marrow of our souls by that great speech of the Boy Orator of the Platte, we never wavered in our faith. It would be Bland. Bland would win.

". . . You shall not press down upon the brow of labor this crown of thorns, You shall not crucify mankind upon a cross of gold!!!"

The Peerless Leader whose voice was as the voice of an angel had appeared. Two days later we knew it was not Bland; it never would be Bland. Our own, our very own, would not go to the White House.

Our candidate was William Jennings Bryan. My brother Joe was in Lebanon, to be with Bland in the hour of his victory. He stayed for a day or two—he was one of the faithful followers of the neighborhood who could not bear so soon to go away from their defeated leader.

Joe took the train to St. Louis to meet Mr. Bland as a gesture of loyalty, and there right on the train from Chicago with Mr. Bland was the Peerless Leader himself! And my brother Joe was right there and saw him and shook hands with him and talked to him. And my brother Joe heard that golden voice that was so intent upon abjuring all that was gold or golden. Joe came right straight home to help me bind and heal my broken heart. So much of the aura of the ineffable presence did he bring with him that almost overnight I was made whole again. I was for Bryan. Maybe we in Dallas County were again become remote, but, if we were backwoodsmen, we had found a champion.

Later, years later, I heard from the lips of men who were in that fight—from Mr. Bryan himself; from Senator James K. Jones of Arkansas, who was the chairman of the national committee; and from my close friend, Urey Woodson, who was its secretary—the tales of that struggle. I likewise have heard from their own mouths the stories of many of the Republican leaders in that fight. I have heard how the battle raged in various parts of the country from participants, each of whom saw his own sector plainest. In later years I have read many a thrilling account of the campaign of 1896. But none of them, it seems to me, was so exciting as what happened to us right there at home in Dallas County when we carried the county for Bryan—the first Democratic candidate for President who had ever carried it—because Dallas County had ever been Whig and Republican, as after 1896 it was ever to be Republican except for the one time in 1932, when it went for Franklin Delano Roosevelt.

What was our situation, our problem, our manifest program? It was, first, that the Republicans were in the majority; second, that most of them would continue to be Republican; third, that our only hope was fusion.

But that word "fusion" was not new to us. The tiny minority of Democrats and the larger minority of Populists or third-party men, once in a while, by virtue of a particularly bad Republican nomination, had managed to squeeze in somebody or other for sheriff or prosecuting attorney. In the state which for so many years had been so safely Democratic, fusion was not so easily tolerated. The question the state Democratic leaders asked was: Why give the Populists anything when we have enough votes ourselves?

Early in 1896, Mr. Bland, with an eye on the national campaign in which he did not doubt that he would be the standard-bearer, took thought. He saw that it was only by the grace of those few states in which some sort of accord had been reached between Democrats and Populists that General Weaver had been able to detach enough Republican electoral votes from Harrison to let Cleveland win in 1892. So he proposed fusion. Mr. Bland himself presided over the

Fusion Convention to which Democrats and Populists adhered and in which Silver Republican support was solicited. Had the Democratic leaders in other midwestern states done the same, the result in 1896 might have been different. In Iowa, for instance, General Weaver, the leader of the Populists, held out the olive branch; but the Democratic governor, Horace Boies, governor in fact by grace of Populist votes, was too loyal to Mr. Cleveland and refused to assent to fusion.

When Mr. Bland gave way to Mr. Bryan as the leader of the Democrats, the Populists were delighted. They nominated him as their candidate for President. They couldn't quite swallow Mr. Sewall of Maine for Vice-President, however, and nominated their own Tom Watson of Georgia for the second place on the ticket. And Tom tried to prevent actual fusion in some states by insisting on a separate list of electors, devoted to simon-pure, middle-of-the-road Populism and, incidentally, to better chances for McKinley.

It was I who in my own proper person found a way out of the confusion of the two vice-presidential candidatures in our county. I was told to print badges for the big Bryan rally that was to be held in Buffalo. We had got some red ribbon, and the printing was to be in silver, naturally. The committee told me to print some of them "Bryan and Sewall" and some of them "Bryan and Watson." I didn't like it. Fusion at the state level had prevailed, and the Populists had nominated the Democratic candidate for governor, Lon V. Stephens, as their own. So I ignored the vice-presidential aspirants and hit a "middle-of-the-road" of my own. The silver type on the red ribbons proclaimed: "I am for Bryan and Stephens." Nobody seemed to mind, and I had got the committee out of a difficulty.

Fusion then was advanced when the Democratic and Populist county committees were merged into one, and a number of Silver Republicans were added to it. That, of course, was the end of the Populists and, for that part of the country, the end of the third party save for the very different recurrence, not in great force, of the Progressive party under Theodore Roosevelt in 1912 and La Follette in 1924. The old-time third parties had become in fact the Democratic party.

The Cleveland Democrats had diminished both in number and in vigor, and after Bryan was nominated there were but four of them. The four "gold-bugs" were centers of controversy. Their erstwhile

A Passion for Politics

Democratic brothers condemned them; the organization Republicans made much of them; they were storm centers. The most vocal one of the four was Tom Brown. Mr. Thomas M. Brown was the president of the older of the two banks, he was a lawyer, he was a contentious and disputatious controversialist; he had a high-pitched voice and a laugh that could be heard, on a clear still night, plumb down to the Niangua River. Better than even the Republicans, he brought to us the gold-standard promise of "the full dinner pail" and the threats of the woes that would ensue were Bryan to be elected and all the factories in the cities to shut down and leave nobody to buy our produce.

Another of the "gold-bugs" was Dr. John George, the dentist, who had worn a white top hat for Grover since 1884, had been postmaster in the first Cleveland term, and who put personal loyalty above all considerations in politics. The third was Mr. Theodore G. Weatherby, the druggist, that rare bird, a Union soldier Democrat from Iowa, who had not got the post office in Cleveland's second term because of the innovation of the direct primary, and whose natural conservatism, which had kept him from voting for Lincoln when he was in the field in 1864, now caused him to shrink from union with the Populists even though that abstention led him straight into the Republican camp. The other "gold-bug" was Adolphus H. Hunt, also a druggist and a member of a large Democratic family. He simply was so much for Cleveland that he just couldn't go back on Grover—and that was that.

I don't think there has been a year of my after life—I almost had said "not a month"—in which in my dreams I have not seen these Dallas County "gold-bugs," whose political apostasy I so severely reprobated. But all of whom, then and thereafter, as long as they lived and as often as I met them, were my close friends, much admired by me, even though I saw in them lost sheep of the House of Israel.

With these four "gold-bugs" I would like to jump ahead of my story to election day in that fateful year. The O'Bannon Republican machine, in control of the county offices and the election machinery, named the judges and clerks for the election. There were nine townships and therefore, at that time, nine voting precincts in the county. Both county committees submitted lists of men to serve as judges and clerks. Both lists were approved and their nominees duly named,

[158]

except in Benton Township. Benton Township included Buffalo, the county seat, and was the most populous of the precincts and, consequently, had the largest number of voters. In Benton Township the names submitted by the Democratic-Fusion committee, names of Democrats, Populists, and Silver Republicans, were ignored. The four "gold-bugs," Brown, George, Weatherby, and Hunt, were put down as the Democratic judges and clerks!

Hardly anywhere in the country did the Palmer and Buckner Gold Democratic national ticket get such recognition. And surely nowhere did the Gold Democrats cause such consternation!

What to do? My brother Joe took counsel with some of his closest friends, Virgil Greever and Frank Morrow in town, Jim and Ed Reynolds, and Jim and Frank Alexander in the country part of the township—all young fellows and very much derring-do. Their whispers were veritable whispers, the conspirators were loyal, not a word leaked. About three o'clock on the morning of election day, while it was yet dark, a hundred—more or less—Bryan men mounted their horses and rode in converging lines on the sleeping county seat. Once there, six horsemen went to Mr. Brown's home, six to Dr. George's, another half-dozen to Mr. Weatherby's, and six more to Mr. Hunt's. They were as quiet as their horses would let them be. They said nothing as each astonished "gold-bug" awakened and peered out into the dusk of the coming dawn. They answered no questions. They sat on their horses in silence.

The rest of the horsemen went to the courthouse, where the election was to be held. They were met there by Joe and by Virgil Greever and Frank Morrow and also by the two Democratic legal lights, John Haymes and Albert Stanley. They raised a mighty shout, and the only man who actually lived on the square, Jim O'Bannon, the Republican chairman, heard the noise in his room at the Laclede Hotel on the corner, dressed, and sleepily walked over to the courthouse to see what the row was about. The four Republican judges and clerks came in, singly, from time to time.

Now the polls were to open at sunrise. The law said, and there were two good lawyers there with books to prove it, that if any appointed judge or clerk didn't show up by sunrise, then it became the duty of the electors then and there assembled to elect qualified persons to take their places.

The four "gold-bugs" were not there. The sun was rising. On

nomination of Mr. Joseph W. Brownlow, the chairman of the Democratic county committee, Mr. James P. O'Bannon, the chairman of the Republican county committee, was duly elected chairman of the assembled electors. And under his presidency the assembly named four good and true Bryan men to take the places of the four Palmer and Buckner Democrats who were so unaccountably absent. Four galloping horsemen sped to take the word to the investing cavalry which had surrounded the homes of the "gold-bugs." There had never been a threatening word. There was nothing to do about it. Nothing at all.

Back of that maneuver, however, there had been one day in the heat of the campaign an incident that almost precipitated a sure-enough riot. By proscription, the Democratic-Fusion committee had chosen a particular day for its final rally of the campaign in Buffalo, and the following day had been set aside for the Republicans. Some time before the great event the Republicans announced that for their big rally they would have the candidate for governor of the state, Mr. Robert P. Lewis, a distinguished man who had exhibited great skill in herding back into the party of God and morality some Silver Republicans who were beginning to forget that it was necessary to "vote as you shot." In other words the "bloody shirt" was to be waved. Old-time Democrats were used to that, but it made some of the Silver Republicans, and Populists, too, for that matter, mighty nervous to be put in the same category as the "rebels."

On the Democratic day, just as the big speaking was about to get started in the courthouse and preparations were being completed for the tremendous torchlight and Roman-candle-shooting parade that was to follow as soon as dark fell; just at that hour in the afternoon when the Bryan forces were at the very top of their bent and ready for anything—something happened.

Mr. Lewis, the Republican candidate for governor, had come. He had been met at the ford of Greasy Creek, a mile and a half to the east, by an escort of a hundred Republican horsemen so carefully recruited from the country that nobody in town found out about the impromptu procession that formed about Mr. Lewis' carriage and trotted up to town, where they were joined by Mr. O'Bannon himself, his more than three hundred pounds buoyed up by a magnificent horse.

The Republicans were stealing our rally day! They were putting on a horseback procession! It was an outrage. As they turned the corner into the west side of the square, Joe went out and took hold of the bridle of Mr. O'Bannon's horse. Mr. O'Bannon raised his right hand and in it a riding whip. A hundred Democrats roared an inarticulate protest. The hand and the whip came slowly down. No blow was struck.

"Jim," said Joe, "take Mr. Lewis to the hotel and don't let these men parade around the square."

"Joe," said Jim, "where do you get the right to give orders?"

"Do you want to find out, right now?" asked Joe, trembling.

"We don't want any trouble," Jim replied, tense with anger but not without his habitual self-control.

Again the roar: "Don't let 'em march!"

Again the roar: "Pull 'im off his horse!"

And Jim said, "All right, Joe; I didn't know they would take it so hard."

That was as near to mass violence as we came in that campaign. I myself heard no cocking pistols click, but maybe I wasn't as close to the source of the sound as were others who did tell me *they* heard those warning clicks.

Election day came on. My hopes were high. In fact, my faith was perfect. I knew that Bryan would win. And whatever doubts I had were resolved that November afternoon when Vic Proctor, the young barber son of the superannuated Southern Methodist preacher who was praying for Bryan, settled the whole thing by necromancy. He stood in a crowd at the hay scales in front of the post office just across the street from the courthouse. His reverend and ancient father was there, as was I. Vic took out his watch, looked at it, and shouted: "It's a sign from God. Pa, your prayers are answered. Bryan has won! Look! It's sixteen to one!" I remember this incident for two reasons. It turned out to be poor augury, and it was the only time on record that Vic ever manifested any particular interest in his father's petitions to the throne of grace.

We won! By early morning, what with riders coming in from the other townships and the ballots of Benton Township being tallied to the end as day was breaking, we knew we had won. We had carried the county. Most of our county ticket was elected. Bryan had carried the county by more than a hundred majority.

A Passion for Politics

I got out my own rooster, the one I had engraved on the satiny smooth boxwood with my own hands. I began to set the type for the already partially prepared tabular returns of the county election. I was still sure that then there was nothing in this whole wide world but victory.

The horsemen came in from the telegraph stations on the railroad, twenty miles away, a little later that morning. Hope breasting high the flood of disaster still hoped against hope. But it was no use. Bryan was beaten. McKinley was elected. My heart was all but broken.

The slogan of the full dinner pail had had its deep appeal. The threat of the closed factories that would lock out their workmen if Bryan were to win had its effect. The "sound-money" parades in the cities had had their effect. And all these were skilfully welded into one great mass effect by that master-politician, Mark Hanna. He had brains. He raised money. And he was a master-hand in strategy and tactics. His candidate, Major McKinley, stayed on his front porch and was discreet, seeking silently the support of all those who were of his party and those of other parties who feared the radicalism of the dauntless Boy Orator of the Platte. There were many.

Mr. Bryan campaigned the country as never had man campaigned it before. He and his committee were hard put to it for money even to pay his railroad fare; but they strove mightily. Never before had such huge crowds listened so intently, cheered so heartily; never before had orator stirred so deeply the feelings of his hearers. Men wise in their generation said then, and still say, that, had that election been held in September, Mr. Bryan would have won. No one knows.

For me, a boy of seventeen, it was the climax of my introduction to politics. Never again was I to feel so deeply that the very life of the world was tied up in my party and in my candidate. I came later to doubt some of the things I so devoutly believed then.

However, I was not alone in my belief that it was an hour of decision and that the decision had been made in favor of money as against men. May I quote from *The Education of Henry Adams,* who indeed is speaking of the decision against silver as of the time it was really taken, 1893, and not of the election of 1896, which confirmed that decision. To him, too, silver was a symbol rather than the crux of the issue. Says Mr. Adams as he leaves the World's Fair in Chicago in 1893:

Did he [Adams] himself quite know what he meant? Certainly not! If he had known enough to state his problem, his education would have been complete at once. Chicago asked in 1893 for the first time the question whether the American people knew where they were driving. Adams answered, for one, that he did not know, but would try to find out. On reflecting sufficiently deeply, under the shadow of Richard Hunt's architecture, he decided that the American people probably knew no more than he did; but that they might still be driving or drifting unconsciously to some point in thought, as their solar system was said to be drifting unconsciously to some point in space; and that, possibly, if relations enough could be observed, this point might be fixed. Chicago was the first expression of American thought as a unity; one must start there.

Washington was the second. When he got back there, he fell headlong into the extra session of Congress called to repeal the Silver Act. The silver minority made an obstinate attempt to prevent it, and most of the majority had little heart in the creation of a single gold standard. The banks alone, and the dealers in exchange, insisted upon it; the political parties divided according to capitalistic geographical lines, Senator Cameron offering almost the only exception; but they mixed with unusual good temper, and made liberal allowance for each other's actions and motives. The struggle was rather less irritable than such struggles generally were, and it ended like a comedy. On the evening of the final vote, Senator Cameron came back from the Capitol with Senator Brice, Senator Jones, Senator Lodge, and Moreton Frewen, all in the gayest of humors as though they were rid of a heavy responsibility. Adams, too, in a bystander's spirit, felt light in mind. He had stood up for his Eighteenth Century, his Constitution of 1789, his George Washington, his Harvard College, his Quincy, and his Plymouth Pilgrims, as long as any one would stand up with him. He had said it was hopeless twenty years before, but he had kept on, in the same old attitude, by habit and taste, until he found himself altogether alone. He had hugged his antiquated dislike of bankers and capitalistic society until he had become little better than a crank. He had known for years that he must accept the regime, but he had known a great many other disagreeable certainties— like age, senility, and death—against which one made what little resistance one could. The matter was settled at last by the people. For a hundred years, between 1793 and 1893, the American people had hesitated, vacillated, swayed forward and back, between two forces, one simply industrial, the other capitalistic, centralizing, and mechanical. In 1893, the issue came on the single gold standard, and the majority at last declared itself, once for all, in favor of the capitalistic system with all its necessary machinery. All one's friends, all one's best citizens, reformers, churches, colleges, educated classes, had joined the banks to force submission to capitalism; a submission long foreseen by the mere law of mass. Of all forms of society or government, this was the one he liked least, but his likes or dislikes were as antiquated as the rebel doctrine of State rights. A capitalistic system had been adopted, and if it were to be run at all, it must be run by capital and by capitalistic methods; for nothing could surpass the nonsensity of trying to run so complex and so concentrated a machine by Southern and Western farmers in grotesque alliance with city day-laborers, as had been tried in 1800 and 1828, and had failed even under simple conditions.

There, education in domestic politics stopped. The rest was a question of gear; or running machinery; of economy; and involved no disputed principle. Once admitted that the machine must be efficient, society might dispute in what social interest it should be run, but in any case it must work concentration. Such great revolutions commonly leave some bitterness behind, but nothing in politics ever surprised Henry Adams more than the ease with which he and his silver friends slipped across the chasm, and alighted on the single gold standard and the capitalistic system with its methods; the protective tariff; the corporations and trusts; the trades-unions and socialistic paternalism which necessarily made their complement; the whole mechanical consolidation of force, which ruthlessly stamped out the life of the class into which Adams was born, but created monopolies capable of controlling the new energies that America adored.

So the jeremiad of the sophisticated, the lettered, the traveled, the aristocratic, the urbane dynast; so Henry Adams and the end of his politics. He could not tolerate a grotesque alliance of southern and western farmers with city day laborers such as had been tried with Jefferson in 1800 and Jackson in 1828.

For me, in the backwoods, unlettered, unlearned, untraveled, democratic, and rustic, a boy of seventeen at his introduction to politics, the issue was as plain and the issue as sharply drawn. But the rustic boy, to drop for a moment into an imitation of Mr. Adams' third person, the rustic boy looked forward with hope to an alliance of farmers and laborers who would make again the attempt that was made in 1800 and again in 1828. The boy was at the beginning of his education in politics, but his path stretched straight before him. For him men, not money. For him who had no sense of class there was no fear of the farmers and the laborers. For him the democratic way. And for him long after, when 1800 and 1828 had been repeated in 1932, for him the leadership of one who, not fearing to prefer his principles even at the cost of deserting his class, said: "We have nothing to fear but fear itself."

PART II

NASHVILLE, LOUISVILLE, AND WASHINGTON

CHAPTER IX

LOOKING TOWARD TOWN

In the winter of 1897 my family and I took stock of my prospects and considered what I was to do with myself. To both Mother and me it was quite clear that the time had come when I should leave home to seek my fortune in a city. I liked to call myself "a printer by trade," but I had learned enough from my tramp-printer friends to know that my acquired skills in combination with my age could at best admit me only as an apprentice. Then also I knew from the *Inland Printer* and the other trade journals that, with the linotype machine sweeping the printers into the ranks of the unemployed, the typographical unions were admitting few if any apprentices. And, besides that, I had neither the intention nor the desire to become an artisan. I was for journalism. If in that day journalism was not quite a profession, by the same token it required no academic training.

It seemed there was but one place for me to go, and that was to Tennessee and to Nashville. There I could stay with my aunt and cousins until I could find a job that would keep me. The problem was to save enough money to buy the railroad ticket to Nashville and to land me there with at least a few dollars in my pocket.

Father and Mother were both teaching school that winter. Father earned thirty dollars a month and mother twenty-five, and there was also the three dollars a week that I was making in the printing office. My brother Walter was launched on his mercantile career in George O'Bannon's store and was making fifteen dollars a month. All this added up to relative affluence. We could and did afford a hired girl, and the savings for my adventure were squeezed out.

On a crisp, cold, sunshiny morning in mid-February, 1898, I lay in the barber chair, and Tom Williamson talked as he shaved me. He would say, after the manner of all barbers and with that air of final authority to which all customers of barber shops have become indurated, that there would be no war, that McKinley was against the war, that Tom Reed was against the war, and that all this war talk was foolishness.

Just a few weeks before, Buffalo had got its first telephone line to the faraway railroad station at Conway, and the marvel of the fact that sometimes whole sentences could be heard over that enormous distance of twenty-two miles was still a matter for awe and wonderment. Such a sentence had been heard, and Vic Proctor, who presided over the other chair in Mr. Williamson's shop, rushed in out of the cold to yell, "The Spaniards have sunk the 'Maine' in Havana Harbor."

Well, we knew then on the instant that Tom Williamson was wrong and that there would be war. For the first and only time in my life since I had abandoned hope of West Point, I ached to become a soldier, but I knew that with my bad eyes and twitching right shoulder I wouldn't have much of a chance.

There was that little chance, however, and I decided without consultation with anyone that the chance would be improved if I were in a city. So I hustled and hurried and worried my mother to write to her sister in Nashville that I was coming now and would not wait for summer as had been planned.

A small trunk was packed with my meager kit—a few clothes, a few accessories, and the rest of the space taken up by my books. There also was a small valise, and on the last day of February, 1898, my trunk and my valise and I were loaded into the mail hack, and we set out on the long four hours' journey to the railroad.

I had decided to travel at night so that I might have a whole day in the glory of St. Louis. Of course, only the local trains, euphemistically called the "accommodations," stopped at Conway, and such trains carried no sleeping cars; but that was a matter of indifference to me, for I would not have spent the money on a Pullman even if there had been one.

I sat up all night under dim oil lights on a red-plush seat on a bitter winter night with a pot-bellied coal stove glowing red-hot in one end of the car. To the accompaniment of snores and the sibilant whispers of mothers attempting to quiet whining babies, in a cloud of odors not made less sickening by the all-pervasive and penetrating smells of stale peanut hulls and banana skins, I put the country behind me, quite consciously dedicating myself to urban living, even if I was not yet aware of what it meant. All of it was frighteningly new, even the railroad, of which I had retained almost no memory from that earlier, childhood trip.

Out of the train at the break of day I clambered in awe-struck bewilderment into the vasty mightiness of the world's largest railway station. Well, at any rate, it was the second largest, for I had read in the newspapers that the Victoria Station in Bombay was a little bigger; but Bombay was in India and St. Louis was in my country, in the United States. St. Louis was my city, from whence my beloved newspapers had come; St. Louis was the city nearest to the heart of America; it was an outrage that Chicago was passing it in population and importance. It was a crime that the capital had not already been moved to St. Louis from Washington, perched so dangerously on the very eastern edge of the continent. St. Louis, I had no doubt, was destined to be the metropolis of the world. That Union Station still is a worry and a puzzlement to me, for now, when I go into it, it nearly always is being added to, and yet it has shrunk unbelievably to a tiny replica of its own self. Its stained-glass windows, then so huge and brilliant, are now murky and dim ornamentations on a dreary landing of a small flight of stairs, if indeed they have survived at all the latest improvements. But in my mind's eye they remain lofty, brilliant, infinitely exciting.

However, that morning there was other exciting business. I bought my ticket to Nashville and arranged to leave that night. I checked my trunk and found out that I could leave my valise in the station. I ate breakfast in what undoubtedly was the largest, the most splendid, the most brilliant dining-room in the whole wide world. It cost twenty-five cents.

Then, bursting with curiosity, electrified with eagerness, I climbed the steps and walked out into my first city street. Not only were there clanging trolley cars, but there were carriages and drays in great numbers, and the six-horse teams of the brewery trucks, and people, people, people.

My curiosity and eagerness collapsed into fright and terror. I was afraid to try to cross the street.

By a supreme effort of will I collected myself and dared to ask someone on the sidewalk how to get to a certain address on Locust Street, where I was to go to see my aunt with whom I was to spend the day. Luckily, it wasn't far away, and I managed to cross the street four or five times and walk the three or four blocks to the boarding-house on Locust Street in which she lived. She was the wife of my mother's brother, Walter, and they had just moved to St. Louis, where he had got a job as a traveling salesman. My Uncle Walter, I knew, was not at home.

I rang the bell, and the door was opened to me upon a long, gaslit, high-ceilinged hall. At one side a red-carpeted walnut-railed stairway seemed to ascend into high heaven itself, and down it came my beautiful Aunt Belle. Her fair hair was piled high on top of her head, and her taffeta skirts swished over her petticoats—a welcome and reassuring sound as she ran down the last few steps to take me in her arms. My fright vanished, and I felt less the little scared boy and more the adventurer which I had set myself out to be.

All in all it was a wonderful day. We rode on a streetcar and saw the outside of the Planters Hotel, and above us the great Eads Bridge stretched across the Mississippi. We walked by the great wholesale and jobbing houses on Washington Street, the names of which were so familiar to me, and saw inside the huge windows the tables piled high with ginghams, calicoes, lawns, and dimities, all the pretty paraphernalia of women's wear not yet liberated from the home dressmaker and purely domestic economy. We went into Barr's store, and there I think that perhaps I trembled a little on my first ride in an elevator.

There was a magnificent luncheon at the Silver Moon, and then, wonder of wonders, delight of delights, my first theater. I don't know whether it was called the Orpheum or the Odeon or what, but it was a vaudeville show, and Aunt Belle had got tickets down very near to the front. It seemed to me that the center aisle was miles long as we marched down it in the semidarkness toward a stage already filled with magic, for we were late and the curtain already had been raised. After that there was hot chocolate at Oakes' and even a box of the marvelous Oakes candy before we went home in the dense darkness of St. Louis winter smog to the boarding-house for supper.

Now, that long boarding-house supper table, laid in the dining-room, which communicated through an arch furnished with sliding doors with the parlor, so completely and everlastingly parlorish with its flowered Brussels carpet, with its red-plush and walnut furniture, with its orange and purple and crimson huge-flowered wallpaper, and all so primly prissed up at the windows with authentic Nottingham lace curtains—all that, if I had but known it, was a preview of the boarding-house parlors and the boarding-house dining-rooms which were for the most part to be my living quarters for many a year to come.

But it was not drab nor dowdy nor *déclassée* to me then as in other times and other circumstances it was to become. Under the gaslit chandelier fitted up with Welsbach mantles, the light was more brilliant than even the best of hanging lamps burning coal oil had ever given. The tablecloth was snowy white to my eyes, and the variegated assortment of napkin rings were to me not so much symbols of the conservation of laundry as they were the sign manuals of the eminent privacy of a city dweller.

There was talk, too—boarding-house talk, war talk. Two weeks had gone by, and the first shocked horror of the tragedy of Havana Harbor had found its verbalization in the slogan, "Remember the 'Maine.' " I was quiet because I was scared, but I was fidgety too because I never before had been present at a conversation with the slightest political content in which I had not cut in. But, when some Republican boarder came out with a sneer at Mr. Bryan, I forgot my fears and did wade in to the very middle of a most beautiful argument. I remember this incident so very clearly because it was the end of whatever feeling of inadequacy in the presence of city people which had so thoroughly frightened me a dozen hours earlier when I stood there so long, too afraid to attempt to cross the horse-filled, trolley-ridden street.

The upshot of the argument was that three of the young men at the boarding-house table, including my Republican opponent, went with Aunt Belle to take me to the Union Station to put me on the train for Nashville. At about nine o'clock on that first day of March, which was raging like a lion in St. Louis streets, I clambered into a day coach to take my second night's sitting-up, nap-snatching, odoriferous railroad journey.

I have been to St. Louis many times since then. I have visited it more infrequently than I have most other American cities, and I have had fewer concerns with it than with most big towns. I did not know it at the moment, but, as my train crossed the bridge and carried me across the Mississippi, I was destined thereafter to look to the south and the east. While actually I did not cut the tie that bound me to the Ozarks until two or three years later, I was already entrapped by the circumstances that the Tennessee to which I was destined had been the birthplace of my father and mother; and to an extent greater than I then knew I thought of it as home.

At about nine o'clock in the morning of March 2, 1898, I got off the train in Nashville into a long, low depot shed that had been built by the Yankees during their occupation of the town in the Civil War and which already was destined to perish with the close of the war with Spain. I stepped off the train to be met with a most enthusiastic welcome by my cousins, Will Vaught, a year or so older, and Amis Vaught, a year or so younger than I. They and their younger brother, Walter, with their mother, my mother's sister Lou, had visited us in Buffalo; and it was Aunt Lou's home that I was to make mine.

The sun was shining brightly. I remember that because of the contrast to the dark and dismal St. Louis of the day before, and it must have been shining very brightly indeed if its rays were able to pierce that smoke and fog which on winter mornings blanket Nashville as deeply as they do St. Louis. My valise, of course, was with me; and Will undertook to perform some sort of a miracle with my trunk check which, he assured me, would get my belongings to me at Aunt Lou's house before the day was done. I am quite sure that I doubted, but I could not but bow to his urban sophistication and so consented to leave the station without seeing my precious trunk.

Of course I knew that Aunt Lou lived at 512 Park Avenue, but it had never occurred to me that a house could house more than one family; and I got a little shock when I found that the Vaughts had only the upstairs of a brick two-story house that was owned by the people who lived downstairs. Yet there was my own lovely Aunt Lou to welcome me, and there seemed to be quite room enough too—a parlor, dining-room all proper enough, three bedrooms, and a kitchen, and something hitherto beyond and outside my experience as a part of a habitation—a bathroom.

Very soon I discovered the genuine hospitality and love for young people that characterized the elderly couple who lived below. Captain Holmes was a Danish sea captain who had retreated to the interior after a battle with the elements that in midstorm he had reckoned to be his last. He had found a wife and a home in Nashville and many other new things to enjoy, not the least of which was to tell sea tales to open-eared youngsters. The tales I have forgotten; I am sorry that I have forgotten, too, just why he came to choose, along with American citizenship, a new name. It seems either that his own name was so beset by umlauts or the other curious diacritical signs with which the Scandinavians compromise the Roman alphabet with their own runes or that he had despaired of teaching anybody how to pronounce it. Somehow or other he had become an admirer of a famous Yankee literary physician, and so he anglicized if not phoneticized his name to Oliver Holmes. The free use of the Holmeses' downstairs parlor soon turned out to be a material advantage to the gang that I shortly was to organize.

Walter, the youngest of my three cousins, was in the country at school. Will and Amis worked in the offices of the Phoenix Cotton Mills, an industrial establishment even then archaic in design and equipment, four or five blocks to the northeast of Aunt Lou's house.

The house at 512 Park Avenue was itself one of the more pretentious buildings to be found in an island of respectability that was chiefly devoted to genteel poverty but from which a few of the affluent had not yet fled. This island, perhaps a quarter-mile wide and almost a half-mile long, was dominated by the eminence on which our house sat; and that eminence in its turn was dominated by a rambling, one-story, antebellum mansion which stood directly across the street from us. In the boom times of the forties this mansion had stood in its own park of a hundred acres or more, a circumstance that had given its name to Park Street, two blocks to the west. Later, when a city street was cut through to run by the very doors of the mansion, the name Park Street was changed, and the new road, the one on which we lived, was called Park Avenue.

Between our house and the intersection of Park Avenue and Line Street there were a number of vacant lots, and diagonally across to the north of Line Street was an unkept, overgrown, city-owned park that once had been a part of the great lawn of the mansion. Line Street, which was the boundary of our island on the north, had a streetcar line; and beyond it, except for a drugstore and a little fringe of cottages, lay the cotton mills and the soapworks, surrounded by their own slums, then the railroad tracks and, then, farther to the east, the great red-light district. Line Street was named, I believe, because once it was the boundary of the city; but its reputation was so encrimsoned that shortly after my advent, in an effort to save the respectability of our island, its name was changed to Joe Johnston Avenue. On the south our hill sloped down to Cedar Street, and just across Cedar Street were the massive stone walls of the state penitentiary. To the westward and only a few blocks away the isle of respectability came to its boundary in some wildwoods and in the campus of Fisk, the great Negro university.

The mansion across the street had at one time been the home of a Dallas who had emigrated from Pennsylvania to Tennessee in the booming forties when James K. Polk of Nashville was President and his own cousin, George M. Dallas, was Vice-President. Now anything that had to do with the family of Dallas had a deep interest for me because of two circumstances—one that I was born in Dallas County, and the other that my cousins were in the office of the cotton mill, the head of which was Mr. Trevanyan B. Dallas. Mr. Dallas was a floridly handsome man, courtly in manner, reputedly rich, and quite consciously an aristocrat. He and his family had long ago left the mansion across the street for a new white-stone mansion on West End Avenue in the new fashionable part of the town.

Mr. Trevanyan Dallas had been twice married, and the son of his first marriage, Mr. Hugh Dallas, was his deputy in the management of the Phoenix Cotton Mills. A tall, spare, pale man in his late thirties, he was very religious, took his work as a member of St. Andrew's Brotherhood most seriously, and expressed that serious interest in work with boys and young men in the YMCA and in helping organize a boys' club for his own Protestant Episcopal Christ Church. He was exceedingly important to me because, before he came to his early death a few years later, he had either directly or indirectly got for me the only jobs that anybody ever got for me.

Now it so happened that my collars were as high and as stiff and as white as any that a city boy could wear, because we had discovered in Buffalo the blessings of ordering collars from St. Louis and sending them all the way back to St. Louis to be properly laundered. But there was an ineffable aura of the bucolic in the cut of my clothing, which too had been mail order but probably designed for the country trade and therefore just a little overdone. The peg-top trousers were too much peg-top, the shoulders a little too shouldery, and the colors a little too colorful. Perhaps the right name didn't come along for nearly fifty years, but as I remember it now I can think of it only as a "zoot suit."

Of course there was no money for new clothes, but fortunately my cousin Will found, and found at once, that I was exactly his height and weight and size. Since Will affected an approach to sartorial perfection in the Nashville mode and thus bought new clothes before his old ones were well worn, I stepped immediately into the possession of an appropriate urban wardrobe.

My two cousins were pleasant fellows, and Will, the elder, also possessed more than the ordinary share of personability; but both were rather reserved, and neither was a good mixer. This lay partly in their reserve, partly in timidity, but a good deal of it proceeded from pure snobbery. And lack of money was no handicap to their feeling themselves to be part of an immutable aristocracy.

On the other hand, I was gregarious, talkative, and driven by a compulsive curiosity to know all that I could about everybody who would let me talk to him. In Buffalo the drugstores, both legitimate and blind tiger, had been the haunt of the grown-ups; the adolescents and the teen-agers had hung about the barber shops. Here, just across the vacant lots on Line Street, was a drugstore. It had no soda fountain any more than did the drugstores in Buffalo, but it already was becoming a hangout for the teen-age boys in the neighborhood. The owner of the drugstore was a middle-aged man with a long gray beard who peered at us doubtfully over his steel-rimmed spectacles and of whom we were all afraid. Perhaps there was no reason for it, but at that particular moment, when I was so desirous of conforming to the ways of my coevals, I had determined to drop what had always been my habit of talking with the elders whenever possible. So I joined with the other teen-agers in that tacit conspiracy of silence and secrecy with which weakness always meets might, as children against adults, as poor against rich, as minorities against majorities the world over.

Mr. Watkins, whom we called "Doctor," as it was then considered the courteous thing to call a pharmacist, had three assistants at the store: one a young man of twenty-three or twenty-four, one his son of about fourteen or fifteen, and another his nephew of my own age, about nineteen, who was even then determined to follow his pharmaceutical training by going to medical college and becoming a doctor. His name was John Stevens, and almost overnight he became my chum. We wangled things so that, when Dr. Watkins was out, we and our gang could take over the drugstore. Of course customers still came in with prescriptions that might be filled, or to buy patent medicines or toilet articles, or without prescription and with no fuss at all to purchase

morphine or gum opium, articles much in demand in the slums surrounding the cotton mills and the soapworks. When Dr. Watkins was
"in residence," so to speak, and, if the time of day were propitious, the
gang came to our house, because I did not have to work all day as did
my cousins.

What we did when we were together was mostly to talk or read.
We played no games, and the frugality imposed by a more or less commonly diffused poverty made buying things to eat or drink out of the
question. All the boys had been to school, and some had even finished
high school, but none had so much as thought of college. Their families
were too poor, and they themselves had to work. Those of us who
used tobacco smoked pipes or rolled our own cigarettes. Furthermore,
John Stevens and I saw to it that even such of the boys of our own
select circle who were musical brought none of their strumming or
singing into our gang meetings, for neither one of us could play or
sing, and neither one of us was ever content to sit in a corner away
from the limelight.

What we talked about was war, history, and books. What we read
was verse. Tops, of course, was war. By the middle of the month
everybody knew that President McKinley was going to call a special
session of the Congress. Before the end of the month everybody knew
that we would be at war with Spain, and to each of us—eighteen,
nineteen, and twenty—the war presented itself in an extremely personal
manner. Each was conscious of the fact that the whole world was looking at him or ready to ask the question, "Why have you not enlisted?"
Each was asking himself in the night and in the morning and at noon,
"Shall I enlist?" And one of us already was a member of the Tennessee
State Militia.

The papers were talking about Theodore Roosevelt and Dr. Leonard
Wood and their scheme to organize the Rough Riders. Already there
was talk about enlisting special regiments from the South to be composed of persons who were immune to yellow fever. Already gray-
clad Confederate veterans were proclaiming their high purpose immediately to don the once-hated blue. (As a matter of fact, with the
exception of Jakes, who was already in the militia, none of us got into
uniform, although three or four did try. In Tennessee, which proudly
called itself the Volunteer State, as in so many other states in that particular war, ten volunteers were turned down to one who was accepted.)

But *Cuba Libre* and the cruelties of the Spanish and even the prospect of war did not keep us all the time. We read much, and we
talked even more about what we read. We read our verse and committed it to memory to spout it before our fellows. We did even more
than that. We set up for ourselves a formal organization, with a written
constitution and a whole set of officers (I captured the presidency). The
name was the Park Avenue Literary Society. We read with what we
thought was sophisticated discrimination. Our analyses of the produc-
tions of Mr. A. Conan Doyle might also have qualified us for the
Baker Street Irregulars of a half-century later; we discussed the variations in Mr. Kipling's style as differently manifested in *Plain Tales
from the Hills* and the *American Notes*. We took the greatest delight
in Mr. Jerome K. Jerome and his *Three Men in a Boat*. We rocked
with poignant sadness with Mr. Barrie as we looked through the window in Thrums, and we felt ourselves forfended in any future verbal
fencing with the fair by our mastery with Sir Anthony Hope Hawkins of *The Dolly Dialogues*.

When it came to reciting verse, my own mastery of the *Poems of
Passion* by Mrs. Wilcox gave me a lead and probably gained for me
the presidency. But all the others were pretty good too. They must
have been, or I would not remember them so clearly and still not without a little twinge of envy. Claud Garland, gifted with a rich baritone
voice, held us in awe as he recited the *Rubáiyát* from beginning to
end; and that to me was a great experience, because I had not known
before of Omar Khayyám and his Mr. FitzGerald.

John Stevens, who had a slightly deprecatory manner and a low,
soft voice, captured and enraptured us with "The Ballad of Truthful
James" and things like that. (Later, when he had become a distinguished psychiatrist, I sat with him at luncheon one day with a group
of his patients. One was Mrs. Steele, the daughter of Francis Bret Harte,
and another was Maurice Barrymore. In order to make conversation,
I asked John to recite "Truthful James." With his deprecatory small
laugh he waved his hand to Mr. Barrymore. Mr. Barrymore arose
and began:

> Which I wish to remark,
> And my language is plain,
> That for ways that are dark
> And for tricks that are vain,
> The heathen Chinee is peculiar.

The paterfamilias of the Royal Family did it well, and Mrs. Steele came out from a three years' silence to talk about her distinguished father. Dr. Stevens was much pleased.)

But all of that was all boy and no girl, and that did not fit into my scheme of things. What bothered me almost as much as the absence of girls was the absence of the older people with whom I had always thought it pleasant as well as profitable to talk.

Out of Buffalo I had brought a simple and effective if somewhat naïve notion that all social relationships naturally centered in the church. Therefore, with my aunt and my cousins, I repaired on Sunday morning to the Park Avenue Methodist Church South, there to be introduced to its pastor, the Reverend Lewis Powell, who was later to become a very close friend indeed, and to sundry of the church people. Among the young people our literary society was represented not only by my cousins, the Vaughts, but also by the Garland brothers; but of course there were other boys and young men and many girls. Without the slightest hesitation I identified the young man who would naturally be the leader of the Epworth League and clove to him as a blood brother. He was William Cassety, and he was by way of beginning forty years or more of work in the YMCA. He had a cousin, a girl, who was agreeable and hospitable, and I found myself seated at the Sunday-night supper table in what Will's father called the "Maison de Cassety." Mr. Cassety was president of the Apex Soap Company, whose smelly establishment stood not far from our island of respectability; he was a short, spare man with a Vandyke beard and so peculiarly formal in a southern fashion that his manners required him still to address his wife as "Miss." The girl, Mrs. Cassety's niece, had a beau, and, wonder of wonders, he was someone I had known in Buffalo, a theological student at Vanderbilt University who came to supper with the Cassetys before all of us went to the church for Epworth League and the evening service.

All of that, of course, was just the sort of thing I might have done at home. But after church, when, according to my standards, we should have gone straight home, Mary and her beau and Will said that I should be introduced into the neighborhood, and they took me calling. We went to see Miss Byrne, in whom Will was evidently interested, and there we found a very gay party indeed, with Miss Byrne and two other girls hanging round Martin Knapp, who was doing perfectly impossible things with the piano. The girls were pretty enough, lively enough, and, being girls, most attractive; but for me the center of interest was Miss Byrne's brother, the Reverend John P. Byrne, a Roman Catholic priest, and the first one I had ever met. Father Byrne was Irish, of course, and furthermore he was an Irish tenor. In that pre-radio, in that even pre-phonograph era, when the "Hit Parade" marched through the parlors of the country and demanded the ministration of amateur instrumentalists and amateur vocalists, light operas were apt to catch the fancy of fashion and be the rage. At that particular moment one such was *El Capitan,* by John Philip Sousa, and Martin Knapp knew all the music. The girls and our Methodistical delegation sang the lyrics, and Father Byrne took the lead. He was not exactly what had been my idea of a Catholic priest, but I liked him very much. I liked his sister, too; and thereafter I was often in the Byrne house.

The reasons that had impelled me not to join the church in Buffalo no longer operated here, and I joined the Methodist church. The pastor, Lewis Powell, was ready to recognize my infant baptism by my uncle, Lewis Amis, who was one of his dearest friends. But in deference to my father's opposition to pedobaptism, although I would not go so far as to defer to his views in the matter of immersion, I was again baptized by sprinkling and received into the Methodist church.

I was living with my mother's sister in this environment of respectable poverty, but of course I had gone almost at once to pay my respects to my mother's cousin, who lived in quite another part of town, who had been wealthy, and who was still a leader of high society. She was Mrs. Mary Paul Johnson Maguire.

On the first Sunday in Nashville I had been introduced into my church, on the second Sunday I joined the church, and on the third Sunday I was commanded by Cousin Mary Paul to accompany her to her church. She was a pewholder in Christ Church, Protestant Episcopal. I was curious to see and hear what went on in a liturgical church, but I still retain some tremors of the terror that engulfed me when she followed the usher and I followed her in a sort of triumphant procession down the aisle to her pew. I did not genuflect. I shared, under her imperious command, her prayer book and her hymnal and with frightened awkwardness stood or sat or knelt as she ordered me. There could be no possible doubt that she was displeased with me, and I am afraid

I was too self-centered in my unhappiness to have got much out of the service or the sermon. Later it turned out that it wasn't so much my trembling; it wasn't so much my unfamiliarity with the liturgy. What Cousin Mary Paul was so impatient with me about was my clothes. Even though I was but nineteen, she didn't like to be seen in her church with a man who hadn't on a frock coat and who wasn't carrying in his hand a top hat. What I couldn't possibly know at the time, but was not very long thereafter to discover, was that she was also annoyed that I had joined the Methodist church, that she had intended to make an Episcopalian out of me, and that on the march down the aisle she had made all the arrangements to have me become an usher; and, of course, to be an usher, I would have to have the appropriate clothing. She had jumped ahead in her plans to what she thought was the proper thing to do to get me in the right church and mingling with the right people.

On the fourth Sunday, impelled by curiosity and my new-found friendships, I again deserted the church of which I had become a member and went alone, for the first time, to a Catholic church—to St. Mary's Cathedral, on Cedar Street in the shadow of the capitol. I had no guide, no mentor, and with difficulty followed the service of the Mass, which was celebrated by my new friend, Father Byrne. I do remember that I was a little astonished by the simplicity of the sermon preached by some other priest, and I also remember that I was not at all offended, as according to my Ozark bringing-up I should have been, by the Latin or by the formalities of the service. Indeed, what astonished me most was that the church was not at all what a Catholic church should have been, according to the things I had read and the pictures I had seen, for it was a plain structure in the Georgian style, and its interior was a simple rectangle. Christ Church on the previous Sunday had given me my first actual experience of a Gothic church with nave, aisles, and transepts.

I was now well set on my travels, and I rarely went back to the Park Avenue Methodist Church, because on every Sunday when I could I went to a new church and, if possible, a new kind of church— Lutheran, High Church Episcopal (Christ Church was Low), the big downtown churches, Presbyterian, Methodist, and Baptist. And one Sunday morning, all by myself, I went to the Howard Congregational Church and found myself, to my surprise, the only white person there.

Looking toward Town

It had been during my very first week in Nashville that Will and Amis Vaught had taken me to see the place where they worked, the Phoenix Cotton Mills. They were proud of it, as they naturally would have been, seeing that they had such good jobs, Will getting seventy-five dollars a month as chief bookkeeper and Amis fifty dollars a month as one of his assistants—big jobs and good pay.

The memory of my first visit to the factory is particularly vivid. It was the first glimpse of the industrialization of which we who lived in the country had but the vaguest notion. Its instant as well as its lasting effect was that of beauty. Surely there was nothing beautiful about the rambling maze of one-story brick buildings and certainly nothing of the sort when I went inside and found myself within a cluster of low-ceilinged rooms that served as the offices.

But, passing out into the factory, I found myself in a great room with what seemed to me to be acres of machines, whirring and thud-thudding looms, canopies of cotton gossamer in patterns of vivid reds and greens and blues, and, among all these machines and finding their way in the maze of millions of threads, a few men and women who at first sight hardly became any part of the picture itself. Then into other rooms where the cotton was carded and spun, where the hundreds and hundreds of big spools were wrapping themselves into what might have been fatter and fatter white candles disposed on dozens of rectangular candelabra—to me truly a beautiful sight. Then the mélange of sight and smell in the dyehouse, where the cotton yarns were being immersed in their smelly baths than ran the whole gamut of color from red to violet. It seemed to me to be something quite unreal, something made of dreams.

It was not so many years later that I came to know that this was an old-fashioned mill, that its business of carding, spinning, dyeing, and weaving all in one factory was an outmoded process, soon to perish before the intensification of specialized processes. Quite soon I was to learn that its machinery was obsolescent, its methods behind the times, and the establishment itself but a marginal venture hanging on to existence out of sheer faith in the conservative traditions of an older generation of textile manufacturers.

Almost at once I was to come to the realization that the price of its existence was inseparably linked with the exploitation of the people who swarmed in the maze of two-room houses that lined the muddy unpaved streets of the slums that surrounded the mill. But at that moment to me, impelled by my overwhelming urge to escape from the country, the picture of the looms, the spinning frames, and the dye vats was beauty—the orderly beauty of repetitive design, beauty in which I recognized the two things for which I was most avid: the city and modern civilization.

A thrill that came to me in those first few weeks, a sensation of novel and almost ecstatic experience, was the theater. Outside of the vaudeville performance that day in St. Louis, my experience with the theater was limited to O'Bannon's Opera House in Buffalo and to two or three evenings with a theatrical company that would adventure that far off the railroad to present for the edification of the purchasers of twenty-five-cent tickets, behind six kerosene-burning footlights, *East Lynne* or *Orphans of the Storm*. Once or twice there had been, either in O'Bannon's Hall or in the church, a traveling stereopticon outfit; but in their case I had been much more interested in the tanks of oxygen and hydrogen that they carried to make the limelight than in the pictures they displayed.

Now, in Nashville, I could go to a real theater, a city theater, all lighted up with electricity and brilliant beyond belief as I looked down upon all the men and women in evening dress, as I heard the overture from the orchestra, and as at length I was rewarded with the make-believe world when the curtain rose.

Will, who had a pocketful of spending money, was most generous. He literally shook with delight as he contemplated my naïve joy and heard my exclamations of wonder. From the goodness of his heart he took me to the theater every Saturday night from the time I got there until I got a job, which, as I worked at night, ended my theatergoing for the time.

But one of my first theatrical experiences stays with me in sharp detail. It was riotous fun, it was fast and furious, it was topical; and, with the declaration of war on Spain but two or three weeks in the future, the waving flags and beating drums and blowing bugles put us in a patriotic frenzy. The show was called *The Governor's Son,* and in it were "The Four Cohans," Father, Mother, Ethel, and George. George waved the flag.

CHAPTER X

NASHVILLE, 1898

I had to have a job, and I was trying to get one. I tried everything. I answered advertisements. I stood in lines. Through my cousins and others I had a network of inquiries laid out. But I had no skill except that of printing, and in that I had not served a formal apprenticeship and therefore was barred. I was not physically strong enough for heavy work. There didn't seem to be any job for me.

One morning I was in a line at six o'clock in obedience to the dictates of an advertisement. I found that I was expected to sell newspapers, yesterday afternoon's papers, and the *St. Louis Chronicle* at that. I was to give the man a dollar for a bundle, and then I was to go to a certain part of the town, sell them, bring the unsold papers back, and keep half of the money I had taken in. I was dubious, but in my innocence my doubt was directed toward myself and my abilities and not, as it should have been, toward the man who was running the shebang. I gave up my dollar and in return got a bundle of papers that I could hardly lift, let alone carry, and staggeringly made my way to a streetcar to set out for my "territory." It was the neighborhood of a cotton mill in the north of the town, very like the one near which I lived.

The poor people who lived in those ankle-deep streets, always ankle-deep if not in mud then in dust; these poor people who lived in two-room shotgun houses lacking utterly the water pipes, the sewer pipes, the gas pipes that to me seemed synonymous with living in the city; these poor people who worked for a pittance when there was work at all, many of whom could not read, were certainly not good prospects for yesterday's St. Louis newspaper. In the middle of the afternoon I went back. I had sold five papers. I had twenty-five cents. I turned it in with my papers. The man pocketed the coins, kicked the bundle of papers into a corner, and told me to skedaddle. I asked for my dollar deposit. He

[183]

threatened to call the police. I stood my ground. He threatened me with a baseball bat. I fled. It hadn't been a job. It was a gyp—my first.

But the events of that day, taken together with what I had seen around the Phoenix Cotton Mills, where my cousins worked, and what I had seen of the inside of the mills, affected me ever thereafter. From that day I was to hate slums, to hate large-scale institutionalized poverty, in a way that I never was to hate my own individual poverty, to hate the system which ground the faces of the poor. Thereafter I was to sympathize with the movements for the amelioration of the lot of the industrial workers, who seemed to me to be so much worse off than even the poorest of the one-room-cabin, hard-scrabble sharecroppers of the Ozarks.

At last Mr. Hugh Dallas, who had interested himself in me from the beginning, found at a meeting of the St. Andrew's Brotherhood of Christ Church that one of his fellows was looking for a young, respectable, honest, reliable man. Mr. Dallas' colleague was Mr. J. A. Daugherty, who leased and operated the cigarstand in the Tulane Hotel. Armed with a note from Mr. Dallas, I went to see Mr. Daugherty, and on the second day of April, 1898, four days before the declaration of the war on Spain, I found myself installed behind the cigar and news counter in the Tulane Hotel, looking out over the chairs in the big lobby to the big glass windows on the crowded corner of Church and Spruce streets. I came to work at seven o'clock in the morning, to be relieved by Mr. Daugherty at eleven o'clock. I came back on duty at seven in the evening and stayed until midnight. And this I did seven days a week. On Sunday Mr. Daugherty did not himself come in but was represented by a substitute who came at ten and stayed until six. Thus I had a nine-hour working day, but split so that it was seventeen hours from my early coming to my late going; and, if I got very much sleep, I had to take it in two pieces, partly in the daytime and partly at night. My duties were to sell cigars and tobacco, to sell postage stamps, to sell newspapers (we did not handle magazines), and to be polite and entertaining to lonesome loafers. Another of my duties was to explain to travelers from other states that it was against the law in Tennessee to sell cigarettes, that we had no cigarettes for sale, but that we did stock a line of "the makin's."

The Tulane was the political hotel. It was the headquarters of the Democratic state committee; it was the place which housed many of the state's political leaders when they came to Nashville. And it was the residence of the former representative in Congress, Benton McMillin, who was by common consent to be the next Democratic nominee for governor. I lost no time in getting acquainted with the politicians, and I am quite sure that some of them found in me an auditor more eager than they were accustomed to encounter. Many of them loafed about my corner of the lobby, telling and retelling their old anecdotes and advising the world in general from their experiences in the Confederate Army just how to lick the Spaniards.

There was Colonel Arthur St. Clair Coylar, in his eighties, a hero of the legal turmoil that followed the Civil War, but a bearer of tales that he had heard from Andrew Jackson himself and which he was then weaving into his biography of "Old Hickory." Two or three times a week there would come that tremendous occasion when the governor, fiddling Bob Taylor, and the governor-to-be, Benton McMillin, would meet at my cigarstand, soon to be joined by a huddle of appreciative chucklers as they swapped the latest.

Not all of my Tulane lobby loafers were politicians. There was François Fogg, the Parisian boulevardier, on an enforced vacation from France to look after his patrimony, tall, bearded, dandified. François may have been a little on the supercilious side, but he too liked an eager ear, and so every day he was at my counter to make my eyes widen and my jaw drop and sometimes my face burn with his peculiar cargo of anecdotes.

Then there were younger people, some of my own age or just a little older, Vanderbilt students, or medicos from the University of Nashville, who were attracted by the fact that we specialized in pipe tobaccos. We had canisters of various sorts and compounded our mixtures, weighed out on the polished brass balances of an apothecary's scale, a ritual into which I put everything that my imagination could evoke out of Mr. James Barrie's *My Lady Nicotine*. With some of these college boys, who were the objects of my special envy, I formed friendships that endured for decades. One of them who used to talk politics with me in the late reaches of the night, Grafton Greene, was for more than thirty years the chief justice of the supreme court of Tennessee.

My favorite then was none of these. My hero of the lobby was Captain Granville Sevier, the great-grandson of John Sevier, the first governor of Tennessee, and at that particular moment a captain in the

Tennessee Militia. He wore every day, with the indulgence of the governor and the adjutant general, a gorgeous uniform, his light-blue trousers blazing with broad stripes of artillery red, his dark-blue cape flashing its lining of that same artillery red, and his black velours hat cocked on one side to conceal but one-third of an artillery-red ostrich plume. Tennessean by ancestry and by birth, actually he had been for many years a New Yorker with a newspaper job in Park Row and a convivial headquarters at the Hoffman House bar on Madison Square, at the then northern outpost of Broadway life. He had come back to Tennessee to raise a regiment and to drive His Most Catholic Majesty's forces, horse, foot, and dragoons, out of the stricken island of Cuba. He seemed to me to embody in one person all the military prowess of our American arms, whether we fought against the British or whether we fought each other in blue and gray.

At my cigar counter I met another, somewhat younger, man who was determined to do his bit for *Cuba Libre*. He was a tall, slender young man, his upper lip adorned with a drooping mustache that matched in color his light-brown hair. He was almost startlingly erect in his carriage, and when his composed and reposeful face would from time to time light up with anger, righteous anger against the cruel Spaniard, his eyes seemed to flash fire. He hailed from McMillin's neck of the woods. He was a militiaman, and he was already raising a company, of which he would be the captain, to fight in the war. His name was Cordell Hull.

Another was Colonel Archelaus Maecenas Hughes. At first he was clad, I had almost said "emblazoned," in a brand-new and beautifully tailored uniform, a gray uniform, the uniform of a colonel of cavalry in the Confederate Army, not so be-ostrich-plumed and gold-laced as one of Jeb Stuart's cavalrymen, but still with yellow moleskin pipings and revers and a yellow silken sash. Colonel Hughes for the next quarter of a century was to me one of my favorite tellers of tall tales, but I must say for him that he began with a small story. He was from Columbia, and his sister had been my mother's classmate in college before the Civil War, which had found him but a stripling. Late in the war, General Nathan Bedford Forrest sent another young Columbian up inside the Union lines, there to recruit a regiment of men, horses, arms, and ammunition which was either to break its way through the lines back to the South or to let its men infiltrate into Alabama by ones, twos, and threes. The man sent to raise the regiment and commissioned a colonel was Duncan B. Cooper, and his first recruit was Arch Hughes. They had "liberated" two horses from the Yankee tyrant, and one night were making their way to a rendezvous for other recruits. Thinly clad, they rode through the dark, and through a dark that was freezing, through a dark in which they were cut by the sleet. Trooper Hughes muttered and mumbled when his smooth-shod horse slipped on the ice and almost fell. Colonel Cooper reined up and waited for him.

"What were you saying? Talking to me or talking to yourself?" demanded the Colonel.

"I wasn't talking to myself, and I wasn't talking to you. I was just telling God that this was the last God-damned country I'd ever love."

After the Civil War Mr. Hughes had become a Republican and a professional Republican politician at that. He had held office under Republican Presidents in Tennessee and in Washington and was now quite willing to display a love not only for the United States but for oppressed Cuba. To the profession of that ardor he brought a special qualification. In the terrible epidemic of 1878 he had volunteered to go to Memphis to nurse those who were stricken by yellow jack. There he had had yellow fever and had recovered. He was immune. And so it went along until the gray uniform was laid away, and he appeared, eagles and all, in the blue uniform of a colonel of the United States Army, the colonel commanding the Eighth Immune Regiment, United States Volunteers.

So excited was I to be in the midst of all this furor and away from my backwoods home that it seems to me now that I must have thought the war a special preserve of Tennessee, of Nashville, and even of the Tulane Hotel lobby, for my recollection that the Congress actually declared the war on April the sixth is in no way personalized. It is just like any other historical fact that happened without my help.

As the spring and summer wore on, I saw more and more soldiers, although Captain Hull, Major Sevier, and Colonel Hughes long since had departed for their posts.

Then the great thing happened. The patriotic women of the city had organized from the first to serve coffee and cake, sandwiches and pie, to the soldiers going through Nashville on their way to the mobilization points in the South. One day we heard that the very next day at noon the train carrying the First Nebraska Volunteers would stop for two hours in the Nashville depot and that they would be served a lunch by the Nashville Chapter of the United Daughters of the Confederacy. I was determined to be there, for it would be my first opportunity to see the greatest hero of my life, the man to whose fortunes I was passionately devoted, the peerless leader, the colonel of the First Nebraskans: William Jennings Bryan. Two years before, when first I had so hated him for defeating Mr. Bland for the nomination and then a few weeks later I had so adored him as the champion of democracy, I had little thought first to see him a soldier and in uniform. But it was my chance. I found out from my cousin, Mrs. Mary Paul Johnson Maguire, who always had a finger in U.D.C. affairs, that the demand for admission was so great that she despaired of getting me a ticket, the tickets being reserved for the great, the good, and the important. But she did tell me where to come so that I could be smuggled into a wagonload of pies and thus get inside the station. I paid a smuggler's fee by helping to unload the pies and lost myself. Boards were thrown across sawhorses, and a table of sorts was made for the colonel, the governor, the mayor, and others of that sort. I squeezed in directly behind the governor, and once, when an efficient and zealous militiaman would have ousted me, the governor, my cigar-counter patron (although what he bought was chewing tobacco), protected me.

So there, in that grimy shed of a railway station, I heard and thrilled to the marvelous voice of him who was, despite his uniform, still the Boy Orator of the Platte. Years later, when he was Secretary of State, I told him about it. He said he remembered the time well, for it was for him also an occasion—it was the first time he heard and thrilled to the oratory of Bob Taylor.

Almost every day in the Tulane lobby I would see someone else who stirred me deeply. It might be Tom Halley of the *Nashville Banner,* or it might be Bob Moorman of the *Nashville American;* but in any event it would be the political reporter of a daily newspaper. Him I envied, him I was determined to imitate; and, in preparation for the great day when I too would be one of that craft, I cultivated my political and martial and journalistic customers. And

I practiced by writing long, long letters about them all, to the one person who would understand and sympathize and encourage—my mother.

II

Having the seventeen-hour stretch at my daily task, even with its eight-hour midday repose, meant that, if I was to get any sleep at all in either of my rest periods, I would have to move from my aunt's house, which was too far away. So I found a place to live with Cousin Sally Perry. She was a first cousin to my mother, a widow who lived with her bachelor son and spinster daughter in a block of row houses only three or four squares away from the Tulane. The house was one of a group even then known generally to its own occupants as Poverty Row. It stood in the shadow of the federal building and, despite its name, was in a neighborhood made up for the most part of the mansions of the well to do and the rich. Cousin Minnie Perry was a stenographer in a railroad office; Cousin Tom, a city salesman for a coffee-roasting establishment. Their earnings were small, but they took me in for room and board for $2.50 a week; and surely no one in all the history of mankind ever got so much good food for so little money. Only a little while after I moved, my Aunt Lou Vaught suddenly sickened and died, her sons moved to the West End, and, except for the young friends I had made, I was cut off from my Park Avenue island of respectability, and I never went back to my Park Avenue Methodist Church.

At Cousin Sally Perry's I was only two blocks away from Christ Church, and when on Sundays I was relieved at ten o'clock I went to that church and sat with Cousin Mary Paul Maguire. Both these women were my mother's first cousins but were not themselves kin. Both were dotingly interested in me; both were indignant that I was being worked to death and being paid a starvation wage. Both of them were very poor, but so far as social standing was concerned they were miles and miles apart.

Cousin Sally stood on her ancestral rights as a member of a good family. She was respectable, she properly despised all "common people," but she accepted her lack of means with fortitude and under no circumstances whatever, with the single exception of a funeral in the family, would she go into any company, much less would she have dreamed of attending a party or a public meeting. She had been accounted rich when she married just before the Civil War. The Yankees and the war had made her poor, and she nursed her resentment in retreat from the world.

Cousin Mary Paul was poor, too, but she never let it get her down. Her father had been rich, one of the richest men in the state, a builder of railroads, owner of coal mines, and a banker. He had lived in a colonnaded mansion that occupied a whole half-square of ground diagonally across the street from the First Presbyterian Church and just west of the square on which was built in the 1850's "Overton's Folly"—the biggest and most luxurious hotel in America —the Maxwell House.

Long before my time that mansion had come down, and its spacious lawn was covered to the very verge of the surrounding streets with business houses and stores, the biggest and best retail stores in Nashville. It was the heart of the shopping center. All that property had been left entailed to Cousin Mary Paul and her two sisters; and, since it was all still in their names, she held herself to be, and in general was accepted still, as one of the rich. The fact that she and her sisters had mortgaged, remortgaged, hypothecated, and otherwise discounted the income from the entailed estate until she was hard put to find enough income to maintain her in a two-room establishment in the neighboring High Street did not interfere with her social activities.

That both Cousin Sally and Cousin Mary Paul were outraged because I had to work such long hours for such a small wage was a mere coincidence, since their reasons for their indignation bore not the slightest resemblance to each other. Cousin Sally was concerned with my health; Cousin Mary Paul was bothered because with such fiendish hours I couldn't go to the places and do the things that she thought a cousin of hers ought to go to and to do. Mary Paul thought it important that I, verging on nineteen, without a dime and with no prospects, should go to the right houses and get acquainted with the rights boys and girls; and she never doubted that she would manage it for me despite all my handicaps. Was I not, after all, a member of her family?

Despite Cousin Sally's good food and despite my joy in a job that gave me a chance to see so many interesting people and leisure enough to talk to them, I did not get enough sleep. I began to lose weight rapidly (and in those days I had little to lose). My right arm and shoulder began again to twitch, and there was a tic in my right cheek.

Cousin Mary Paul took me to a doctor, and he sent me to an oculist. Both Dr. Buist and Dr. Graddy thought that some of my symptoms might be related to uncorrected astigmatism. And so on came the spectacles that for fifty-five years afterward I never had off except to sleep. But it was not enough, and I had to quit work.

Thus it came that by the time of my birthday at the end of August I was back in Buffalo, my adventure into the city ended, my physical health apparently more precarious than ever. There was even doubt as to whether or not I could control my right arm sufficiently to go back to the printing office and set type. My older brother, whose business in Buffalo had all but collapsed, had moved with his frail wife and two little children to the Indian Territory; and there I was, a burden on the family whose fortunes were never high, at a time when they were never lower.

But I cannot recall that I was for a moment either discouraged or dismayed. My optimism was not justified by any facts, but it was fed and warmed by the fun I was having and undoubtedly was based on the fundamental fact that I never had had any health, I never had had any money, and therefore I had no actual appreciation of the absence of either.

The fun consisted in telling everybody all about the wonders of the city. I resumed my place in society and my avocation as a writer of letters, although this time they nearly all went to Tennessee. I resumed my place in Sunday school and church, in the political and other arguments around the square and in the courthouse. And in these resumptions I assumed an air of authority that ought to have been extremely offensive but which for some reason inexplicable to me was not so regarded. I still retained the privilege of being an odd fish. During that summer and autumn I rested. The relief of eyestrain afforded by spectacles undoubtedly helped, and I was about to go back to my old job in the printing office when a letter came that changed all my plans.

The letter was from Mr. Daugherty. In addition to the Tulane Hotel cigarstand, he had acquired the cigarstand at the Maxwell

House. He wanted me to come back. My hours would be better. On one day I would have the seven-to-eleven in the morning and the seven-to-twelve trick at night, to be relieved at midday by Jim Greene; but the next day Jim would have the long, and I would have the short, hours. The pay, he explained, could not be more; it still would be five dollars a week. But, if I would come, he would send me the money to pay my way to Nashville.

When that letter came, I realized that I had indeed feared that I would never get out of the country again. Neither the pleading of my parents nor the warning of physicians could stay me then.

During the autumn my brother's wife had come back to Buffalo, ill, had given birth to a baby girl, and then had died, leaving my mother with the care of a newborn baby, a girl of three, and a boy of six. My brother could not leave his business in the Indian Territory, which was barely making ends meet; and, if ever I was needed at home, I was needed then. But Mother, with the patient resignation that accompanies deep and distressful poverty, possessed also an imagination that gave her confidence that somehow, if I had only the chance, I would break the chains of poverty.

So the first of December, 1898, found me back in Nashville. But now I had a purpose. It was not merely to see wonders and to meet people; it was to get a job, and a particular job—that of a reporter on a daily newspaper. I changed my environment. The Maxwell House was a much more impressive establishment than the Tulane. It was, it is true, not quite the fashionable hostelry that it once had been, for at that time the smaller and less architecturally pretentious Duncan Hotel was considered to be at the top of the mode. Nevertheless, the Maxwell House still in certain circles retained its vogue, and it certainly had an air.

When John Overton set out to build in the flush 1850's the finest hotel in the United States, he did not necessarily confine his standard to America. And indeed there was something to be said for those who asserted when it opened its doors that it was the handsomest, the most luxuriously appointed, the most brilliantly lighted, the most beautiful, and the grandest hotel in the world.

The Civil War came, and "Overton's Folly" was degraded to the rank of barracks. It was filled with Union soldiers who, with that insouciant disregard for enemy property which has characterized all soldiers in all wars, broke up its rosewood furniture to burn in the fireplaces under their marble mantels; while a breed of brigands, euphemistically known at that time as army contractors, managed to find means to requisition and take away the drop crystal chandeliers and many of the gilt-framed mirrors. Between them, high and low, the place was wrecked, and it was a long, long time after the war before it could be refurnished and reopened. And even then it was still the grand hotel and was held by travelers to exceed in beauty and elegance the Astor in New York, the Palace in San Francisco, the Parker House in Boston, or the St. Charles in New Orleans.

With the exception of its great Corinthian façade that has been ripped away to make room for widening what is still a narrow sidewalk in a narrow street, the Maxwell House still has a certain grandeur. Looking down on it from an upper floor of a new hotel across the street in the summer of 1946, my eye was struck first with the complexity of its maze of chimneys, each with its multiple array of chimney pots, all telling the story of the glory that once was advertised as a fireplace in every room. At the same time my eye was compelled to admire the sheer beauty of the façade, perhaps not so much marred by tearing away the colonnade as one might think. Built of brick, long before the days of steel, the Maxwell House walls still bear testimony to the skill of the artisans who built them. The brickwork under its patina of nearly a hundred years is so satisfying in design and in detailed execution that, if for no other reason, I think the Maxwell House should be preserved as a national monument to the skill of mid-nineteenth-century bricklayers—bricklayers who were not only artisans but artists as well as being Negroes and slaves.

To me at nineteen, again reprieved from the backwoods, as I stood at the cigarstand behind its tall counters of mahogany and plate glass, with my back to huge glazed cabinets of mahogany and polished brass, and looked out over the great lobby, it seemed that here was one of the greatest works of man. The expanse of the tessellated marble floor was interrupted by huge round columns which thrust their way upward to bear at mid-height the balcony off which opened the parlors and the great dining-room. Across the lobby from me were the desk and offices, elaborate in mahogany and brass, the whole lighted by a great chandelier hanging from the center of the ceiling, whose flaring open gas flames no longer had to be lighted by hand. Each bracket and arm of the chandelier was wrapped with wire, and the wire came to the orifice of each gas jet. One had only to turn on the gas and press a button, when lo! the marvel of an electric spark lighted each and every jet.

Around the walls of the lobby, broken only by the doors and other openings, ran a wainscoting of pink and white marble lightly veined with turquoise. It was so strikingly beautiful that strangers always asked whence it came, and in my day, 1899, all of us were firmly convinced of the truth of the tradition that the quarry had been a secret one and that Mr. Overton, when he built the Maxwell House, had had it sealed up and the traces of it destroyed so that never might any other building have such marble. That such a fanciful thing might be done in Tennessee, where the hundreds of marble quarries discovered scores of colors and varieties, is not beyond the bounds of probability. That pink marble is not the pale pink of the Tennessee marble from Knoxville with which the National Gallery of Art in Washington is built. It is not one of the pink marbles of commerce, some of which have either a brownish or a grayish tinge. The Maxwell House wainscoting is a pink marble of flaunting and shameless pink. And all this marble was joined with elaborate filigree of brass that has now triumphantly withstood nine decades of daily polishing.

On the balcony floor the high-ceilinged parlors, opening through wide, high archways one into another, were multiplied into infinity by their opposing mirrors, which turned their equipment of wrought-iron filigree into a maze relieved only by the great carved white-marble mantelpieces. On one whole side of the balcony there was the grand dining-room.

Unfortunately, some of the biggest and best examples of this pink marble are not open to general public view. They are the huge slabs that form the walls to the stalls in the men's room. I do not know whether or not the motif was carried into its opposite number. However, it is a fact that the Maxwell House had bathrooms and hot and cold water and all the other plumbing conveniences when it was first built. Of course it did not have a bath with every room, as it had a fireplace in each, but there was provision of a sort then quite unusual. It is a pity, it seems to me, that not enough attention has been paid to the history of our modern conveniences, although perhaps I should not say that, since I have made no intensive researches into the subject. Thanks, however, to the enterprise of *Life* magazine, I did see in reproduction some of the drawings which accompanied the report of the first Japanese mission to the United States, members of which acknowledged in their communication to the Mikado the cordiality of the reception tendered them at the White House by President Buchanan but seemed to exhibit more interest in the description and sketches of the bathtubs and the water closets in Willard's Hotel.

In my day, as the nineteenth century was drawing to a close, the dining-room was not all bare shoulders, satin and crinoline, not all wide mustaches, imperials and gray uniforms. Indeed, it was none of that. Also it was not all pink-marble walls and a mahogany reredos to conceal its kitchen doors. It was a very lively place where the guests of the house and guests from without came for breakfast, dinner, and supper. As the somewhat cheaper Tulane was the headquarters for the politicos, including the governor of the state, the Maxwell House, more expensive and more fashionable, was the habitation of those who found that they had business with the politicos—the representatives of the railroads, the insurance companies, and the banks. It also was the place where the great lawyers who had business with the courts were accustomed to come and stay. And so far as the dining-room was concerned, it still had its clientele of Nashville people who, because of some dire domestic disaster, were compelled to endure the social disgrace of eating in a public eating place.

Of course there were occasions when a visiting family from Louisville or Memphis might come with a debutante daughter to grace the coming-out of some Nashville girl, and while they stayed at the Maxwell House parties might properly be given by them. But for local society by that time one could hardly entertain in a hotel unless in the summer at the springs, in the mountains, or at the seashore.

One approached the dining-room to be met by Archy. Archy was old, timelessly old. He was slender; he was slight. His hair and his mustache were gray. His manners were formal, and he bowed from the waist with the dimmest hint of a smile on his face as he took one's hat and placed it on a shelf in one of the huge mahogany racks that stood on either side of the dining-room door. He had had no predecessor, and there he had stood and there he had bowed and there he had taken hats from the day the doors of the hotel were opened. Never had he given any check, and never had he forgotten to whom belonged the hat, the coat, the fur, the wrap, or whatever might have been left with him.

Leaving the impeccable Archy, one entered the wide door to be received by Banks. Banks too bowed from the waist, which in his case was quite something to do, for his figure was as rotund as his smile was ingratiating. He was quite dark, almost black, and his manners were those that one might impute to a grand vizier of some oriental court. He showed one to one's chair with an air that left no doubt that Banks had been saving the best table and the best chair for this particular most honored guest. Indeed, he could by a slight cock of his head and a slight twist of his smile indicate that he had spent hours in keeping persons of less importance away from that particular table. Then, hovering just back of the chair, Banks would communicate in a confidential manner his notion as to what was the best thing on the menu before rising to his full height and peremptorily, almost brusquely, ordering a waiter, "Serve this gentleman."

Not that I often got up on the balcony and into this marvelous dining-room. I was too poor for the likes of that, but once in a while someone would invite me to be a guest at dinner or at supper, and so I came to know the gorgeous ritual.

The food was something else again. If the meal was the midday one, it would be dinner. The napery was fine and white, but the china was that heavy sort of queen's ware that for a time was thought to be necessary for hotels and restaurants. There would be a soup and after that a main dish, pot roast or fried chicken or chicken and dumplings. When it was served, the waiter would dispose to the left of one's plate three small heavy oval boats, each laden with a different vegetable, while at the right at the tip of one's knife he would put a cup of frozen sherbet. It was the frozen sherbet that made it a dinner. There would be a bread-and-butter plate, and both hot biscuits and hot cornbread, and of course the coffee for which one might substitute either sweet milk or buttermilk. After that was over came the dessert—pie or an apple dumpling or a pudding, and ice cream. I don't mean *or* ice cream; I mean *and* ice cream.

The charge was seventy-five cents. Of course the Duncan House, which was a little more fashionable, was then charging a dollar for a dinner, but the Maxwell House had not raised prices and was sticking to its old customs. As far as the cooking was concerned, I must admit that it was not of the order of the beauty of the place or the grand manner of the servitors. It was at that time indeed quite second class and especially so in Nashville, where domestic cuisine always has been at high tide.

Consciously, however, I not only savored but seemed to share in the departing glories of the Maxwell House, and from my observation post in the cigarstand I seemed to be able to sense the varying life about me. In the embrasure of the window looking out on Cherry Street was an easy chair; and there were long, long times when no customer demanded my services and I could sit in that chair and look out on the narrow street across to the town's best restaurant, the Utopia, and glimpse between the great fluted Corinthian columns of the portico the gilded saloons and gambling establishments, the Climax and the Southern Turf. Just outside my window would come every afternoon an old gambler, Alf Burton, to stand between two columns and look out on the passing throng. In mild weather when my window was open I could hear him. If he had won the night before, he would sing, *sotto voce,* gospel hymns. If he had lost, he would curse himself most vilely out of the corner of a twisted mouth. Young boys and some not so young used to half-hide themselves around the other columns to hear Alf Burton at his vespers. Not only did I see the street scene, but through a close friendship soon formed with Frank Davis, the head clerk, and J. Knox Hume, the cashier, I soon was admitted to a share in the goings-on (those public, those not so public, and those particularly private) within the hotel.

The shift arrangement whereby I had one long day and one short day not only gave me more time, but my relations with Jimmy Greene, my relief, were so friendly and cordial that we could make exchange of time so that either of us was able to go places and do things, although of course not together. However, we did overlap our time because of our common interest in reading. We discovered down the street in the same block a bookstore owned and run by a man who soon became, as he remains today after full fifty-five years, one of my closest and dearest friends, Reuben M. Mills. He was a young fellow then, of course, only five or six years my senior, but already Mills' Bookstore was a center in Nashville not only of the literati and the intelligentsia but of that much more numerous and much more miscellaneous lot of persons who happened at the time to be young and who liked to read.

Greene and I pulled a good many young men who were accustomed to hang about Mills' Bookstore into loafing with us at the Maxwell House; and, because some of them did not have to work, Jim and I made them into messengers who brought to us from Miss Mary Hannah Johnson in the beginning Nashville Public Library some of the books we had tasted on Reuben Mills's counters and which, of course, we could not afford to buy. Among these "messengers," and most sedulously cultivated by me, were two or three newspaper reporters, Dudley Glass, who ran a column of literary criticism in the *Atlanta Constitution* for forty years, and David Rankin Barbee, then a dramatic critic and later for years an editorial writer on the *Washington Post*.

When I came back to Nashville, my domestic arrangements and my social life were completely changed. Cousin Sally couldn't take me because a granddaughter had come to Nashville to work and had my old room, so I went with my cousins Will and Amis Vaught to the West End, where one great mansion had been converted into a boarding-house, the first tiny spot of the blight that later consumed what then was the most fashionable section of the town. Of course we did not recognize ourselves as being the forerunners of the blight, but we did like to live in the neighborhood and among the nice people. And we formally changed our church membership from Park Avenue to the West End Methodist Church, which had a congregation made up half of the socially elect and half of the faculty families of the neighboring Vanderbilt University. Once again I plunged into church work, taking my alternate Sundays for active leadership in the Epworth League and the Sunday school and extending my acquaintances rapidly among the university people, students and members of faculty families, who were approximately my age.

The pastor of the church was Edwin B. Chappell, a learned and scholarly man of a broad and liberal mind. He interested himself in me because I had had no formal education, and, discovering by means of patient examination what I had and had not read, he undertook to supply some of my deficiencies by lending me particular books. It was his theory that Christianity had nothing to fear from science unless it were the obscurantist tendencies of some Christians to insist upon ignorance. So it was out of his library that I read *On the Origin of Species* and *The Descent of Man*. It was he who led me to read Le Conte, the American geologist, as being perhaps a bridge between Hugh Miller and Darwin. It was he who gave me an essay on Descartes, by whom I do not remember, and urged me to read Henri Bergson to demonstrate the fact that in this world some philosophers were mathematically exact and found solace in equations while others found their salvation in the *élan vital* and in persuasiveness of total truth rather than in precise measurement of a particular truth. And it was he who, having learned of my early adventures with the *Homilectic Review,* talked with me about the *Methodist Review,* the scholarly quarterly of which he was co-editor.

Dr. Chappell was not only my pastor; he was a great teacher who, seeing how poignantly I regretted my inability to go to school and college, made himself my beloved professor. In his later career as one of the leaders in Southern Methodism, he exhibited in the educational work of that church the same broad and liberal spirit and the same Christian devotion that so completely won me, heart and mind.

When I had lived with Cousin Sally, she had had a good breakfast for me so I could get to work by seven o'clock; but that couldn't be done in my West End establishment. Neither could my long-day, short-day shift be fitted into the meal hours of the boarding-house, so for the first time I was thrown on the business of eating out. Of my weekly wage, $1.50 went for my share of the two rooms that I occupied with the Vaught boys and with Charley Colmore. That left $3.50 for everything else. It was easier to skip breakfast than to pay for it. On the days when I could, I ate supper with Mrs. Thomas where we lived, but most of the time I ate at Pappas' Place, a Greek establishment more distinguished for its reasonable prices than for either its cleanliness or its good cooking. My hours were not so cruel as they had been at the Tulane; but, with insufficient food and, almost as a matter of course, no vegetables or fruits, I again began to lose weight, to feel again the twitch, to see again in the eyes of others their discomfort as they saw the tic in my cheek. I was too ill to work, and once again I had to give up and again to go back to Buffalo. It was a most dispirited young man of twenty who took the train on the eleventh of December, 1899, back to Missouri, back to the Ozarks, back, as it seemed to him, to a life in the backwoods.

CHAPTER XI

HOME, FOR A WHILE

In mid-December, 1899, when I got back to Buffalo, it was evident that times were better and that even Dallas County was sharing in the rising economic fortunes of the country; but for me and my family there was no share in it. My older brother had not made a go of his harness and saddlery store in the Indian Territory and was in Kansas City looking for work. Although Mother had the care of his three little children, we were fortunate indeed in that we had persuaded Miss Lizzie Humphrey to live with us to care for the children; and that left Mother free to teach school again. For two years Father had been so ill that he hardly ever left the house, but he did more than his share in helping with the babies. My younger brother had work in O'Bannon's store, but it was all very hard sledding. My old newspaper, now the *Buffalo Record,* had passed into new hands and was being published by Mr. O. H. Scott. He was shorthanded, and there was a job for me at once, with the familiar and standard three dollars a week attached.

Better times had enlivened the social life of the little town. More and more of the teen-age youngsters were going away to college, or at least to normal schools and business colleges. The livery stables had new surreys and side-bar buggies, the horseflesh was better, and indeed almost every aspect of life was rosier than it had been in the deep darkness of the hard times of 1893–96.

Mr. Scott's son Clyde, who was perhaps two years younger than I, had been for years one of my most intimate friends. He also worked in the *Record* office, and there were my old friend, Bernice Marshall, and one or two other printer girls.

In Nashville my well-nursed ambition to get to be a reporter on a city paper had caused me to study with great care the Nashville newspapers. In the *Nashville Banner* I admired greatly the society column, then edited by Miss Sue Porterfield. I had come to know Miss Porterfield, and I thought her the most charming, the wittiest, and altogether the most delightful person I had ever known. She had promised Cousin Mary Paul to help me get a job on the *Banner*.

So when I got back to Buffalo and back on the *Record,* I proceeded to set up a society column. I was sure that somewhere in the laws of the Medes and the Persians there had been an edict that only a woman could be a society editor, so I did not want to sign my name. I attempted to persuade Nelle Pittman, the reigning beauty and belle of the town, to be the editor. She declined because she said she wouldn't sign what I wrote, and there was no doubt that I intended to do the writing. That all resulted in a compromise. The column was headed in 24-point Bradley "In Society," and it was signed by the initials of my first name and hers, "L. and N."

Not content with recording the news of things that happened, I intervened to make them happen. This intervention took the form of the organization of a literary and public affairs discussion club which was called the "Round Table." In that enterprise one of my principal aiders and abettors was Mrs. James E. Ballard, who had been my good friend since the time when I had worked in the post office with her and whose lively intellectual interest I had known since we had read books together in the Chautauqua Literary and Scientific Circle back in 1889.

Together we whipped things up. Membership was made desirable and hard to get by a limit of twenty-five members, and new applicants were kindly but firmly told that they would have to wait until there was a vacancy in the club's roster before their pleas could be considered. Then, too, we met every Monday evening. The Round Table reflected in its organization my own notion that adults were also people, and it was not confined as most things of the sort were in that day and time to one age group. Some of its members were more than fifty years old; one at least was under fifteen. I am indebted to Miss Lascelles Rush of Buffalo for lending me a scrapbook in which she had pasted the clippings of that old society column, thereby incidentally saving the record of the Round Table.

In deference to the traditions of the literary societies of an elder day, we sometimes had readings of poems and short stories, but for the most part the old clippings show that we were engaged in discussing current affairs. There were regular weekly reports on what had been done in the Missouri state legislature in the previous week and on the progress of the Boer War. There were reviews of the magazines to which the club subscribed and which were circulated among its members by its librarian, Clyde Scott. The liveliest things, however, were the informal debates. There was the Boer War. Some of the members were on the English side; some were on the side of the Boers—I was a champion of Oom Paul. We discussed the trusts. The Round Table included Liberals and Conservatives. One of the Conservatives was destined in later life to be for many years the dean of education in a state university, and another to become the dean of the medical college of another state university. I, one of the Liberals, was to devote myself to public administration. My stay in Nashville among the Conservatives had not undermined my liberal faith, and every Monday night we fought over some phase of the never ending battle of the Left against the Right. It was at a meeting in January, 1900, in the last year of the old century that I committed to print what may have been my first admission that it may never be settled. Here is a paragraph from my report:

Mrs. O'Bannon read Edwin Markham's famous poem, "The Man with the Hoe." As was to be expected, this precipitated a lively argument. The fact that the Hoeman of this hideous type does exist in the person of the drudges of the sweat shops and mines was tacitly admitted, but the question was, "Who is to blame?" Some thought the fault was in the rulers, the political and social government, others that no one was to blame but the Hoeman himself.

It already has been set down that in Buffalo in my earlier teens there was no dancing. The church had frowned. Round dances were unthinkable, and even the square dances had to be played as "games," with the music furnished by the players' own singing, for a piano or even a guitar would have brought the whole business under the ban. But I discovered that, while I was away in Nashville growing up, a whole change had come over the place. Bob Furth had come back from a couple of years in St. Louis, and he appointed himself dancing master in ordinary to our crowd. When I came back from Nashville, I found everybody waltzing, and those who were not were performing in the dance orchestra between times. I was shocked, not because of any puritanical objection to dancing, because I had none, but because here was something going on which definitely did not include me. I was too awkward, and after a few essays it was the unanimous opinion of the girls that, whatever else might happen to me in my life, I could never be taught to dance.

Our crowd began to dance, and my only recourse, in order not to be left out entirely, was to set myself up as a pirate. I dived straight through the seventeen-year-old outfit into the "frying size" and went with first one girl and then another. It was tremendous! I had no idea of what power an "older man" would be able to exercise in this particular field! But my triumph was short lived. Dean Stanley, who was of the set older than our crowd, dived through two generations and taught Lascelles Rush to dance. The "frying size" took up the new mode of life, and I was left high, dry, and alone.

However, I had a short period of revenge. I reasserted my leadership and took command of the situation in the name of the church, not that I attempted to restore the puritanical ban on sinful diversions but that I introduced something new into the church life of the town itself, which, for a season, did restore me to what I thought my proper place. The only churches in the town were Methodist, Baptist, Christian, and Presbyterian. There were no Catholics. There were no Episcopalians and no Lutherans. And there never had been any observance of Lent. Now, in Nashville, I had learned about Lent and knew that even in its gayest society that season put an end to dancing. So, though I had done justice to the Valentine's Day Ball of the Terpsichorean Club, at the same time I stopped the thing thus:

Buffalo society is, we are glad to say, going to church just now. There have been no parties or entertainments and all the young people are more or less interested in things of far greater importance and every night finds most of them at the revival meeting. Altho it may be said that worldly amusements are never the best, yet it is eminently fit that during Lent, the season of forty days before Easter, the day we celebrate the Resurrection of our Lord, spiritual things should receive our attention to the exclusion of the world, the flesh and the devil.

It was a losing fight, though, and I knew it. I never again could be a leader of the crowd. My leadership never had been sufficiently respected anyhow and was, perhaps, acknowledged only by me. Now, even I could not pretend. The dance had won.

Not only had it won, but the town had a song for it. From that time until this very day it is a prime article of faith stoutly held by every native of the county seat of Dallas County, Missouri, that there is a song that was written in the town by a native and that when sung elsewhere it is sung only by thieves who have no proper respect for property rights:

> Buffalo gals, won't you come out tonight,
>   Come out tonight,
>   Come out tonight,
> Buffalo gals, won't you come out tonight
> And dance in the light of the moon.

Perseverence and persistence are not commonly attributed to me by either family or friends, but after a fashion and with long lapses in between I did keep at this business of dancing. In the winter of 1904-5 in Washington, when I lived in an apartment hotel, four girls who lived there undertook to teach me to dance. They kept at it all winter. In the spring they gave me a diploma which certified that I never had known how to dance and that I could not be taught how to dance and that I never would learn to dance and that this certificate ought to be accepted as final judgment in the matter. It was not until I was fifty-seven years old that a family friend who was also a dancing teacher took me in tow, guided me into Arthur Murray's, and, lo! and behold, I did learn to dance. But by that time it could be only for my own enjoyment and in no way to advance my social progress.

Then, also, other things were happening. Boys and girls in our crowd were getting married. Sometimes they married one of our own. Sometimes they found a mate abroad. One of the earliest desertions was my first sweetheart, Alice Weatherby, a girl whom I had loved so desperately but who always succeeded in keeping me dangling while she carried on her more serious affairs with more acceptable beaux. At nineteen, in 1899, she "jumped over the broomstick." Others were following.

Here again I was excluded. In the first place, I had not the slightest intention to marry and settle down, because I had not yet become a reporter on a daily newspaper and also because I was too poor. Actually, I never even thought of it for me.

Suddenly in April, 1900, my whole situation was changed. My elder brother was offered a job in a wholesale harness and saddlery establishment in Springfield, Missouri, a business in which he eventually became partner and then principal owner and which he conducted until the end of his days. He got a job for me, and I went to Springfield.

There began my only experience with hard physical labor. It began at seven in the morning and ended at six in the evening, with an hour for dinner in the middle of the day, and through the six days of the week—in other words, a sixty-hour week. The pay was good. It was double what I had been getting in Buffalo. It was six dollars a week. I was a man of all work. I was janitor; I was stockroom boy; I was shipping clerk; I was freight-elevator operator (a freight elevator operated by rope and manpower). I was busy with hard, backbreaking work, practically all of which was far beyond my physical strength, for all of the ten working hours of the day save one. That one was at midday dinner time when Mr. Hermann, the president of the company, and my brother left for their meal, and I stayed on to watch the front of the store in which a retail business was carried on. There were few customers at that hour, and there was no objection to my sitting down, none to my reading, and none, in fact, to my doing as I pleased except that I was supposed to keep a wary eye out for a customer, make a sale if I could, and, if I couldn't, to use all possible arts and wiles to detain the prospective buyer until Mr. Hermann or Joe got back.

I didn't make many sales, but one that I did make I would have closed; and, had I had five minutes longer, it would have been rung up on the cash register to my everlasting glory as one of the greatest saddle salesmen of all time. It was just too bad that Mr. Hermann came back from dinner just in time to take over after the sale had been closed and take the money, one hundred and twenty-five dollars in gold, which the customer was willing to pay for a beautiful saddle, a cowboy saddle with a high cantle, hand-stamped intricate designs by our eighty-year-old saddle-maker, and, moreover, a saddle with a sterling-silver horn. It would have been glory enough to have sold such a beautiful saddle for such a handful of gold pieces to any customer, but it was beyond the reach of dreams to have sold it to this customer.

He was Frank James.

In the course of looking over our stock of saddles, the man had mentioned casually that he lived in the Indian Territory, but there was no occasion then to ask his name. It was only when Mr. Hermann had intervened and the gold was passing and the silver horn was passing that I (and, praise the Lord, it was I) said, "Would you like to have your initials stamped on each side of the pommel in this space (*indicating*) which has been saved for that purpose?"

The man asked, "Is there room for my whole name, the first name on one side the last name on the other?"

There was.

Then he told us. I am not sure who turned whiter, Mr. Hermann or me, but both of us blanched.

We began to talk. We talked for an hour, and Mr. Hermann never even noticed that I was staying in the front part of the store when I ought to have got back to my work.

That was not to be, however, the end of my adventures with the famous James boys. Before I left Buffalo I had been chosen as a delegate to the Democratic state convention which was to meet in Kansas City in June, just a month before the Democratic national convention was to hold its 1900 session in that same city. I would not be twenty-one until the next August, and I desired above all things to go to that convention. My brother Joe was willing, Mr. Hermann was complacent, and I joined the Dallas County delegation, headed by my good friend Mr. Frank Furth, at Bolivar on their way to Kansas City. It was a delegation of seven or eight, larger than any Dallas County ever before had sent to a Democratic convention, because it had been fixed in proportion to the vote cast in 1896, when Bryan carried the county. In Kansas City, established in accordance with the economic necessities of most of the delegation in a third-rate hotel, we prepared with tense excitement for the great day; and I was honored above all men because, still too young to vote, I was made the spokesman for the delegation and was to respond to roll calls, make appropriate nominations, and the like.

We met in a great new auditorium which was being prepared for the national convention but which unluckily burned before the big show opened. There was a great gathering of the Democratic elder statesmen, those who had been for Bryan, those who had openly opposed him, those who had gone fishing in 1896; and there were also the old men who had left the party thirty years earlier to be Greenbackers and Union Laborites and Populists and all such left-wingish things and who now were welcomed back into the bosom of the reunited family. There was more than a sprinkling of Civil War veterans—Grand Army men some of them, but a goodish number ex-Confederates.

On the first day after the convention was called to order and after the prayer was heard, there was a tremendous excitement in the rear of the hall, and somebody with a voice of Stentor called out, "Mr. Chairman, I have the honor to present Jesse James, Jr.!"

And Jesse James, Jr., flanked on either side by a Confederate veteran and tailed by a yelling retinue, marched down the main mid-aisle.

The performance shocked me to the marrow of my bones. Already I had come to look on the James boys as nothing more than the train-robbers they really were, but my sense of shock was ameliorated by the fact that I knew that, for most southern sympathizers in the state, the James boys were enshrined in a Robin Hood tradition. They had been driven by Unionist persecution to their career of depredations. They were desperadoes because they had been excluded from the amnesty which was extended to regular Confederate troops at the end of the war. Their sins were forgiven them because they were heroes. I felt all that emotionally when young Jesse marched down the aisle, as I did when I almost sold the saddle to his Uncle Frank; but, intellectually, I knew better.

However, except that from time to time I arose to announce the vote of Dallas County, that incident of the introduction of Jesse James, Jr., remains in my memory as the one highlight of the state convention in which I participated as a delegate before my majority.

Back from that excursion, I continued to struggle with the job in the harness and saddlery factory which was too much for me. My brother and I had a room together, and we ate at a boarding-house. As I remember it, there was enough food, and my hunger was sufficient sauce to make it appetizing enough. Its quality and range, however, probably would have outraged a modern dietitian. As for me, I had all sorts of internal troubles. I was visited with a plague of boils.

I grew weaker physically instead of stronger and, as the autumn came on, was on the very verge of collapse.

My reprieve from the backbreaking work came from Nashville. While there I had not permitted my activity at the Methodist church to interfere with my familiar and friendly relationships with the Episcopal church. The rector of Christ Church, the Reverend William T. Manning, but lately from London and not yet even dreaming that he would be the bishop of New York, patronized the boys' club which Mr. Hugh Dallas had organized; and I was one of its active participants. The clubhouse was on a downtown shopping street in a suite of rooms over a busy store and was available for reading and rest during the day and for games and conversation in the evening. Mr. Manning, discovering my curiosity about books, my wide-ranging taste in reading, and my lack of schooling, once went so far in his generosity as to offer to lend me the money to enable me to go to preparatory school and college. However, although it was not expressed, there seemed to be implied in that offer an obligation that I would at least consider carefully preparing for clerical orders. I was grateful, but I declined. I could support neither the explicit financial obligation of the loan nor the implied obligation to enter the church.

One of the men in Christ Church active in St. Andrew's Brotherhood, himself the son of an Episcopal bishop and the brother of another, was Joseph Gray. I had come to know him well in the club. He was a good friend of my indomitable cousin, Mary Paul Maguire. He was also secretary to Major E. B. Stahlman, the owner and publisher of the *Nashville Banner*.

So one day in Springfield I got a letter from Gray. He told me that it had been decided to add two or three reporters to the city staff of the *Nashville Banner* and that he thought that, if I came to Nashville, I would have a good chance to get one of the jobs. The terms were that the applicant was to be willing to work for nothing during a training period, and then, if he were able to pass muster, he would be put on a salary which Gray thought would be five dollars a week. I had scrimped and saved a little. I could borrow a very little more. But nothing could have kept me from going to Nashville.

At the same time I delayed going for a reason that under the circumstances, with an opportunity at last to realize my ambition to be a reporter on a daily newspaper in the city, must have seemed a little odd to anyone else. On August 29, 1900, I had become twenty-one. The letter from Gray came on the first of October. I delayed going until the first Wednesday after the first Monday in November because I could not, even to achieve my dearest wish, forego the opportunity to cast my first vote for the Peerless Leader of the Democracy, William Jennings Bryan.

On that Wednesday, dismayed by the defeat of my hero at the polls but determined to carve out for myself a career in journalism, I took the train for St. Louis, there to change again for Nashville.

CHAPTER XII

MR. MORTON AND THE "BANNER"

For me Nashville was *the city!* And just to be there once again would have assuaged my sorrow over the second defeat of Mr. Bryan by Mr. McKinley. But to get there with the prospect of getting a job on a daily newspaper seemed to make my cup of blessings overflow.

I moved in with my two cousins and, bright and early, went to the office of the *Nashville Banner* to see Joe Gray, secretary to Major Edward B. Stahlman, owner of the paper. Mr. Gray told me that there was nothing else he could do but send me upstairs to the third floor to see the managing editor, Marmaduke B. Morton. He warned me that Mr. Morton was a ferocious devourer of young persons, a very volcano of profanity, a merciless taskmaster, but a very good newspaperman. What he said did not alarm me, but the fear and awe in which he held Mr. Morton did. Subsequently I was to learn that Joe never could be comfortable in Mr. Morton's presence, although he had for so many years adjusted himself to the much more vigorous and explosive personality of Major Stahlman. I also was later to find out that he did not know that only a few weeks earlier Mr. Morton had foresworn swearing, that he was ever thereafter to keep his vow not to be profane (except in cases of the most extraordinary emergency), that he was even at that moment attempting to accustom himself to nice little parlor exclamations as substitutes for his old expletives, and that he was having some very rough going indeed. For Marmaduke Morton to be limited to "Dear me!" or "Mercy me!" was a miraculous manifestation of the power of will over habit, well buttressed by a diamond-hard sense of obligation not to break a promise. He had made the promise to the pastor of the Tulip Street Methodist Church. He kept that promise, but I am sure that he never confessed to the pastor that for a

[211]

long time his feelings were those of Samson after Delilah's shears had deprived him of his locks.

But of all this, that morning, I knew nothing. I climbed the stairs, asked someone where I could find Mr. Morton, followed the indication of a jerked thumb, and was suddenly at the very elbow of the great man. He sat at a roll-top desk in the corner of a room in which four or five other men and one woman also were sitting at plain deal tables, all busy. Over his desk was an open-burning gas jet, the flame turned low. Even sitting down he gave the impression of being very tall—in fact, since his legs were short, he seemed taller sitting than standing. His hair, reddish-yellow, cut in the then prevailing masculine pompadour, now called a crew-cut, bristled with the warning, "No foolishness!" Icy-blue eyes dominated a thin face in which a thin nose and thin lips offered no challenge to the power of an iron jaw line. That face had been taught impassivity at many a poker table; and it was a mask which hid a seething sea of almost ungovernable emotions. This could be guessed only by the rapid swinging of his right foot as he sat with his legs crossed.

He was smoking. He was always smoking. He smoked a corncob pipe. The second left-hand drawer of the roll-top desk was innocent of papers and had a far higher function. It was filled with smoking tobacco, a mixture made only by a Morton to be smoked only by a Morton, since no one else could have survived it. The tobaccos came from the strongest strains to be found in the Kentucky Black Patch and were the result of an annual expedition which he made to his native Russellville, Kentucky, for supplies. The only compromise he permitted was the addition of some handfuls of the even blacker perique which was bought for him by a New Orleans friend from some Louisiana plantation which boasted that it grew the strongest of the strong. This mixture, like most good pipe tobaccos, was difficult to keep burning, so the great man, with forethought, had provided himself with a whole pigeonhole full of spills rolled from sheets of copy paper; and, whenever he had a spare moment, new spills were rolled to maintain the supply.

I stood. He neither looked up nor spoke nor seemed to know that I was there. It is possible that my questioning "Mr. Morton?" was inaudible—but I doubt it. It had been ignored. I raised my voice. He turned and in the mild manner of a May morning said, "Do you want to see me?" A chair was kicked around, and I sat down. He pulled out the working slide of his desk, laid on it a bunch of copy paper and a pencil, and said, "Are you the boy Joe Gray told me wanted to get a job?" Being reassured on this point, he went on. "Can you write your name so that a human being can read it?" He put the pencil in my hand. I wrote my name on that pad of copy paper. A quarter of a century later Marmaduke Morton was heard to assure all and sundry that never thereafter had I ever achieved such a marvel of legible chirography.

Then more questions. Where was I born? Why did I want to be a newspaperman? Why did I think I could be? And was I willing to work? Then a spill from the pigeonhole, a long arm-reach to the gas jet, the reignition of the tobacco in the corncob pipe, a deep inhalation, and a frightening sequel that would have done credit to a dragon. The interview was done. He had not cussed once.

Then he said: "You go to work in the morning at seven o'clock. You will work for nothing. You will work for nothing for eight weeks, and then, if I don't fire you before that, at the end of eight weeks I probably will fire you. But, if I don't, we will talk about wages then."

He stood up, and, grasping the bowl of his pipe in his hand so that the stem stood out between his first and second fingers, he used it as a pointer and said: "And seven o'clock means seven o'clock. It does not mean seven-fifteen, as Jim Clark thinks it means [*pointing at one of the men in the room*]. Nor seven-twenty, as Tom Clarke thinks it means. Nor eight o'clock, as Bob Miller thinks it means. Nor any time at all, like Alex Sears thinks it means. And most of all not nine o'clock, like Miss Porterfield thinks it means. It means *seven o'clock,* by [*swallow—swallow*] 'Jimminy crickets'!"

As he exploded these several names, their individual owners looked at me, smiled, and nodded in recognition of an introduction which he completed by picking up the sheet of copy paper on which I had written my name and, it seemed to me, screaming, "This cub's name is Louis Brownlow." In a recess in another corner of the room there was another roll-top desk piled mountain-high with newspapers, and at it was a man, his back turned to me, leaning over, writing busily. Mr. Morton's pipe stem did not point him out, did not indicate him, nor did he turn to acknowledge the introduction. Later, I came to know that he was Richard H. Yancey, associate editor and, quantitatively, the principal editorial writer.

As I started for the door into the adjoining room, the man at the table next to it, James B. Clark, the city editor, halted me. He said, *sotto voce:* "Don't worry. You'll be all right. I'll give you some assignments in the morning and will take you around myself. I know you know my daughter Elsie."

I escaped into the next room, my entire being fixed upon the hour of seven o'clock the next morning, my entire body rigid with fright, my throat constricted, and my mouth as dry as the Sahara. I saw a water cooler. I made for it. I filled the common drinking cup—those were the presanitary days. As the cold water revived me, I heard voices from the other room and knew that its inhabitants already thought me well down the stairway. In the room where I stood at the water cooler there were four tables whose accompanying chairs were unoccupied and one roll-top desk over which a man was bowed hard at work. He was, I later came to know, Lee J. Hampton, the telegraph editor. As the water revived me, my eavesdropping was rewarded but not in the classical manner, for this is what I heard:

Marmaduke Morton: "That kid didn't scare worth a [*gulp*] hoot."

Tom Clarke (*amid general laughter*): "You can't scare 'em any more, Morton, with that new milk-and-water vocabulary of yours."

Alex Sears: "He was scared enough, all right, as it was. If you'd have cussed, he probably would have fainted."

Miss Porterfield: "He has very black eyes."

Mr. Morton: "Maybe I can't scare 'em any more, but I sure can work the [*gulp*] out of 'em."

As the water quenched my thirst, so this conversation swept fear from my soul. I went out of the room into the hall on tiptoe and was careful to make no noise going down the steps. I floated up Church Street on the clouds and turned in on High to see Cousin Mary Paul Maguire and tell her the great news. The "Old Lady," as she was known not only to her kin but to all other Nashvillians of my generation, was happy but somewhat reserved because of the fact that I had committed myself to working for nothing, without any guaranty that there ever would be a salary attached. But, sensing my great elation, she soon was able to congratulate me and then came out with this: "What are the perqs?" I didn't have the faintest idea what she meant, and said so. She said: "I mean the perquisites. What will you get any-how without a salary? I know you will get streetcar passes and theater passes and passes on the railroads. Indeed, there ought to be all sorts of perqs."

Thus solacing her disappointment at what she evidently thought was my selling myself into slavery, she gave me her blessing, and I went around the town visiting some of my old friends to tell them what a wonderful thing had happened. All of them—Reuben Mills in the bookstore; all the clerks and cashiers at the Maxwell House and the Tulane; my pastor, Dr. Chappell—all shared my joy, but all seemed to have some question about how I would be able to live on a salary of nothing a week. As for me, I thought that my secret hoard of forty dollars, so nicely calculated at eight times five, would suffice for that eight weeks.

My room with my cousins was on the third floor of a four-story row house on Belmont Avenue, directly across the street from the side en-trance to my church and but four or five doors away from Demoville's Drugstore, which was the social center of that community—a com-munity of mansions sheltering the rich and the socially high-placed families of the town but into which boarding-houses had already begun to infiltrate. My cousins and I were the only lodgers in this house, which was maintained by Mr. and Mrs. George E. Blake, who lived there with their young son and daughter. Mr. Blake was a regular con-tributor to the *Nashville American* under the by-line "Blake of Tennes-see." Mrs. Blake was the sister of the very distinguished and handsome William S. Morgan, then secretary of state for Tennessee, and herself a free-lance writer. I told the Blakes the glad news. I must have told it as though it were the most important news since the foundation of the world, because later that day, just as I came in from supper—I took my meals at Miss Lellyet's boarding-house around the corner on Hayes Street —the two children came to me—Morgan, aged seven, and Gladys, aged five—each with a piece already written which I was asked to be certain to see was published in the next day's *Nashville Banner*. That I was not able to do. But, as a matter of fact, it was but a few weeks later that I began to take regular contributions from Gladys to the "Satur-day Children's Page"; and for both the Blake children it was the begin-ning of long and useful lives as journalists.

After supper I went to the drugstore and there announced the news of my great good fortune to some of the assembled "jelly beans," the name then current for what later became "drugstore cowboy." One of them already was a reporter on the *Banner* at nothing a week. I had not known it, but Theodore Duncan Rousseau some three weeks earlier had got the same kind of job I had just landed. There was another who frankly envied us. He wanted that kind of job, too, and he was soon to get one. He was Grantland Rice.

It was early home and early to bed for me. There was that deadline to meet. I must be there at seven in the morning. A faithful alarm clock that never had failed us was so suspect that I tried it three times, then set it for half-past five despite my cousins' grumbling protests. Perhaps I slept a little but not much, for in the morning I turned off the alarm before it rang, dressed in a hurry, and started to walk to the *Banner* office, something on the order of a mile and a half. There were no nickels to waste on streetcars, and, besides, streetcars were few at that early hour. My first objective was Pappas' Place, the Greek restaurant just across Church Street from the Tulane. Nick Pappas and his four brothers, who were the cooks and the waiters and the entire staff, were friends of mine; and there I had my usual breakfast of three fried eggs, a piece of ham, and two hot biscuits for fifteen cents. There was no tipping. I don't suppose anybody ever tipped in Pappas' Place, at least not in those days when three eggs for breakfast was standard operating procedure.

Thus fortified, I made for the *Banner,* wondering if the doors would be open. They were. And at exactly 6:50 by the office clock I was in the room in which the great thing had happened to me only the day before. Nobody else was there. Five minutes later, in came Mr. Morton. He stared, flipped me a copy of the morning paper, the *American,* from a pile under his arm, and told me to find a table in the next room and to read the paper until Jim Clark came. A little after seven, the others began to come in. In the room where I was were Duncan Rousseau, whom I had seen the night before; Haynes McFadden, also a cub on nothing a week; Tom Halley, the star reporter who did the state capitol; and Lee Hampton, the telegraph editor. Rousseau made the introductions. I read and fidgeted.

By eight o'clock, all were gone on their assignments, and then Jim Clark called to me. "Come on, Brownie. Have you got a pencil and some copy paper? Come with me." Ever thereafter I was to be

"Brownie" to the *Banner* and all its staff. Mr. Clark had got the name from his daughter Elsie. Elsie, in turn, had picked it up in the Sunday-school class of which both of us were members, a teen-age Sunday-school class which, for some occult reason, had decided that every one of its members should be known only by a nickname. "Brownie" thus I became and "Brownie" have I always been, with the exception that to my newspaper friends and colleagues in Washington I was "Louie."

Now Jim Clark was not only city editor; he was also a star reporter. His city editorship consisted only in giving assignments to the other reporters. There was no U-shaped copy desk or, indeed, any copy desk. A rewrite man was an unheard-of thing. Mr. Morton, the managing editor, read all the local copy; Lee Hampton, all the telegraph copy; Tom Clarke, all the state correspondence. Mr. Gideon H. Baskette, the editor-in-chief, who had sanctuary in a tiny little room opening into Mr. Morton's realm, read the editorial copy. Each of them sent it upstairs to the composing-room in a hand-operated, rope-pulled dumbwaiter contrivance. Galley proofs came to Mr. Morton.

The telegraph editor and the state news editor wrote their own headlines, and, since Mr. Morton was always so crowded, he required that each reporter also write his own headlines. This, I was later to think—and I believe I still cling to that naïve faith—was an ideal arrangement. At any rate, it did make possible an intimate relation between the text and the headline which somehow or other never seemed to survive the modern copy desk. However, this scheme was daily disrupted when toward press time Mr. Morton disappeared upstairs into the composing-room to make up the paper. Then, with nobody there, each reporter read his own copy, wrote his own heads, and sent it "boiling hot" to the composing-room. The scheme wasn't much for co-ordination, and it doesn't precisely fit into what later became my moving passion for orderly administrative management; but it did afford great opportunity for individual self-expression.

Jim Clark took me that day on his regular beat. It was intensely interesting to me, but then at that time I suppose any beat would have been almost as interesting. But not quite. For this particular beat brought in politics, and I had always breathed politics. Whether taking that beat that morning was for me merely a coincidence or whether it was a determinative fact, I cannot know.

We went first to the city hall, from there to the county courthouse, and from there to the federal building. We did not go to the state capitol, since that was Tom Halley's territory. The omission of state government on that particular day probably would not have bothered me even if I had sensed it, for did I not already know the governor of the state and his predecessor? Did I not already know all the heads of the state departments? Did I not already know the leaders of both houses of the legislature? Else, if I did not, how had I been wasting my time as a cigar clerk over the better part of two years in the two political hotels, the Tulane and the Maxwell House?

Jim Clark, forty-odd, fattish, jocular and jovial, almost as disorderly as his handwriting was illegible, compassionate to all human frailities, fiercely intolerant of social change, restive under and resentful of his poverty and his all but intolerable burden of work—Jim Clark was one of those who most profoundly affected me in my later life. His black eyes still snapping, but his black hair already turning to snow-white without intermediate shadings of gray, he had arrived at the roaring forties as a member of a family long servants of the *Banner* but never owners, maintaining his always insecure foothold on the pay roll as a result of a series of personal triumphs. His brother Battle Clark was head of the advertising department. His brother Martin Clark was head of the circulation department. Jim was city editor. He was not managing editor, because Mr. Morton had been imported from Louisville for that job partly because Jim was so high-tempered, so irascible, and felt himself by heredity so much a part of the *Banner* establishment (his father had been editor-in-chief) that he had more than once defied Major Stahlman, the owner, to his face. Not only that, but he had been offensively profane, worse apparently than Mr. Morton ever had been, and his city-room talk had offended the delicate ears of the first woman society editor. Moreover, upon occasion or upon no occasion, he got drunk. Worse than all this, he had read certain books; he had gone to hear Colonel Robert Ingersoll lecture; he was suspected of being an infidel.

Something of this purple past I already had known through my associates in the church. Now I was to know that he had overcome most of these obstacles to his career. He was a devout Methodist. He was a teetotaler. He had abjured profanity long before Mr. Morton had done so. But his past hampered him; and, despite indefatigable industry and eager performance, he was destined not to rise.

He took me to the city hall upstairs over the lively city market and introduced me there to the news sources—to the mayor, James M. Head; to the chairman of the Board of Public Works, George W. Stainback. And I found in the city clerk's office Bob McKay, one of my Park Avenue gang of 1898.

Jim Clark took me to police headquarters a little more than a block away from the city hall, and there I met the handsome chief of police, Thomas Curran; another man, heavy in flesh but lively in visage, Robert L. Sidebottom, chief of detectives; and another fat man, dull-eyed and heavy-lidded, but who I afterward was to learn was great of heart, a former policeman, now police judge, James Buchanan.

Then in a swift lope that put even my thin legs and thin body to the test to keep up with him, Jim Clark took me to the courthouse to meet more of the great. I met the county judge—the administrative head of the county, the presiding officer of the county court—the "lame miller," Judge McCann; the attorney-general (Tennessee for "prosecuting attorney"), Andrew Jackson Caldwell; and then, higher up, clerks of the circuit court, clerk and master of the chancery court, judges of the circuit court, including William Hart sitting on the criminal bench, and, most eminent of all, and by a coincidence that is comparable only to the conjunction of the planets, two chancellors—Chancellor Cooke of Franklin and Chancellor East of Nashville, each of whom reached back into that now nebulous past that was still at that time so recent and so tangible, the ante bellum South, the days before the war.

From time to time my mentor stopped me, here sitting at a table, there standing at a high desk. I wrote the news stories that I had gathered. Mr. Clark claimed but few of them for himself. Mostly they were mine. He gave me a copy of the *Banner* of the day before and told me how to count the letters and spaces for the headlines; and, while once or twice he giggled, he said nothing to restrain me as, in deck after deck of headline, I exaggerated the importance of the news story.

Then back to the *Banner,* he at a lope and I at a run, stopping often to greet his friends and to introduce me to them, rushing in only to the business office on the ground floor of the *Banner* and sending our stories, headlines and all, up to the third floor, where Alex Sears would grab them out and put them on Mr. Morton's desk. And thence on a half-mile to the federal building.

And there to meet news sources again; prominent persons whose names I had read but who had seemed to me to be a little alien to the scene as being at once federal officials and Republicans. First, Major Andy Wills, the postmaster, politically interdicted as a carpetbagger and a Yankee officer, but a society leader and the pre-eminent *bon vivant* of the town; Abram Tillman, the district attorney, dignified, able, our meeting the beginning of a close friendship that endured until his death well into the days of World War II; Colonel Doak, the clerk of the Federal District Court, classicist, wit, and salty raconteur.

Thence, again at a lope and a run, back to the *Banner*. It was past noon. I was hungry. I tried to say so, but I was afraid. Just opposite the *Banner* we turned at the same rapid pace into an alley, and suddenly we were in the Little Gem Restaurant on a corner where two alleys crossed. There, two huge haunches of beef and two men with the longest and sharpest knives that I had ever seen. In that hideaway only half a block from the Maxwell House the working people in a hurry came for lunch. A swift deep cut and a thin slice of the juicy rare beef came on to a plate. I grabbed from a mound near by a single cornbread muffin. There was, I subsequently found out, a place in a corner where one could get a mug of coffee or a mug of milk, but we had no time for that. We swallowed our rare beef and our cornbread, each paid the ten cents demanded for the lunch, and, pace accelerated, dashed to the *Banner* and raced up the steps. There, the managing editor gone, we scribbled our last stories, wrote the headlines, and sent them upstairs.

There was a letdown. Nobody paid any attention to me. I was tired, very tired. The excitement had run out, and I was sure that I had failed. There was nothing to do.

After a while there was a rumble in the cellar, and in a few minutes up came Alex Sears with a bundle of papers. One he threw on the table in front of me. I could not breathe. My heart seemed to stop. There on the front page, three stories of mine with headlines just as I had written them. And, turning the page, ten more—thirteen on the first day. Jim Clark had given me the breaks.

So, happy as could be, I waited for congratulations. Rousseau and McFadden were too busy to speak to me. Other people ran away. Mr. Morton was nowhere to be seen.

Mr. Morton and the "Banner"

Jim Clark called me in. "Well, Brownie, you made the front page. Here is something for you." And he gave me a book of streetcar passes. That morning he had discovered that I was passless, an ignominious condition far below the deserts of any newspaperman. He had taken care to repair that omission.

Thus, no longer compelled to walk because nickels were too scarce to spend for streetcar rides, I took a streetcar and went to the Phoenix Cotton Mills to see Will Vaught, my cousin, taking with me, quite naturally, the *Banner*. I found him, neat and tidy, his green-baize apron protecting his waistcoat from ink stains, black or red, putting down figures in his neat bookkeeping style. With him was his associate, Walter Akin. I took up a blue pencil and marked first on the front page and then through the paper the stories I had written that day. Will was delighted. Walter said he didn't believe a word of it.

Looking over these thirteen stories which I got printed, three of them on the front page, on my first day as a reporter on a daily newspaper, I can now seen plainly that even according to the standards of that day they were inordinately inflated. More than one of them was a twice-told tale that somebody in city hall or the courthouse had palmed off on a new reporter in order to get his name in the paper. Perhaps no one of them justified the license afforded me in self-estimation when the privilege was given me of writing my own headlines. It seems that, in taking the *Banner* of the day before as my model, I was unable to see any of the small headlines. That night at Miss Lellyet's boarding-house I monopolized the conversation.

Then to bed, and again reality. It had been too close a shave at 6:5C that morning. The alarm was set for 5:15.

There was in all Nashville, I am sure, no human being as happy as I. Here I was just turned twenty-one, a reporter on a daily news-paper, and my stories were being published, some of them on the front page. To be a reporter on a daily newspaper had been my deepest desire, and the fact that I actually was one fulfilled my highest hope. The little matter that I was a cub working for nothing, without even a promise of a regular job, or of a place on the pay roll, mattered not at all.

But there was one little thing that pulled me down from the clouds and kept my feet on the ground. It was that Marmaduke B. Morton, the managing editor who had hired me, had made my eminent position somewhat insecure by a not-at-all-veiled threat to fire me instanter if I were not on the job at seven o'clock in the morning.

The first day I had got there ten minutes before the deadline, but to my dismay Mr. Morton himself showed up at five minutes before the hour. On the second morning, which was November 14, I was there a full quarter of an hour before the office clock over Miss Porterfield's desk struck seven. Mr. Morton came in at ten minutes to. On the third morning I was there at 6:40. He came at 6:45. He said nothing. I said nothing. All other members of the staff found us there when they came; but, of course, they did not know how long we had been there.

So day after day, morning after morning, I shoved ahead the alarm clock, I wakened before it went off, and I headed for the office determined never to let him beat me there. I had to stop at the Union Station lunch counter for breakfast because Pappas' Place was not open. But earlier and earlier I came. Earlier and earlier he came. But I always beat him by a few minutes.

There was a Sunday, and it was a day of rest. I had worked every day and all day and sometimes into the night. My devotions to the *Banner* included Vespers as well as Matins; but, when Sunday did come, I did an outrageous thing. I slept straight through the morning; I did not go to Sunday school or church, and that despite the fact that the church was just across the street.

The new week came, and there was no letup in the contest. And so it happened that on Thursday morning, November 22, I arrived at precisely five minutes to six, and Mr. Morton came in at six. I had not seen the morning paper—the newsboys were not on the corners. But Mr. Morton had one, and there on the front page under what was for those days a big headline—three columns wide—was a meager story about a tornado that had devastated the little city of Columbia, sixty miles to the south of Nashville. It said that many were killed but gave only three names. One was that of a Miss Farrell. There was an explanation that all wire communication with Columbia had been lost. Mr. Morton knew what I did not, that Miss Farrell was a sister of the *Banner* correspondent in Columbia, Ernest Farrell. He knew he had to get someone to Columbia to cover the story. He had not seen the morning *American* until he picked it up just at the *American* office a half-block away on his way to the *Banner*. There

was no time to get a regular reporter. There was no time to find anybody but me. His voice was strained as he called: "Brownlow."

I rushed in.

"Get to Columbia. Catch the seven o'clock train. Get the number
of the killed and injured. Get their names. Don't write any fancy
cyclone stories. We can do that in the office. And, for God's sake,
get those names back to us as quick as you can, any way you can."

"Yes, sir," was all that I could find to say.

"Have you any money?"

I fished. "Seventy cents," I reported.

He fished. Two half-dollars and a dime. It was all laid out on the
desk—a total capital of $1.80.

"Don't buy a ticket," he yelled. "Beat your way if you can. Get out
of here! Get the heck out of here!"

I ran down the steps. There was no streetcar. So I started out on a
trot. I ran most of the way to the station.

Almost breathless, I ran into the then new Union Station in time
to hear a stentorian call, "All aboard! Franklin—Columbia—Decatur
—and way stations." It was good that there was then no gate guard
with the power to demand to see and the duty to examine a passenger's ticket, for I had no ticket. Down the long, long steps in a scurry-
ing crowd I made for the train. Its three coaches soon were jammed.
Not only was every seat filled, but also every arm of a seat on the
aisle and every available bit of standing room. Groups packed tight
around the tall, unlit coal stoves at the end of each car. Open platforms at the ends of the cars filled until it seemed that on every curve
at least a few passengers would be spilled off.

The news of the cyclone had spread. The extent of the disaster was
unknown. Everybody who had heard about it and who had kin in
Columbia was on the train.

The train itself was an institution that quite literally lived up to
its cognomen. It was an accommodation train because it accommodated
every passenger aboard by stopping wherever anyone asked it to stop,
and it accommodated every potential passenger not on board by
stopping wherever a signal required it. There were not only whistle
stops and flag stops but even crossroads stops in response to quite
informal and casual signals. Nevertheless, the train did run in accordance with traffic rules. These rules, quite general in character, were

as a matter of course known to every railroad man and pretty well known to all the passengers. They contemplated the operation of the trains by telegraphic "orders" which the conductor was bound to pick up at every telegraph station and communicate by means of carbon copy in writing to the engineer.

So, under telegraphic orders, the train proceeded from Nashville southward to Franklin, stopping, of course, at all the little way stations where there were no telegraph keys and consequently no orders. At Franklin there was both dismay and delay. Since the wires had gone down at about eight o'clock the night before, no telegraphic orders had come in. The conductor, the engineer, and the station agent decided to go forward by dead reckoning. That meant that the average speed of the train, which had been around fifteen miles an hour from Nashville to Franklin, was slowed down to, say, ten miles an hour.

The cinders and the soot from the puffing engine blackened us all. But, in my excitement, I ignored that. The standing in the crowded aisle of the swaying car added to our discomfort, and I ignored that. The fact that in the hustle and hurry of the crowd the conductor never found me, and my $1.80 was intact, might have encouraged me; but under the weight of one overwhelming circumstance I ignored that, too. The only thing that mattered was that the train was too slow. For I realized that I was that greatest of heroes, not merely a reporter, but a staff correspondent on disaster duty, obligated under penalty of the direst doom to get the news and get it back to the paper before the deadline.

Columbia, the stricken city toward which we were crawling at a snail's pace, had a population of about six thousand. But so important was it in the scheme of things and so accommodating was the Louisville and Nashville Railroad that it boasted two stops—a suburban one at the United States Arsenal and a principal one at the depot. Knowing this, I spent entirely too much time worrying about where to get off. When the train stopped at the Armory, there was no question at all. Houses torn into jackstraws, trees uprooted, and all sorts of debris showed too plainly the path of the tornado as it swept through the Arsenal grounds.

I got off there. Almost the first person I saw was Will Fleming, a boy about fourteen years old, who was a distant cousin of mine. He was equipped with a Kodak and, as the first question demonstrated, was full to the brim with information. He led me straight to the building that was being used as a morgue. I walked in. There were many dead bodies on the floor, and others were being brought in. For, although it was now nearly ten o'clock in the morning and the storm had struck more than twelve hours before, the work of taking the dead and the injured up from the wreckage was still going on. I had no difficulty in attaching Will to my side, and he required no persuasion to take pictures with his Kodak. From the first temporary morgue to another, then to a temporary hospital and on in toward the center of the town, traversing the path of the storm, talking with survivors and members of rescue parties.

I arrived soon after eleven o'clock at the Western Union telegraph office with what I had been told to get—a list of the dead and injured. My list showed twenty-four dead (by the next day the number was up to thirty-five) and more than fifty seriously injured. The lone telegraph operator was busy at his key and before him was a thick stack of telegrams of the general tenor, "I am safe. Mary." He told me he could not possibly get through that stack and take my message before four or five o'clock in the afternoon. I put up the argument of my life. I told him that, if my message went out, then everybody would know and that in the public interest he really should take my dispatch first. Happily my arguments were supplemented by those of William S. Fleming, young Will's father, who had been made chairman of the relief and rescue committee. Young Will had seen my difficulty and had dashed out to bring in his father, then perhaps the leading lawyer of the town. There was but one wire, and that south to Birmingham. The operator finally decided to ask the Birmingham manager, received permission to take my message, and started sending it. All the names that I had listed as dead went over the wire. About half of the list of injured was telegraphed when that wire, too, went dead. I went to the depot and found that a railroad operating wire had been restored, but nothing could persuade the railroad operator to interrupt his task of restoring traffic order. As a part of his job, however, he said he was going to send a locomotive over another line to Decherd and that the engineer would take the message and try to get it telegraphed in from Decherd, a small town twenty-five or thirty miles to the east on another branch of the railroad. I copied my list and gave one to the engineer.

Then, in desperation, I decided to try the telephone. Telephoning over such great distances as sixty miles was then a chancy thing at best, but my task was much greater. When I got to the telephone office, I found that there was only one wire, and that, too, ran south to Birmingham. And then Birmingham would have to make a con- nection with Nashville either to the east by Chattanooga or to the west by Memphis, a feat which in the opinion of the manager of the Columbia telephone office had never been accomplished and in all probability never would be. But in the excitement he was willing to try.

About a quarter to one in the afternoon the miracle happened. I got through to the *Banner* office.

Now the *Banner* editorial office had one telephone—a contraption fixed high on the wall and complete with jangling bells and hand- turned crank. The person who answered the telephone was one I had never met. He was Ed Stahlman, the son of the owner, having the title, I think, of "news editor." He had returned to Nashville only that morning after a two-week absence. For Mr. Ed Stahlman, ordinary, everyday life went on at a constant and stable level. It was just one explosion after another. In times of stress, however, he deserted this plane and went far, far above it into bigger and better explosions. I could not know at that time that, when he had come into the *Banner* office and had found that Mr. Morton had sent only a young, untried, ignorant, eight-day cub to report the Columbia cyclone, he had reacted with a new, all-time, record high in Stahlmanic explosions.

When he answered the telephone, and I managed to say through the buzz and whir and squeaks and squeals of that remarkable round- about connection that I wanted to speak to Mr. Morton, he informed me with emphasis and profanity aplenty that I would tell him and no- body else what I knew, if anything. Through it, though, I gathered that none of my telegraphic dispatches had got through. I began to read him my list, and he calmed down while I tried to spell out the names. Suddenly there was a change in his voice, and then I heard him shout that both the message from Columbia and the completion from Decherd had just come in. They had the list. It was in ample time for the two-thirty o'clock deadline. I was saved.

Then I went back to work. There were new names to be written on the lists of the dead and of the injured. There were stories to be gathered, and there was also the matter of the photographs. Will and I did not get around to that until late in the afternoon. We had to have the films developed. Only recently the advertisements had been talking about Velox paper on which photographs could be printed by artificial light. We searched the town. We found some. The films were developed, the pictures were printed, and four or five of them were good.

Now, in those days the reproduction of photographs in newspapers was a rarity. But I had seen a few in the *Banner* and knew that it could be done. I did not know that it could be done only for the Saturday issue and only after several days' work of making the halftone plates, curving them to fit the cylinders of the press, and actually inserting them as inlays on the stereotype plates. But, nevertheless, I had my pictures.

The next day after a very early breakfast I went with my copy ready to catch the train for Nashville. So great had become my sense of my own importance that it never occurred to me to buy a ticket. I just got on the train. I still had my $1.80, having had no occasion to spend any money for anything. The Western Union had accepted my messages collect, and Major James T. Williamson, the vice-chairman of the relief and rescue committe, an old beau of my mother's, had paid for the telephone.

"Captain Kidd" was the name of the train that left Columbia early every morning, dropped people off at way stations and took them aboard, arrived in Nashville about nine in the morning, stayed there all day, and then went back to Columbia late in the afternoon. The train took its name directly from its conductor. Captain Kidd knew everybody in middle Tennessee and was known by everybody. His glory was a tremendous beard which he wore parted in the middle as pirates were said to have done and, as of that time, in the fashion affected by Admiral von Tirpitz of the Imperial German Navy.

Captain Kidd found me and demanded a ticket. I told him somewhat loftily who I was and what I was doing and that I had had no time to get a pass. He knew as well as I knew that it was immoral for a newspaperman to pay cash money to ride on a train. So he said, "Pay me some other time."

Back in Nashville and then, as fast as streetcar and legs would carry me, to the *Banner* and up three steps at a time to the third floor, not for an instant thinking that I had done anything wrong. I had written and written the night before. I had written and written on the train coming up. And I had a bulkish sheaf of copy paper. I had even contrived some headlines for the main story and for a feature—the freaks of the cyclone—and I had the photographs. I rushed in.

"What in the Sam Hill are you doing here? Why aren't you in Columbia?" shouted Mr. Morton as I dumped my bundle on his desk.

In from the next room came Ed Stahlman. "Why in the blankety-blank, blankety-blank did you come back?"

After Mr. Morton had tackled the pile of copy, Ed Stahlman and Tom Clarke gathered round; and then the bent figure of the associate editor arose, and I was introduced to him, Mr. Richard H. Yancey. Mr. Morton threw the freak-story part of my copy to Tom Clarke. They were all busy, but they calmed down so far as I was concerned and told me to get back to Columbia to cover the follow-up on the story and to stay there until they told me to come home. There was, of course, a lot more writing that I had to do that day and a lot of questions I had to answer; and, when Mr. Jim Clark and the reporters came in, all the tales to tell over again.

There was no doubt about it. I was a hero. But it seemed to me that I wasn't quite as much of a hero as I ought to have been. I was sure that Richard Harding Davis himself, with Gallegher's help, could not have done more. There was eagerness in the questions from the other reporters. My copy was displayed in the paper that afternoon. My story had a line over it, "From a Staff Correspondent." But no word of praise from Mr. Morton or Mr. Stahlman or Mr. Jim Clark—only objurgations and grumblings because I had left the scene.

There was only one little thing. Mr. Morton himself at lunchtime said, "Come along." We went together to the Little Gem, and he put down twenty cents, paying for both our lunches. I had offered to return to him the $1.10 he had lent me Thursday morning, but he said, "Wait. Wait."

Not long after lunch, Mr. Morton handed me a pass on the Louisville and Nashville Railroad. That afternoon I embarked with Captain Kidd on the return voyage to Columbia.

On the road back to Columbia, I had with me, of course, a copy of the *Banner*. In it I read over and over again the things I had written— the list of the dead and injured; the note that explained why Mr. Lee Farrell, the regular Columbia correspondent, had not been able to report the disaster, because his two sisters were killed and he himself was injured; and then I would read the running story.

Lady Luck had certainly been with me in letting me have my first real fling in Columbia. Columbia was the capital of Maury County, and Maury County was my mother's home, the locale of the golden age of the tales I heard in babyhood. It already had a poet laureate in the person of John Trotwood Moore, who had rechristened it "The Dimple of the Universe." I had so many kinsfolk there, and through them so many friends, that I had had, as I already have told, help in my first assignment that no utterly strange twenty-one-year-old could have hoped for. And then also I got from them far too great a draft of the heady wine of praise that comes all too soon to young newspaper folk.

After another day in Columbia a wire came from Mr. Morton telling me to come back on Monday. I got to the office at midmorning. I put my stack of copy on Mr. Morton's desk. He looked up, took his pipe out of his mouth, and said, "Mr. Grigsby wants to see you."

"Who is Mr. Grigsby?"

"He is the cashier down in the business office."

"Shall I give him this note of what we owe Major Williamson for the telephone call?"

"No, give it to me. Mr. Grigsby wants to see you."

I went downstairs to the business office, into which I had not theretofore ventured, and asked where I would find Mr. Grigsby. He was the cashier, the bookkeeper, the accountant, and, incidentally, at his particular level, the dictator of the *Banner*. He stood at a high desk in the proper costume of a bookkeeper—in his shirt sleeves with his vest protected by a green apron.

I said, "Mr. Morton told me you wanted to see me."

"Who are you?"

"Louis Brownlow."

"Mr. Morton told me to give you this," replied Mr. Grigsby, and he handed me an envelope. He turned to his books. The interview was ended.

I started to leave.

"Congratulations!" said Mr. Grigsby, apparently to his ledger, since he did not look at me.

I opened the envelope. In it were five five-dollar bills! Twenty-five whole dollars all at once!

I ran up the steps and rushed in to Mr. Morton. His pencil was plowing through copy. I touched him on the elbow and said, "Thank you."

He whirled around, took his pipe out of his mouth, pointed the stem at me, and said, "You did some hard work, and that's your pay for it." Another draw or two on the corncob, and he fastened it in his hand and laid down the law to me with the stem, emphasizing every word. "That's your pay for it," he repeated; "but don't let that swell your head. On the different papers where I've been, all told, I've broken in one hundred and two cubs; and you're the most unlikely of the whole lot. But, if you want to work for nothin', come in the morning at seven, and I'll give you something to do until the first of the year, and then I'll probably fire you."

"Yes, sir," was all I could manage in reply.

The next morning Mr. Morton and I collided on the sidewalk at the entrance to the *Banner* office. It was 6:59. The war was over.

CHAPTER XIII

A YOUNG REPORTER

So I went about the business happy in my poverty, consoled by the twenty-five dollars that I had earned on the cyclone story, and supremely confident that I would not be fired come January.

In the six weeks that yet remained of the year 1900, I was put to do a variety of things. I sometimes covered the city hall and the courthouse, sometimes the markets, sometimes the churches, sometimes other things. I was the newest cub on the paper, junior of a few weeks to Theodore Duncan Rousseau and Haynes McFadden, but yet so fresh that the lowest of all tasks—the compilation of the daily grist of obituaries—was mine. And usually, also, for the same reason, the weather.

Once in a while during that period the state capitol reporter, Tom Halley, would be ill, and then I would get to climb the hill and the great steps to the capitol and there to cover the news of the state government. I was not slow to let my fellow-reporters, as well as my superiors, know that my greatest interest was in the city hall, the courthouse, and the state capitol. I had an infallible method of carrying that conviction into the realm of demonstration by volunteering to take any night assignment in the field of politics or government that might be given to any of the other reporters. There was not one of them who would not willingly turn over a night assignment, and there was no night assignment in that field that I was not eager to take. Inevitably, therefore, the city editor, Mr. Clark, and the great man, Mr. Morton, would know that it was I who was doing most of the work in politics and government.

On the day after Christmas Mr. Morton called me in and said he wanted to have a talk with me. He said that he still thought that I would never make a reporter and that I wrote too much and was inclined to follow my own fancy with respect to style rather than the accepted canons of the *Banner* which he had brought intact from *The Courier-Journal*. He had accepted those canons as immutable under the tutelage of the great "Marse Henry" Watterson himself. It was unthinkable that they should be changed. Now, it must not be imagined that Mr. Morton used this language in communicating to me this lack of faith in my ability to adopt a correct journalistic style. He said it in short words, quite vigorously, and with as much bowdlerized profanity as could be managed by a reformed cusser who could no longer use the words but certainly could carry the tune. And then he said: "Now I'm going to give you your chance. I'm going to put you on the pay roll at eight dollars a week, and, when the legislature meets, I'm going to let you cover the senate."

Thus it came about that at midnight five days later I, kneeling in prayer in the West End Methodist Church, welcomed the twentieth century with a happy heart and with the utmost unfeigned faith that it was to be my century. I was twenty-one. I had a job on a daily newspaper. I was writing things every day, and they were being printed the same day. Not only did I write for the paper but I read the newspapers.

The Boer War was in full swing, and for the first time it seemed that the Boers were breaking and that the British might win; and London had staged a great reception for Field Marshal Lord Roberts when he had come back to see Her Majesty, Queen Victoria. On the very last day of the nineteenth century the Chinese emperor accepted the demands of the Western powers, and the Boxer Rebellion was over. On the third of January Mr. Hay, with the backing of President McKinley, said that the United States would insist on the "Open Door" in China. The *Nashville Banner* itself was carrying on a campaign for the Nicaraguan canal, but the United States Embassy in London was having difficulty getting the Hay-Pauncefote canal treaty reopened; Paris was convulsed by a rumor that Captain Dreyfus would demand a reopening of his case; and Washington was jubilating over an utterly false report that Aguinaldo was killed and that the Philippine insurrection was virtually at an end.

The biggest headlines were concerned with the hazing of Cadet Oscar L. Booz at West Point; and the military court of inquiry had called before it two suspected culprits, Ulysses S. Grant, grandson of the President, and Douglas MacArthur.

As the old century died, William Jennings Bryan announced that he would run for President again, and a committee of the Congress began an investigation of the disfranchisement of Negroes.

In that first week of the new era, Eugene Field published *Sharps and Flats,* and the *Atlantic Monthly* began a series on "Reconstruction in the Southern States," with an article written by Professor Woodrow Wilson.

On the eighth day of January, the anniversary of the Battle of New Orleans—Jackson Day—the legislature met. Tom Halley was assigned to the house of representatives and I to the senate.

The senate chamber was a rather small room, large enough for thirty-three senators, with some room at the ends and at the back of the chamber for chairs and benches to accommodate those who, although not senators, had the privilege of the floor. There also was a very small gallery.

The senate was presided over by a speaker selected from among its members by their own vote. He sat on high, and in front of him there was a desk to accommodate the clerk and the assistant clerks of the senate. In front of them, on the floor itself, was a large table for the accommodation of the newsmen.

The techniques employed by a reporter in his daily business were very different then from those that now prevail. In the first place, since the *Banner* had no copy desk, only one telephone, and no such thing as a rewrite man, reporters could not telephone in their stories to be written in the office. They had to be written *in situ* at the place where the reporter was assigned; and, if the assignment were to cover an especially long period of time, the reporter would be visited periodically by a copy boy, who would take his stuff straight back to the *Banner* office. The *Banner* had no typewriters. All copy was written with a pencil, and, when the stuff did get back to the office, it received frequently but a cursory glance from the managing editor before it went directly to the composing-room. In fact, Mr. Morton depended more on reading the galley proofs to catch outrageous violations of his canons of English and possible libel suits than he did upon any pre-editing.

Up until that time it had been the custom for the *Banner's* two reporters in the two houses of the legislature to write a running, chronological account of what happened without attempting to give any emphasis to any occurrence, to any speech, or to any measure other than that inherent in giving some additional space to the more interesting

items. The arrangement was strictly chronological. The reporter wrote.
The copy boy came. The copy went back to the office. It went into type
and was printed that way. Never did any story of the doings of the
legislature begin with any other paragraph than that announcing that
the chaplain had opened the session with prayer. Nor did any story
conclude except with the statement that the senate or the house then
adjourned.

The regular routine had priority, and most of the time I reported the
doings of the senate in the approved fashion, stressing chronological
sequence, setting down every bill introduced, every resolution proposed,
and every motion made with meticulous care and with no differentiation in the running report between the important and the unimportant,
the interesting and the dull. Outside that running report and supplementing it, I discovered I could have a great deal of fun with my new-
found freedom. Whether or not the senate chamber in the capitol of
Tennessee in 1901 was the best school of journalism in the country, it
was certainly the best available to me. In retrospect, however, after a
half-century, I doubt its efficacy as an instrument of education in the
field either of the theory or of the practice of journalism, although it
had its instant advantages for a neophyte.

As a school of politics and history, on the other hand, it was an admirable institution. The senate chamber itself was an inner room in a
great building which was placed on a high hill in a capital city of a
state. That state itself was a reflection of the institution and the growth
of the American republic, a beginning and a development which was
mirrored in what was to be seen by my youthful eyes and which to an
astonishing degree was evident in the personalities of the public men I
met in that room, in the corridors of the capitol building, in the hotels,
and on the streets of the town.

The capitol building itself was the result of the upsurge of self-
confidence and pride of the people of Tennessee in their position of
leadership among the states of the Union. This leadership seemed to
them to be assured when their own Andrew Jackson had become not
only the President of the United States but the successful leader of a
democratic revolution in which the western, the truly American, the
nonsubservient, element had come into control of the government of
the United States. It was General Jackson, former President Jackson,
who had engaged the services of his protégé, William Strickland of

Philadelphia, the most distinguished architect of his time, to design the capitol. If fate decreed that General Jackson was to die before the final completion of the building, it was the same fate that was to decree that one of his successors, another of his protégés, his choice as head of his party, was to become the President of the United States in his turn, at just about the time the structure was finished. Not only was the body of William Strickland, the architect, to lie forever entombed in the walls of that building but hard by in the grounds was to lie the body of Jackson's successor, another Tennessean, James Knox Polk, who was the President of the United States in the year of decision which took the American flag to the Rio Grande and to the Pacific.

In the library across the corridor from the senate chamber, my fancy was caught by a huge set of volumes that I could not read because they were printed in French. It was a file of the *Moniteur,* published in Paris in the years of the Revolution and presented to the state of Tennessee by Napoleon Bonaparte, first consul of the Republic of France. In the corridor immediately outside, of much more intimate concern to me, among the battle flags of the Confederacy, both those returned by northern states from the captors to the captured in the administrations of William McKinley and Theodore Roosevelt and those that never had been captured, was one Confederate battle flag of special meaning to me. It was among those never captured. It was the battle flag of the Third Tennessee Infantry, Confederate States Army. It had been carried at Fort Donelson by a color-bearer who was shot down in action. It had been picked up from his fallen hands by my father, a color guard. He, in his turn, had been wounded, and it was picked up by another color guard, George Washington Hubbell. It had been carried by him next to his body, under his shirt, through a term in prison in Chicago. And, after many adventures in many battles, it had been taken back to Lynnville in Giles County, Tennessee, by Private Sullivan, the last of the color-bearers of the "I" Company of that regiment, finally to find its place in the cabinet on the wall of the corridor just outside the senate chamber.

In the library there was another lesson in history of particular interest to me, the portrait of William Gannaway Brownlow—Parson Brownlow—the pro-Union, proslavery governor of Tennessee. He had fought the Rebels with all the vigor of word and deed that formerly he had devoted to theological disputes, and he had died after completing a full term in the United States Senate as a Republican, being succeeded by a former President of the United States, Andrew Johnson, who as a Democrat had fought Parson Brownlow as a Whig in the days before the Civil War.

In the city I found persons who could link me, through their own recollections, with the times that stretched back almost to the very beginnings of the state and more than one who, in his memories, treasured personal acquaintances and sometimes political connections with the very founders of the state. The most venerable and ancient of these was Miss Jane Thomas. While what she had to tell me was connected in no way with the senate chamber, it was because of my interest in the past that I evidenced as a reporter of the state senate's proceedings that I was given the assignment to interview her on the occasion of her one hundredth birthday. Miss Jane lived in a very old house on Cedar Street, three or four miles west of the capitol, where Cedar Street at some time imperceptibly became the Charlotte Pike. She was a tiny wisp of a woman, lively and energetic and very proud of the fact that she had rounded out a full hundred years in Davidson County, Tennessee. She had lived from 1801 to 1901, the full stretch of the nineteenth century.

What seemed to me that day the best of the tales she told, and the one to which I gave the most space in my report, indeed united two of the great events of the nineteenth century. She told me that, when she was nearing sixteen, there had been tales of a new contrivance—a steamboat—that could come upstream almost as fast as the log rafts hitherto had floated downstream. She also said that she had heard that these monstrous new machines heralded their approach by a screaming steam whistle that was fit to scare a catamount. One morning, so Miss Jane said, there was an unearthly scream, something more than could be credited to a single "painter" or any other varmint of the woods. Her father promptly mounted his horse and rode as rapidly as possible into Nashville. He was there in time to be at the wharf when the first steamboat ever to come up the Cumberland to Nashville arrived. With that packet there came from New Orleans copies of the New Orleans newspapers which contained a tremendous item of news. It was the report of the defeat of Napoleon at Waterloo. You may be sure that my imagination prompted Miss Jane to tell whether or not she actually remembered how that news was carried at once to "The Hermitage," where, in temporary retirement, rested Andrew Jackson, who, a few months earlier, at New Orleans, had defeated Pakenham and the veterans of Wellington's peninsular campaign, just as now Wellington had ended the career of the mighty Napoleon.

And there was James D. B. De Bow, Jr., the son of that De Bow, a protégé of James K. Polk, who was the director of the Census of 1850 and the editor of *De Bow's Review,* perhaps the first journal devoted to the field of economics and political science regularly to be published in the United States.

Even within the walls of the senate chamber itself there was a chance to discover interesting links with the historic past. The rules of the senate permitted the presence on the floor of former members of the legislature, and two of these oldsters were of very special interest to me. One was John Houston Savage, who gloried in the sobriquet, "Old Man of the Mountains." He was old. He was born in 1815 and, therefore, was eighty-six on those occasions when he hobbled into the senate chamber, crippled by arthritis, and yet keenly interested in every current phase of politics. His hands were knotted and gnarled, and he had but one greeting for everyone who came near him. That greeting was a snarl, "Don't try to shake hands with me! Whatever you do, don't try to shake hands with me!" But, once he had established immunity from the handshake which, to him, was so painful, he became genial and loquacious and was never averse to telling a tale, either a little tale or a tall tale.

Mr. Savage was a friend and a supporter of Andrew Jackson, under whose command he had served as a captain of infantry in the Seminole War. After being elected prosecuting attorney for his home district, he broadened his experience in public life as a clerk in the White House in the administration of James K. Polk. He added to his military record by serving as a major in the United States Infantry in the war with Mexico. Then, from service in the White House and at the fighting front, he was elected to Congress. He served two terms in the House of Representatives, beginning in 1849; he declined a third term but changed his mind and went back to Congress in 1855 and served until 1859. At the outbreak of the Civil War he was commissioned a colonel in the Confederate Army but was wounded and was invalided home from military duty. He became a member of the Confederate States Congress, and then, after the Civil War, served several terms in the state legislature. He was full of stories, but most of them were about obscure events in the political history of the state—some of them the feuds between the pro-Jackson and the anti-Jackson Democrats, between the Democrats and the Whigs, in the two decades from the 1840's to the 1860's, when Tennessee was a doubtful state.

Another former member of the legislature who frequently came in was an equally picturesque figure but as different from Colonel Savage as night from day. He was Emerson Etheridge. Erect in carriage, dapper in dress, no one could avoid seeing instantly that he was a man of parts. He wore tight doeskin trousers, a silk vest of variegated colors, and a broadcloth coat. In his lapel there was always a rose or a carnation. And his black slouch hat, indoors or outdoors, was usually carried in his left hand, while his right grasped a gold-headed ebony cane. His head had a flowing mane of white hair, his upper lip a tiny waxed mustache, and his face was crisscrossed with lines that seemed to accentuate the smoothness of his yellowish, parchment-like skin. At that time Mr. Etheridge was eighty-two years old, but he didn't look it, and he didn't like very much to talk about it except that his love of tale-telling was continually tempting him into the recital of memories that could not do otherwise than date him.

As Mr. Savage was unapproachable, Mr. Etheridge was exceedingly affable. Mr. Savage had been a Democrat in the days of Jackson and Polk; Mr. Etheridge in that same period had been a Whig, an enemy of Jackson, an opponent of Polk, and a devoted admirer of Henry Clay. His first public service was as a member of the state house of representatives, elected in 1844 on the anti-Polk, Whig ticket from that part of western Tennessee which was then Whig in sentiment and a very large part of which to this day continues to be Republican. He was elected to Congress in 1852, and again in 1854, but was defeated in 1856. He was re-elected to Congress, however, as a Whig in 1858. On the expiration of his term in Congress, on March 3, 1861, he stayed in Washington and when, after a delay of some months and after the beginning of the Civil War, President Lincoln called the Congress into extraordinary session, Mr. Etheridge was elected clerk of the House of Representatives, a position which he held until March, 1863. That a Tennessean, a former representative from one of the states that had seceded from the Union and was in open rebellion against the authority of the United States, should have been elected clerk of the House of Representatives is a sufficient tribute, perhaps, to what the young Emerson Etheridge must have been. When I knew him, he gloried in the fact that he was the last member of Congress who set the party designation "Whig" against his name. Although in the beginning of the twentieth century he was still voting the Republican ticket, as he had done for forty years, he was quite clear in his own mind that he was the sole, surviving Whig in the United States.

Emerson Etheridge had stories to tell of the political conflicts that raged in Tennessee between the Unionists and the Secessionists of both parties. He had found himself, in 1861, ranged not only with his old Whig comrade, Parson Brownlow, but with his old Democratic adversary, Andrew Johnson, on the side of the Union. But these friendships were temporary. In 1867 he had been a candidate against Brownlow for governor and had suffered defeat at the hands of his old Whig colleague. As a member of the state senate he voted against Andrew Johnson as a candidate for the United States Senate when the former President was chosen by the legislature for that office to succeed Parson Brownlow.

The senate in 1901 was made up of thirty-three members, twenty-six Democrats and seven Republicans. Some of them were veterans of many stormy years of political life, and others represented a familial connection with the early days. One of the Republicans was Roderick Random Butler, a Republican from eastern Tennessee. A Whig, he had got his first political appointment from President Fillmore as postmaster of his home town. He had been a soldier in the Union Army. He was a delegate to the Union National Convention in Baltimore in 1864, which nominated Abraham Lincoln for President and Andrew Johnson of Tennessee for Vice-President. He had been elected to Congress in 1866 and had been in and out of Congress for four or five terms —an interesting individual whose political career was not unscathed by scandal but whose ability as a speaker and as a raconteur was unexcelled.

Then there was William C. C. Claiborne of Haywood County, well along in his seventies, bent under the weight of his years, his face given a saturnine expression because of a cast in one eye. He affected long white hair and wore a beard. He looked like the ancient of days. He was the grandson of that William Charles Cole Claiborne who had one of the most romantic careers of all the statesmen and politicians of the early days of the Republic. Senator Claiborne knew a great deal about his grandfather and was perfectly willing to pour his old family tales into my receptive ears.

His grandfather, who was born in Virginia in 1775, grew up in New York during the Revolutionary War, was admitted to the bar in Tennessee, and was a member of the constitutional convention which adopted the first Tennessee constitution in 1796. Then he became a judge of the supreme court of Tennessee but, after serving only a year on the bench, was elected to Congress from Tennessee. He served two full terms, from 1797 until 1801, the remarkable thing being that he served both of those terms in the Congress before he had reached the constitutionally eligible age of twenty-five. As a member of the first constitutional convention of Tennessee, as a judge of the supreme court of Tennessee, and as a member of Congress, he had been a colleague, in all three positions, of Andrew Jackson. He was a friend and a protégé of Thomas Jefferson, who appointed him governor of the Territory of Mississippi in 1801. And then, two years later, he was named one of the commissioners to take possession of the Louisiana Purchase, which President Jefferson had acquired from France. He was the first governor of the Territory of Orleans, the first governor of Louisiana, and then was elected to the United States Senate from Louisiana, but he died in 1817 before he took his seat, being then all of forty-two years old.

While here in these contacts I had been brought in very close touch with the political events of the past leading back to the very foundation of the state of Tennessee, the things that were going on naturally looked to the future, and there were young men there, sitting senators, who were greatly to influence me. One was a senator from Davidson County, from Nashville, who was serving his first term in the senate. He had been, in the previous legislature, the speaker of the house of representatives. It so happened that his seat was nearest to that corner of the reporters' table at which I sat. He was Joseph W. Byrns. The other of the two Nashville senators was an elderly man, John Thompson, with gray hair and imperial beard, the perfect picture of a cartoonist's idea of a southern colonel. He was the leader of the farm bloc.

Mr. Byrns was the leader in his home county, and to a degree in the state, of a reform element that carried on intermittent war with the dominant powers of the Democratic party in the state. He was not in open opposition to the governor, but he represented what was considered to be a threat to the orderly carrying-on of the affairs in the legislature by the gentlemen who thought they were permanently cast in the role of the dominant faction of the majority party. A few years later, in 1908, Mr. Byrns was elected to the Congress, in which he served twenty-eight years. Near the beginning of the administration of Franklin D. Roosevelt, he, a strong supporter of the New Deal, became majority leader of the Democratic party in the house and then was elected speaker in the Seventy-fourth Congress, serving until his death in June, 1936. My friendship with Joe Byrns, which began on the senate floor in Tennessee in 1901, served me in good stead, indeed, when, as chairman of the President's Committee on Administrative Management in 1936, I dealt with President Franklin D. Roosevelt and first with Leader Byrns and then with Speaker Byrns in the establishment of the joint committees of the two houses of the Congress to which the report of our committee was presented and out of which came the bills that led up to the enactment of the Federal Reorganization Act of 1939.

There were other young men in that senate who were later to carve out careers for themselves. But, as it always is easier to recognize a has-been than it is to identify a will-be, I am not at all sure that I paid enough attention to some of the younger ones.

As a reporter, however, it was my business not to look so much for those who had been and those who were yet to be but rather to identify those senators who, in positions of leadership or opposition, were shaping the course of events from day to day. The speaker of the senate (there is no lieutenant-governor in Tennessee, and the presiding officer of the senate is chosen from among its own members) was Newton H. White. Unquestionably he had ambitions for a political career. A successful farmer, or perhaps a planter, he was particularly interested in improving the educational facilities of the state with more especial emphasis on agricultural education and the better utilization of the state's natural resources. He looked forward, too, I think, to being governor and perhaps senator. Neither he nor any of his colleagues nor any of the observers there present knew that he had then already reached the peak of his political career.

The floor leader of the Democratic majority, John Isaac Cox, was an extremely capable and clever individual who actually was but on the threshold of his career. A few years later he was to become speaker of the senate and then, when the sitting governor, James B. Frazier, was elected by the legislature to the United States Senate, Mr. Cox was to become governor.

In the conduct of the affairs of the senate it soon became evident to me—young and naïve as I was—that the senate was really managed by three men, John Isaac Cox and two able lieutenants, Edward T. Seay and James J. Bean. They had, of course, other lieutenants who served them ably and well in the conduct of particular discussions and particular questions; but these three men, it seemed to me, were running the show.

Then, exploiting my new-found liberty of getting away from routine reporting, I began to write little pieces about them and gave some accent to what I wrote by calling them the "Triumvirate." With the benefit of the capital *T,* I soon got a great deal of publicity for the Triumvirs. And, although at the time it seemed somewhat strange to me, no one of the three seemed averse to seeing his name in the paper, and no one of the three seemed to object to being set down in the public print as a "boss"—in fact, all three of them seemed rather to like it. And, to the degree that they liked the publicity, they seemed to like me. At any rate, I soon found myself in the confidence of Mr. Cox and his two lieutenants and frequently was given in confidence, of course, advance briefings on what was about to come up and, more particularly, a very definite and, I must say, always accurate prediction of just what the senate would do.

Here in the course of my education in politics and public life, I found that there could be some differences of opinion as to just who was running what. It was none of my business to visit the governor's office or the offices of the heads of departments of the state capitol. That was reserved to Tom Halley, the statehouse reporter, who had been on that assignment for years and who currently was also covering the house of representatives. But I was a frank admirer of Governor Benton McMillin and his career. Years and years before, when I was just a youngster, I had been an ardent McMillin man in the contest for the Democratic nomination for the speakership of the national House of Representatives. Without knowing anything about it, of course, but emotionally, at that early age, I was a low-tariff man; and Benton McMillin was, in my estimation, a convinced free-trader. He had been twenty years in the Congress, most of that time on the Ways and Means Committee.

Also, for most of that time, the Republicans had been in control, and he had had little opportunity for leadership except in opposition. He represented that same Tennessee district which later sent Cordell Hull to the Congress, and in a way he may be said to have been Mr. Hull's mentor and guide—at least in Mr. Hull's younger days.

One day, after I had established the Triumvirate as the controlling factor in the senate, and by implication in the state government, I met Governor McMillin in the corridor. He asked me to come with him into his office. There he made me feel at home and told me two or three good stories. The preliminaries over, the Governor leaned over, put his hand on my knee, and said, "Louis, have you got anything against me?"

Of course I hadn't, and I told him so. Not only that, but I told him how much I admired him. Then he said, "Louis, do you know that you are doing me an injury?"

And of course I denied that, asking him, "What do you mean? What makes you ask such a question?"

Then he said: "Well, every two or three days you are writing stories about three men in the state senate whom you have dubbed the 'Triumvirate,' and you are giving the impression to the public that these three men are running the state—or, at any rate, that they are the ones who make the principal policy for the Democratic legislature and for the administration.

"Now, Louis, I just want to tell you that I am the governor of this state and that I consider myself the leader of the Democratic party in Tennessee, and it is I who make the policy and set up the program. It is I who chose John Cox to be the floor leader of the senate. It is I who suggested to Cox that Ed Seay and Jim Bean would be his ablest lieutenants. Now what they are doing is that they are carrying out my policies, and they work very closely with me. But, because of this new way you have of reporting in the *Banner* about the things that go on in the senate, the average reader probably thinks the state hasn't got a governor."

That was my introduction to what perhaps is the most puzzling phase of the eternal problem of American politics—the delicate relationship between the executive and the legislative branches. Thereafter, I found ways and means of communicating with Governor McMillin on particular occasions without too great risk of violating the jurisdictional line that separated my assignment from Mr. Halley's. Accordingly, while I did not desert the Triumvirate, which really was in charge of the senate, I also discovered that my three leaders were not particularly appreciative of my dragging in, from time to time, the name of the governor.

When contrasted with the program that any legislature of any state in the Union now has to deal with, the business before the state senate of Tennessee in 1901 seems to be petty indeed. There was, of course, the basic problem of revenue and appropriations. Both the revenue measures and the appropriation bills were developed in the committees of the two houses after consultation with the department heads and, more by grace of the acknowledgment of his primary position as party leader than by recognition of the chief executive, after some consultation with the governor. That was before the days of the executive budget; and with respect to the revenue act and the appropriation bills there was much pulling and hauling, although the sum total involved seems, in the mid-twentieth century, very, very small.

Aside from these perennial questions, which plague every legislative body in all times, there were in that opening year of the twentieth century two principal issues that divided the opinions of the public and brought about conflicts in the senate. One was liquor. The other was the railroads.

As to the liquor question, the sentiment for prohibition had been increasing in Tennessee ever since the resumption of government by civilian authorities after the Civil War. The attack against the saloon as the symbol of the retail distribution of liquor had begun in the rural districts and had the support of rural opinion, led, in the first place, by the ministers of the Protestant churches, which, in turn, had the support of the vast majority of the population of the state. That movement had resulted in the passage of the "Four-Mile Law." The "Four-Mile Law" forbade the sale or the licensing for sale of any spirituous, malt, or vinous liquors within a distance of four miles from any church or schoolhouse except in the theretofore incorporated towns and cities of the state. The "Four-Mile Law," the origin of which I have forgotten, became a state-wide institution through the agency of the Peeler Bill, so named for a member of the house of representatives who still was in the state capitol in my day, or perhaps Mr. Peeler only gave his name to some later revision of the act.

The movement for prohibition, however, went on and on, and in the smaller incorporated places a strong sentiment began to be manifested for the extension of the provisions of the Peeler Bill to particular communities. That was accomplished by the process of electing to the legislature representatives and senators who would introduce and support bills for the surrender of the charter of an incorporated place. Once the charter was surrendered, the town or city became unincorporated, and then the "Four-Mile Law" applied. The next step was to go to the legislature and get a new charter. But, since the provisions of the Peeler Bill applied to all places thereafter incorporated, this double-shuffle arrangement would make the town dry. There had been no provision in the Tennessee constitution of 1796 for the incorporation of municipalities, and that process had been undertaken by the legislature itself with the blessing of the state supreme court. While there had been a general municipal charter bill, it was for various reasons not utilized, so every town and city went to the legislature and got a charter all its own. Now the state constitution forbade the passage of special acts, but the legislature got around that by using some language which would make the act apply to any municipality within the state of Tennessee having a population of not less than 24,752 and not more than 27,756, as determined by the United States Census of 1900. That language, according to the supreme court, excluded the measure from the constitutional clause forbidding the enactment of special laws.

Both houses of the legislature proceeded under rules of legislative courtesy. If in the senate a senator introduced a bill repealing or changing the charter of a city or town in his district, all other senators would vote for it as a matter of course out of senatorial courtesy. The same custom prevailed in the house. Therefore, if in any particular town the senator and the representative were agreed, the action by the legislature was a foregone conclusion. In some instances, where the drys had elected a member of the house from a particular county and had not been able to win the senator from that senatorial district, conflict arose.

In my time the conflicts arose naturally most often in the senate, because the representatives, coming from smaller constituencies, were more likely to represent the current political sentiment; whereas the senators, from larger constituencies, and some of them from quite large cities, were opposed to the prevailing trend toward prohibition. There were some lively times over these Peeler Bill contests. There were charges of bribery. There were investigations by committees. There were all sorts of the things that usually go on with respect to legislative conflicts and hot floor fights in legislative bodies.

The other great issue was usually not brought out quite so openly. It concerned the railroads. The railroads had had a dominant position in the politics of the state and in the control of the legislature for many years—something that was true in the latter half of the nineteenth century not only in Tennessee but in many other states. The particular issue in this session of the legislature, on which depended the fight against railroad domination, was the statutory repeal of the Fellow-Servant Law, which made it impossible—or practically impossible—for an employee of the railroad to recover damages for personal injuries occurring in the course of his work, since the damage was ruled to arise not from an act of the employer but from that of one of his fellow-servants.

This movement for the repeal of the fellow-servant rule had been going on for some years in many of the states and had been consistently fought by the railroads. It was, of course, the forerunner of the later workmen's compensation acts and presented a question that within the decade was solved, so far as the railroads and other interstate carriers were concerned, by federal legislation. Actually, by 1901, the complete domination of the legislatures by the railroads was already on the wane —partly because the railroads for the most part had what they wanted, partly because the feverish era of competition among rival railroads was beginning to diminish, and partly because of a rising change of attitude on the part of the people. As yet, however, the great flood of what may generally be regarded as social legislation had not yet manifested itself—at least not in Tennessee, where I was getting my education.

The other major factor in the diminution of railroad domination was that Tennessee, as had most of the states, had shared in the great movement of the 1870's and 1880's which resulted in the organization of state railroad commissions. Tennessee had established such a commission, and, since its very existence had reduced the necessity for particularistic legislation about individual railroad problems, not so much came to the legislature. Yet, there still were in the background the great figures who had had so much to do with politics and, over all, the shadow of one particular railroad—the Louisville and Nashville—whose president, Milton H. Smith, sat in Louisville and seemed almost to dare any legislature to do anything that he did not desire it to do.

One of the methods—not the only one, of course—by which the railroads had maintained their hold on the legislative processes was by the liberal use of free passes. Many of the senators who sat in the room where I was taking notes had in their pockets blank books of passes. Anyone who desired could go to any one of these senators and ask for a pass. If the applicant was considered to be "right" or "regular," the senator would write out a pass which would entitle the senator's friend to a railroad trip without cost within the state of Tennessee. These blank books of passes which many of the senators—I think, perhaps, *most* of the senators—carried with them were not valid outside the state. However, the intrastate provision actually did not exclude interstate travel if both the point of origin and the point of destination were within the state. Thus, a senator could give one pass from Nashville to Chattanooga on the Nashville, Chattanooga, and St. Louis Railroad, even though a part of that journey might take him out of Tennessee and into Alabama and back. Furthermore, if the friend of the senator was "right" enough, the senator could easily get him a pass beyond the borders of the state; but that involved a note or a telephone call to the central railroad headquarters and sometimes took the better part of a day to accomplish. Pullman passes were even a little harder to come by, and that process sometimes took as much as two full days to accomplish.

But even the railroads were not co-ordinated, and sometimes it was a little hard to get a pass from a railroad that did not operate in Nashville. Because of that circumstance, I was forced to suffer what seemed at the time to be a great humiliation.

The senate had appointed a committee to investigate some scandal that had arisen in Knoxville in the state deaf and dumb asylum. That was before the days when a more sensitive public conscience had changed the name of the institution to the school for the deaf. It also was in the days when legislative investigating committees sometimes betook themselves to far-distant parts of their jurisdiction to conduct investigations, because it seemed to be more convenient than to bring the witnesses to the state capital. That process was interpreted by the ungodly as being a legislative desire for junkets at the public expense. At any rate, an investigating committee was sent to Knoxville, and in the natural order of business I was assigned to go with it. The *Banner* had no difficulty whatever in getting me a pass from Nashville to Chattanooga on the Nashville, Chattanooga, and St. Louis Railroad. But since the decision to take the trip to Knoxville had been made suddenly, and I had to leave within a few hours, it was impossible for the *Banner* to get me a pass on the Southern Railway from Chattanooga to Knoxville because of the fact that there was no pass-issuing office of the Southern in Nashville, and I was forbidden to ask one of the senators to accommodate me.

I boarded the train that night. It was my first ride on a Pullman sleeping car. I was instructed to give the conductor my pass, Pullman and railroad, to Chattanooga and to request him, when the train stopped around two or three o'clock in the morning in Chattanooga, to send out the porter to the ticket office, where my pass for the remaining part of the journey would be waiting for me, that matter having been arranged by the paper over the Western Union Telegraph lines without cost to the *Banner* by means of a Western Union frank.

I went to bed in a lower berth all athrill with the adventure of actually undressing and going to bed to sleep on a train. My wallet, containing a very large and generous amount of expense money—twenty-five dollars, in fact—I stuck under my pillow. Then the Pullman conductor told me that a new rule had been promulgated by the Pullman Company in Chicago. It forbade the employees of the Pullman Company from going out of the train on errands for passengers, even when the Pullman car was parked for a considerable length of time in a station. He told me that there was nothing to do but for me to get up in the middle of the night and go out and get my pass for the rest of the journey. He said the porter would wake me. The porter performed his function promptly. I dressed, at least as much as I thought was necessary, for a 3:00 A.M. appearance in the Chattanooga railroad station. I went into the station. I got my railroad and Pullman passes to Knoxville and returned, went to my berth, and went blissfully to sleep.

In the morning, on arrival at Knoxville, I dressed and got my things together and went to the Farragut Hotel along with the members of the committee. I ate breakfast with the senators in the dining-room, and one of them generously paid for my breakfast. Then, walking into the lobby, I went up to the cigar counter—a place that then had, and still has, a very special interest to me because of my early experiences at the Tulane Hotel and the Maxwell House. There I invited the senators to have a cigar on me. They all accepted. I took out my wallet to pay for the cigars. There was no money in it!

I was dumfounded! I had been robbed on the train! While I was out in the station, somebody had taken my twenty-five dollars!

However, I had in my vest pocket a Western Union frank. I could telegraph without paying out any money. I went immediately to the Western Union counter and sent a telegram to Mr. Morton, telling him of my disaster and asking him to telegraph me some money. Then one of the senators came up to me and said, "Well, until you hear from the *Banner* office, perhaps you might need some money and please permit me to lend you ten dollars." It was the first time anybody had ever sought my permission to lend me money. I was overcome with gratitude, and the possession of the ten-dollar bill helped my morale no little. Still, I was dissatisfied. I wanted to pay it back as quickly as possible and wanted to be spending the *Banner*'s money, not some senator's. Late that afternoon I got back to the Farragut Hotel, after being with the senate committee all day, and there found a telegram addressed to me.

It was a telegram that could have been sent only by a man with a cold heart. It seemed to me the expression of a cynical person who had no faith in human nature. It was a terrific blow. The telegram read: "In future avoid legislative poker. Signed, M. B. Morton, Managing Editor." The only poultice that I could apply to my bruised and wounded spirit was the sudden realization of the fact that there would be more from where I had borrowed the ten dollars that morning.

It wasn't long after that until one of my favorite senators happened to be talking to me about things in general and said something about Atlanta. I told him I had never been to Atlanta. He said: "Well, why don't you take a trip down there? I'll be glad to give you a pass. Is there anybody you would like to go along?" I told him that I thought one of my cousins, with whom I roomed would like a trip. And so, without any difficulty apparently, the next day there were two railroad passes from Nashville to Atlanta and return, accompanied by two Pullman passes.

The trip to Atlanta was enjoyable, entertaining, and instructive. But it was only the beginning of a particular sort of instruction for me.

A few days after I got back, my senatorial friend who had made the Atlanta journey possible asked me to leave out of my report any mention of his handling of the senate's action on a certain measure. I am glad to be able to report that I did not accede to the senatorial request. On the other hand, I am not so sure that I am now proud of the fact that I gave the particular measure and his particular part in it about three times the space that ordinarily I would have given it— or, perhaps, even that I do not so greatly regret. One thing it taught me. Never again did I accept a pass from a senatorial friend. Of course, for years thereafter I continued to ride on passes, but never except on one that had been obtained for me by my employers in what was then considered the ordinary course of business and never on one which I had personally solicited.

In fact, both employer and employee on a newspaper at that time accepted the business of free passes and other perquisites as a part, at any rate, of the compensation of the worker. My free passes on the railroad when I went on trips for the *Banner* seemed to be just a part of an expense account. But, when I went home to Missouri on my vacation, I always got a free pass on the railroad and a free pass on the Pullman car, and I felt that it was just a part of my pay. So, too, with the passes on the streetcars, the passes to the theaters, and the free entrance to almost any sort of entertainment for which other persons paid cash money.

When the legislature recessed in mid-term, as is the custom in Tennessee, my work was rewarded by a raise. My weekly salary was hoisted from eight dollars to ten dollars, and I was furthermore and most signally honored by being put on a general assignment. That is to say, I no longer was required to do one of the regular runs except to fill in when another of the reporters was ill or on vacation. Mr. Morton wanted me to follow up what I had done in my change of pace in the legislative reporting to see what I could glean from roaming the town, as he said, "high, wide, and handsome." However, just to keep me from getting the "swell head," still using his words, he tied me down to two regular chores. One was the lowest estate that can come to any reporter—doing the undertakers. The other was a field which I found I could occasionally exploit for a real news story —doing the hotels.

This freedom from routine gave me a chance to run around the town, to try to develop new sources of news, and to add to the number of men and women with whom I sought to get acquainted. Most of all, it gave me an opportunity to extend my education along the lines of my predilections. I was interested in politics. I was interested in government. And it turned out, years later, that even then I was interested in the processes of public administration.

At the political level the hotels gave me a chance to see the people and, without many restrictions, to write political gossip. It was not necessary in writing a hotel column always to quote the person who gave voice to a bit of gossip. And, without the necessity of quoting anyone, I soon discovered that anonymity gave me a chance to quote myself.

It was a little later, after the legislature had adjourned and when the political machinery was beginning to turn toward the nomination of the members of the next legislature, that I had a lot of fun trying out this game of gossiping with myself. But I also discovered that it was a dangerous game and one that two could play.

First, in my hotel-gossip column, I began to talk about a revolt in the Democratic party of Davidson County which had for its purpose the overturn of the legislative delegation from the county. I discovered and printed rumors that another organization—antimachine— was being formed. Later on I dubbed this purely imaginary organization with a name. I called it "The Reformers." After a while I created so much interest that actual persons began to give interviews, not only to my paper but to the other newspapers, about "The Reformers." Then I began to sprinkle in the names of persons who were being considered for nomination for the senate and for the house of representatives by "The Reformers." Some of these persons were quick to refuse the crown. Some were pleased but noncommittal. Some were avid for the honor.

So much interest was created that Mr. Morton began to take my pieces about the antimachine organization out of the hotel column and run them as separate news items under special headings. That, of course, I played up to and began to write them as news. So much curiosity was excited that people began in various ways to demand to know who were these reformers.

One morning I dropped in at the office of a lawyer friend of mine and found three other persons there, all well known to me. I explained my predicament to them. I said that I had now reached the stage where I was compelled to bring forth an organization. These three men—Allen G. Hall, Myles P. O'Connor, and Verner Lewis Jones—already knew about my project. We had talked it over frequently at our luncheon meetings at Pappas' Place, and each of them had contributed something toward what he considered to be the great joke of the organization of the antimachine reformers. Now they recognized that I was up against it, and they agreed, after some discussion, to let me use their names as members of an organizing committee that was engaged in setting up "The Reformers" party. It happened to be too late for me to write the story for that day's *Banner,* so we agreed that tomorrow would be the big day when I would unveil the mystery of "The Reformers."

Alas and alack! It was too late! The next morning when I came downtown, there in a vacant store on Cherry Street was every evidence of bustling activity, and on the window was a sign: "The Reformers' Organization."

I was nonplused and struck dumb. I walked in. Inside, there was a redheaded, red-mustached, red-bearded gentleman who was well known to be in close sympathy with the regular organization of the Democratic party. He had been, in the past, a state comptroller. He was by no means one of the reformer type. He was a clever politician with one personal handicap—he stuttered. And through his stuttering, when I came in, he led me over to a chair in the corner and told me, with great circumstance and in the most minute detail, how the organization had been set up, who had inspired it, just what its purposes were, and also suggested a few of the names that might be on the slate in the coming Democratic primary! Then, with more of a stammer and a stutter than ever, he demanded, with a great show of indignation, that I give him the name of the traitor within the ranks of "The Reformers" who, over the past several weeks, had been feeding me information about the new movement that he said was confidential and was not to be made known to the public until an appropriate time and until they had gathered together enough means to set up this office and headquarters.

I had had a lot of fun, but it cured me of faking about politics. At the same time it undoubtedly reduced the readability of my hotel-gossip column. I was forced back on facts, which, unquestionably, are a handicap in that particular field of journalism.

CHAPTER XIV

AN EARLY EDUCATION
IN POLITICS

Nashville, then as now, had a public square, but the buildings in it were of an entirely different character from the present ones. The courthouse stemmed from the 1840's—a gray-stone building, ornamented with façades of Corinthian columns, the acanthus leaves of their capitals being covered with wire netting in a vain effort to do something about the pigeon problem. In another part of the square was a red-brick structure which was the city market on the ground floor and, above that, the city hall. I liked to go to the city hall, since the best and cheapest meals to be had in the town were in the city market, where one could always get a breakfast for ten cents, a luncheon for fifteen, and a dinner for a quarter.

Inside, I found other interesting things. I found a mayor. Now, I had never seen a mayor before. In Buffalo, Missouri, where I grew up, we hadn't got that far along. That particular mayor was a most impressive individual named James M. Head. He was in his early forties, a vigorous and a handsome man. He possessed also another qualification which I always have liked in public men: he was a raconteur of parts, and in those days the anecdote was in its full flower as a most highly appreciated form of art in America. In Tennessee only artists could win elections.

I didn't know anything about city charters, and I suspect that I was naïve enough to think that the Nashville system was a system common to all cities. In fact, the Nashville charter was unique, although I didn't yet know it. It provided a government consisting of a mayor and a council. The mayor was responsible to the general public through the electoral process. The council was responsible to the electorate in the particular wards by which its individual members were elected. But the principal powers of legislation and of appropriation and of administration were vested not in the mayor and council but in the Board of Public Works, which was not directly responsible to the people, its members being chosen by the mayor with consent of the council for fixed overlapping terms which made it practically independent. It was in this complex atmosphere that I had my introduction to the study of municipal administration.

In some way I seemed to sense the fact that the people who were doing the work in the city hall were swimming upstream. They seemed to be trying to do their best but under very adverse circumstances. That feeling set me apart from some of the other city-hall reporters. I am not quite sure out of what circumstances these variant attitudes arose, but most of the other city-hall reporters—Mr. Clark on my paper and those on the opposition papers—seemed to me to demand of the city hall perfection in all things. When by chance the event was something less than perfect, they lambasted those poor officials for not delivering the goods. On the other hand, I was always looking at their troubles and giving consideration to their handicaps, the barriers that made it so difficult to do the things they set out to do. I began to write with sympathy on the efforts of the city officials to do their work.

It must be remembered that Nashville was still in the horse-and-buggy days. There were only two or three automobiles in the town, and they were home-built affairs, put together by one Duncan Currie, who actually tried to start a horseless carriage factory in Nashville but found the industrial atmosphere so chilly and the paving so bad that he betook himself to St. Louis before he actually got into production —a production which perhaps turned out three or four cars a year. The mayor kept at it, however, and at last prevailed upon the Board of Public Works to start paving. All the blandishments of the Barbour Asphalt Company had been resisted, by what alchemy I do not know; and it was discovered that there was less resistance to the similar blandishments of the Warner Brothers of Boston. I reported that battle between those two great paving trusts sympathetically. I didn't know that there was any other way to do it, and I was strongly in favor of paving the streets of Nashville.

That incident made me a very close friend of the mayor. He generously gave me part of the credit for getting a paving program under way. He also said that his whole plan might very well have lost out if the *Banner,* my newspaper, had not handled the matter constructively. The quarrel about who was to get the contract was a lively one, and, had the public attention been focused on that rather than on the fact that the macadamized streets were inefficient, dusty, and expensive to maintain and that the city could afford to embark on a long-term plan for modern, asphalt paving, the mayor never would have been able to get the consent of the Board of Public Works. And, also, he thought the manner in which I had handled the matter about the contract had resulted in a considerable reduction in the price and a considerable saving to the city treasury.

The friendship with Mayor Head stood me in good stead on another occasion. The street-railway franchise had expired, and there was a great dither and to-do about the terms upon which it should be renewed. Actually, the street-railway company was bankrupt and in receivership, but the receivers were attempting to get an extension of the franchise to form the basis of a reorganization. The two receivers were Major Eugene C. Lewis, who was the owner and publisher of the *Nashville American,* the esteemed and most heartily disliked contemporary of the *Banner.* The other receiver was a gentleman named Mr. Percy Warner. Now the *Banner,* my paper, was owned by Major Stahlman. It so happened that the two majors did not like each other. At one time or another, both of the newspapers had existed for the primary purpose of controlling the legislature in the interest of the Louisville and Nashville Railroad. Major Stahlman was no longer the head of that interest, but Major Lewis was.

For many, many reasons, perhaps some of them prudential, the reporters on the *Banner* did not ordinarily regard Major Lewis as a fruitful news source. I had been attempting to find out what really was going on with respect to the street-railway franchise and the many accompanying differences between the city and the receivers of the traction company. Because of Major Lewis' position, I was reluctant to go to Mr. Warner. And at the same time I knew quite well that my friend Mayor Head would be reluctant to talk to me about the matter or to give me any real news on the subject, because that would involve my getting a scoop on the *American* and, in all probability, infuriating Major Lewis.

One day, in the course of my visits to the hotels, I happened to walk into the Duncan House, and there I saw a very important person enter the building from a side door and go rapidly to the elevator to be whisked upstairs. It was Mayor Head. A few minutes later another important gentleman effected his very quiet entrance into the building through the same side corridor, and he promptly was whisked upstairs. *He* was Mr. Percy Warner, one of the receivers for the street-railway company.

I said nothing. I wrote nothing for the newspaper. I had enough, of course, to have made a very sensational story about a clandestine meeting between the mayor and the street-railway receiver. But I also had other fish to fry. In my opinion the interests of the city would best be served by a compromise on the street-railway issue which would involve the granting of a new franchise containing greater safeguards for the public interest than had been included in the older charters of various companies that had been merged into the one now bankrupt and in receivership. Also, there was the question of a piece of property, owned by the street-railway company, which had been the site of the Tennessee Centennial Exposition of 1897. If that plot of land could be acquired by the city for a park, I thought that it would be an excellent thing for the town and that it would also be a permanent memorial of that exposition which, although I had not seen it, still amounted to a great deal in the life of Nashville and was regarded as a high light in the memory of most of the people in the town. Then, also, I wanted the story of whatever settlement was to be made, and I knew very well that in the ordinary course of events the story would be given to Major Lewis' own newspaper and that the *Banner* would be left out in the cold—that neither I nor any other *Banner* reporter had any chance to break the real story. I also knew that I had enough now to write a story that would in all probability disrupt the whole negotiation.

So that night I paid two calls—one on Mayor Head at his residence and one on Mr. Warner at his residence. And then there were some telephone conversations between these two gentlemen. The upshot of it was that we made a deal. I promised that I would not print anything until the story was ripe, until after the city authorities and the receivers had agreed on the terms of the new franchise, and until after the receivers had made the necessary dispositions in order to deed Centennial Park to the city. In turn, they promised me that I should have the story exclusively and that they would do everything in their power to prevent leaks to the other papers. I was very nervous about that, because I knew that, if the *American* did get the story first and then it was discovered that I had had most of for a long, long time and had sat on it, my position with the *Banner* would be—to say the least—most unpleasant. Thereupon, after some further conversations upon my demands for security, Mr. Warner telephoned Major Lewis. He told Major Lewis that I had the story, that I had talked both to him and to the mayor, and that if I printed it now, before the lawyers had got done with their work, the chances were that the whole compromise would be in danger. Thereupon, Major Lewis gave his word that, even if an *American* reporter did get wind of the deal, the *American* would not publish it.

Another story went back to the Tennessee Centennial Exposition, when the Fine Arts Building was erected as a replica of the Parthenon. It was done in lath and plaster, and, except for the interior walls which had been solidly built of brick in order to protect the paintings and loan exhibitions from fire, it was falling to pieces. In front of the building there had been a heroic statue of Pallas Athene, also in lath and plaster. One day some boys lighted a fire, and Pallas Athene burned. She was highly combustible, and the interior of the heroic statue made a good chimney. I was sent out to write the story. Actually there was nothing to write. The statue had burned up. There was nothing but a little debris. Although I had not seen the exposition, as I have said, it was a matter of so much moment to so many people that I deemed it necessary to invent a story.

So I interviewed Pallas Athene in her funeral pyre. And, through me, she implored the people of Nashville to restore the Parthenon as a permanent memorial to the exposition. Major Lewis was then chairman of the park commission. That afternoon he stopped me on Church Street and said, "I read your piece about the burning of the statue. Will you come to the meeting of the park commission tomorrow?" That, of course, ended my vicarious enmity with Major Lewis, and thenceforward I was, I think, as good a friend of his as I was of Major Stahlman's. The result of my interview with Pallas Athene was that the Parthenon was restored, and there it stands today, not on a high hill, as it should, but on the plain of Centennial Park.

My roving commission gave me opportunities to learn about people and things in many walks of life, the people and their interests that went together to make up the complex of the urban society which, to me, a country boy from the backwoods, was so intensely interesting, and all of which led, of course, to my general interest which later became concentrated in local government administration.

In one way, Nashville offered unique opportunities for study in church administration. Right on the public square there was a great institution which attracted me. It was the publishing house of the Methodist Episcopal Church, South. Then also, in Nashville, there were the headquarters of the missionary efforts of the Southern Presbyterian church and of the Southern Baptist church and, in another part of town, the publishing house of the Cumberland Presbyterian church. My connections with the Methodist church were close, since I continued my active membership in the West End Methodist Church and maintained my close association with its pastor, the Reverend Edwin B. Chappell. Furthermore, at the boarding-house to which I had moved soon after I found a place on the *Banner,* I had another special connection with Southern Methodists. There were two dining-rooms in Miss Lellyet's boarding-house, one of which seated ten or twelve persons, while the smaller one accommodated five members of a family. They were the Reverend and Mrs. James Atkins, their daughter and two sons. Since there was a vacant place at that table, Miss Lellyet asked me if I would move in with the Atkinses. I was happy indeed to do so, because I admired Dr. Atkins and liked his daughter, Miss Love Branner Atkins, very much, indeed. Dr. Atkins at that time was the Sunday-school editor and, therefore, had editorial supervision over the numerous Sunday-school journals issued by the Methodist Publishing House.

Through him, I soon discovered that there were many news stories that could be discovered if a reporter were assiduously to cover the publishing house, which contained the general offices of the denomination. Thereafter, I made it my business, as often as opportunity presented itself, to visit the various headquarters of the churches that happened to be established in Nashville.

Then, too, through these two men, Dr. Chappell and Dr. Atkins, I found means to extend my acquaintance at Vanderbilt University and, through Vanderbilt, to the other colleges and schools in the town. This, for me, was indeed a rich experience. As I had not had any formal education, I knew nothing of schools beyond the visits to the rural schools in my native Ozarks. Not only was I tremendously interested and impressed but I soon developed ways and means through frequent visits to find news stories which I could exploit in the *Banner*.

In these ecclesiastical establishments, as well as in the universities and colleges, I was primarily looking for news. It so happened that the discoveries that seemed to me to be newsworthy usually had to do with the administrative aspects of the work of these institutions. So it came about that I sought out those persons who could give me information about what went on administratively in these churches and schools.

Dr. Atkins, later Bishop Atkins, had a special interest in ecclesiastical government and was then engaged in writing a book entitled *The Polity of the Methodist Episcopal Church, South*. Dr. Atkins discussed that book with me over and over while it was being written, and, through him, I began to make the acquaintance of the bishops of the Methodist Episcopal Church, South, some of whom always lived in Nashville, and all of whom came to Nashville once or twice a year for meetings of the College of Bishops.

It happened at that time, also, that the College of Bishops of the Southern Methodist church were trustees of Vanderbilt University, then a denominational institution. At the university I sought out the chancellor, James Hampton Kirkland, in his office, where I soon began to make regular visits. He discovered that, when he told me something about what was going on administratively in the university, it would turn up as a news story published in the *Banner*. Then, being a good administrator, Chancellor Kirkland began to tell me to go to see the deans to find out what was going on in some of the departments. In that way I came to know very well indeed the deans of some of the departments in the university and, curiously enough, especially the dean of the biblical department, Dr. Wilbur F. Tillett, who also had an interest in church government.

At that time the University of Nashville, which included the George Peabody College for Teachers—now long since consolidated with Vanderbilt—was a separate institution with a campus in South Nashville. There, on that campus, I soon discovered in the person of Dr. Wickliffe Rose a news source of unparalleled interest to me, since he would willingly and even eagerly enter into my quest for news and then ask me to keep his name out of it. Sometimes the news he gave me ranged far beyond the campus of the University of Nashville and frequently into the general educational situation in the state, especially with respect to the public schools and teacher-training. This interest, of course, was what later enabled him to become the great educational statesman who guided the Rockefeller Foundation in its early and formative period. And, for me, it was the beginning of an association with Dr. Rose which, in later years, was to have a very great effect upon my own interests and work.

Another group of persons with whom I became acquainted and in whose work and views and programs I became intensely interested were the labor unions. Of course, there had been no labor unions in my Ozark home; but, because of my father's political views, the political newspapers and magazines which I read, and my Populistic and Bryanistic leanings, I had already a deep sympathy with what I thought to be the aims and purposes of union labor. My own experience with long work weeks had made me an ardent supporter of their movement for shorter hours. Then, too, I had observed in the legislature that the best parliamentarians, not only in the senate, which I reported directly, but in the house of representatives, which I visited frequently, were those who had come from a labor-union background. For years, spending Sunday afternoons in meetings of central labor-union councils, they had learned every little device of the parliamentarian and could use all their knowledge, as well as all the tricks of the trade, in either advancing or delaying parliamentary action.

Attracted to some of the local labor leaders—at that time the labor-union movement in Nashville was confined almost, if not quite exclusively, to the building trades—I found ways to get news and then found myself assigned frequently to meetings of the central trade-union council. If there was any labor trouble in the town, it usually fell to my lot to report it.

In the course of this work I learned to sympathize with the problems of some of the labor leaders, but at the same time I discovered that it was not always wise for a reporter to assume that there was but one side in a labor dispute. In fact, I discovered by actual experience in the field that it was equally wrong to assume that there were two sides to a labor dispute. It was when I found what seemed to me unmistakable evidence that, although a plumbers' strike had been called by the union, the real prompter of the trouble was the central organization of the employers, that the master-plumbers were in cahoots with the journeymen plumbers, and that the object of the whole dispute was a joint effort to raise wages a little and prices more.

These circumstances caused me to develop a cautionary approach to my reporting of labor disputes and the routine work of the labor unions. As I have said, only the building trades were strongly organized in Nashville at that time, and the labor movement affected really only a small part of the population. It was not considered big news. However, when anything *did* happen in that field, it was my job.

A coal strike in the western Kentucky coal fields affected Nashville and its industries and might possibly have spread to the Tennessee coal fields, which more intimately concerned our town. Therefore, when violence broke out in the strike in western Kentucky, I was assigned to cover the story. I went to Madisonville, Kentucky, which was the headquarters of the strikers, of the coal operators, and also of the Kentucky National Guard, which had been called out by the governor of Kentucky to maintain order in the region. It was my first assignment to anything that might remotely be called a continuing shooting affray. There had been a clash between union and nonunion miners in which several persons had been killed before the National Guard arrived on the scene, and even thereafter there were sporadic violence, shooting almost every night, and occasionally a fatal shooting or a serious wounding of a mine guard or strikebreaker. On the other hand, sometimes one of the strikers would be the victim of a pot shot fired from ambush.

I seemed to feel that I needed some personal protection. So for the first time, the last time, and the only time in my life I packed a pistol. I obtained a revolver from a fellow-employee of the *Banner* and actually carried it in my hip pocket. I am sure I was never comfortable about it, and I am also quite sure that the small essay at target practice which I discreetly carried out gave me no added confidence in my own ability as a wielder of a shooting iron. Still, I thought it was necessary, some of my colleagues thought it was imperative, and I went forth armed.

In Madisonville I found a friendly person in the clerk of the hotel where I stayed. He was a gregarious man of few prejudices. He was friendly to the coal operators. He had friends among the striking miners. And he was regarded as a top aide by General J. Tandy Ellis, the most genial commander of the National Guard. It was he who told me that an important decision would be taken by a committee of the strikers that might possibly lead to a settlement of the dispute. This miners' meeting was to be held at Earlington, another small coal-mining town about four miles from Madisonville. I heard about the meeting around noon and also, at the same time, that it probably would be finished about three o'clock. I went to the livery stable and hired a rig. It was a side-bar buggy, and in the shafts was harnessed a mare who gloried in the name of "Brown Bessie." She was quite a stepper and was regarded, so my friend behind the desk in the hotel told me, as the best piece of horseflesh to be had for hire in the whole community.

My pistol on my hip and my unpracticed hands on the reins, I drove to Earlington. I was not happy. I never had liked either fire-arms or horses; and I was afraid of both. The prospect of trying to get into a closed meeting of striking miners was not one that greatly attracted me. Nevertheless, duty called, and I responded.

I got to Earlington, and, after a few false moves, I discovered just where the miners were meeting. It was impossible to get in, of course, and there was nothing for me to do but to hang around until the meeting broke up and then see what I could find out. The meeting went on and on. The sun set. The moon did not rise. It was dark. I was hungry. I was far from comfortable. I stuck it out, however, and about half-past ten the meeting broke up. I found two or three of the men willing to talk guardedly for publication and managed to get a story—a story that indicated that, under certain circumstances and hedged with all sorts of conditions, the strikers would be willing to consider an offer made by the operators. There was a prospect of peace.

Then I started out for Madisonville. It was the longest four miles I ever experienced. And the fact that Brown Bessie was a stepper didn't particularly add to the comfort of that lonely night ride, for, as she trotted along the macadamized road, whenever her hoofs struck fire on a piece of flint, there was always—or, at any rate, very frequently—an answering shot from one side of the road or the other aimed at that spark. I regret that Brown Bessie's speed was not clocked on that occasion. I am sure that, if my urgings had any effect upon her, it would be found that on that night ride she broke all her previous records.

Actually, I got her and the buggy safe into the livery stable at Madisonville. Then I got myself safe into the lobby of the hotel. And there I turned over to my hotel clerk friend the pistol that I had been packing. So far as I know, it is still there.

But, from this incident and others that arose during the two weeks that I stayed in Madisonville, I discovered that the real news in a strike situation was not confined to the shooting and the threats of shooting but was to be found, rather, in the small groups of the representatives of each side who were in almost continuous huddles, planning the strategy and directing the tactics which would be most advantageous to the particular side. Furthermore, I discovered that the most important part of the news was to be found somewhere among those who were in the middle and who were attempting, in one way or another, to bring about a cessation of hostilities. In this particular instance I found the conciliator where I least expected to find him. I found him in the person of the commander of the National Guard.

General Ellis was a large and jolly person who didn't enjoy being on strike duty and who was particularly interested in the feelings of the men under his command, no one of whom liked either to be shot at or to shoot at anybody else. Primarily a politician by profession, General Ellis made great use of his talent as a raconteur and a hail-fellow-well-met. On this particular occasion, although I was not permitted by the seals of confidence that were placed upon me to tell the facts at the time, what really happened was that General Ellis discovered who among the representatives of the coal operators on the scene was most interested in a game of draw poker. Further research developed to his satisfaction the name of the person on the strikers' side who was most interested in the possibilities inherent in a little game of draw. It was at one of the resulting poker parties, where both of these gentlemen sat in, that the bridge between the two sides actually was constructed and the basis for the negotiated settlement arranged.

Still later, in other coal-mining difficulties, including one of a revolt among the convicts of a state-owned mine in Tennessee, I was to discover that the adjutant general, or the commander of the National Guard, frequently was more important and influential as an administrative official than as a military commander.

So it was that I began to discover, identify, and segregate for special interest the administrative aspects of many of the activities which came up in the news of the day and which fell to my portion to report. Not only in the statehouse, the courthouse, and the city hall, but in the park commission and the school board, not only in the publishing and business establishments of the churches and in the organization of the colleges and in the conduct of the labor unions, but, almost as a matter of course, what then went on within the newspaper office itself. There I found a control descending from a publisher and owner through three streams of hierarchical authority: the business office, the editor-in-chief, and the managing editor. Likewise, I saw that, because there were three such lines of authority, it was not always easy to find out, even within the family itself, just who in any particular situation was the top boss. Certainly the editorial policy was determined by Major Stahlman, the owner, and was formulated in editorial pronouncements by Mr. Gideon H. Baskette, the editor-in-chief, and his assistants. Certainly prime matters with respect to advertising and circulation were within the province of Edgar Foster, the business manager. Quite as certainly, the whole business of the news to be printed, local and telegraphed, the features to be admitted to the columns of the paper, the business of makeup, and the general appearance and physical character of the paper were clearly within the province of its managing editor, Marmaduke B. Morton.

But since there then were none of the co-ordinating devices that already were coming into use in the great newspapers in the larger cities of the country, it was still possible for anyone down the line, even to the lowliest reporter, to get things in the paper on his own, reflecting his own views and containing his own interpretations of events. The city editor was in only nominal control of his staff and was himself a reporter.

In the governmental establishments, as well as in some of the business firms with which I had contact, I had noticed this same lack of centralized supervision and direction. It was the day of the individual who might regard his attachment to the hierarchy of employers or a congeries of co-workers with whatever degree of attachment or detachment seemed best to him. The consequence was that I absorbed out of the very atmosphere around me an idea that one's loyalty as a man at work ran chiefly to the person who was his immediate superior, who was his actual employer, and to whom he was accustomed to answer in person for his deeds or misdeeds, the things done or the things left undone.

This must not be taken, however, to mean that there was not at the same time a clearly developed sense of institutional loyalty which made me, as it made my fellows of the time, almost fanatically devoted to the institution which we served. When I was a reporter on the *Banner,* I was a partisan of the *Banner.* When I found myself in disagreement with the editorial policies of the *Banner,* which so far as concerned national politics was practically all the time, I deemed it my bounden duty to keep my mouth shut. So far as the *Banner* took a publicly proclaimed and clear position on local affairs, I was loyal, whatever might be my own personal views. This loyalty did not in the least prevent me from exploiting the freedom that was mine, and which stemmed directly from the lack of a centralized supervision, to play on my own in the realms where my superiors had laid down no lines of guidance. That was a wide area indeed, and, in playing within it, I learned many lessons, and, as has already been indicated, I got some very sharp comeuppances.

Nashville had been my first city. The range of personal contacts that I found there was very great. Even the first lowly jobs I had there at the cigar counters in the hotels brought me in contact with the politically great of the time and place. And then on the newspaper not only did I discover the special interest in government institutions which centered in the state capitol, the courthouse, and the city hall but also I followed the police into the highways and byways of the town and saw its contact with crime and with vice. In the police court and the criminal court I had firsthand knowledge of the seamy side of life in the city that was at once to me the center of culture and religion.

Then, too, I began to taste now and then a little of the heady wine of public notice and public praise and occasionally the dregs of that cup in the form of public blame. This publicity increased as the knowledge spread among the news sources of just who it was who was handling a particular line of news in the paper. The by-line at that time and in that particular newspaper was never used for a local reporter; but, whenever one was sent out of the city, the stories at publication were labeled either "By a Staff Correspondent" or by a by-line with the name of the reporter. As time went on, I was given more and more out-of-town assignments; and the line, "By Louis Brownlow," began to appear at the head of my articles. The out-of-town assignments were various. Two of them in particular, which now, some fifty years later, seem to be a little odd, arose from the *Banner*'s custom of sending a special correspondent each year to the annual reunion of the United Confederate Veterans. Two such assignments fell to me. One was in 1901, when I went to attend the reunion in Memphis. There I saw the marching Confederate Veterans, thousands of them, many in gray uniforms, break ranks to rush up with tears streaming down their faces to shake the hands of two generals who were in the reviewing stands. Both of them were in blue uniforms. One of them was Brigadier General Joseph Wheeler, who had been a lieutenant general in the Confederate Army and who had exchanged the gray for the blue when he went into the service in the Spanish-American War. The other was one who had always worn the blue, Major General Frederick Dent Grant, the son of Ulysses S. Grant. The striking resemblance he bore to the portraits of his father at the time the elder Grant was President of the United States was such that every man in the column recognized him. They also recognized Joe Wheeler. The discipline of the 1860's perhaps was not very strict, but Hardee's *Tactics* and the controls demanded thereby were by that time forgotten. The lines broke as the veterans rushed up to the reviewing stand and demanded handshakes from the reviewing generals. My stories of this reunion not only got me a good deal of praise among my friends and acquaintances in Nashville but also brought me an offer of a job on the *Memphis Commercial-Appeal;* and that, in turn, got me a raise in salary from the *Banner.* I went up to the dizzy height of fifteen dollars a week.

A year later I went on a similar mission to Dallas, Texas, and there I had the great pleasure of an entirely surprise meeting with my father. I had written to ask him if it were not possible for him to go to Dallas to the reunion. My mother had replied that he would like to do it, of course, but that he really was not physically able to make the trip. At the last moment, however, his precarious health seemed suddenly to improve, and, without letting me know, he journeyed with his fellows of the Springfield, Missouri, Camp of the U.C.V. to Dallas.

And on this occasion I improved the shining hour by interviewing a half-dozen of the surviving generals of the Confederacy. Among them, I recall especially John H. Reagan, "Texas Tiger" Reagan, who had been born in Gatlinburg, Tennessee, who had been a member of the Confederate Congress, a general in the Confederate Army, and postmaster-general in the cabinet of Jefferson Davis. It was that same John H. Reagan who, in his later service in the House of Representatives of the United States, introduced and carried through to passage the act creating the Interstate Commerce Commission. My stories got me an offer of a job on the *Dallas News* and, in turn, a raise in salary to eighteen dollars a week.

Perhaps, however, it was the by-line on the stories I wrote of the coal strike from Madisonville, Kentucky, that affected me most. One of the stories was mentioned by General J. Tandy Ellis to Graham Vreeland, the assistant managing editor of *The Courier-Journal* of Louisville. Mr. Vreeland in turn spoke to Brainard Platt, the city editor of *The Courier-Journal,* and, as a result of that, Mr. Platt wrote me without benefit of any of my Christian name. The letter read:

LOUISVILLE, Nov. 13, 1902

Mr. Brownlow
Reporter
Nashville, Tennessee

DEAR SIR:

The Courier-Journal staff is in need of a man and Mr. Graham Vreeland has recommended you to me. If you care to change your condition, I should be glad to hear from you at once.

The opportunities of getting on in the newspaper business here are much superior to those in Nashville and conditions are now more favorable in Louisville than they have been for years.

Hoping to hear from you without delay, I am

Yours truly,

BRAINARD PLATT

The resulting correspondence showed that I was to be welcomed as a member of the city staff of *The Courier-Journal* at the princely salary of twenty dollars a week.

For once, Mr. Morton did not attempt to meet the competition. For Mr. Morton, himself, had once been city editor of *The Courier-Journal*. He believed that *The Courier-Journal* was the greatest of all newspapers, and he thought that any young man who had a chance to go on its staff, to work under "Marse Henry" Watterson, to know the Haldeman Brothers (who were the principal owners and publishers of the paper), and to know the other men who made up its staff was an opportunity not to be despised. He bade me go with his blessing.

As I left the *Banner* to go to Louisville early in December, 1902, I was even then conscious of the fact that I was leaving the sheltering care and the almost paternal protection of a man who had influenced me perhaps more than had any other person, aside from my own parents. He had schooled me in his particular style of journalistic English. He had instilled in me his high standard of personal conduct. He had transmitted to me his own unswerving institutional and personal loyalty. He had kept me on my toes. He had been ready with caustic reprimand and with smiling praise. And, above all, he had taught me that news was news, that it was the duty of a reporter to get the news and to write the news as he saw it, not fearing any man or favoring any. At the same time he gave me to understand that, so far as my opinions of men and things were concerned, I was free to follow my own conscience; that, while I was in duty bound to listen with tolerance to the disagreeing opinions of others, I was compelled in simple honesty to be true to myself. Therefore it came about that, on nearly every essential matter in the realm of politics, economics, and social activity, we found ourselves poles apart but each respecting the other and each bound to the other by undying bonds of affection.

CHAPTER XV

"THE COURIER-JOURNAL"

It was on a Sunday that I reported at the office of *The Courier-Journal* at Fourth Avenue and Green Street in Louisville. It was cold. It was drizzling rain; and the town was all but submerged in fog. I had been told that I should report at one o'clock in the afternoon. I also had been told by my old chief, Marmaduke B. Morton—and this loomed most importantly in my mind that day—that I was to do one thing and not to do another thing. The one thing I *was* to do was to take whatever assignment might be given me. The thing I was *not* to do was to ask the city editor anything whatever about *how* or *where* I was to carry out that assignment.

So with these precepts and warnings foremost in my mind, I was determined to do whatever Mr. Platt might tell me to do. And I was equally as determined not to ask him a single question.

It was just a few minutes before one o'clock when I made my way up the unmanned stairway into an uninhabited second floor where I discerned a dim dusty sign that indicated the "City Room." Walking in, I found it, too, unguarded, open-doored, and uninhabited. It was furnished with six or seven desks and, at one side, a table on which rested *the* telephone and also an unabridged dictionary. A telephone instrument on a table was something new to me. I had not theretofore seen one that was not fixed to the wall, as had been the single telephone instrument in the editorial rooms of the *Banner*. Then, also, I saw that each one of the desks was furnished with a typewriter. Now this was something for which Mr. Morton had not prepared me—in fact, I suspect that he didn't know that *The Courier-Journal* had admitted mechanization into the editorial department after he himself had been its city editor. In the *Banner* office in Nashville there were but two typewriting machines (so far as the editorial rooms were concerned), one of which was manipulated by the Associated Press operator who, listening to the dots and dashes of his Morse machine, translated them into the written words upon his typewriter. The other was an antique Remington Number One, which my colleague Haynes McFadden used, not for any copy prepared for the *Banner,* but for the weekly communication that he wrote for a trade publication, the *Modern Miller.* I had not used it. Nor, indeed, had I so much as touched a typewriter since the very early days when there was but one in Buffalo, a Smith-Premier with a double keyboard well fitted to my then childish fingers and the pick-and-hunt system. Also lying about in the litter and scatter of these desks were little bits of copy, and the realization swept over me that I would be expected to write my reports on the typewriter. This meant, in short, that in one cold, rainy, foggy day I was to meet and master a new and strange city, a new and strange manual skill, and a new and strange administration of my affairs.

Shortly after one o'clock another reporter drifted in. He looked at me curiously. I introduced myself, and he grunted a welcome, saying that he had heard that a new man from Nashville was on the way but didn't know when he was to arrive. He was courteous in manner but grumpy in tone, and I didn't know whether or not I was cordially welcomed as a new member of the staff or whether I was detested as an intruder. His name was Isaac Harcourt.

Since he was not the city editor and, I was willing to assume, was a colleague of but little seniority and of something near equal status, I was willing to question him. I asked where Mr. Platt's office was. With a jerk of a thumb, he indicated a small room opening off the city room in which there were two desks. And then he startled me by saying that Mr. Platt would not be there that day; that it was his Sunday off; and that, in his stead, I would meet Mr. Wakefield, the assistant city editor. At the other end of the room was another small room with two desks in which reigned the managing editor, Mr. Arthur Y. Ford, of whom I had never heard, and Mr. Graham Vreeland, the assistant managing editor, who was in the first instance responsible for my being in Louisville at all. Two or three other reporters drifted in, and Ike Harcourt introduced me to Perry Farnsley, to Eustace Williams, to Anthony Woodson, and to Lewis Johnson. And then, at about two o'clock, there was a hustle and a bustle, and everyone was on the alert. John Dunlap Wakefield, tall, slender, dark, sedately dressed (he might well have been a cleric), the assistant city editor, had arrived. He seated himself at the big desk, which really belonged to Mr. Platt, and busied himself with paper and pencil. After a while he began to call out names, and the reporters, as their names were called, disappeared into the little room. There something went on, the nature of which I could not know, but I assumed it was the giving and receiving of assignments for the work for the day and the night. At last, when all the others had gone, he walked into the city room and asked if my name was Brownlow. He gave me a cordial handshake and asked me to come in.

I was embarrassed. It was a long, long time after this that I learned that Mr. Wakefield also was embarrassed. He had not known that the new reporter from Nashville was to turn up on this particular day, and he had had no instructions from his immediate superior as to what to put me to doing. So he seated himself and talked with me cordially, inquiring about Mr. Morton, who had been his city editor when he first started as a reporter. He quizzed me, incidentally, about the kind of work I had been doing on the *Banner,* and you may be sure that I did not depreciate my value nor did I underestimate the importance of the work I had done. It is also quite natural that I made some special reference to Madisonville and the coal strike, since it was through General Ellis and Mr. Vreeland, who had read my reports of that event, that I had got my new job. And of course I was able to carry special personal messages from his old chief—his hero and mine.

Wakefield was a curious combination of an extremely kindly and gracious person with a hard-boiled outlook on life that sometimes seemed to be tinged with cynicism. But on that occasion I saw nothing but his kindliness, and I suspected nothing whatever of his devilish cynicism as he gave me three special assignments for the day.

One was to go and interview some people in a colony of houseboat dwellers on the Ohio River at the eastern edge of the town and discover whether or not there was any truth to the story that he had heard to the effect that this particular colony of houseboaters had decided that they had been mistreated in Louisville and in Jefferson County and were going to move their headquarters down the river to Paducah.

Another was to go to the west end of the city and find out whether or not there was any truth to a rumor that he had heard to the effect that the machinery of the locks of the Louisville and Portland Canal had broken down and that there was danger that the locks would be closed and would constitute an impediment to navigation on the Ohio River for the next week or ten days.

The third assignment was to go to the Old Fort, which turned out to be at the south end of the town, and there interview the king of the gypsies and discover whether or not a rumor concerning an approaching war between two gypsy tribes was founded in fact or in fancy.

I was so innocent and so naïve that I did not at the time suspect that all three of these assignments were made up out of pure moonshine; that they were gags; that they constituted a trial and represented not so much a reasoned test of my industry and ability as they did a protest that Mr. Platt had neglected to let Mr. Wakefield know that a new man was coming on the job and had failed to tell him what he ought to do with me.

Mr. Wakefield in the goodness of his heart had volunteered that the houseboats were at the east end and that the canal was at the west end of the town. He left for me to find out where the Old Fort would be. A stranger in a strange land! I knew nobody nor where I ought to turn. Immediately across Fourth Avenue there was a drugstore— Buschmeyer's Drugstore. I turned to it as a place where I might perhaps gather my wits while reviving my body and spirit with what then was my favorite beverage—hot chocolate. Warmed by that draught, I found that I was expected to pay for it at a cashier's desk. Behind the cash register sat a comely, buxom blonde. I turned to her instinctively as perhaps one who would help. Since the information had been vouchsafed to me that one of my assignments would take me to the extreme eastern end of the town and the other to the western end, I asked first where the Old Fort was and how one got there. She seemed to be so astonished by the inquiry that I told her I was a new reporter on *The Courier-Journal* and that I had never been in Louisville before and didn't know how to get anywhere. She responded at once with sympathy and information. She told me how to take one streetcar, how to transfer to another, and how to go to the end of the line, walk up a hill, and there find the Old Fort at the very southern edge of the town. It dawned on me then that I had to go east, west, and south. At that particular moment I doubt if I was sufficiently grateful that I had not been sent north into the Ohio River. Since the young lady was so informative about the Old Fort, I asked her what streetcar to take and how to approach my eastern and western quarries.

I think she knew then—much sooner than it dawned on me—on what sort of a fool's errand I had been sent. At any rate, she did tell me that there was little use in going down to the canal, because her uncle was the locktender, and that I could telephone to him and find out whether or not the machinery was in order; and then she told me how, by another complicated streetcar journey, I could reach a place where perhaps I could find my way down to the river's edge and see my houseboaters. There was a telephone in the drugstore. The nickel in the slot had not been dreamed of, and the use of the telephone was offered freely to customers. I got the number, and I telephoned the young lady's uncle and found that the lock machinery was all right. There was no story there in the west, for the Portland Canal locks were functioning. I had not that journey to make. Then another conference with the blonde cashier, and I started on my journey: first to the east.

I managed, by talking to streetcar conductors and an occasional passenger, to find my way to the river and to the end of a car line, and there I got off and walked. It was muddy. The drizzle had ended, but it was damp and cold. I walked or, rather, I slipped and slid down the bank to a place where I saw some shanty boats. There, fortunately, I found on the bank a gathering of four or five men, and I went up to them and asked whether they lived on the boats and, if so, whether they were deserting a hardhearted Louisville for Paducah. They were astonished by the question. It turned out that they had no such general grievance or such a plan. Even if they had, they wouldn't have the money to put their boats through the locks of the canal, and they wouldn't be able to steer their shanty boats through the rapid waters when the river was up. They gave me some needed instruction in the problems of navigation of the Ohio River and then let me absorb the information that shanty boats were cheap places to live but that they were not particularly suited for long voyages. Then came the story.

What they were doing there on the bank together was to discuss what to do with a family of a father and mother and two children who had lost their home the night before when one of the shanty boats had burned to the water's edge. It wasn't much of a story. But it was a story. I took my notes of the names of the persons and their great distress and the means by which their fellow shanty-boat dwellers were sharing from their meager funds the essential things required to tide the family over. The father of the family was there. He expressed his gratitude, but I had my story.

Then, back by the unknown route, still asking questions, to the Brook Street car line, out to the end, and up the hill—another muddy, muddy walk—to the Old Fort. The Old Fort wasn't much to see. In fact, if I hadn't known that it was an old fort, I couldn't have recognized it as such. Louisville was not under direct attack or in very grave danger from the Confederate forces during the Civil War, and the fortifications that were erected about it were sketchy, to say the least. It had none of the impressiveness of the Civil War fortifications to which I was accustomed in Nashville and nothing like the majesty of Fort Negley—that permanent monument to the Battle of Nashville which stood well within the incorporated limits of that town.

But my reward was that there was a gypsy camp at the Old Fort. Another reward was that there was a slight clearing in the western sky that brought a flash of light just as the sun disappeared over the horizon, and in that flash of light against the setting sun I saw a young gypsy girl. At that moment I was talking to two or three of the tribe. They pooh-poohed the notion that there was war or a threat of war. Tribes there were, of course. But they said they had come, as had several others of their tribes of kin and kindred, to Louisville to attend a Mass to be sung for the soul of one of their departed chieftains—one whom they called "King." He had died many months before in Alabama, but they had had a sentimental attachment to Louisville and had arranged for the Mass for him to be said at the Louisville cathedral. They gave me names and were quite willing indeed to tell me all about their travels and their journeys, and I am sure they embroidered their tales just as richly as their women embroidered their kerchiefs and their skirts.

I made my way back to *The Courier-Journal* office. It was late Sunday afternoon. There was nobody in the city room. None of the reporters was there. No one was in the city editor's room. No one was in the managing editor's room. I was alone. I chose a desk and a typewriter at random and began to experiment with the infernal machine. It took me some little time to learn the trick of inserting the paper and controlling the margin. It took me longer with the hunt-and-pick system to write my tales. I wrote about the shanty boats; I wrote about the gypsy camp—and in both of them I dressed up the story no little. I tried a sob-sister, tear-jerking approach for the family whose shanty boat had been burned out and for the gypsies, of course, romance. I painted the picture of the beautiful damsel standing silhouetted against the setting sun, her arms akimbo, the embodiment of Romany Rye.

I pounded out my copy, read it, edited it, and was face to face with the problem of how to write headlines in *The Courier-Journal* style. I picked up a copy of *The Courier-Journal* of the day before, turned to it, and wrote quite modestly, of course, number-one heads over each of my two stories.

Then famished, frightened, and very, very lonely, I went back across the street to the drugstore and consumed another cup of hot chocolate —that was long before the days when soda fountains were also restaurants. I supplemented the hot chocolate with ice cream and let that do for my supper.

I had laid my offerings on Mr. Wakefield's desk. I came back to the office and found one or two reporters there, pounding away at the typewriters, ignoring me. After a while in came Mr. Wakefield. I darted to his door and pointed to my stories lying on his desk. He picked them up.

"What!" he said. "Did you write the headlines?"

"Well, I always have!"

He looked quizzical and then glanced up at me and said, "You wrote number-one heads?"

"Yes," I said. "I thought the stories good enough."

"But," he said, "you have written the wrong kind of heads. We have only one deck for the top of number-one heads on *The Courier-Journal*."

"Well," I said, "I looked at yesterday's *Courier* and found a double-deck head there." I ran back to the desk I had used and brought the paper and showed it to him.

"Oh," he said, "you looked on the sporting page. They do use the double decks there but nowhere else in the paper. See—." And he turned and showed me the standard.

I was abashed, but he said nothing more, put the stories to one side, and asked me where I was staying. I told him I was registered temporarily at the Fifth Avenue Hotel, a modest hostelry only a short block and a half away from *The Courier-Journal* office, which had been recommended to me by Mr. Morton. He asked whether I had had my supper.

I said, "No."

"Well, you had better get something to eat and then come back."

I didn't know where to go at that time of night, but I didn't ask him. I was true to my instructions. Instead, I went in and asked a reporter. One of them told me to go around the corner on Jefferson Street to the English Kitchen. There I went and, having supped, returned to the office. Mr. Wakefield said nothing. I sat down and waited. He was busy editing the copy of the other reporters. It should be said parenthetically that the copy desk had not yet reached Louisville, as it was still utterly unkown in Nashville. I waited a long time and then went to ask him if there was anything else that night.

He said, "No. I think you had better go on home and report tomorrow afternoon when Mr. Platt will be here and will give you your assignments." Not a word about my stories.

I went back to the hotel. I had attempted in one day to learn something about the new job in a new city, where I knew not one human being. I felt sorry for myself. I could not help but run over in my mind the sad and touching plight of the girl who had thrown herself into the Thames, and I applied some of Hood's verses to my own state:

> Was it not pitiful?
> Near a whole city full,
> Friend he had none!

Up betimes on Monday morning, I set out to find a place to live. Ike Harcourt had told me the night before that some newspapermen lived at an establishment called Coker's at Eighth Avenue and Chestnut Street. There I went. Coker's I found to be unlike anything I had ever seen or heard of. And I must say, fifty years later, that I have never seen anything remotely resembling Coker's! It was an establishment where rooms were let to male paying guests. I saw and took a room, since fortunately there was a vacancy. I agreed to pay for it at the rate of two dollars a week, and I paid a week in advance. The room had in it a narrow bed and across from the bed a little table. The distance between the bed and the table was approximately a foot and a half. I think the room could not have been more than six feet wide or more than eight feet long. Down the hall there were some communal bathing and toilet facilities, but the room, the little cubicle, had the advantage of a door leading onto the hall that could be closed. It did have privacy. It was mine. There was no closet or storage room, but at the foot of the bed a small spindly chest of drawers. I went to the L. & N. Railroad station, got my trunk, which fortunately was of the variety then called "steamer," and had it sent to Coker's. Thence I went to the Fifth Avenue Hotel, where I paid my bill of $1.50, got my handbag, and went back to Coker's. The trunk opened, a few of the things stowed in the shaky chest of drawers, the trunk shoved under the cot, and I was at home.

It was now a little after twelve. I had to be in *The Courier-Journal* office at one. I found a little restaurant. I ate a hasty lunch; and at one o'clock I was on deck.

It was the end of my first twenty-four hours in *The Courier-Journal* establishment. It was the end of the longest day of my life. As I walked into the city room, where already, it being a weekday, two or three reporters were gathered, I was utterly disconsolate. I sat down at a desk near the door of the city room which somehow or other the day before I had discovered was unoccupied. One or two of the men who had been in on Sunday spoke to me, but they were busy with their own concerns. I sat there. I looked in the door and saw Mr. Wakefield. And then in came a person I had not seen before. It could be only Mr. Platt.

"What's doing, John?" asked Mr. Platt, for indeed it was he.

"Nothing much, but that new fellow from Nashville showed up yesterday, and you forgot to tell me what to do with him."

"Oh, I am sorry I forgot. What did you do with him?"

Wake proceeded to tell him. Platt slapped his thigh and laughed aloud. "What happened?"

"Well," said Wake, "he turned in a couple of stories. I don't know whether he faked them or not, but he wrote his own headlines, and number-one heads at that, and I ran them that way."

"What!" said Platt. "He wrote his own headlines?"

"Yes, he said that he always had."

"Did you have to change them much?"

"Only the top deck. He took that out of the sporting pages, and I had to change it to our style."

"Well, what do you know! Let me see those stories."

Wake handed him the paper, which Platt had not yet read. The first one was about the gypsies. Then I heard Platt giggle and say, "Think of it! A reporter on *The Courier-Journal* who would dare to write 'a damsel with arms akimbo.' Think of it! Something new under the sun!"

There was something in his tone, in his amused little laugh, though I could not see him, which lifted a great weight from my soul. The winter of my discontent burst into a promise of a verdant and a flowering spring. Within the hour it was made glorious summer by that some mighty city editor, B. Platt.

One by one he called in the other reporters and gave them their assignments. At last he called me. I went in. He arose from his desk, extended his hand, and with no little formality introduced himself. His face was illumined by a slight half-smile which later I learned was a characteristic that accompanied his every move and was no more a telltale of what was going on in his mind than would be the most deadpan poker face. At that time, though, it seemed to me to be warm and friendly.

First of all he had to go over with me his recollections and mine of our common mentor and patron, Marmaduke B. Morton. He even wanted to know what Mr. Morton thought of his hiring me away and explained that he had been careful not to mention Mr. Morton or their former relationship in his letter to me. I told him that Mr. Morton had always kept me from taking any other job which was offered but that, when it came to *The Courier-Journal,* he had told me that it was my chance and had bade me depart with his blessing. Then Mr. Platt went over in considerable detail the kind of work I had been doing in Nashville. I am inclined to think that perhaps, as on the day before with Mr. Wakefield, I was none too modest in my appraisal. Quite naturally, however, I accented the jobs that had interested me most—the courthouse, the city hall, the state capitol, as well as politics in general. He said that he had a good regular man on the courthouse, another good one on the city hall, and that, all in all, he thought he would give me a tryout on the Main Street run. Now I didn't know what the Main Street run was. He told me without the necessity of my asking any questions that it involved three factors. One was to look after the business news in the banking establishments and in the great wholesale establishments that in Louisville at that time were located along Main Street from the Galt House at the east to the Louisville Hotel at the west. Then also I was to cover the railroads. That was a task with which I had had some experience in Nashville. I was to do the hotels at night and write a hotel column. That of course was an old, old task to me. He told me that Wake had said my stories were pretty good and that, while reporters were not required to write headlines, if one felt so disposed, it did no harm, although the city editor might not at all agree with the reporter's notion of the importance of the story or the nature of the head.

And then he spared me the necessity of asking questions. He took at least an hour to tell me how to go about the Main Street assignment, where to go, the names of good news sources at one place or another, and he also told me to watch out for news of mergers.

I left the office a little late to go on my first run, but I was elated. Now in this town of Louisville I had two friends—Mr. Wakefield, won by a volunteered headline; Mr. Platt, won by a phrase, "arms akimbo." I was sure not only that the world was my oyster but that I would make short work of the conquest of that part of it that lay in Louisville and Kentucky.

Vivid as is my memory of that first long lonely Sunday, now thereafter the days and hours crowded together, and there was little distinction with respect to time as I began the great adventure of learning a new city. Each workday began at one in the afternoon. There was one day off a week. Ordinarily, one was expected to finish one's work by a quarter of one at night. At least once a week, however, one was expected to stay on the "dogwatch" until the paper was printed at three or three-thirty in the morning. The long hours were oppressive from the beginning, and, of course, I had to learn entirely new habits for my hours off duty, few as they were.

I soon learned that my breakfast would be other people's lunch and that it was best to take it at Miss Jennie Benedict's wonderful restaurant just across the street from *The Courier-Journal* office. There at the long table in the rear of the room I discovered a group of young men, mostly young lawyers or young businessmen and one or two other reporters. The twenty-five-cent lunch was delicious. The talk was stimulating, and the atmosphere was friendly. I was admitted on what appears to have been the nomination of Perry Farnsley, who showed me the place, and never thereafter did I feel the least bit of strangeness.

Then there was the excitement of meeting the new people on Main Street, learning a new job, and also the experience of the midnight bull session with the other reporters and the midnight or one o'clock supper-breakfast in the English Kitchen or the American Restaurant, or sometimes at the free-lunch counter of one of the open-door saloons. This, however, of the earliest day I recall with a mingled sense of pride and shame. Shame because I did not quite understand the lifted eyebrows of the other reporters when they found out that I had been put on the Main Street run; pride because I soon discovered that the Main Street assignment had been Mr. Wakefield's and before that Mr. Platt's, and it was considered the prize of the star reporter on the paper and one that ought not in common decency to have been given to a raw rookie. It was fortunately some little time before I realized what a prize I had plucked, and therefore, not understanding some of the offishness of some of my new colleagues, I perhaps was not sufficiently resentful but accepted their slightly scornful attitude with deep humility. At any rate, we were soon all good friends.

Thus it was I came to face a new life. Everything was new and strange, but there was one quality of absolute difference which theretofore I never had experienced. Although I had made, I thought, two friends in that first long and dreary day, yet there were no old friends here nor, what amounted to more, no one who by any stretch of the imagination could be considered kith or kin. There was none of my family here. It came to me with a sudden shock of realization how much I had depended on my family and home and on my kin in Nashville and how much I prized the very fact that they were there to be sought out when I needed them, quite irrespective of the fact that most of my friends and associates were outside their circles and that most of my interests from day to day were with the friends and not with the family.

And here again, in the new life, I was to encounter a new city; I was to find my friends among total strangers. I was to have no support from anyone who thertofore had known me or any of my family; these of necessity would have to take me for myself alone. Then there was the geographical change which had plunged me so suddenly into a town the physical characteristics of which I knew nothing except what I had discovered in two and a half hours of streetcar rides and muddy walks in pursuit of those gag assignments of the first day. The new life was to be in a new city of whose business, political, and social patterns I knew nothing. And, most important of all, it was to be centered in the new job which I was compelled to learn, almost from the bottom up.

I did not know then, of course, that my time on *The Courier-Journal* would be limited to six months. If I had known that, perhaps, I would not have been so overcome with the sheer weight of the physical difficulties of the long, strange hours—the odd and alien business of turning day into night and night into day. As I went about this reorientation of my life, this learning of new ways, I think that quite unconsciously I divided the task into three tolerably distinct parts: one, and it seemed the most immediate, was the need of friends and associates; the next, and an immediate concern in ascending order, was the need to know the city; the third, and to me the most important, was to make good on the job.

The first problem, then, was how to seek friends. First at hand, of course, were my associates on *The Courier-Journal* and immediately thereafter, and almost simultaneously, the other newspapermen on the other papers in the town—the rival morning paper, the *Herald,* and the two afternoon papers, the *Times* (which was an adjunct and an affiliate of *The Courier-Journal,* printed on the same presses and published in the same place), and the *Evening Post,* its rival and implacable foe. *The Courier-Journal* men and some of those on the rival morning paper were wont to gather at midnight meals in such cheap eating places as the American Restaurant and the English Kitchen, or, as I have said, sometimes in the saloons. These midnight eating places had nothing whatever to recommend them but their cheapness and the fact that the food was food, however unappetizingly prepared and however unattractively served. The only thing that made them tolerable at all was the company—the conversation, the shop talk, the tales that were told, the jeers and the jokes that were exchanged, the brags and the lies that were bandied and bantered about. Most agreeable was the breakfast at Miss Jennie Benedict's, which was lunch to all of us except the morning newspapermen and which from the first brought me in touch with some of the younger men of the town who liked to eat at Miss Jennie's not only because the prices were low but also because the food was good and the service far above the average of restaurants we encountered in those days.

At six o'clock in the evening there was supper at Miss Benedict's. Then the long table at the rear of the room became the exclusive property of the newspapermen, all of them who came from all the papers. It was the mid-meal of the day for those of us on *The Courier-Journal* and the *Herald*. It was supper for such of the *Times* and *Post* reporters who did not go home or perhaps had no home to go to for their evening meal. Most of those who gathered at that evening meal were young, most of them in their twenties. I myself was twenty-three, and, for some reason as yet unknown and perhaps unknowable to me, I was then, as ever since I have remained, exceedingly fond of the company of persons younger than I and those older than I. I liked, of course, my coevals, but I was not content to have only associates of my age. Here I was sure that, in the ordinary course of my work, I would meet older people; but I longed to know younger ones. Most of all I missed knowing any girls. From my earliest boyhood I had spent much time with women and girls. I liked their society, and here I soon began to miss their company sorely.

It was natural with my background in Missouri and Tennessee that I turned to the church as a place in which I would be certain to find those friends young and old and of both sexes with whom I might soon find myself on easy and familiar terms, sharing a common background, sharing a common code, and acknowledging a more or less common destiny. But here I was up against my peculiar schedule. I brought my church letter from the West End Methodist Church in Nashville and duly joined the Walnut Street Methodist Episcopal Church, South, in Louisville.

But my hours defeated my purpose. Even if, as I now suspect it was not, the church had been organized to meet the needs of such young strangers as I, I could not have met the timetable of the church. On Sunday mornings I did get up in time to go to the eleven o'clock service, although that meant no breakfast and, on the mornings when I had not got to bed before four and not to sleep before five, a very real sacrifice of my necessary sleep. The Sunday school at nine, which might have been the place in which I could have made some of my desired social contacts, was impossible for me. And then the Young Peoples' Meeting, then called the Epworth League in the Methodist church, meeting early on Sunday evening, was of course impossible for me, because I always had to go to work at one in the afternoon and never could be through by six or seven. Gradually, as the weeks went on, I began to sleep late Sunday mornings rather than to go to church. The church had not fulfilled my desire for new friends; and it was not enough in a nonliturgical church, where the principal feature of the Sunday-morning service was the sermon, to go and sit among strangers to hear a strange man preach, no matter how good were his sermons—although I do remember that that particular preacher was a good preacher indeed.

What, then, was left to me of the church? Only this: that, since my day off was Thursday and I always worked on Sunday, there were those times when on a Sunday evening there was a particular reason for the city editor to assign me to report a particular sermon by a particular preacher. This did take me into many churches of the city. But, then, that was all a part of my work and, while in that way I got acquainted with some very excellent men and managed to expand my knowledge of the town and its ways, and to expand my knowledge of the different customs of the different denominations, it was all a part of the job and but little more.

On *The Courier-Journal* there was one woman reporter. She was the society editor, Nancy Czapski. It was her desk and her typewriter that I had appropriated on that first Sunday and Monday of my work, days when she was not there. Miss Czapski was bright of eye, light of spirit, sparkling with wit, and overflowing with vivacity and the joy of living. A society editor, she was by definition a gossip; but, if at times her gossip seemed slightly tinged with malice, its maliciousness always seemed in part atoned for by an amused sidelong glance and a little crooked smile with which she always seemed to apologize for the sharpness of her tongue and beg the hearer's forgiveness—which could not fail to be granted. The only woman working in a room with seven or eight young men, the only woman working in the whole editorial rooms with twelve or fifteen men, she literally ruled the roost; and she did that, I may add, by the simple device of keeping herself to herself. The fact that she afterward fell in love and married one of the reporters later to come, Haynes McFadden, could in no wise have been predicted by the standoffishness of her attitude toward all the others.

The only other young women I could come to know in those early days were working just across the street, the comely blonde cashier at Buschmeyer's Drugstore, who had given me my first help in Louisville, and her brunette sister, who spelled her at the cash register. They came to be my good friends. And then, above all, there was Miss Rose Clelland, the cashier at Miss Jennie Benedict's Restaurant. She not only was my friend but was a friend indeed of all of us impecunious reporters. It was our custom there, as soon as we got our pay, to buy a meal ticket which was good for a certain number of dollars and cents (I think it was five dollars) and so arranged that Miss Rose could punch out the price of each meal as one took it. At times the ticket did not suffice, and then it was that Miss Rose would give us another meal ticket, with the hope that we would come up with the necessary five dollars on the next payday. Most of us did, but sometimes there were long delays. And then sometimes I suspect, in the goodness of her heart, when for one reason or another our poverty was too evident, she would punch out only twenty-five cents when thirty-five cents was indicated. Sometimes indeed, I suspect, she felt so deeply sympathetic to the hardworking, poorly paid newspapermen that she forgot to punch at all.

And, over and over again, it came to me that, while I liked my job, while I liked all the new things I was seeing and doing and learning, how I hated the dreadful hours! That long, long fourteen hours from one in the afternoon until three in the morning! The meagerness of any possible normal recreation at the times when one did have a little leisure or when the work did end early—say, not later than one in the morning. What good in any normal fashion is a two-hour release from the chain gang when it comes between one and three in the morning?

So there was the open-door policy of the Louisville saloons of that period. No wonder that all of us at times and many of us far too often found solace there. One of them, Hummler and Nolan's, boasted that there was no lock on the door and consequently no key. It was open twenty-four hours a day, three hundred and sixty-five days in the year, except during leap year, when the doors swung wide both ways for three hundred and sixty-six times the revolution of the earth. There was around the corner Sullivan and Brach's, where the free lunch if anything was better than it was at Hummler and Nolan's. Across Green Street from *The Courier-Journal* office, there was Al's, a German bar in which the Würzburger and the Pilsener flowed freely, the imported beers not entirely supplanting the Louisville brews and those of St. Louis and Milwaukee. Here one could meet Al Stein and others of the staff of the German morning paper, the *Louisville Anzeiger,* the offices of which were just over the saloon. And here always, if one were hard put to it, there were the fried oysters and the tartar sauce that could be consumed ad libitum and without question if one had five cents for a glass of beer. If one didn't have the nickel, as not infrequently happened to the young men of our profession in those days, what easier than to ask the amiable bartender, whose first name was a part of my professional perquisites, to put it on the cuff? Indeed, I think some of our boys did that more often than not, and it was astonishing how far some of them could push their luck without getting a comeuppance.

But the saloon then was not a coeducational institution. There were, of course, I knew, along Green Street, stretching far to the west, many *maisons de tolérance,* but these were not my province. Nor indeed did I ever see anything much of that Louisville that Eliot Paul visited only a year or two later and wrote so well about in his after years. There was indeed, in so far as I knew, but one place in town where a nice girl looking for a drink might go unaccompanied and be served. That was in the rear dining-room of Seelbach's Hotel on Main Street, later to be known as the Old Inn. Here on occasion we found another newspaperwoman, one who worked on the other morning paper. She was a person of keen mind and vaulting ambition who, frustrated by having to do society news, was wont to seek her own counsel away from women and men alike and drown her sorrows in drink. The drink that she particularly affected was absinthe frappé. One morning about two o'clock, Lewis Johnson and I walked through that back room. The only person there was this girl. We walked over to her.

"Girlie, you oughtn't to drink that," Lewis said. "That will make you drunk tomorrow."

She looked up at him with large, round, sad, blue eyes and said, "Mr. Johnson, I am in no particular hurry."

So, while I did not despise the company I found in the open saloons, and while I remember some good times there, I found there not what I most sought.

Indeed, there was another place of similar but at the same time quite dissimilar character that I found more to my liking. It was August Hollenbach's *Weinstube* on Lower Third Avenue. Here there was neither hard liquor nor beer. Here there was only wine, and for the most part the wines were those of the Rhine. August indeed would serve champagne, but, of course, none of us had the money for that. He would, if urged, serve the wines of France; but for the most part his wines were as German as he and as German as were most of his customers. They sat about at little tables, smoking, playing chess or checkers, and talking. There I remember no roistering, no boisterous talk even. And there I came to know, when I had discovered the possibility of stealing a little time after writing my copy and before supper, a little time between five and six in the afternoon, the *Rötemit* —a large glass half-full of Assmannshäuser and topped off with Seltzer water. There at those tables over a leisurely glass of wine and water, I found two good friends. One was the dramatic and literary critic of the *Louisville Evening Post,* Charles Musgrove; the other was the assistant editorial writer of the *Louisville Times,* Charles Dobbs.

These captured late-afternoon half-hours or hours were precious to me. Not the less so because perhaps I felt that they were stolen. Usually, of course, I had tried to get my afternoon stint of work done and my copy in, but ofttimes I was conscious of the fact that I was hurrying because I looked forward to an encounter with Dobbs or with Musgrove at the *Weinstube.* Sometimes of course an older man, Young E. Allison, then the editor of a fire-insurance trade journal, would drop in and join us. The reason that I liked the place so much was not, I think, the slow sipping of the wine and water, agreeable as that was, not the kindly ministration of the old German host, not the atmosphere of *Gemütlichkeit* which pervaded the place, but the fact that here in Dobbs and Musgrove and Allison I could commune with other rebellious spirits. I had always thought of myself as a rebel and rabid. It was true that, from the early days of poverty in those Ozark Hills, I had channeled that rebellion into a protest against the things of the political world. It was equally true that I had found a very occasional fellow-rebel among my coevals in journalism either in

Nashville or in my new city of Louisville; but here were three rebels together, although the things they rebelled against and the revolutions that they would set up were of entirely different characters.

Musgrove wrote verse and felt deeply as he read his own verse that it was not poetry. His frustration caused him to lash out at his generation of writers. He dreamed of greater things. He thought each week that some of his verse, deadly dull as it seemed to him, would catch the lambent fire and be translated into the glory of the stars of poetry. Of his poverty he complained not, because poverty was the lot of poets. Of his physical ailments he complained not, because they were a part of what he considered his due meed of suffering. His rebellion was against himself and his own inadequacy, and he found his consolation only in reading and in quoting the poets. Not only those of the eighteenth and nineteenth centuries, with whom I had so closely associated, but also the more obscure and less-read seventeenth-century poets and those then moderns who were just coming into recognition.

Mr. Allison was a rebel, too, but in a different way altogether. He was older. He was already quite deaf, and one had to shout to make him hear; and he, on the other hand, dropped his voice and spoke so softly that his hearers had to cup their hands to hear him at all. He wrote novels and just at that time was completing a delightful little book called *The Secret Vice*. That vice, one discovered on reading into the manuscript, was novel-reading. He was addicted to the novel, and yet he thundered against it. He was addicted to the novel, but he cried out against the novelist and at the same time longed to be a novelist and tried and tried and tried. Cynical in a rather good-humored fashion, he was apt to dart out at the frailties of his fellow human beings; and he declined quite simply but completely to accept the prevailing values in the field of literature, as he did also in other realms than the talk I had wandered into.

Dobbs was the only one of these three rebels who shared my particular striking-out at things as they were. His was in politics. However, unlike me, he thought of politics as controlled by economics; but, as I took the historical view, I was inclined to think that, if the politics were properly set up, the economic benefit would flow naturally from an improvement in governmental structure. He had read Karl Marx. I had not. He was a determinist. I was not a determinist then, as I never was to be. He was a member of the Socialist party. Indeed, he was a friend of Eugene Debs and was himself a perennial candidate on the Socialist ticket for such offices as governor of Kentucky or representative in Congress. (That, of course, was long before the time when candidates for the United States Senate presented themselves to the people. The members of that august assembly then were elected by the state legislatures.) The three rebels and I, slowly sipping our wine and water, knew little of the fact that our rebellions were our individual struggles against the times and were directed in quite different directions. We did not think of co-ordinating them. What really was the reason, I think, for my delight and perhaps for theirs in these little get-togethers in the *Weinstube* was that it not only gave us a chance to talk out our troubles and attack the world as it was but also gave us a haven of refuge from a circumambient atmosphere in which at that time all the talk was of money, riches, business, or getting on in a material way.

The twentieth century had just come in so far as the calendar was concerned; but, beyond the argument as to whether it began in 1900 or in 1901, we certainly knew nothing of its portent. The widow of Windsor had died but yesterday, and nobody expected that under her son, who had so long been the Prince of Wales and must now be called, unfamiliarly, Edward the Seventh, anything possibly could happen to that empire. Leo XIII still wore the triple crown of the Holy See at Rome and seemed to be as eternal as the city of his see. Japan had not yet struck at Russia to inaugurate the revolution in which Asia was to resist the effort of the Western world to write it down as a civilization of peoples and countries subordinate in power and in skill to western Europe and the Americas.

No doubt, here and there, voices were raised in warning. No doubt there were prophets of woe as well as those who had read in their crystal balls of dire events to come in the new century. But we knew little or nothing of them, and, what little we knew, we ignored.

Allison and Musgrove's troubles were within themselves. Dobbs and I saw the world as external to us, but each of us would go about its reform in a different way. I was a Democrat and believed that with a sufficient popular education in the old American way, according to the American political process and in the ways prescribed by the American Constitution, the voters would find the means to correct the evils that beset a country in which the rich were getting richer and the poor were getting poorer. Dobbs would undertake to change that situation by quite other means; but even his Marxism was colored by the rule of the Fabian Society, and he was a believer in the inevitability of gradualness. He was a rebel but not a revolutionary. He always was at great pains to make it quite clear that his socialism had nothing whatever to do with its violent manifestation that had crept up in some parts of the world. This, he was very apt to say with more labeling than argument, was not Socialist at all but real anarchy.

It must not be taken from this that all the persons in Louisville who at that time were writers were either such failures or were so frustrated. In fact, there was Thompson Buchanan, who had but recently left *The Courier-Journal,* despising the very Main Street beat on which I was now engaged. He had flitted to New York, and there later he was to become a successful playwright. There was Cleves Kincaid— we called him "Piggy" Kincaid—over on the *Louisville Post,* too, who was to become a successful playwright. There was right on the staff of the *Louisville Times,* the afternoon edition of our paper, Madison Cawein, minor poet of considerable talent and deep feeling. There was Cale Young Rice, another poet whose published volumes were received with approbation by the critics of the day. There was also his wife, Alice Hegan Rice, who was the author of what then was a best seller, *Mrs. Wiggs of the Cabbage Patch.* But these creative writers, these more determined and more successful literary characters, I had at that time little opportunity to know.

If I had known them, I probably would have thought of them as living in another and to me an unapproachable world. They might have seemed to me just as did the rich. They lived on the same planet but, so far as I was concerned, in a separate civilization. I did not envy the rich. I did not envy the successful writers. It was simply that I had no notion that I could ever be admitted to either of those higher categories. With my background of poverty, it seemed to me a miracle that I could keep a job and be paid regularly, twenty dollars once a week. I was satisfied. Of course, I hoped that I would rise gradually in the profession, but that profession to me was bounded on all sides as well as beneath and above by a newspaper office. When I thought of my rise within that cubic container, I thought of it as being slow and gradual. My rebellion was a rebellion of the intellect only. It had no emotional repercussions. I did not strike out blindly, and, more than all, I lacked the ambition that would have given me the drive to permit me to force my way upward by conforming to the rules of the game.

The one thing and the only thing against which I was in open rebellion was the long hours. From one o'clock in the afternoon to three o'clock in the morning was intolerable. The upshot of that one piece of rebellion was that I began after only a few months to long for the day when I could again get a job on an afternoon newspaper. Even on such a paper, I would not have minded twelve or even fourteen hours if those hours could be accommodated to the rising and the setting of the sun.

Above all, I was a conformist. I wanted to be like other people and do what other people did. Among all my newspaper friends in Nashville, there was none who failed to accept as right and proper the current doctrines of the American government as headed by William McKinley. It is true that Theodore Roosevelt had succeeded McKinley, but as yet he had not begun to rock the boat. The *Nashville Banner,* which had been a Democratic paper, had refused to support William Jennings Bryan and free silver in 1896. *The Courier-Journal,* which was a much more important Democratic paper and whose editor, the great Henry Watterson, was one of the leaders of the Democratic party in the nation, also had balked at Bryan and free silver and in 1896 had been a leader in the support of the bolting national Democratic candidates, the "Gold Bug" candidatures of Palmer and Buckner.

Of the seven or eight reporters on *The Courier-Journal* at that time, none was over thirty. None was married. All were of an age when one might expect to find a radical spirit. But there was not one who did not share fully and wholeheartedly in *The Courier-Journal's* opposition to Bryan, free silver, and all the radicalism the mention of the very names entailed. There was not one who was not for the things that were going on in the country at the time. Most of them—I think, all of them—were Democrats except Lewis Johnson, who was a Republican. The only issue with respect to national politics on which they differed was the tariff. The Democrats were inclined to be for a low tariff; Lewis Johnson was for a high protective tariff. Mr. Watterson had been one of the major prophets of the low tariff, if not, indeed, of the free-trade school of thought; and I think perhaps most of the reporters thought that it was heresy to have a political position

different from that of the great editor of our newspaper and different
from the exactly similar views held by General William B. Haldeman
and Mr. Bruce Haldeman, who were its owners and publishers.

So it was, too, with the young lawyers and young businessmen with
whom I ate lunch at Miss Benedict's at midday. They, as were all
my associates on the newspaper, were content with things as they
were. Not only did they and my newspaper associates regret the descent
of the Democratic party into the abyss of radicalism with Bryan and
the Farmers' Alliance but also they all devoutly believed that the radical Democrat, William Goebel, who had been a free-silverite and other
reprehensible things and who had been assassinated at Frankfort, was
a man who would have led the state into a demagogic revolution in
which property rights would have been sacrificed to purely personal
political greed for power. But, with fourteen hours a day at work,
there was little time to search out other associates; and perforce I
spent all of it that could be called "leisure" with newspaper friends.

As I went about my work, I could not fail to learn the ways of
the new city. It was a river town and a railroad town. It was an agricultural market center and a manufacturing city. It had a background
of tobacco and whiskey and horses. It was the metropolis of Kentucky,
which had a special aura among the states of the Union. One explored
it by streetcar—that is, if one were not rich enough to turn out a horse-
drawn equipage or on occasion to hire one from a livery stable. The
half-dozen automobiles in the city were not to be reckoned with and
indeed were themselves chancy vehicles, each one entering upon a new
and untried adventure any time it left its stable, which was already
beginning to be called a garage. One was never certain whether or not
it would get there. And, indeed, I had very few opportunities to ride
in one of the contraptions at all. If one were to venture beyond the
limits of the city as determined by the ends of the street-railway lines,
then there had to be recourse to the railroads or to the interurban lines
to the east. Across the river, in the two Indiana towns of New Albany
and Jeffersonville, there were also the beginnings of manifestations of
the satellite towns which later were to be included in a metropolitan
area from which they were cut off by the political boundary of a state
line as well as the waters of the Ohio.

Even the geography of the town, however, was tinged with politics.
A marvelously handsome gentleman, General Castleman, reigned at

the head of a park commission. He had, by various methods, founded three great parks for the city. One at the east had been dubbed "Cherokee"; that at the west, "Shawnee"; and the other at the south, "Iroquois." Since General Haldeman did not like the persons who had given these names to these parks, in *The Courier-Journal* we called two of these same parks "Eastern" and "Southern"; and, as far as Iroquois Park was concerned, we called it "Jacob" in honor of a man General Haldeman thought had had more to do with the acquisition of the park than had General Castleman himself.

The great ports of entry were three: one railroad station serving the Chesapeake and Ohio at Seventh Avenue and the river; one, the Louisville and Nashville at Tenth and Broadway; and one, the wharf at which an occasional steamboat still stopped, although the days of the passenger boat on the river already had gone.

Incidentally, one of the things about the job was to learn some tricks not only in *Courier-Journal* style but in *Courier-Journal* taboos. With respect to *Courier-Journal* style, I had already been instructed by Mr. Morton, who was a graduate of the Wattersonian school, and I knew that it was a crime of the first order to spell "whisky" with an *e* or "traveler" with two *l*'s. But the taboos were something different. I soon discovered that the name of Mr. John H. Whalen, one of the Democratic bosses of the town, once a partner and now an enemy of General Haldeman, could never be mentioned; nor could the name of his private business establishment, the Buckingham Theater, a burlesque house, be admitted to the columns of our papers. There were other persons about the town whose names could not be mentioned in print in our paper, no matter what they did. Of course it was not primarily the reporter's responsibility to enforce these rules; but the city editor and his assistant were quick and ready to impart the information, because they desired no slip-up, nor did they wish to have to deal with some commitment some reporter may have made in conversation outside the office. It had seemed better to the regime to punish its local enemies by sending them to Coventry than by giving them publicity by horrendous verbal attacks in print. That in itself was perhaps unconsciously a change from what had been the habit of *The Courier-Journal* and its predecessors under the ministration of the great editor, George D. Prentice, to say nothing of Mr. Watterson, who in his earlier days had not spared invective.

Occasionally I would get to the courthouse or the city hall. I discovered soon that the peculiar form of municipal government I had known in Nashville was entirely different from that prevailing in Louisville. But still I knew so little about it that I was not prepared for the discovery I later made that the Louisville charter was itself unique and that it bore little resemblance to that of most of the cities of the country. Louisville was governed by a mayor and a board of aldermen, but there was the interposition of a board of public works and a board of public safety between the mayor and the board of aldermen, on the one hand, and the operating departments, on the other, that made for confusion and also made it quite difficult for a newspaperman seeking news. There were so many ways to duck and pass the buck.

The tribe of those journalists and former journalists who once worked on *The Courier-Journal* with Mr. Watterson, diminishing in number, is perhaps still engaged in the pleasant pastime of compensating for its gradual disappearance by remembering more and more about the great man. This is also true, I have no doubt, for those who worked with Dana on the *New York Sun,* those who worked with Pulitzer on the *World,* and those who not only worked with James Gordon Bennett on the *Herald* but traveled with him as his secretaries.

It is a commonplace that the great days of personal journalism, those just before and after the Civil War, ended practically with the nineteenth century. It was about that time that the publisher became more important than the editor-in-chief. Indeed, in the earlier days of the mid-nineteenth century, it was the editor who became the publisher; and it was toward the end of that century that the business process of publishing a newspaper began to take precedence over the more artistic process of editing one.

One night in the city room about half-past one in the morning, seven or eight reporters were sitting around. All of us, as I have said before, were in our twenties. None of us had had the advantage of a college education. We knew little of science, and that little we had absorbed, I suspect, from the Sunday magazine sections and from the periodical press, with more particular attention to the marvelous little steps that were taken toward the revelation of the secrets of the universe. But we had heard about molecular movement, and we had heard about the atom. More particularly we were enraptured at that time by Sir William Crookes and his kinetic theory of matter. One of the things that came up about that time was the matter of the measurement of the degree of cold that could be equated with absolute zero. We divided in our dispute perhaps four on one side and four on another. Four of us maintained that the advance of science would be such that, at some time in the future, it would be possible to measure absolute zero and that we would be able to know at how many degrees the ordinary zero on the Fahrenheit scale or the centigrade scale that point would be. The other half maintained that that would be utterly impossible, because any instrument capable of measuring absolute zero would depend for its readings upon molecular motion; and, since absolute zero was that point at which all motion ceased, the instrument inevitably would go out of business before the measurement could be read.

Mr. Watterson came into the room. He was quiet, and nobody noticed him. He listened for a while, and then he touched Perry Farnsley on the shoulder and asked, "What are you boys talking about?"

"Well," returned Farnsley, "we were talking about Sir William Crookes and the kinetic theory, and we were arguing about whether or not the scientists would ever be able to measure absolute zero."

"Nonsense," said Mr. Watterson. "The cold of absolute zero has been measured years and years ago. Absolute zero is that degree of cold which is maintained always at the point of contact between the editorial rooms and the business office of any daily newspaper in the United States!"

This business of touching the shoulder was a habit with Mr. Watterson, since he was so very nearsighted that it was difficult for him to recognize persons without peering into their faces. Within the precincts of *The Courier-Journal* editorial rooms that of course was not necessary. Therefore, for his shortsightedness, he substituted a short-armed jab to the shoulder, usually accompanied by the peremptory question, "Who is it?"

One morning about three o'clock when I was on the dogwatch, I was using the solitary telephone for the dismal business that the reporter assigned to that task was forced to do toward the "30" deadline—call up the various homes of the prominent citizens whose deaths were momentarily expected and ascertain whether or not we should use the obituary, which, of course, was in type and always ready. I

[294]

was trying to get the house of Basil Doehoefer in the West End, and I was turning over idly the pages of *Webster's Unabridged Dictionary,* which lay on the desk where the telephone was. As I waited and waited, I turned the pages. Mr. Watterson came through. He jabbed me on the shoulder. "Who is it?"

"Brownlow," I replied.

"What are you doing?" Evidently Mr. Watterson did not see the telephone at my ear, or else he chose to ignore it, so I thought the better thing to do was to tell him what I actually was doing at the time instead of what I was waiting for. So I said, "I am reading the *Dictionary,* Mr. Watterson."

"Skip the adjectives," he retorted. "Skip the adjectives! I will have you to understand, young man, that on this newspaper adjectives are the sole prerogative of the editor-in-chief."

Although at that time few if any college graduates could be found on the city staff of a newspaper in almost any part of the country, the threat of their intrusion already had been recognized, and those of us who were not collegiate banded together instinctively to resist the invasion. One of the tales we liked to tell each other was about a young man from Harvard who got a job on *The Courier-Journal.*

A new cub reporter on *The Courier-Journal* was always put quite naturally on the lowest rung of the ladder. In the city-room hierarchy a police reporter was the lowest order of animal life. The police beat was divided into two parts, the East End and the West End. The West End was much to be preferred, for within its precincts were the city hall, with the headquarters of the Police Department and of the Fire Department, the red-light district, most of the hotels, and, generally speaking, the greater number of news sources.

The East End was meager in its prospects. There was an East End Police Precinct, there were one or two hotels, and there was the ghetto, which was well behaved. There was almost no chance for juicy murder, and there were relatively few big fires. The East End was drudgery. Yet the beat had to be taken, and there always the newest reporter was placed, and there as a matter of tradition the cub was introduced into the mysteries of the business. At one time—it was before my day—the East End beat was assigned to George Middleton. By the time I got on *The Courier-Journal* he had left the paper and was beginning to be a Blue Grass racing-stable magnate, in which capacity he attained prominence and wealth.

Some friend of Mr. Watterson knew a young man who was being graduated from Harvard. He asked Mr. Watterson whether his young Harvard protégé might not get a job on *The Courier-Journal,* as he felt himself destined for journalism. And, among other things, he told Mr. Watterson that this young man had a command of the German, French, and Italian languages and he thought that he might be very useful to Mr. Watterson in translating editorials and leading articles from the journals of those European countries. Mr. Watterson promised to take care of him. June came, and the young man got his degree at Harvard and entrained for Louisville.

Mr. Watterson was as good as his word and did give him the European exchanges for the purposes of translation. At the same time "Marse Henry" was mindful of the ordinary workings of the newspaper in that day, and so he sent him down to the city editor to be educated not according to Harvard standards but according to newspaper stand-ards of the time. The resentment of the city editor, the managing editor, and the entire corps against the intrusion of a college graduate was massed behind the decision to put him on the cub reporter's job. He was assigned to assist Mr. Middleton in covering the East End.

One night shortly after the educated young easterner had been fol-lowing Mr. Middleton around through the darkness of the East End, they wandered into the Galt House. The Harvard young man was thirsty. The Harvard young man was well heeled with pocket money. Mr. Middleton was busted. Mr. Middleton also was thirsty. The Har-vard man, perhaps hoping to overcome some of the enmity and re-sentment which doubtless he felt, asked Mr. Middleton to come into the Galt House bar and have a drink. Mr. Middleton without too much hesitation accepted. In the sacred precincts of that bar they met an elderly gentleman who had known the Harvard man's father and grandfather in Boston. He was delighted to see him. He asked, "What are you doing here?"

"Well, I am working on *The Courier-Journal.*"

"Oh," said his friend, "you are going into journalism."

"Yes, and I am an assistant to Mr. Watterson."

"Oh, what could be better than to begin your work under the aegis of the greatest editor in the newspaper world. And just what are you doing on *The Courier-Journal?*"

"I am the European editor," said the young man. "It is my business to translate for Mr. Watterson the leading articles from the Italian, the French, and the German journals."

"Excellent! Excellent! I am sure that all of your father's and grandfather's friends will be delighted to know of your good fortune." And then, remembering his manners, the elderly gentleman turned to Mr. Middleton, to whom he had been introduced, and asked, "Are you also on *The Courier-Journal,* Mr. Middleton?"

"Yes, sir."

"And what do you do on *The Courier-Journal?*"

"I am the Oriental editor. I handle the East End."

And in those days we were naïve enough to believe that that tale could stop any college man from ever trying to get a job on *our* newspaper.

Mr. Watterson's great editorials were written by him with pen and ink in handwriting that was undecipherable. Only the few could read it. We believed in the office that after it was cold—say, a week later— even Mr. Watterson would not be able to read what he had written. Its translation into type depended upon one or two printers who had come over from the hand-set days and who, despite their age, painfully had learned to operate the linotype; but even they guessed. The final authority for reading Mr. Watterson reposed in an elderly proofreader. He had a long pointed beard, a long pointed nose, long pointed eyebrows, and a disposition that was the reverse of amiable. His name was Lynch, and quite naturally he had early in his career earned in lieu of a Christian name the sobriquet of "Judge." Judge Lynch could read Mr. Watterson's handwriting. Judge Lynch corrected the proofs, and we believed that once in a while Judge Lynch modified Mr. Watterson's editorial policy. We were equally certain that, if Mr. Watterson discovered something in print that he had not intended, it was sufficient to say that Judge Lynch had read it that way. Mr. Watterson dared not question the authority of that high court of his last resort.

Mr. Watterson's style, distinctive as it was, was not one that could not be copied. The associate editor, Mr. Harrison Robertson, who served on *The Courier-Journal* also for a half-century, wrote many and many an editorial that was quoted by newspapers all over the country as typical Watterson pieces. Later Tom Wallace also wrote editorial after editorial that in quotation was credited to "Marse Henry."

But that does not mean that his style was not his own. He was the product of his generation. He shared with the rhetoricians of his day, whether they were statesmen, military officers, littérateurs, humorists, or poets, the American and especially the Mississippi Valley faith in emphasis by exaggeration. If put to it, and he was often put to it, Mr. Watterson in an editorial could depend as much upon that particular form of emphasis as did Mark Twain or the folklorists who invented Paul Bunyan or John Henry. Indeed, at that time, the emphasis of understatement was but beginning to be observed in the higher literature of the mother-country of the language, England. Dickens, Thackeray, and Trollope, no less than Scott and Bulwer-Lytton, had known how to draw a long bow. Sir Robert Peel and Mr. Gladstone and Mr. Disraeli knew no less than did the two Pitts and Burke the cumulative effect of peroration.

In the editorial style of the American newspapers from Bryant to Greeley and Dana onward, the peroration was the essential part of a smashing editorial. Indeed, the peroration was what gave the very word "smash" to the vocabulary of the editorial dissertations. Mr. Watterson could write of the Democratic party about to renominate Mr. Cleveland: "It is marching through the slaughterhouse into the open grave!" He could at the beginning of World War I create and carry at the masthead of his editorial page the motto: "To Hell with the Hapsburgs and the Hohenzollerns!"

And never could he have understood the revulsion against emphasis, of the distaste for peroration, that has brought after his time a whole generation of writers to worship at the tail end of diminuendo, the diminishing finish of any article, so that every book review ends with either "It lacks an index" or "Its index is inadequate"; so that every public speech ends with an apology for having transgressed on the time of the listener; and so that every editorial ends, if not explicitly, implicitly with a sentence or so which seems to me to say: "At least this is our tentative view for today; but, if you will kindly read our editorial page tomorrow, you perhaps will find out we have admitted our error of judgment." Now one is expected to discuss both sides of a question. Then also, perhaps, there were but two sides: my side—right; your side—wrong. And as Mr. Watterson would have said and, in fact, did say: "Under which flag, bezonian?"

CHAPTER XVI

LOUISVILLE AND "MARSE HENRY"

It was the day of mergers. Trusts were forming. No matter that the Sherman Antitrust Law had been passed as long ago as 1888 or that the Hearst papers were fulminating against the trusts. Homer Calvin Davenport was drawing dollar marks all over the outward habiliments of Mark Hanna and the rich clothing of that fatted corps of Milk Trust, Sugar Trust, and Steel Trust. Every little while some company, a distillery or a tobacco concern, was being purchased by one of the great trusts; and there was news to be had in Louisville and, for not a few of its people, money to be made. There was, over and above me but not in direct hierarchy, the financial editor, Mr. Watkins, who kept up with the stocks and bonds, who pursued the doings of the bulls and bears, so that I was not expected to do anything in my work concerning the rise and fall of stock values or to pay particular attention to financial transactions. It was my business to look sharp to see that no new distillery was acquired by the trust, that no tobacco concern was being absorbed, and that no news or rumors of further mergers were left out of the news columns of *The Courier-Journal*.

It was also the heyday of railroad control of industry, and it was by virtue of the ukase of railroad presidents that cities rose or fell. And, in turn, it was the railroads which were being controlled more and more by the great concentration of banking power in Wall Street. It was my business to keep up with the railroads to see what was going on and to see how they were getting on in their twin activities of competition and consolidation. They were competing furiously with one another, but strings were also being pulled by financial interests above. They also were co-operating with one another. It was the day of the railroad-rate rebate and of preferential freight tariffs.

It was, in short, three or four years before the passage of the Hepburn Act, which gave the Interstate Commerce Commission at Washington the power to fix freight rates and control railroad tariffs.

The dominant railroad in Kentucky was, as it had been in Tennessee, the great Louisville and Nashville. It was as much in control of the legislature in those two states as was the Southern Pacific in California or the Burlington in Iowa. It was as influential with respect to the industrial establishments of its territory as was the New York Central in the Empire State or the Pennsylvania Railroad in the Keystone State. It had as much to do with the social evolution of the region which it dominated as did the New York, New Haven, and Hartford in New England.

At the head of the great Louisville and Nashville was the implacable, the indomitable, the mysterious, and the unapproachable Milton H. Smith. It was well known that he had never given a newspaper interview. It was well known that he despised newspapers and that he, unlike most others, feared them not. It is true that, through subsidiaries and agents, he controlled not one but several newspapers; but, seemingly, the more he was able to control, the greater his contempt for them and for their hirelings. It was my duty, however, to try to see Mr. Smith. I did try conscientiously. I never saw him. Mr. Smith was not only a despot in his system but an autocrat. He disdained even a private secretary. However, outside his office there sat an individual known as an executive clerk, and to him, always grave, always courteous, and nearly always utterly uncommunicative, I came every day. He was Wyble L. Mapother, later himself to succeed the great Mr. Smith in the presidency of that railroad.

Once in a while, almost furtively, and with an air that not only besought but compelled confidence, Mr. Mapother would give me a tip. I remember with a sense of triumph how, following one of these most casually dropped intimations, I went to Mr. Evans, the vice-president in charge of operations, and got what then seemed to be a tremendously big story—indeed, it was played up on the front page—of the purchase of fifty new and improved locomotives, a purchase that ran well into the millions of dollars.

Perhaps the best series of stories I got out of the railroad world is illustrative not only of the manners and morals of the time in the business world but also of that peculiar relationship which newspaper reporters have ever held sacred and have ever exploited to the full—that of the confidential guardianship of the secret leak.

At that time the Southern Railway and the Illinois Central Railroad had begun to compete for shipments of tobacco from the Kentucky Dark Patch—shipments designed for export to Europe. These shipments were sent from three great centers: Paducah and Owensboro on the Ohio River to the west of Louisville and, in a smaller degree, Louisville itself. The tobaccos of the Dark Patch, from these towns, and from Russellville, Kentucky, and Clarksville, Tennessee, were purchased in the main by governmental tobacco monopolies of Austria-Hungary, Italy, and Germany. The resident buyers from these governments established at these centers made their purchases and then consigned the shipments to the ports where they usually were picked up by ships of their own nationality.

The competition of these two railroads to the ports of New Orleans, Louisiana, Mobile, Alabama, and Brunswick and Savannah, Georgia, began to annoy the railroads which were served by the great ports of New York and the scarcely smaller export centers of Philadelphia and Baltimore. Acting under orders from above and beyond the immediate environment of Louisville, the freight agents of all the railroads formed a tobacco export-rate committee. That committee met in the office of Mr. Fitzgerald, a general freight agent of the Southern Railway. Now Mr. Fitzgerald was an amiable gentleman, white-haired and white-mustached, of courtly manner, and, as I had ordinarily known him, as uncommunicative as Milton H. Simth or the Sphinx. I was conscientious about my work. I went every day, no matter how unrewarding, to every person the city editor had told me I ought to see; and so every day I went to see Mr. Fitzgerald. He always saw me; he always asked me to sit down; he always offered me a cigar—but he never told me any news.

One afternoon as I went into his office, perhaps an hour later than usual, I was astonished to see there several gentlemen all fairly well known to me, at least by sight, leaving his office. They were the freight agents of a good many of the railroads. After they left, I was dumbfounded when Mr. Fitzgerald's secretary told me in the hearing of some of the men that Mr. Fitzgerald had no news and was too busy to see me. I was dismayed, but there was nothing for me to do but to leave. I went down in the elevator with Mr. Newman of the Monon Route and Mr. Ryan of the Baltimore and Ohio. I asked them for news, because I had missed them in my afternoon rounds. There was no news.

That night after supper I was summoned to the office telephone. Now the telephone was not used very much in those days as a news-gathering piece of equipment. It was not trusted, for one thing, and the telephone habit had not grown upon us. A lady's voice at the other end asked me if it would be possible for me to come out to a certain house at a certain number on Third Avenue to see Mr. Fitzgerald. I said that I would be glad to come. I went out and was received in the drawing-room of a fairly sumptuous mansion by the urbane Mr. Fitzgerald. He offered me the inevitable cigar and the invariable invitation to have a seat. Mr. Fitzgerald asked me if he could rely upon my discretion. I told him that he could. He asked me if he could rely upon my confidence to the extent that I would not disclose to anyone in authority at *The Courier-Journal* that he had sent for me and wanted to talk with me. I told him that I certainly would keep the secret. Then he unfolded the tale. It was that all the freight agents, acting under orders, and all of them but two acting quite willingly, were elaborating a new scheme of rates for export tobacco which would make it all but impossible for the Illinois Central or the Southern Railway to handle through shipments of tobacco and would cut off the southern ports entirely from the traffic. One or two technical questions were involved wherein competitive railroads were struggling over details of the scheme; and there was implicit the rivalry of New York, Philadelphia, and Baltimore, all standing together at the expense of the southern ports, but, of course, each trying to do the best for itself in the arrangement.

The next morning I had about a column and a half on the front page of *The Courier-Journal.* I was not prepared for the consternation that it had caused when the next afternoon I went from railroad office to railroad office. I discreetly went into Mr. Fitzgerald's office as usual and was told that Mr. Fitzgerald was busy and could not see me. I could hear voices from behind the partition, and I suspected that the freight agents were again assembled. Again, earlier in the afternoon, I had seen two or three of them, and each had cross-examined me about the story, each had tried to make me believe without directly saying so that somebody was joking with me, and each had tried to give me the impression that the story was utterly untrue. But that night I went out and had another talk with Mr. Fitzgerald. Again the front page. And so on for more than a week. After four or five days the stories got to be juicy indeed. I told exactly what went on at the meetings. I told how the finger of suspicion as to the informer had shifted from one to another; how Mr. Newman of the Monon had been accused of talking to me and how indignantly he had denied it; and how Mr. Ryan of the Baltimore and Ohio had fallen under suspicion because he had been particularly friendly with me and how the redheaded Mr. Ryan had erupted with indignation. But never— not once—did any of those there suspect that it was the grave and reverend seignior who sat at the head of the table who was the source of the leak.

The upshot of it all was that the effort to instal the new export tobacco freight tariff was abandoned, and the Illinois Central and the Southern kept their share of the business. I have no idea whether or not the higher-ups in the Southern Railway ever knew just what Mr. Fitzgerald had done. I am sure that until this moment I have never disclosed it to anybody; but now, after fifty years, it will do no harm.

This business occasionally got me into trouble. One day I went into Mr. Ryan's office, he of the Baltimore and Ohio. He picked up the telephone and conducted a long conversation in which he let it be known that there was something going on that would make a juicy bit of news so far as railroads were concerned. I was completely convinced that he had done it deliberately in my hearing so that I could write the story and yet to be able to say that he had not directly told me. I did it. Mr. Ryan was outraged. He said that I had violated a confidence. He complained to the city editor and the managing editor, and I could only plead my interpretation of what went on at the time. Later, although Mr. Ryan was perfectly furious, he did admit to me that, perhaps in view of other things that had happened, I was justified in believing that he was deliberately revealing a story to me. However, the instance so shocked me that I thereafter was careful to make sure that accidental leaks were consciously given, and I never thereafter took advantage of an accidental disclosure such as that.

Once one of the great whiskey dealers on Main Street who shall be nameless gave me a story about the purchase of a half-dozen Blue Grass distilleries by one of the huge companies that was engaged in assembling plants for the whiskey trust. He asked me not to use his name and to keep his part in it quite confidential. Of course, I respected completely this character's request for confidence. Mr. Platt asked me where I got the story. He was not entirely uninterested, because he had considered buying some of the stock of one of the distilleries involved in the deal, and he knew that the publication of the news would put the price out of his reach. Nevertheless, he used the story, and I kept the secret.

A day or two later, to my great astonishment, the man who had told me the story made a complaint to Mr. Ford, the managing editor, saying that I had abused his confidence, that he had told me an unsubstantiated rumor of the proposed distillery deal, and that I had gone all out and printed it as a fact. It subsequently turned out that he had been suspected and accused and in his fright had thought that I had betrayed his name. At any rate, he confessed his fault and tried to put the blame on me. It was unfortunate from the point of view of the promoters of the merger, because, after the news got out, some of the smaller stockholders were unwilling to sell at the shakedown prices. When I explained the matter to Mr. Platt and Mr. Ford, they were convinced. I promptly marched myself down Main Street, walked into his establishment, and, standing in the aisle between the great barrels of whiskey, properly bawled him out regardless of the fact that he was a much older man than I, a rich man, and a most eminent and prominent citizen. The next day there was delivered to me at Coker's a case of a dozen quarts of excellent whiskey. I am glad to say, although it cost me a dollar to employ a colored expressman, the whiskey went back within the hour. That was one place that I was supposed to go on my daily rounds that I never saw again.

What now strikes me after a half-century as peculiar is that it never once occurred to me, as it had to each of my predecessors, that in this Main Street swirl and whirl of mergers and dollars I might make some money. My predecessors all had benefited from information that they had received and tips deliberately given and perhaps deliberately sought. They had put very small sums of money saved from their very meager salaries into these speculations that had

worked out for them very well indeed; and, above them, Mr. Vreeland, the assistant managing editor, and Mr. Ford, the managing
editor, also were well aware of what was going on and did not
neglect their business opportunities. It must have been that I had
no mind for business. It may have been that I had no interest in
speculation. It may merely have been that, when I was born, the
gaming spirit was left out of me utterly. I never liked to play a game.
I never liked to see a game played.

I well remember in that spring of 1903, when the great classic,
the Kentucky Derby, was to be run at Churchill Downs, the day
of the great race came on my day off. I was the envy of every reporter on the paper. All the others had to work. I was free to go
to the races, and, of course, as in all things of that sort, it would have
cost me nothing, because I could get a pass. One of the reporters,
Howard Robinson, was acutely depressed by the fact that he could
not see the race—he was Kentucky-born but never had been in Louisville before on Derby day. I went to Mr. Platt and bowled him over
by asking if I might swap places so Robbie could see the race. He
sat down suddenly, blanched, and looked up and said, "Yes, but my
God!" And that was why I never saw a Kentucky Derby. And that,
or something like that, is the reason why I never thought of using
the information I gained or the acquaintances I made on the Main
Street run in order to improve my personal fortunes.

I went to work on the Main Street job at one o'clock in the afternoon. I tried always to finish my calls by four. I tried, if possible, to
finish writing my notes by five and then to steal the hour between
five and six, or what was left of it, for my cronies at the *Weinstube*
or some other *divertissement.*

After supper, if there was some unfinished copy, I made away
with that and then started out on my night run of the hotels. I would
go to the great Galt House, eastward on Main Street at the very
extremity of the business district, but approached at night through
block after block of dark whiskey warehouses, banks, and office buildings, a little island of light in a sea of gloom. The Galt House had
been and still was, in a way, a great hotel. Built before the Civil
War, it was not so grand and glorious as the Maxwell House in
Nashville, but it had great pretense and a great history. Charles
Dickens had immortalized it, Harriet Beecher Stowe had patronized

it, and Mark Twain knew it and wrote about it. Then, long blocks to the west through more gloom of the closed wholesale and financial district, to Seelbach's and the Louisville Hotel. Thereafter, I went to some of the smaller ones, such as the Fifth Avenue Hotel. When I had done all I could by interviewing the clerks, by hanging about the lobbies, by examining the registers, and by talking to persons chance-met in the bars or in the lobbies, I had the material wherewith to make up my column. It wasn't very good, even as hotel columns then went. It certainly was bounded too much by matter-of-factness. I occasionally threw in a pseudonym for a man who did not care to be quoted personally, but I was too much on the conscientious side with respect to pure invention. Yet, Platt said that it was all right, and he seemed to like it. It must have been better than my predecessors had made it, for it attracted the attention of Mr. Watterson.

Mr. Watterson was born in the District of Columbia in 1841. His father at that time was a representative in Congress from Tennessee, the district that centered in Maury County and in Columbia, the home of my maternal ancestors. Mr. Harvey Watterson was born in the adjoining county of Bedford and grew up to the practice of law in Shelbyville. He served in the Twenty-sixth and Twenty-seventh Congresses. He was a Union man with southern sympathies during the war, one of a great number so mixed up. After the war he was appointed by President Andrew Johnson to serve on a commission to investigate "conditions in the states lately in rebellion," and thereafter he practiced law in Washington. In 1880 he moved to Louisville and became a member of the editorial staff of *The Courier-Journal,* of which his more distinguished son was then editor-in-chief.

When young Henry was eighteen, he got a job on the *Washington State,* a Democratic newspaper, which he served for three years. In 1861 he became the first and the sole correspondent of the newly created Associated Press in Washington. It was in that capacity that he stood on the platform on March 4, 1861, when Abraham Lincoln was about to take the oath of office as President of the United States; and it was to the young Watterson that Mr. Lincoln handed his hat to be held during the solemn ceremony.

But young Henry Watterson was a southerner, and it was but a matter of weeks after that great event that he left Washington to enlist in the Confederate Army. He was too nearsighted to be a combat soldier, even if his arms had not been too short to admit of drill according to Hardee's *Tactics*. So he became a staff officer—a prototype of a psychological warrior of the twentieth-century ruthlessness. He served on the staff of several distinguished generals but returned to his vocational love to edit the *Chattanooga Rebel*. After the war he went to Louisville, and in 1868, with Walter N. Haldeman as partner and monetary angel, he purchased the *Louisville Journal*, consolidated it with the *Courier*, and became the editor-in-chief of *The Courier-Journal*, in which position he served for a half-century, until his death in 1921.

While he spent his boyhood and youth mostly in Washington, he kept up with his Columbia associations and his Nashville friends. Although he had worked on a newspaper in Washington, he did not consider journalism to be his vocation. He played the piano, and it was his ambition to become a concert pianist, and that despite the fact that he was extremely nearsighted and that both his arms were so short as to give him almost an appearance of deformity. Playing the piano in Nashville, he fell in with the younger musical set of the town. Among them at that time, in 1861, just after the war drums began to thrum, was a very lively redheaded, green-eyed girl who sang.

Mr. Watterson was very much taken by Miss Fannie Johnson, and she was much intrigued with his conversational charm as well as his musical skill. One thing led to another quite naturally, and Miss Johnson, who had just broken an engagement with a recent graduate of West Point because he, an Ohio boy, had declined to resign his commission and join the Confederate cause, was quite ready to accept another swain, as the saying was, "on the bounce." Henry Watterson and Fannie Johnson became engaged to be married. Thereupon Miss Johnson's father, John Johnson, a builder of the Louisville and Nashville Railroad, a rich man, and one who believed that wealth was the product of hard work and who had little use for the arts, struck in with a thunderous note. "I will not let my daughter marry any God-damned piano-player in the world!"

Perhaps the attachment had been only an affair "on the bounce." Perhaps young Henry, too, was not too deeply engaged. Perhaps it was only that the war came on and the young man left for the army. And maybe it was because Miss Johnson's father was able then to exercise the authority that he arrogated to himself by his action. At any rate, the engagement was broken off.

Now it so happened that Miss Fannie Johnson was my mother's first cousin. She was a sister to Mrs. Mary Paul Johnson Maguire, who, as I have set down in these recollections, was my mentor and sponsor in Nashville.

As soon as I went to Louisville to work on *The Courier-Journal,* Cousin Mary Paul wrote to Cousin Fannie, then Mrs. James Y. Leigh of Norfolk. Cousin Fannie promptly sat down and wrote to Mr. Watterson that her cousin had deigned to honor *The Courier-Journal* by accepting a position as a reporter on that newspaper and she trusted that Mr. Watterson was sensible of that situation and would see to it that I was treated as one of my family lineage would necessarily deserve.

One morning I was summoned into The Presence. It was not Mr. Watterson's habit to send for cub reporters or to talk with the very newest addition to the staff. It somewhat startled the city editor, Mr. Platt. Mr. Platt asked me if I knew why in the world "Marse Henry" was sending for me. Of course I didn't, and I must say that I went in fear and trepidation.

It took but a moment for him to put me at my ease, and I spent more than a half-hour with him. All the time was devoted to giving him the news of his old flame. He had not heard of her or from her for years, and he wanted to know all about her and her older sister, Mary Paul, and her younger sister, Ida Gordon. When I told him that Cousin Fannie, according to family gossip, was still engaged in singing in the choir and in fighting the Civil War as the treasurer-general of the United Daughters of the Confederacy, he began to overflow with anecdotes and with reminiscences and utterly astonished me by the story of his early ambition to be a pianist, something I had never heard. There was a wistful quality in what he said, and he seemed to pour out from an old spring a spate of words that jokingly but nonetheless seriously expressed his frustration and disappointment that things had turned out so that his great career as a pianist had been interrupted by what at that particular moment, and that moment only, he attempted to write down as a much lesser career as a journalist. The upshot of it was that I became in a way a sort of pet of "Marse Henry." Once in a while he sent for me to give me a tip on a story that he thought was worthy of the news columns. Once in a while, not often, he invited me into those little discussions with his great friend Mr. Macauley of Macauley's Theater.

Once, I remember, I went to him in pursuit of a news story. A new hotel was projected on Fourth Avenue by the Seelbach brothers, and they had decided to name it "The Henry Watterson." Mr. Watterson promptly rejected the honor. I was assigned to write the story and went directly to "Marse Henry" to ask him why. He said that he didn't believe that a hotel ought to be named after a living person and that he had suggested to the Messrs. Seelbach that they name it "The William Preston." Naturally, I asked, "Why did you suggest William Preston?"

Then I felt the full force of his outraged wrath. He railed at me and said that I, like every other new reporter, thought the world began the day I got a job on a newspaper; that I knew no history; that I knew nothing whatever about what happened day before yesterday, let alone last week. Then he proceeded to tell me in great detail who William C. Preston was—what a great name he had left in the annals of the state of Kentucky—and stormed at me as an ignoramus.

I stuck to my ground, although I really think I would have preferred to flee. But, when he was through, I was able to tell him that I did know about General Preston but that I asked the question simply to find out from him why he, Henry Watterson, had selected William Preston as the Kentuckian to be honored in the name of the new hotel rather than some other of the great Kentuckians. He was mollified and gave me the story.

In the course of time my hotel column attracted Mr. Watterson's attention. He asked me about it several times and once or twice suggested as a good subject for an interview the name of some person who had come to town. Some of these interviews turned out very well; and, when they did, Mr. Watterson was pleased, for he liked to have his newspaper honor his personal friends. His was the era of personal journalism in the sense not only that the editor-in-chief transmitted his personality to the columns of the paper but also that those columns reflected very frequently his personal likes and dislikes.

One afternoon Mr. Ford, the managing editor, and Mr. Platt, the city editor, and I were asked to come to see Mr. Watterson. He told my superiors that he had been noticing the hotel column and that he thought it could be greatly improved if it were not so narrowly confined to the actual reporting of things that I discovered on my nightly rounds of the Louisville inns and hostels but that it might be the conveyance for other chitchat and gossip. In other words, he said he would set aside a column on the editorial page for me, and, what is more, he had the title for that column.

It was "On Dit." It was the perfect caption for a gossip column. It gave me a great thrill. I thought at first that here was the place for me to try my wings and display my wares as a writing man. I did put in a good many things that had no relation whatever to the hotels. But the city editor and his assistant didn't like it. It wasn't news. It was outside the scope of what they considered the business of the city room. And so these gossipy inventions I essayed were blue penciled and failed to find their way into the column.

I was so orderly in my hierarchical relationships with my bosses that it never occurred to me to go over the head of my immediate superior. I submitted the column, and, while the headline still read "On Dit," it was nothing more than it had been before, simply the news of the hotels. Thus I had my chance to become one of the first gossip columnists in the United States. I had that chance under the sponsorship of one of the greatest journalists of the time. But I lost it because I was well disciplined, because I was obedient, because I lacked the flare for adventure in the written word. I submitted to the traditions of the city room as they then existed.

In recording that failure some fifty years after the event, I feel pretty sure that I share the feelings that were expressed to me by Mr. Watterson on the first occasion when I met him, his wistful yearning for his lost career as a concert pianist. Of course the chances are that I, with my puritanical upbringing and my discipline of obedience and conformity to custom, would not have made very much of a gossip columnist. He then saw, and I now see, only that our great careers had been interrupted by a chance circumstance and not by reason of our own inadequacies.

As the summer came on, I grew more and more weary. The long hours told on me. I did not get enough sleep. I did not get enough recreation. And, I fear, I was beginning to be affected by a sort of self-pity.

[310]

One day in June, 1903, I got a telegram from Buford Goodwin, the managing editor of the *Nashville News,* an afternoon paper and a rival of my own beloved *Nashville Banner.* He offered me twenty-five dollars a week to come to Nashville to become city editor of the *Nashville Daily News.* I accepted by return wire, resigned my job to Mr. Platt, and told him I was leaving for Nashville just as soon as he would let me off. That turned out to be in just one week. Platt knew that I was suffering greatly from the long hours and forgave me at once.

The increase in salary of five dollars a week was not unwelcome, but what meant most to me was that I was going back to Nashville, where I had many friends and many kinsfolk, to a place that I knew. But, more than that, I was going back to an afternoon newspaper.

CHAPTER XVII

BRIEF RETURNS TO
NASHVILLE AND LOUISVILLE

Back in Nashville I was faced with two problems. One was how to overcome the supreme distaste for me and my activities exhibited by my old chief, Marmaduke B. Morton. He had no use whatever for the *Nashville News,* which was the rival of the *Banner.* He didn't think it was quite cricket for the *News* to have set up its offices directly across the street from the *Banner,* and he particularly condemned the habit of the *News* in attempting to recruit staff members from among the employees of the *Banner* and its alumni. The other problem was how to live up to the title of "city editor" when my staff was so small as hardly to justify the dignity and when my duties ranged over a much wider area than the title of the job indicated.

Despite these troubles, I was inordinately proud of the job. I was glad to be a city editor. I thought it was the beginning of my upward march into the higher realms of journalism. Actually, although I had the task of assigning particular tasks to the three or four reporters whom we had, there was little to do, because each of them had all he could possibly manage in covering ordinary routine assignments. Then also I discovered that the reporters on that particular paper were not so eager to take night assignments as I had been in my early days and, indeed, of late afternoons and evenings, they mightily liked their ease.

I found, too, that I was to be telegraph editor as well. The *News* had no regular wire service. It depended upon a "pony" report that was filed in Cincinnati by somebody (connected with the United Press or its ancestor) in the office of the Scripps-McRae newspaper, the *Cincinnati Post.* Sometimes these pony reports were simply skeletonized dispatches which it was my duty to expand. Sometimes, when the person in Cincinnati was too rushed or too lazy to condense, he would file in full a sufficient number of items to make up the daily grist, which, as

I recall it, was only a few hundred words. That meant, then, for that day we could have a few items of news from the outside world; but the method of their selection was most curious and spotty, and we were apt to be scooped by the Associated Press across the street on some of the most important happenings. Nevertheless, it was my job to pick up these pieces of "flimsy" as they were dropped on my desk by a messenger from the Postal Telegraph Company and to try to make out of them something that would resemble, faintly at least, a wire news report for the day.

There was another trouble that I had not anticipated. The *Nashville News* was on the financial rocks. Its managing editor, Buford Goodwin, a good friend of mine, was energetic and industrious and had a bulldog determination to make good. But money was hard to get, and pay rolls were exceedingly difficult to meet. The *News* had been founded by Colonel Jere Baxter to support the subsidy sought from the city of Nashville for the Tennessee Central Railroad. After succeeding in that venture, Colonel Baxter characteristically turned his attention to other things, and the *News* languished.

Colonel Baxter had brought to Nashville from Paris an editor-in-chief, a man who greatly impressed the town as he greatly influenced me. His name was Anthony Van Leer Polk. He was a member of the great Polk family of Maury County, the family that had turned out Presidents, bishops, generals, and leading citizens of all the professions, including journalism. Mr. Polk had lost interest in the *News*. He rarely came to the office but wrote his editorials in greater comfort up at the Hermitage Club. My salary was twenty-five dollars a week. Buford's was thirty dollars. We paid the editor-in-chief thirty-five dollars for a few editorials, such that Buford and I thought we could throw together in odd moments. So in solemn conclave, we—the managing editor and the city editor—decided to fire our superior, the editor-in-chief.

We provided ourselves with railroad and Pullman passes from Nashville to New York. With the greatest of difficulty we got together three weeks' pay in advance. Then, one afternoon, just as soon as the paper was put to bed, Goodwin and I proceeded to march up Church Street, turn in at High, and invade the sacred premises of the Hermitage Club. There we found our editor-in-chief quite at ease.

Buford opened up along this line: "Mr. Polk, as you know, the

News is in very sore straits. We are not at all sure we can continue publication. It is extremely difficult for us to pay the printers, the stereotypers, and the pressmen, let alone the editorial staff. We have regretfully come to the conclusion that it would be to the best interest of the *News* if you were to resign."

Then came the astonishing reply. "Buford, I have been trying for several weeks to invent an excuse. I am tired. I want to go."

Then Buford said, "Mr. Polk, I can arrange to get you a railroad pass and a Pullman pass to New York, and perhaps I could not only pay you this week's salary but scrape up another week's."

"Don't trouble yourself, Buford. If you would just get the passes for me and pay me this week's salary, it will be quite enough. I can manage, and I will be delighted to turn everything over to you. I believe you can do a better job of it than I have done."

So, in a wondering haze of excitement and great accomplishment, Buford and I left. The passes we had. We had needed only one-third of the $105.00 we had raised. The *News* was $70.00 to the good.

One day precisely three weeks later the Postal Telegraph messenger dropped a piece of flimsy on my desk. I picked it up. It was one of the days when somebody in Cincinnati was either very busy or very tired. The dispatch was in full. It had not been skeletonized. It read: "Kiel, Germany.—The Emperor William II embarked today on the Imperial yacht 'Hohenzollern' for a six weeks' cruise in the North Sea. His only guest was Mr. Van Leer Polk of Tennessee." The yell I let out would have done credit to any Rebel soldier or Comanche brave. It brought Goodwin running. We hardly could believe our eyes, but there it was.

Polk's father, as the Civil War threatened, had prudently invested a considerable sum in English sterling and French francs, so that, when the war was over, he was in funds, something quite unusual for even a rich southerner of that day. During the war a French military attaché, the Comte de Charette, had accompanied Hood's army on its march northward to its final defeat and dispersal in the Battle of Nashville. On that journey through Maury County the young French officer, a person of great charm and wit, met a Maury County girl, also witty and charming as well as beautiful. She was Antoinette Polk. Shortly after the war ended, the Polk family went to France, and Miss Antoinette Polk became the Comtesse de Charette. She took up her residence somewhere on the Riviera in a place where mediatized members of former royal houses maintained establishments to which the young princelings of the reigning royal houses frequently were sent for holidays.

The Comtesse de Charette's younger brother, Van Leer Polk, grew up there and spent his adolescent years in that atmosphere. As a matter of course he became very well acquainted with other boys of his own age, particularly with Prince Wilhelm of Germany and Prince Humberto of Italy; and he also had an opportunity to meet some of the older generation and became a very close friend of Albert Edward, the Prince of Wales, and Leopold, the crown prince of Belgium.

After Polk had reached manhood, he occasionally would come home to Tennessee and get a job on a newspaper or sometimes run for the legislature or take some other part in politics; and then, after a year or two in his home state, he would go back to Europe again to associate with his royal and imperial friends. There is more, much more, to the saga of Van Leer Polk, but to me personally he stands out as the only boss I ever fired.

There was another editor on the *News*—the sporting editor. He had been a friend of mine since even before my journalistic days when we both used to hang around the soda fountain at De Moville's Drugstore. When he was a reporter opposite me on the *Nashville News* and I was on the *Banner,* we occasionally used to engage in some surreptitious dickering. He would be assigned to some political meeting or other, which he heartily hated, and I would be assigned to cover a sporting event, which, to say the least, did not in any wise engage my interest. So we used to swap jobs quite unbeknownst to our bosses, and he would cover the sporting event for me and I would cover the political meeting for him. Now I found him sporting editor and nominally subject to my jurisdiction as city editor. Needless to say, I never gave him any instructions. In the first place, I knew that I was incompetent in that field. In the second place, it would have done no good whatever. He was a man who was then at the beginning of a long and successful career. As a sportswriter, as a versifier, and in time—then far, far in the future—as a showman of sorts—Grantland Rice.

One thing about the *Nashville News* I did like. It was an afternoon newspaper. Sometimes I had to work late in the afternoon, it was true. Sometimes I had to go out and cover night missions. But ordinarily, when the paper was put to bed, I was through except for an hour or two's chores getting ready for tomorrow's deadline. Then I could go home, or I could visit with my friends, or I could relax; but, more than that, I could go to bed early in the evening and sleep without any danger of interruption until the hour of six next morning.

But it was not to last long. In fact, it lasted only four weeks.

Then I got a letter from General William B. Haldeman, one of the two Haldeman brothers who owned *The Courier-Journal* and its afternoon edition, the *Louisville Times*. General Haldeman offered me the job of city editor of the *Times*. The salary was no more than I had been getting, twenty-five a week; but I had a feeling that in Nashville the regularity of that stipend was precarious, to say the least, and that in Louisville it would be monstrous regular. I accepted. I resigned. Buford said he didn't blame me, and in a month's time I was on my way back to Louisville. Thus ended the *Nashville News* interlude.

II

I was going back to Louisville to become a city editor. For about four weeks I already had been a city editor, but the situation on the *Nashville News,* as I had intimated, was cozy and private, even if insecure and undistinguished. The responsibilities laid upon me as an executive were slight, indeed, since the responsibility of every pencil mark I made was shared with the managing editor, Buford Goodwin.

The first intimation I had that my presence was desired on the *Louisville Times* came in the form of a letter from Robert J. McBryde. I am afraid that, when I was on *The Courier-Journal,* I paid not too much attention to the affairs of its prosperous and lively afternoon edition, the *Times*. I knew, of course, that the Brothers Haldeman were the owners of *The Courier-Journal* and therefore necessarily of the *Times*. I presume that I knew that General William B. Haldeman gloried in the title of "editor" of the *Times,* just as Henry Watterson did in the title of "editor" of *The Courier-Journal*.

I had heard that General Haldeman was engaged in upsetting precedents and, indeed, that he had supplanted the great Emmett Logan and his assistant, Charles Dobbs, with a youthful college graduate, Robert J. McBryde, lately from the University of Virginia, who had been put in charge of the editorial page. Long editorials, that is, relatively long editorials, began to prevail over the pert paragraphs that had been the speciality of Messrs. Logan and Dobbs. And it was from Mr. McBryde that I first heard that my presence was desired on the *Times*. Bob wrote to ask me if I would be interested in coming to Louisville as city editor and that the job would pay twenty-five dollars a week. I replied that I would be very much interested, indeed, but that I was getting twenty-five dollars a week in Nashville and that I thought the Louisville job was worth thirty.

Of course my trouble with my health, my difficulty in contending with the long hours which had driven me to the verge of exhaustion, was something known not to me alone but to others. The response I got from my gentle insistence upon as much as thirty dollars a week came not from Bob McBryde but from the great General Haldeman himself. He stuck firmly to twenty-five dollars and put up to me the question of my health. His letter read in part:

> Those who know best as to your newspaper capabilities refer to you most highly, but there has been a doubt expressed to me as to whether your health was sufficiently good to stand the wear and tear of the work that devolves upon the City Editor of *The Times*. I wish you to write me frankly as to your own belief in this matter. You can have the place if you think you can stand the pressure and the salary comes to what you will expect. Mr. Baird receives $25.00 a week and that salary will be paid to you.

In my naïve way I accepted every word in this letter at its face value. But it was not long after I got to Louisville that I found there were things that I should have seen between the lines. For instance, there was no mention in it of Mr. Robert W. Brown, known to me as the managing editor of the *Times,* and therefore in the normal course of events a person who would have a good deal to do with the hiring of a new city editor. In view of the phraseology of the letter, it is perhaps natural that I did not know that Johnny Baird was not retiring voluntarily from the position of city editor but that he was being pushed out. Nor did I so much as suspect that my coming would be a matter of very grave disappointment to the assistant city editor, Mr. Isaac Marcosson, who long had confidently counted upon succeeding Mr. Baird.

Nevertheless, I acted at once. I accepted the job at the prescribed salary and wrote to Mr. Haldeman that I was sure my health would permit me to stand up to the pressure and that the only trouble I had, really, was on account of the long hours imposed by the morning newspaper work. With respect to that particular item, I was able to refer to one of my few chance conversations with General Halde-man, when, over a glass of beer at Al's, he had quite generously ex-pressed his sympathy not only with me but with all persons who had to slave the fourteen hours or more a day required by morning news-paper work.

When I got to Louisville and turned up for duty bright and early at seven o'clock on a Monday morning, I felt as though I had blun-dered into a funeral. Mr. Baird was standing, not sitting, at his desk. He turned it over to me with the sad, sweet smile which characterized almost his every action but which at that moment seemed to me especially intended as a gesture toward me. He took a place at a table near by to which seemingly he had been assigned—or rather consigned—to a position of innocuous desuetude, a forced retirement without diminution of salary but also without definition of duty. Ike Marcosson barely spoke to me. Some of the other reporters who were in the room came up apparently for their assignments. They all knew that I knew nothing whatever about the established routine. I saw at once that it was now or never with me. I sensed that, if I did not take command and that instantly, I would be forever lost. Summoning as much of a mask of *savoir-faire* as I could command to conceal my genuine dismay and fright, I said: "Mr. Marcosson, hereafter the assistant city editor will give the reporters their ordinary assignments. In case of any difficulty or dispute, please refer the matter to me."

In all the long years that the gentle Baird had sat in that desk he never had given an order. In all the long years that Ike had been assistant city editor he had never received an order. He, too, was nonplussed and set back. He, too, had to make an instant decision. He blinked rapidly behind his thick-lensed pince-nez, began to stam-mer something, swallowed, and then came out sputteringly and stut-teringly with, "Very good, sir!" And you may be sure that for the next thirty minutes I was all ears listening to a disgruntled assistant giving the new boss his primary and elemental lessons in the routine of a job for which the assistant was convinced the boss was unfit and unprepared.

That over, I glanced in the next room and saw Mr. Brown, the managing editor, bustling about. I walked in to see him. He looked up. He did not smile. That in itself was something to be remembered, for Bob Brown was a professional smiler. He was the hail-fellow-well-met who had a cheery word for everybody.

I mean up until then. He had no cheery word for me. He did not ask me to sit down. He had said, "Hello, Louis," in his first non-smiling address; but, that over, he deserted the use of my first name and said: "Brownlow, you know very well that you are not here by any act of mine. You ought to know that I disapprove of the whole business. I don't think Johnny Baird ought to have been put on the shelf. I don't think Bob McBryde has any business interfering with my running of the paper. I am sure you will regret having been bumped into taking this job by Bob McBryde."

Dismayed, but at bay, I responded that I had been offered the job not by Mr. McBryde but by General Haldeman himself. That took Bob aback. He had thought that perhaps my coming had been a part of the usurpation of his job undertaken by the tall, handsome, and far-too-well-educated McBryde. While he had known, of course, that General Haldeman had approved, he had not known that General Haldeman had personally intervened. I showed him General Haldeman's letter. Then he smiled. But it was a wintry smile. And I knew that I could expect no support whatever from my managing editor, technically my immediate superior and according to all the orthodox tenets of journalistic hierarchical arrangements my absolute boss.

If I was thus confronted by disapproval from my immediate subordinates as well as my immediate superior, you may be sure I fared little better at the hands of the reportorial staff. They, all of them, adored Johnny Baird and with excellent reason. A lovable man, mild-mannered and gentle, he sympathized with them in their troubles. He rarely raised his voice at all and never in reproof. He liked his boys, and he did not suspect that in many ways he was the prisoner of their affections. There was Ed Fitzpatrick, who did the city hall, a stolid and thoroughgoing reporter noted for his accuracy as well as for the lack of spark in his writing. There was Roger Burlingame, a rough-and-tumble police reporter. There was his elder brother, Paul Anson Burlingame, the top general reporter and the holder of the title of "star." There was poor discouraged Mrs. Gregory, the society reporter. There were others. They were willing to take the routine assignments Marcosson had given them. They shuffled out on their rounds, but there was no spirit in them. My being pushed into the position of city editor by the editor and owner without the consent of the managing editor and over the heads of all others had filled them with deep resentment, which was not at all relieved by the fact that there was a great rivalry between the *Times* and *The Courier-Journal;* and the imposition of a *Courier-Journal* man, or rather a mere boy, over the local staff of the *Times* was in itself an offense, an injury hardly to be forgiven.

The style of makeup of the *Louisville Times* was peculiar. The *Times* boasted of having the largest circulation of any afternoon paper in the South. Its style was to have no style at all. It was a paper exceptionally devoted to headlines; but, unless there was some terrific calamity or catastrophe, its heads were always one column wide. We broke a column rule only for a national catastrophe. And yet anybody writing a headline was free to write just as he pleased. There was no orderly style. There were no number ones, number twos, number threes. There were no single-line, no double-line decks. One wrote just whatever popped into his head, and then the composing-room set it up in whatever style any particular hand-set printer might desire, for at that time the *Times's* heads still were set by hand.

That meant that anybody could write heads, and write them rapidly. On the first day, then, after seeing pieces of copy dumped first on Ike's desk and then on mine by reporters a little bit puzzled as to where they should go, I seized a pencil and began what to me was the hideous task of writing irregular headlines and editing a very large part of the local copy myself, leaving Ike free to do his other work. For, besides being assistant city editor, he also was dramatic critic and book-reviewer.

The copy was all written in pencil. The typewriting machines that had invaded the city room of *The Courier-Journal* were yet few in number in the city room of the *Times*. It is true that Ike wrote his dramatic criticisms on the typewriter and that Mrs. Gregory pounded out part of her society news on another. But most of the copy was written at the city hall or at the courthouse or on the fly. Reporters brought it in themselves or sent it in by messenger boys who had been dispatched to points of collection.

It was not difficult for me to discern that I was in the middle of a bad fix. It was obvious that there was some justification for the resentment. At the same time, I was convinced that there must be some good reason why General Haldeman had upset the applecart. Perhaps that was a conclusion all the easier reached by me because I most certainly was one of the beneficiaries of the turnover. Therefore, I set about as promptly as could be to discover what was the matter.

In a way, I already knew. From the vantage point of *The Courier-Journal* city room, with my wits sharpened by the jealousies that always existed between morning and afternoon newspapers, especially when they were under the same ownership and published in the same plant, I had noticed that the opposition afternoon newspaper, the *Louisville Evening Post,* was creeping up on the *Times.* I deduced that perhaps General Haldeman had noticed that. With that disdain that we of the editorial staff then looked upon the business office, I did not inquire with respect to circulation. I did not inquire with respect to advertising. I only looked at what happened to the news columns.

The *Evening Post* was edited and, I believe, owned by Richard W. Knott, a conservative Gold Democrat who was gradually but not too slowly becoming a Republican. Its managing editor was Boyle Gilbert Boyle, "Gil" to all and sundry. Its city editor was Lewis Humphrey. On its local staff it had some notable reporters. There was Cleves Kincaid, who was the opposite number of Ike Marcosson. There were Charles Musgrove and the industrious self-driving, meticulously accurate Tom Wallace.

In short, the *Post* was making things hot for the *Times.* Maybe that was something that General Haldeman wanted me to handle. I sought in vain for some counsel from Bob McBryde. He was having enough troubles of his own. Charlie Dobbs, his paragrapher, had not yet left for the *Insurance Field,* and he, McBryde, was up against Dobbs's sulky rebellion in the same way that I was up against that of my staff and my managing editor. It became increasingly clear to me that something had to be done and that it was up to me to do it.

Now, I had found out something of a scandal when I was on *The Courier-Journal;* and, while I may have deprecated its existence, I must confess I did not do much about it, for I did not want to get into a position of responsibility with respect to reporting police news.

But I had known while I was on *The Courier-Journal* that the police reporters of all four of the Louisville papers were saving a good deal of shoe leather and no little hard work by faking police news. This exercise in creative fiction certainly produced some pretty good stories. It certainly saved a lot of time and hard work. There was no overt agreement with respect to the practice. Indeed, every one of the reporters on all four of the newspapers, if he happened to run into a good tale, would endeavor by every means short of mayhem and manslaughter to keep it exclusive and thereby to score a scoop. But what was the use, so they seemed to have argued to themselves, of going out into the highways and the byways to discover news when one could find good stories within one's own head. However, this contrivance did require some sort of connivance above and beyond the profession. For instance, if *The Courier-Journal* came out in the morning with a whopping big tale, certainly both the afternoon newspapers would assign reporters to the follow-up. Therefore, even the fake story had to have an anchor outside.

A sample of such an anchor, and there were many such, was a certain physician down west in Portland who, despite the proclaimed ethics of his profession, was not adverse to such little advertising as might come his way if he got his name in the paper. So if one of the morning-paper reporters ran an item about a shooting or some other police story, the reporters of the succeeding newspapers would go into that particular doctor's office to see him. The good doctor always would have some fresh and additional details which would make the story stand up and which he had thoughtfully saved for the next round.

There was the time when Ike Harcourt of *The Courier-Journal*, being hard up for news, invented a tale about a man who was discovered unconscious on a street in the West End. He was carried by a passer-by into the office of the good doctor, whom I will call "Hamlin," which was not his name. There, after a careful examination, Dr. Hamlin discovered that the old gentleman, who was well dressed and apparently a man of circumstance, had been rendered unconscious because of the slow infiltration of a bullet into the cerebral cortex. On recovery of consciousness, the old gentleman was able to tell the story: The bullet was one that he had received from a rifle leveled by a Union soldier when he was serving in the Confederate Army in the Battle of Fort Donelson. All through Ike's story the boys in gray marched again. All through Ike's story the Stars and Bars waved again, and tears were squeezed from any reasonably good southern eye.

The next morning around eleven o'clock, when Ike arose and was preparing for breakfast, he discovered his father was in the act of putting on his hat and coat. Ike's father was an elderly man, a veteran of the Confederate Army, who had been confined to the house for many weeks by the infirmities instinct upon old age. Ike was astonished to find his father preparing to go out.

"Where are you going, father?"

"Well, I read in the paper this morning about an old comrade-in-arms who was found in the street and was taken to Dr. Hamlin's office. I am going down there to see him. I was standing by his side when that bullet hit him."

That cured Ike Harcourt, but it did not cure the disease.

As city editor of the *Times,* I soon made up my mind that it would be necessary for me to import some new reporters from other cities who not only would support me out of sheer loyalty as the boss who had given them the job but who also could be depended upon not to join the tacit conspiracy of faking. I calculated that a good hotfoot reporter getting about town and really hunting for news might be able to put over a considerable number of scoops. "Scoop" was the word we then used. It was some years before the old word gave way to "beat" and long before the paper publicly labeled their scoops or beats as "exclusive."

In the meantime I had picked up enough from Ike Marcosson, my resentful assistant, and from Johnny Baird, my mild and gentle predecessor, to know how to run the city room according to its ancient routine. I then made it my business to establish a new order in which the old routine would give way to a new one of which I would be the improviser and inventor and by that token the sole arbiter. In other words, I knew that I had to get on top of my job or lose it. What the *Louisville Times* had suffered from was an excessive degree of mildness. Mr. Brown, the managing editor, was usually concerned with things outside the office. He was a public relations man par excellence, but he was content to let internal affairs manage themselves. Mr. Baird, the city editor, never raised his voice, never pounded the table, and, as I have said before, never issued an order; and, therefore, he never had subjected himself to the inconvenience of having one of his orders disobeyed. I have heard tall tales of the "tough" city editors. I had myself experienced the administration of a not-too-gentle mentor, Marmaduke B. Morton. I made up my mind to get tough!

One day about a half-hour before the deadline for the city edition (it was in the summertime, and the windows were open) I heard a great clatter and commotion in Green Street just below the second-story window which was open at my back. I looked out. There had been a collision between a horse-drawn spring wagon and a street-car. The wagon had been filled with green groceries, which were spilled all over the street. A crowd was collecting. Someone was lying on the pavement, and it was evident that there had been an injury. I looked about the room. Not a single reporter was in sight, so I said, hardly thinking what I did, "Ike, run down there and get that story. I think we can make the city edition with it. Someone's hurt."

Ike drew himself up, glared at me through his thick lenses, and said, "I am the assistant city editor. I am not a reporter."

I looked at him blankly. I ran down the steps myself, got the story, came up, wrote it, and sent it to the composing-room. Then I said, "Ike, I want to talk to you."

He rose. I rose.

"Mr. Marcosson," I said with a summoned formality, "you are discharged. You will receive one week's extra pay. Your connection with the *Louisville Times* has already ceased."

Now, when this colloquy took place, the room was practically filled. It was only ten minutes until the deadline, and everybody was there. Marcosson said not a word. I resumed my seat. He stood staring and then silently turned to his desk. I said: "You may take all the time you want to clear out your personal papers from the desk. I will let Mr. Offutt know about the week's salary." He did not reply.

Twenty or thirty years later, when Mr. Marcosson was at the height of his popularity as a contributor to the *Saturday Evening Post* and pursued a most successful career in journalism and finance and was rated not only as the Little Brother of the Rich but one of the Rich himself, Ike told me that nothing that had ever happened in his life had been so fortunate as the fact that I fired him.

"Brownie"
1898

To Lewis Brownlow and a friendship that lasts throughout the years affectionately M. B. Morton

MARMADUKE B. MORTON OF THE *Banner*

HENRY WATTERSON OF *The Courier-Journal*

STAFF OF THE *Louisville Times* ON A SUNDAY PICNIC, SUMMER OF 1903

(*Left to right*): *seated:* Charles Dobbs, Editorial Writer; *bottom row, standing:* Edward Fitzpatrick; Mrs. Edward Fitzpatrick; Mrs. Charles Dobbs; Henry V. Escott, Jr.; Theodore Duncan Rousseau; Miss Clara Haldeman; William Waller Hawkins; Miss Kathryn Payne; (*peeping through*): Anthony H. Woodson; Mrs. Elizabeth Gregory; Mrs. William B. Haldeman; General William B. Haldeman; Mrs. Robert W. Brown; John A. Baird; Robert W. Brown; *rear row:* Roger Burlingame; Harry Bell; Louis Brownlow; Charles E. Johanbocke; Robert J. McBryde, Jr.; Paul Burlingame; Mrs. Henry Y. Offutt; Miss Ada Cain; Miss Lizzie Haldeman; Henry Y. Offutt.

Brief Returns to Nashville and Louisville

The Marcosson incident gave me a vacancy in the position of assistant city editor as well as in that of dramatic critic. I resolved for the time being not to have an assistant. The upshot was that I imported Theodore Duncan Rousseau, one of my old colleagues on the *Nashville Banner*. I also brought in two other reporters, one stolen from the *Louisville Herald* and another from the *Louisville Evening Post*. I had anticipated something of the need for new blood, and during the week's vacation that I took just before coming to the *Louisville Times* I went to my home in Springfield, Missouri. There I found on the staff of the *Springfield Republican* a young reporter on whom I had had my eye for a year. His name was William Waller Hawkins. Hawkins came to the *Times,* and I at once put him on police. He turned up thirteen headline scoops against the *Louisville Evening Post* on his first day. That ended for all my time, and for all I know for all time, the conspiracy of fakery on police news in Louisville. It also earned for Hawkins the sobriquet of "Hawkeye," by which he was known during all his Louisville career and still is known to the survivors among his old Louisville colleagues. Later on, he dropped the "Waller" from ordinary usage and became William W. Hawkins, the "Bill" Hawkins who after a career in the United Press became second in command to Roy Howard at the head of the great Scripps chain of newspapers and finally retired to end his days in a fashion appropriate to great wealth and great accomplishments in the salubrious climate of California.

I am afraid that I did get tough. I am afraid that I went too far in bossiness to have been a really good boss. Partly, as I now look at it in retrospect, this was because the paper had suffered, especially in the city room, from the lack of firm direction. On the other hand, I am sure that I went too far simply because I was uncertain of my own position; and, out of the depths of my insecurity, I asserted myself too much. It is no wonder that I made enemies. As I think it over, after a half-century, I am inclined to the belief that perhaps it was a good thing that I had to make those decisions. I long since have abandoned the old doctrine credited to Tom L. Johnson that a good executive is one who decides every problem promptly and occasionally correctly. At the same time, I must say that the experience of fifty years has convinced me that a good administrator is one who does decide.

Certainly, once I had asserted myself and once I had imported and infused some new blood into the organization, the resentment among the old-timers melted away. In the space of two or three months the whole organization of the city room had been knitted together, and never did a city editor anywhere have a more loyal, more conscientious, or more hard-working staff than I was privileged then to command.

When Rousseau came from Nashville, I set my head to find a way to get a job for Haynes McFadden, the other of the "three musketeers" who had started out together on the *Banner* in the summer of 1900. McFadden already had demonstrated that his particular skill was in business news, and there was no reason for me to displace Paul Burlingame, who was our Main Street reporter and who was alert and conscientious, well known and well liked in the business community of Louisville. Still I wanted Mac to come to Louisville, so that, when I heard Mr. Platt still was looking for a man to take the place that I had left on *The Courier-Journal* two months earlier, I persuaded him to send for McFadden.

Even before I had left Louisville for the *Nashville News* I was desperately tired of Coker's and had found refuge in a room rented from Carl Owsley, a colleague on *The Courier-Journal* who was married and had an extra room in a very nice apartment. To that I returned when I took the job on the *Times,* but it was available for only two or three weeks, because some member of the Owsley family was about to come to Louisville and had been promised that place.

Out of this circumstance arose a very delightful series of happenings. Mr. Harrison Robertson, the associate editor of *The Courier-Journal,* had a two-room apartment on the ground floor of a two-story house owned by Mrs. Martin. I had resumed with Mr. Robertson the habit of taking a late Sunday-morning breakfast at the Old Vienna— a breakfast of *croissants,* of Viennese coffee with whipped cream, and that sort of thing. Mr. Robertson told me that Mrs. Martin's upstairs two-room apartment was vacant. I seized upon it; and, together with Rousseau and Hawkins of my staff and McFadden of *The Courier-Journal,* we set up our *ménage chez Martin.*

While I was always at my desk by seven in the morning and rarely left it before six in the evening, still I did have the evenings free, and I was relieved of that dreadful pressure of morning-news-paper hours. All four of us plunged at once into the social life of the town. Rousseau already was acquainted with some of the people in the higher society brackets. I knew a few youngsters just emerging from the high-school set. Hawkins was at once admitted by virtue of family ties into the highest social circles of the town. McFadden knew no one in Louisville, but that didn't bother him even a little bit.

On the day he arrived it was I who took him in and introduced him to *The Courier-Journal* crowd. Among others in the room was Miss Nancy Czapski, the witty and attractive society editor. Within an hour after I had introduced McFadden to her, she came into the *Times* office, rushed up to my desk, and said, "Where in the world did you get that lovely Mellin's Food baby?" (Mellin was a baby-food manufacturing company whose sign manual was a blue-eyed, laughing, golden-haired baby.) That was too good for me to keep. I told the tale, and poor Mac, with his flashing blue eyes, his pink cheeks, his sunlit blond hair, was soon dubbed "Mellin's Food." Miss Czapski no longer was able to keep herself to herself. Pretty soon she was engaged to McFadden; and now, as I write this in 1954, they have been happily married for nearly a half-century.

Hawkins met his distant cousin, Margaret Wright, a charming girl with a crinkly smile and a halo of reddish-golden hair—dainty, sweet, and altogether lovely. Later Margaret Wright became Mrs. William Waller Hawkins.

Rousseau had a very good time, but he didn't settle down in Louisville. And, as for me, I had three or four different lightsome affairs, one of which came very near becoming an engagement, but none of which resulted in anything other than a very happy mingling with a very charming set of young men and young women, hardly more than boys and girls.

It should be said, perhaps, that we four were little more than boys. All of us had had to go to work in our teens; none of us had finished high school. I was the oldest but not yet twenty-four; Mac and Rousseau were twenty-two and twenty-one; and "Hawkeye" was only twenty years old. All four of us, I fear, maintained a half-joking but still an emotional sense of loyalty to the lost cause of the Confederacy. After all, we were young, our parents had been through the holocaust of the Civil War, and in point of time we were then nearer to the Civil War than I am, as I write this in 1954, to the end of World War I.

But it was not to last long. I took over the city editorship of the *Times* in July. In January the editor of the *Louisville Evening Post,* the opposition paper, took up by correspondence with Mr. Morton of the *Nashville Banner* a scheme to get rid of me and get me out of Louisville. It was that the *Louisville Evening Post* and the *Nashville Banner* join together and employ me as Washington correspondent at the dizzying salary of thirty dollars a week. The temptation was too much. I could not withstand it. I decided to go to Washington.

CHAPTER XVIII

A WASHINGTON CORRESPONDENT

Thrilled by the prospect of what I then considered to be a great promotion, and even more excited by the fact that I was to go to Washington—the center of that political activity in which I had been so intensely interested—I boarded the train on that February night at Louisville. I had expected to get to Washington in the daytime, but a freight-train wreck delayed us for nearly twelve hours. Of course, dark comes early in February, and the next evening, I cannot now recall the precise hour, I got off the train in Washington at the old Pennsylvania Station at Sixth Street, the one that then was famous as the site of the assassination of President Garfield.

With a satchel in one hand and a valise in the other, I made my way through the station and out into the dark. I didn't know where to go. Somebody had told me that near the station was a hotel called the St. James. I asked someone where it was. He pointed diagonally across the street.

It was dark, but something was wrong in the sky. All over a great quarter of it there was a glow—not like that of a sunrise; not like that of a sunset; but a peculiar glimmering glow. I had known, of course, the day before in Louisville that Baltimore was on fire, but I had been isolated from news for nearly twenty-four hours. I did not know that Baltimore was burning. However, the glow that I saw in the sky as I debarked from that train and made my way across Seventh Street in the semidarkness to the St. James Hotel was Baltimore still on fire.

My stipend of thirty dollars a week, which was five dollars more than I ever had had, did not stretch by any sort of reckoning to living in a hotel. Indeed, I hadn't even thought of such a thing. It was

[329]

my task to find a boarding-house, but it also was my first order of business to establish myself as the Washington correspondent of the *Nashville Banner* and the *Louisville Evening Post*. When I wakened next morning and had absorbed the *Washington Post* and had concluded that the Baltimore fire was under control and that it was no business of mine, I set out to do my job.

My first port of call was the Wyatt Building at Fourteenth and G streets, which housed the Western Union Telegraph Company and the offices of a goodly number of newspaper correspondents. Among them was the office of Albert Halstead, who had been for a number of years the Washington correspondent of the *Nashville Banner* and the *Louisville Evening Post*. His remuneration in that august position had been seven and a half dollars per week from each newspaper. I was getting twice his salary, and I was supplanting him. Of course Halstead had a number of other newspapers on his string, principally the *Brooklyn Standard Union* and the *Philadelphia Evening Telegraph,* which paid him a real salary—I do not know just how much. But these southern newspapers were simply little things which he had added to his principal job. Halstead in turn was the successor in the joint job of the *Louisville Evening Post* and the *Nashville Banner* of a very urbane gentleman named Archibald W. Butt. But by this time Archie Butt had become an army officer by way of the Spanish-American War and was assigned to the White House as an aide to the President. He was to go on in his clever combination of the suave gentleman with the skilled journalist to be a principal aide to President Taft, was doomed to perish when the "Titanic" went down, and eventually was to be commemorated by a monument all his own in the grounds south of the White House. Archie was an individual applauded, envied, and ridiculed by the fellows of his profession. His full name was Archibald Willingham deGraffenreid Butt. Charlie Edwards used to say at Shoomaker's Bar that he was the only man in the world that had a name that sounded exactly like a trunk falling down stairs.

His successor, my predecessor, Albert Halstead, was as tall and spare as Archie was short and rotund. Halstead was trained in urbanity but never had been able to conquer an innate tendency to the acidulous. He was entirely conscious of the fact that he was the son of the great journalist, Murat Halstead of Cincinnati. He was acutely conscious that no Democrat possibly could be qualified for any position that required the slightest exercise of intellect. And at the same time he had been so well schooled socially in the art of not hurting other people's feelings that he received me with that precise degree of hauteur, condescension, and kindliness that was to fit him for a long career in the consular service. It is a pity that he lived too early to experience the later amalgamation of the consular and diplomatic services, for, in my opinion, he would have been one of the most correct of the diplomats who ever essayed to represent the United States of America in a foreign country.

Mr. Halstead was kind to me and told me in considerable detail what was necessary for me to do to get accredited to the press gallery. Over and above that, he said he would be delighted to take me around and introduce me to those persons he thought would be useful sources of news for the papers in Louisville and Nashville. At the same time he confessed that his concern with general news and with the affairs in the East had caused him to neglect getting too well acquainted with some of the men that perhaps I would like to know. He said that he knew all the members of the House and the Senate from Tennessee and Kentucky but that there were persons in Washington whom he hadn't had time to cultivate who might be useful to me, now that both of the newspapers were embarked on a program of using more Washington news. No more generous gesture could have been made, and I was deeply touched by his consideration.

At the same time I knew, or thought I knew, where I was headed. I left Halstead after making an engagement to meet him early the next morning and made my way to the Treasury Building. My goal was the office of John W. Yerkes, commissioner of internal revenue. Mr. Yerkes was a Republican leader in Kentucky. He was an intimate friend of Richard W. Knott, the owner of the *Louisville Evening Post.* He was greatly admired by Major E. B. Stahlman, the owner of the *Nashville Banner.* He was a hero to Boyle G. Boyle, managing editor of the *Post,* and a hero also to my own mentor, Marmaduke B. Morton. His heroic stature arose from the fact that he had been counted out as a Republican candidate for governor of Kentucky at the election of 1902. He had been a candidate against John Crepps Wickliffe Beckham, the Democrat who had succeeded to the governorship by virtue of the fact that he was lieutenant-governor when William Goebel was assassinated. The Goebel contested election case had made news throughout the United States. It had split the Democratic party in Kentucky, and, generally speaking, those Democrats who had been against Bryan and for Palmer and Buckner; those Democrats who had favored gold against silver; those Democrats who had not stopped halfway but had gone over to McKinley in 1896 and again in 1900, had been against Goebel and had regarded Beckham as an upstart.

Now it so happened that I had been swimming upstream in the newspaper offices in both Nashville and Louisville. I had been a Bryanite; I had sympathized with Goebel. At the same time I had conceived a distrust of Mr. Beckham, and I was convinced that Mr. Yerkes, if the votes had been counted honestly, would have been elected the governor of Kentucky. So I approached the office of this Republican leader with a high degree of personal admiration and also a belief that he had been deprived of his just rights. I knew also that his secretary was a newspaperman who was reputed to have a great understanding of the desires as well as of the deficiencies of young reporters. And there at Mr. Yerkes' door I asked to see Harry Giovannoli. I was admitted instantly. It was then a little after eleven o'clock in the morning. The messenger took me to Giovannoli's desk. Harry arose and welcomed me most cordially. Both my managing editor, Mr. Boyle, and Mr. Morton had written him that I was on my way. At once I was at home. After a little chat he said, "Come in and meet Mr. Yerkes."

He showed me into the long room where Mr. Yerkes sat alone reading a newspaper. Mr. Yerkes was graciousness itself. He asked me to sit down. He leaned back. He talked about Dick Knott and Gil Boyle. He talked about Mr. Watterson. He talked about all Kentucky. He asked if I had ever been in Washington before. He paid very little attention to what I said, but he told me what he thought about Washington, and he regaled me with a tale or two out of his political past. It was very evident that the commissioner of internal revenue had very little work to do, that he was lonely, and that anybody who came in who would listen to a new story or an old tale was very welcome indeed.

Then Harry took me into the next room and introduced me to

his stenographer, Miss Alexander, and into another room and introduced me to Arthur Hayes, counsel. These four constituted the upper staff of the commissioner of internal revenue. As far as Washington was concerned, the whole bureau occupied only the rooms on the second floor of the north wing of the Treasury Building. Of course there were collectors in the various districts whose job it was to sell stamps for whiskey and beer and tobacco and cigars and cigarettes. Of course there was a clerical staff which looked after the returns from these field offices. And there were problems that arose, such as searching out moonshiners and breaking up illicit stills in the mountains, and naturally a great many problems of a legal character that came up with respect to the enforcement of the internal revenue laws. The liquor and tobacco taxes were small. There was no income tax. The Bureau of Internal Revenue was a very small show.

My main quest, however, at that moment was for a boarding-house. Harry said he didn't know very much about them but would telephone to a friend of his who worked in the State Department to come by on his way to lunch to see if he could help me out. So Mr. James H. Dorman soon dropped in.

We swapped tales, newspaper stories, and the like, speculated on what would happen in Baltimore, and even got around to some consideration of problems in Washington—principally speculation as to who the Old Guard Republicans would put up against "Teddy" Roosevelt now that it was known that Senator Mark Hanna was very ill and could not possibly recover. Mr. Dorman was a very formal gentleman, young (I think still in his thirties), bald-headed, short, and slender. He was a Kentuckian from Owen County—"Sweet Owen," as he always was careful to say. He was an avid pursuer of college degrees. That was something that I had never before encountered. In fact, I fear that at that time I had no notion whatever of what a college was like, much less a university. I had had my only contact with institutions of higher learning at Vanderbilt, and there I had seen students and professors, but I had not yet come to know the nature of the prizes so eagerly sought. Mr. Dorman had a Bachelor's degree, as became apparent the first few minutes of conversation. He also had a Master's degree and was eagerly out to become a Doctor of Philosophy. All that was Greek to me. Harry seemed to understand it. Even I sensed that in part Jimmy, as I later was to call Mr. Dorman, was endeavoring to impress the Washington correspondent of the Louisville newspaper with some sense of his importance.

Actually he was a clerk in the State Department. Actually what I wanted of him was help and guidance in discovering a boarding-house. Mr. Dorman impressed me greatly. He wore, as all of us did then, a high stiff collar and detachable stiff cuffs. But the distinctive badge of his superior social standing was the fact that he kept a handkerchief within the cuff of his right sleeve, drawing it out from time to time to touch his lips or to flourish it in the air and then tucking it back in his cuff to emphasize the carefully chosen periods of his carefully enunciated and precisely articulated sentences.

Jimmy said that he thought he could get me in the boarding-house where he took his meals—which, he said, was unquestionably the best in Washington—but that I would have to find a room somewhere in the neighborhood, as Mrs. Bocock's boarding-house on Q Street was filled to overflowing. He told me he thought the best thing for me to do was to go up to see Mrs. Bocock around three or four o'clock in the afternoon and see what I could do. He gave me a scribbled note of introduction. He then asked me to lunch with him. We went across the street from the Treasury Building to my first Washington luncheon. I had had breakfast that morning in the dining-room of the St. James Hotel (a breakfast was included in the American plan price of $2.50 for room and three meals a day)—a breakfast consisting of oatmeal, bacon and eggs, potatoes, and unlimited coffee. The luncheon was different. I knew that I had to pay for it at the St. James, but here I was a guest. Ford and Graham's was a popular place. The menu was strictly limited. There was a choice of Maryland biscuits whole or split with a sliver of ham between them. There was a choice of milk or coffee. That was all. Jimmy and I had Maryland biscuits whole without benefit of ham and a cup of milk. He insisted on paying for the lunch. The tab was twenty cents. No tip.

That afternoon I duly presented myself at 1714 Q Street and met Mrs. Bocock, a hearty, buxom woman with a generous smile and a certain eye for business. She said that there was one vacancy at her table and that I would be welcome to come to supper tomorrow night. She served for those who did not live in the house only breakfast and supper. Midday dinner was reserved for those who had rooms in her house, and there was no vacancy. She suggested several places in the neighborhood where I might find a room and said that there would be a place if I came back to supper the following night; and she thought I would like it and that any friend of Mr. Dorman's, she was sure, would be welcomed by her other guests.

Then, taking the list of three or four places that she gave me, I made my way around in the next street, then called Madison Street, now Church Street, and found at Mrs. Shinn's a back room on the third floor that she was willing to let for five dollars a month. I was to have the privilege of a bath on the second floor, and I was also to furnish my own soap and towels. Mrs. Shinn said that it would be ready for me the following morning. So, desiring above all things to be settled, I went by to see Mr. Halstead and postponed my engagement with him for my introductions in order that I might get settled and stop the outlay of $2.50 a day at the St. James Hotel. Although that $2.50 a day did include three meals, it was still too steep for me. The next morning, with some help from the hotel porter, I sent my trunk (which was checked at the station) and my valise and satchel by an express wagon driven by an old colored man out to 1755 Madison Street, and then via the Mount Pleasant streetcar I got to Mrs. Shinn's before my goods and chattels arrived.

Duly installed in the rear room on the third floor, I found noontime approaching and dinnertime. I had come out to this place on the Mount Pleasant streetcar, from which I debarked at Du Pont Circle. I inquired about transportation and decided to adventure on the Fourteenth Street car line, my new home being approximately midway between. I walked through Q Street to Fourteenth and decided that I would save streetcar fare. I already had discovered that carfare, even at the rate of six tickets for a quarter, soon would pile up. In Nashville and in Louisville I always had free passes on the streetcars, and it hurt to pay my way—just as if I were not a newspaperman.

Not being in any particular hurry, I decided to walk. A few doors south of Q Street on the west side of Fourteenth, I saw a restaurant. I went in. There were not very many people there. I took a seat. A waitress came and took my order. It was only then that I looked around as other customers came in and discovered that I was the only white person in a restaurant that was run by and for Negroes. Not only that but, just as my food had been brought to me, the restaurant had filled up, and the headwaiter brought another customer, a young Negro man, and sat him down across the table from me.

This was a great crisis. I had thought that I had achieved a high degree of tolerance. But to eat with a Negro, according to all the standards to which I was accustomed, was to descend to depths so low that there never could be recovery. Yet, I had committed myself to pay twenty-five cents for dinner. I was partly through with it, and I am proud to this moment of the fact that I don't think I showed in the slightest my discomfort. Nor did anybody else there seem embarrassed. Certainly I managed an informal chat with my tablemate. Now, with greater knowledge, I am perfectly sure that nobody there thought I was white. They simply thought that I was a light-skinned Negro, else in those days I would not have been in that restaurant. But, for me, it ended forever a vain and foolish prejudice.

I wandered around that afternoon, dropping in again to see Mr. Giovannoli, not caring again to disturb Mr. Halstead. I walked around the White House. I walked around the Washington Monument, and then, being overcome for the first time with loneliness, I found my way to my room. There I had an acute attack of fright. I theretofore had thought that nothing was beyond me. But now the inadequacy of my twenty-four years, the consciousness that I was not only in a strange city but in the Capital, the consciousness that not merely was I expected to scribble or to type things of greater or less consequence but that what I was to report would be sent sometimes by telegraph and sometimes by mail and that I was expected to produce a quality of news as well as a quantity that was superior to that furnished by the older and more experienced correspondents formerly employed on a part-time basis by the two papers—all this crashed in upon me at once. I was crushed. It was with the greatest difficulty that I managed to pull myself together to present myself at Mrs. Bocock's for supper at six o'clock.

Washington at that time was a city in which the boarding-house exerted a powerful and permeating influence. In 1904 there were at least three distinct groups recognized by others as being in high society. There was officialdom. There was the diplomatic set. And there were the old Washingtonians, the old Georgetownians—the cliff-dwellers. And there were also, of necessity, the purveyors of goods and services—the people who ran the stores and shops and markets, the people who served those who served the government. But, over and above all, there were the boarding-houses. In the boarding-house one found the people who made the wheels go around. One found here the gossip that was the lubricant for the machinery, and one discovered the ambitions and identified the energies that were to shape events to come.

Mrs. Bocock's, I am still persuaded to believe, was properly characterized by Mr. Dorman as one of the best. The tables were set in what had been the parlor and the dining-room of a row house on the south side of Q Street. The boarders were ranked strictly as ever protocol established the precedence for a diplomatic reception at the White House or a garden party at Buckingham Palace. In the parlor at one long table presided an elderly lady who had to be lifted from her wheel chair and who was attended by her daughter. At the next table, a little smaller, there was a middle-aged gentleman, handsome, debonair, elaborate in manner, accompanied by a perky, snub-nosed, redheaded, sixteen-year-old daughter who was always more than a little willing to cut under her father's pretensions as a captain in the Confederate Army and a collateral descendant of George Washington.

The last long table in the dining-room, and the one to which, by common consent, Mrs. Bocock routed the lower orders, was the one to which I was assigned. Mr. Dorman sat there oposite me. On my left was a man I later learned to be Charles C. Clark, who not until 1950 was retired from the position to which he later ascended as chief clerk of the Weather Bureau. On my right was a plump young woman from Georgia, a clerk in the War Department. She was Jessie Dell, later to be a member of the United States Civil Service Commission. Across the table from me and next to Mr. Dorman was Mr. J. Fred Dearing, a fellow-Missourian who then was deeply immersed in his studies of the Russian language—something which utterly astonished me at the moment but which was to prove a steppingstone to him in his career in the foreign service, from consular clerk to ambassador. Also, there was Mrs. Beckwith, who later I was to know as one of the secretaries of Mr. Taft when he was Secretary of War and with whom I was to be associated rather particularly during the second occupation of Cuba by the United States.

But not all were young and on their way up. There were two older people at the table: Willard Warner, a clerk in the Treasury Department, who had been a United States senator from Alabama, a Republican, and a relict of the reconstruction era, and, most important of all, Mrs. Maria Donnelly, already an elderly lady, already a crusader for the church—the Protestant Episcopal church—and, from her position in the office of the auditor for the War Department, a mighty warrior for the Lord, the Republican party, and all that the superiority of both could connote.

Mrs. Bocock's boarding-house not only had a forward thrust into the future represented by the careers-to-be of those who sat at her tables but also had its roots deep in the past and was the focus for reminiscences of the old, old days as well as problems of the present and the hopes for the future. The elderly lady who, attended by her daughter, queened it over all from her wheel-chair throne was full of stories about the time when her sister was the first lady of the land and the mistress of the White House. She was Mrs. Casey, born Miss Dent, sister of Julia Dent, wife of Ulysses S. Grant. Mrs. Casey was tremendously interested in politics and a violent partisan. She was a Democrat who believed that no good ever could come of anything that was remotely connected with the Republican party. She made exceptions occasionally in favor of her distinguished brother-in-law, but she was fond of reminding everybody that, after all, General Grant was born and brought up a Democrat. She also liked to tell the story of how General Grant was the last slaveowner in the United States. According to Mrs. Casey's tale, her sister went to Burlington, New Jersey, during the Civil War to live, taking with her the three or four slaves owned by the Dent family. The Emancipation Proclamation did not extend to New Jersey. New Jersey, which had decreed early in the nineteenth century a gradual emancipation by freeing all the infants born in slavery, had never established complete emancipation. The rest of the states did abolish slavery immediately after the Civil War, but, since there were so few slaves left in New Jersey, the New Jersey legislature just didn't bother. Therefore, when the Thirteenth Amendment to the Constitution was adopted ending slavery throughout the United States, the only slaves to be freed were those belonging to General Grant, the victorious leader of the Union Army which had conquered the Confederacy. I never tried to check up on this tale. Maybe the "slaves" were only servants. But Mrs. Casey wouldn't have it that way.

I think I have already said that the boarding-house dominated the scene in Washington. Washington was then, as it had been from the beginning, a place where government was the chief industry and the most important concern. Persons who then were employed in the federal government, unless they had very high positions, were known as "clerks," regardless of the character of their duties. What is now a "G-Girl" was then a clerk. What is now an administrative assistant was then a clerk. The clerks, on the other hand, never spoke of themselves as being attached to a particular department. They invariably referred to their own status as being "in office." "I have been in office more than thirty years," said Mrs. Donnelly.

"I am in office," said Miss Dell.

Even those in the State Department destined to be ministers and ambassadors spoke of themselves as being "in office." A necessary concomitant of the status of being "in office" was to have a particular congressional patron and protector. Miss Dell reposed safely in the shadow of the huge senatorial rock of Senator Augustus O. Bacon of Georgia. It made no difference that the administration was Republican, and few, if any, had any notion that it would ever be anything else but Republican. Even the Democratic representatives, certainly the Democratic senators, had their quota of patronage and were entitled to place some of their supporters "in office." Of course there was a civil service law. It had been enacted just twenty-one years before. But it didn't apply to a great many positions, and its protection was not fully relied upon by any but the newest, the most naïve, of those "in office."

As for such a thing as a governmental employees' union, I am sure that every person in the boarding-house would have dropped dead with horror at the very thought of such a thing. They looked upon themselves as superiors, far, far removed from the category of persons who had banded together in organizations such as the carpenters, bricklayers, and plumbers, or even the printers.

Yet they were eager to improve their status, and most of them were eager to exploit the possibilities of Washington as a place in which they could, without too much expenditure of money, add to their educational equipment. Georgetown University and Columbian College, later to become George Washington University, offered opportunities for those who sought education in the law, in medicine, in dentistry, pharmacy, engineering, and the like. The hours of all government departments were from nine to four, and the colleges and other schools opened their doors at four-thirty, so that whole platoons and battalions of those "in office" attended these schools, and many were graduated into the professions. In this process they were differentiated from the others "in office" by a generic appellation of "sundowners." Such a "sundowner" was my friend and introducer, Mr. James H. Dorman. Such a "sundowner" was Fred Dearing, working assiduously at his Russian.

The remuneration of government clerks was generous and handsome and gave those "in office" a considerable advantage over other persons struggling in the Washington scene who were employed by newspapers, such as I, or by banks, stores, and other establishments. Many of the clerks got as much as nine hundred dollars a year; a considerable number of them got salaries as high as twelve hundred dollars; a few as much as eighteen hundred a year. And then, of course, there were those up toward the top of the bureaus who got as much as twenty-four hundred or thirty-six hundred or even four thousand a year—approaching but not quite reaching the high level of the salaries fixed for members of the cabinet, senators, and representatives at five thousand dollars a year each.

As a matter of course at Mrs. Bocock's boarding-house, there was no room for any but the aristocrats. Here those "in office" had big jobs—fifteen hundred, eighteen hundred, or two thousand dollars a year. Even I, the newcomer, was in the money at thirty dollars a week or fifteen hundred and sixty dollars a year.

Most of us were not compelled to go to the boarding-house for our midday meal, as were the rank and file of the clerks "in office." The day's work began at nine; there was a full hour for lunch, so that the clerks could go home on the streetcar to their boarding-houses for the midday meal. We, in our aristocratic and more affluent circles, ate lunch downtown and assembled again only for the meal that some of us still called "supper" but which Mrs. Bocock was beginning to call "dinner."

Drugstores were all but universally equipped with soda fountains but not with lunch counters. Restaurants were few and far between and catered very largely to a noon-luncheon trade or to tourists and visitors from out of town. There were, with one or two exceptions, no first-class restaurants outside the hotels. People ate at home; if they had no home of their own, they ate in boarding-houses.

Governmental gossip flowed freely, and the talk was always of politics. Most of the time it was merely office politics. The gossip was about this chief clerk and his undue favoritism to some particular clerk. There was gossip about what were the probable relationships between a certain senatorial protector and a very charming person who seemed to be "in office" without any particular clerical qualifications. There was gossip of a partisan type concerning the quadrennial convulsion of presidential elections. Most of the people in these boarding-houses were Republicans. The Democrats were few and, if they were "in office," were inclined for prudential reasons to be quite quiet about it. Most of the Republicans "in office" were also anti-administration.

In my fifty years in and around Washington, I have never known a time when most of the gossip among governmental employees was not anti-administration. I believe that the record of those who in the neighboring states of Maryland and Virginia have an opportunity to vote will show that government employees usually are anti-administration. I am fully conscious that this runs counter to the currently received doctrine that everybody on the government pay roll of necessity votes for the party in power in elections and for particular persons in power in primaries. I do not believe that that doctrine will stand up under careful examination.

Certainly most of the government clerks then "in office" had one thing in common with their muted Democratic fellows. They did not like Theodore Roosevelt, President of the United States. They were quite sure that the Republican party, come June, would recover its sanity and would nominate somebody other than the wild man who was plunging the country rapidly into the abyss of socialism.

Now, I didn't like Theodore Roosevelt. I was a Democrat. I was a states-righter. I believed that Mr. Roosevelt had flouted the Constitution. I was sure that he was wrongheaded about many things and that his liberal sentiments occasionally proclaimed were entirely blanketed by his devotion to the interests of the trusts, the protected industries, and the financiers of Wall Street, who were, in the words of my hero, William Jennings Bryan, reducing the American people to a state of economic slavery. So we at Mrs. Bocock's boarding-house looked forward hopefully—the Republicans to the fourth of the following March, when a safe and sane Republican would replace "Teddy" in the White House; the Democrats, to the off-chance that perhaps we could find a Democratic nominee who could win the election.

On the morning of my second day in Washington I reported at the office of my predecessor, Mr. Halstead. He and I walked the mile and a quarter up to the Capitol, he showing me on the way points of interest and giving me instructions on how to proceed with my application to join the press gallery, on the minutiae of filing telegrams and of meeting the mails, and things of that sort. We went first to the Senate press gallery, and there he introduced me to the custodian, James D. Preston, one of the few men of that day who still serves in the Capitol and now (in 1955) in semiretirement in an honorary position in the office of the secretary of the Senate. There I filled out the requisite form of application for membership in the gallery; there I was sponsored by Mr. Halstead and by two other correspondents whom he captured and introduced to me and who were quite willing to sign their names.

Then we went down onto the Senate floor. Few senators had yet come in, but he told me all about the rights and privileges of a correspondent and then walked me through the Capitol, past the Supreme Court, through Statuary Hall, over to the House of Representatives. There he took me up to the press gallery and introduced me to the custodian there, Mr. Charles H. Mann. He told Mr. Mann that I had already filed my request for admission with Mr. Preston at the Senate end. Both Mr. Preston and Mr. Mann immediately admitted me without waiting for formalities to be passed on by the Standing Committee of Correspondents, and I was given free run of the press gallery.

Then down the elevator and into the rooms of the House Committee on Appropriations, where a gentleman very well known to me maintained a desk, although he was not the chairman of the committee. He was my distant cousin, Walter Preston Brownlow, a Republican member of Congress and a man whom I already had known very well in my Nashville days. Walter was glad to see me and promised his help; and, of course, I knew it would be a part of my duties to see him every day.

On the floor of the House, where the members of Congress were coming in and where it was not necessary for us to leave until one minute before the clock struck twelve, I met several of the ten members of Congress from Tennessee and the eleven members from Kentucky, nearly all of whom already were known to me from my Nashville and Louisville days. One of them, a representative of Tennessee, also was a distant cousin of mine. His name was Thetus W. Sims, but at that moment I had no idea that he was in time to be my father-in-law.

Also there on the floor I met the representative from Louisville, Swagar Sherley, and his secretary, John D. Wakefield, who was the assistant city editor who received me on that dismal, dreary December afternoon when he gave me those three impossible assignments on my first day with *The Courier-Journal*. We were happy to see each other. For him I was a link to the newspaper world which he had deserted and to which he longed to return; and for me it was somebody in Washington of my own craft, well known and well liked.

From that day forward I attended most assiduously to my duties with respect to the Congress. If it were in session, I was in the Capitol every morning not later than half-past eleven. I saw every member of the Kentucky and Tennessee delegations every day. Nevertheless, the intensive concern with the delegations from my own states did not at all prevent me from pursuing my acquaintance further, and, by the time that Congress had completed its work for the year and adjourned, I had made the acquaintance of nearly every senator and more than three-fourths of the members of the House of Representatives. I had attended meetings of every important committee that held an open hearing. I flattered myself that I had become intimately acquainted with the members of Congress.

One day, as I was walking across the plaza from the Capitol toward the Library of Congress, I met a representative from Texas, James L. Slayden, who I already accounted a rather close friend. He was accompanied by an elderly gentleman of distinguished appearance, his father-in-law, Colonel Maury. Mr. Slayden said to me, "I have got to get over to the House to vote on that District of Columbia school-board row. What do you know about it? How do you think I should vote?"

"I haven't the faintest idea," I responded. "I suppose it is just another one of those school-board rows. I never knew any school board that wasn't in a row, and apparently it is usually about nothing at all. It does seem to me that somewhere, sometime, merely by accident, a school board would be set up that was composed of persons of some sense that would try to run the schools without being in a continual ruckus."

"You are absolutely right," Mr. Slayden said. "I never heard of a school board that had a member on it that had enough sense to come in out of the rain."

Up piped old Colonel Maury: "Jim, I think you are taking in a little too much territory. I knew a school board once that I don't think you could say such things about. My father was a member of that school board, and once I attended one of its meetings. One day, when I was about nine or ten years old, I was walking on the street with my father. We met three other members of the school board. We stood on the street corner, and my father stated the business and said that the other member was out of town. The decision was made, and my father was instructed to record it in the minutes as a regular meeting of the board. The other three members were Thomas Jefferson, James Madison, and James Monroe."

Forty years afterward I asked Maury Maverick, then a representative in Congress from Texas, a nephew of Mr. Slayden and a grandson of Colonel Maury, what school board that could have been. He said that it was the committee in charge of the construction of the University of Virginia at Charlottesville. The meeting was in Charlottesville.

Another discovery that became a favorite daily haunt was the Library of Congress. That great institution had two branches in the Capitol, one serving each house. The library for the House of Representatives was presided over by three individuals, and one of them was another distant cousin of mine, John F. Brownlow, a grandson of Parson Brownlow. Jack, a year or two younger than I, was possessed of a remarkable memory and was an avaricious reader; and through him I could get any book that I liked out of the vast repository of the Library of Congress. That helped me a lot, but it did not keep me from going almost every day to the library itself to read, to browse, and to become acquainted with its infinitely rich resources. The main library building then was but newly finished, its flamboyant decor had not yet fallen under the criticism of the moderns, and it was widely and all but universally proclaimed as one of the most beautiful buildings in the world.

While thus devoting a large part of my time to the workings of the legislative branch of the government, I by no means neglected that other great branch of the government ensconced in the Capitol building itself—the judiciary.

The marshal of the United States Supreme Court was Major J. Montgomery Wright. My friend, William Waller Hawkins, whom I had brought to Louisville to become a reporter on the *Louisville Times,* was a distant kinsman of Mrs. Wright; and the great Wright mansion on Tenth and Broadway in Louisville was but a little distance from the establishment of Mrs. Martin, where Hawkins, Rousseau, McFadden, and I had lived. I had soon come to know one of his daughters, Margaret Wright, very well indeed. She later married Hawkins. So, when I got to the Capitol, I went to see Major Wright and sat through one of the Monday opinion days of the Supreme Court. I had a letter of introduction from the owner of my Louisville papers, Richard W. Knott, to one of the justices, John Marshall Harlan of Kentucky. Through the intervention of Major Wright, I had an early opportunity to present that letter. In retrospect, I must confess that my career as a Washington correspondent was not crowned with any great glory. I didn't climb very high up the ladder in that particular activity. However, I am sure that I can boast, as the old orators used to say, without fear of successful contradiction, that I am the only Washington correspondent who ever filed an absolutely accurate telegraphic report of a decision of the United States Supreme Court. It came about this way.

I had an instruction from the *Louisville Evening Post* to watch the United States Supreme Court for a particular decision in a much-battered-about lawsuit that had been up and down in both the state and the federal courts. Therefore I was present every Monday at noon to hear the opinions delivered. One day Mr. Justice Harlan hunched his great bulk across the bench and read out the decision in the case that I was looking for. I listened attentively, but the language was so extraordinarily legalistic and technical that, when the end came, I did not know which side had won. That was all I wanted to know, so that I could send an immediate telegram the details of which would have been worked out in the office in Louisville. But I couldn't even guess. So I made my way around to Major Wright and asked him which side won. He said, "Well, I don't know. I heard Mr. Justice Harlan read the case, but my attention was distracted, and I didn't hear the decision."

"Will you send up a note?" I asked.

"Yes, I'll be glad to."

So I wrote a note to the Justice in which I said that I was under instructions to telegraph the result of that particular case but that, while I had listened, I did not have sufficient legal knowledge to know which side won, and I asked if he would please tell me.

Then I saw the Justice lean forward, take a pen, and write. I thought he was answering my note directly. The page came back with the note. It read:

A Passion for Politics

You came to court forgetting your legal lore. I came to court forgetting my chewing tobacco. If you will go down to Engle's at New Jersey Avenue and C Street, N.W., and buy me a ten-cent cut of Graveley's Natural Leaf chewing tobacco, I will endeavor to have your dispatch written by the time you get back. J. M. H.

I broke all pedestrian speed records getting down to Engle's. I bought the plug of tobacco. I came back. I presented myself to Major Wright's desk and sent up the little package. The page took it to the Justice, and the Justice in turn handed him several sheets of paper. He had written:

> *Evening Post*
> *Louisville, Kentucky*
> DAY PRESS RATE
> THE SUPREME COURT TODAY . . . [and so on and so on, complete with signature] BROWNLOW.

All I had to do was take it out, rush down the hall to the Western Union desk, and file the dispatch. I didn't even read it.

It was some years later that I had occasion to cultivate my acquaintanceship with the members of the Supreme Bench. The state of Georgia had filed a suit against the state of Tennessee, a case in which the Supreme Court took original jurisdiction. Georgia said that the state-owned copper mines at Ducktown, Tennessee, were operating their smelters in such a way as to send poisonous fumes across the Georgia line, killing the forests of Georgia. The Court, having taken jurisdiction, appointed a master to hear testimony in Chattanooga. The master, having no process-server of his own, called on the sheriff of Hamilton County, Tennessee, to serve his writs. The sheriff, acting on the advice of attorney-general of the state of Tennessee, declined to do so. Thus was presented to the Supreme Court of the United States the case of the contumacious sheriff of Hamilton County, Tennessee. By that time I had become also the correspondent of the *Chattanooga News*. This was a hot story in Chattanooga, and I went to the Court every morning to see the assistant clerk, Mr. Stansberry, to find out what the Court was going to do about our sheriff. One morning while I was in Mr. Stansberry's office, Mr. Justice Harlan came in. With him were Chief Justice Melville W. Fuller and another justice later to become Chief Justice, Edward Douglass White. Mr. Stansberry in a joking mood said, "Gentlemen, I haven't got your sheriff for you, but I have a correspondent of a Chattanooga newspaper. Why don't we take him and hold him as hostage?"

There was a little laughter, and a day or two later I saw Mr. Justice Harlan again. He said, "The Court has had your case under consideration, and we have had quite a little difficulty. We don't know whether to have you hanged, drawn and quartered, or merely boiled in oil."

The joke kept up, and a day or two later the Court decided to do nothing whatever with the sheriff. One afternoon I encountered Justices Harlan and White as they were about to leave the Capitol and walk down Pennsylvania Avenue. Justice Harlan hailed me and said, "The Court has decided that, because of my advocacy, you being a fellow-Kentuckian, we will punish you as was the Duke of Clarence, who, you will recall, was drowned in a butt of malmsey. Malmsey is hard to come by here in sufficient quantity; but, if you will come along, my Brother White and I will drown you in a butt of bourbon." We went to Mades' Hotel, and the sentence of the Court was duly executed.

Members of the House of Representatives at that time, unless they happened to be chairmen of committees, had no office space. The great office buildings of the House of Representatives and the Senate were yet to be constructed. Senators who were chairmen of committees had their committee rooms, but all senators were provided with some office space, the nonchairmen being tucked away in odd corners all over the Senate wing of the Capitol, while a few (naturally those of the minority party) were housed in a tumble-down walk-up apartment building a block away from the Capitol on a site long since razed. My four particular senators, Blackburn and McCreary of Kentucky and Bate and Carmack of Tennessee, were housed quite variously. Senator Blackburn was in a tiny room in a subbasement of the Senate, and Senator Bate was tucked away in what was known as the library wing of the Capitol, the portion of the Capitol Building west of the great dome in which the Library of Congress was housed before the library building was constructed. Senators Carmack and McCreary were in the old apartment house on New Jersey Avenue and B Street. To see all four of them every day thus became a considerable walking chore.

Members of the House, having no offices at all, had the habit of coming onto the floor quite early, and usually I could see nearly all of them before the House convened. Those I had missed, I would send for later and ask them to come to the corridor. On the Senate side the members of the press gallery then had the privilege of the Marble Room behind the Senate chamber—long since reserved solely for senators and those who have the privilege of the floor of the Senate. Here it was possible for the newspapermen to gather in little knots, send in cards, and bring in senators for conversations, long or short as the case might be.

The business of checking up with every member of two congressional delegations every day seemed to be an inescapable part of the standard routine, although it usually was quite unproductive of news. However, one never knew just when and where a story would break.

A picture of what went on in those days may be gained by considering what went on in Senator Carmack's office. He had one secretary, who did all the typing and filing and acted as receptionist. But his office every morning was filled with a half-dozen or more persons and, late in the afternoon about four-thirty, sometimes with a considerably larger crowd. These persons were government clerks who hailed originally from Tennessee and, despite the legal protection of the civil service law, felt acutely the need for senatorial patronage and protection. A good many of them had had their day in politics. Some had been successful as candidates for county and city offices; some simply gloried in the reminiscences of the time when they "made the race" for county trustee, sheriff, or whatnot. Carmack, a tall, red-haired man of distinguished appearance, had been a newspaper editor and was as well known for his caustic wit as he was for his campaign oratory. Actually he was a kindly soul, and he suffered all these hangers-on, listened over and over again to their oft-repeated tales, and seemed never to be annoyed. He was quite naturally, I suppose, since he had been a newspaperman himself, my best news source. He not only talked to me about things important to Tennessee that he knew would justify telegraphic dispatches but also was helpful in suggesting news stories that could be sent by mail as well as stories that had nothing in particular to do with the current events of the day but which enabled me to write interpretative pieces about the problems of the Congress. He was a Democrat of the Bryan school, a passionate "free-trader," but at the same time a thoroughgoing sentimentalist with respect to the South and its past glories. After his one term in the Senate, he was later to die, shot down by an assassin on the streets of Nashville after he had returned to a position as editor of a newspaper.

General Bate, the other Tennessee senator, was elderly, a cripple because of a Civil War wound. He had been a major general in the Confederate Army and was taciturn to the point of gruffness. The old gentlemen had courtly manners, but he distrusted all newspapers and had short shrift for newspapermen.

The two Kentucky senators were both characterized by great urbanity. Senator McCreary was a very model of punctilious politeness; but, if he ever knew any news, he didn't tell me. Perhaps he was keeping it for Colonel O. O. Stealey, the elderly correspondent of *The Courier-Journal,* which was a supporter of Senator McCreary, whereas my paper was opposed to him.

On the other hand, Joseph Clay Stiles Blackburn, gray-haired, gray-mustached, wearing always a red Windsor tie, was ever gracious and polite. He was the greatest raconteur I ever knew. He was the darling of his fellow-senators, and, although a Democrat, when at last his services in that great body were terminated by the voters of Kentucky, a Republican Senate unanimously put him in charge of the building of the Lincoln Memorial, a sinecure which enabled him to live in Washington until the end of his days. Long after, when he was stricken with years and hardly ever left his home, in good weather he always sat out on the little stoop in front of his house. It was not far from where I lived, and I had a habit of dropping in to see Senator Blackburn every afternoon to hear him tell a tale. Always the anecdote was ready; always the story was good; and never, unless by my earnest request, did he tell the same story twice.

Members of the House of Representatives, having no offices, nearly all—unless they happened to be chairmen of committees—worked at home, although a few rented space in office buildings downtown. One such was Swagar Sherley of Louisville, and his office was always my first port of call in the morning. There I could see John Wakefield and go over the gossip of the day, and there I would have my talks with Mr. Sherley, an earnest, studious, hard-working man who had just come to Congress and was at the very beginning of his distinguished career which brought him at last to the chairmanship of the great Committee on Appropriations during World War I. After the morning visit to Mr. Sherley's office, then my next stop was to call on Mr. Yerkes, who was always free to see me and who was an excellent news source.

A Passion for Politics

The year was 1904, and the winter was drawing to a close. It was, of course, a presidential year, and already all conversation everywhere in Washington, in the Capitol, in the departments, and in the boarding-houses, was all about who would be President.

The one man who was looked upon as certain to get the Republican nomination despite all the efforts of Theodore Roosevelt, the incumbent President, was Mark Hanna. Within a week or two of my arrival in Washington, Senator Hanna died in his house on Lafayette Square. Instantly there came the question of how to agree on somebody else who could beat the irresponsible "Teddy" in the Republican Convention. For lack of a more obvious man, for the time being, the anti-Roosevelt Republicans tended to rally around Joseph B. Foraker, who had been Mr. Hanna's colleague from Ohio in the Senate; but there was a general understanding that he was what has come now to be popularly known as a mere caretaker candidate to hold the fort until somebody more likely to win could be chosen. Such great leaders as Senators Quay and Penrose of Pennsylvania, Aldrich of Rhode Island, Platt of New York, and Platt of Connecticut—indeed, all of the big-wigs of the Republican party—were certain that Roosevelt was leading the country to destruction and the party to ruin and were convinced that at all costs he must be replaced.

This group of senators, strongly supported in the House by such leaders as Sereno E. Payne, Nelson Dingley, and John Dalzell, and at times, it seemed, by Speaker "Uncle Joe" Cannon, were known as the "Allies." The Republican race was on, and it was the "Allies" against "Teddy." Washington, so far as it was vocal and so far as a neophyte correspondent could discover, was almost unanimous in its opinion that the "Allies" necessarily would win.

On the other hand, the Democrats, who had been wandering in the wilderness with Mr. Bryan for years and who had all but lost any hope of winning an election, began to perk up. Most of the Democrats whom I met were at one in saying that the Democrats would have to get rid of the incubus of Bryanism and the imputation of radicalism and nominate a conservative. They disagreed with their Republican colleagues. They said that "Teddy" would be able to force his own renomination, and they thought that "Teddy," of course, would be easy to beat provided the Democrats only had sense enough to put up a conservative.

Just who they wanted was a matter of debate, but one thing was pretty sure. They had nominated Mr. Bryan twice, and Mr. Bryan twice had been defeated, and they wanted no more of him. These Democrats remembered that they had won the presidency but twice since the Civil War and also that they had won with a New Yorker. New York, with its great block of electoral votes, seemed to be the state from which they should choose their candidate. At the same time, while desiring the support of the Tammany-controlled city Democrats, they wanted no candidate who was a Tammany man. That had been the description of the anti-Tammany governor, Cleveland, with whom they had won twice. Already by that time, therefore, support began to develop for Judge Alton B. Parker. One of his most ardent supporters was the member of Congress from Nashville, John Wesley Gaines; another was the congressman from Louisville, Swagar Sherley. So it was natural from the very beginning that, with my two particular congressmen in the lead, I was kept *au courant* with the Parker boom.

The presidential press conference, which was invented by Woodrow Wilson in 1913, was then something utterly unknown to the Washington of 1904. Indeed, there had been a pressroom only about a year. "T. R." in a general renovation of the White House (which was not characterized by very good engineering, since its careless destruction of bearing walls and other safeguards led eventually to the collapse of the presidential mansion, requiring it to be entirely rebuilt) built the West Wing, and the President's offices had been moved into it and out of the White House proper. One cold winter day the President came across Bill Price of the *Washington Star* standing in the sleet outside the door of the White House waiting to interview callers on the President to gain from them what news he could. The President took pity on him and moved him into the White House offices and established a pressroom, and thus began for the first time any official presidential recognition of the existence of Washington correspondents. Until this day, however, any official accolade conferred upon a Washington correspondent is under the control of a standing committee of the press galleries of the House and the Senate.

Since there were no presidential press conferences, a correspondent who desired to see the President had to seek an appointment as best he might and take his chances. The great advantage was that, when he did see the President, he would frequently see him alone. Of course

[351]

there were occasions when the President would invite a favored few of the newspapermen in to see him, and those often singled out for the honor came to be known to their less fortunate colleagues as the "fair-haired boys" or, even in more derogatory parlance, as "cuckoos."

Theodore Roosevelt was the first President I ever knew. My memory of my first meeting with him is vivid. I had been in Washington but a few weeks. I was twenty-four years old and regarded with awe the White House wherein had lived all the Presidents but Washington; and I stood in even greater awe of the man, the President of the United States, who to me was most of all the personified symbol of the Republic. I was too much a party Democrat not to have marked reservations with respect to Theodore Roosevelt the politician, but Theodore Roosevelt the President commanded my whole respect. I was not a little frightened and not a little nervous when I was shown into the Cabinet Room by Mr. William Loeb, the President's secretary, and asked to take a seat. Hardly had I done so when I sprang from the chair as the door opened and in burst not the President of the United States but "Teddy" himself, flying coattails, flying eyeglass cord, gleaming teeth, squinting eyes, outstretched hand, and "*Dee*-lighted!"

He sat at his place at the head of the table and, waving at the customary seat of the secretary of state, said, "Take Mr. Hay's chair." In a moment I was at ease and under the spell of his charm. Then he asked me what in that day and time were the inevitable questions addressed to me by anybody acquainted with political history, "What relation are you to Parson Brownlow? What relation to Congressman Brownlow?" I hurriedly explained not only that the cousinship was distant but that my father had not, like his distinguished editor-preacher cousin, stayed with the Union but had gone to the South and had served four years in the Rebel Army. This permitted him to claim kin with Georgia and the Confederate Navy through Admiral Bulloch. I think I even managed to squeak out that I personally was a Democrat, but he swept that aside, because I was of much more importance to him, naturally, as the Washington correspondent of two papers, one of which, the *Louisville Evening Post,* was actively supporting his candidacy for the Republican nomination. The "Allies" still hoped to prevent Roosevelt's nomination, still hoped to hit upon someone who would be more amenable to the orthodox Republican party command which Mr. Hanna had captained.

There was still some question how the Kentucky delegation would vote.

Theodore Roosevelt, the party candidate, appeared and jumped into the middle of things. "I want you to let Dick Knott know that I am looking to him for leadership in winning Kentucky. If I had my way, I would wipe out the present Republican leadership and reorganize the party under the command of such men as Dick Knott and Basil Duke."

I do not think he could possibly have said anything that would have been more distasteful to me. While I was a Democrat, I had the very highest respect for Mr. John W. Yerkes, who was then the leader of the regular Republican party, and while I had a high professional esteem for the owner and editor of my own paper, Mr. Knott, the fact that he was a Gold Democrat rated him low indeed in my political scale. As for Basil Duke, he was to me not only a renegade Gold Democrat but also the very personification of the railroad lobby in Frankfort, Kentucky. Of course, I loyally transmitted Mr. Roosevelt's message to Mr. Knott, my editor; and my paper did valiant service in winning for Roosevelt the support of the Kentucky delegation—which, I am persuaded, Mr. Yerkes would have given to him anyway. And, of course, I never told Mr. Yerkes what "Teddy" had said.

I saw Mr. Roosevelt many other times in the White House, sometimes—as, for instance, during the struggle over the Hepburn Bill extending the powers of the Interstate Commerce Commission—quite frequently. He never again talked party politics to me; but, from that first White House interview of mine with a President, I have realized that party politics is and must be one of his prime concerns. He would not have got into the White House without it; he cannot stay there without it; and, without it, when he comes to leave, he cannot expect any of the policies he has worked so hard to establish to be continued. But, if the President maintains his political leadership, he has the opportunity, in some measure, to do the three things people expect of him as President: first, to manage the machinery of government; second, to engineer the economy of the nation; and, third, to represent the opinion of the people.

It was late in February, 1904, when I sat down in the Cabinet Room in the White House for my first talk with a President of the United States. He was the first of the eight Presidents I have known, most of them very slightly indeed; a few of them quite well.

CHAPTER XIX

"T. R." AND THE SAGE OF ESOPUS

In the spring of 1904 all Washington, including me, became utterly absorbed in the oncoming campaign—the great quadrennial presidential sweepstakes.

It was a matter of considerable concern that the Congress was dillydallying and dawdling in its business and showed every sign of not being willing to adjourn in time to get the campaign really under way. The general belief expressed by the speaker of the House, "Uncle Joe" Cannon, was that the Congress had no business staying around after the middle of April. Actually, however, it did not adjourn until May 6. In those dim and distant days before the adoption of the Twentieth Amendment, each Congress had two sessions. One, the long session, began on the first Wednesday in December and continued until adjournment; the other, the short session, also began in December but was always held after the next election and terminated with the expiration of the terms of office of its members on the following third of March.

Those were the days when Washington in the summertime was almost a deserted village. Rarely had a long session lasted until June. It was unthinkable that all the supply bills for the fiscal year beginning on July 1 would not be passed in ample time to meet that deadline. In 1904, however, a very considerable number of Republican members of Congress still hoped to find a candidate to pit against President Theodore Roosevelt, who, according to their notion of things, had succeeded only by accident to a position for which they deemed him unfit. After Senator Hanna's death in February, the "Allies" tried their best to find a candidate; but it soon was evident that the popularity of "Teddy" was too great, and it was almost certain that he would be nominated at the Republican convention.

On the other hand, the Democrats had rising hopes of success. Witnessing the internecine strife of the GOP and believing that the time had come for the party to swing away from Mr. Bryan and his vagaries, they thought it necessary only to nominate a strong conservative candidate who would capitalize on the unpopularity of Mr. Roosevelt in his own party in order to win. By the time the Congress adjourned, the principal candidate of the conservative Democrats, at least of those in the Congress, was Judge Alton B. Parker of New York.

The two newspapers that I represented then divided. The *Louisville Evening Post* determined to support Mr. Roosevelt for the nomination and the election. The *Nashville Banner,* on the other hand, was an ardent supporter of Judge Parker and believed he would be nominated and elected. That left me in a precarious state. There was little news to be had in Washington during the summer and especially in a year when the campaign would take most of the political activities away from the Capital. So a new arrangement was made. I went off the pay roll of the Louisville paper. The *Nashville Banner* undertook my whole salary of thirty dollars a week and assigned me to cover the campaign.

The Republican National Convention met in Chicago on the twenty-first of June. I got there the day before. It was my first visit to the great city where many years later I was to spend a great part of my life and do a great part of my work in the field of public administration—a field which at that moment, I am afraid, held no interest for me whatever. Ten years earlier I had envied those few persons from my native town of Buffalo who had been able to go to Chicago to see the great World's Fair. And here at last was I!

Fortunately, my cousin, Walter P. Brownlow, a Republican member of Congress from Tennessee, was a member of the Republican National Committee and the head of the Tennessee delegation to the convention. He had a suite of rooms on the Michigan Avenue side of the Auditorium Hotel Annex, which has since changed its name to the Congress Hotel. I had a bedroom in a much smaller, less pretentious hostelry, the Kaiserhof, at Clark and Van Buren streets, but I was able to make my daytime headquarters in the palatial Annex. The windows opened on Michigan Avenue and the Lake, the lake whose waters then lapped the Illinois Central Railroad tracks only a stone's throw from the hotel. There, a little to the south, was General Logan on a bronze horse atop a rounded mound waving a bronze flag. A little to the north was the Art Institute, built on a promontory that extended out into the lake. There on the avenue below me was the traffic of a mighty city, the hansom cabs in which the delegates were driven from hotel to hotel or from the hotels out to the old Coliseum at Twenty-second Street and Michigan Avenue, where the convention was to be held; there the smart traps and high-stepping horses of the well-to-do and rich citizens of the Windy City; there the great commotion and clatter; there the central artery of a great city pulsing with vigorous life.

Walter Brownlow was far from being an ardent Roosevelt man, but nevertheless he was a loyal Republican. He was convinced that Roosevelt would be nominated, and he was chiefly concerned with Republican politics in Tennessee, fighting to thwart the ambitions of a rival leader, Henry Clay Evans. And also he believed that the time had come to break the Solid South. He thought that the conservative southern Democrats were tired of Bryan. He indulged the hope that the time had come when he would carry his own state of Tennessee for the Republican presidential candidate. Because of his leadership in the party and because of his vigor in the campaign to win at least a part of the South away from the Democrats, his suite became a rallying place for Republican leaders of sorts from all over the South; and he himself was visited by not a few of the leaders from the rest of the country. He had been temporary chairman of the Republican National Convention which met in Minneapolis in 1892. He had been chosen a member of the National Committee in 1896 and had had a prominent part in the councils of the party for many years. His rooms gave me an excellent vantage point from which to witness the inside workings of the convention.

By that time the opposition to Roosevelt's nomination had all but vanished, and the newsmen's principal concern was about the second place on the ticket. Mr. Brownlow was for Charles Warren Fairbanks of Indiana, and with my distinguished cousin I went to call on Senator Fairbanks. I already knew him fairly well, and I soon was intensely engaged in following the course of his campaign, one which resulted in an amazingly easy victory. What I thought about it all at that time I duly recorded in my dispatch to the *Nashville Banner* on the opening day of the convention. I telegraphed:

The choice of a candidate for Vice-President—the one thing graciously left to the delegates by the imperious and imperial Roosevelt—is not of enough importance to stir emotions and when questions are asked the reply is generally, "Fairbanks, I suppose—if he will have it."

The rank and file of the delegates appear to look on the game as from the viewpoint of a rank outsider and appear to be wondering what they will be commanded to do next.

The convention opened in the old Coliseum. It was a large hall, much too large for the voice of a man unaided by microphone and public address system. The temporary chairman, Mr. Elihu Root, could hardly make himself heard, even on the floor, much less in the galleries. Mr. Cannon, Speaker of the House and the permanent chairman of the convention, was forced to rely more upon the noise made by his gavel than upon his own unaided vocal apparatus. Thus the galleries were not attractive to many persons, and for the most part they were largely empty. People who struggled and wangled to get tickets stayed a little while and left. They could see, but they could not hear. The convention itself, my first national convention, was distinctly dull, distinctly disappointing. My older colleagues in the press gallery agreed that it was the least exciting performance within their memory.

One man in the press gallery I sought out above all others. He was William Jennings Bryan, then acting as a correspondent for the *Omaha World Herald*. He was a center of interest not only to newspapermen but even to the Republicans, who had already twice defeated him but still had for him that lingering admiration accorded to a fallen foe. This the delegates manifested by cheers and applause, which he beamingly acknowledged by rising and bowing from his press table.

Furthermore, and contributing not a little to the dulness, there was the fact that, while there was no question that the delegates were going to nominate Mr. Roosevelt, a very great many of them, perhaps even a majority of them, did not like him and did not approve of what he was doing. Some regarded him as a dangerous radical, and some even suspected him of socialism. And they were being compelled against their will to support him. It was a dull meeting.

"Teddy" in Washington must have heard of this, or he must have sensed it, for he came to a realization that he must do something to wake up the crowd. Therefore he sent a telegram. That message, which enjoyed a brief season of fame, was nicely calculated to fit the headlines. It read: "Perdicaris alive or Raisuli dead!"

The convention was electrified. No longer was it dull and drab. No longer was even the slightest speech greeted with a mere polite patter of hands. Everybody whooped it up for another war against the Barbary pirates. But now, around fifty years later, the message carries no meaning for most Americans.

Ion Perdicaris was said to be a naturalized American citizen of Greek birth. At that particular time he was a prisoner of a Moroccan chieftain named Raisuli. The United States through its ordinary diplomatic channels was demanding that he be freed. That demand had crept into the news but had made no particular uproar on either side of the Atlantic. But when dramatized as "T. R." knew how to dramatize it, acutely atuned to the headlines, it transmitted the spark to ignite the otherwise cold and emotionless gathering of Republicans into a militant swashbuckling orgy of patriotism.

Perdicaris was released. The incident lapsed into what Mr. Cleveland used to call "innocuous desuetude," but it did not entirely die. Years after, when Mr. Root became secretary of state, he used to tell with an amused air how angry the then secretary of state, Mr. John Hay, became when it was discovered that, after all, Perdicaris had not been naturalized and was not an American citizen—or at least his papers were not in order, and his status was most doubtful. Nevertheless, Perdicaris was alive, Raisuli was not dead, and neither was the convention.

The business of nominating Mr. Fairbanks for Vice-President went off smoothly. There were no exciting fights over the platform. The convention gave a rousing welcome to Harry Stillwell Edwards of Georgia, a short-story writer who predicted that the Solid South was breaking and that never again would the Democrats reign undisputed in a territory that once had been the Confederate States of America, an institution that had been liquidated at Appomattox less than forty years before.

For me it had been a most interesting experience. I had seen a national convention. I had observed the lassitude of the Republicans. I saw that the professional politicians were not particularly interested in their candidate. And I had had a chance to meet and talk with my own particular hero, Mr. Bryan.

From Chicago I went back home to Buffalo for a week with my father and mother and to shine in courthouse and street-corner con-

versations as the great authority on the Republican convention, something which was of intense interest to the overwhelmingly Republican citizens of my home town and county. I am afraid that I was
just a little bit of an exhibitionist and that, except for the kindly
generosity of my old friends, I must have been quite an insufferable
creature.

St. Louis, where the Democratic National Convention met on the
sixth of July, was not so new to me as was Chicago, but never before
had I seen the town so crowded, so gay, and in such a jubilant mood.
The Louisiana Purchase Exposition, the World's Fair, was on in
Skinkers' Meadow. Even without the benefit of a national convention,
the hotels were jam-packed, and there was an over-all and pervasive
spirit of common joy.

Here in the Democratic convention there was none of the lassitude,
no trace of the lethargy, that had plagued the Republican assembly
in Chicago. There was an air of excitement. It seemed to many of
the delegates, to the professional politicians and even to a good many
of the newspapermen, that the times were ripe for a change. If only
the Democrats had the gumption to nominate a strong conservative
candidate; if only the convention had the courage to put Mr. Bryan
in his place; if only the convention would remember and return to
the halcyon days of Cleveland—everything would be well. The dangerous radical Theodore Roosevelt would be ousted from the White
House, and the country would be safe and sane—at least it would be
safe from the Republicans. However, that feeling was not shared by
all the Democrats or indeed by all the delegates to the convention.
Mr. Bryan was there, now not as an observing note-taking journalist,
as I had seen him at Chicago, but as a delegate from Nebraska. Mr.
Bryan and his not inconsiderable following were unwilling to see
the party turn back to the conservative position represented by the
old Cleveland tradition.

That indeed was the very idea against which Mr. Bryan had led
the revolt of 1896. That revolt, it was recalled by everybody in St. Louis
that hot July week, had marked a milestone in the history of party
politics in the country. Only three times in the sixty years preceding
had any President been re-elected: Lincoln, Grant, and McKinley.
Indeed, aside from these three, but two Presidents in office had been
renominated—Van Buren in 1840, only to be defeated by William

Henry Harrison; and Grover Cleveland in 1888, only to be defeated by Benjamin Harrison, the grandson of "Tippecanoe," the old Whig general. Mr. Cleveland had been nominated by the Democrats for the third time, as had no one before him, and in 1892 he had in his turn defeated Harrison. That made history by way of being the only time that any President had served two nonconsecutive terms. Only Cleveland was "in again, out again, in again."

At the very outset the second Cleveland administration ran into foul economic weather. The panic of 1893 was on. The country was in distress. The blame was heaped on Cleveland. So, when the Democrats did meet in Chicago in 1896, the money question was paramount. For right or wrong, for weal or woe, everybody seemed to think that the root of the evil and the cure for it lay in the money issue—something difficult to recall in the mid-twentieth century.

Cleveland had stood for the gold standard. Many, perhaps most, Democrats were for free silver. The issue was drawn. The Silver Democrats, under the leadership of Richard P. Bland of Missouri, Joseph C. S. Blackburn of Kentucky, and John R. McLean of Cincinnati, were determined to oust the Clevelandites and write a free-silver platform. Mr. Bryan, young, magnetic, a great orator, seized the leadership of the silver hordes, dominated the convention, got the platform he wanted, and was nominated for President.

In that convention there sat at the head of the New York delegation David Bennett Hill, sometimes governor, sometimes senator. Mr. Hill had not been friendly to Mr. Cleveland, but he was for gold. Mr. Hill and three hundred delegates loyal to the administration of the sitting President of their party did not bolt but sat through the shouting and the tumult and abstained from voting.

Now here in St. Louis in 1904, after Mr. Bryan had suffered his second defeat in 1900 at the hands of McKinley, the forces that had met in battle in 1896 again were arrayed against each other. The Cleveland wing of the party was in the ascendant, and to lead it there was David Bennett Hill. Mr. Hill, when Cleveland had been nominated against his opposition, was asked if he would vote for him. His reply was, "I am a Democrat!"

Thereafter every cartoonist always caricatured Mr. Hill with a feather in his cap on which was emblazoned that slogan. When Cleveland was nominated the third time against his opposition, Mr.

Hill was asked the same question. Mr. Hill replied, "I am still a Democrat." In 1896, after Hill got back to New York from Chicago, he was asked if he would support Mr. Bryan. His reply was, "I am still a Democrat—very still." But here in St. Louis in 1904 he was far from still. Indeed, he was quite vocal, and he at once seized the leadership of the convention.

As so often happens, the first grave battle was in the credentials committee. There were two rival sets of delegates from the state of Illinois. The Cleveland conservative wing had let it be known that its members would support Judge Parker. The rival delegates were for "not turning back the clock."

Mr. Bryan, again with his marvelous voice (he was one of the few who could ring the rafters and reach the ears of everybody in the great hall), made a tremendous fight on the seating of the Illinois delegates. Bryan was defeated by a vote of 650 to 300. That crucial test indicated that the convention had more than two-thirds of its members ready to swing to the conservative side. John Sharp Williams of Mississippi was made temporary chairman, and Champ Clark of Missouri permanent chairman. Bryan had lost.

But the great fight had not ended. Now it centered in the committee on resolutions. John Sharp Williams of Mississippi, the brilliant minority leader of the House of Representatives, had a scheme that he thought would unite the party. It consisted essentially of a watered-down money plank which meant very little, indeed, but which, he thought, might satisfy Mr. Hill and not be too offensive to Mr. Bryan. On the other hand, to help Mr. Bryan (whose faith in the unitary paramountcy of the monetary issue was slipping), he proposed a plank recommending an income tax—something new in the history of political parties in the United States.

The resolutions committee met in secret. I myself knew most of the members of the subcommittee on drafting, but I couldn't get a word out of any of them. So also with the other newspapermen. They got nothing but silence. Nobody would talk. At the same time with every edition of a newspaper carrying Associated Press dispatches there appeared what seemed to be an authoritative story of the actual debate in that secret room. It was a long time after that convention adjourned that we discovered that James T. Williams, Jr., of the Associated Press, had found a way to climb down a fire escape from an upper floor and perch himself just outside the open window of the hot smoke-filled room in which that big ruckus took place.

The upshot of it all was that it was decided to duck the money question altogether. Mr. Bryan would have none of the Williams compromise on the money question. Mr. Hill would have none of the Williams offer to Mr. Bryan on the income-tax plank. So it was decided that, as these matters were not "paramount issues" in the present campaign, the platform should be silent about them. The platform as reported and as adopted dealt only with what the committee regarded as "live issues": the usurpation by the Executive of the power of the Congress and the courts; a stern warning against the erratic and reckless methods of Theodore Roosevelt; a vigorous condemnation of official corruption in the federal service accompanied by a demand for exposure and punishment of the evildoers; a good old Democratic line with respect to the tariff and the trusts—and that was all.

Then Parker was nominated. Mr. Bryan himself made the motion to make the nomination unanimous, winding up with a peroration in which he said: "Must we choose between the God of War and the God of Gold; between militarism and plutocracy!"

Parker was nominated; everybody was pleased; and victory was asserted, assumed, and seemingly assured. But the next morning before the convention met to choose a candidate for Vice-President a shocking rumor spread throughout the hall. It was that Judge Parker had sent a telegram to William F. Sheehan of the New York delegation taking a firm stand for gold.

This was a blow not only to the Bryan and free-silver element but also to the moderates and the compromisers. John Sharp Williams said, "We have adopted a platform on which both Bryan and Grover Cleveland can stand, and the situation ought not to be disturbed by reckless statements." There were denials that Sheehan had got such a telegram. Nobody had seen it. Speeches, and furious speeches at that, came from delegates from all parts of the country.

Later the telegram was made public. Judge Parker had wired to Mr. Sheehan:

I regard the gold standard as firmly and irrevocably established and shall act accordingly if the action of the convention today is ratified by the people. Inasmuch as the platform is silent on the subject, I deem it necessary to make this communication to the convention for its consideration, as I should feel it my duty to decline the nomination except with that understanding.

The convention was thrown into an uproar. There were angry demands that the nomination be withdrawn.

Mr. Bryan, who three times earlier had spoken to the convention and had reached with his voice every nook and cranny of the huge hall, had a bad throat. He was hoarse. It was announced that he would see the newspapermen at eight o'clock the next morning at the Jefferson Hotel. The phrase "press conference" had not yet been coined, but this certainly was a forerunner of the now familiar gathering, with the exception that Mr. Bryan did most of the talking. The questions were few, and, indeed, since he was quite voluble and quite candid, they were hardly necessary. He was free in his denunciation of the candidate for having repudiated the platform, but at the same time he was cagey enough not to demand the withdrawal of the nomination. He was husky. His shirt collar was open. His neck was swathed with a red flannel bandage which gave evidence to the eye and to the nose that it was well soaked in kerosene. He said he would attempt to get the floor at the convention that morning.

He did. The voice now was not golden. The throat now was not silver. It was rasping. The neck was still swathed in the surplice of red flannel. But even with his hoarseness he managed to let everybody in the convention hall, casual auditors as well as delegates, know that he disapproved of Judge Parker's telegram and that he considered that the candidates of the convention were irrevocably bound by the declaration of the party in its platform and that therefore he would not demand the withdrawal of the nomination. The platform was not amended. The convention hurriedly nominated Henry Gassaway Davis, a quite solvent octogenarian from West Virginia, for Vice-President and adjourned.

The Democrats had met in an aura of victory. They adjourned in the twilight of doom. The radiant confidence which seemed to be shared by all the Democrats there assembled on the sixth of July had utterly disappeared when the convention adjourned on the tenth. Indeed, the very air seemed to be permeated with the direful predictions not only that Parker would be defeated, not only that Roosevelt would be re-elected, but that even the Solid South might be broken.

From St. Louis, at the beginning of the Democratic convention, I "poured it on" in my dispatches to the *Banner* that the Democrats were sure of victory. At the same time I am glad that I retained enough sanity and balance to wire the following:

> As was said in these letters from the Chicago convention, the Democrats will do well not to base too much hope on the lack of enthusiasm displayed by the Republican delegates. It may be said with equal truth that the Republicans need not be too much alarmed over the remarkable and unprecedented display of enthusiasm here.

Then, as the Democratic delegations left for home, I wired my paper:

> Friday [the day before the Parker telegram was received] it was the common belief that the Democrats of the country were on the eve of a great victory; but Sunday, as the delegates left, they were much at sea. "I don't know," was the usual response to all questioners.

I managed, I think, to keep my gloom and pessimism out of my dispatches to the *Nashville Banner,* but I was quite sure that two other men from Nashville in attendance at St. Louis, my managing editor, Marmaduke B. Morton, and Major E. B. Stahlman, the owner and publisher of the *Nashville Banner,* secretly shared my doubts. Major Stahlman was more furious with Bryan than ever he had been, even in the days when he had deserted the party to support Palmer and Butler, in 1896, and, in 1900, Mr. McKinley himself.

Then, for me, a delightful interlude. I stayed on in St. Louis for a week. My mother came up to see the fair. Her brother and two of her nieces from Tennessee met us there, and we saw the fabulous show, took our first ride in a contraption which was then called the "horseless carriage," and generally had a big time.

Also I was extremely happy because Mr. Morton and Major Stahlman had talked my assignments over with me and had decided that, as soon as the campaign got under way, I ought to go to New York and cover the New York national headquarters and Judge Parker's campaign tours.

I never had been in New York. This was my key to the great gates of the great city. But there was a catch in it. I was simply to move my base from Washington to New York on the first of September to cover the campaign, but there was to be no expense account. The *Banner,* as usual, would provide me with the necessary railroad passes so that I could follow the candidates or cover as much of the territory as I desired; but I would have to pay my own expenses, as I had to pay for my board and lodging and the like in Washington. I was so delighted by the prospect that I couldn't bring myself to protest, although I knew of course that the expenses would be greater than my simple boarding-house–rooming-house life in Washington. Mr. Morton came to the rescue with a five-dollar-a-week increase, and I was all set with thirty-five dollars a week.

Back in Washington from Missouri, I celebrated alone my arrival at the mature age of twenty-five on the twenty-ninth day of August, and the next day I set out for Manhattan. I saw it first as a traveler from the South invariably did in those days—from a ferryboat. It already was overpowering with its upthrusting skyline, and I was thrilled in every nerve with the expectation of the great career I was about to carve out for myself in the field of journalism.

I knew exactly where to go. It was to 61 Washington Square South, the rooming-house presided over by Mme Blanchard. During most of my Louisville days there had been a hegira of Louisville newspaper-men to New York, and Mme Blanchard's was always their first port of call. There had been Thompson Buchanan and Cleves Kincaid, who were to become successful playwrights. There had been Clarence Axman and Howard Robinson, both of whom had found their niches on New York journals.

I had written to Axman, and he had invited me to share his room at 61 Washington Square South. My arrival there was celebrated by a reunion of a half-dozen Louisville newspapermen, and I was ap-prised of the niceties of living on nothing a week in the Bohemia of Greenwich Village. And it soon turned out that thirty-five dollars was not quite enough to meet the requirements of nothing a week. I found myself on short-commons.

But what difference did it make? There were the sights to see: the Village itself; Wall Street and Trinity Church; the great reaches of Fifth Avenue and Broadway; the iron steamboat to Coney Island; the dignified passage northward from the square in the horse-drawn Fifth Avenue coaches; the clanging rides up Broadway on the trolley car; the thundering clatter of the "L," on which one could take passage to far places such as the zoo in Bronx and the aquarium at the Battery. There were the teeming groups of shoppers in the great retail stores on Sixth Avenue. There were the theaters stretching along Broadway and its debouching streets all the way from Union Square to Herald Square and beyond. There was talk of the subway that was to open sometime very soon and which no one seemed to foresee would change the pattern of New York life.

In addition to all these things, there was my job. My work centered on Thirty-fourth Street across from the Waldorf Astoria in the upper floors of the Century Building, whose ground floor was occupied by the already doomed Knickerbocker Trust Company. There was the headquarters of the Democratic national committee presided over by Chairman August Belmont. To that suite of rooms I attached myself with eagerness. It was part of my job to do everything I could to report the campaign but also not to neglect any opportunity to do what was possible to help along the Democratic candidate, Judge Parker, who had such enthusiastic support from my newspaper.

In a way this was not altogether to my liking, because I still had an abiding affection for my boyhood hero, William Jennings Bryan, and it did not seem to me that he had been fairly treated in St. Louis. However, this objection was overcome by Mr. Bryan's support of the candidate and more so by the discovery at the headquarters office of a kindred soul. He was Urey Woodson, the editor and publisher of the Owensboro, Kentucky, *Messenger,* the secretary of the National Committee, and an ardent Bryan man who was bending every effort for the ticket. He introduced me to the head of the publicity division, George F. Parker, who had been a secretary to Grover Cleveland and who was indeed the father and founder of the great tribe of press agents and public relations counselors—although perhaps that honor has been imputed more often to his then assistant, a young man from Georgia who was to reap the rewards of both fame and fortune in this new field. His name was Ivy Lee. And it was Ivy Lee who greeted me daily and who helped me with my task.

However, there also was Tom Taggart of Indiana and blue-eyed Billy Sheehan of New York, and all of them, including Woodson, I regarded as my old friends, since I had met them and had known them in my Louisville days. Mr. Lee, a Georgian, seemed genuinely on fire in his enthusiasm for the "Sage of Esopus," as we were attempting to persuade the public to call Judge Parker. He was also shorthanded, and so, when he found that I had had a background of experience in my youth as an editor of a country newspaper, he put me on the pay roll at ten dollars a week to assist in getting out what later was known as a clipsheet of ready-made editorials for country weeklies and also of material to be made available to the concerns that furnished patent insides and "boiler plate" for the rural press. The weekly newspaper job was in charge of another Missourian, John Carradine, a tall, slender man about my own age who looked exactly like his father, a militant Methodist evangelist I had known in Missouri and who was to be succeeded by his son and his very spit and image, the John Carradine of Hollywood and the movies.

That ten dollars a week I found of very present help indeed. However, the job lasted only six weeks, and it was the only time in my life that I ever was on the pay roll of a party committee. I have never had occasion to regret the experience, especially since it brought me in even closer touch with Urey Woodson, with whom I went over every piece of copy I wrote. Mr. Woodson, with his background of Kentucky small-city journalism and his indefatigable industry, kept a close eye on the firm of Parker, Lee, and Carradine and insisted on clearing all our copy himself. That meant a daily conference with the genial Kentuckian which was the beginning of a friendship which was later profoundly to affect my career. And, incidentally, it brought me many lunches at the Waldorf with Mr. Woodson and his close friend, Tom Taggart. Once or twice a week I would be picked up by them and taken across the street where I was introduced to the splendor of the then greatest hostelry in town and there experienced the administrations of the great Oscar himself in an initiation into a gastronomic world of which I had not the faintest notion and which, so far as my resources were concerned, was certainly not to be contemplated by me as a way of life.

I was quick to discover, of course, the possibility of passes to the theaters and therefore spent most of my evenings with my own Washington Square crowd, one or two of whom always would wangle passes for some show or other even if it were only Proctor's Vaudeville.

Yet there was more time for one as eager as I to sample the delights of the city. Just as Fifth Avenue marched away from Washington Square, there was the Brevoort Hotel, and living there Van Leer

Polk of Tennessee. I would occasionally pick him up, and we would walk up Fifth Avenue to Madison Square bound for his favorite haunt, the bar of the Hoffman House. Not infrequently on the way we would see the one-legged Daniel E. Sickles, a survivor by grace of the "unwritten law" of a trial for the murder of Philip Key in Lafayette Square in Washington, a survivor at the price of a lost leg of the Battle of the "Peach Orchard" of Gettysburg in the Civil War, and a survivor by royal favor of an affair with the queen of Spain. In the very next block we would see the white-haired Mark Twain coming down the steps from his house, also ready to walk up the avenue. And on two notable occasion, most memorable, Mr. Polk, who was well known to Mr. Clemens, joined him; and I walked with them both all the way up to Madison Square and into the Hoffman House bar.

There one would find of an afternoon such cronies of Mr. Polk as Colonel Duncan B. Cooper, whom I also had known in Tennessee; and a younger man who had been a member of my Saturday luncheon table at Fauçon's in Nashville, now assistant attorney-general of the United States, temporarily on duty in New York and living at the Hoffman House. He was James Clark McReynolds, later to become attorney-general of the United States and an associate justice of the United States Supreme Court. Here, I heard tall tales, and here, since cocktails were still two for a quarter even at the Hoffman House bar, I was able to hold up my end and buy a drink or two. Occasionally I made so bold as to venture to invite Mr. Polk to go with me to dine at Bartholdi's or, farther down Broadway, to the delightful Luchow's, where we were served our favorite Pilsener. By going without suppers for a day or two, I was able to manage that once in a while, no doubt to the gratification of Mr. Polk, who was almost as broke as I was.

My gastronomic education was being furthered despite my poverty by more than one fortunate incident. For instance, Mr. Watterson came to the city. He stayed at the Manhattan Club, but I ran into him at the Hoffman House, and we had a delightful reunion of a sort at the end of which he invited me to dine with him at Delmonico's, then at the height of its fame. A day or two later I accompanied him up to the Democratic headquarters, and thereafter he took me to luncheon at Moquin's, a famous French restaurant down-town. "Marse Henry," despite his identification with Kentucky, was never a devotee of the wine of that country. He rarely drank bourbon or any other kind of whiskey. What he really liked best of all was beer. But, on such an occasion as a dinner at Delmonico's or a luncheon at Moquin's, he disclosed himself to be the gourmet that he was. He held long conferences with the headwaiter and the captain. He held animated and intimate discussions with the wine steward, and, as a result, I was given an opportunity to learn what it was to be served with food properly prepared, accompanied by exactly the right wine. Then also there was the great banquet given by Messrs. Muschenheim on the occasion of the opening of the Astor Hotel, which marked the advance of the Great White Way northward into what is now Times Square, a dinner that would have delighted the soul of Vattel.

My first subterranean journey, also, was a thrilling experience. Mr. August Belmont, himself, invited me—of course along with a good many other newspapermen who were hanging around his head-quarters—to ride with Mayor George B. McClellan on the first sub-way train. I remember the dedication of the silver control handle, which was presented to the Mayor at the city hall, the assemblage marching down into the brand-new and gleaming subway station, and the clanging journey northward under Broadway. (Many a year later I rode on the first subway train in Chicago with Mayor Edward J. Kelly at the controls—I being the only person who took the first subway journey in the first subway train in both New York and Chicago.)

Among other things, I took advantage of the opportunity of being in New York to extend my acquaintance in other directions. For instance, I looked into the matter of the Socialist party. I am sure that neither Eugene Debs, then its candidate for President, nor anyone else thought that the party had a chance; but Charles Dobbs had been such a close friend of mine in Louisville and had so earnestly endeavored to convert me to his creed that I had sufficient interest to pursue an inquiry into what the Socialists were up to. Charlie Dobbs wrote to me and inclosed a letter of introduction to the then New York City leader of the Socialists, Morris Hillquit. I met Mr. Hillquit and a good many others of his associates on the Socialist newspaper

Forward, and I listened with interest and sympathy to their arguments and plans. But I was not convinced.

It soon became apparent that the Parker campaign was not going well. "Teddy" was too popular. From the days of the Spanish-American War and the Rough Riders onward through his lively career, he was a figure with an appeal which our worthy, solid, solemn Judge Parker could not match. Mr. Taggart and Mr. Woodson decided it was necessary to persuade Mr. Bryan to go actively to work. A speaking tour in Indiana and other mid-central states was arranged for him.

All in all, it had not been an exciting campaign. After the dust had settled and the flurry of excitement caused by the two conventions was over, the whole affair drifted into the doldrums. Judge Parker was duly notified of something that perhaps he already knew by a delegation that went to see him in Esopus and formally told him that he had been nominated by the Democrats. Mr. Roosevelt received a similar delegation at Sagamore Hill. The two national chairmen, August Belmont and George B. Courtelyou, agreed that the active campaign need not start until the middle of September; a little later, by consent, that date was postponed until October 1. Judge Parker did not issue his letter of acceptance until the last week in September, and it was not an inspiring document. Thus it turned out that, if anybody was going to put any life into the Democratic campaign, it would be up to Mr. Bryan. Much was made of his speeches, and, while he loyally supported the nominee, even he could find little basis for his particular brand of enthusiastic oratory in any of the pronouncements of the candidate. But Tom Taggart wanted to "redeem" Indiana, and he believed the best way to carry his own state was to let Bryan do the work. Thus it was agreed that he was to take a ten-day trip to the Indiana hinterland, making speeches in the large cities and rear-platform talks at every stop.

I joined the train at Indianapolis and for two or three days had a perfectly wonderful time riding in the red-plush day coach which was Mr. Bryan's equivalent of a special car. A good many reporters and correspondents were with him, and at almost every stop local newspapermen got on and rode until the next stop. He was charming. He amused his visitors by his sleight-of-hand tricks. He astounded us all by his ability to fall asleep instantly, and he explained to us that it was that method of resting that enabled him to keep at the task with such vim and vigor.

Although I was adequately provided with railroad passes, the expense of the hotel stops was a little too much for me, and so, after Indianapolis and one or two other stops, I was on my way back to New York. By that time I had no confidence in Judge Parker's ability to beat "T. R.," and, I suspect, some of my pessimism was filtering through into what were necessarily my optimistic dispatches to one of the newspapers so heartily supporting the New York judge, one that so heartily disapproved of Theodore Roosevelt and all his works.

So back to New York, where I made what, I am sure, was a dismal report to Mr. Woodson. Then, at the very end of October, the committee began to bestir itself and to demand that Judge Parker do something. So, late as it was, Judge Parker began his campaign on the last day of October with a speech in New York. That he followed as late as November 4 by a journey to Hartford, with speeches there and in three other Connecticut cities. I went with him on that trip.

Judge Parker was a man of great dignity. Despite his urbanity in personal communication and his gentleness in conversation with even us newspapermen, of whom he seemed to be afraid, it was difficult if not impossible for him to unbend. He did not have the common touch. At the theater in Hartford where he made his great speech, he did manage enough denunciation of "Teddy" to rouse the audience to some enthusiasm, and it was rather pathetic to see how eagerly he took to his bosom the encouragement of that applause. The denunciation not only was of Mr. Roosevelt's radicalism but took the form of charges that the Republican National Committee was illegally and corruptly using money to influence the election. This provoked from the White House a characteristic reply from the President and a riposte from Judge Parker on the Saturday before the election. Whatever might have been the effect of an earlier start and a more vigorous campaign, it now was too late.

The election date, Tuesday, November 8, 1904, rolled around with its inevitable result. My friend James Clark McReynolds, nearly twenty years older than I, possessed a dignity of carriage and manner which I never could hope to achieve and, in fact, to which I should never aspire, shared with me on the eve of this election day a common interest. We were curious.

A Passion for Politics

He was born in Kentucky, and I in Missouri; he in a small town, I in a still smaller and more remote village. We had met first in what must have seemed for diverse reasons a principal city. It was Nashville. It was a principal city because not only was it the capital of Tennessee but, to Mr. McReynolds, it was nearer than any other urban center, closer than Louisville, bigger than Frankfort, and more nearly a capital for his native Elkton in the social sense (despite political geography) than any Kentucky city could be. He was a lawyer. He was a university man—an alumnus of Vanderbilt and Virginia. He was, as such things went in those days, affluent and independent. He was handsome, unwed, affable, and witty, and so he cut a swath in Nashville society wider than was warranted by his imagination. Few of the dowagers and maidens, few of his legal fellows at the bar and on the bench, and fewer still of the bankers, the industrialists, and the rich knew that his emotional life already had ended. Few, indeed, knew that there was a day in each year when he repaired alone to the cemetery in the outskirts of Louisville to lay a sheaf of roses on the grave of the girl he loved—the only girl he ever would love. And, of the few who were apprised of that poignant secret, I am persuaded that not one, not even James Clark McReynolds himself, knew that in her grave were buried all his hopes for the future; not one, I believe, so much as suspected that ever thereafter he would look backward, never forward, and that ever thereafter he would yearn for yesterday.

I, younger, eager, not having tasted the satisfactions of wealth and position, and having no notion of the deprivations that the death of a loved one may bring to the privileged, was all set for the future. To me the past was but poverty and privation.

But McReynolds and I had, as I have said, one thing in common. It was curiosity. We had discovered that common trait in each other in our Saturday lunches at Fauçon's in Nashville. Aside from this common curiosity, McReynolds and I had certain common concepts. We were both Democrats. We were both Jeffersonians. We were both Jacksonians. Each of us believed that country people were apt to be better than city people. Each of us was profoundly Christian, he a Calvinist and I an Arminian.

In that particular year, for reasons that were not only dissimilar but contradictory, we were for Parker and against Roosevelt. He was, by appointment of Theodore Roosevelt, an assistant to the attorney-general of the United States. He had been, under the "T. R." Square Deal, launched on his career as a trust-buster. And, not only because he held high office under a Republican President but also because in 1896 he had bolted the Democratic party, I could not quite trust his politics. In 1896 he had stayed by Cleveland. He had been for gold. He had supported Palmer and Buckner against Bryan and Sewall. Not only all that, but he actually had been the "Gold Bug" candidate for Congress in the Nashville district. Despite this heresy, the lengthy vinculum of party tradition stretched over us both. I had held no high office and no low one either. But I was still vaguely afraid of "T. R." and what his Square Deal was about to do to the sacred cause of state rights. McReynolds was afraid of any change. But, for a moment, we were one. Not only were McReynolds and I both for Parker but we were both fearful of what the amorphous, agglomerate, polyglot population of the big cities might do.

We were agreed that, whatever happened, it would happen on election day. Overt rebellion and revolt had perished at Appomattox. McReynolds believed that, the fewer who voted, the better the verdict would be. I believed that, the more who voted, the brighter the hope. I was for votes for women. He was against it. I doubt if we then thought very much about votes for Negroes. At any rate, at breakfast at the Hoffman House on Monday, we decided that we should see for ourselves what an election in New York was like. We decided to look at it as adventurers from another sphere; to see if we could detect the evil machinations of Tammany—the "evil" at that particular moment being a current belief that Tammany was supporting "T. R." by giving only half-loyal lip service to Parker—in the common parlance, that Tammany had made a trade to knife the Democrats.

We were up at five in the morning, and, when the polls opened at sunrise, we left the elevated at South Ferry and began our peregrinations from polling place to polling place. We veered northwestwardly through Canal Street as far as Avenue A; back toward the west; at noon we had a hearty lunch at Lorber's great kosher restaurant on Grand Street; again we thrust to the northwest, through Washington Square to the Hudson, thence northeastwardly from precinct to precinct to the Gas House District.

There was not time enough to do it all; and I am afraid that, at that time, even four full years after the consolidation of Greater New York, to both McReynolds and me, New York meant only Manhattan. When the polls closed, I left him tired and footsore at the Hoffman House and forced myself to go on to Thirty-fourth Street.

There I went up to the headquarters of the National Democratic Committee. It was yet hardly dark. The extra papers had given us the doom of our hopes in their headlines, but as yet there was no real news. The headquarters was empty. There was no Urey Woodson in the secretary's office. There was no J. T. Fanning in the campaign manager's office. There was no Ivy Lee in the publicity office. No stenographer, no typist—not even an office boy. But, far back in what had been the inaccessible sanctum sanctorum, there was a man.

He was August Belmont. He was the chairman of the National Democratic Committee, and he stood, like Mrs. Heman's youthful hero, alone on the burning deck. I walked in, saw who it was, murmured, "Excuse me," and attempted to beat a hurried retreat.

"No," said Mr. Belmont, "come in. You and I are apparently all that's left of the Democratic party. Won't you please join me in a bite to eat?"

Overwhelmed and grateful, I managed a more or less articulate assent. We went down the elevator. We walked straight across Thirty-fourth Street into the Waldorf. We found a table. Oscar himself came. There were oysters. There was lobster Newburg. There was champagne. "T. R." was in, and the name of Alton B. Parker had been inscribed forever on the roll of those "who also ran."

CHAPTER XX

AN IMPORTANT MEETING
AND AN INTERLUDE IN PADUCAH

The Sims family then lived at the Varnum Hotel, only one block away from the Capitol on the site now occupied by the new House Office Building. The family consisted of Judge Sims, his wife, and seven children, five girls and two boys. But I was not to meet all of them on the occasion of my first dinner with them. There were, in fact, at the table only the three eldest daughters—Edna, the eldest; Tom, whom I already knew; and Elizabeth—with their father and mother. Kent, the older son, was away at college in Vanderbilt University. The three youngest children had had their supper and were gone. Mrs. Sims was a strikingly handsome matron, and her daughters all were beautiful girls. It was a grateful and a warming experience to be welcomed at that board and into that family as a kinsman.

The dinner over, the two elder girls instantly disappeared on affairs of their own, and so did Mr. and Mrs. Sims. That left me alone with Elizabeth. I was glad to have a chance to get better acquainted with my newly found blue-eyed cousin, who had, I thought, looked at me with an amused and slightly quizzical smile. I had no idea that it was my first meeting with my sweetheart and wife-to-be.

Formally introduced by her mother as "Elizabeth," she had been called "Bess" and "Bep" and "Liz" indifferently by her father and sisters. I was left in a state of mild confusion with respect to what her first name was; but of course even in the case of a kinship, in that day, I would not have dreamed of addressing a young lady on a first meeting by her first name unless she had been a first cousin, and then I would have been sure to have said "Cousin Elizabeth." As it was, I called her "Miss Sims."

Miss Sims, it turned out, had been home but a very short time from Randolph-Macon Woman's College at Lynchburg, Virginia, where she had got a little more than halfway through her second year when an illness compelled her to leave college. She had recovered, but she had not yet gone about very much; nor was she anything like as busy as her two older sisters. That made for a chance for me. It wasn't long before I discovered the reason for that quizzical smile. She knew I did not know her, but she knew entirely too much about me. I asked, of course, if she knew a student at Randolph-Macon who was an old flame of my Nashville days. It turned out that Miss Sims did know her. It also had turned out that she had been told a great deal about me—maybe too much. So that, when she met me, she looked me over to see if the rest of me matched the scalp that she had been shown hanging from the belt of one of my old girls.

Miss Sims in a short time became "Miss Bess," and I discovered that we had a great many things in common. In the first place, she had been born in the little town of Linden, Perry County, Tennessee, which was in some respects much like my own birthplace, Buffalo, Missouri. It was a county seat of a county that had no railroad. It was even a little smaller than Buffalo. There she had lived until she was twelve, when her father was elected to Congress, and she moved to Washington. There in Linden, as I in Buffalo, she had had an intense interest in politics from her earliest childhood. Her chances for a superior education in that field were greater than mine. From the time she got to Washington at the age of twelve, the moment her school was out, she made a beeline to the Capitol to sit in the gallery of the House or the Senate to hear the debates. She knew by sight every member of both houses of Congress. She was a Democrat, a liberal Democrat; she was inclined to a hero worship of Mr. Bryan; she had not approved McKinley, nor did she entirely approve his successor, the redoubtable "Teddy," then in the White House. We found that we had many things to talk about, but most of them turned out to be political.

She had no notion of accepting me as a beau, nor did I have any idea of such a relationship. It was cousinhood. That in a way was a considerable advantage, because I could go to see her when I liked without too much formality of arrangement; and then I could ask her to go about with me on very simple excursions that were better fitted to my poverty and yet which would have been beneath the dignity of a beau.

For instance, one of the things that then could be done on a hot summer night without too great an expenditure of money was to take a trolley ride. A streetcar ticket (then sold in pasteboard strips of six for twenty-five cents) gave access to open trolley cars whose transverse seats ran from side to side, with access from a "running board" outside the car. There were very few automobiles in Washington then, and only the very rich could afford them, as only the well to do could afford a carriage or even a horse and buggy. So the trolley car was socially acceptable.

I soon discovered that social customs in Washington differed very greatly from those in vogue in Nashville and Louisville. For instance, I found out not only that a young gentleman asking a young lady to go to the theater with him had to appear in full bib and tucker of white tie and tails but that he was expected also to furnish a corsage, not to mention, in many cases, a third theater seat for the chaperon, and, of course, a carriage.

One hot summer night I asked Miss Bess to go with me on a trolley ride to Chevy Chase Lake. There were two streetcar companies in Washington then, and each of them maintained an amusement park at the end of the line: one at Glen Echo, which still exists, and the other in Chevy Chase, Maryland, long since abandoned. The streetcar tickets were cheap, of course, and I did manage to have a dollar or two in my pocket to take care of such emergencies as lemonade or popcorn when we got to the park. We arrived there delightfully cool from the long trip in the open car. We took a walk. We stopped for a moment at a shooting gallery. If there was one thing in the world that did *not* interest *me,* it was that. I had never had any truck with fire-arms. On the few occasions that I had attempted target shooting with a .22 rifle I had been unable to hit anything. I had been told that I couldn't hit a barn door with a scatter-gun, and I believed it. Just as we walked up, a young girl was shooting at the targets—some stationary ducks and a row of moving white ducks. She didn't hit anything. She asked her escort if she might try it again, and he bought her another rifle: She fired all fifteen shots. She hit nothing at all. They turned to leave. The young fellow in charge of the gallery spoke aloud, ad-dressing the world: "It makes me sick to see women try to shoot. None of them could ever hit anything on earth no matter how long they tried."

Miss Bess turned to me and in a quiet voice said, "Buy me a gun." Utterly astonished, I laid down a quarter. She picked up the rifle. One, two, three, . . . and so on . . . fifteen of the *moving* ducks were shattered! I shall never forget the look of amazement on that young man's face, and I am sure that, if he had looked at me, he would have found there registered in my whole attitude not only amazement but infinite respect.

So when in early November the shouting and the tumult of the campaign were over, and my first go at the glamour of New York was behind me, I came back to Washington confident in the belief that here I would spend the rest of my days; that here, with my feet on the bottom rung of the ladder, I would have an opportunity to climb to the highest peaks of my chosen profession of journalism. And naturally, too, for me, I looked forward to rejoining the family of my Washington kin.

I discovered that the Sims family had made a move. They had left the Varnum Hotel and set up a new ménage in a house at 1538 Seventeenth Street, N.W., within half a block of where I lived. That would have made things altogether delightful except for two new circumstances. Invitations were already out for Edna's wedding on November 29 to Mr. William Lewis Beale, who had been for some time the most favored of her many beaux. Bess was apparently herself recovered, but the doctors didn't think that she should go back to college. Her sister, Tom, had a persistent attack of bronchitis, and it was decided that Bess should go with Tom to the Southwest for the winter. They left for California on the fifth of December. But that did not at all deprive me of the Sims home and the Sims household as a second home. I already felt on very close terms with Judge and Mrs. Sims, as I did with the three smaller children: Paul, Marie, and Enid. And, in the summer before, after the close of the college year, I had met Kent, who had but one more year in Vanderbilt. So, very often indeed, the evening found me in the midst of the Sims household even after Edna had moved into her own home and Tom and Bess had gone west.

Even that pleasant retreat was not long to be enjoyed by me. My notion of permanency in Washington was but an ephemeral dream. During the Christmas holidays I was delighted to meet Urey Woodson one day in the corridor of the Capitol. I had seen him nearly every day in the New York headquarters of the party during the campaign. He was a liberal Democrat, and so was I. He asked me to come down to the Willard Hotel for dinner. That night at the table we went over the dismal record of the campaign, the fiasco of the Parker nomination at St. Louis, and the debacle of the succeeding campaign and election. We agreed that the party must turn once again to the leadership of William Jennings Bryan.

Then after dinner he said he wanted to talk to me about my own future. He said that he thought I ought to have a chance at a top editorial position and that he would like me to come to Paducah to be managing editor of the *Paducah News Democrat,* in which position I would serve directly under him and not only be responsible for the ordinary duties of a managing editor but could try my wings at editorial writing. He said that he would be in Owensboro nearly all the time and would come to Paducah once or twice a month and that therefore I would be in complete charge of the paper. He also told me that his present managing editor, Irvin Shrewsbury Cobb, a brilliant writer and an excellent managing editor, had not seen eye to eye with him with respect to politics and that, therefore, when Mr. Cobb had received an offer from the *New York Sun,* he had encouraged him to accept. He wanted me to come to Paducah to take Cobb's place. The salary wasn't very large—only thirty-five dollars a week—but it was five dollars more than the combined salaries paid me by the *Nashville Banner* and the *Louisville Evening Post.* The opportunity seemed great. I said "Yes," and that meant that at the end of January, 1905, I was leaving Washington, bound again for Kentucky.

II

Thus it came about that early February, 1905, found me back in Kentucky, the state I had left exactly a year earlier to go to Washington. My predecessor, Irvin Shrewsbury Cobb, already had a wide reputation as a wit and a raconteur. I had met him myself during my early days on *The Courier-Journal.* But Cobb had been so intent upon his Paducah home and his Paducah neighbors that he seemed to be a home-town fixture. When he left to go to New York, I am sure that very few persons thought his place could be filled, and I am sure that I, under the blandishments of Mr. Woodson's persuasive conversation, had an altogether too exalted opinion of my own ability to do it.

Nevertheless, I was welcomed in Paducah with open arms. I found a room in the home occupied by the four Misses Morton, cousins of my mentor, Marmaduke B. Morton, next door to the Cobb family home. And I found a place at the table, Irvin's own place, with his mother, Mrs. Cobb. Throughout his long and prolific life Irvin Cobb wrote many books on many subjects and filled the magazines with articles and stories, but throughout all of them there ran one theme— it was an echo from Cobb the gourmet; it was an indication that Cobb might also be a gourmand. I had not had his place at his mother's table for more than a day or two until I could well understand her elder son's obsession. He had been brought up on the best food in the world. It was Mrs. Cobb's boast that she had never been in her kitchen, which actually did occupy a somewhat detached little building reached from the main house through a covered passageway. Whether or not her boast was to be taken literally, I do not know. There is one thing that was sure, and that was that the cook came to Mrs. Cobb and that Mrs. Cobb directed all the culinary procedures: the preparation of the menus, the marketing, the serving. It was superb!

My job, I found, was a heavy one. I was at my desk at six-thirty in the morning to get things started, to send the early copy to the composing-room, to give assignments to my three reporters, and then, when the day's work was under way, to walk back the three or four blocks to Mrs. Cobb's for breakfast. The lunch hour was more a matter of chance, but I usually was able to make it, and my working day ended at six-thirty in the afternoon after everybody had left but me. It was then I pounded out one or two editorials for the next day. That would not have been so bad, perhaps, had it been only a six-day paper, but the trouble was that the *News Democrat* also had a Sunday-morning edition, so that on Saturdays my day began at six-thirty in the morning and never ended until four the next morning. It was a terrific grind.

I also was telegraph editor. The *Paducah News Democrat* had a pony Associated Press report, which was supplemented by me with clippings from the metropolitan papers of Louisville, St. Louis, and Memphis; by clippings daily provided from Owensboro by Mr. Woodson; and by the use of "mats" (matrices) carrying pictures from the then newly organized Newspaper Enterprise Association which enabled us to keep up in a way with the course of events of the Russo-Japanese War and whatever was going on in Washington, New York, and the great outside world.

Yet, at the same time, it contributed no little to my education. It brought me into direct contact with the business office, and I found myself concerned as I never before had been with problems of advertising and circulation. It brought me into direct contact with the foreman of the composing-room, John Curd, and with the foreman of the pressmen, John Meloan. It gave me an opportunity for daily personal contact with everybody who had anything to do with the paper from the front office through all the mechanical departments up to the absent editor and owner.

The three reporters were Miss Ora Leigh, thirtyish, who was not only the society editor but a general all-round news hound and a good one; Richard Lovelace, a tall and handsome youngster, who was responsible for business news and principal assignments; and John Cobb, Irvin's diminutive younger brother, who did the police and sports. Needless to say, all three were very busy persons. Only Lovelace used the typewriter. Miss Leigh's handwritten copy was legible and required little or no editing. John Cobb's handwriting was easy enough to read, but he had extremely peculiar notions of sentence construction as well as an unfortunate habit of intruding personal opinions in straight news stories which required me to edit his copy with great care.

As I have intimated, Mr. Woodson had ideas about the place the *Paducah News Democrat* should have in the political life of Paducah and of McCracken County, of which it was the seat, and of the First Congressional District, of which it was the metropolis. The sitting congressman was Ollie M. James, a huge mountain of a man who recently had succeeded Charles K. Wheeler of Paducah. Mr. Wheeler was an excellent lawyer and a distinguished man who had made his mark in Congress, but he had been loyal to Cleveland and to the gold standard and therefore had been repudiated by the Bryanites. Ollie James, on the other hand, was a devoted follower of the Peerless Leader. The immediate problem, however, was to be centered in county and city politics. The county attorney (as the prosecuting attorney is known in Kentucky) was a Democrat, a genial soul, a handsome man about town, an intimate personal friend of Irvin Cobb, and another great storyteller. However, he was not distinguished for his diligence in prosecuting some malefactors, especially those who had to do with gambling, and, what may even have been worse (from Mr. Woodson's point of view), he, too, was suspected of not being an entirely loyal Bryan man.

The mayor of the city was an eminently respectable retired physician who owned one of the most successful drugstores in the town. He was a tall, handsome, bearded man who seemed to Mr. Woodson and me to be entirely too complacent about certain goings-on. In retrospect, I must admit that he did not have very much power under the archaic system of municipal government then prevailing in Paducah, but, nevertheless, he had assumed a certain responsibility for the conduct of municipal affairs. It was very evident that the police department was lax, to say the very least, in its law-enforcement activities, and many of the other municipal functions were carried on seemingly on a hit-or-miss basis. Indeed, from my office, which was on the second floor of a small brick business building, I could look into the open windows of a second-story room directly across the street where a gambling establishment was in full operation without any attempt at concealment.

Given my background and my interest in news about law and order, it required no pressure whatever to induce me to begin a campaign to clean up Paducah police-wise and especially with respect to gambling. That meant that I was soon in a bitter public fight with the city administration, which had its defenders in the opposition afternoon paper, the *Paducah Sun,* and in the morning paper, the *Register.* It was a slam-bang, old-fashioned journalistic set-to. I found, however, that I had a great deal of popular support not only from the clergy, the church people, and the unco guid but also from the business element. Presidents of banks, owners of wholesale establishments, retail merchants—all assured me that they were behind me, and all encouraged me to go ahead. This sort of thing, of course, has happened in so many cities and in so many places and under circumstances so similar I perhaps will be forgiven for saying that I was not nearly so successful as I thought I would be or, indeed, as I pretended to myself that I was.

Among the businessmen in the community was a banker who was a leader of civic thought, Mr. James C. Utterback. He, while applauding what I had to say about the municipal government, also pointed out to me that, unless we got better support for law-enforcement programs from the county attorney, we would not get very far. Mr. Woodson always talked with Mr. Utterback when he came to town, and the three of us decided that the time had come to find someone else, some Democratic lawyer who would be a candidate in the Democratic primary for the position of county attorney.

There was a young lawyer who had just come to Paducah from the neighboring town of Mayfield. He was personable. He could make a good speech, and, what was even more to the point in Kentucky politics at that time, he was an admirable storyteller. He announced his candidacy. The *News Democrat* backed him heartily. He won the nomination. And, as a matter of course, he was then elected county attorney of McCracken County. His name was Alben W. Barkley, and that was the beginning of a political career that carried him into the House of Representatives, into the Senate, into the leadership of the Senate, and into the vice-presidency.

The many incidents of newspaper life, spectacular murder mysteries, toward solutions of which the newspapers helped, and the ordinary grist of the news made life exciting every day. Of all my newspaper adventures in Paducah, one stands out distinctly in my memory because it could well have meant the termination not only of my career as a journalist but of my existence on this earth. It might be called the "Case of the Murderous Mother."

Miss Ora Leigh in the pursuit of her duties as society editor and general reporter made a habit of meeting the passenger trains at the distant Illinois Central Station, a considerable trolley-car trip beyond the outskirts of the town. The trains from Louisville to Memphis and from Memphis to Louisville passed each other in Paducah around one o'clock in the afternoon. She was always there to see the comings and the goings and to collect not only gossip for her society column but any odd bits of news. When she came back to town at two o'clock, she always went by the undertakers to pick up the latest mortuary news. As I have said, Miss Leigh's handwriting was legible, her English was good, and I had learned that it was not necessary for me to go over her copy very carefully. On this last run, when she got to the office around twenty minutes past two and we went to press at three, I simply sent her copy to the printer at once.

One afternoon when the paper came out I read one of Miss Leigh's stories that brought me up with a jolt. She had found at an undertaker's the bodies of three little children. Their simultaneous deaths had given Miss Leigh some reason to suspect that all was not well, and her raised eyebrows were clearly reflected in the news item. She came as near as possible without actually doing so to accusing the children's mother of having murdered them.

Now this was at the time of the white-hot fight I was carrying on against the police department and the city administration. I was very much afraid that this story would cause me trouble. I called in Miss Leigh and discovered that she had almost nothing to go on except suspicion voiced by a very young and therefore irresponsible attendant at the undertaking establishment. I could only hope that nothing would come of it.

My hopes were doomed the next morning when the *Register,* a very peculiar newspaper, came out with a front-page blast against me and against the *News Democrat,* which it called a "yellow journal," winding up with a very thinly veiled invitation to the populace to rise and drive me out of town. At my desk at six-thirty with the *Register* before me, I was at my wit's end to know how to proceed. I knew I could get no help from the police. I didn't know where to turn. At the very depth of my puzzlement I heard a noise behind me. I turned. A suitcase dropped to the floor, and there stood my old friend, Howard Robinson. Now, Howard had been a star reporter on *The Courier-Journal* and after that had gone to New York, where he had built up quite a reputation as a detective-reporter on the staff of Mr. Hearst's *New York Journal* and was later to cover himself with considerable journalistic glory in his report of the Harry Thaw–Stanford White murder trial. He was, he said, on a vacation at his old home of Guthrie, Kentucky, and had decided to come over and spend a few days with me. He was a gift from heaven. What he got immediately was an assignment. I told him the story and told him to go and get it!

About two-thirty in the afternoon I looked across the street, and in the gambling establishment I saw a crowd five or six times as large as usually could be observed there in the afternoon. Then also groups of loiterers walking along the street came to a pause directly opposite the *News Democrat* office. It wasn't at all difficult to see what was going on. John Cobb came in and told me that he had been nosing around and that he was sure, if the *News Democrat* did not come out with a retraction and an apology, some of the hotheads might incite the mob to attack us. The fight was that hot.

I waited and waited and waited. Not one word from Robbie. Lovelace, Cobb, and Miss Leigh had been unable to find out anything. They couldn't even find out where the mother of the children was. The undertaker, if he knew, wouldn't tell. We knew her name. We knew that she was not at her home where the three children had died. That was all. We were completely at sea. And not a word from Robbie.

I waited as long as I could. I decided to miss the early edition, which we sent south by train and which was put to bed at twenty minutes past two. Three o'clock was press time for the city edition. I decided to wait at least ten minutes. I stood by. All the pages were stereotyped, and the casts were on the press with the exception of the front page. That page was made up but made up in such a way that I could pull a three-column headline and two or three inches of type for a bulletin. Three o'clock came. Five past three! Ten minutes past three! I kicked the turtle away from me to John Curd, the foreman, and I said, "Let her roll."

At that instant the telephone on the wall rang. I ran to it. It was Robbie. He said: "Hold everything. I have her and her signed confession. I will be there in fifteen minutes."

We pulled the three-column headline. John ran to set it. I dictated the bulletin directly to Louis Head at the linotype machine, and, less than fifteen minutes late, the *News Democrat* burst onto the street with the screaming headline: MOTHER CONFESSES MURDER OF THREE CHILDREN!

The mob, and by this time it had become indeed a mob both in size and in temper, evaporated.

Robbie came in. He had run up an enormous bill at a livery stable for a carriage. He had gone to find the mother at her home and had taken her in a closed carriage to the home of one of her kinsmen and had talked to her all morning. She had confessed in the presence of witnesses, including the minister of her church, and had signed the confession. With that, an hour later, we were on the street with an extra and the full details.

That ended the talk about running the yellow journalist out of town. Robbie stayed with me three or four days, and we had a good time.

My relationships with the mechanical department were very cordial. While of course, the compositors were members of the typographical union, they were not very strict in their rules. Since all our heads were hand-set, I found myself frequently at the case, setting type for the headlines. One of the compositors, a redheaded, tobacco-chewing wit named Louis P. Head, also, despite union rules, actually taught me to operate the linotype machine. While I never became skilful, I could cast a few slugs when necessary or for my own amusement. I was still close enough to my Ozark country printshop to revel in that sort of thing. Louis Head was tremendously interested in politics, and he counseled and advised me about the editorials I should write with respect to the local political fight. He got around the town. He knew all the other printers, and he helped me a great deal by bringing me in pieces of information that I could use in my news stories and my editorials. It was that newspaper fight over the city administration which marked a turning point in Head's career.

After Paducah he went to Dallas and got a job as a linotype operator on the *Dallas News*. After some years his interest in municipal affairs became known to the city editor, and he was translated from the composing-room to the editorial room. There he became an expert on municipal affairs. He was the first journalist anywhere in the United States to apply William Bennett Munro's criteria of city government to an actual administration. He successfully campaigned for the establishment of a city planning commission, and toward the end of his career he conducted successfully the campaign that caused Dallas to abandon the commission form of government and adopt the council-manager plan.

I found also in my evenings off a delightful social life in Paducah. I met a great many men and women both young and old and thoroughly enjoyed myself in their company. I was not entirely insensitive to the fact that my position in the town in a way was an open-sesame to all sorts of circles, and at the same time I am as sure now as I was then that the people of Paducah were as considerate and as kind to the stranger within their gates as ever had been the people of any community. Furthermore, I discovered that among them were many cultivated, sensitive souls with whom one could be at home in discussion of literature, current events, philosophy, religion, or whatever.

Then, too, I extended my education in another way by attempting to supplement my meager staff by giving apprenticeships for nothing a week, or for a very few dollars a week at most, to young men just leaving high school. Three or four such boys worked for me, and at least two of them there began successful journalistic careers.

But the difficulty was that I did not have enough physical stamina to withstand the rigors of an eighty-two-hour week. So, when the hot weather came, I wilted. It was more than wilt. I had had the symptoms of that sort of thing before, so one day in September, when Mr. Woodson came down, I told him I was too tired. I would either have to have a vacation or else! He agreed with me that I might turn the paper over to Lovelace for a couple of weeks and that he would come down more often than usual and keep closer tab on things and let me take a rest. In that way I got two weeks off. And, considering the shortness of my tenure and the customs of the time, it was astonishing that it was two weeks off with pay.

III

With two weeks and a railroad pass, I might have gone home to Missouri, but I did not. I decided that this would be a good time to explore another part of the world. The Sims family, I knew, was at home that autumn. "At home" meant that they all were at the family seat at Linden on the Buffalo River, the county seat of Perry County, Tennessee. It was still considered necessary in those days that a representative in Congress should spend half of his time at home. The long session of Congress usually ended on the thirtieth of June, because at that time the two houses of Congress still had some sort of feeling of responsibility of getting through the appropriation bills by the end of the fiscal year. Crisis government had not yet been admitted or even envisaged, and so congressional families were not very apt to spend the entire year in Washington.

Linden, I knew, was a small town, even smaller than Buffalo, Missouri; but there was a likeness: Linden was the capital of a county which had no railroad, but, unlike my native Dallas County, it did have on its western border a great navigable river, the Tennessee. And the town itself on its eastern border had another river, also flowing northwardly, the Buffalo. The very word "Buffalo" meant a great deal to me nostalgically, and so I began to think of Linden in the hyphenated form as Linden-on-the-Buffalo.

It seemed to me that, if I could have a vacation, I would rather spend it with the Sims family than anywhere else. I wrote to my Cousin Bess, and she said it would be all right for me to come down. I negotiated the distance by way of the Illinois Central Railroad and the Nashville, Chattanooga, and St. Louis Railroad and got as far as Perryville on the west bank of the Tennessee River. There I was rowed across the river in a skiff and embarked on the hazardous journey of twelve miles to Linden over crooked and almost untended roads by way of the familiar mail hack of my youth.

I joined Judge Sims and Kent at the hotel. The rest of the Sims family, with the sole exception of Edna, were with Mrs. Sims's sister, Mrs. S. A. Macdonald, only two blocks down the street. So in Linden I found Kent, Tom, Judge and Mrs. Sims, the three little children, but, more importantly, Bess. She still was looking at me with a quizzical smile. She still was "Cousin." But somehow or other, just on account of the simple daring of having joined the Sims family and just because the Judge and Mrs. Sims had taken up my nickname and called me "Brownie," I at this stage dropped the "Miss." The girls were "Tom," and gingerly, I think—at least there was a little bit more timidity—a choice between "Bess" and "Bep." Others had called her "Bessie," but I knew she hated that, and her sister Tom had called her "Liz," and I knew she hated that, so I began to call her "Bep."

There wasn't an awful lot to do around the town, but we managed to keep busy day and night. There were pianos, and Tom, who had already had six months in the Sargeant School of the Drama in New York, found places to do impersonations. There was a girl named Gus Dodson who not only could and would but did play the piano, and there was always a gathering of the teen-agers and those just over their teens, as were Kent and Tom and Gus and Bep and me.

There were horses around, and it turned out that I never had ridden a horse in my life. So one morning Kent came up with a horse that did not seem to be so tremendously large to me, and he asked me actually to pat it on the neck. The horse didn't seem to mind, so Kent said, "Well, you ought to learn to ride. Now, this horse is tame. All the children in town ride him. Why don't you try it out?"

The whole family happened to be assembled that morning at the hotel. I was so ashamed that I overcame my fears, and with help, and considerable help at that, I most awkwardly got into the saddle. I could barely reach the stirrups with the tips of my toes. Kent pulled up the skirts of the saddle and said, "Well, the girths are laced, and it would be too hard a job to shorten them. Nevertheless, this is just a tame cat. You ride him around, and it won't make any difference."

So I ambled off. Now it so happened that at that particular time there was in the town one of those country circuses—a traveling circus that avoided railroads, disdained steamboats, but went by country road from town to town. We knew very well that later on that morning there would be a circus parade around the square. We knew very well that all of us were going that afternoon and again that night to see the circus. But the coincidence of my attempting my first horseback ride and the presence in the town of the circus certainly escaped me, and I acquit Kent of any guilty knowledge of what later may have been considered a conspiracy.

At any rate, I was on the animal. I had enough sense to guide him to the right or the left by the use of the bridle reins, and I rode him away in triumph at a slow walk down one side of the square, turned to the left, then to the right, and out toward an eminence which gloried in the name of "Nigger Hill." There I thought I had gone far enough, and I succeeded in turning him around. On the way back to the square, however, I passed the tent which was in process of being pitched for the circus, and there something terrific happened.

The circus band struck up! My horse pricked up his ears. He quickened his steps. My feet lost the stirrups. He frightened me to death. I seized the saddle horn, and at the same time I relaxed my hold on the bridle reins. Now, I had no notion that this was a horse that had had its early education in Texas. Still less did I know that graduates of the Equine Curriculum of Texas Horse Colleges had been taught from their youth up that relaxation of the reins was a signal to go. He went! He went rapidly.

By that time it was getting close on to ten o'clock in the morning, and the people who had come in from the country were already lined up around the square, awaiting the circus parade. They could hear in the distance the circus band. They knew that the great hour was approaching.

Then something happened that not one of them had expected. A trick rider appeared, the vanguard of the circus! The faster that animal ran, the more I clung to the saddle horn and the more I let go of the reins. For some reason or other he decided to execute a series of left turns which would take him all around the square. We went around the square. I lost my spectacles on one turn. At each concentric circling of the square he automatically shortened the radius, and at long last he raked me off against a hitching post on that side of the square where the hotel was and deposited me, spectacle-less, torn, and somewhat bloody, at the feet of my charming cousin, Bep.

The quizzical smile with which she had met me in Washington faded away. She doubled up with laughter. I might have been ashamed except for the fact that I doubted if I would live. I was certain that all my bones were broken, and I was sure that it was my last hour. Whereupon out from the side lines came one of the spectators, one of those who at first had thought that this was the greatest trick circus rider they had ever seen, until on the third time around the square they discovered it was just a town boy who didn't know how to ride a horse.

This person who came out to me was Bill Taylor. Now, Bill Taylor was a character. At the time of the Civil War he had been a Loyalist. His family was Whig. He had been for the Union, and he had no use whatever for Jeff Davis or the southern Confederacy. However, he had been drafted into the southern army and had been taken away to the eastern theater of the war, where in a gray jacket he had been put in the lines against the blue-coated Yankees. When he got home, Bill always said: "Of course I stayed with them until Appomatox. They all knowed I was a Union man, and, in spite of my Union sentiments, I got up there in the front line, and them Yankees shot at me, and, damn them, I shot back at 'em."

It also so happened that Bill had never learned to read and write, but nevertheless he was a philosopher. He was the one who picked me up. He was the one who said, "Maybe you need some arnica."

When Kent and the others rushed out to help me, Bill said to me, "Young feller, so you ain't never rid a hoss before, has ye?"

I answered, "No."

"Well, young feller, let me tell ye this. Don't never trust no literary hoss. The next time you get on a hoss, you look him all over, and, if there is any writin' on his hindquarters, you stay offen'm. Ye can't trust these literary folks—peoples or hosses."

It was apparent that the horse in the course of his early education in Texas had been branded on his hindquarter. He was literary. Bill was not. It was my first and last horseback adventure.

My spectacles were found, with the bows bent but fortunately with lenses intact, in front of Dr. Daniel's drugstore. Various articles from my pockets were collected from various points around the square. The suggestion of arnica was admitted. I retreated to my room off the veranda, made such emergency repairs as could be made in a bowl-and-pitcher economy, and came out most shamefacedly to stand with Bep and review the circus parade as it went around—band, clowns, trick riders, and all the rest of it.

As we stood on the veranda with our hands on the rail and I more uncomfortable than I ever was in my life and more ashamed than I had ever been, I experienced a great thrill. She reached over with her left hand and patted me on my right hand.

Peace came unto me.

After seven or eight days delightfully spent with the Sims family and much of it with my cousin Elizabeth, I left with all of them to go to Jackson, the metropolis of Judge Sims's congressional district, where he was to set up his campaign headquarters. From Jackson, yielding to nostalgia again, I set out for an old home week in Nashville.

There not only did I see my numerous kinsfolk and many of my friends but, of course, I went straight to the office of the *Nashville Banner,* which was, after all, my alma mater. I had a long talk with Mr. Morton about what I was doing. He thought I was getting a rich experience, but he also intimated that I might be paying too much for my education.

"Brownie," said Mr. Morton, "you are a very nervous and sensitive youngster, and I don't believe you can ever stand long hours. The morning-paper grind is terrible, and you couldn't take it on *The Courier-Journal.* The twelve-hour, six-day week, with ten hours extra tacked on for the Sunday edition, of an afternoon newspaper is too much. If I were you, as soon as I could find a good replacement, I would talk to Mr. Woodson and leave Paducah."

"But where would I go? How could I get a job?" was naturally my rejoinder.

"Well," he said, "I have been thinking it over, and the *Banner* would like to have you go back to Washington; and this time I wouldn't go to the trouble we had with Gil Boyle and the *Louisville Evening Post.* You can go for the *Banner* alone, and I will pay you as much as you are getting now, and perhaps you will be able to pick up something else on your own. I would like to have you back in Washington, and Major Stahlman [the owner and publisher] would like it too."

[391]

That settled it in my mind. So, while I was there, I went to see my old friend, Buford Goodwin, managing editor of the *Daily News,* then on its very last legs. He told me that the paper would fold within a few weeks. I asked him if he would consider taking my job in Paducah. He said he would, because he had nowhere to go.

So, back in Paducah, I picked up the reins again. I waited for Mr. Woodson to come back from a vacation up in the Great Lakes area, and, when he came to Paducah, I told him the story. He said he was very sorry, but he also agreed that I was not physically able to stand up to the job. He did want a little time, however, to look into Mr. Goodwin. The upshot was that he had Buford come to Owensboro to see him, and, after another delay or two for one reason or another, Buford came to Paducah around the first of November. I stayed with him a week putting him onto the ropes, although that was not at all necessary for such a capable managing editor as he.

Then a trip home to see my family in Missouri and back to Washington for the opening of the Congress at the beginning of December.

Thus came to an end my brief but richly rewarding experience in Paducah. That Mr. Woodson must have been satisfied is manifested by the fact years and years later in a sketch in *Who's Who* he included a statement of a type I have never seen in any other biographical note of the kind. It reads:

> Editor and Publisher—Paducah (Ky.) *News Democrat* 1901–1912 employing successively Irvin S. Cobb, Louis Brownlow, and Buford Goodwin as managing editors.

Surely never was an employer to leave a more gratifying testimony of his regard for three of his hirelings than was that.

CHAPTER XXI

MR. HASKIN ENTERS THE PICTURE

When I found myself back in Washington in November, 1905, I felt at home. I assured myself that my wanderlust had been conquered and that I would try no more experiments. In addition to the *Nashville Banner,* I managed to get the *Knoxville Sentinel,* edited by George Fort Milton, Sr., and the *Birmingham News,* edited by Rufus N. Rhodes, to put me on their pay rolls at five dollars each. That permitted me to break through the ceiling that hitherto had always held me under the two-thousand-dollar-a-year goal that I had set for myself. That also permitted me to take a one-room-and-bath apartment at the Westminster, an apartment hotel at Seventeenth and Q streets in the neighborhood of my former boarding-houses; and I set myself up with my own lares and penates. Breakfast and dinner were served in the hotel, and I was on my own for lunch. I established myself in an office in the Metropolitan Bank Building with only one other occupant, Walter Edward Harris, of the *Richmond Times.* I no longer considered myself confined to writing for the wires only localized state news. I decided to be a full-fledged Washington correspondent and send, at least to the *Banner,* the news that I could collect and the observations that I desired to make on what was going on in Washington on a national and even on an international scale.

This transition was made all the easier by the fact that in the first week in December the new Fifty-ninth Congress was to assemble. This was the Congress which had been elected in 1904 when Theodore Roosevelt had won the presidential election in his own right and after a campaign in which he had made a considerable number of definite promises to the people respecting great reforms. It was the Square Deal. The Republicans had a great majority in both houses.

There was no question that the leadership of the majority party would remain in the hands of the old guard of those who had supported McKinley, of those who had regretted the rise of the formidable "Teddy," many of whom, at any rate, were patiently willing to see him and his Square Deal program scotched. "Uncle Joe" Cannon was re-elected speaker of the House without question, and in those days the speaker had powers with respect to the appointment of committees which supervened the seniority system and had powers of recognition which enabled him practically to dictate the course of legislation in the House.

In the Senate, Republican leadership, nominally under the control of Senator Orville H. Platt of Connecticut, was shared with Senators Aldrich of Rhode Island, Allison of Iowa, and Spooner of Wisconsin. More of the defeated Democrats (under the leadership of John Sharp Williams of Mississippi in the House and of Bacon of Georgia in the Senate) were inclined to the Bryan wing of the party than were amenable to the Cleveland influence, which, indeed, had all but entirely disappeared.

Two major struggles were soon under way. One was concerned with the effort to amend the Interstate Commerce Act so as to extend the powers of the Interstate Commerce Commission in several ways but most importantly to include the rate-making power, which up until that time it had not possessed. It also extended the commission's jurisdiction to include express and sleeping-car companies, oil-pipe lines, terminal facilities, ferries, and bridges. It contained provisions sharply restricting the issuance of free passes, increased the membership of the commission from five to seven, and contemplated stricter enforcement.

The other struggle was the contest concerning the terms of a proposal to set up, under the aegis of the interstate-commerce clause of the Constitution, a federal pure food and drug law. After a half-century these reforms, then so vigorously fought for by the progressive and liberal elements of both parties, seem to be mild indeed, but then they were resisted not only by the vested interests which would be affected but by conservative-minded people who were more afraid of change than they were hopeful of benefit from the radical proposals of "Teddy" Roosevelt.

The result of the election was still fresh in the minds of the members of the House, however, and the railroad-rate reform bill got away to a quick start. The Committee on Interstate Commerce in the House of Representatives, under the chairmanship of William P. Hepburn of Iowa, wrote a rate bill which received the unanimous support of the committee, Democrats as well as Republicans. I faithfully attended the hearings that were held on the Hepburn Bill. Perhaps fifteen or twenty other correspondents would be in the room. There was no dais. The members of the committee sat around the table in their cramped quarters on the gallery floor of the House Wing of the Capitol. There was no fanfare, and, for the most part, there were no auditors except the newspapermen.

On one occasion, however, nearly all the members of the press gallery crowded into the room, most of them, I am sure, confident of seeing a member of their own cult thrown to the lions. Mr. William Randolph Hearst was a member of the Congress, and he had introduced his own railroad bill, more radical than the Hepburn Bill and directed toward government ownership of the railroads. Many of us were sure that the young captain of yellow journalism was not his own bill-writer and was not his own speech-writer. We were sure that, when the committeemen got after him with questions, he would flounder in disgrace despite the imposing figure he cut in his flowing, full-skirted Prince Albert coat.

Never were those of us who came to gloat and to giggle more completely disappointed. Mr. Hearst, without notes, first made an oral presentation of his ideas on the problem and the solution that he had proposed in his bill. Then the questions began to come. No doubt most of the members of the committee had had the same notion that I had, but Hearst was too much for them. He knew his subject—from his point of view, of course—and he answered easily, quickly, succinctly, and in very good humor. The chairman, after the first few rounds, left most of the questioning to the Democrats, to Mr. Adamson of Georgia, the ranking minority member, and Mr. Sims of Tennessee, the next in line. Neither of these gentlemen believed in Mr. Hearst's ability. Both were lawyers who asked him searching questions if not, sometimes, those that might verge upon entrapment, but Mr. Hearst took care of them both; and after a little more than half an hour they abandoned the field. Of course the Hearst Bill had no chance, but Hearst's stock among his colleagues in the House of Representatives and among the members of the press gallery rose immeasurably.

The Hepburn Bill passed the House by an overwhelming majority.

Then, in mid-March, the issue was joined in the Senate. There it was a different tale. The Senate Committee on Commerce, composed, of course, of a majority of Republicans, met under the chairmanship of William B. Allison of Iowa. The Hepburn Bill, or rather a Senate version of it, could find no real support from among the members of the President's party. No hearings were held, as I remember it. The situation was unprecedented and, so far as I know, remains unique. The committee was willing to report the bill to the Senate for consideration and debate, but not one Republican member was willing to undertake the responsibility of its conduct. So, in a gesture of defiance to "Teddy," the committee gave the bill to the ranking minority member, "Pitchfork Ben" Tillman, the one-eyed radical from South Carolina, and authorized him to report it to the floor. Mr. Tillman and the President were enemies. They did not speak to each other. The President had publicly declared that under no circumstances would Senator Tillman be permitted to enter the White House as long as he, Mr. Roosevelt, was its occupant.

Then began the spectacle of the principal enemy of the President attempting to put through the Senate the principal measure of the President's program! Senator Tillman, rated by many as a dangerous demagogue, was nevertheless a man of great ability and of great strength of character and mind, which were matched by great powers of physical endurance. His principal assistants in support of the President's measure were two other Democrats, both of whom had been forbidden to enter the White House grounds by the President. One was Joseph W. Bailey of Texas, a handsome, clever, and able lawyer who had been the minority leader in the House of Representatives. The other was Senator Carmack of Tennessee, a redheaded orator of the flamboyant style who was distinguished by two features of his political life: the effort to break the hold of the railroads on the state legislatures and the throwing-out of Theodore Roosevelt from public life.

On the other side of the aisle the opposition to the essential features of the President's bill were Spooner of Wisconsin, perhaps the ablest lawyer in the Senate; the canny, quiet, and resourceful Allison; the brilliant and eloquent Foraker of Ohio; and most of the other Republican leaders. The debate ran on for weeks and weeks. The galleries were always crowded. The press gallery was always full, and I, like many others, never voluntarily missed a word of it.

The issue centered on whether or not there was to be what was called a "broad court review" or a "narrow court review"—on whether or not the rates established by the Interstate Commerce Commission were to stand without court review unless there was some substantive question of improper procedure or whether every rate decision might be appealed to the courts. The President was for the narrow court review. The opposition was for the broad. Because of the fact that the President was not on speaking terms with any of the senators who were conducting his fight, a secret liaison was set up. Former Senator William E. Chandler of New Hampshire was the go-between. He saw the President every night, and then every morning he saw Tillman and Bailey.

At long last the President, however, managed to find some weak spots in the Republican opposition, and he authorized Mr. Chandler to approach the Republican leaders with a face-saving compromise which, however, did leave Mr. Roosevelt in command of the field of battle. This compromise was entered into without the knowledge of Tillman, Bailey, or Carmack. It caused them to fulminate in a final outburst against the outrageous Roosevelt, but Roosevelt had his way. The bill passed the Senate. And, after the differences between the two houses had been ironed out in a conference report that gave the President even more of a victory, it was passed on the last day of the Congress and was signed on June 29, 1906.

It ranked in importance perhaps with some of the great constitutional debates that took place in the early days of the Republic and with those that later were centered on the question of state rights versus centralized control, especially as thrown up in the great slavery issue which led to the Civil War. Politically the struggle was remarkable because the Republican President found his strongest support among the members of the opposition party. Yet, because of his great political skill (the Democrats of that day called it by a more opprobrious name), he managed to win a victory for this principal item of his program. At the same time he kept his party leadership and prevented, or at least postponed, the split that was not to develop until six years later.

Another great fight was on over the pure food and drug issue, which was another part of Mr. Roosevelt's Square Deal program. Here, however, he did have the support of a greater number of the members of his own party, and the measure, which passed the House rather early by a comfortable majority, saw its principal battle in the Senate. Here the bill was in charge of the chairman of the Agriculture Committee, Senator Redfield Proctor of Vermont; but Mr. Proctor, for whatever reason, delegated the conduct of the floor fight to an intimate friend of the President, Senator Albert Jeremiah Beveridge of Indiana, who was contemptuously called by the conservative Republican press and by some of his elder colleagues "The Grand Young Man of Indiana." Here, too, the battle joined at the end on a narrow issue—whether or not packers should be required to put the dates of packing on every can or receptacle of processed or preserved food. That fight raged furiously for a considerable length of time. Then one day Mr. Proctor went to the White House, came back to the Senate, arose, and in a mild voice withdrew the dating amendment. Mr. Beveridge had not been advised. The Indiana orator was furious, but nothing could be done. The bill was passed. But again it also had had a more hearty support in the early and critical stages from the Democratic minority than it had from the Republican majority.

It so happened that I was not in the Senate gallery when Mr. Proctor made his astounding proposal, because at that particular time I was over at the House end trying to get some news out of the House Appropriations Committee concerning rivers and harbors appropriations that would affect my Tennessee-Kentucky-Alabama area. While I was there, in walked Walter Preston Brownlow. The room was abuzz with gossip. Why did Proctor do it? Did "Teddy" let Beveridge down? And so on. . . .

Mr. Brownlow spoke up and said, "Don't worry. I done it. I done it myself."

"You done what? You done nothing!" came back Mr. Bankhead of Alabama.

"Yes, I did," said Brownlow. "I just was tired of this fight, and I just slipped over there on the floor of the Senate, and I just moseyed up to ole Proctor, and I said, 'Proctor, if you get this bill passed, and you get this food too damn pure, what's going to happen to all them tombstone quarries you got up in Vermont?' That settled it."

The proposal to date packaged goods has been revived from time to time in the last five decades, but never has it been seriously considered. It does remain a fact, however, that one of the dates most frequently falling under the eyes of Americans is the date of the adjournment of the Fifty-ninth Congress in the familiar labeling: "According to the Food and Drug Act of June 30, 1906."

Mr. Haskin Enters the Picture

While for the seven months of that session of the Congress I spent nearly all my time at the Capitol, I did not neglect by any means the other end of the avenue. I still kept in touch with my news sources in the departments, principally the Treasury and the Post Office. I occasionally went to the State Department, and I not infrequently had an opportunity to see the President.

Newspapermen who were more or less friendly to his program could manage to see him sometimes alone, more frequently in small groups of five or six. Very frequently these sessions were held in the late afternoon after the adjournment of the two houses of Congress when the President was preparing to leave his office and go over to the White House to dress for dinner. This was the time of day when he was shaved by his valet. A more skilful barber never existed. "Teddy" in an ordinary armchair would be lathered, and, as the razor would descend toward his face, someone would ask a question. The President would wave both arms, jump up, speak excitedly, and then drop again into the chair and grin at the barber, who would begin all over. Sometimes these explosions interrupted a shave ten or a dozen times. It was more fun to see than a circus, and it did bring a few of us who were not the correspondents of the great metropolitan papers but who occupied (to make the best of it) but the marginal fringe of the profession in close contact with one of the most dynamic men ever to occupy the White House.

As soon as the Congress had adjourned, I was ordered home to Nashville to become the state political editor of the *Banner,* with the special duty of covering the gubernatorial campaign then about to begin. This involved giving up my two little papers and a cut in remuneration, but there was nothing else to do but to obey orders. So I went back to Nashville and, in order to compensate for the loss in salary, took up my quarters in the home of James B. Clark, my old city editor, where I shared a room with a newly arrived reporter, William P. Hoffman. However, most of the time, or at least a great deal of the time that summer and early autumn, I was in the field, traveling on an expense account, and that helped matters along.

At the end of May the Democrats had nominated Malcolm R. Patterson, formerly a representative in Congress from the Memphis district, for governor. The Republican convention was to assemble in Nashville, and I was to report it. The Republicans had high hopes of carrying the state, but unfortunately they were torn in an internecine

[399]

warfare between the "easy boss," my cousin, Walter P. Brownlow, and a rival leader, Henry Clay Evans of Chattanooga. The convention was a lively, almost riotous, occasion; and its members acted as if there was no doubt that, relying on incipient factionalism in the Democratic party, they would be able that fall "to redeem" Tennessee from Democratic rule. The Brownlow and the Evans factions fought it out. But Brownlow had been away in Washington too much and too long, and he had made too many patronage appointments and had created too many ingrates and a tremendous number of enemies. Evans won the nomination, and Brownlow returned to his own First District, where he had a red-hot campaign on to save his own seat in Congress. The upshot was that the Republican split advantaged the Democrats, and Patterson was elected, albeit by a fairly narrow margin of only twenty thousand votes. The campaign, however, contributed greatly to my own education, because it took me into all parts of the state and gave me an opportunity to visit all the large cities as well as many of the remote county seats and even little villages where the favorite Tennessee sport of political debates was being carried on.

During the summer I had several talks with Mr. Morton and told him that I thought it would be better if I were to stay on in Washington regularly whether or not the Congress was in session and that he ought to get someone else as state political editor who would be on the job all the time. That decision was to give me an unlooked-for and at the time unrealized great opportunity which years later was to prove of great significance in my life. As I went around the state, being commissioned thereto by Mr. Morton, I talked to reporters and finally decided that one man, a political reporter on the *Clarksville Leaf-Chronicle,* was the man we needed. I recommended him to Mr. Morton. He came to Nashville. Mr. Morton liked him. He was employed, and then it was agreed that he would come on and travel with me and overlap with me for four or five weeks. That he did, and in return I was supposed to instruct him in the involved mysteries of local and state politics, partisan, factional, regional, and whatnot.

His name was Joseph Ruggles Wilson. Then one day in October he and I went to Chattanooga together. The occasion was not a political meeting. It was merely a dinner given by the Chattanooga Princeton Alumni Club. The occasion was a visit from the president of Princeton University. He was Joe Wilson's brother, Woodrow Wilson. Joe and

I had several long talks with his distinguished brother, and I had a chance to get acquainted with the president of Princeton.

Then also during that fall I took time out for a visit to my father's home county seat, Pulaski, on the occasion of the dedication of a statue to Sam Davis, a local hero of the Confederate Army, a man who had been hanged by the Union soldiers as a spy. Sam Davis, a Rebel Nathan Hale, had been captured at my aunt's home and had refused to give information as to his aides and confederates. One of them in the very first degree was my own aunt. Another, though operating some thirty or forty miles away and perhaps at that time unsuspected by the Union commanders, was my mother. My sentimental interest in the Sam Davis story, the visit to my ancestral home, and the meetings there with many of my close relatives were in themselves exciting enough.

The election over and Joe Wilson installed, I was soon on my way back to Washington. Thus ended the last phase of my newspaper career in Tennessee, where it had begun only five years earlier.

II

One thing I told myself when I got back to Washington was sure, and that was that I was there as the correspondent of the *Nashville Banner* and would stay there. Hardly had this resolution been hardened and communicated by letter to Mr. Morton when temptation too great for my strength of resistance came my way. The temptation was to travel and see the world. The wanderlust of which I thought I had been cured returned in a more virulent form.

The temptation came from one Frederic J. Haskin. I had known his name from seeing it in the *Banner* and other papers signed to a weekly Saturday or Sunday feature story about odd and curious things in many parts of the world, principally the Orient. These feature stories were a preview of the sort of thing that Ripley later exploited so successfully in drawings in "Believe It or Not." Here in Washington I found Mr. Haskin in the flesh. He said that he had decided to start up a daily syndicated article and that he wanted help in writing it. The articles were to be published under his by-line, and he would supervise and edit all of them, of course, but he wanted primary help in running down the material and preparing the articles. He would be very busy, he said, a large part of the time in selling the product, but he was sure he would be able to make a success of it. For anybody who helped him, he could promise, with almost absolute certainty, travel not only to different parts of this country but to Europe, Asia, Africa, South America—in fact, to all the places in the world where stories of interest to American newspaper readers might be discovered.

This project he had decided to launch in January. He had written a half-dozen or more articles himself for the beginning, but he needed help and needed it quickly. Now, it so happened that, while I had my *Nashville Banner* job, I had been, temporarily at any rate, dropped by the *Knoxville Sentinel* and the *Birmingham News;* and, in order to keep up my standard of living, it was necessary for me to pick up a few odd dollars. So I proposed to Haskin that I begin work for him on a part-time basis and see how we got along. That I did.

When the "Haskin Letter," as after many years it came to be known, was launched in mid-January, 1907, I furnished the signature "By Louis Brownlow" for the opening article, which told the story of Mr. Haskin's career, beginning, as mine had begun, on a country newspaper in Missouri and leading up to his foreign travels and his present decision to change and expand what had been a weekly feature story into a daily letter. Thereafter, for two or three months, I had a dual personality. I kept up with the news and sent my daily wire dispatches and three or four mail stories a week to the *Banner,* and I began to write pieces for Mr. Haskin. I soon discovered that he didn't edit them very much except to see to it that they conformed to standard length and fitted into his general notion of what the newspapers would buy. That meant that they were not to be news, because they would be written sometimes weeks in advance of publication, but they were to have whenever possible some relationship to things that were going on in the world. It was a variant of a type of daily newspaper letter that had been published for years by William E. Curtis and with something of the flavor of the travel letters of Frank G. Carpenter and a little of the old Haskin insistence upon the odd and the curious.

The syndicate prospered. Mr. Haskin picked up additional clients, more by virtue of his unexcelled qualities as a salesman than because of the intrinsic merit of the articles. It was soon evident, however, that even so much work as I was putting into them would require help. I was working only part time and on a piecework basis, being paid so much (ten dollars, to be precise) for each eighteen-hundred-word article. Help was needed. Haskin told me to get it. I turned to a good friend of mine, a girl reporter (they were scarce in those days) on the *Washington Post,* Ruth Hale. She was a fellow-Tennessean and the daughter of a redoubtable female journalist of an even earlier day. Her mother, Mrs. Annie Riley Hale of Rogersville, Tennessee, was always perfectly certain about everything and never wrong. In her complete one-sidedness, she managed to sell a few pieces to the papers and magazines. Her daughter Ruth was determined also to be a journalist, but she prided herself on seeing two or ten or twenty sides to every question. She, too, usually came up with the one definite, final, and absolute answer. Ruth needed the money, and she wrote a few of the ten-dollar pieces; but she was unhappy with enforced ambivalence of what already I had begun to call "Haskinitis" and even more unhappy with the sacrifice of her by-line. She quit.

(Ruth, with whom I ran around a good deal in my salad days, later married and still later divorced Heywood Broun. Her mother, Annie Riley Hale, finally rested her absolutes on a three-legged stool: anti–Theodore Roosevelt, anti-Negro, and anti–medical profession. One morning, years and years later, I picked up the *New York World* to read, as was my daily wont, the Broun column. It was divided neatly into three parts, exactly equal in length, entirely disparate in content. First was a defense of the medical profession; then a defense of the Negro; and, finally, an apostrophe to the memory of "T. R." I clipped the column, pasted it on a sheet of paper, appended the query, "Mother-in-law visiting you agin?" and sent it to Heywood Broun. A day or two later the clipping and my question came back to me. At the bottom he had written: "She is." Then he had struck that through with blue pencil and substituted, "She am!")

After a few similar adventures (high, wide, and handsome) in search of piece goods, Haskin decided that it would be necessary, especially if we were to get in any travel and risk the hazards of long mail delays, to have a permanent, salaried staff. The task of organizing it Haskin turned over to me. I succeeded in recruiting two other writers. One was Tom Wallace of *The Courier-Journal,* who in my own Louisville days had been on the staff of the *Evening Post;* the other was Miss Anna B. A. Brown of the *Memphis Commercial-Appeal.* Both were old friends of mine. Both, I knew, were eager to get out of a rut, to go places and see things. Both were willing to abandon, at least for the time being, their own by-lines.

[403]

At first we did all our work in our rooms at the Westminster, where I had found quarters for Haskin and for Miss Lora Brooker of Haskin's home town, Quincy, Illinois, who was to be secretary, bookkeeper, mimeograph operator, and office manager. Tom Wallace joined the Westminster group. So did Miss Brown.

Then Mrs. Haskin came to Washington from Quincy and took a house and moved into it. She was a charming lady, a Missourian by birth whom Haskin had met and married in Japan. It was a big furnished house, the home of an admiral, and into it came not only Miss Brooker, Miss Brown, Tom Wallace, and me, but also our friend James H. Dorman of the State Department. It made a merry and a happy household. Mrs. Haskin lost no time in engaging two competent servants. The food was excellent. The furnishings were luxurious, and, while the boarders (as we called ourselves) undoubtedly helped Mr. Haskin with expenses, we were all happy about it. Mrs. Haskin was an accomplished pianist. Miss Brooker, Miss Brown, Mr. Dorman, and Mr. Haskin made an admirable mixed quartette. Neither Wallace nor I could play nor sing, but we could enjoy and applaud. And all of us were happy in the homelike atmosphere in which the admirable Dolly Haskin enveloped us.

Pretty soon Miss Brown, Wallace, and I were writing all of the letters, and Haskin himself was busy on the road selling. After a few months it dawned on both Haskin and me that it would be a good deal better if I could do some travel and devote more of my time to the "Letter," as we had begun to call our daily product. Thereupon, I regretfully resigned from the staff of the *Nashville Banner* and suggested that my place be taken by my office mate, Walter Edward Harris. So I became to all intents and purposes a full-time employee of Mr. Haskin, albeit at a salary slightly larger than I ever before had enjoyed.

My odyssey began without my leaving the District of Columbia. Within its boundaries I discovered a new world. It is true that I had frequently visited the Library of Congress before that time and had learned how to seek out there a reply to a specific inquiry. But now I discovered what the Library of Congress really was, with its vast depository of all sorts of material which would reward the seeker of knowledge richly for his every effort.

I had theretofore no notion of research. I had had no contact with anybody who ever had engaged in research as such, and, if I did, I had no idea what they were about or how they proceeded with their work. Here in the Library of Congress I plunged into a new world of daily delights. Here I could wander at will through the current world or transport myself backward in time to elder days and spend hours in happy amusement. And with almost no trouble at all I could turn up every week with three or four jewels of knowledge sparkling to me in my ignorance that I could turn into the "Letters" that I was expected to produce.

III

Then came the summer. I was to try my wings seeking out stories to write, not from books, the newspaper files, the magazines, the trade journals, and the like, which had yielded me so much pleasure and perhaps a moderate profit, but I was to begin to travel, to go places, and there to interpret the things I saw in the peculiar style of the articles I was hired to write. That meant I was to keep my eyes and ears open for many things that perhaps I should not like. Nevertheless, I was to travel. As far as Mr. Haskin was concerned, he was paying me a salary and my travel expenses, and he undoubtedly thought that my principal concern and interest was production of the "Letter." I thought otherwise. I was about to set out to see the world!

My first voyages were wholly within the United States—a trip to the Carolinas and there to describe the new burgeoning industry of western North Carolina and retell old historical tales of sleepy Charleston. This was soon to be followed by a journey to an old part of the United States, to a new state. I went to explore the Indian Territory and the Oklahoma Territory in order to have "Letters" ready to be published on the occasion of the admission of Oklahoma to the Union, the addition of the forty-sixth star to the flag. I interviewed the prospective Democratic governor-elect of the new state, Mr. C. N. Haskell, and at greater length the two men certain to be elected by the new state legislature to the United States Senate. Of them I wrote:

"The two United States Senators chosen are as different as men can be different. Robert Latham Owen is an aristocrat of aristocrats. In his veins flows the blood of the two most aristocratic peoples in America—the Virginians and the Cherokees. He is one-eighth Indian and a member of the tribe, but he was born and educated in Virginia. He is a lawyer of great ability and has distinguished himself by earning a fee of $150,000 in a single case. He is reserved and dignified and he is that type of politician known as a 'conservative thinker.'

"The other Senator, Thomas P. Gore, is the first blind man ever elected to the Senate. He lost his sight when a boy in Mississippi. He declared that when he left home a penniless blind boy he told his mother that he would never come back until he was a United States Senator. His vaunting ambition will be realized as soon as the legislature of the new state convenes and then he will go back to Mississippi to visit but not to see his old home. . . . Gore is a radical of the radicals. He appeals to the poor man as a poor man. And he does it in speeches of wonderful oratorical power."

I remember clearly how greatly impressed I was by Senator Owens. In view of the fact that later he became co-author with Carter Glass of Virginia of the Federal Reserve Bill, I can also recall something that happened to me in Oklahoma City on that trip.

It was the time that later was to be known as the "Banker's Panic of 1907." The annual difficulty of getting funds in the western banks to move the crops was being experienced, and the rigors of the money market were extraordinary. The banks of the new state were very hard put to it, and the new governor, exercising an authority given him in the new constitution, proclaimed a bank holiday for ten days which froze all the funds in all the banks all over the state. Now this new constitution had been acclaimed by Mr. William Jennings Bryan as the greatest document of its kind in the history of mankind. The President, Theodore Roosevelt, had said to newspaper reporters that his opinion of the new constitution was not fit to print. But under it Governor Haskell took a radical action that had a tremendous repercussion throughout the country.

It so happened that I received a telegram from my home in Springfield, Missouri, saying that my father was desperately ill and asking me to come at once. In those days I always traveled with cashier's checks drawn on New York banks by a cashier of a Washington bank in denominations of fifty dollars. This was Mr. Haskin's scheme to provide funds. In later years he used traveler's checks. I didn't have enough money to buy a ticket on the Frisco Road back to Springfield. I went to the president of the largest bank in town, a man whom I had already interviewed, and told him of my plight. I showed him the three fifty-dollar checks drawn on New York, so he knew that I was in funds. But he said he didn't have enough cash of his own to buy a ticket, and he didn't know of anybody who did have. It was Saturday. A train would leave for Springfield that afternoon, but there was no chance for me to get enough money to buy a ticket. Finally, the banker said: "I tell you what we will do. You come to the First Christian Church tomorrow to Sunday school and to services. I am the superintendent of the Sunday school and one of the elders of the church. I don't know how much there will be in the collection plate tomorrow, but I hope there will be enough to give you the money to buy the ticket. Anyhow, all that comes in, I will let you have, and perhaps you can get on the Frisco tomorrow afternoon for Springfield."

I was at the church bright and early for Sunday school. There wasn't quite enough money in the collection plate for me. I stayed for the church service, and then, with the blessing of my banker friend and the other elders, I got enough money to take me on my way. Fortunately, when I got to Springfield, my father was much better, but I did stay there for several days.

The banks in Missouri were open, and one morning I went to one of the banks and handed one of my fifty-dollar checks to a cashier, Claude Woodruff, a young man of my own age whom I had known for years. He promptly handed me out fifty-three dollars! New York exchange was at 6 per cent premium in Missouri that day. That was the type of thing now unknown in this country; and, while we have had bank holidays since that time, a dollar has been a dollar, so far as exchange is concerned, within the continental confines of the United States ever since the then Oklahoma senator-to-be and his Virginia colleague, Carter Glass, got through the Federal Reserve Act under the administration of Woodrow Wilson.

The world had been shaken in 1904 and 1905 by the Russo-Japanese War. It was not merely that it had been ended at Portsmouth, New Hampshire, by the intervention of Theodore Roosevelt, the President of the United States, as mediator. It was not merely that a new factor had been introduced into the thinking of American and European peoples with respect to Asia. It was to many minds the fact that the world might expect great disturbances, since an obscure and relatively young (young, that is, in the sense of modern industry) nation of Asiatic origin, culture, and locus had defeated, at sea and on the land, one of the great empires of Europe. The yellow race had triumphed over the white race.

It was more than that. In 1906, because of the discrimination with

respect to landholding in the state of California against Asiatics, the
Japanese Empire, flushed by its victory over Russia, had all but threatened war against the United States. To most Americans the threat
was the acme of absurdity. I believe that to a great many newspapermen
in the press gallery—I still was there by courtesy—it was nothing more
than evidence of idiocy. I shall never forget being beckoned from the
Senate gallery by Senator Carmack, who pointed to the Marble Room.
I went down there. He was very grave. In fact, I had never seen him
possessed of such a serious mien. He said: "Louis, don't let any of
your prejudices get the better of you. This threat of the Japanese is
serious. Of course you know the President doesn't speak to me, and
I don't speak to him. But I have heard from Mr. Root. This is a time
of danger. We must be circumspect."

Then he went on to tell me that the President was so much concerned about the threatened action of the California legislature with
respect to land tenure that he had abandoned hope of approaching it
except indirectly and that he had consulted Senators Jones of Arkansas,
Stewart of Nevada, Teller of Colorado, and Tillman of South Carolina,
and Carmack himself, as Democratic leaders, to ask them if they could
not persuade William Jennings Bryan to go out and see whether he
could not pour oil on the troubled waters in Sacramento. (This may
perhaps have been the beginning of Mr. Bryan's career as a crusader
for peace, the genesis of his lecture-platform success, "The Prince of
Peace.")

Certainly it was by that means that the normally Democratic newspapers in the country were put in the state of "Shush! Shush!" I have
no doubt that it was just as difficult for the President and Mr. Root
to reach the Republican newspapers through the miasma of doubt and
ridicule.

However, the President had taken decisive action with the virtually
unanimous concurrence of both houses of Congress and of all the
members of both parties. His riposte to a Japanese threat was to send
the United States fleet on a voyage around the world. The fleet assembled at Norfolk, then under the command of Admiral Robley D.
Evans, was the greatest armada of all times. It had to make the long
journey around Cape Horn. The Panama Canal was yet but an engineer's dream, a French company's unsuccessful adventure, and a
football of American politics. I have no doubt that Mr. Roosevelt's

action at this particular time in sending the fleet around the world resulted in two things: it stopped the Japanese threat and it induced the American people to support the Congress in going sufficiently in debt to build the Panama Canal despite all the difficulties—engineering, biological, and political—that intervened.

The fleet had rounded the Horn. The fleet had been in Asiatic waters. The fleet was to come back to San Francisco in the spring. It seemed the timely thing to have some Haskin "Letters" from Japan. This was very agreeable to Mr. Haskin, himself, who had been to Japan, who had found his wife there, and who had also discovered a ready market for his Sunday feature articles based on his experiences there. It looked like a good notion to have something ready that could be printed in the Haskin style in the newspapers that subscribed to the Haskin Service by the time the fleet got back. It is true that the Japanese threat seemed to have stopped. There was no more talk of war, but certainly there would be a revival of interest in all things that had to do with Japanese-American relations by the time Admiral Evans dropped anchor in San Francisco Bay come the spring of 1908.

It was settled. I was to have my great adventure. Everything was arranged that Haskin and I were to go to Japan. We were to leave in January. The tickets were purchased. The funds were arranged. The advance sales were made. And for me it was at the moment a great happiness.

That happiness was to be interrupted by a personal sorrow. Ten days before I was to leave Washington for San Francisco a telegram came, telling me of the sudden death of my father in Springfield. By that time I had left the Haskin ménage and was living again at the Westminster. With the help of the Haskin staff, I hurriedly packed for the long voyage, my first to take me outside the United States. There was a great deal of gear to be assembled. I was distrait, and only because of the actual and manual assistance of Mr. Haskin and Miss Brooker did I ever get packed.

My father had been in bad health for several years and had been compelled to abandon his occupation as a teacher. It was as my own teacher that he meant a great deal to me. In my preoccupation with politics and public affairs from my childhood, he had influenced me toward the liberal or radical point of view, just as my mother had tended always to curb my extremism by her more conservative attitude.

However, it was from him that I got other things than merely political interest and insight.

That his was a gentle and a generous soul was exemplified in a letter of condolence received by my mother from one of their oldest friends, Frank Furth, the head of the only Jewish family resident in my native town of Buffalo. Mr. Furth wrote:

> I learn with regret and sorrow, the death of your beloved husband. You have the deepest sympathy of our entire family, for no one has a right to know the loss of a good neighbor or the stern good qualities of a citizen, than those who enjoyed his companionship as long as we had. There was nothing so good, that was too good to divide with his friends. His cheerful disposition and his ready wit like gentle breezes would vanish gloom into sunny smiles.
> "Bob," that familiar name so often heard on the street or in gatherings of church and society . . . a man with strong character, a noble heart and generous disposition, hatred nor wrath never entered that big heart of his.

While I attempted to console Mother in her inconsolability, even in that hour I can remember well how she told me that she had warned me during the Russo-Japanese War that it was never right always to be on the side of the underdog. I had been for Japan; she had been for Russia. Just a few years earlier I had been for the Boers; she had been for the Britons. A good many years earlier she had been in the service of the Confederate States Army. Her inclination to the weaker antagonist had been conquered by her conviction that in the Civil War the other side had been right and that her side had been wrong. It was from her that I had got my sensitivity in politics. It was from her even in this hour that I got a warning that I was not to take things always just as they seemed. It was from her that I got the advice, on that significant first journey beyond the confines of the United States, that I was to hear as well as to speak, to listen to all and then to make up my own mind, and to try to subordinate prejudice and preconceived notions to the ultimate judgment that could come only from long questioning and deep inquiry. My mother was not only a politician. She was a stateswoman.

Thus bound westward from Springfield, Missouri, to Kansas City, to San Francisco, and on across the broad Pacific, I had achieved the ultimate in that deliberate and conscious exchange in which I had traded my right to a by-line for the adventure of travel. I plunged deep into the abyss of anonymity.

PART III

AROUND THE WORLD

CHAPTER XXII

WESTWARD TO JAPAN

Kansas City had a snow, then a cold rain, followed by sleet and more rain. The temperature dropped to zero, and the streets were a glare of ice. Yet I was beyond notice of the weather. I was on the way! I was to see the Rocky Mountains, the Pacific Ocean, and not only to see it but to set sail on it for my first ocean voyage bound for that faraway, mysterious Japan for which I had been entirely too romantically prepared by my reading of Lafcadio Hearn.

Not very long after I had settled myself in the Pullman, a gray-haired middle-aged woman across the aisle from me spoke cordially and asked me where I was bound. "San Francisco," I replied. "Where are you going?"

"Well, I am going somewhat farther than San Francisco. I am going to China."

"And I am going to Japan."

So in a very few moments we discovered that we both were booked for the Pacific Mail Line Steamship "Mongolia" and that, perforce, we would be traveling companions not only for the four days on the train to San Francisco but for the eighteen days' sea voyage before I would debark at Yokohama. Her accent betrayed her southern origin. Her gray hair was combed severely back and twisted in a tight little bun at the back. It turned out that she was a medical missionary who had spent many years in China; that she was going to join her husband, a Methodist ministerial missionary, in San Francisco; that her home was in Soochow, where she was one of the physicians attached to the University of Soochow, in which institution my first cousin, Walter Nance, was a member of the faculty. In almost no time at all we were chums. Mrs. Fearn knew also a great deal about Japan. She was, however, pro-Chinese and by that token anti-Japanese, and she undertook to correct in some degree my excessive romanticism about Japan and the Japanese.

On the train with her was her fourteen-year-old nephew, Harvey Johnston, son of Oscar Johnston of St. Louis, a great mercantile tycoon of the time, the head of one of the great St. Louis shoe-manufacturing establishments. Harvey had been ill of a heart ailment and was going home to spend a year with his aunt in China in the hope that, under her ministrations and in the new environment, he would recover his strength.

Mrs. Fearn had crossed the continent many times. She was an alumna of Jefferson Medical College in Philadelphia—one of its earliest woman graduates. Hen medics were few in those days, and why she, the daughter of the wealthy Walter family of Holly Springs, Mississippi, decided to take up medicine and then to devote her life to missionary work was made understandable only perhaps by the unfortunate effects of the smallpox which in her early teens had so definitely disfigured her. With Mrs. Fearn and the young boy there was no loneliness on that long railroad trip, and I looked forward with the keenest pleasure to seeing a great deal of her on the long voyage across the broad Pacific.

San Francisco still showed many of the signs of the great earthquake and fire that had devastated it less than two years before; but the St. Francis Hotel, new and most modern, offered me the most palatial haven that I had ever experienced. With just a little guidance from the two Doctors Fearn (her husband had joined us there), I saw the sights of the city and was introduced to its marvelous restaurants.

Mr. Haskin was to join me there; but, since he was coming down from Portland, Oregon, and would get to San Francisco only on the day of sailing, it was left to me to make all the necessary preparations. One had to do with money. I had cashier's checks drawn on a New York bank, and Haskin wrote to me to be sure to get three hundred dollars in currency, so that we would not be bothered to draw drafts against the letter of credit which he would carry. That didn't seem to me to be a very difficult task, but it was.

Almost the first thing that struck me in San Francisco was the hard money. There were silver dollars, and there was small change, although no one-cent pieces. A nickel seemed to be the lowest denomination in the coinage of the country, and many of the older people seemed to prefer the tiny silver half-dimes to the nickel. And, as for anything above the silver dollar, there was gold—two-dollar-and-a-half coins, five-dollar, ten-dollar, twenty-dollar coins—everything was gold. It didn't take me long to discover why some of the old-timers preferred the half-dimes. Feeling in my pocket for a nickel by size only, I paid a rapidly disappearing newsboy five dollars for the morning paper. After that I could understand the reluctance with which some of the San Franciscans accepted the nickel piece.

However, I thought it would be a simple matter to get the three hundred dollars in currency. I took my checks to the cashier at the hotel, and I said I wanted currency. He said he didn't have any. He would give me gold. I didn't want gold. So I went down to Montgomery Street and went into bank after bank after bank. Not one of them could scare up three hundred dollars in currency. Not one could cash even one of my three one-hundred-dollar cashier's checks. Finally, at the very extreme end of the financial district, I went into the Sub-treasury, and there, after much hustling around, they did manage to produce two hundred dollars in excessively old and dirty bills. That was the best I could do.

Then came the big adventure. Haskin came, and we boarded the ship. I never before had been so excited, nor have I ever experienced such a thrill of anticipation. I greatly feared that I would be seasick. I even had some little trepidation about the possibility of disaster at sea. Yet, for all of that, I was all atingle.

The ship sailed out through the Golden Gate into the eye of the setting sun. Soon the "Mongolia" began to rise and fall as the long, slow Pacific swells passed under her. That sensation of motion was utterly new, but to my astonished delight I found it extremely pleasant.

Haskin had taken our passage on the "Mongolia" so late that we could not get a first-class or even a second-class cabin, although we were paying first-class passage. We were consigned deep down in the hold to a somewhat segregated cabin in the third class furnished with four bunks but reserved for us. There we had to dress and sleep, but for the rest of the time we were first-class passengers. That inconvenience, we knew, would last only until we got to Honolulu, when the ship would discharge a very great portion of its passenger list, and then we would have a first-class cabin. It was hard to dispose of all our luggage in that cheerless hard-bunked cabin which was just off a 'third-class hold filled with Asiatics, principally Chinese, going home. Haskin had eight or ten pieces of baggage, and I had thirteen bags, hatboxes—for each of us carried a silk hat to be ready for ceremonial calls. We carried evening clothes, both tails and tuxedo, a roll containing our steamer rugs, which in those days every passenger carried on his own, and, in addition to all that, a typewriter. It was as near to being a portable typewriter as was then available, but it weighed nearly thirty pounds. Yet it was the one absolute essential piece of my baggage and one that Mr. Haskin regarded as if it were the apple of his eye. It was on this machine that I was to pound out the "Letters," which he already had sold, the monetary produce of which would pay us for the voyage. We dressed for dinner every night after the first day out and then had to make our way from the depths of the hold, where the odors were not exactly those associated with the fragrance of Arabia, up to the first class, where we could find our fellows.

The next day the passenger list appeared. I discovered on it the names of Mr. and Mrs. Robert M. Wilcox. That evening at dinner, when everybody was all dressed up, we saw a short and plump individual dressed in white tie and tails, his bald dome surmounted by a blue tam-o'-shanter with a red pompon. When he came into the smoking-room for cocktails with a distinguished-looking lady by his side, his headgear caught every eye. It turned out that he was Mr. Wilcox, and his wife was Ella Wheeler Wilcox, the poet.

That evening after dinner Mrs. Fearn and I stretched out in our deck chairs, looking out over the ocean lit by a full moon. We gossiped about our fellow-voyagers. The Fearns had been placed at the surgeon's table (she was a surgeon), while Haskin and I were seated somewhat farther below the salt with the purser. The Fearns had not been in the smoking-room for cocktails, so I proceeded to tell her about the spectacular tam-o'-shanter and that Mrs. Wilcox was Ella Wheeler Wilcox, the poet. She said that she didn't know anything about Mrs. Wilcox except that she had written:

> Laugh and the world laughs with you,
> Weep and you weep alone.

Then up I came with the boast that at one time I had known all the verses of Mrs. Wilcox's volume of *Poems of Passion* by rote. I confessed that my memory might fail me now, but nevertheless I started in at the beginning of the book, and I went all the way through it with only a few gaps and fumbles. Mrs. Fearn seemed to be entranced, or at least highly amused, as I went on and on. At the end, a figure lying stretched out in a steamer chair under a steamer rug near us arose, dropped the rug, crossed to us, and said, "Young man, I don't know who you are, but this is the greatest compliment I have ever received in my life!"

It was Ella Wheeler Wilcox! So, from there on until they left us at Honolulu, the Wilcoxes, the Fearns, Haskin, and I were nearly always together.

Very early one morning we saw the unimaginable beauty of Oahu, of Diamond Head, and we were in Honolulu. While the ship was to be there not quite forty-eight hours, Haskin and I went ashore, took up our quarters at the Alexander Young Hotel, and went to pay our call of courtesy (and, so far as Mr. Haskin was concerned, of commercial hopes) on Mr. Thurston of the *Pacific Commercial Advertiser*.

Mr. Haskin had been known as a feature writer concentrating on things curious and odd. He had sold these weekly feature letters to the *Commercial Advertiser*. Now, in the process of changing the "Letters" from a weekly to a daily contribution, he had decided to expand their content. Therefore, as I have said heretofore, he had added me to his staff. While the "Letters" were signed "Frederic J. Haskin," Mr. Haskin did not pretend to his newspaper customers that he was writing all of them. On the contrary, he made much of the fact that he was employing a staff assistant. This was evidenced by an item published in the *Pacific Commercial Advertiser* of February 6, 1908, which read as follows:

CORRESPONDENT HASKIN IN TOWN
YESTERDAY

Fred J. Haskin, whose letters from the Orient were features of the Sunday *Advertiser* some years ago, is on the Mongolia with his assistant, Louis Brownlow. They are going to supply syndicate letters on the Japanese political and international situation, supplementing them with letters from Hawaii and San Francisco. Mr. Haskin will drop off at Honolulu in March to attend the local end of the enterprise leaving Mr. Brownlow to finish up in Japan.

While we were still in Honolulu, we arranged that, on the return voyage, Haskin would go straight to San Francisco and that I would drop off and spend ten days or two weeks in the Hawaiian Islands, an arrangement that I in no wise resisted but which was to be credited to Mr. Haskin's superior skill as a salesman. He took on the *Advertiser* as a client.

Having discharged a great many of our passengers in Honolulu, the ship set sail again. Haskin and I moved up into a first-class cabin, and the last long leg of the journey to Yokohama began. Then we had some weather. It wasn't a terrific storm, but it was rough enough that very few persons indeed showed up in the dining-room for meals. I was one who was one of the chosen few. My fear of seasickness was gone. In fact, it is a sensation I never have known save once. That was several years later when, for some unexplained and inexplicable reason, I got that queasy feeling in New York on a ferry voyage from South Ferry to Staten Island.

II

In Yokohama, for the first time I trod the soil of a foreign land. I was excited by the burst of color in the costumes of the people and by the haggling with the swarms of ricksha men and porters and the host of noisy importunates on the pier. We intrusted all our bags to the head porter of the Grand Hotel—that is, all but one piece. Haskin insisted that I hold on to the typewriter. Then, on a cool, crisp mid-afternoon, with a few flakes of snow in the air, I had my first adventure in a jinrikisha, with that thirty-pound typewriter in my lap, clattering up from the pier to the hotel! Soon we were settled in our rooms. We were shown where the bathrooms were down the hall; we were given menus; and we were literally showered with attention.

The first order of business before it got dark was to go across the street to a Chinese tailor, well known to Haskin from his previous voyages to Japan, each of us to order a new tuxedo, which, to my astonishment, the tailor assured us would be delivered the next afternoon. That evening, since we had to leave our old tuxedos, both of which happened to be pretty well worn, we dressed for dinner in white tie and tails and found that we were by no means alone. Such was the formality of the times. Everybody in the whole dining-room was in evening dress. And the dinner was prepared by what turned out to be

Chinese cooks with notions of French cuisine and served with perhaps more strict emphasis on correctness than upon the gross matter of the food itself.

There Haskin had attended to the matter of changing some of our dollar bills into yen. Haskin, with his familiarity, rapidly inducted me into the customs of the country, and in the bar I discovered that one did not pay for his cocktail but signed a chit for it. There in the bar I was introduced by Haskin to a fellow-journalist, a man I never had seen before, a distant acquaintance of Haskin's. However, we had one thing in common. All three of us were Missourians: Haskin from Shelbina, Thomas Fairfax Millard from Rolla, and I from Buffalo.

It was only a matter of minutes before I discovered that Millard had an interest in government, politics, and international affairs which I could share and which, for the most part, left Haskin cold. So, while Haskin and I were working together, it also turned out that a greater part of my leisure time in the bar and in the lobby was spent with Millard; and I found myself with him at nearly all the meals in the dining-room. He was a Sinophile and as anti-Japanese as anybody could be. He began at once his efforts to indoctrinate me, and he followed the path of Mrs. Fearn in getting out of my head the pro-Japanese notions that I had absorbed. It is not quite accurate to say that most of them came from Lafcadio Hearn. In preparation for my visit to Japan, I had also read a history of Japan by Captain F. Brinkley. And, much more than that, during the two or three years before, during the war between Russia and Japan, I had been, as were most Americans, a sympathizer with the Japanese. That sympathy grew out of my prejudice against the Russia of the czars. It stemmed from reading George Kennan's articles in the *Century* magazine about the terrors of the Siberian prisons and the sufferings of the Siberian exiles. It had support from the belief that Russia was dominated by a tyrannical, cruel autocracy. It also gained support from the fact I believed that the Japanese were one Asiatic people who had taken unto themselves Western civilization, were adapting their civilization and culture to Western ways, and especially had adopted constitutional practices and were conforming to democratic political theories.

My mother, as I have said, was for the Russians against the Japanese. She used to say, against all my arguments, that she felt that the Japanese could not be trusted. The disaster to the Russian arms she looked upon as an evil omen for Europe. In 1906, throughout the Japanese threat of war against the United States, she used to write me that she had been right about the Japanese and that one day she was sure the time would come when the Japanese would attempt a war against the United States. I was completely frustrated in my efforts to tell her how absurd was the very thought of such a thing.

I didn't believe that the Japanese threat was serious, and I listened with considerable incredulity to Tom Millard's indictment of the Japanese naval and army officers as conspirators against the peace and especially as the enemy of China and the United States. The Japanese occupation of Korea was indeed a stumbling block, but I was inclined to set it aside. Much more was eventually to come out of my conversations with Millard. But at the moment the greatest thing to me was the thrill of my first adventure in a foreign country. And the next morning after our arrival I set out to see, to listen, and to learn.

The sightseeing was undiluted joy, an afternoon to see the Great Buddha at Kamakura, visits to all the great shrines and scenes, and then, after a week, moving to Tokyo, where Haskin and I found ourselves well put up in the Imperial Hotel—that wooden structure which later gave way to the Frank Lloyd Wright building.

I visited more shrines and temples. I wandered through the parks. And then, thanks to a simple discovery, I found myself walking, walking anywhere I pleased, becoming utterly lost yet never being afraid. The discovery had to do with what at that time was a passionate desire on the part of young Japanese boys to learn English. In one of my earliest walks out from the hotel, I found myself in a park and sat alone on a bench overlooking what obviously was a baseball diamond. As I sat there, out came two teams dressed in regulation A. G. Spaulding baseball uniforms, with the exception that the umpires were in kimonos instead of the familiar blue uniform and blue cap. I was rooted to the spot. I was eager to see, and especially to hear, a baseball game in Japanese. The pitcher wound up. The ball left his hand. The batter stood steady. The catcher caught the ball. The umpire sang out, "Ball one." The game was played in English!

Just about that time two young boys came along dressed in a distinctive costume of wide trousers which already had been identified to me as the uniform of a high-school student. They stopped by my bench. I asked them a question. They answered in English. One of them already was quite fluent in the language, and he told me that all the high schools were teaching English. Thereafter, whenever I went for my long walks and got lost, all I had to do was to spot a group of boys in high-school uniforms. They invariably were courteous; they invariably insisted on walking me either back to the hotel or to a tramway that would take me close to the Imperial; and all they expected in exchange was an opportunity to practice their English. By courtesy of these high-school boys I saw a great deal of Tokyo, even side streets and obscure places that I never could have seen had I depended on a patter-spouting tourist guide.

In the very center of the city was the Imperial Palace—not open to visitors, of course—surrounded by its wall and moat, a veritable symbol of the mysterious East. Then, too, there were evidences of the adaptation of Western ways: the new railroad station, the beginnings of the great avenue of the Ginza, and even, in some cases, paved streets. Tramways, or streetcar lines, were everywhere; but, as yet, the automobile was more rarely to be seen than it was in those days even in Washington.

It was necessary for me to write some of my "Letters" about the sights to be seen pitched at the "look-see" level, but from the beginning my interest was centered in political, governmental, and economic development of the country. In the first place, I talked with as many persons as I could about the history of Japan, adding to what I had read in preparation of the voyage and trying to get the feel of things. In this endeavor I was greatly helped by a newspaperman, the foreign affairs editor of the *Jiji Shimpo,* Mr. K. W. Kawadzura. I met him at the hotel on my first day in Tokyo and visited him frequently in his office. I sat at his desk while he edited the cable dispatches that came in from Reuter's, the British news agency, and tried to answer his questions about the United States as he so kindly was answering mine about Japan. This developed into a very rewarding friendship, since he was kind enough to give me letters of introduction to persons high in the government whom I could interview, and he also took me on personally conducted tours through such buildings as the House of Parliament, the House of Peers, and other governmental establishments to which otherwise I could not have been admitted. The Diet was not in session, but I did see the meeting chambers and got some idea from him of the legislative processes and procedures in Japan.

He also gave me running translations of the editorials not only from his own newspaper but from other newspapers, explained to me the cartoons that were carried, read to me some of the comic weeklies, and gave me a general idea of the division of the country into two groups—not necessarily to be associated with the formal political parties, but two schools of thought: one imperialistic, military, and reactionary; the other democratic, liberal, and peaceful. One was resolved on a firm foreign policy; the other, on conciliation and friendliness with other nations.

Most of all, of course, my interest was centered in the question of whether or not there was in reality a threat of war which Japan would force on the United States. The opening "Letters" of my series from Japan discussed this in some detail. I wrote:

"Japan is making the most extraordinary expenditures on its army and navy ever undertaken by any nation of like resources in time of peace. The United States is sending to the Pacific Ocean the most powerful Armada in the history of navies. Despite assurances from Washington and Tokyo that there is no serious quarrel between the two countries, these are concrete facts for the acceptance of which it is not necessary to take any one's word. Does this mean war? . . .

"It is manifestly the purpose of Russia to obtain control over China and to exclude from this vast territory the other nations of the world. If this policy had triumphed, Japan would have been dwarfed and its commercial progress stopped. . . .

"Occupying a position absolutely unique in modern statescraft, the elder statesmen of Japan exercise an influence that is all but supreme in the affairs of their country. This remarkable group of old men has no legal status and their existence is not recognized by the constitutional form of government. They are the survivors of the young Nipponese patriots who 50 years ago undertook to bring their country into the family of nations and induce their people to adopt western civilization. . . .

"The most interesting of the living Elder Statesmen are Prince Ito and Count Okuma, the one supreme in power and the other insistent in opposition. Prince Ito is better known to foreigners than any other Japanese statesman. . . . It was Ito who wrote the Constitution by which Japan is governed today, and it was Ito who guided the ship of state through the storm of wars with China and Russia. He retired once but the late war again brought him into activity, and he is now conducting affairs of Japan in Korea, acting as resident general and practically autocrat of the effete Korean Empire. . . .

"Count Shigo-nobu Okuma is the great commoner of Japan. . . . He is peculiarly interesting to Americans because it was he who led the Japanese protest against the United States when the San Francisco school question and the immigration agitation first came up. As leader of the opposition, Count Okuma undoubtedly seized upon these questions as clubs with which to belabor the government but at the same time he did not compromise with his conscience to do so. He holds that the Japanese people are racially the equal of other people, or rather, that there is no difference of degree inherent in different races. . . .

". . . it is not strange that Count Okuma came to admire the great American Democrat, Thomas Jefferson. When he learned that the Declaration of Independence had been written by Jefferson, he set about studying the career of that statesman. He read several biographies and some extracts from Jefferson's own writings and became familiar with his principles. Three years ago William Jennings Bryan was a guest of Count Okuma. When Mr. Bryan went back to the United States, he sent Count Okuma the complete collection of Jefferson's works which now occupy a position of honor in the old Count's library.

"The influence of Jefferson on Count Okuma's life is marked. As Jefferson in his old days placed the University of Virginia above every work of his life as his most worthy deed, so Count Okuma is prouder of his position as founder of the Waseda University than of all his political accomplishments. . . .

"In the concluding chapter of Count Okuma's new work, 'Fifty Years of New Japan,' he frankly says that the Japanese nation has not arrived at the level of civilization employed by other nations. He declares that Japan is still in school and must stay at its studies until the tasks are all finished. Then he thinks Japan will be equal to any nation on earth. While recognizing the inferiority, he denies it is inherent or permanent. Therefore he is opposed, heart and soul, to the Japanese government adopting a policy by which it pledges itself to accept the right of mandate of another nation that Japanese people shall not go where they please, just as foreigners are allowed to come and go in Japan.

"It is in support of this doctrine of national pride and dignity that Count Okuma voiced the anti-American sentiment that stirred Japan a year ago. Although he used the issue to hammer the heads of the cabinet knowing that the issue is no longer to be used as a policy cry, Okuma and all his followers have ceased to talk. Count Okuma will declare as all Japanese will 'The United States is Japan's best friend and that trouble between them is unthinkable.' Count Okuma adds, as other Japanese do not, that the United States must treat the Japanese as an equal in every respect. . . ."

III

My visit to Japan was in the fortieth year of Meiji, the Era of Enlightenment. "Meiji" was the name given to the time of the reign of the Emperor Mutsuhito, for he, the then young Mikado in 1868, had been brought from the sacred retreat in which he was little more than a prisoner and restored to the throne as a ruling emperor.

To me, a young journalist on his first voyage outside his own country, Meiji also was an era of enlightenment. A little of the Japanese history I already knew, but this was my first opportunity to learn at first hand about the Japanese people or, indeed, any other people than English-speaking Americans. Not the least interesting little incident was to see Prince Tokugawa, the last of the shoguns, the one who had been overthrown from his position as "mayor of the palace" in order to restore the youthful Mikado to the throne of his ancestors. I saw the last of the shoguns come out of the House of Peers, take some bicycle clips out of his coat pocket, wrap his trouser legs around his ankles, apply the clips, mount his bicycle, and ride away in peace, if not in glorious ceremonial. Much as this incident contributed to my pleasure and amusement and no doubt to my education, my own particular enlightenment came from other quarters. Interested as I had been in the politics, national and international, of Japan as expressed by some of its leading statesmen and journalists with whom I had an opportunity to talk, my early city-hall, court-house, and state-capitol experience had inclined me toward an insatiable curiosity about administration. From these great men and from the journalists concerned more with international affairs than with anything else, I got little. But I was persistent, and, finally, my search was richly rewarded.

I arranged to meet Baron Makino, then minister of education. It was from him that I not only learned a great deal about administration in Japan but obtained perhaps my first insight into the problems of differentiated and comparative administration as professed and practiced by different nations having different historical backgrounds and varying cultures.

Makino was one of five or six young boys who, shortly after the visit of the Japanese mission to President Buchanan in 1858, were selected to go to the United States to be educated. The Philadelphia public schools were selected then as the best in this country. The Philadelphia school authorities were hospitable to the idea and promised to take care of the young boys. Makino was eight years old when he went to Philadelphia. He told me some interesting tales of his boyhood there, of some of his difficulties with the language, of his even greater difficulties with the strange customs, and of his inculcation into American history, Anglo-Saxon customs and laws, and the Christian culture.

Then, when I asked him to give me his opinion with respect to the tremendous progress made by Japan since the Restoration, he began a lecture which lasted for more than an hour and was resumed two days later for another two-hour session. He told me that, after the decision was made to adapt Western ways to the exigencies of Japanese customs, laws, and culture, the Japanese had sent missions to all parts of the world to assess what they found to be best suited to their purposes in the administrative practices of many countries of the world. He, then a young man with a background of education in the United States, was chosen to go on several of these missions.

In essence, he said that the Japanese were an eclectic people and that that quality had been illustrated in their history from the earliest times. They had taken their written language from the monosyllabic Chinese, although their own language was polysyllabic. They had absorbed arts from Korea and China and then had adapted them in such a manner as to make them particularly and peculiarly Japanese. So also they had embraced Buddhism and then adapted it to conform with Japanese ideas of ancestor worship. Eclecticism was at the very

[425]

base of the Japanese mind. Japan took what it thought it needed from wherever it could find it and then reshaped it to fit its own purposes.

So, in government, Japan—and in this case it seemed to be quite natural—had taken its public school system from that of Philadelphia and had adapted it to fit its own requirements. The army took the German model; the navy took the British. In local government the police systems were an amalgam of three models: the French *sûreté* and its customs and regulations had been the basis for its detective work; the German police, for its identification system; and the London "bobby," for its patrol work. The local taxation system had been based on the German model; the land taxation, on the British. The archival institutions borrowed freely from Spanish sources. The higher educational system of colleges and universities was a welding-together of the German and the British models—a process that, indeed, was going on at the very same time in the United States itself.

Baron Makino, endowed with many honors and titles, lived long. He became one of the *genrō,* and, at the time of the surrender of Japan on the battleship "Missouri," he was the chancellor of the imperial household. He had lived and wrought through many phases of Japan's history.

Seeking to learn something more about Japan's great industrial expansion than was evidenced merely on the surface by observations of the control of its finances by the imperial family and two or three great companies, I was assisted by the good graces of one of the managers of the great Mitsubishi Company, who introduced me to Mr. Fuji, a manager of one of the cotton factories in Tokyo. He took me to a cotton mill. I knew very little indeed about industrial establishments in the United States, and the only type with which I was at all familiar was a cotton mill. As I walked through the weaving mill, I noticed that practically all the machinery was from Draper and Company of Hopewell, Massachusetts. That prompted me to ask him why they had selected American machinery. He said: "It is very simple. It is midway between what the English machinery is and what the Japanese will be." Then he went on, in essence, to say:

"The British build their textile machinery to last for forty years, and it will last for eighty. The Americans build theirs to last twenty years, and it will last for forty. That means that the English mills already and the American mills presently will be burdened by obsolescent machinery too antiquated to keep, too good to scrap. What we Japanese intend to do is build textile machinery designed to last two years and so fragile that we hope that under no circumstances will it last longer than four. That will mean we can undersell the British and Americans in the markets of the world even if the time comes, as it will come, when we will not enjoy the terrific advantage that we now have in low labor costs."

Mr. Fuji undoubtedly was exaggerating; but, even as he drew the long bow, he gave me an insight into Japanese methodology which in later years permitted me the more easily to understand some of the reasons why the Japanese industrialists were able to reach so far out into the markets of the world.

The time came for me to leave Japan. When I got on the ship bound for Honolulu, I felt greatly rewarded by my initial adventure abroad. I had seen much. I had heard much. I had learned much. And for me it was indeed an era of enlightenment.

CHAPTER XXIII

A REVOLUTION IN VENEZUELA

I sat in a chair on the marble terrace of the Mark Hopkins Hotel atop Nob Hill in San Francisco in May of 1908. I was twenty-eight years old. The green California hills dipped into the waters of San Francisco Bay. And into the bay through the Golden Gate steamed the mighty armada of the great white fleet. Admiral "Fighting Bob" Evans had brought it home. Battleships, cruisers, destroyers—all gleaming with fresh white paint; all ablaze with bunting; all alive with white uniformed sailors; all of them all dressed up. And all San Francisco was there to see the spectacle and to share in the great uplift of patriotic feeling that this parade of invincible strength had demonstrated as the complete assurance of peace and power for the United States of America.

Just to be there, on that terrace with the notables of the city and state, seemed to me to be the very apex of success. Had not Kipling himself written of "Fighting Bob":

> Zogbaum does things with a pencil,
> I do things with a pen,
> But you sit up in a conning tower
> Bossing eight hundred men.

Had not the British, who alone among the nations of the world had a greater fleet than ours, had not even they been gracious enough to congratulate the admiral and the commander-in-chief on that great cruise? True, it had not yet ended. The fleet again was to go around the Horn, and it would be some months yet, after again visiting many South American ports, before it would put into its home waters at Hampton Roads. But its work had been done. The show of might and skill had been made. Whatever threat of war there may have been from the Japanese militaristic empire had subsided, at least so far as the United States and its possessions were concerned.

I had just experienced a great change in my own life as a result of my first sea voyage. I had had some weeks in Japan seeing my first foreign country. I had left Yokohama for Honolulu on a Japanese ship, had had a pleasant and profitable voyage, and by now felt myself a sailor and never happier than when at sea. I had had two delightful weeks in Honolulu writing articles not only about the things to be seen but about the people, their history, and their political institutions. There were stories of their kings, of the missionaries, of sugar, and of the heterogeneous peopling of the islands and prediction that the beginnings of a naval base at Pearl Harbor would eventually develop it into an impregnable bastion of American naval strength. There were stories of the Hawaiian aspirations for statehood, and, of course, stories about the hibiscus hedges, the slashed-*ti*-leaved skirts of the hula dancers, the yellow leis, and the beach at Waikiki.

Then I had had two weeks of California: a week in the great city of San Francisco and a week in the then smaller but rapidly growing City of Our Lady of the Angels to the south. I had written some pieces about the extremely complicated and most controversial political situation in San Francisco. And I fancied myself to be, albeit anonymously so, a rising young general correspondent.

And on that May 6, when the fleet came in and at the great city banquet to Admiral Evans and his officers the next evening, I was sure that I had chosen the right way; that it was my good luck that would, within the next year or two or three, permit me to see most of the rest of the world. I was sure that as a journalist I had achieved the world viewpoint, that my utterly boundless curiosity would be satisfied, that I had set aside prejudices and predilections, and that I already had attained the tolerance if not the fulness of the wisdom of the sages. Untouched by the anxieties of a desire to make money, too cocksure—in a word, so young—I sat on top of the world.

After San Francisco I went to Missouri to visit for a week or ten days with my mother. She listened eagerly to my tales of adventure but was much more interested in the political stories I had to tell, the reports of my interviews with statesmen and high personages, than she was with any of the ordinary tales of travel, although she did have a most intense concern with what I told her about the missionaries, with many of whom I had had such long and rewarding conversations.

It seemed at the time to be perfectly natural, after my visit with my mother in Missouri, that on my way back to Washington I should stop in Tennessee. I was bound this time, not for Nashville, but for Monteagle, a resort in the Cumberland Mountains where the Sims family maintained a summer cottage. I wanted to see Bess. When she met me in the railroad station in Monteagle, it was quite evident that I was not merely dropping in for a chat with a cousin. I was a suitor.

Here again, and in surroundings that enchanted me, I found Bess to be interested most in the things that most interested me. She listened responsively to my tales of the political and governmental observations I had made on my first trip abroad and with tolerance, to say the least, to my boasting of my prowess as a sailor, adventurer, and world journalist.

Generous as Mr. Haskin was in the matter of vacations, the time came when of necessity I had to report in Washington. What would be next, I had no idea. It turned out, however, to be another series of adventures in the Library of Congress. It was 1908. It was a presidential election year. I was assigned, not to cover the events of that particular campaign, which certainly were beyond the scope of a mail syndicate such as the Haskin Service, but to review for our clients and our readers the presidential campaigns of the past. Very hurriedly I threw together a few articles about past political conventions. They turned out to be so successful that I was given the task of writing a series of twenty-two articles on past presidential campaigns, beginning with 1828, the first election in which there was anything like popular participation.

It was Mr. Haskin's genius to insist on the odd and the curious. Therefore, I was to write about the things that had happened in these presidential campaigns which were not ordinarily known or had been missed in the condensations of historians. That meant that my first task was to read the books that had been written about these campaigns. Then I set myself to dig into the newspapers and other contemporary documents to see what I could find that had been missed by historians, at least by those most popularly read and by those most generally used as textbooks in schools and colleges. It was a fascinating game.

It was difficult indeed to discover anything that some of them, let us say, McMaster in particular, had missed. Here, indeed, perhaps I cheated a little, because it was McMaster, especially in his footnotes, who guided me to many of the contemporary sources. But here also it was easy to pick out of the same sources that he had used odd and curious even if irrelevant events that that meticulous historian had rejected so far as his text was concerned. Mr. Haskin was able to sell articles because they did reflect the odd and the curious; but, in order to get in those irrelevancies, however interesting, I had to tell the overall tale of each succeeding campaign. Whatever of good was reflected in the pieces that were printed, and I am glad for my own self-comfort that I have not read any of them since, the assignment did give me an extraordinary opportunity to immerse myself in the political party history of the country and sharpen the interest in the institution of the presidency, which ever after was to engage me as a matter of prime concern.

I was eager for more travel, and Haskin had found that the travel letters were salable. There was trouble in Venezuela. Diplomatic relations had been suspended not only by Great Britain and France but also by the United States and even some of the Latin-American countries. The dictator, Cipriano Castro, had flouted American, British, and French claims and still later had gotten into trouble with the Netherlands by objecting to the transshipment of cargoes bound for Venezuela at the port of the Dutch colony of Curaçao, an island very close to the Venezuelan port of La Guaira. The Dutch had sent an ultimatum demanding Castro's compliance by November 1. They threatened a naval blockade of all Venezuelan ports. So it was decided that I should go to Venezuela.

One afternoon in Shoomaker's Bar, where journalists and politicians were wont to foregather for refreshments and conversation, I ran into Count Seckendorff, a German nobleman, then an editorial writer on the *Washington Post*. I told him of my contemplated voyage. He said: "My cousin, the Baron Seckendorff, is the German minister in Caracas, and, since now Germany is the only European country that has not broken off diplomatic relations with Castro, you might find it useful to know him. At any rate, I shall be happy to give you a letter to him." That letter was to prove almost literally a lifesaver. The Baron Seckendorff, a career diplomat in the German service, later in 1914 was to find himself German ambassador in St. Petersburg at the time of the outbreak of World War I and also to find himself there deceived by his own government, a virtual prisoner of his military and naval attachés, just as were the Kaiser's ambassadors in London and Washington.

Stopping in New York for a few days before boarding the "SS Zulia" of the Red D Line for the voyage to Venezuela, I dropped in what then was known to the cognoscenti as "the Forty-second Street Country Club." To the general public it was the bar of the Knickerbocker Hotel, a bar that was distinguished by a great painting by Maxfield Parrish of King Cole, his pipe, his bowl, and his fiddlers three—a mural that found a dismal storage somewhere during the long years of prohibition to be rescued by Vincent Astor to grace, as it continues to grace, the bar of the St. Regis Hotel. There I found my friend Tom Millard, with whom I had enjoyed so many conversations in Yokohama and Tokyo; there I found sundry others of my newspaper friends; and there, my mission to Venezuela being known, I was introduced to Thomas R. Ybarra, already, I believe, on the staff of the *New York Times*. His father, General Ybarra, at that time was in hiding, and Tommy intrusted me with a letter to him. Now, I had little knowledge of any kind about conditions in dictatorships, nor could I conceive of the nature of a Latin-American dictatorship in a time of revolutionary tenseness. I accepted the letter, and it did not occur to me at the moment that it was at all odd that he suggested to me that I show it to no one but turn it over quietly, when nobody was in the room, when I should have an opportunity to meet and talk with President Castro's foreign minister, José Jesús Paul. Tommy said that Señor Paul was a graduate of Yale, that he spoke English well, and that he was sure that he would be delighted to receive me, although the United States had severed its diplomatic relations with Venezuela.

I had to get a passport to go to Venezuela. At that time only three countries in the world required passports of American visitors: Russia, Turkey, and Venezuela. I made my formal application to the Department of State for the passport, which I obtained on September 14, 1908. An American passport in those days was not bound in a little book. It was just a sheet of parchment paper containing the essential text. Actually the grant of a passport to a country with which we were at odds was such an important event that I received the passport personally in the office of the Secretary of State and saw with my very own eyes the Secretary, Mr. Elihu Root, sign it.

Then in New York I had to get a visa from the Venezuelan consul-general. That turned out not to be such a routine matter. I had not had a fresh smallpox vaccination. No other inoculation was required—in fact, few if any then were known—but I found a doctor, I got the vaccination, I waited until it "took," and I had a very sore arm. And then I got my visa. I was the only passenger on the good ship "Zulia." She was a peculiar craft, one of two that had been built with double keels for very shallow draft navigation over the bar in Mara-caibo Bay, a greater convenience in loading coffee for the return voyage to Brooklyn.

Despite the fact that it was September, the hurricane month, the voyage was smooth and uneventful, and my mess with the captain and the chief engineer quite delightful. We put in for a day at Ponce, the Puerto Rican port, where I had my first little glimpse of that island which then had been under the United States flag for a little less than a decade. Then on to Curaçao, where we stayed a whole day. The pontoon bridge across the narrow mouth of the deep port was thrown open, and the "Zulia" came to an anchor within the harbor. I was put ashore and of course began to pick up materials for a story about this little bit of an island in the tropics, with its houses that looked as though they had been copied from a Dutch story-book and with its extremely black people, spattering, not, as it seemed to me, in the Dutch tongue, but rather, as I later discovered, in a patois of Dutch, French, English, Spanish, and whatnot. However, for the occasional tourist—there were very few in that day—there were comforting signs painted on white boards put up at various places. They were green arrows, with the legend: "This Way to the Irish Consulate-General." That, of course, was long before the Irish Republic and long before there were any formal Irish consular or diplomatic representatives anywhere in the world. But I followed the arrows. They led to an establishment presided over by Mr. Patrick Kelly, whose ancestors were from Ireland but who himself hailed from Brooklyn. The establishment was a bar and a restaurant. I liked Mr. Kelly very much.

Thence on to La Guaira, the hottest seaport on earth. From the sea at La Guaira the mountains run up almost perpendicularly more than a mile in height. Thence, only eight miles from the sea itself, nestling in a depression in the mountains, was the capital city of Caracas. The route then led from the very hot tropics up that mountain through all the variations of climate manifested in the flora to the capital city itself, with its oak and maple trees, a detached part of the temperate zone. The journey could be made only on a narrow-gauge railroad that made its way up the mountain with much noise, clatter, steaming, and puffing, to stop only once at the siding named, appropriately enough, from the chief characteristic of the railroad itself—"Zigzag."

Once in Caracas, I found myself established in the Hotel Klindt in a suite consisting of a bedroom, a parlor, and a balcony overlooking the Plaza de Bolívar, the great central square of the capital. It was a park distinguished by an equestrian statue of the Liberator, Simón Bolívar. I had not expected to occupy luxurious quarters, but the cost was so little that I did not complain. Here I dug in. I didn't have much baggage, because we had decided that in Venezuela, traveling through troubled times, it would not be necessary for me to bring the regalia required by formal calls and entertainment such as I had lugged to Japan. However, I was a little bit astonished when an English-speaking Negro servant appeared. It turned out that he was to be my valet, my chambermaid, and, in the dining-room, my waiter. There were few other guests in the hotel. I had arrived late in the afternoon, and, after refreshing myself from the stains of the journey from the hot port below the mountain, I went to dinner. There were perhaps a half-dozen persons in the dining-room. My own particular English-speaking servant saw to it that I had an excellent dinner. I felt a certain tenseness in the air. I resolved that I would not attempt to take an evening walk. I was afraid. I waited until the morrow to explore the town.

At that time all the great offices of the state of Venezuela were grouped around the Plaza de Bolívar. The Casa Amarilla, or "Yellow House," was the residence of the president. The capitol, the meeting place of the Congress, was there, as well as the general post office, the war department, and the like. Near by was the cathedral and the art gallery. I found everything practically within walking distance.

It didn't take me long to discover, partly through the help of my *valet de chambre,* that there was one man in charge in the all-but-closed American legation. I went to see him. He was John Brewer of Rockville, Maryland, a consular clerk and a nephew of William W. Russell, who was the accredited minister to Venezuela but who was absent in Washington until such time as diplomatic relations with that republic might be resumed. Mr. Brewer told me that there were only three American citizens besides himself in Caracas. One was a missionary, Mr. Pratt; another was Mrs. Pratt; and the third was an American portrait painter, Charles Johnson Post, who was engaged in painting portraits of the president, the foreign minister, and other notables. Mr. Brewer said he thought I would find Mr. Post also at the Hotel Klindt. Mr. Brewer was glad, almost excessively so, to see and talk to an American. We arranged to have lunch together, and he told me that he thought, so far as my interview with the foreign minister was concerned, it would be better if I made the approach directly by a letter to be sent by messenger.

I wrote the letter. My faithful servant volunteered to act as messenger, and within a few hours I received an invitation to call on the foreign minister at his office. I was received with courtesy, even with a little ceremonial grandeur. When I was seated in Señor Paul's office and everybody else had left the room, I gave him my letter to General Ybarra.

"How long have you known Mr. Thomas Ybarra?" he asked. "I never met him but once," I answered.

Señor Paul burst out: "Isn't that just like him that he should have the effrontery to ask me, of all persons, to deliver this letter. Nevertheless, I will do it. And I will let his mother know that I have done so. However, may I ask you under no circumstances whatsoever to tell anybody in this country what you have just done."

Of course I promised. Then Dr. Paul gave me a lengthy dissertation on the troubles of Venezuela with the rest of the world; how Venezuela was right; how all the other countries were wrong. He was the correct diplomat. At the end of the lecture he invited me to a luncheon at his home, an invitation which of course I was delighted to accept.

What caused me to hold my tongue and not to ask him about the American portrait painter, I have no idea. However, I was glad that I hadn't mentioned him, for, when I got back to the hotel, I found that Mr. Post had a suite on the same floor with mine. I called on him. He was a portrait painter, it was true; but he was there to paint portraits only because that was an available masquerade for his true mission, which was that of a correspondent for the *New York World*. Under wraps and therefore attempting to file nothing of news, he was there awaiting what a great many people had predicted—the inevitable overthrow of Castro. He was not writing anything, but he had been all around Caracas, and he had been in other parts of the republic. He was generous enough to give me much of the material which he had gathered but which at that time he could not use. (This adventure was worth much more to me when, after some years had passed, I found out that Mr. Post was the son of Louis F. Post, then the editor of *The Public,* a liberal weekly published in Chicago. Louis Post was later to be the first assistant secretary of labor under Woodrow Wilson.)

I also found my way to the Pratts, the lone Protestant missionaries still in the country. From them I learned a good deal about the customs of the country and something of the sad situation of the common people under the oppressive rule of the dictator and of the sorry state of affairs in which Venezuelan industry and commerce had practically come to an end.

Both the foreign minister and Mr. Post had advised me not to attempt to seek an interview with the president. Mr. Brewer had declined to give any advice at all. But, before I could make up my mind what to do and in the belief I still had two weeks or more to see and do things, my whole plan was upset.

I was at dinner one evening in the Klindt Hotel. Alone at the table, with my servitor hanging over my shoulder, I was interrupted by a messenger in the uniform of a German soldier. He handed me a letter. It was from the Baron Seckendorff, to whom I had sent my letter of introduction and from whom I had asked an interview. I had had a reply setting a date well into the next week, but I had not yet met the Baron. Here was a second letter from him. It said: "Whatever you are doing now, stop it at once, go to your room, pack your bags, and come with this messenger at once to the German legation. I suggest that you ask no questions."

I arose from the table. I told my servant to pack my bags at once. I paid my bill. Within an hour I was in the German legation. Baron Seckendorff was a most courteous host. He said: "Please do not ask me how I know, but I do know that you were to be arrested at midnight tonight. I didn't think you would like to languish in a Venezuelan jail. The Red D Line ship "Zulia," on which you came down from New York, is back from Maracaibo and will sail from La Guaira tomorrow. You will stay with me here tonight, and tomorrow morning I will give you a guard to take you down to the port."

That night I slept in safety under the red, black, and white flag of the German Empire. The next morning, with a sergeant and five soldiers in German uniform, I was duly escorted to the "Zigzag" train and established in a special car engaged by the German minister. Not only was I taken down to the port but I was escorted with great ceremony onto the deck of the "Zulia" herself. There I came under the protection of the Stars and Stripes and safety.

The "Zulia," it turned out, would spend more than two days in Curaçao. When I got there, the Irish "consul-general," Mr. Kelly, kindly introduced me to a Dutch naval officer who in turn invited me aboard his small cruiser for dinner. Then, it being established that I would have the whole day in port, I had my only voyage on a naval vessel, in and out of the port of Willemstad. It was a genuine treat not only because of the naval atmosphere but also because it was my first experience with the lavish richness of Dutch provender. The food and the drink were all that any Dutchman could wish, which is saying much.

Then, on the "Zulia," we set out for New York. I thought I was the only passenger. No one had appeared after we had left La Guaira. However, when we were safely out of Willemstad, another passenger did show up. He was General Carmelo Castro, major general in the Venezuelan army, a brother of the president and dictator. Unlike his distinguished brother, he was possessed of a fair knowledge of the English language. I asked him whither he was bound. He told me he was going to New York for a vacation. He said that he had gone to school in New York when he was a young boy and that ever since he had hankered to see the city again. I asked him how long he would stay. He didn't know. If I had been half as good a newspaperman as I then fancied myself, I would have sensed at once that he was running away and that the end of the Castro regime was at hand.

Steaming north, off Cape Hatteras, we ran into a hurricane. We were blown far out to sea, far to the east. We lost one of our screws. The green water was deep in the waist of the little ship. She tumbled and wallowed. General Castro was sick. I was not. We had no wireless. We limped into Brooklyn four days late. I had not had sense enough to be afraid.

Four or five days later, walking down Broadway, I met the captain and the chief engineer of the "Zulia." I hailed them. I liked both of them very much, indeed, but I was astonished to see them.

"Why are you here? I thought the 'Zulia' was to sail back today."

"She is due to sail today," said the captain, "but without us. We decided that we would never again go to sea in that tub." Then they told me how they had thought that we would not survive that storm off Hatteras. The captain said he had bought a farm near Lynchburg, Virginia. The chief engineer said he had bought a farm out in central Iowa. Both of them said that they never expected to go to sea again. That was when I got scared.

None of these adventures crept into the pieces I wrote about Venezuela. As good luck would have it, and good luck frequently did seem to keep Haskin under a special guiding star, just about the time my series of articles on Venezuela was printed, running the last twelve days of October, just as the Dutch ultimatum of the first of November rolled around, just in time to make the story stand up, the news came that Cipriano Castro, president of the Venezuelan Republic, had set sail from La Guaira on a Spanish ship bound for Madrid, where he hoped to obtain the medical care that would enable him to recover from a mysterious disease. It was the end of Castro.

I have one souvenir of that voyage. As the "Zulia" neared New York after the storm, limping along on one screw, General Carmelo Castro told me with most elaborate politeness that he had greatly enjoyed my company on board and that he would like to make me a present if I would deign to accept it. I graciously assured him that I would be delighted. He went to his cabin and brought forth a sword—a highly ornamented (but not bejeweled) sword—which, he said, had been worn by his distinguished brother and had been given to him on the occasion of his promotion to the rank of major general. I still have Cipriano Castro's sword.

While I managed to turn out a respectable measure of some twenty-five or thirty "Letters" about Venezuela and Curaçao, I began to sense that I had not been a howling success as a correspondent. I had got most of my information from Charlie Post. I had stubbed my toe in wandering around through the mystic mazes of a totalitarian regime about to collapse. I had not fully realized either its strength or its weakness. I came back to New York somewhat sadder but, I trust, a little wiser young man. I was not nearly so cocky as I was on my return from Japan. In retrospect, what I wrote then about Venezuela and Curaçao seems now to be written about some other world. Indeed it was, for then there was no oil. Venezuela was not yet rich. Curaçao was not then one of the great centers of the Dutch petroleum industry. I had no crystal ball and knew nothing about what would happen, but I felt quite keenly my own inadequacy to meet the situation of the moment. While grateful to the German minister and that squad of German soldiers for getting me out of Caracas safely, I was quite sure that I got into the trouble through my own fault, a result of my own rash, know-it-all attitude.

But all that made little difference in Washington. Very soon I was again on the road. This time it was Georgia, Florida, and Cuba. First there was a stop in the historic Georgia port city of Savannah and then the thrilling adventure of the Flagler railroad down the east coast and over the Keys on the way to Key West.

There were feature stories from Jacksonville, a thriving metropolis; from St. Augustine, the oldest city in the United States; a stop at West Palm Beach, a tea at "Whitehall," the Flagler mansion on Palm Beach itself; and thence on to Miami. What I wrote about Miami was principally about its amazing growth. I was perfectly willing to give it the sobriquet invented by its chamber of commerce, "The Magic City." It had risen in 1896 on the ruins of Fort Dallas. It now had a population of five thousand and claimed ten thousand. There were glass-bottomed boats that took one out over the then crystal-clear waters of Biscayne Bay toward the mangrove-covered island that now is Miami Beach. Here I was bold enough to predict, and luck was with me, that Miami would in time become a favorite place not only for the winter tourists but for an all-the-year-round population. I said that it looked more like an Oklahoma boom town than one could expect to find on the Atlantic Coast. I wrote paeans of praise that would have done credit perhaps to some of Miami's later press agents.

Then on down the railroad, the seagoing railroad, which was leaping over the Keys toward Key West. The effective terminal then was

Knight's Key, whence I took a small boat to Key West. My prediction of through Pullman sleeping cars from New York to Havana never quite materialized, since the sea train that was to ferry the Pullman cars from Key West to Havana never actually came into being so far as passenger cars were concerned, although of course for years there was a great freight traffic by that railroad-car ferry. That the railroad itself would perish in a hurricane and that it would be replaced over its own bed by a highway that would carry many, many more persons to Key West by automobile than ever the railroad could carry, I had no notion.

Then Havana. Here was my second adventure into a Spanish-speaking country. Havana was already a great city. The second American occupation was about to end. I was there in December, and the United States occupation was due to end on January 28, the birthdate of José Martí, the great leader of the Cuban Revolution. Tremendously impressed by the beauty of Havana, I wrote about its great success in the improvement of sanitation; the mosquito control that had ended the threat of yellow fever, which for centuries had held back the growth of the city; and the world trade that floated in and out of its great harbor. I wrote, I fear, from a strictly United States point of view. I was not very successful in meeting many of the Cuban leaders. There were too many Americans still about, many of whom I had known in Washington. It was but natural that I spent a great deal of time with them and that I reflected their views. I also met old friends whom I had known in my very earliest days in Nashville, old friends who were established in businesses in Havana and who greatly feared the second withdrawal of the Stars and Stripes. Yet, from the few Cuban statesmen I did manage to meet and with whom I was able to talk, which means I met some of them who spoke English, I made some effort to correct what otherwise would have been a fall into the trap of envisioning another, a third, and perhaps a permanent, United States occupation of the island. As it was, I went only so far as to support the claim, still advanced, that the Isle of Pines was in fact a permanent American territory under the terms of the treaty of peace and should not revert to Cuban rule.

Actually the event in Havana that made the most lasting impression upon me had nothing whatever to do with my profession, with the United States, or with Cuba. There I met Mrs. Beckwith, an elderly lady who had been a fellow-boarder at Mrs. Bocock's on Q Street. She was a clerk in the War Department and had been assigned to the staff of Governor Magoon in the second occupation of Cuba. She spoke Spanish fluently. She lived in a pension where she was the only English-speaking person. She invited me to dinner. I enjoyed that greatly. After dinner, at her urging, I settled down with her into a poker game. Never adept at cards, never a lover of games, I had quit once and for all playing whist while I was still in Nashville. That was in the days of duplicate whist—long before auction whist or contract whist was thought of. But I still thought it incumbent upon me to play poker occasionally, as I had in Louisville and in Washington. That night in the Havana pension after dinner we sat down to poker—it was penny ante—and I bought a dollar's worth of chips. Mrs. Beckwith could speak Spanish. No one else spoke English. Mrs. Beckwith chose to speak Spanish. She was too much immersed in the game to remember my linguistic handicap. After four hours at the table, no one speaking English to me, it got to be one o'clock in the morning. Nobody else seemed in the mood to stop the game, but I was. I rose. I cashed in my chips. I had lost one cent. I had worked four hours desperately to lose that one cent. I decided never again to play poker. I have never broken that pledge.

CHAPTER XXIV

EGYPT AND PALESTINE

Between times, in between these various excursions to one country and another, I continued to press my suit and became engaged to be married to Miss Elizabeth Virginia Sims. Mr. Haskin had a plan in mind which not only would increase my salary but also would enable me to save a little more than I had been able to do. The Haskin plan was a trip for me through the Orient. So Bess and I set the wedding date for late in 1909. In the meantime Bess and her sister Tom were going on a trip to Europe while I would be in Asia.

Haskin was loath to send me alone into the lands where sicknesses lurked, partly because of his humanitarian kindness, no doubt, but partly because a series of daily letters once begun in publication was not to be broken into. I suggested that we call Tom Wallace back from *The Courier-Journal* on the notion that Wallace could get a leave of absence and would be glad to take the trip and serve without salary if his expenses were paid. Wallace's illness in 1907 had taken him back to Louisville, and he had become an assistant to Henry Watterson. This proposition was made. It was heartily approved by Mr. Watterson, who believed that Tom Wallace's ability as an editorial writer would be enhanced by a trip to the countries of the Eastern world.

In January, 1909, Wallace and I went aboard the North German Lloyd Steamship "Koenig Albert" to sail for Naples, then to change to another ship for Alexandria, Egypt. We stowed our gear—twelve or thirteen pieces of luggage for each of us—for we had to take not only that inevitable Wellington typewriter but all sorts of ceremonial costume on the chance that we might be able to see some great dignitaries. We had tuxedoes and we had swallow tails, we had cutaway frock coats and we had silk hats, as well as white linens and accouterments indicated for the hot countries.

Next we began to explore the ship. Tom was particularly happy. He was one who took his social obligations and responsibilities most seriously. Until this day he has never been known to be twenty-four hours late with a bread-and-butter letter to a host. He never has been known to violate in the slightest degree the canons of social conduct that were set for him in his youth in Shelbyville, Kentucky. Happy to be free of his social responsibilities for once, he said, "For the next six months I shall not have to do anything that I do not want to do merely to be polite."

We continued to explore the ship. Soon we ran into one of the owners of *The Courier-Journal,* General William B. Haldeman, with Mrs. Haldeman (who was brought up in Shelbyville, Kentucky) and their daughter, Miss Lizzie. Within the space of an hour we also ran into Mrs. Madison Cawein, the wife of a Louisville poet who was also a dramatic critic for *The Courier-Journal;* and, also, Miss Lizzie Greene of Falls of Rough, an old friend of the Wallace family. Then we encountered Mrs. Augustine Ballard of Louisville, who also had connections in Shelbyville. In short, by the time we got back to our stateroom Tom had discovered that there were at least three different sets of Shelbyville society folk aboard, and his dream of independence of social obligation rudely perished.

I, more gregarious and, I fear, much less polite, was delighted to see these people, because I already knew the Haldemans, Miss Lizzie Greene, and Mrs. Cawein. It seemed to me to be a very nice Kentucky crowd, and so it turned out to be. Within a day or two we were out of the cold weather bound for the Azores. We touched Gibraltar and Algiers for sight-seeing. We were a little late in getting into Naples, and, instead of having twenty-four hours ashore as we had hoped, we actually transshipped by lighter in the harbor. We were not able to "see Naples and die," although the murky clouds lifted just after we sailed to give us a little glimpse of Vesuvius. All the Kentuckians had intended to debark at Naples, but the weather was so cold and raw that the Haldemans decided to go on with Tom and me to Egypt and postpone their European journey until better weather.

A few days later Tom and I with the Haldemans arrived at Shepheard's Hotel in Cairo. The next morning Tom and I were standing with General Haldeman on the terrace when a carriage drove up and discharged three passengers, all from Shelbyville. They were Cale

Young Rice, the poet; his wife, Mrs. Alice Hegan Rice, the author of *Mrs. Wiggs of the Cabbage Patch;* and her aunt, Mrs. Fannie Macaulay, the author of the then current best-seller about life in Japan called *The Lady of the Decoration.* They had been in Japan and China and India and were on their way back to the United States across the Atlantic. That made two Shelbyville sets in Shepheard's Hotel. Late that afternoon after tea, Wallace and I walked out on the terrace, and suddenly we heard a little scream of pleasure, and Wallace was embraced by a dazzlingly beautiful young woman all in purple gloriously set off by a Gainsborough hat complete with plumes. She also was from Shelbyville and was a divorcée.

The very next day Thomas J. Felder of Kentucky and Nashville; his wife, the daughter of Milton H. Smith, the president of the Louisville and Nashville Railroad; and her young cousin Alice Smith from Nashville also arrived at Shepheard's. They were not exactly from Shelbyville, but they were certainly Louisville and Nashville. Poor Tom's social obligations and responsibilities were resumed. He had been, in his youth, the president of the Shelbyville Hop Club, and it was a tradition that the holder of that office was condemned to a life of bachelorhood, leadership of cotillions, and a devoted career as a squire of dames. It remained for Tom, years later, to marry and break that tradition.

We saw the streets of Cairo; we visited the Sphinx and the Pyramids. We saw the museums; we looked in at some of the big mosques; we visited the great university of El-Azhar. But both Tom and I managed to get in a little work and a few interviews with important persons in the government, mainly those connected with the British residency. We learned a great deal about Lord Cromer and his significant administrative work in Egypt. We learned a lot about the operation of the Suez Canal. We also began to learn a little about the restlessness of the Egyptians, especially in the presence of the fact that the country, under the suzerainty of Turkey, was seething with discontent and powerfully activated by the revolution then in progress in Turkey, where the Committee of Union and Progress was conducting an attack on the sultan, Abdul-Hamid II, a movement that in popular parlance was called the "Young Turk Rebellion." We had little notion that we were witnessing the breakup of the Ottoman Turkish Empire, much less that the discontent we observed was the beginning of a great Near Eastern revolution.

Our plan was to leave most of our goods and chattels in Cairo and to take a side trip through Palestine. We were so intrigued with Egypt, with the monuments of its old civilization, and with the evidences of that ancient life preserved in the museums, so much occupied by our delightful social contacts with all the Kentucky and Tennessee visitors in Cairo, that I fear neither Tom nor I kept up very well either with the seething unrest in Egypt or with the news from the rest of the world. Certain it is that, when we journeyed to Port Said to get a ship for Jaffa in Palestine, we took no reckoning of the state of affairs in the eastern Mediterranean. We did not so much as ask what the nationality of the ship was we were to take. We did not know that it was an Austro-Hungarian vessel out of Fiume; and much less did we know that the Turkish government in Constantinople had formally boycotted Austria-Hungary and that, therefore, we would not be permitted to land in Palestine.

The next morning when our little ship dropped anchor off Jaffa, where we expected to be met by rowboats that would take us ashore, we were greeted instead by a cannon ball fired from an ancient gun mounted on an ancient Turkish fort. The skipper hoisted his anchor and set a course for Fiume. None of the dozen or more passengers on board had any wish to go to Fiume. We were all for Palestine. A Dominican monk, possessed of the command of many languages and a most charming personality, had entertained us the evening before, after dinner, by a marvelous performance on the piano. He gathered the passengers together and said: "I know the Turkish governor at Haifa, and I also know he is bribable. If we take up a collection, and each of you put in a gold sovereign, I will try to persuade the skipper to stand in at Haifa, and I think we can make an arrangement with the Turkish governor there to permit us to go ashore."

The monk had soon collected a purse of golden British sovereigns. We saw him go on the bridge and talk with the Austro-Hungarian captain. Whether or not the purse was lighter when he came down, I do not know, but he brought with him the good news that we would stand in at Haifa. We did. There were signals, and a boat came out. There was a conversation with the captain and the monk, and then the signal that all was well. Very soon other boats came out, and all of us were put ashore at Haifa.

Tom and I had reckoned only to go up to Jerusalem and its environs, with a possibility of getting some kind of transportation that would take us over to the Jordan. We had not reckoned on northern Palestine, but here we were. With us were three Australians, a Methodist minister and his wife and young son, bound for a visit "home" to England.

Being in the north, we thought of Nazareth, even of Damascus. But here we found revolution. The railroad had stopped. No trains had run from Haifa to Damascus for weeks. The problem was to get back to Jaffa and on the road to Jerusalem. We committed ourselves to the kindly ministrations of the ubiquitous Thomas Cook & Son. They said there was no way to go except by wagon. They could furnish us a wagon which would take the five of us to Jaffa in a two days' journey, but unfortunately there were no drivers who could speak English. There were drivers who spoke German, French, Arabic, Italian, and even Spanish, but none who knew English. However Cook's said they could furnish a good driver with written notes who could manage our journey.

That arrangement being made, Tom and I set out to walk up to the monastery on top of Mount Carmel, the bold profile of which had been etched in my memory from childhood by way of the pictures in my Sunday-school literature. It was a longish walk, a steep climb, and we were pretty well tired when we got to the top. There we stood looking out over the sea. A tremendous blow had come up. We saw a small ship in the roadstead which evidently was in trouble. The fury of the gale from the west increased, and suddenly that ship, carried over the sharp edge of a reef, broke in two. Against the black western sky, rain not having begun, we could see members of the crew jump into the water.

We hurried down the mountain. The darkness increased. The wind off the Mediterranean whipped up a gale. The rain came. Finally we stumbled into our hotel almost as wet and bedraggled as the survivors of the shipwreck who were there ahead of us. It turned out that all hands of the small Italian freighter were accounted for. All either had been able to swim to shore or had been carried in by the very fury of the storm that wrecked their vessel. The dinner that night with the survivors was enlivened by the presence of the Italian skipper, who had lost his ship but was so happy over losing no lives that he made a great deal of entertaining the five English-speaking persons, his English being very good indeed.

The next morning, long before daylight, the three Australians, Tom, and I were perched on our seats in a huge wagon drawn by two horses. We submitted ourselves to the care of the driver, who spoke no English. The storm had abated. As we drove in the darkness along the road that skirted the foot of Carmel, the driver stopped. There was beginning to be a dim light. We could see that he had halted at the mouth of a cave. He called aloud, "Abdul! Abdul!" He called again. There was no answer. He dismounted and went into the cave. Soon he emerged in the dim light with another Arab dressed in Arabic costume, not as our driver, who was in western European clothes. There was a long and earnest conversation in what we presumed to be Arabic.

Five lonely, frightened English-speaking passengers were silent, but each, as it turned out later, was overwhelmed with the conviction that we and we alone were the subjects of that conversation. When at last our driver returned and we started on our journey, we were tre-mendously relieved but already touched by anxiety. As we turned the promontory and went southward into what, at least to our unpracticed eyes, was the roadless and trackless Plain of Sharon, still traveling at the very edge of the sea, the sun came up and flooded with light the beautiful ruin of the castle of Athlit, a castle built at the very edge of the sea by the Crusaders. The Gothic ruin was guarded by an Arab wearing a long robe and armed with the longest rifle we had ever seen. The driver stopped. There was a conversation. By signs they made it known that we were to give the guide some coins and that then he would admit us to see the castle.

It seemed the better part of valor to accept the situation. Inside the wall we could see better than ever the medieval Gothic church and, for an added effect, great balls of seafoam that the wind, still from the west, was picking up from the churning surf of last night's storm. The white foam balls wafted through the broken Gothic arches of that visible reminder of the great Crusades, which, I am afraid, meant to me not so much the preaching of Peter the Hermit and the res-toration to Christendom of the tomb of Jesus as it did the adventures of Richard Cœur de Lion and his great adversary Saladin in the twelfth-century seige of Haifa.

On and on we went inland, over the roadless plain, seeing only occasionally in the distance a tiny village, all of us overcome by the beauty of the spring flowers that here had bloomed in early February, the anemones that Jesus had called the lilies of the field, excited once in a while by an antelope or a deer breaking into our field of vision. About five o'clock in the afternoon we came to the Zionist colony Zircon-Jacob. We were driven to a door over which there was a sign "Hotel de Graf." Out bounced a short, round character who exclaimed, "Get right out, gentlemen, get right out. I know you're from New York. I'm from Brooklyn myself. I think William Randolph Hoist is the greatest man in the woild."

Whether or not Tom and I shared our host's evaluation of Mr. Hearst, whether or not the Australians knew what he was talking about, we were delighted to hear Brooklynese; and I, at any rate, felt great relief. Our host put us up in our rooms and then took us to see his wine cellars and vineyards. He talked to us about the great success of this colony, which was the first of the Zionist colonies established under the munificence of the Baron de Hirsch.

After the sight-seeing there was a most delicious dinner. While we were at the table there was a great commotion outside. Into the great hall, which was lobby, reception hall, and dining-room in one, came three men. By their speech we knew they were Americans. They were bloody. Hurriedly they told of a brush with some Bedouins in the desert. They had been beaten about the head and shoulders but escaped to make way to this haven. We helped to wash and bandage their wounds, none of which, fortunately, was serious. One turned out to be Professor Robert Harper, head of the department of archeology and brother of William Rainey Harper, the president of the University of Chicago. With him were two young students. One was president Harper's son, Paul. Long afterward I knew him very well in Chicago, where at the time of his unfortunate and sudden death he was a law partner of Adlai Stevenson.

Glad as we were that the two Harpers and the other young student had not suffered serious injuries, it was with a certain amount of trepidation (at least on my part) that we set out the next morning in the care of our non-English-speaking driver destined for the second day's overland journey toward Jaffa. Just before noon that second day we came upon something that I had never expected to see again—a road. Three wagons just like ours were coming from Nazareth to Jaffa. As the sun crossed the meridian, we stopped at an ancient well. An English-speaking driver of one of the other wagons told us we could rest the horses and take time to eat the excellent lunch which had been prepared for us by the Zionist host of the Hotel de Graf.

Thence to the southwestward from the well, the road was much better. Through the English-speaking driver we told our own driver that we, Tom and I, would walk on ahead to get some exercise. As we walked, we were utterly astonished to find ourselves on a good macadam road. We were amazed to see concrete culverts over the beds of little streams, now dry, but probably subject to freshets. We walked on around curves, up hills, and down dales, forgetting to look backward at all. In fact, we never looked back. We were secure in the bosom of Father Abraham, alias Thomas Cook & Son.

On a little rise we met two men coming toward us. Both of them were in the Bedouin costume of the desert. Each had slung over his shoulder an extremely long rifle. In the brilliant sunlight we could see the mother-of-pearl inlay on the gunstocks. We could see that they were very old guns, but we were not at all certain that they were not still quite efficient. If this were not enough, each of the two carried in his right hand not a staff, although he used it as a staff, but a spear.

I was frightened out of my senses. I think Tom was, too, but Tom had a resource, an inner defense mechanism, that I never possessed. It was one of desperate, dry humor. As we saw these two gentleman and remembering my terror at the mouth of the cave in Carmel, I heard Tom say, "To think that I, once a dramatic critic in Louisville, Kentucky, and once a 'super' in an opera, should ever meet somebody seriously carrying a spear."

I giggled. He giggled. But it didn't do us very much good. We met the two gentlemen. We were unarmed. They stopped us. We held parleys. Since the beginning of time, certainly since the adventure of the Tower of Babel, it has happened that persons attempting to converse in unknown languages incline to believe that understanding comes by raising the voice, the rise in ratio of decibels being proportionate to the lack of understanding. So Tom and I shouted at our captors. Our captors, also moved by the same human quirk, shouted at us. We were sore in trouble. We looked backward (we had arranged that the English-speaking driver and wagon would be the first to come when our caravan reassembled itself), but there was no succor.

Over a little rise in the direction of Jaffa appeared two other gentlemen. They also were in Bedouin costume, but each of them was accompanied by an ass. These burros had slung over their backs great burdens—so heavy that their masters were walking. They stopped. There was a long, long conversation in some unknown language, presumably Arabic. As the upshot of the conversation, in which Tom and I did not participate, the two gentlemen lately arrived turned the heads of their pack animals back toward Jaffa, and then by signs they invited us to mount the asses. Unsuccessful in that tactic, they jettisoned the caroges of the two burros and again invited us to get astride. Again sign language failed, so far as the nuances were concerned. We, that is, Tom and I, were sure that we had been captured by Bedouins of the desert. We were also sure that we were being held for ransom, since there were no threatening gestures with either spear or rifle. We were also uncomfortably certain that there would be nobody to ransom us, nobody even to know we were lost. We were acutely aware for the first time that we were traveling in a revolutionary country. We had never before paid very much attention to the Turks, and we realized suddenly that we had paid much less attention to the Young Turks than was their due.

A long parley ensued. Signs failed. Tom and I kept looking backward. Our two captors and their two adjunct confreres accompanied by their burros were very, very eloquent, both with tongue and with gesture. The more they shouted, the more we shouted. The more the two sides shouted, the less each understood the other. Then our captors decided to take positive action. They turned the heads of the two asses back toward Jaffa, and then two of them took hold of me and two of them took hold of Tom, and they endeavored to lift us up on the backs of these animals. Then we knew that we were doomed.

Just at that time there was a clatter from our rear, and here came our caravan. Fortunately, in the van was the driver who spoke English. He came up alongside. Tom and I shouted to him. I think our voices were still too high, for we were still thinking we were talking at cross-languages. He asked, "What is the matter?" There followed what seemed to be an interminable conversation in Arabic. Finally it boiled down to this:

The English-speaking driver of the Thomas Cook & Son wagons, Nazareth-to-Jaffa-bound: "You gentlemen have been mistaken. These men met you and thought that you were walking toward Jaffa, and they knew that you could not get there by nightfall. They were afraid that the night would come upon you and that you would be devoured by wild beasts. They tried to tell you that you should not go forward. Then the two men came along with the donkeys, and the first two men said you were Americans and therefore very, very rich, and, if they would turn the donkeys around and give you a ride back to Jaffa, they would be richly rewarded. They objected that they had bags of wheat. [That was when they had thrown the cargo overboard.] Then they did turn the animals around and thought that, if they could take you back to Jaffa in safety and protect you from the wild beasts and from desert bandits, you would reward them and make them rich for life."

When this was translated to Tom and me, we laughed, not heartily, I think, but with the high giggle of relief. By this time our own driver had come up. The three Australians were both perplexed and distressed. They had not walked ahead with Tom and me. Our driver had the English-speaking driver explain the situation to them. He did. They were slightly comforted, but nevertheless they resumed their hopes to live until they got to Jaffa.

Then followed a long parley. How much would these gentlemen, the Bedouins, accept as a gift from us, now that our wagon had come along and there was no doubt that we would be able to get to Jaffa in safety. The result was that we (Tom and I) gave each of our two original captors and each of our mounted saviors a souvenir. Somebody had told us that, if we got into trouble in certain parts of the Near East, we should have with us some silver dollars, preferably Maria Theresa dollars, but, in lieu of that, a United States of America silver dollar. Tom had paid no attention to that advice. I had weighted myself down with six silver dollars. They were in my right-hand trousers' pocket. I bestowed upon each of the four Bedouins one silver dollar. Thereupon a great change shot through the assembly. Our four captors and would-be guardians not only beamed and smiled but bowed to the ground. Tom and I received our first salaams.

Then on. As dusk was gathering, our caravan—we had picked up two or three other wagons in the meantime—made its way into Jaffa. The fact that there was a road in this all but roadless wilderness impressed us both. Our curiosity was so aroused that the next day in Jaffa we asked why the road was there. We were told that it had been built a few years before for Kaiser Wilhelm of Germany in anticipation of his visit to the Holy Land on the chance that he might desire to see that part of the country which sometimes in the event of an infrequent rain was swampy. The Kaiser, so our informants told us, actually didn't use it. I put it down as a useless expenditure to meet the off chance of a royal and imperial whim. Wallace seemed to agree.

It is certain that neither of us newspaper men in our adventure on that road ever so much as dreamed of suspecting that that very road traversed the only low and soft ground between the Damascene Railhead and the Suez Canal or that within less than a decade it would actually be used by German and Turkish artillery in the effort to cut the lifeline of the British Empire. If we had suspected it, we probably would not have written anything so seemingly fantastic. And, if we had written, I am sure no newspaper in the United States would have printed it.

At Jaffa we were deposited at a hotel, an establishment favored by Messrs. Cook & Son. There I made our non-English-speaking driver, who had guided us through two days of peril and terror, rich by giving him my two remaining United States silver dollars. Never before and never since have I seen such an expression of gratitude on the face of any human being.

The hotel was an adventure in itself. I don't know what the population of Jaffa was at that time, but it was a small town that had not changed appreciably since it had been, by some transliteration or some transitory exchange of pronunciation, differentiated from the Joppa of biblical days, which I had known so well from my early childhood. The hotel had I don't know how many rooms, but certainly the first thirteen were not numbered. They had names. The rooms were given the names of the tribes and half-tribes of Israel. Each was a little cubicle with a single bed and was furnished with the austerity of a medieval monastery. That night I slept in Dan. Tom slept in Gad.

Refreshed a little from a wash-up out of the bowl-and-pitcher combination to which both of us had been accustomed from our early youth, we ventured with not much confidence into the great hall, which actually was a very small hall but which served, as seemed to be then the custom of the country, as reception room, lobby, dining-room, and all the rest of it.

The supper we were served about eight o'clock that night of our arrival in Jaffa was probably one of the greatest gastronomic events of my career. It was a soup. It was a roast of mutton. It was a salad of cabbage and orange. It was accompanied by a rough red wine. As it was in Haifa, so it was in Jaffa, the bread was better than any bread I had theretofore tasted. (It was years afterward that I discovered, or at least I heard from an expert of the Department of Agriculture, that the wheat plant is native to Palestine and that bread is better in its native habitat.)

However, Jaffa for both of us was just a place to get off the ship. Our objective was Jerusalem. We were delighted to learn that the railroad from Jerusalem to Jaffa was still operating. We also discovered that it would be very much better if we waited for two days in order to have adequate accommodations on the single coach which had re-served seats (a sort of parlor car) that would assure our getting to Jerusalem in comfort.

Tom and I decided that we would not attempt to travel farther in such troubled times in such polylingual areas without having retained the services of an interpreter and guide. Naturally we consulted Thomas Cook & Son. Also we were still conscious of the fact that we had work to do. Tom went out to see a new Zionist colony which was devoted to citrus growing and which was the source of the famous pear-shaped Jaffa orange, the most delicious of all oranges. Meanwhile I was look-ing around Jaffa to find out something about its municipal government. Here I ran into a gentleman who told me that the town was so crowded that people of the well-to-do class had almost nowhere to live. He told me that a group of forty or fifty well-to-do Jews had decided to build a new suburb and that on the next day the cornerstone of the first edifice in this subdivision would be laid. I was interested, and so on a crisp, brilliant, sunshiny morning in February, 1909, I imposed myself on a group of some fifty or sixty persons who were proceeding in carriages out of Jaffa to a spot on the treeless, plantless sands of the Mediterranean.

There I saw the laying of the cornerstone of a schoolhouse—the first building to be erected in that new subdivision. Already forty-six persons had chosen by lot the site of the homes they intended to erect once the school was completed and ready to receive their children. That school was the first building in Tel Aviv. Now, nigh on to fifty years later, Tel Aviv has a population of more than four hundred thousand persons and is the chief city and the metropolis, if not always the political capital, of Israel.

Messrs. Cook & Son turned up a guide-interpreter for us. He met us at the hotel. He wore a fez, a red fez with a black tassel, but also he was accoutered with the square-cut, square-tailed frock coat known as a Prince Albert. He assured us in excellent English that he was a Christian. Perhaps that didn't register sufficiently with either Tom or me, whereupon he asseverated with great emphasis that he was not only a Christian but an Episcopalian. We were not so much interested in his religion, ignoramuses that we were, as we were in his ability to speak English. He gave us examples of that. We found him extremely fluent. He assured us that he could speak all the other languages that there were.

We heard rumors of trouble in Jerusalem, but we were naïve enough to believe that trouble would never trouble us. We got on the train in a reserved compartment. It was a combination freight, caboose, and observation car. There was room in the compartment at the rear end of the train only for six passengers. There were but four: Tom and I, our guide-interpreter, and another individual. As we started to climb the grade up from the Mediterranean sea level toward Jerusalem, our guide started a patter about Er Ramle, Ain Ger, and the other places; but Tom and I shared an antipathy toward the repetitious patter of guides, and we shut him up. From then on he engaged in earnest conversation with the other passenger, who also was attired in a red fez and a Prince Albert coat. The other passenger seemed to be very anxious about his luggage. He had a suitcase which he kept in his lap all the way.

At long last we came near Jerusalem, and our guide told us we would soon be in the station. It was then that he told us that in a private car just ahead of our car was the new Greek Orthodox patriarch of Jerusalem who recently had been chosen by the Holy Synod in Athens, a Greek who had never been in Palestine and whose selection was much resented by the Orthodox community in Jerusalem. We took that to be just a matter of everyday gossip. It seemed not to concern us at all.

[454]

As we drew into the railway station in Jerusalem and the train slowed down, we heard great tumult and shouting. We looked out and saw the whole station surrounded by armed Turkish soldiers with fixed bayonets holding off an enormous crowd, shouting words which we could not understand, but the emphasis and inflection of which showed that they were deprecatory and defiant. As the train slowed down, our guide's unknown confrere dropped the suitcase he had nursed so carefully in his lap into the arms of a man running along. He muffed it. The suitcase fell on the platform. It burst open. It was full of revolvers and ammunition.

Here was a pretty how-do-you-do. The train came to a stop. A Turkish sergeant came aboard and immediately collared and arrested not only the man who dropped the suitcase but our own guide. I said to Tom, *sotto voce,* "We are only about three hundred yards from a place where a very great saint once made a great denial." When the sergeant asked us if we had anything to do with either of these men, I am proud to say that neither of us overtly lied, but we covertly did. We did not admit any connection whatever with the Episcopalian Christian gentleman who had been given to us by the Messrs. Cook & Son.

Now, deprived of an interpreter, getting off the train in the midst of a riot, and feeling ourselves but insecurely protected by the Turkish soldiers against the onslaught of an infuriated Christian mob, we managed (merely because we were foreigners) to get an escort of a corporal and three soldiers who took us out of the station to the near-by King David Hotel. As we walked into the hotel, other Turkish soldiers dragged out the bodies of three gentleman who had been but freshly killed.

We went through the motions of getting ourselves registered. The manager said that he would have to ask us to stay in our rooms until the American consul-general could come to see us. He wasn't long coming. His office, it seemed, was just across the square from King David's Tower. He stormed in. He was a political appointee, in that day, of course, a Republican. He was from Iowa. He was a member of a celebrated Iowa family. His surname was Wallace. His first name, by coincidence, was Tom—the same as my companion. He was in an ugly mood. He upbraided us. "Why are you two kids coming into a country like this at a time like this when everything is so dangerous?

[455]

Why are you coming here to involve me in trouble? Why are you coming here when your presence may cause an international incident which will require action by the State Department?"

We attempted to assure him of the innocence of our errand and the fact that we were ignorant of the political and revolutionary situation, but he was quite deaf, and it was sometime before we were able to convince him that we really were on the level. Then he told us that the Young Turks were rising in Palestine, that the old Turk governor of Jerusalem was being beseiged, and that he would have to confine us to the hotel. He came up to the rooms assigned to us and discovered that they had outside windows. He saw the manager and had us moved into one interior room looking out over a court. There we were imprisoned for three days and nights. By some international courtesy he had persuaded the Turkish governor to post a guard at the doors of our room. Even if we had desired to break out, we would have been forcibly prevented. The management provided meals. Not only that, but after the first day there was a vacant room on that floor, and all the prisoners, that is, Tom and I, an Anglo-Indian lady, and an Italian merchant, were permitted to go into a sitting-room for rest and recreation. It was indeed recreation, for the Anglo-Indian lady had a black bird with a yellow-bordered beak, a myna bird, the first I had ever seen or heard. The myna bird spoke several languages, could whistle a good many tunes, and could even sing a lay or two. It helped.

It didn't help much, however, when even in the inside room of that hotel all night long we could hear the tramp, tramp, tramp of marching soldiers, rifle fire, and an occasional cannon shot. We did not know exactly where we were except that we were in Jerusalem. We did not know what we were except that for the moment we were prisoners. We did not know what would happen to us. But we were appreciative of the excellent service and the truly wonderful cuisine. And, furthermore, we realized at last that we were in a revolution.

Around midnight of the third day the firing increased in intensity. Suddenly there was a great commotion in the hall. Our Turkish guards were overwhelmed by superior numbers, or perhaps by discretion, since no one was hurt. The Young Turks took over. The old Turkish governor's defense had collapsed. The Committee of Union and Progress was in control.

That night in some respects was the greatest night of my life. The

Young Turks had attracted to the support of the Committee of Union and Progress the youth of all three religions: Moslem, Christian, and Jew. That night the site of Solomon's Temple, the Mosque of Omar, the sacred place for all three religions, was thrown open, and the young people of all three faiths swarmed onto the plane, we two innocent Americans with them. Toward morning the Jews began to bring in their old people—the old bearded Jews and the old bewigged mothers of Israel who for years and years had spent their lives at the Wailing Wall and never again had hoped to be admitted to that sacred eminence. The world seemed that night to come together. Indeed, that night it did come together, so far as these three religions were concerned. The fact that it didn't last long, that within a week the Jews were excluded, the Christians subjected to severe controls, and the mosque returned to its Moslem sovereignty, has made little difference to me in the four decades or more since that night. I had then a glimpse of the unity that might possibly be conceived among those who hold to the Greco-Judean-Christian ethic.

A pseudo-peace having been arranged, we visited the Garden of Gethsemane, and we went into the Church of the Holy Sepulcher in Jerusalem and the Church of the Nativity in Bethlehem. We saw the signs, but so confused was the situation that we had little opportunity, if any, to talk to any persons in high governmental station; and we dared not press forward into the regions beyond. We abandoned hope of traversing the road to Jericho. We abandoned hope of seeing the Jordan.

CHAPTER XXV

THE ASIATIC AWAKENING: CEYLON

Back in Egypt for a few days, taking stock of my adventures in that turbulent fortnight in Palestine, I began to prepare for what was emerging as a much more difficult task than I had anticipated. While the very fact that Wallace and I were on the assignment was due to disturbed conditions in Asia, I fear that I, at any rate, had thought of the journey in terms of seeing the sights and writing about them in the manner of a travelogue. The significance of what I was to see and hear and its effect upon my own political and social views was but dimly discernible.

In Cairo we bade goodbye to General and Mrs. Haldeman and their daughter, Miss Lizzie, who set out for Paris, where their trip was to have a tragic end in the death of Miss Lizzie, their youngest daughter, a victim of appendicitis. We also bade goodbye to the Cale Young Rices and Mrs. Macaulay after getting from them careful and precise instructions about how we were to travel and behave in India and China and, even more important, the address of a "bearer" or Indian servant who had served them so well during their stay in India. For my own preparations, I bought several books on oriental problems to be read on the ship en route to Ceylon.

Also I began to take a much greater interest than I had theretofore in the Coptic churches and the Islamic mosques in Cairo itself. The events I had witnessed in Jerusalem and my intense interest in the holy places I visited there and in Bethlehem had had the effect of rekindling my great curiosity about religion. My observations were superficial at best. They extended no further than an attempt to hear as many of the different liturgies as possible, to observe as many of the customs of worship as I could manage, and to fix in my memory at least a dim appreciation of the different symbols of the several faiths as well as those of the intrafaith divisions.

My study, of course, could not be profound. I had neither the time nor the scholarly equipment to do more than to witness exterior manifestations. In Jerusalem and Bethlehem I took care to visit as many establishments as possible, such as the chapels of the Church of the Holy Sepulcher and the chapels and altars of the Church of the Nativity, in which I either witnessed the ceremony or met some of the clergy of the various divisions of the Orthodox Eastern church along nationalistic lines—Greek, Russian, and the like. I also saw some of the obscure and ancient rites of the Jacobites, Marianites, and the Copts and even got a glimpse of a vestige of the Nestorians in the person of a priest who claimed to be of that rite. In the Church of the Nativity there were, of course, Latin, or Roman Catholic, and Orthodox as well as Coptic priests in attendance. There was a huge caravansary for Russian pilgrims in a monastery outside the walls of Bethlehem. There were the ceremonies of admission sans shoes at the Mosque of Omar on the very site of the temple. There was the opportunity to see the Jews praying at the Wailing Wall, reputed to be the last vestige of the foundation stones of the Temple of Solomon. Naturally I learned only a little, but I did get, somewhat hazily and doubtless inaccurately, the spirit of the differentiations of the manifestations of the symbol of the Cross, the differing cuts and colors of the vestments of the priests, but enough to have implanted in me a deep respect for the historical and cultural roots out of which have sprung the divisions of the several faiths and which are continued in their various symbolisms. There was no time for more, but I began to look forward with eagerness to India and China, where I would have a chance to see other religions not a part of the Judeo-Greco-Christian-Islamic world, in which so many differences were counterbalanced by so many likenesses that spring from what originally was a more or less shared history and philosophy.

It took the little German ship on which we embarked two full weeks to reach Colombo in Ceylon. The Red Sea was hot. The ship's company was small, but there was time to read and, indeed, to make some acquaintances which later turned out to be most rewarding for our work.

Perhaps I got more from Lord Cromer's *Modern Egypt* than from any other book I had read. It was for me at once an introduction to the science and art of administration as contradistinguished from the more directly political aspects of government. It also served to warn me of the danger of attributing to a particular word a connotation that arose from my own limited experience and my own wide and deep prejudices which could not with any justice be applied to the use of the same word in a different context by a different person with a different background.

Two such words were "empire" and "imperialism." "Empire" had meant to me the subjection and subjugation of weaker peoples by a stronger nation with the purpose of ruthlessly exploiting the small peoples in the interest of the big. "Imperialism" meant to me the very summation of the evils instinct in empires. This I reckoned to have arisen out of my interest in the domestic political scene in the United States in the years following the end of the Spanish-American War. The United States, whatever the immediate occasion, had gone to war to free Cuba from the evils of Spanish imperialism. The war had been extended to take away from Spain not only little Puerto Rico but the great Philippines and thus to destroy the colonial system of Spain with the exception perhaps of a few small colonies in Africa. When that war was over, there was some indication that some people in America thought it would be a good thing for the United States to do its part in the imperial contest then taking place among the great powers—to divide up among themselves, with the greatest share to the strongest and most ruthless, the undeveloped portions of the world.

Albert Jeremiah Beveridge, senator from Indiana, termed contemptuously by the *New York Sun* "the Grand Young Man," had clearly indicated, although he carefully refrained from advocating, the necessity for the United States to get into the great game. I had read his articles in the *Saturday Evening Post,* later brought together in a book, *The Russian Advance.* There he had set out the story of the Russian advance over the centuries ever reaching toward a warm-water port, struggling to get to the Mediterranean, struggling to get to the Pacific, its seizure of its own sphere of influence in Manchuria, and its taking of the seaport of Port Arthur, which the Japanese had fondly thought had fallen to them along with Formosa as their share of the spoils of their successful war against China in 1895. He discussed not only what the Russians were doing in Asia but the great rivalry of the British and German empires and the French imperialist republic in the cutting-up of Africa in the last two decades of the nineteenth century—the extirpation by the British of the three republics of South Africa in the Boer War and, by implication, the necessity for the United States to protect itself by seizing for itself what, if anything, was left.

In the presidential campaign of 1900 the Democratic candidate, my hero—William Jennings Bryan—had deserted the sacred cause of free silver in order to make "imperialism" what he termed the "paramount issue of the campaign." In that campaign Mr. Bryan led the Democrats to demand immediately the independence of Cuba, the eventual independence of the Philippines, and the repudiation of any imperialistic purpose on the part of the United States in Latin America, in the Pacific, or elsewhere. There was perhaps really no reason to believe that Mr. McKinley thought otherwise, but even some Republicans shared the Democratic distrust of what might be going on in the turbulent and ambitious mind of the Republican candidate for Vice-President, Theodore Roosevelt. As a side issue, the Bryan group also tended to criticize what was going on in the threat to the independence of the Boer republics and to set up American notions of the inherent right of nations to self-determination with the implied condemnation of the activities not only of Japan and Russia in the Far East but of Germany, France, Italy, and England in Africa.

Mr. Bryan had taught me that imperialism was an unmixed evil and "empire" another word for mass slavery. Lord Cromer gave me the other side of the picture. I had myself witnessed through the newspapers the extirpation of the South African republics and their absorption into the British Empire. I had witnessed in the same way the unheralded attack of the Japanese upon the Russians at Port Arthur and the utterly unexpected victory of the little Japanese over the great empire of the czar. In one of those wars my sympathies were with the Boers. In the other my sympathy was with the Japanese.

But Sir Evelyn Baring (later Lord Cromer) as the British resident in Cairo gave me facts in his simple and beautiful English which compelled me to see the other side of the coin. The Turkish Empire was rotten to the core. The Sublime Porte was truly the sick man of Europe. The efforts to wrest Egypt and Palestine from the Turkish sway by the French under both the greater and the lesser Napoleons had come to naught. Other French essays in Africa had been disastrous with the exception of De Lesseps' adventure in cutting and opening the Suez Canal. Whatever I might have thought of the rights and wrongs of the British occupation of Egypt in the 1880's, it was manifest that the British residency, maintaining its strict regard for the symbolic trappings of the caliph of Egypt and his suzerain, the sultan of Turkey, had brought many blessings to the Egyptian people. It was also manifest that this had been done by wise administration, by the effort of the British occupation to interfere as little as possible with the customs of the country, but by pressure and general suasion to bring the leaders into a position where they paid more attention to the wants and needs of the great mass of the people, thus mitigating the cruelties of despotic exploitation. Not least among the methods employed by this great administrator was the effort to introduce, as far as he could, improved educational processes and the acceptance as far as possible of some of the technological advances made possible by modern science. Damming the Nile added millions of acres to its fertile valley, stabilized in timing and in levels the beneficent annual flooding of the valley and its delta, and introduced at least the elements of a desire to take advantage of modern technical devices.

On board ship there were several persons who greatly broadened my educational horizon. There were a Mr. Colebrook and his sister, both English. Miss Colebrook was a minor novelist who had published several fairly successful works. Her brother had been in the diplomatic service all his life and now, aging and not in good health, was en route to what would be his last assignment in Tokyo before his retirement. He had spent many years in Constantinople on the staff of the British legation there. He had himself shared in many of the negotiations that were continually arising between Lord Cromer and Egypt and the Sublime Porte. Well informed, he had the knack of telling me about his experiences without at all ruffling my egalitarian, American, anti-imperialistic views.

Another passenger was Miss Winifred Crabbe, who had been "home" to England and was returning to her native Australia. A granddaughter of the English poet, Crabbe, she was a nurse and in her work had done a great deal in furthering public health. She was an Australian, and she put me promptly in my place when I ventured to say that Australia ought to secede from the British Empire, be independent, proclaim itself a republic, and get rid of the king. Voluble and well informed, she also showed me something of the other meanings of the word "empire," for in it she saw for her own country of Australia not subjugation and subjection but a sharing of the benefits of modern civilization among a great family of peoples with consequent rewards in education, health, and mutual protection.

Still another passenger from whom I learned much was a young man, just turned twenty-one, on his way home to his native Ceylon. He had been in England at school since his twelfth year. He had taken his degree at Oxford. He was on his way home to enter the public service. He told me that his father was the highest native in the civil service of the colony of Ceylon and that there was an increasing opportunity for young men trained in England to assume positions of influence and power in the government of the island. He did not dissemble his dissatisfaction with some of the restrictions placed upon his people by the British rule, but he also more than counterbalanced this by his praise of what the British had done for his people. He endeavored to impress me with the great magnificance of Colombo, his native city. I recall several times warning him that, since he had been only twelve years old when he left home, he must be prepared to see the buildings shrink in size, the streets to be narrower, and the trees less tall. In short, I attempted to soften in advance what would be the inevitable visual impact of his homecoming and its disturbance of his nostalgic dreams. He would have none of it.

His name was P. Mahadeva. His father was P. Arunachalam. Both were Hindus of Tamil nationality. I believe I tried to discover why a father and a son did not have the same surname but had to content myself with discovering that he thought the common initial *P* was sufficient identification.

Another passenger on the ship also contributed to my instant confusion but ultimately to the clarification of my education with respect to empires and colonies. He was a Dutchman on his way to Java, a middle-aged businessman, a stockbroker, a linguist who had a perfect command of English and, so I was given to understand, of German and French as well as his native tongue. He was a hail-fellow-well-met, gregarious and hearty in his social contacts, and, withal, absolutely set in his notions of politics at home and abroad, determined in his opinions, and never hesitant about expressing them.

He was kind and gracious and jovial, but he did not disguise the fact that he hated the United States and that he deprecated the influence of Americans. He forgave individuals such as I only because he thought it became a product of a superior civilization to be kind to the semisavage. To him it was a matter of *noblesse oblige*. He told me that he had lost a great deal of money because he had mistakenly revived faith in the United States despite his father's and his grandfather's injunction to the contrary and had, therefore, been a loser in the United States panic of 1907. His grandfather, who had founded his brokerage house, had transmitted to his son and his grandson one injunction. It was: Never invest in a revolution! He told me that his grandfather had lived to a very great old age and was reluctant to turn over to the next generation his business; but, at long last when the family convinced him that it was time for him to retire, he said he would do it, provided only that the inner office of the head of the firm would be decorated by him to suit his taste and that for at least four generations that decoration should be preserved. That unusual request met with family approval perforce. So the front office was papered on all four walls and ceiling with bonds of the Confederate States of America!

The business had descended to the son and then to the grandson, who was telling me the story. The grandson said that he began to think that grandpa was unreasonable and perhaps the United States had at last become stabilized and no longer should be regarded as a revolutionary country. So he bought some stocks. He lost money. That was the end of his faith in the United States.

While a lot of this was mere joking, there was a kernel of conviction behind the jest. We were unhurried on that German ship sailing through the hot Red Sea, and there was a bountiful supply of Würzburger and Muenchner Hofbräu. Gradually it came out that my Dutch friend's real opposition to the United States was to the policy it was pursuing in its colonies, although I resented his use of the word "colony" in that connection. We had given freedom to Cuba. We had already indulged the Philippines in entirely too much self-government, had half-promised them independence, and already were guilty of teaching English to the Filipinos. That, he said, was bad. It would give the natives false notions of equality—arguments for independence—and it could lead to nothing but disaster.

The Asiatic Awakening: Ceylon

The Dutch, he said, had much more sense. They did not attempt to teach their language to the natives of their colonies. Their colonies were rich. Their people were well fed. Their people were content. The Dutch policy was to leave them undisturbed in their various religions, unaffected by European science, and to keep them subservient and, in the Western sense, ignorant. Free rein was given to the development of their own native cultures. The English, he thought, had made the mistake of introducing modern culture into colonial areas, thus destroying the future of the empire.

The ship's surgeon, the most sociable of the ship's officers, often joined some of the passengers in the smoking-room. He listened, and he laughed. He said that only the Germans knew how to deal with the peoples of the East. It is true, he admitted, that there had been only a few attempts at colonization. The Germans depended most on the peaceful penetration of commerce. Were not all the better ships flying the German flag? Did they not have more control of essential mining and agricultural operations in the Dutch East Indies than did the Dutch, more profitable business in French Africa than the French? At the end of one of these long arguments the surgeon said: "If only the Germans would continue to put their trust in the merchant marine and never again turn over their empire to the army, the Germans, with their inventive skill, mercantile acumen, and industrious pertinacity, would conquer the trade of the world. And, what else," he asked, "is there to conquer?"

So with this preparation, or lack of preparation, I came for the first time face to face with imperialism in Ceylon. Here indeed was color—color and variety. Wallace and I established ourselves at a hotel in the center of the town and then, at the quay, joined with seven or eight of our fellow-passengers to pick up the ship's surgeon and take him to a luncheon at the Galle Face Hotel, a mile or more away, to which we were whirled in carriages drawn by gaily caparisoned horses driven by most decorative coachmen. The colors not only were those of variegated dyes of raiment and of various pigmentation of skins but were also those of the exuberant and exotic flora—giant bamboos whose feathery fronds swept the heavens, great spreading sacred bo trees with their heart-shaped leaves, sacred because Buddha had rested under the shade of the bo.

Perhaps even more startlingly indicative of the mixture of population that was Colombo was the seemingly infinite variety of head-dresses: Sikh policemen with their handsome towering turbans; pig-tailed Chinese coolies trotting between the shafts of rickshas; pillbox-capped Bengalese Hindus, greatly outnumbered by the Tamils from southern India, who constituted the major part of the population of the city, with their peculiar headdress; Singhalese, more numerous, descendants of the original Ceylonese, each bareheaded with his long black hair done up in a bun at the back of his head and kept in order by a semicircular tortoise-shell comb; shaven-headed Buddhist monks in their yellow robes which left the right arm and shoulder free and bare; and then the utter undress of the small fry of every color of skin from pale cream to ebony black.

Wallace and I and Mr. Mahadeva were the only passengers whose destination was Colombo, and late that afternoon we saw the North German Lloyd ship, the "Zieten," sail on toward the East. Early the next morning Mr. Mahadeva came to see me. He was stricken in spirit. He came to confess that, as I had predicted, everything in Colombo had shrunk in size. I gave him what comfort I could. He said he was grateful for my warning despite the fact that he had dis-regarded it, and he offered his services to help Wallace and me in any way he could during our stay in Ceylon.

That led to an introduction to his father, Mr. P. Arunachalam, the highest native civil servant in the government of the colony. He was most gracious and gave me a great deal of time in which he also ex-tolled the virtues of British imperialism. Then he gave me the benefit of his own view with respect to what he called "the awakening of Asia." Among the imperialists, he said, the British were the best, the Dutch the worst, but the United States in Cuba and the Philippines had set up a new standard of conduct by recognizing the essential in-terests of the native inhabitants. In his discourse I was astonished to discover the marked differentiation in emphasis that he placed upon the government as a part of an imperial political concept and the government for the colony which he interpreted in terms of adminis-tration. Not entirely content with this political interpretation, we asked for more, and he readily gave us guidance with respect to the sights we ought to see, persons who could help us interpret the econ-omy—the agriculture and business enterprises of the island—and, for me, he gave me invaluable help with respect to my interest in the religions.

Mr. Arunachalam, being a Tamil, was a Hindu in religion. When I broached the subject of my interest in the religious groups of the colony, he responded with enthusiasm. Since it was a matter in which he shared my curiosity, although confessing an innocence almost as naïve as my own with respect to the basic philosophies of the different sects, he did understand their impact on the governmental, social, and economic life of the colony. He told me that there was one man in the island I should see by all means, although he would have to find some Buddhist friend who would get me the necessary introduction. Within a matter of hours that introduction came. It was to the abbot of a Buddhist monastery situated only a few miles from Colombo. He was called the "Prince Priest" because, at least so the story went, he had renounced the succession to the royal throne of Siam in order to devote his entire life to religion.

I drove out in a carriage to the monastery compound, was met at the gate by two young yellow-robed monks, was taken to a small building, and was told that anyone who approached the Prince Priest was asked to spend at least a half-hour in meditation and prayer in this chapel. I went in. The doors closed behind me. The room was lighted by turquoise glass windows around the four walls near the ceiling. It was empty save for a golden statue of Buddha at the opposite end of the room from the door and in front of which was a golden bowl of water bearing a single lotus flower. In that dim religious light and in that solitude, I think that even the most irreverent and the most cynical person would have felt a spiritual uplift. At the end of the time the door was opened, and the two monks said that they would conduct me to the Prince Priest. I found him lying on a rattan couch under a thatched roof supported only by pillars. Near the couch was a stool. I was asked to have a seat. The two other monks withdrew. The Prince Priest, then well in his eighties, was the perfect picture of the ascetic devotee. His skin, parchment-like, adhered to his cheek bones, and his shaven head gave him an aspect of one barely in the land of living. His shrunken right arm accentuated his appearance. He opened the conversation with, "Well, young man, why do you want to talk to me?" In my embarrassment all I could do was to compliment him on his excellent English. He thanked me and said that he had taken up the study of English when he was seventy-five years old and had found it rewarding and, in some aspects, amusing.

When I asked him to tell me of some of his views about religion, about the state of the world in general, and particularly what he thought of the United States of America, he launched into a free and easy discourse, his face illuminated by what almost might be described as a ghostly but friendly smile.

"I would like to say something that heretofore I have not had an opportunity to say, partly because I see so few Englishmen or so few Americans, and partly because my English has been acquired only since my seventy-fifth year. It has puzzled me to know why you in the Western world have been so much more fruitful in the matter of invention than we, while at the same time you seem to be so backward in things spiritual. It has puzzled me why you can invent machines and at the same time in your preoccupation with the present still seem to forget that eternity stretches infinitely into the past and infinitely into the future.

"At last I have decided that the reason lies in your religion. In fact, one of your English poets expressed the thought, if not the religious source, from which your culture has derived when Robert Browning wrote: 'A man's reach should exceed his grasp.'

"So, I think, it comes back to the matter of religion. It is possible, I believe, for a man to be a good religionist. It is quite easy, relatively speaking, to be a good Moslem. One has but to live up to a few external maxims of material conduct. It is very easy indeed to be a good Taoist. Indeed, even a subhuman animal can be a good Taoist, his actions responding only to his fears; his hopes bounded only by the prospect of food and a mate. It is entirely possible for a man to be a good Hindu. Here he has but to recognize certain ephemeral and transitory material and human limitations and at the same time to free himself from the concept that his spiritual life was begun here or will end here.

"It also is possible, although extremely difficult, for a man to be a good Buddhist. I believe that in Buddhism lies the highest human hope. I believe it is the greatest of all religions. I believe this because at the very core of every worth-while religion there is a renunciation of self. The religious impulse in its highest spiritual realization implies selflessness. It is only complete renunciation—a concept introduced by Buddha and the ethical and moral principle that guides every true Buddhist—which perfects that self-renunciation in life after life in complete observance of karma, the practice of religion ending in the complete absorption of self in Nirvana, the un-self of the God Substance.

"So, while it is possible to be a good religionist in any one of these faiths, the reason that you who call yourselves 'Christians' are so restless, the reason that you are so spurred onward, the reason that you are always troubled and so must invent things to help you in this life, the reason that you neglect the life that your soul had before you were born, the reason that you so frequently forget the life that will come after the death of your body is that you are Christians.

"It is impossible for any human being to be a good Christian. Jesus at once set up a standard of perfection so high that no human being ever could attain it, and at the same time he expressed it in such simple terms that every human being might aspire to it. Impossible!"

So from an aged Buddhist priest, I heard one of my most impressive Christian sermons. Nonetheless, I recognized the fact that not all American newspaper readers shared, or would care to share, my religious curiosity. I was, perforce, writing primarily of politics. I could not stray into the field of comparative religions. Tom Wallace could, and did, write of the sights, the sounds, and the scenes of our odyssey. But it was my job to keep my eye on the ball.

So the first "Letter" I wrote from Ceylon, printed as it was in American newspapers in July, 1909, was entitled "The Asiatic Awakening."

"COLOMBO, CEYLON.—The awakening of Asia has stirred the blood of the happy native of prosperous Ceylon no less than it has thrilled the more unfortunate Asiatic of countries to which Nature has been less bountiful and Man more cruel in oppression. . . . The Ceylonese has liberty, he has plenty to eat, all he wants to wear, the blessings of education and almost unlimited opportunities for personal advancement. But he shares in the unrest of his continent, and he is set upon Reform for the sake of Office.

"The victory of Japan in the war with Russia awoke the embers of a long-smouldering fire and kindled the blaze of Asiatic patriotism which is now sweeping over the oldest and the greatest of continents. In

Ceylon the interest in that war was intense. . . . All over the island the people joyfully celebrated each successive Japanese victory. . . .

"Touching Ceylon, another factor contributed to the present unrest and agitation. The United States had gained possession of the Philippine Islands, where Spain had ruled with medieval harshness for four centuries. The Americans had promised ultimate independence. Finally, they granted an elective legislative assembly. That gave the Ceylonese his clue. . . .

"The native press, of course, urges the reforms in season and out. But it is temperate in tone, protestant of its loyalty to the Empire, and does not even consider the possibility of a severance from England. The Ceylonese know, all too well, that their little island is one of the richest prizes of the sea and that if England was driven away some other nation would come in and seize it. Much as they gloried in an Asiatic victory, they fear Japanese control beyond anything. So far as the press is concerned there is not the slightest protest against English domination; it is only against the method of administration.

"But, in private—and this is the reason why the average Englishman is so eloquent in discussing what he calls the American failure in the Philippines—in private, many Ceylonese will declare that they would like nothing so much as to come under the wing of the American eagle. It is impossible for them to understand that all the United States is not a unit for imperial aggrandizement, but if their flag is changed at all they would ask for the Stars and Stripes. The Philippine administration is responsible for this feeling, and it must be admitted that the educated Ceylonese knows vastly more about the American rule in the Philippines than does the average educated American.

"Another effect of the Asiatic awakening in Ceylon is social rather than political. Many of the most prominent men are leading a movement for a return to purely native social customs and costumes. The teaching of ancient Ceylonese history in the English schools—practically every school in the island is English—is one of the recent results of this agitation. . . . The awakened Ceylonese is proud of his history, but he is warned by his knowledge. Unless he knows exactly what is before him he will content himself with English rule and permit his racial patriotism to blow off steam in reform movements and the everlasting chase for Office."

CHAPTER XXVI

THE EMPIRE OF INDIA

From Ceylon it was but an overnight journey on a small steamer to Tuticorin, where we debarked on Bishop Reginald Heber's "India's coral strand." What little I knew of India was mainly the India of Rudyard Kipling's verse and romance and the much earlier India of Lord Macaulay's "Essay on the Trial of Warren Hastings." I had read little else, and even what I had read had not prepared me for what I was about to experience.

Entranced as I had been with Mr. Kipling, he had by no means eradicated from my mind the boyish, almost the infantile, prejudices that I had stored up against England and the British Empire. The very reason that Wallace and I were here at all was because the American newspapers, having only the sketchiest communications with Asia, already had sensed the great unrest in India and its portent for the possible cracking-up of the British Empire. Hence my entrance into the teeming polyglot, polychrome subcontinent was perhaps colored in my mind by my overweening desire to see the Indian patriots triumph in their cause—albeit a cause which was but vaguely defined in my mind.

At the ship's side we were received by Abdul, our bearer, who had theretofore served the Cale Young Rices and Mrs. Macaulay. Immaculate in his long white coat, crowned by an impeccably wound turban, his black beard barbered to perfection, he made us in an instant feel at one and the same time that we were gods condescending to visit India; that we were his masters to whom he had devoted and would continue to devote a life of servile humility; but that also we were expected to do the things he wanted us to do, to visit the places he wanted us to visit, and to see the things that he thought fit for us to see,

Here, for ten dollars a month, we had found the perfect servant, just as our Kentucky friends in Cairo had predicted we would.

We were not to see much of southern India, spending just a night and a part of a day in Madras. There Abdul showed me what he said was the outside of a Christian church that I wanted to see. There was not time to go inside, and I have never been quite sure that the building he pointed out was the one I had hoped to see, a church of the Christians of St. Thomas, who devoutly believed that their church was founded in the year of the destruction of Jerusalem, A.D. 70, by St. Thomas the Doubter, and thus was the oldest apostolic church in Christendom. I have ever been regretful that I did not stay a little longer in Madras to see more of that establishment as well as the headquarters of the magazine, the *Theosophist*.

We already were behind our schedule, so we set out on the long railway journey of two or three days and nights northwestwardly across the country to Bombay. It was hot. The pith helmets that we had acquired in Colombo and our white clothes were in constant requisition. We were hardly prepared, however, for the railroad travel and found it to be more comfortable than we had anticipated. On every train we, as first-class passengers, had a four-berth compartment which traversed the entire car, giving out on doors either to the right or to the left. At one end of the compartment was a door which led to a shower bath and toilet, and at the other end a door opening into a tiny compartment in which Abdul, carrying his own bedclothes and gear, rode in the daytime and slept at night, if he really did sleep, ready at an instant's notice to respond to a tap on the connecting door. At mealtimes we got out at one station, went to the restaurant wagon, and then waited until there was another stop when we could dismount and come back to our own compartment. This was in 1909 and long before there was an air-conditioned Pullman in the United States, but here we had a sort of primitive air-conditioning. Each window into the compartment had four drops, one of glass—an ordinary window—one an ordinary window shade, one composed of slats something like a fixed Venetian blind, and the other, a tatty—a window covering made of coarse cocoa matting. When it was pulled down, one could turn a cock above it, and a tiny trickle of water from a reservoir on top of the car would dampen it. That had the effect of straining out much of the dust and dirt and also, because of the rapid evaporation, of reducing materially the temperature in the car. We did not suffer too much.

In Bombay we were struck by the horror of an epidemic of the plague. Hundreds were dying every day. The United States consul told us we had no business to come there. He had lost a member of his family and one or two members of his staff to the plague. He and many of the English and Europeans still remaining in the city were terrified. Yet we managed to stay on long enough to see some of the sights before we set out through ever increasing heat toward the northeast to see the sights of Baroda and Jaipur, to go on to Agra and worship at the shrine of beauty of the Taj Mahal, to see Delhi—New Delhi and Old Delhi—but not of course the New Delhi which later became the capital of India and which then did not exist. Then onward southwestwardly through Allahabad, with a stop at the sacred city of Benares, and thence on to Calcutta, then the capital of India—the India that was a seething cauldron of political unrest.

My interest in politics, Wallace's interest in the country and its customs, did not keep us both from seeing all we could and having a great deal of fun and not a few adventures as we crossed the country. It is true that I had little opportunity to gratify my curiosity with respect to religions. Abdul saw to that. Whenever we got to a new city, willy-nilly, we had first to go to the zoo. Abdul had a passion for zoos. He had no notion that there was anybody in the world who would not prefer to see the animals in a zoo to anything else. He had also to be restrained almost by force from using the somewhat elongated swagger stick that he carried for whipping Hindu small fry out of our paths. We were sahibs. It seemed to be his notion that everything and everybody ought to bow down before us. Under pressure Abdul would conduct us to a mosque. In fact, while he had no inhibitions about permitting us to see some monument of the great Mogul Empire, he definitely was opposed to our visiting Hindu temples and shrank from conducting us even in Bombay to see the Parsee Towers of Silence, where the adherents of that religion expose their dead to be consumed by vultures. Despite the reluctance of our ten-dollar-a-month conductor and despite the ravages of the plague during the few days I was in Bombay, I did have a chance to talk with two distinguished members of the Parsee community, gaining from them, however, much more information about politics and the economic situation than I could about their Zoroastrian religion. However, one of them did introduce me to a Jew, a member of the Ben-Israel tribe of Bombay. I had mistakenly thought that he was one of the Indian Jews who, according to their own beliefs, had been established in India since the very beginning of the Diaspora, at the time of the destruction of the Temple, but I found that he was one of the colony of oriental Jews settled in Bombay some two centuries ago under the patronage of the great Sassoon family. However, there were Hindu temples and Hindu shrines, and of course from some of the very leading Indian politicians I met I could get some glimpse of their attitude toward their own complex religion.

But mostly we were occupied with seeing things. There was Jaipur, with its pink and blue and yellow buildings disposed under strict architectural control to make of the whole city in the burning sun of late March a confection worthy of a Parisian *pâtisserie*. Then in Delhi and, above all, in Agra and its environs, there were the great architectural remnants of the fine flowering of the Mogul Empire crowned by that jewel of jewels, the Taj Mahal of Agra. My camera was our constant companion, and I was forever taking pictures, some of which turned out to be fairly good.

Actually, it took us only a little while to get accustomed to what at first seemed the infernal business of early breakfast—chota hazri—hot tea and a banana at five o'clock in the morning. An adjustment more difficult than this was to learn to take, in the middle of the day, a siesta.

Then there hung over us the shadow of the bubonic plague raging in Bombay. Fortunately there is something in my physical makeup which is considered to be not-nice by a flea. Parties of fleas I have known have sometimes engaged in a superficial survey of some parts of my anatomy, but none has ever remained to bite. Poor Tom Wallace did not have this protection. The fleas were biting, and therefore he suffered much more than did I from dread of the plague. As we crossed the country and told travelers as we met them in hotels and other places that we intended to stop in Benares, we always got earnest advice. It seems there were two hotels in Benares; one traveler recommended one; the next, the other. It turned out invariably that the recommendation was to go to the hotel which was not the one in which our informant had stopped. I think our choice finally was dictated by flipping a coin. When we arrived, we were shown to a room on the ground floor which was furnished with two large beds and flanked by a bathroom. The bathroom had a concrete basin or tank, and it was filled with water brought in by a cleaner—one of the lowest-caste Indians, actually an outcaste or pariah, who filled it from a goatskin water bag which gave us a feeling of kinship with Mr. Kipling's Gunga Din.

Our gear was piled in by the procession of bearers who had brought it from the station, an army commanded with disdain by Abdul, the individual members of the phalanx being rewarded from his purse by a few annas and pice. It was the custom of the country that one person could carry only one piece of baggage; but, since we had managed to consolidate our gear so we had only eighteen pieces, we always were preceded by a procession of that number.

As soon as we were alone in the room, we heard a great noise which apparently came from underneath one of the beds. We stooped down to see. There it was. A great trap had caught the biggest rat we had ever seen in our lives. We made up our minds not to tarry too long in the sacred city of Benares.

In the next two days, however, we did see a very great deal of that holy place, its temples, some of its religious rites—some of which seemed to be outlandish and some of which seemed to be in keeping with the mystery that is India—and its many holy men and fakirs. But most impressive of all the sights, of all the things we saw with respect to the Hindu religion, were the hundreds and hundreds of people bathing in the sacred Ganges, wading into the water, lifting the sacred fluid in their cupped hands, pouring out libations to the gods, and cleverly undressing and dressing with a minimum exposure of flesh, and all of them seemingly, with rapt and reverent faces and gestures, attaining through the symbolism of that bath a step toward a higher life.

Then, too, we saw death, the funeral pyres of wood with the corpses on them being consumed by fire on the burning ghat, as were called the stone steps that led down to the river. Occasionally at the very end we witnessed the taking-up by the mourners of the residue of ashes and the casting of them upon the broad bosom of the holy river.

Perhaps the greatest religious assemblage I ever witnessed was on a great plain not far from Delhi. It was a hot day under a burning sun, and, according to the estimates made by the police, more than a hun-

dred and twenty thousand persons had gathered there to make propiti-
atory sacrifices to the goddess of smallpox. Wallace and I saw that
huge mass of humanity, but we had little opportunity in our uncomfortable horse-drawn vehicle to get near enough to the center to see
anything of the ceremonies. What we did see, however, on the very
fringe of the crowd was a small company of the devotees of quite
another religion engaged in an enterprise which was destined inevitably
to be subversive of the worship of that particular goddess. It was a
little group of Seventh-Day Adventist medical missionaries from Ta-
koma Park, Maryland, in suburban Washington, engaged in vacci-
nating against the smallpox every person they could reach and persuade to subscribe to the possibilities of preventive medicine, that
magic of Western science.

At many places I had a chance to talk with missionaries from the
United States, most of them Baptists, with a few Anglican missionaries
from England and with several Roman Catholic priests. It seemed to
me that they were making little progress indeed with respect to con-
versions but also that, in the field of education, of health, and of breaking down the intense conservatism of a predominately contemplative
people, they were making a great contribution toward energizing the
whole mass of people in their desire for self-expression and self-rule.

By the time we had reached Calcutta, merely by reading the newspapers, merely by talking to chance-made acquaintances among the
travelers, I had begun to modify my views about the British rule. Since
Wallace had not shared that prejudice at all, perhaps he also exercised
a moderating influence upon me. Nevertheless, it was my business to
report on the unrest and its causes and to speculate as to its outcome,
and that I set myself to do. The British point of view reached me very
largely through acquaintances I made on the staff of the great newspaper, the *Statesman of India,* and also from a few British officials
whom I had the good fortune to find accessible—but they were few
indeed. The Moslems with whom I came in contact took a much less
violent approach to the problem and seemed to fear the Hindus more
than the British.

The Indian patriotic point of view I heard from the editor of the
great newspaper, the *Amrita Bazaar Patrika.* I was introduced to him
by a young Irishman from Chicago who was in Calcutta installing a
Hoe web perfecting press in the printing establishment of the *States-*

man of India. It was he who took Wallace and me one night to a distant part of the city where the native patriotic newspaper was published, and there we met the editor, an Oxonian who was busy at work clad only in a white dhoti, or loincloth. It was from him that I got the letters of introduction which enabled me to meet two of the great leaders of India. One was Surendranath Banerjea, who was the organizer of the then new Indian National Congress. Mr. Banerjea was gracious, gave me a great deal of time, talked with me about the Indian case, and made only the condition that I would not quote him directly. Then also I met Mr. Romesh Chundra Dutt, the distinguished historian who had been councilor to the enlightened Gaekwar of Baroda and whose patriotic aspirations for self-rule for India did not at all obscure his level-eyed assessment of many of the great benefits that had come through British rule. It was he, I think, who first convinced me that the British Indian civil service, built on the foundations laid by Lord Macaulay and his nephew, Sir George Trevelyan, after the Mutiny and the assumption of direct rule of Queen Victoria over the Indian Empire, had many beneficent effects. Yet, at the same time, he protested the exploitation, as he found it, of India and the Indians by their imperial masters. He gave me an autographed copy of his own book, *Victorian India,* and cited to me various other documents and helped me no little to get what I fondly thought to be an understanding of some of the great political, economic, and social movements of this great subcontinent of more than three hundred million souls. He, unlike some of his Hindu compatriots, believed that it would be possible for the Hindu and the Moslem communities to dwell together in peace and amity if the Indian Empire were set up as an autonomous self-ruling member of the British Empire.

Another leader of the Indian patriots was Arabinda Ghose. Him I did see, but I was not able to talk to him, although I read many of his proclamations and his articles. I saw him in the dock along with some twenty-five or thirty others who were being tried for a conspiracy which had for its purpose the end of British rule by the direct method of assassination. Whether Mr. Ghose was guilty or not, I did not make up my mind; but certainly he was a most impressive figure and a writer of very great skill.

What struck me then was that the entire patriotic movement was being carried on in the English language, since there was no lingua franca which would reach all parts of India, with its scores and scores of languages and hundreds and hundreds of dialects. So it was basically the English language which was the tie that bound one group of the Indian patriots to another.

The upshot of these things was that, while I continued my sympathy for the Indian aspirations, I took a much more charitable view of the British rule and came at least to a tentative conclusion that the better solution would be a gradual one; that the reforms then being proposed by Lord Morley would form a basis for a gradual improvement in the situation which might eventually lead to autonomy. In any event, the terroristic approach would be nothing but self-defeating. That, of course, was a long time before Mahatma Gandhi and long before the initiation of a policy of passive resistance. It seemed to me that the British rule, the British raj, had on the whole been beneficial, and that the unrest was a healthy sign of a people predominantly contemplative turning toward a more energetic exercise of its social power.

The series of letters that Wallace and I sent from India had a running title of "The Empire of India." The very first, which happened to have been published in the United States on July 5, 1909, I called "The Great Unrest." In it, and subsequent articles, I attempted to draw a picture not only of the discontent of the people but of the sincere and even strenuous efforts being made by the British to correct the cause of the trouble. In those articles I made bold to predict that India would become a self-governing nation within the framework of the British Empire but that, once it achieved that goal, it would break into two nations, one Hindu and one Moslem. At that time I wrote:

". . . The Indian patriots do not wish to secede from the British Empire. They know that they would be at the mercy of other great maritime powers were England to withdraw. What they do wish and what they are demanding, is autonomy. . . . The Morley 'Reform Scheme' is accepted as a first installment of the grant of self-government. It will have the effect of quieting the people for a time, but as soon as India believes an opportune moment has arrived to insist upon further concessions, the unrest will manifest itself again. . . .

"Both 'Swaraj' [home rule] and 'Swadeshi' [boycott] are manifestations of the great Asiatic renaissance which is now remoulding the whole social and political fabric of the Mother Continent. The cry of

'India for the Indians' has been heard from the lips of a few scholars and officials ever since Queen Victoria promised the Indian people a share in their own government in her epochal proclamation of 1858.

"But it was not until after Japan, an Asiatic nation, had met and defeated one of the most powerful nations of Europe in the greatest war of modern history, that the cry 'Swaraj' burst from the throats of the millions. One of the leading men in India, a Bengal Hindu who has held high office under the English and who has been a professor of Oriental history and languages in the universities of England said: 'The plucky stand made by the Japanese against the advance of the Terror of Europe—against the Bear that had already devoured the heart of Asia—called forth the deepest admiration of every Asiatic.' And when that war resulted in victory for the Japanese, every man in Asia felt that a new and brighter day had dawned, and that the long centuries of bondage had come to an end. It gave every Asiatic a sense of pride and self-reliance which he had not possessed before.

"Every Indian one meets unhesitatingly and voluntarily declares that the Japanese victory was one of the chief contributing causes to the independent movement in India. With equal unanimity, every Englishman one meets declares that the Russo-Japanese war had nothing whatever to do with the 'unrest.' The native newspapers, printed in English, are full of the praises of Japan as the leader of the great movement which will make all Asia free. But the Englishmen, except the police inspectors, do not read the native press. There are two prominent native daily papers in Calcutta, printed in English. They were the first newspaper offices in India to install linotype machines. But the average Englishman doesn't know of their existence except from the comments in his own papers, and it is impossible to find a copy of either for sale in the European section of the city.

"It is this English habit of declining to know anything about the natives that has contributed no little to the present unrest. The Englishman is but a bird of passage in India. He comes here to stay three years or five years or ten years. He is always going 'home,' is always thinking of 'home.' He looks upon India only as a place from which money may be extracted. He lives with his own people, he knows nothing beyond his club and his sports. He declines to consult the wishes of the Indians either in governmental administration or in business. Therefore he must now face the problem of a great discontent in the political world, and the rapid rise of two great rivals for his trade. The Germans and the Japanese are crafty merchants. They have gone to the Indians and have asked what the Indians wanted. They have made and sold goods according to the Indian notions, and they have never made the British mistake of attempting to force English goods of English patterns upon a people who wanted something else. Take the instance of scissors. English scissors are made with the thumb and finger hole of the same size. Indian tailors demanded scissors with a larger aperture for the thumb. The English factory even upon the advice of their agent in India, declined to humor the foolish whim of the absurd barbarian. Whereupon India now buys its scissors from Germany. The British merchant will not change his ideas of business to suit Indian ideas, any more than he will change his woolen underwear and yarn socks to meet the differences between the climates of London and Madras. . . .

"The contemptuous treatment of Indians by English residents in India is cited as another cause of discontent. Not only in matters of government, but in every other aspect of life, the Englishman proclaims his superiority with every act. He will not associate even with the pure-blooded Englishman who had the misfortune to be born in India, even as he will not admit that an Australian or a Canadian is quite his equal. The Indians resent this attitude on the part of the English, although the orthodox Hindu would rather cut his own throat than to accept an invitation to dine with an unclean Christian. In this matter there is much to be said on both sides. The Brahman proclaims his superiority over all men, treats the low-caste native with indignity, and then, with naive inconsistency, demands that the Englishman shall treat all men as equal.

"It is, after all, a matter of education. The English have taught the Indians their language. And with that language came the stories of the great reforms and revolutions of the western world—the names of Hampden, Burke, Russell, Grey, and Gladstone, as well as those of Washington, Mazzini, and Garibaldi. Every Bengali student knows the history of parliamentary reform in England as well as he knows the events of the week in Calcutta. He knows that England could not keep Canada and Australia for a fortnight if it did not grant those colonies the right of self-government. He knows the story of the revolution in America. He has been educated and he cannot be turned back. . . .

"Englishmen in office in India, those who have studied the needs of the country and the aspirations of the people, believe that the Reform Scheme will bring about internal peace and prosperity. The Viceroy, the Earl of Minto, and Sir Herbert Risley have been the 'men on the spot' who have formulated the Scheme after taking stock of the opinion of all shades of men in India, native and European. Lord Morley, in London, has given the Scheme the stamp of his broad-minded Liberal views and has insisted upon the essential representative principle.

"Other Englishmen in India, the commercial class, are divided in opinion, but many of them believe that the Reform Scheme will send the country to the demnition bow-wows. They are opposed to giving the native Indian any rights whatever, they cry out against education, they oppose any Indian gaining prominence in affairs and are generally to be classed as radical Indophobes. Their attitude is something like that of the wildest anti-Negro agitators of the United States.

"The Indians receive the Reform Scheme only as an installment. It is good, they say, as far as it goes, but it stops short. The more progressive leaders say they will decline to quarrel with the restrictions imposed so long as the Scheme recognizes the long-denied right of representation as a right. In this particular the Morley Bill is epochal. The Indians believe that it is the first installment of a series of constitutional reforms which will in the end bring about the day of self-government in India—the long prayed for Swaraj.

"Whatever the reason that impelled the British government to grant the Reforms, they came at a time when India believes the 'unrest' brought them forth. That fact gives India the key to the future. There will be no end of the unrest in India until the Morley Reform Scheme has been amplified and carried to its logical conclusion—the government of India by the Indians. . . ."

CHAPTER XXVII

THE SUN NEVER SETS

One morning, after saying goodbye to our faithful Abdul, Wallace and I went aboard the British East India Steam Navigation Company's steamship, the "Lindula," bound for Rangoon in Burma. As that vessel made its way slowly and cautiously down the sluggish reaches of the muddy Hooghly toward the Bay of Bengal, I was depressed. I had a sense of being overcome by the confused and contradictory impressions made upon me by the things I had seen and heard during those weeks in India. My visit had been too short, my vision too circumscribed, my interviews too few to give me any sense of having understood the significance of my experiences. At the same time that depression was alleviated by the simple fact that I had recognized that it was incumbent upon me to throw off childish prejudices, to recognize that in this world there were millions of people who looked at life in quite a different way from us Americans, and that the myriad aspects of life in the great Indian Empire would permit a multitude of interpretations of its people, its problems, and its politics. I was uneasily aware that I could not fully understand the awakening of Asia, but I recognized it as a great fact that probably would affect hundreds of millions of people in the course of the twentieth century, although I had not the slightest notion that the Asiatic awakening could ever be a matter of genuine concern to the people of the United States.

Burma, to which we were destined, Mr. Kipling had taught me, was a cleaner, greener land. I certainly hoped that it would be so, for the "Lindula" certainly was not clean, and in that terrific heat the waters of the great bay seemed hardly to be green under their blanket of haze. The "Lindula" was propelled by steam engines whose boilers were fired by coal of the most inferior quality. Its stacks belched more cinders than smoke. The weather was terrifically hot, Most of the passengers, including Wallace and me, slept on the open deck wrapped in rugs to awaken in the morning to shake off thick, black snow of cinders and soot. The food was bad. I never had greatly enjoyed English cooking as I had encountered it in the Indian hotels, but here that cuisine interpreted by Lascar cooks was even more impossible. I am certain that never voluntarily would I choose such a breakfast as we had every morning. It afforded a small variety of dried and smoked fish, centering around a *pièce de résistance* served on the table in a huge casserole, a sort of half-baked, half-soupy vegetable hash given the glorious name of "bubble and squeak."

Uncomfortable as were the first-class passengers on the "Lindula," our sufferings were as nothing compared to those of the steerage passengers, whom we could see so well from our vantage point high above the foredeck. They, a motley crew, were always on deck, always trying to get a breath of air; and it was here that Tom Wallace anticipated me in my researches into some aspects of comparative religions. He spied and pointed out to me two yellow-robed Buddhist monks among the steerage passengers, monks who evidently were not Orientals. The yellow robe was there, the bare right arm was there, the begging bowl hugged by the left forearm against the body was there—but the men unquestionably were Europeans. A Buddhist monk is supposed to eat only the food that is given him in his begging bowl and nothing whatever after the sun reaches the meridian. Wallace suggested that we tempt these two men into telling us their story. I held back, thinking of some of the American and British Buddhists I had met in Ceylon, for I was afraid they might be insulted. Wallace had no such scruples. He managed to scrounge two ham sandwiches and two bottles of beer and made his way down to the foredeck. When I happened to look down there, he was squatting on the floor with the two monks, who evidently were enjoying the feast. I joined them. Here were two Americans, beachcombers both, engaged in exploiting the East. Both of them had been far to the north into the borders of Tibet. There they had managed to get from a lamasery an old document inscribed in the sacred Pali language on slats of bamboo which they were taking with a letter to some great leader in Siam, or so they said. They had high hopes that they would be richly rewarded and that their mission would yield them enough money to pay their passage back, or at least part way back, to America. One had been a sailor who tarried too long at his cups and was left by his ship. The other had been a ship's barber who had suffered the same fate. They had been together only a few months; and they told us astonishing tales of their adventures, some of which may have been founded partly upon fact. They said that they had worn the heavy raiment of the northern Buddhists when they got near the Tibetan border and had changed to the yellow robe of the southern Buddhists only when they got back to Calcutta and were ready for the voyage to Burma.

The barber said that, when his ship left him, he had nothing except the clothes he stood in and his razor. He was hungry and sought succor from a Buddhist monk who happened to speak English. His plight was so sorry that the monk took him to a monastery where the old abbot took him in. The monks' heads are shaven, and it very soon turned out that the abbot was very much more comfortable under the ministrations of the San Francisco barber with his keen razor than he had been under one of his own men. All the other monks seemed to like it, too. They gave him a cubicle, and through some of the English-speaking brothers he persuaded the old abbot to get for him a small kerosene stove so that he could heat water to make the shaving even more comfortable.

Thus he was housed and fed and clothed, but the food, while plentiful, was monotonous. The rice and bananas that the faithful gave him in his begging bowl, or which he shared from the bowls of the other monks who wandered through the town, were monotonous. In the courtyard of the monastery was a fountain in which swam a great many sacred fish. One night under cover of darkness the barber-monk captured a fish. He took it to his cubicle. He lighted his oil stove and proceeded to boil his fish. In his great excitement over his anticipated feast, he became so agitated that he kicked over the stove. It set the house afire. The monks came running; the abbot was brought. Discovered *in flagrante delicto* in the act of cooking and preparing to eat one of the sacred fish, he was expelled from the monastery, but the very religion of his hosts prevented a more direful punishment. Then, after other adventures, he finally decided that the Buddhist racket was a good racket. He had picked up the other American beachcomber, and the two together were exploiting their luck.

[484]

But they did like the ham sandwiches. They not only liked the beer but wanted more. There were no Buddhists among their fellow steerage passengers, all of whom were Hindus or Moslems, so they had no shame in breaking their fast. Two more outrageous rapscallions I have never met—or, by the same token, two better storytellers.

When we did get to Rangoon, I was happy to discover that it was in fact clean and that it was green. I forgave it its high temperature. As usual, our first call was on the American consul. There Tom Wallace happened to say that the most unpleasant thing about India was the fact that there was no safe drinking water and that all the water one drank came out of bottles, water heavily carbonated. He said that he had got to feel as if with every glass of water he was swallowing a handful of fishhooks. Whereupon the consul exclaimed: "Come to lunch with me today. I want to talk with you both, and I want to give you a treat."

A little later we presented ourselves at the consulate to receive a hearty welcome. The consul asked us to come with him. He unlocked a door. We walked in. He locked the door behind him. It was a spotless room with white walls and ceiling and a linoleum flooring. Against one wall was a huge refrigerator. In the middle of the room there were two or three mysterious-looking mechanical contraptions.

"I never admit any person in this room unless he is an American citizen," said the consul. "No native has been in it since I set it up. The refrigerator gets its ice from a door that opens into a hall where the native servants put in the ice, but none of them is permitted in here. This device," he said, turning to the center of the room, "is a still. Its purpose is to distil water." From below the mouth of the retort, he picked up a glass container of perhaps a gallon capacity which was a little more than half full of clear liquid. "This is distilled water." Then, turning to another little machine, he said, "This is a revolving churn. It has been sterilized by me this morning with boiling distilled water. I shall now pour this water into the churn." He set it revolving with a hand crank, saying, "This is for the necessary aeration to make the water palatable." Then from the refrigerator he took a large pail of ice, sunk the closed churn into the ice, and said, "Now, a half-hour later, when we have lunch, I will give you the greatest treat you have had since you left home—a glass of plain still water."

The consul told me that there weren't any particular political problems in Burma, that the people had enough to eat and were content, that their reliance on their faith in Buddhism sustained them, and that I wouldn't find any politics there. Nothing whatever, he declared, except the troubles that ordinarily beset a boom town after the discovery of oil. Whether or not he was entirely accurate, I do not know, but certainly Wallace and I turned in for seeing sights and writing travelogues. We saw the Burma girls and their whacking white cheroots. We marveled at the massive pure-gold-encrusted Shwe Dagôn, towering three hundred and sixty-eight feet above the place in which lay buried the relics of Gautama Buddha, himself. The streets were colorful with their shops and their people and the colors of their raiment. The women were gay in their variegated costumes, and everywhere were the yellow-robed Buddhist monks with their begging bowls. We saw the "elephants a-piling teak" and had, even in the great heat, a chance to relax. Then, on another ship, a cleaner one this time, on to Penang.

One day we passed a tiny gunboat. It flew a flag on which one could easily see the figure of the white elephant. It was, the ship's officer told us, the entire Siamese Navy. Here, I felt a pang of disappointment that Siam was not on our schedule. First I had learned of it in my earliest boyhood from Ernest Baldwin, who had been an American consul in Bangkok during the first Cleveland administration, and latterly I had heard much of it—a great deal about it, in fact—from John Barrett, the director-general of the Pan American Union, who has been American minister to Siam. But Bangkok was not for us.

There was a brief visit to Penang, a memorable and colorful trip, when we were carried in chairs on the shoulders of sweating coolies up to the top of a mountain along a narrow road bordered by the lush and exotic flora of a tropical forest.

Then Singapore. Here a mixture of all sorts and conditions of men, a mixture even more marked in its extremes than that of Colombo, a veritable crossroads of the world betwixt the East and the Far East and situated almost on the equator, a meeting place of the Northern and Southern hemispheres. Burma, Malaya, and the Straits Settlements constituted a grouping of lands and peoples which it was difficult for me to realize had been comprehended together in the geographies of my childhood under the single name of "Farther India." And here in Singapore I had a chance to renew my acquaintance with two interesting young Englishmen whom I had met crossing the Pacific on my first voyage to Japan two years earlier—young men representing the business side of British imperialism. They were complaining of the inroads being made upon their trade and commerce by the Germans. They were critical of the government in London for its free-trade policy. They were supporters of Mr. Joseph Chamberlain and his "tariff-reform" program—"tariff reform," which had always meant to me in the United States the Democratic party and lower tariffs, here, it seemed, meant protectionism and higher tariffs.

In between seeing the sights, we crossed the narrow straits and visited the sultan of Johore. We had some conversations with some American adventurers, mainly from Hawaii, engaged in establishing rubber plantations in the peninsula, and we chatted with Australian travelers and with Germans. From one long talk with a Chinese merchant prince, I learned something about another aspect of the British imperialism which at one and the same time seemed to confirm my prejudices against its exploitative manifestations and also to extend my horizon with respect to its beneficent influence in the establishment of far-flung trade routes and the stimulation of commerce, transportation, and education. Of these things, I wrote at the time:

"Harsh critics of the Imperial policy of England have not hesitated to assert that the British appetite for square miles extends to every foot of land and sea of whatever description. But it must be admitted that the British palate is particularly tickled by a bit of land which lies hard by a 'narrow passage of water connecting two large bodies of water,' known to the geographers as a 'strait.' Take a map of the world and look it over for straits. Wherever there is a strait, nine times in ten, there will be a British possession alongside. Gibraltar, Malta, Hong Kong, the Bahamas, Jamaica, Trinidad, Ceylon, Falkland Islands, Aden, and others of lesser importance, not to speak of the occupancy of Egypt and the control of the artificial strait of Suez, are links in the chain of British Empire 'upon which the sun never sets.'

"One of these colonies has the name 'The Straits Settlements,' and, however inconvenient for daily use, the name is full of meaning and suggests the secret of the dominancy of the British Empire. The Straits Settlements controls, in both the military and business sense, the Straits of Malacca. . . .

"Until recently the paramountcy of Great Britain as a trader in the East was an established fact, and that she would remain in possession of her trade was unquestioned. Conditions unexpected ten years ago by students of the commercial equations of the Orient have developed, and the English are anxiously asking one another to what extent the German advance will go. If there is one word that will adequately tell the secret of Germany's rapid acquirement of an important part of the business she is seeking, that word is 'adaptability.' . . ."

From Singapore to Hong Kong our passage was booked on the North German Lloyd steamship, the "Kronprinzessin Cecilie," a luxury liner that had been in the transatlantic trade and had but lately been transferred to the Asiatic run as a part of the general German effort to expand trade and prestige in that region of the world. Compared to the other ships we had been on, it was indeed a paradise. The ship's company was mainly European and consisted very largely of German businessmen, although there were not a few Englishmen who frankly said they preferred the superior accommodations of the German shipping to those of their own Peninsular and Oriental Line.

Here, while enjoying excellent food and the best of beer, I became acquainted with one or two German merchants. One of them in particular talked with me at great length about the Orient and what was going on in the great stir that had followed the Japanese victory over the Russians. He said that everywhere the German traders were prospering, that they were defeating the British in their competition, and that they were forestalling the Americans, who had largely confined their trade thus far to Japan, China, and the Philippines. He repeated the hopes and fears that had been outlined to me by the surgeon of the "Zieten." He said that, if only the Germans would keep their military men under control, then German industry and commerce would encompass the world. When I asked him what he thought of the English policy of keeping the ports of their far-flung empire open to all sorts of trade, he took the liberal view, asserting that the British were wise, that theirs was the only way to encourage trade, and that, in the end, the German competition that they were now feeling so sharply would induce them to adopt better methods. The closed port, he said, was a failure. He criticized the high protective tariffs of the United States, but in particular he pointed out that the one German colony in China, that of Tsingtao, despite all the money that had been spent on its port facilities, was languishing, since no ships but German ships were permitted to come into the port except upon payment of ruinous fees, and that the whole place was tied up with the red tape imposed by a Prussian bureaucratic system. He was a Hamburger, and his very use of the word "Prussian" made it sound as though it were a swear word. So, again from a German source, I got a broader and more liberal view of some of the British imperial policies.

In Hong Kong we were to stay but a day or two before taking passage on a small steamer for Manila, that outpost of the execution of an American policy which I had found deprecated by all the Europeans I had met on the long voyage save perhaps a few of the Germans. On that little ship in its three- or four-day voyage to the Philippines it turned out that, although a great many of the passengers were Germans, here for the first time the preponderance of numbers actually was American. One German, a representative of a Hamburg mercantile establishment, had been transferred from a post in Colombo to Manila. With him were his wife and daughter. The daughter was a young girl of perhaps fourteen who had lived two years in Colombo and had devoted herself to learning English. She spoke it very well, indeed, almost without accent; but she was determined to learn even more of it, and she entreated both Wallace and me to teach her idiomatic American English, which, she thought, would stand her in good stead in the coming years she intended to live in Manila.

One day, while Wallace and I were lolling in our deck chairs, I happened to say, expressing some preference for some inconsequential thing, in terms well understood to him as a Kentuckian, "If I had my druthers, I would do so and so."

Out of her chair the girl came, "What is that idiom? What does that mean?" If any two southerners ever had a hard time explaining a local idiom, it was to try to tell that girl that there was no such word as "druthers," that it was a corruption of "would rather," and that "rather" in its turn was a purely American expression for "preference" and so on, and so on.

Next day the three of us were standing at the rail looking out over a choppy sea which a cross-wind had beaten into whitecaps as far as the eye could see. The little German girl then piped up, "I have conquered an idiom: Look at the waves. They wager like muttons in the pasture." Our turn came. We demanded to know what she meant by that. It turned out that she had heard an English idiom and translated it through her dictionary. What she has intended to say was, "The whitecaps gambol like lambs on the green."

Also on this little ship there was a young German on his way to Manila in pursuit of some commercial adventure. He had left the army only recently. His face was disfigured with dueling scars; his figure and bearing were those of a soldier. I scraped up his acquaintance only to discover that his attitude was entirely different from that of the other Germans I had been talking to. He, in his turn, thought that the United States had made a colossal error in giving the Philippines even limited self-government, in teaching the English language to the Filipinos, and in promising eventually to give the islands their independence. His view was that Europeans were a superior people, that the event of the Russo-Japanese War was a calamity, and that Americans were causing entirely too much trouble in the Orient with their lax ways and their hopeless endeavor to teach democracy to "the lesser breeds without the law."

CHAPTER XXVIII

ON TO THE PHILIPPINES

Up betimes, thrilled by the Gibraltar-like appearance of Corregidor, impressed by the very nearness of Cavite, we came into Manila. I doubt if either Wallace or I had concerned ourselves very much with the problem of the Philippines and the Filipinos before we set out on our journey except of course to know that Manila was an important place on our itinerary. He, with his distaste for politics, had not considered it as being so much of a symbol of a change in the American way of life as had I. However, from the time we landed in Egypt, with the exception of the turbulent weeks in revolutionary Palestine, we had heard more and more and more of the American carryings-on in the Philippines. From British and German and Dutch and, generally speaking, all Europeans, we had listened to expressions of grave concern in different degree and expressed in different ways. Almost all of them had agreed that the United States was undermining the very existence of order in Asia. The Americans were transferring out of the abundance of their ignorance their own institutions to a people not prepared to receive them; we were blindly introducing democratic methodology among a people unfit for self-rule; and, so the agreement ran, while it might be our own business in the Philippines, it certainly was no business of ours to upset the orderly process of imperial government and international trade and commerce as carried on by the British, the Dutch, the French, and the Germans. All this prepared us in a way for much more questioning of what we were to see in the Philippines than otherwise would have been the case.

Now it so happened that I had been outside the borders of the United States more than once—Tom Wallace never. I was a loquacious liberal; he, a close-mouthed conservative. I was given to the use of extravagance for emphasis; he, to understatement. As we came to Manila Bay and saw there the Stars and Stripes, our emotions expressed themselves willy-nilly. Certainly I had not been born in the Philippines. But Wallace had never before experienced an entry into his own country. I had.

First of all, of course, we were welcomed, if that be the word, by a customs officer. On our journey we had seen several of that ilk, but, with the exception of the Egyptian who impounded our type-writer as a sort of infernal machine when we landed in Alexandria (although we did reclaim it without difficulty when we left Port Said), no other customs officer had done more than wave a polite wand over our baggage in the perfunctory manner of the British civil serv-ant. Here, "at home," so far as the flag was concerned, the United States customs officer went through our bags, bag by bag, shirt by shirt, handkerchief by handkerchief, in a most thorough and business-like demonstration of the American way of life. Wallace was manifestly discouraged. I was inured. But, despite that dash of cold water, even Wallace bubbled over with patriotism an hour later when, quartered in a hotel—not by any means the best we had experienced underneath the Star-spangled Banner—a waiter in the dining-room, all unbidden and without any apparent scorn, brought a glass of clear, still ice water to each of us. As Wallace wrote at the time: "To him who has known not the taste of plain water but once for months; to him who has choked down impossible hygienic soda, vile bottled lemonade, and bitter tonic water; to him who has almost forgotten (but not quite) the appearance of ice in a glass; to such an American traveler the Manila welcome was a godsend."

So before the first day was done we felt ourselves at home. Never-theless, we were not unmindful of the adverse comments that we had heard from so many of our European friends during the voyage. Both of us, certainly I, at any rate, had begun to doubt that the Ameri-cans were one-half so good, one-half so liberal, one-half so forward-looking as we had heard from the Asiatics—Moslem, Buddhist, or Hindu; Egyptian, Ceylonese, or Indian. It is true that I hoped to find some foundation of fact for their roseate democratic dreams, but, be-cause of their very coloration, I had become suspicious.

Here it was 1909 and but a few weeks more than eleven years since Admiral Dewey in Manila harbor had said, "You may fire when ready, Gridley," and that Pacific outpost of the empire of his Most Catholic

Majesty, the King of Spain, had fallen. And here I was in Manila only a few weeks after William Howard Taft had been inaugurated President of the United States, only a few months since he had defeated William Jennings Bryan in that "Peerless Leader's" third unsuccessful attempt to win the presidency, after a campaign in which a liberal Philippine policy had won the tacit consent of both the Republican and the Democratic parties.

Only eleven years after the Battle of Manila, and I already knew what I had not known when I left New York—that the United States in a little more than a decade had done things which had been greeted with profound regret by the European proconsuls and with great applause by the Asiatic spokesmen of the Near and Middle East. It is true that that American attitude was always bracketed in one way or another with the Japanese military defeat of the Russians, which had destroyed in the Asiatic mind the myth of European supremacy. That very bracketing, however, had induced a hope of a greater political independence stemming from the American Philippine policy, social, economic, or political.

Here, talking to Americans resident in Manila and the Philippines, I discovered among them a difference in attitude. Most of the Americans whom I talked to stressed the tremendous value of the great improvements that had been made in the eleven years of American occupancy and rule; but some of them, and not by any means the worst informed or the most unintelligent, expressed a longing for what was then currently known as the "days of the Empire," those early days when the American rule was absolute and military; and they deplored the action when, under the first civilian governor-general, William Howard Taft, those political promises to the Filipinos were made which had brought so much praise from all Asiatics.

Military and mercantile veterans alike found their feelings about the "little brown brothers" expressed in the lines of the song:

> He may be a brother of William H. Taft,
> But he ain't no brother of mine.

As I tried to look at the facts (perhaps I saw them through rose-colored glasses), I did see things which tempted me to look on the optimistic side. Not only was there that glass of ice water freely tendered at the table but there was a drugstore complete with soda fountain; there was a daily newspaper with the news displayed on the front page and the advertisements relegated to the rear; there were moving-picture houses—hardly yet a part even of American life—and there was a general atmosphere which seemed to be not only American but liberal and democratic. And, over and above all that, the people seemed to be busy and happy.

Leaders among the Americans confirmed that optimism. First of all, there was Martin Egan, the editor of the *Manila Times,* an old newspaperman whom I had known in Washington and who had spent much of his life in foreign countries. With Martin was his altogether charming wife, Eleanor, also a journalist, who had roamed the world in search of news. There was the governor-general, W. Cameron Forbes, who enthusiastically supported the Taftian policies. There were many others I met at the club and at Egan's home. And very importantly there was a young Filipino of my own age, Manuel Luis Quezon y Molina, who had been a lieutenant under Aguinaldo in the insurrection against the Americans but who had just now been elected the first resident commissioner of the Philippine Islands to sit in the House of Representatives in Washington, of course without vote, but with voice, in the same capacity as did the delegates from the then territories of New Mexico and Arizona. (This was the beginning of a close friendship with Manuel Quezon, first president of the independent Philippine Republic, that was to continue until his death at Saranac in 1944.) I wrote at the time:

"It is only a little more than eleven years since Admiral Dewey fought the Battle of Manila Bay, it is not quite eleven years since the occupation of Manila by the American troops, and it is only eight years since American civil government was established in the Islands. The achievements of American rule in that short time have revolutionized the life of the Islands from the topmost circles of society in Manila to the everyday life of the dog-eating, head-hunting savages of the mountains. More has been done in a decade than Spain accomplished in over three centuries.

"America found a subject people which had absolutely no part in the government, and which for years had been in a constant state of insurrection against the authorities. . . . Today the Philippines enjoy a tranquillity never before dreamed of in the Islands. The Filipinos have been granted almost complete autonomy in municipal affairs, and a large share in the legislative, executive and judical government of the Islands. The lower house of the legislature is entirely Filipino, there are three Filipinos in the cabinet of seven and of the seven justices of the Supreme Court three are Filipinos. . . .

"America found ninety percent of the people in absolute ignorance and a school system which offered no hope of bettering their condition. An American public school system now reaches a half million pupils out of the total population of seven million. The percentage of illiteracy is still large, but the next generation will see it greatly reduced. The English language has already become common in many parts of the islands and it is spoken by a greater number of natives than is Spanish. . . .

"America found the mountains inhabited by wild tribes who knew nothing of civilization, and which were constantly at deadly war with each other, seeking heads of the enemy as trophies. The Americans have reached out among these people, have persuaded them to cease their war-like habits, have stopped the practice of head-hunting, and are bringing the wild tribes into touch with the civilization of their Christian brothers in the lowlands. . . .

"America found a judiciary system sadly in need of reform. Litigation was protracted, expensive and uncertain. . . . The Americans have established a new judicial system, from the justice of peace to the supreme court, although they have maintained in force the Spanish and Roman system of law. The trial courts are presided over by Americans and Filipino judges, and all are of the highest integrity. Appeals to the higher courts are a matter of right, and the old summary injustice is a thing of the past. . . .

"America found a people which naturally divided itself into two classes, the aristocrats who looked upon work as degrading, and the masses who worked only enough to supply themselves with the most meager necessities. The Americans have been endeavoring to teach the Filipinos, of high and low degree, that honest labor is not disgraceful. To some extent this effort has been successful. The Americans have taught the people to want more things, and they must work more to have them. But ten years is too short a time to make over the habits of a race which has run in the same groove for ages.

[495]

"America found the Philippines eleven years ago. The accomplishments of that brief period are wonderful—yet the march of progress there is considered hardly well under way."

The first session of the first Philippine National Assembly was opened by Governor-General Taft in 1907. The second session of that body adjourned on May 22, 1909, just before I reached Manila. The establishment of the Assembly was the most interesting and the boldest political experiment made by the United States in the effort to educate the Filipinos in the task of self-government.

"The Filipino people aspire to national independence. This is not an unnatural aspiration on the part of any people, it has been known as 'patriotism' in some countries, and even in the Filipinos it is not altogether wicked. This natural aspiration has fed on rich food from Washington. The party which has been in power in the United States ever since the Philippines came into American possession has repeatedly assured the Filipinos that they would be given independence as soon as they were fitted for it. The party in opposition has lost no opportunity to demand the immediate independence of the Islands. Individual Americans assert that the flag will never be hauled down in the Philippines, but their word counts for little with the Filipinos, in view of the repeated assurances from the government and continual agitation by the opposition party leaders.

"Therefore, on the tongue of the Filipino, no matter what doubts may linger in his brain, there is but one question concerning independence, and that question is: 'When?'"

So I wrote in 1909. Whatever may have happened in the decades since my enthusiastic appraisal of the civil government in the Philippines, whatever may be the present view of what the Filipinos have done with their independence, I am quite sure that my democratic predilections with respect to the political views of the Philippine Islands as a semi-independent or independent republic have been at least as much justified by the event as what I wrote at the time with respect to the military meaning of the United States occupation of the Archipelago. For that, lest there be some thought that I am permitting present knowledge to color the convictions of 1909, I quote verbatim what I wrote then:

"If present plans are advanced with reasonable expedition, a very few years will find Manila the Gibraltar of the East—fortified against attack and sheltering a naval base upon which will rest the far-flung battle line assuring American marine supremacy in the Pacific Ocean.

"There was a time when the most common objection to the retention of the Philippines by the United States was expressed in the sentence: 'We couldn't defend them in case of war.' Nowadays one hears, in the Orient at least, the remark: 'The Americans must keep the Philippines as a military base to protect their interests in Asiatic waters.' This also implies the growing conviction that the United States has other and greater interests in Asiatic waters, and in the Pacific Ocean than the Philippine Islands. In other words, the Philippines 'no longer present an army problem of defense, but a navy problem of offense.'

"That military epigram, lately used by a well-informed writer on Pacific affairs, is subject to the qualification that a naval base at Manila, however well fortified against attack by sea, must depend upon the army for protection from an invading land force. The island of Luzon is almost as large as England and an invasion might easily be accomplished.

"Manila Bay, within which is located the naval station of Cavite which someday will be equipped as a great naval base should be equipped, is already well fortified. The fort on the Island of Corregidor, a huge rock in the middle of the narrow entrance to the wide bay, is not completed, but it is even now one of the most formidable defenses in the Orient. The details of its construction and armament have been properly kept secret, but it is already known as 'the American Gibraltar of the Pacific.'. . .

"In the event of a war between the United States and Japan, a conflict which is highly improbable in the near future, the Philippines will be either the greatest strength or the greatest weakness of the American arms. If the plans for defense are carried forward with dispatch, if there is a naval base here which will give a fleet all the advantages which it could have at San Francisco, and if the fleet maintained in the Pacific is of sufficient strength, there is no reason why the Philippines should not be, in a military sense, as close to Japan as Japan is close to the Philippines.

"If, on the other hand, the plans for defense are permitted to drag along, if the naval base here is not adequately equipped, and if the Pacific fleet is not fully as strong as that of the possible antagonist—

then an invasion of the Philippines might be expected, and a long land warfare on the other side of the world might be precipitated.

"In view of the liberality with which the United States is spending money on fortifying Manila Bay, it is difficult to conceive of the possibility of a retrogressive American policy which would leave the other measures of defensive and offensive preparation unprovided for."

The crystal ball did not then reveal to me the events of 1941. But ever thereafter I looked West as well as East.

CHAPTER XXIX

CHINA

We left Manila, greatly impressed by the success of the United States in its Far Eastern adventure. In a few days we were in Hong Kong, the British colony, the entry port of South China, which we had barely looked at on our earlier visit. Now we were concerned with China and the Chinese Empire.

Primarily, however, we were concerned with an extremely personal matter. We had first encountered the chit system in Egypt. We had taken it up all too eagerly and continued to practice it through Ceylon, India, Burma, and wherever we went, including the somewhat startling experience of encountering it under the American flag in Manila. The system meant that one rarely or never paid cash for anything. A meal, a drink, or a pack of cigarettes in the hotel or on shipboard always simply was signed for. When settlement day came, as it did inevitably on the day of departure, the chits added up to so much more than one had expected. Then of course there was the inevitable loss in exchanging the currency of one country into that of another, so that we got the notion that the chit system was really a saving, and I didn't bother so much about the big bills. But in Manila we signed too many chits. On the little ship coming to Hong Kong we signed too many. Settling up on the ship, we discovered to our amazement that we were practically broke. We went to the hotel, signed a chit for the carriage and the tips to the porter, and took stock. Not far away was a cable office. Arriving there at about half-past six in the evening, we composed a cablegram to Mr. Haskin in Washington explaining our position and asking for money at once. We hadn't enough money to explain why we were busted. In fact, after we had negotiated the cablegram, our combined capital amounted to less than a dollar if translated into American currency. There was nothing to do but to go to the hotel and wait. We speculated and worried. We wondered whether Haskin would be in Washington. We wondered, if he weren't, whether anybody in the office would take the responsibility of sending us some money. If he were away from Washington, would the office write him or telegraph him or telephone him. We imagined all sorts of dire things, and we condemned ourselves to imprisonment within the hotel and its precincts where we earnestly hoped and prayed our signatures on the chits still would be good. We went to bed.

The next morning, shortly after seven, there was a knock on the door. I opened it. There stood a well-dressed Chinese young man. I invited him in. He said, "I am a messenger from the comprador of the bank. We have received a cable authorizing us to issue a letter of credit to you for one thousand dollars American gold." If we had been in Baltimore and had sent a telegraphic message for succor, money could not possibly have reached us in such a short time. Such, we discovered, was a virtue of the difference in time between Hong Kong and Washington, and the promptitude of Mr. Haskin.

Then there followed sight-seeing in Hong Kong; a renewal of our interest in the German advance by looking over the great German shipping installations at Kowloon, which were so much more impressive than those of the British; and some very delightful luncheons and dinners with members of the staff of the American consulate and, through them, similar meetings with some of the British officials and members of the staff of the German consulate. Then followed a voyage up the Pearl River to Canton, slightly frightened that the river pirates might attack us. We spent a few days there in the great southern Chinese city, safe and comfortable in the foreign concession, with full liberty to roam, to watch the teeming millions of the Cantonese in the narrow streets of their very great city, and to wander with the benefit of a motor launch through the pathways of the thousands of Chinese who lived in the boats on the river.

From Hong Kong we took passage on a French ship for the three-day voyage to Shanghai. The French ship was a different world. It was so utterly different from the German, the British, or the American ships of my acquaintance. The food was superb. I am sure there must have been some sort of refrigerator on board, because the white wine was chilled; but that ship's company would have none of your refrigerated food. On the deck at the rear of the ship there were milch cows and beef cattle, sheep and chickens, turkeys and geese and ducks—all sorts of domestic animals which may or may not have been quite comfortable in bad weather but which were there to insure that the chef would have available for the delectation of the passengers the fresh meat and poultry that enabled him to demonstrate his skill and artistry. The passengers also in the main were French. There were several French colonial officials who had boarded the ship at Saigon, and one or two of these spoke English. Getting acquainted with them, I found myself being upbraided for not having visited the French colonies in China; but there was not one word of complaint about what we were doing in the Philippines. After probing, I discovered there was no complaint because our experiment there, which had so nettled the British, German, and Dutch, seemed to be utterly unknown to the French colonial officials.

Then there was a group of a dozen or more young novitiates under the chaperonage of Jesuit missionaries who after a season in Saigon were being taken to a mission in the interior of China. All but one of the novitiates were young men from France. The other was an Annamese. A few of these youngsters spoke English, and, being eager to improve their command of that tongue, they were ready and willing to talk. None, of course, with his vocation, could confess to homesickness; but it was very touching to see how much they used of their English to describe their homes in France and their families and how with equal enthusiasm they were looking forward to spending their lives in their work for the church and Christianity in mid-China.

Then Shanghai, the Paris of the East, the metropolis of modern China, one of the greatest cities on earth, a crossroads of every civilization, a city devoted to trade, to pleasure, to education; a city having no formal political significance but nevertheless a city in which was stirring even then the evidences of the Asiatic awakening and, if I had had but the wit to discern it, the prologue of the great revolution of 1911, so soon to come. But I had neither the wit to discern the symptoms nor the clairvoyant quality which would have enabled me to see into the future. And, besides that, Wallace and I were just entirely too busy seeing things and going places in the most exciting and fascinating metropolis we had encountered.

[501]

A Passion for Politics

All the way from New York until we actually got to Shanghai, from time to time, I would tell Wallace how eagerly I was looking forward to China when I could renew my acquaintance with the Doctors Fearn—husband and wife, both Methodist missionaries, both physicians, and both, as I knew, then living in Shanghai. Despite anything I said, Wallace was cold. But I must say that, until we got on the French ship and Shanghai was our next port, he had been as polite as he was cool. On the day before we got to Shanghai he gave me distinctly to understand that I could go with my Methodist missionaries but that he did not intend to get mixed up with them in any sort of social contact, although, of course, in the line of duty, he was prepared to interview a missionary as well as any other creature. Once installed in the Hotel Astor, I immediately telephoned to Mrs. Fearn. She was in. She asked us both to come to dinner that night. I accepted for myself but pleaded a slight indisposition on Mr. Wallace's part. "Let him come along," she said. "Dr. Fearn [referring to her husband] will come for you and show you how to get here." There was no saying nay to her. After a while Dr. Fearn was announced. I prevailed upon Wallace at least to go down to the lobby to meet him and make his own excuses for declining the dinner. He reluctantly agreed, and we went to the lobby. There to my astonishment was Mrs. Fearn. Her husband had been busy, and she had decided to come and get us. In less than sixty seconds Tom Wallace's indisposition had miraculously disappeared. He joined us at dinner. That was the beginning of a series of luncheons and dinners at the Fearns and with friends of theirs, some of them missionaries, some of them Chinese, some of them journalists. It was also the fortunate beginning of an acquaintance with Dr. Fearn, who volunteered to conduct us on sight-seeing tours through the city—sight-seeing tours that Wallace was more than a little astonished to discover were placed on the itinerary by a Methodist missionary.

Thus chaperoned, we saw the famous Foochow Road, with its lights and color. We went even farther into the dark dens of iniquity, into opium joints, where Dr. Fearn lectured the habitués in Chinese; we explored the three Shanghais: the International Settlement, the French Concession, and the Chinese native city.

In the old days the several nations had had separate concessions and built each its own town. When I saw Shanghai, all of them but the French had been consolidated in the International Settlement, at that time the largest and most important part of Shanghai. Along its Bund, or water-front street, which was the principal artery of the city's life, the skyline monotony was varied by the magnificent bank and club buildings. The Bund continued into the French Concession, the dividing line being a small canal. On one side of that canal English was the language, and the customs were British. On the other, everything was French. Not far away, but carefully hidden from view of the Bund, was the walled Chinese city which was there ages before the red-haired barbarians of Europe descended upon these happy Chinese to make trouble. Two ridiculous cannons of the fashion of millennium before last were mounted over the gate, and a horde of wise and greedy guides waited under them to entrap the unwary tourist.

The International and the French cities were the same to the eye. The Chinese city presented the contrast. Wide paved streets, electric car lines, electric lights, well-kept parks—this was the European part of the city. Streets four feet wide, dirt, noise, smells, but also color—this was the native Chinese city.

But the greater part of the modern city, too, was inhabited by the Chinese, and it was here that one saw how the Celestials adapt themselves to the conditions of Western city life. Imagine a wide avenue, well paved, flanked by rows of business houses of uniform color and size. Each shop proclaimed its character to the Chinese wayfarer by means of huge signs hung out over the sidewalk. Every sign was of the same size, preserving the uniformity of the houses. Letters of gold shone out from black-lacquered backgrounds on every one. The shops with their plate-glass windows, their electric lights, and their display of wares were no whit different from small shops in any Western city. But the fact that their signs were all uniform and all in perfectly good taste transformed what might have been a dismal business street into an avenue of remarkable beauty.

Then there was Foochow Road—the street given over to pleasure and to sin. The houses were modern and European in construction. All the rest was Chinese. The long rows of three-story buildings sheltered shops on the ground floor. The two upper stories had open verandas running their whole length, and the walls were but windows to be pushed aside in pleasant weather. At night millions of incandescent bulbs made the whole street as brilliant as Coney Island. Five of every six houses were devoted to the business of selling tea in cups. The other house was the home of dramatic art as the Chinese saw it.

Thousands of night-singing birds, hanging in gilded cages along the verandas, furnished a background of shrill music to the chattering of the multitude which crowded the streets and overflowed the balconies. Broad flights of stairs led up to the teahouses. Here one found a huge room filled with tables and chairs. Men leaned on the tables and sipped the scalding tea, varying the excitement once in a while by nibbling at a melon seed. It was about eight o'clock in the evening, and there was an air of expectancy in the place.

Then came the pitiful procession of the painted girls who helped to make the fun. One little girl, she was as like all the others as one pea to all those in a peck measure, was not more than fifteen years old. She was dressed in a purple coat of heavy satin and trousers of light-blue silk. Her tiny deformed feet were thrust into thimble-like shoes covered with jewels. Her long black hair, heavy with oil, was carefully coiled on the back of her head and fastened with a pin of silver and jade. Her neck and arms were weighted down with jewels. Her feet were so small that she could scarce walk without assistance, and she was carried up the stairs on the shoulders of a porter accompanied by an old woman, her amah, in dull-colored clothes. No girl was ever seen without her amah, or maid.

Her face was painted thickly—eyebrows plastered with black, forehead white as death, cheeks pink as peach blooms, lips scarlet as geraniums. She looked as if she never smiled, never thought, never lived. She seated herself at a table and, in a moment, was joined by a silk-clad young Chinese. She knew her duty and, instantly, began to talk and laugh and be amusing. There was tea to drink and, perhaps, "chow" to be eaten. Maybe the silk-clad man loafed to another table and another painted plaything. There were twenty thousand such as she within a stone's throw of Foochow Road. Splendid with its lights, joyful with its myriads of birds, jubilant in its pleasure and fun—the two rows of magnificent buildings of Foochow Road screened from the eye of the passer-by the miserable warrens where these painted playthings lived out their days in squalor, suffering, and sin.

In some of these teahouses there were other rooms. In them one found k'angs, that article of furniture which was a combination of couch, chair, bed, and table and which in the northern part of China also did duty as a stove. On these, men were lying in all stages of that intoxication produced by smoking opium.

Mrs. Fearn took us driving in Bubbling Well Road, where between five and six o'clock in the afternoon one not only could see prerevolutionary Shanghai, its people, but could feel Shanghai, its charm. Bubbling Well Road was a stage setting worthy of a pretty scene, and no one who loved life, color, and the pursuit of happiness could be disappointed in its daily pageant. Here could be seen in sharp contrast the various types of the lordly white man as he was when he lived far away from his own people and his racial home. Here could be seen, also, the types of those Chinese who would ape their occidental brothers in manners and customs whether it were for salvation or for gain. Here could be seen, in epitome, a moving picture of the great human comedy, albeit, colored with the rose; for on Bubbling Well Road even pinching poverty and sordid sin wore gay livery.

Europeans, Americans, Chinese; bankers, society leaders, gamblers, beachcombers, clerks, missionaries, family men; rich, well to do, poor—they all drove. And, when we got back to the Astor House for dinner, we half-believed what the big Sikh policemen knew all the time —that all the world, for all the ages, was portrayed in the pageant to be seen every afternoon, of a fine day, from five to six o'clock in Bubbling Well Road.

It was all exciting. It was all fascinating. There was talk of maladministration in Peking, of the decadence of the Manchu regime, of distrust of the Japanese. Here, however, it was not that the Japanese had demolished the myth of European invincibility by defeating Russia; it was that the Japanese themselves were a threat to China. The disastrous war of 1895, in which the Chinese had been so signally and so suddenly defeated by the Japanese, had had its great effect among the Chinese by liberalizing their attitude toward the foreign devils, foreign machines, and foreign learning. Many Chinese with whom one talked were proud of their progress. In fact, the whole series of articles that Wallace and I turned out in China had the running headline, "In Modern China."

I talked with a good many representatives of the great British trading concerns, English style, and great American organizations—Standard Oil Company and the American Tobacco Company. They without exception were optimistic with respect to the Chinese; almost without exception they were suspicious of the Japanese; and without any exception they agreed that, so far as the Chinese Empire was concerned, Russia was no longer to be feared.

I must confess that, just as we had overspent our funds, so had we overstayed our time; and in Shanghai we found ourselves up against the tribulation of meeting a deadline, however far distant it might be measured. The mails now of course were going eastward across the Pacific. The publication of our articles had begun. They had to appear daily, and we were increasingly conscious of the difficulty of getting our stuff into Washington on time. So, in Shanghai, Wallace and I decided to separate. I, at any rate, had a feeling that I knew China, and I certainly had no sense of my profound ignorance of that great people. I already had visited in Japan, and Wallace had not. So the decision was made that he would go from Shanghai to Korea and thence to Japan, while I would go north to Peking to pick up the threads of my political story in the Chinese capital and then join him in Yokohama for the voyage across the Pacific to San Francisco. This arrangement gave both of us the inestimable advantage of a little longer time for doing things and seeing things that were not strictly necessary in the pursuit of our mission.

For me this especially was welcomed. It gave me the opportunity to spend a week in Soochow. My first cousin, Walter B. Nance, the son of my mother's eldest sister, a graduate of Vanderbilt University, an ordained Methodist minister, an accomplished linguist who in 1894 had put in a year at the newly established University of Chicago studying Hebrew under the first president of that institution, Dr. William R. Harper, had gone to China to be a missionary. Later another linguist, also a graduate of Vanderbilt University, Florence Keiser, also a Tennessean, had gone out to China and had become Mrs. Walter B. Nance. Walter had begun his ministry in Soochow, then approached from Shanghai only by canal but now connected by railroad. I arranged to spend a week at Soochow University with my cousin, then a professor on the faculty of that institution, whom I had not seen since I was five and he was fifteen, and, of course, with his wife, whom I had never met, and with his three young sons, my second cousins, equally unknown to me.

China

That visit was the highlight of my Chinese experiences. Here, not in a port city, I had an excellent guide to show me through the maze of streets that within the walls of that old city gave me a picture of Chinese civilization and manners quite different indeed from that in the gay international port of Shanghai. Here I had an opportunity to meet the president of the university, Dr. Anderson, and his wife, the members of the faculty, other missionaries from other denominations than Methodist, many of the students in the college, and not a few Chinese with whom I could talk only by virtue of my cousin's skill as an interpreter.

Walter took me to a Taoist temple. He took me to one or two shrines that had some significance in the Confucian philosophy. He took me to see, although not to enter, a Mohammedan mosque. Soochow, for some reason or other unfathomable to me, since it is a city far from the sea, for centuries had been a center of the pearl trade. Walter took me to see a Mohammedan pearl merchant. There I spent some hours in the ceremonial approaches to the central theme of the merchant's existence—tea, courteous exchanges of honorifics, and at last the display of his gems—one pearl at a time laid in the center of a black square of velvet, which in turn had been discovered only by folding back a larger, then a larger, then a larger square of silk— yellow, blue, purple, and vermilion. I had no money for pearls, but fortunately Walter had a commission to buy one for some friend, so that the visit turned out to be quite legitimate.

I was utterly overcome by the linguistic ability of my three young cousins, Keiser, Dana, and Francis, but especially that of Francis, who then at the age of three seemed to know all languages. He would address me in some dialect of Chinese, probably Soochow; discovering I didn't know that, he would come at me with Mandarin; and, finally, probably writing me down as one of the more ignorant creatures of this world, in English. That short visit effectively erased from my mind the notion that I had gained in gay Shanghai that I knew something about China. I now decided that I knew nothing whatever.

(After Walter had been president of the university for some years, the revolutionary government decided that all foreigners were to be deposed from the highest titles in the universities of China, although the new title of "Western Adviser" probably carried more authority than did that of "President," subject as it was to the limitations not only of faculty committees on the grounds but of distant boards of missions operating in New York. There Walter stayed, with occasional sabbatical visits to the United States. The boys went to Vanderbilt, and all three became surgeons. Florence died, but Walter stayed on in Soochow. That is, he stayed until the Japanese took over China. They imprisoned him. Getting out of prison by virtue of the Swedish ship "Gripsholm," through the Red Cross, he came back to the United States until the war with Japan was ended. Then he went back to China on a special mission, living in Soochow and Shanghai until the Communists crossed the Yangtze River. Then again he was imprisoned, again to be rescued by way of the "Gripsholm."

Then back in Oak Ridge, Tennessee, living with his son, Dr. Dana Nance, in 1952 he received a petition from some eight hundred alumni of Soochow University, now refugees in Formosa, asking him to come to Formosa and organize a university in that last stronghold of Nationalist China. He ardently desired to go, but his friends and his family persuaded him that it was not absolutely true that life begins at eighty-five.)

Now having learned in Soochow that all was not well within the Chinese Empire and that all China did not consist of either Foochow Roads, Bubbling Well Roads, or the long, long bar in the Astor House, I went back to Shanghai and took ship for Tientsin on my way to the northern capital of Peking.

II

When Alfred, Lord Tennyson, wrote the line, "Better fifty years of Europe than a cycle of Cathay," it is to be feared that his point of view, if not British, at the very least, was European. He gave to the world "cycle" its European connotation, perhaps blissfully in ignorance of the fact that in China a "cycle" is sixty years. Even then the differential of ten years does not seem to carry out the great poet laureate's meaning. But if one occasionally hesitates, as I do, to look backward to that year of 1909, when I went to Peking, the word "cycle" takes on anew significance. Surely at that moment I had thought of my own United States as a stable, civilized, settled country. Yet a half-century earlier statesmen in my country were endeavoring to find some way to settle or at least to postpone the quarrel that only two years later would eventuate in the Civil War in the United States

—the bloodiest war in all the history of mankind up until that time. A little less than fifty years before I set foot in Peking, China had experienced in the 1860's, in the Taiping Rebellion, a civil war which was the rival in fury to the one then raging in the United States.

I was content in my own mind to think of the United States as well established and to give due weight to its three particular dates: its independence, its establishment, and its stabilization—1776, 1787, and 1865. At the same time I could and did reach backward through my English forebears to such things as the Norman Conquest in 1066, the grant of Magna Carta in 1215, the discovery of America in 1492, and even to the bloodless but glorious revolution of 1688 which so aptly served Lord Tennyson's thought.

But it was hard for me to accustom myself to what very quickly I sensed in the conversation of the Chinese—that each of them considered himself to be a product of a much older civilization than any of us Westerners knew. That the Chinese could and would adapt some things from the West, they not only admitted but asserted. But back of all their talk of "modern China," of "the new education," of the progress that they were making, of the great things that they intended to do, there was instinct the notion that "this, too, will pass away." Later, many years later, I was destined to find what I had deemed to be some of my original discoveries in the field of public administration logically set out in the works of Wang An-shih (*ca.* A.D. 1066) and my notions of public personnel administration succinctly stated by Lioa Shao (*ca.* A.D. 200).

Established in the Grand Hôtel des Wagons-Lits in Peking, I made my customary call at the American legation to find things there in rather a dither because our minister, W. W. Rockhill, was leaving, and things were all upset. In fact, it took me several days to arrange an interview with Mr. Rockhill, but I did find a lively young American student attaché in the embassy. I remember him as "Gale," but, when I met him forty-odd years later, he was Professor Esson Mc-Dowell Gale of the University of Michigan. He was very kind. He had not been in Peking quite a year. He was busy learning the language, but he did give me a great deal of good advice about where to go and what to see and, much more than that, found me a young Chinese student who would, for a very modest consideration, act as my guide and interpreter. Turning as I always did to my journalistic colleagues, I found in Peking two who were willing and able to instruct me. One was Joshua K. Ohl, the correspondent of the *New York Herald,* a Georgian whom I had known in Washington. The other was Mr. Li, a young English-speaking Cantonese who had but recently established in Peking an English-speaking daily, a four-page tabloid affair called the *Peking Daily Times.* Mr. Li did not speak Mandarin or any other Chinese dialect but his native Cantonese and in the North was as much at the mercy of an interpreter as was I. Fortunately, the English-speaking interpreter I had engaged could speak this Cantonese dialect. So, in going about, seeing the sights, and interviewing Chinese civil servants, Mr. Li was my constant companion.

More important to me, however, was the presence of an old friend of mine from Washington in the person of Major George M. Barnett of the United States Marines and his charming and beautiful wife, Lelia Gordon Barnett. After the Boxer Rebellion in 1900 the United States, as well as the other great powers, kept armed legation guards on duty in Peking to protect their missions. The detachment of the United States Marines was established in its own compound under Major Barnett, he who was later to become major general in command of the entire Marine Corps. At the Barnetts, I had breakfast, I was invited to tiffin, to dinner, to tea, and in that way I managed to meet a great many more of the members of the diplomatic and foreign colony than otherwise would have been at all possible.

Everywhere and by everybody, it was recognized that China was in a state of transition. The disastrous defeat at the hands of the Japanese in 1895 had seriously disturbed the Chinese complacency and had caused a great many of the wealthier Chinese to permit their sons to be exposed to Western education and particularly to Western science. Only five years before my visit the Japanese defeat of the Russians had introduced Japanese power into the mainland of Asia and was causing great concern to the Chinese, who recognized that, in the Russo-Japanese struggle for dominion in Manchuria, the Chinese were the real losers. The Manchu dynasty was coming to an end. The old empress dowager who had ruled for so long was dead. The young emperor had died. The Son of Heaven was a baby only three years old. The child emperor's father, Tsai Feng, Prince of Chun, was regent and all but the absolute ruler of the Empire. The then ranking Chinese statesman, Yüan Shih-k'ai, had graciously been permitted to retire to his home to treat his sore foot. Recalling Sir John Tenniel and his cartoon in *Punch* remembering Bismarck, I called this incident "Dropping the Pilot."

The new regime had recognized that new things must be done and had promised constitutional government, a constitution that was to be proclaimed in 1917—the intervening eight years to be devoted to its preparation. The effective control of the ports, the customs, and the salt revenue by the British inspector-general of customs and by the Western-dominated salt gabelle in the meantime were the principal props of an uneasy stability.

Not even the radical liberal editor, Mr. Li, so much as suspected at the time that within three years the Manchu dynasty would come to an end, that China would be proclaimed a republic, or that Yüan Shih-k'ai would be recalled to be its first president, only to yield a little later to Sun Yat-sen. Nobody so much as suspected that the queues would be cut, that nice girls' feet would come to be big, that this "Awakening of Asia" would become a social as well as an economic and political revolution in China.

It was clear to me then that Prince Chun promised infinitely more for the constitution than the empress dowager had contemplated when she made the original announcement in 1906 or when a year later the date of the constitution, 1917, was announced. The original program did not contemplate giving the Parliament entire control of the finances. On the other hand, it was expressly provided that the power of finally determining the budget would lie in the emperor, as it did then in the kaiser in Berlin, the czar in St. Petersburg, the sultan in Constantinople, or, for that matter, President Porfirio Díaz in Mexico.

In the same edict the prince regent denounced corruption in office, a denunciation he repeated almost daily after his accession to power. It seemed to me then that if he seriously attempted to purge Chinese officialdom of corruption, if he seriously engaged to abolish the "squeeze" system of graft, Prince Chun had undertaken the greatest task one man ever assumed. But also I was naïve enough to believe that a determined attitude upon his part, and a ready use of his power to chop off official heads, would do much to correct the grosser evils which beset the country.

I wrote then: "The chief danger in the path of the young prince is the pitfall of racial and dynastic jealousy. He, of course, is a Manchu and he is not insensible to the agitation among the Chinese that it is high time to overthrow the alien dynasty and set a Chinese upon the Throne of the Son of Heaven. This agitation is sporadic, and it is to be doubted if it is based upon a very widespread or deep-rooted sentiment. The Boxer organization of ruffians started out as an anti-Manchu movement and ended in disgrace as the tool of the wisest of Manchus—the old Empress Dowager.

"Yet Prince Chun, the avowed friend of reform and progress, has disgraced the leading Chinese of the Empire, Yüan Shih-k'ai, and has not taken pains to bring a Chinese successor into high place. It is difficult to analyze this situation, but there are many in Peking who believe that the Prince's zeal in support of the Constitution is partly a result of his conviction that it is the only method to perpetuate the Manchu dynasty. . . .

"The power of the essential democracy of China is so formidable that the government would not dare to do anything against the wishes of the people. For centuries this has been true, and when the government has gone contrary to public opinion it has been only because of ignorance. The system of memorials and censorial reports by which the belief and desires of the public have been made known to Peking is absurdly inadequate in this day of quick action, and the Chinese government recognizes that fact. But it is even more inadequate in another sense, in that there is practically no machinery whatever by which the government may make its wishes known to the public, present its arguments and reasons for its position, and endeavor to convince the people of the soundness of its attitude. This is the essential weakness of the Chinese form of government, the centripetal forces of democracy not having the necessary balancing effect of centrifugal authority. . . .

"Let him who doubts the genuineness of reform and progress in China journey to the modern city of Peking and there be convinced. Not only is there reform in spirit, but there is actual progress in the adaptation of western ways and the old order is rapidly giving way to the new. Go to the 'Arcade' in the evening and see the cinematograph show. The moving picture machine has accomplished what generations of teachers and preachers have failed to do—it has introduced the western idea of men and women appearing in public together on a plane of equality. The Chinese ladies have been secluded from the gaze of all men other than their husbands for centuries. The moving picture show has broken the purdah, and the tourist from New Jersey devours the face of the Chinese lady of high degree the while she looks on the antics of a wonderful made-in-France magician.

"Go to the Grand Hôtel des Wagons-Lits at five o'clock in the afternoon. There in the center of the hotel lobby, enduring the critical inspection of rude foreign ladies from America and Europe, sits a group of Manchu princesses, gossiping over their afternoon tea. The tea is poured from a pot with a spout on it, into a cup which has a saucer, and the dainty fingers toy with an alien spoon and try to like the tea which they have spoiled with an alien lump of sugar. Their faces are painted as thick as ever Hamlet saw, and redder with rouge than ever Hamlet dreamed of. Their long tight-fitting silken gowns suggest the fashions yclept 'directoire' and 'sheath,' yet their style has not changed in three centuries. Their jewels are pearls and jade, modestly magnificent. Each wears her national head-dress, a curious contraption consisting of a board fastened on the head over which the hair, or black silk yarn if the hair is not long enough, is smoothed down in the fashion of an enormous butterfly bow. Under and around this bow are gay and gaudy artificial flowers.

"Spectacular as they are, these Manchu women of noble birth were never to be seen by profane foreign eyes until within the last two or three years. That they come now to a foreign hotel to take tea for recreation is a sign of the times. . . .

"The streets of Peking, that is the main thoroughfares, are as wide as the avenues of Washington—in startling contrast to the streets of other Chinese cities where one may touch both sides with extended arms. The Manchus who lived in the wide, free plains, planned Peking and they used plenty of space. (That plan was made just as Columbus was setting sail from Palos to discover America.) Even off the main avenues, where the streets are quite narrow, each house has an enormous compound and there is always wide breathing-room.

"The original plan of Peking was an admirable one as the foundation scheme of a City Beautiful, and it will not be many years until it will come into its own. From the top of the ancient Drum Tower in the heart of the Tartar City one commands the magnificent vistas of the broad, tree-flanked avenues, each leading to some monument well worthy of the setting. The substantial beauty of the temples and palaces of Peking is so impressive that one is inclined to regret the advent of western methods of building, despite the advantage of the occidental systems of architecture in point of convenience. But the Chinese, even the most conservative among them, are not deterred by any such sentiment.

"This is the same Peking, the capital city, in which less than ten years ago the Imperial government with a degree of treachery and breach of obligation unmatched in modern history, laid seige to the legations of the various nations of the world. It is less than ten years of actual time since the Boxer War, the seige of the legations, the capture of Peking by the Allies, and the violation and sacking of the Forbidden City, but in progress and change it is more than a century for Peking.

"The uniforms of a score of nations are seen in the streets, and the powers maintain a garrison against the possible recurrence of the horrors of 1900. But everybody knows, or believes he knows, that there is no such possibility. The capture of Peking in 1900 was the beginning of a new era in China. The change has been felt in all parts of the Empire, and has manifested itself in many ways, but in ancient and conservative Peking the tangible progress is most marked."

Not all my time in Peking was so devoted to the problems of the seething caldron of Asiatic politics as what I wrote then would indicate. I was having the time of my life.

The railroad running northwestwardly toward the Kalgan Pass into Mongolia was new then. Those hardy pioneers of comfortable travel, the Messrs. Thomas Cook & Son, were as usual forehanded. They had arranged tours—one to Nankow at the inner gate of the Great Wall into Mongolia and another at Kalgan at the outer gate into the vastnesses and the fastnesses of Outer Mongolia and Siberia.

I signed up for both. To Nankow I had as fellow-travelers Felix Fuld of Bamberger's, Newark, New Jersey; his sister and brother-in-law, Mr. and Mrs. Morse; a wide-ranging stockbroker (specializing in gold and silver mines) from Denver; an aging but adventurous baroness from Budapest; and a young Prussian army officer. We made a party to Nankow. Arriving at night after dark, we settled for a cold supper and some excellent Pilsener beer; we arose while it was yet dark; we were herded; we were fed; we were mounted—each of us quite separately—on little donkeys' backs.

Thus we saw the tombs of the Ming emperors. Thus we traversed the amazing avenue to that goal betwixt the stone counterfeits of elephants, tigers, and the like. My fear of horses still pursued me, but, if the quadrupeds of my nightmares were but thus manifest in tiny burros, I was even more afraid of the ridicule of Messrs. Cook & Son and my fellow-travelers than I was of the animals. I took photographs. It was a twice-welcome relief—to my mind and my body—when at midday we had an elaborate luncheon atop the Great Wall.

Here at Nankow the Mings had built into the more ancient wall a wing gate, loops and loops of walls. And here had been set inns in which the caravans that kept open the trade lines across Asia for centuries had found "accommodation for man and beast." And here in a scene set back centuries amid a cacophony almost unbearable, amid stenches undreamed of, we saw and heard, and smelled, two caravans: one on its way east; one on its way west. The eastward-bound camels were laden with brass samovars and bowls and also with Western woven woolens and a great quantity of cheap ornaments and imitation jewelry—a very brummagem bill of lading. The westward-bound camels were laden with silks and tea, woven cloth and ribbons— tea compressed into dark-brown bricks that looked to me very like plug chewing tobacco. The camels of the caravans were keeping on across the deserts, the steppes, the plains, and the mountains of Asia—a parlous link between East Asia and West Asia, between Marco Polo and St. Mark's, between Peking and St. Petersburg—the competition of the Trans-Siberian Railway notwithstanding. The Middle Ages had not yet surrendered to the twentieth century.

My companions I left in Nankow—all but the questioning and questing Prussian officer. He and I went on to Kalgan, where there were fewer camels in the caravansaries but many more locomotives in the railway yards. I, the American romantic, regretted the decline of the camel; he, the Prussian realist, quite evidently did not share my sentiments.

But the Chinese knew in 1909 that Russia and Japan both looked upon them and their great empire, the great masses of their people, and their great natural resources as fair game. As I sized up the situation in 1909, it seemed to me that Manchuria was the stake in a great game of empire in which the whole world was vitally concerned.

Manchuria was a wheat field about the size of the German Empire, with enough left over for beans and pasture to cover half of France. It was almost twice as large as Texas, and its opportunities for agricultural and mineral development and exploitation were the greatest in Asia. The question of the world's bread supply would become more and more vital as the years went on, and two or three generations hence Manchuria would be called upon to help feed the world. Under what flag it would come into its own was the question.

Manchuria was a part of the Chinese Empire, bearing a relation to China proper about such as the territory of Alaska bore to the states of the Union. China's sovereignty in Manchuria was admitted by the nations of the world, was confirmed by solemn treaties with interested powers, and was indicated by coloring on the maps. As a matter of fact, about two-thirds of Manchuria was ruled by the Russians and the other one-third by the Japanese. In questions affecting the more important functions of government and development the Chinese had no voice whatever. They even depended upon the friendships of foreign powers, such as the United States, to get a hearing for their grievances. Mere administrative functions were left to the Chinese, unless there was some particular reason for Japanese or Russian interference.

The principals in the struggle for the control of this rich territory were China, Japan, and Russia; but indirectly Great Britain, Germany, France, and the United States were involved. The development of this enormous tract of practically virgin land would mean the establishment of a large trade. The European industrial nations were in direct connection with Manchuria by railroad, and the United States was interested as a Pacific power. If China's rights in Manchuria were respected and the "open door" was maintained, all these nations would have equal opportunities for trade development. If Russian rule became paramount, the development would be along Muscovite lines, an outlook not particularly encouraging for commerce. If the Japanese achieved complete victory, all industrial enterprise, all commercial development, and everything worth having would be exploited by the Japanese for the Japanese.

Russia's presence in Manchuria was the result of the ruling passion of Muscovite ambition of centuries—the everlasting and unwearying struggle to gain an ice-free port. The settlement of the Pacific coast of Siberia, the gradual descent upon Chinese territory, the hitching southward of the whole Asiatic Russian boundary line, the activity in Korean affairs, the building of the railroad and the exploitation of resources southward of the Amur—all were a part of what was known as "the Russian advance." The world trembled before the specter, "Adam-zad—the Bear that walks like a Man!" China piteously appealed for help from its stronger friends. Britain fairly wept for the safety of its India; and Kipling dreamed of marching with redcoats or without them, as in his tale, "The Taking of Lungtungpen," into St. Petersburg.

In the meantime Japan was busy getting ready for war. The Japanese had defeated China in 1895 and had obtained a foothold upon the mainland by the cession of the Liaotung Peninsula, including Port Arthur. Under pressure from the Powers, Japan was forced to retrocede the peninsula to China. Then Russia obtained Port Arthur by "lease," and the Bear laved his paws in the warm waters of the Yellow Sea. Japan was struggling for the control of Korea, and Russian corruption and intrigue were met at Seoul by Japanese cunning and deception.

Finally the crash came; Japan attacked Russia without warning. For the information of the world the Japanese government solemnly announced that the purpose of the war was to save Korea and to drive Russia from Manchuria, so that China might have complete control of its own territory. The "open door" in Manchuria was one of the chief causes for which the Japanese said they were fighting.

The war resulted in the annihilation of the Russian navy and in Japanese victory on land. The Battle of Mukden was the greatest battle of historic times, measured by the number of men engaged and the extent of territory actually in the battle zone. The land war had been fought altogether in Manchuria, in the Chinese territory which Russia had been occupying and which the Japanese contended must be restored to its rightful owners.

The evacuation of Manchuria by both Russian and Japanese troops was technically accomplished after two years' delay, but as a matter of fact the soldiers of both empires remained on Chinese soil in the guise of "railway guards." The Chinese authorities resumed administration of petty affairs, but they had no voice in general policies in the higher functions of government. Japan, by treaty, engaged not to obstruct China's plans for the development of the country, yet the Japanese would not permit the Chinese to build railways in their own territory. The Japanese promised not to use their railroad for strategic purposes, and, if the word be confined strictly to its military sense, they perhaps kept faith. But it was notorious that they used the control of the railway to tighten their grasp upon the native residents and the Chinese authorities, to further Japanese business schemes to the exclusion of the trade of other nations, and, in short, to keep shut the fabled and mythical "open door."

Long-suffering China found the Treaty of Portsmouth, signed in the state of New Hampshire under the aegis of the President of the United States, to mean almost anything except what it said, so far as Manchuria was concerned, and was forced to negotiate directly with Japan and Russia. With the Russians the Chinese were fairly sucessful. They had the aid and advice of the Washington government, and St. Petersburg then was inclined to be liberal and fair, permitting the Russian claims to be limited to the actual business requirements of the Russian railroad, to which no one objected.

Japan, on the other hand, was more grasping than ever Russia had been. The practical triumph of the Japanese was as certain as death and taxes, for China could not resist the military power of Japan when no other nation could afford to espouse its quarrel, and Japan curtly declined to submit the issues to arbitration. The Russian advance, so I said then, had been checked but not stopped. The Japanese advance was now on the march. Another seemed inevitable.

As I prepared to leave Peking, I was thrilled with a great and stirring new ambition. I desired above everything then to come back to China as soon as I could, to establish myself there as a correspondent in order to witness what it then seemed to me to be sure would be the next great act in the drama of a developing world. But more of that later.

Actually I left Peking in good company. Our minister, Mr. W. W. Rockhill was leaving. I was fortunate enough to get passage on the ship that was to take him from Tientsin to Nagasaki in Japan. I had had one interview with him at the legation. He was then, it seemed to me, somewhat distrait. He evidently had not anticipated his recall. He didn't like it. But, of course, he was far too good a diplomat to say anything of that to a wandering journalist such as I.

But on that little ship I found a way to get better acquainted with him. He usually sat on deck all alone, telling his beads. They were amber beads, the beads that he had brought back from a lamasery in Tibet. Why he was forever fingering these beads no one quite knew. A few persons thought that he was actually saying his prayers in the fashion of the Northern Vehicle of Buddhism in a manner that would have been considered orthodox in Lhasa. Others, including some of the younger persons on the legation staff and my friend Gale, thought that he told his beads in order to have something to do with his fingers so as to cut down on his cigarette-smoking. I do not know.

My approach to him on shipboard was to take advantage of the little formal conversation I had had with him at the legation and then to tell him that as a young boy I had followed him through the pages of the *Century* in his explorations of Mongolia and Tibet. Perhaps because he was bored, perhaps because he recognized the fact that I would be so persistent that it would be useless to discourage me, he asked me to sit beside him. That began a series of long lectures. I was an eager listener. Mr. Rockhill had things to say that had been pent up for months, perhaps for years, by the discretion imposed upon him as a diplomatist. Once again he was the explorer, and I had the delightful experience of hearing from his own lips, repeated again and again, many of the tales of adventure which he had in part written years and years before and which I had read in my youth.

However, he did not confine all his conversation, once barriers were down, to his ancient explorations. The things I wrote about China were written mostly after I got to Japan, and, mistaken as I may have been, wrong as events have proved me, I can comfort myself that my opinions then formed and my views then set down in writing were confirmed by my conversation with one of the greatest authorities on eastern Asia, whose whole career had been devoted to an effort to master the mystery of China, Mongolia, Tibet, and Manchuria.

I joined Tom Wallace in Tokyo. He was busy writing his experiences in Korea. I was similarly occupied with my Chinese notes. We postponed what little we would have to write about Japan until we embarked for San Francisco.

I am sure that I, at any rate, never dreamed that, when I got on the ship in Yokohama harbor to sail for home, never again was I to set foot in the Orient. And I am equally sure that ever since, in one way or another, I have profited by the things I saw, the things I heard, the things I learned, and have been penalized by the things I failed to learn in my oriental odyssey.

Actually my dream of going back to China was twice within a hair's breadth of realization. After my return to Washington the articles that I had written, albeit signed by the syndicate name of Frederic J. Haskin, were at once attributed to me; and, because they seemed to be so definitely pro-Chinese, I was given a great luncheon by the Chinese minister in Washington at which the then secretary of that legation, Dr. W. W. Yen, made much of what I had written. Through Dr. Yen I became acquainted with Charles R. Crane of Chicago, an industrialist of great wealth who had a very great interest in all Asiatic problems. In 1911 President Taft appointed Mr. Crane to be our minister to China. Mr. Crane thereupon asked me if I would go to Peking, not as an official attaché of the embassy, but as a personal aide to him to be paid out of his own purse and to serve as what nowadays would be called a public relations adviser and ghost writer. I agreed. The arrangement was to become effective shortly after he would get to Peking. Unfortunately for me, if not for Mr. Crane, the new minister to China on his way out to Seattle to take ship for his post made a speech. That speech was entirely too pro-Chinese, too anti-Japanese, to meet what then was considered the requirement of discretion in a diplomatic officer. President Taft recalled Mr. Crane before he took ship. That was the end of my near-diplomatic career, but not the last for Mr. Crane. In 1920 President Wilson sent him to China as the United States minister. The Senate declined to confirm him, so that, when Mr. Harding came to the White House, he, too, was done. Mr. Crane, however, kept up his interest in Russia, China, and Czechoslovakia, and his educational benefactions exercised a powerful influence on later phases of the Asiatic awakening.

Later, in 1911, Thomas Fairfax Millard, whom I had known so well in Japan, came back from the East to make arrangements for the establishment in Shanghai of an English-language–American-owned daily newspaper—the *China Press*. I engaged to go with him as managing editor. I helped him get his incorporation papers in Delaware and helped him buy presses and typesetting machines, and I was all ready to move to Shanghai and there to make my home. But my mother was ill; my wife's mother was ill. Our families pleaded with us not to go, and the familial difficulties so greatly multiplied that my wife and I finally yielded, and I sent my resignation to Millard in Shanghai by cable. His reply showed that he was somewhat upset. He did not wish to delay the beginning of publication, so that, in lieu of my coming, he demanded that I find and engage the services of a young man who in my opinion would make a top-flight managing editor. I made the deal with a friend of mine, Phillip H. Patchin, whom I knew very well as a correspondent for the *New York Sun* in Washington. The *China Press* expired in 1917, to be continued in a weekly edition called *Millard's Review* for some years thereafter. Mr. Patchin, so he told me later, had a great deal of fun establishing the *China Press*. However, that incident ended his journalistic career. He went into diplomacy and after a successful career in that field switched to business and found excellent connections in China, and, when he retired in the 1940's, he had been for some years the president of the Standard Oil Company of California.

These two near-misses determined for me that never was I to have my name enrolled in the great list of Americans known as "Old China Hands."

CHAPTER XXX

A HONEYMOON IN ENGLAND

Late in July I saw the Golden Gate and home again. So industriously had Wallace and I applied ourselves to our typewriter during the long voyage on the Pacific Mail Company's "SS Mongolia" that, once in San Francisco, we mailed our copy to Haskin, and I awarded myself the luxury of a vacation, bade Tom Wallace "goodbye," and turned my thoughts to other things—other things of much greater importance and much greater personal significance to me than the awakening of Asia.

On the way East I stopped in Springfield, Missouri, for a week's visit with my mother and brothers, a week in which the terrific Ozark heat of the early days of August was assuaged by finding myself again in the bosom of my own family and in the familiar atmosphere of my native Missouri. Mother accompanied me on a visit to Buffalo, where she had spent so much of her young married life and where Walter and I were born. That was fated to be perhaps not her last visit to Buffalo but the last when I was with her. It meant much to me. Not only did I regale the friends of my childhood with tall tales of my travels but, with Mother's freely voiced blessing, I told my old friends— girls and boys alike—of my engagement and my approaching marriage. It was a happy announcement for me to make, the more especially because my mother was almost as happy about it as I was.

Thence to Nashville—the Nashville which still seemed a second home to me. Seeing the *Banner* city room was the equivalent, I suspect, of an old grad's visit to the campus of his alma mater. Here was my mentor, my great teacher, Marmaduke B. Morton, still the active managing editor on the newspaper on which I had started out as a cub. And here, instead of interviewing, I was interviewed. Instead of writing about other people, I was written about. The chalk-plate artist did a little cartoon of me, and I was permitted to talk in type about my adventures in what then was an unfamiliar Far East.

I write this in the mid-twentieth century. It is almost impossible for one to recapture the sense of far-distant places that was the common experience of nearly all Americans when they thought of Asia in the days when instant communication by radio was undreamed of, long before the airplane had shrunk the world so that India and China would be only half as far as was San Francisco then from Washington. In retrospect, it is almost as though the traveler's tales were accorded an importance and perhaps even a credulity that was much nearer to the experience of the European awakening from the Dark Ages when communication was largely intrusted to the troubadours, the palmers, and the jongleurs—a reliance reflected in the literature that even down until the nineteenth century set so much store on the word-of-mouth accounts of the elect few who had been to far places and had seen strange things.

Then eagerly I went on to Monteagle, Tennessee, a mountain resort where the Sims family had had a cottage for many years and where they were accustomed to spend their summers, there, of course, to see my affianced bride. And there to feel at home, really at home, in a new and enthralling sense; there to be received by her father and mother, by her brothers and sisters, and by her maternal grandmother as one of the family. There again I experienced to a fuller degree than I theretofore had known that close communion which had brought us together in the first place and which, as I write this, has been sustained with ever closer correspondence for over five-and-forty years.

Bess was a beautiful girl. Her blue eyes in lively fashion reflected her interest in all things. Her delicately beautiful hands were indicative of her sensibility to the finer things of life and her high aspirations for what it would bring not only to her and to me but to everybody. She had been but twelve years old when her father was elected to Congress in 1896. The next year the family moved to Washington. They lived at first in a hotel very near the Capitol. Bess went to a public school only a few blocks away. The moment school was out, Bess made a beeline for the gallery of either the House or the Senate. Her interest in politics and public affairs had been enkindled when her father was a successful candidate for presidential elector in the interest of Grover Cleveland and the Democratic party in the campaign of 1892. Tennessee is one of the few states in the Union where it has always been the custom for candidates for presidential elector to canvass the state, make speeches, and take a lead in active politics. Bess was only eight at that time when her father began his first political tour of the state, and she associated herself with him, his fortunes, and, to a very large extent, his party opinions.

When I first met her in Washington in the spring of 1904, there was an instant rapport based on our common interest in politics and public affairs; an instant kinship of the spirit that we set down at first to our distant blood kinship; a common interest that, as it ripened into enduring love, was the most fortunate circumstance of my life.

Here two travelers matched their tales. Bess and her sister Tom had spent the summer in Europe. Bess had seen in Europe the great monuments, the cathedrals, the public buildings, and the museums that represented European history and culture as it had unfolded itself down to the beginning of the twentieth century, but at the same time her curiosity had not been satiated by these monuments of the past. She had kept her eyes open, had read the newspapers avidly, and had informed herself with respect to political and social conditions as she could see them in England, France, Switzerland, and Italy. I had had the same experience in the Near and the Far East. We determined that, if it were at all possible, we would travel together and see with each other more and more of the world.

And then, for me, it was back to Washington and back to work.

As September, 1909, came along, it meant many things to me, but a great many of them must be reserved to a later chapter. If I now desert the chronological order and the sequential arrangement for the topical and the consequential, it is because I am taking first things first.

The first thing to me, of course, was my approaching marriage. Mr. Haskin had known, I am quite sure, of my engagement, but not until I got back to Washington did he know anything about when the wedding would take place. Haskin was all for us. There was immediately not only a reward for past performances but, as he put it, an earnest for the future in the form of a small increase in salary. The late summer wore on. The autumn came. The Sims family came back to Washington, and I was to be found every late afternoon, and every

[524]

evening at dinner, with my soon-to-be new family at 1410 Massachusetts Avenue.

There I was enveloped in an atmosphere of love and acceptance. There I was to find a great many things that I liked: talk about politics; talk about old times in Tennessee; talk about history not only of the immediate past but of ancient times; talk about the emerging problems of the country; and now, enlarged by both Bess's and my travels, speculations of the future for the world. Furthermore, there was something else that I liked very much. It was the cuisine. Bess's grandmother, Mrs. Kittrell, was an inspired cook. Her daughter, Mrs. Sims, had a way with a recipe. Bess failed to share that ancestral trait, although she did appreciate the results of the skills. I had been brought up in my own family tradition. My mother lacked interest in cooking, my father being a good cook. There were no girls in our family, and so I had come to believe that only men really could cook unless it were an occasionally specially gifted woman or naturally endowed servant. Here in this household then was Alice, a Negro cook who was the complete mistress of the secret art of making perfect hot biscuits—an art in which she excelled whether that particular item of southern cooking was of the buttermilk-and-soda variety or the more simply constructed and easily turned-out baking-powder kind.

Bess had a younger brother and two younger sisters. So completely was I accepted in the family that I suspect the younger children thought of me in my original capacity as a cousin rather than as a future brother-in-law. At any rate, one afternoon I took the three younger ones, Paul, Marie, and Enid, to a vaudeville performance at Chase's Theater on Pennsylvania Avenue. We sat in the front row of the balcony for a Saturday-afternoon matinee. I was then on the verge of thirty, and I suppose it must have been a little bit unusual to see one of my years coming in with three young children. At any rate, an elderly lady who sat behind us in the intermission leaned over and said to me, "Are these your children?"

"Naw," Paul almost shouted, "he's only a cousin."

Then Mr. Haskin took a hand. There was a crisis in Europe. There was a deepening of the chasm betwixt Britain and Germany. There was an armament race. There was the threat of war. And on top of that there was a political crisis in the United Kingdom which was sure to result in a general election.

Mr. Haskin, participating at second or third hand in our plans for our wedding, determined to have his say in setting the date. He also decided what he would give us as a wedding present. He told me that he wanted me to go to England and Germany and write a series of articles about the impending crisis. His wedding present to us, he said, would be to pay all the expenses for my wife on the trip, in addition to my small salary increase. It was not hard to agree to this arrangement, since both Bess and I wanted to see more of the world. It was not hard, in view of the new obligations, to accept even the tiniest increase in salary. It was a generous gesture, and I trust it was accepted with good grace. At any rate, Mr. Haskin participating, the date for the wedding was set for December 22, 1909. Mr. Haskin had engaged passage for us on the Cunarder "Lusitania" due to sail from New York on December 29.

It was to be a home wedding. It was to be an evening wedding. It was to conform in a modest way to the mode of the time. There was to be a minimum of ceremonial entertainment, but all the family connections and our journalistic and political friends were to be invited.

Of course, Bess with her mother and two older sisters had a great deal to say with respect to the trousseau. I was not unmindful of my obligations in that regard. We were to go to Europe in the dead of winter. My brother Walter, who was in the women's wear business in the days when it was quite important for impecunious younger persons to "get it wholesale" if they could, helped us out. Through his skilful introductions Bess got a fur coat, and I got a fur-lined coat. Bess got a velvet hood. I outfitted myself as best I could in a local haberdashery. My outfit, of course, was built around the white tie and tails necessary at the wedding itself, the frock coat and striped trouser uniform necessary for my journalistic and diplomatic explorations in Europe, and sundry other comforts which my ocean-going experience had taught me might come in handy.

Bess, perforce, chose white satin for her wedding dress. But, her taste, being better than that of either her sisters or her mother, triumphed in her selection of the other articles for her trousseau. Blue, copenhagen blue or delft blue, for her eyes for afternoon dresses; a severely tailored cloth suit; that peculiar purplish red then universally known as "American Beauty" for an evening dress; fur-lined carriage boots for cold evening rides in the horse-drawn carriages that must needs take her to evening parties; and so on.

My interest in women's clothes matched hers in men's clothes. I discovered then, even before we were married, that ever thereafter it would be more convenient if I were to let her select my clothes, my hats, my neckties, and my accessories. At the same time, partly because of my brother's influence, I was able to persuade her that thenceforth it would be better if I were at least to be consulted with respect to her clothes—in fact, it wasn't long after we were married that many times she left to my sole selection what she was to wear.

So, politically and sartorially, we were well matched. As the wedding day approached, I got "nervouser and nervouser," and so did she. I was thirty. She was twenty-five. Each of us was older than our age in respect to history and politics. Each of us was younger in respect to what is ordinarily known as "society." Each of us was completely and comfortably sure of the other, but each of us shared that trepidation which so many young persons experience when the time approaches for what in those days we used to call the ceremony of "jumping over the broomstick." But both of us were happy.

Came December, and on December 1 my fiancée's birthday, and, as December went on, more and more of the preparations not only for the wedding but for the honeymoon voyage across the ocean and the honeymoon to be spent in that Europe for which I had so eagerly yearned and which my bride-to-be had so recently experienced.

It is, I assume, not unusual at the time of critical events in one's life to have etched indelibly upon one's memory things tangential, not central—events adventitious, not necessarily of consequence. So it is of my marriage. Four days before the wedding day, into my office in the Haskin Syndicate walked a very tall, handsome young woman. She brought me a letter of introduction from Charles T. Wilder, the editor and publisher of the *Colorado Springs Gazette*. Attached to it was a note from Mrs. Wilder, the former Maude Mitchell, one of the summer visitors to Buffalo with whom I had kept up a desultory correspondence over the years. Mr. Wilder was a Republican, as was his wife, Maude. Both Mr. and Mrs. Wilder were editorial writers. So was Miss Hazlitt. Miss Hazlitt was a descendant, whether direct or collateral, I do not now remember, of William Hazlitt, the great British essayist. She had been in Colorado Springs for several years, having gone there from her native England in search of a cure for tuberculosis. In England she had been secretary-stenographer to Mr. Joseph Chamberlain, at the time that that once great Birmingham Liberal had joined forces with some of his once-hated Tory rivals in opposition to the Liberal leader and prime minister, Mr. Gladstone, and his support of home rule for Ireland. Mr. Chamberlain, who in his native Birmingham had been once regarded as a dangerous socialist because of his establishment of municipal milk depots for undernourished children, had, after his severance with Mr. Gladstone, become the protagonist of a revival of a protective-tariff system for England. That revival was known in England as "tariff reform," the very appellation in the United States that Mr. Tilden, Mr. Cleveland, and Mr. Bryan had given to their advocacy of lower tariffs, freer trade, and opposition to protectionism. Miss Hazlitt had been the redactor of many of Mr. Chamberlain's tariff speeches. She was an ardent protectionist. During her convalescence in Colorado Springs she had found a kindred soul in Charlie Wilder, an arch-Republican of the pre-McKinley, pre-Canadian reciprocity, strictest school of high-protective-tariff advocates. She had got a job with him as a stenographer-secretary. She had remained to write editorials.

Miss Hazlitt had not theretofore been in Washington. She was on her way to England to visit her mother and sisters. Charlie and Maude had given her letters to me. The *Colorado Springs Gazette* was a patron of the Haskin Syndicate. I was supposed to show her around. I was to be married four days hence.

I took all this in my stride. I did show her around the town. I introduced her to my bride-to-be. I was captivated by her personal charm, although neither Bess nor I hesitated to oppose her political views. I took her to the Capitol, to the Library of Congress, and to the Supreme Court and generally showed her the sights. Of course, under the circumstances, Bess and I made an engagement to see her in London. It was arranged that, as soon as we were settled, we would let her know where we were and arrange a meeting. That was one tangential circumstance.

The other that stands out so sharply in my memory and, so I have been assured many and many a time, also in my wife's memory, albeit

[528]

we recall it in an entirely different connection, happened just at the very time of the marriage ceremony itself. So far as I had known up to that time nobody by the name of Brownlow had ever been tongue-tied. Nearly all the Brownlows I had known had suffered a common curse. Some fairy godmother had endowed each of us with a memory of the type that it was then common to label "photographic." It was the curse of total recall. At the same time another fairy godmother had touched each baby Brownlow's tongue with the wand that induced the magic of loquacity. All Brownlows could remember everything. All Brownlows could recall every tiny detail, and no Brownlow had been lacking in willingness to retell to every listener all that he could remember or recall.

The house at 1410 Massachusetts Avenue had on its first floor a great drawing-room, a wide and spacious central hall, and beyond it a large dining-room, all three of which could on occasion be thrown together. This expanse of parquet floors and rugs was dominated from above by a descending stairway in two flights, a white stairway, a wide stairway; a stairway on the occasion of a bridal procession of frightening dimensions. Just behind this stairway on the second floor was a large room devoted to desks and books—the library.

In attendance was an elderly cousin of mine, Colonel John Bell Brownlow, a son of "Parson" William Gannaway Brownlow. John Bell Brownlow was a colonel in the Union army, a representative of the Whig and Republican wing of the Brownlow family, just as I was in my youth a representative of its Democratic branch. He liked to tell stories. So did I. He liked to hear stories. So did I.

Everything was in readiness. I was attempting to collect myself from my nervousness. Colonel Brownlow, with kindly intent, perhaps with the compulsion of the unsuppressed anecdote, began to tell a story. The hour struck. The wedding march began. The bride was poised to begin her slow descent of the stairway. All eyes looked up toward her. She, for all her apparent calmness, was just as nervous as was I. But where was the bridegroom? He did not appear. Messengers were sent.

It was, Brownlow-like, utterly impossible for the bridegroom, a Brownlow, to leave a storyteller, a Brownlow, until he had finished the anecdote! Thus it was that I was a full minute late at my own wedding!

Mr. Haskin was a managerial person. He was an arranger of his own business as well as an arranger of all the affairs of everybody else within the compass of his influence. He had taken a bridal suite for us at the Belvedere Hotel in Baltimore. Two days later he had a similar suite for us at the Hotel Astor in New York. He had engaged our passage on the "Lusitania." He had endeavored and, I am sure except for my utter rebellion, would have succeeded in arranging for us a hotel accommodation in London. There I drew the line. Bess and I both were determined that, once we got across the ocean, except for my obligation to get my work done, we would be free and on our own.

There was a goodly company present on that December night when at eight o'clock Elizabeth Virginia Sims became Mrs. Louis Brownlow. There were representatives of congressional and journalistic families. It was a gay party and, of course, the customary shower of rice, but there was none of the boisterousness of the charivari. My brother-in-law, William L. Beale, husband of Bess's elder sister, Edna, accompanied us in a horse-drawn carriage to the Union Station. In the Sims household, according to the custom of the times then prevailing, there had been no liquid refreshments that contained what then were described in legal documents as "spiritous, malt, or vinous" liquors. Mr. Beale, getting us to the Union Station some little time ahead of the departure of our train, took us into the restaurant and there gave us what he thought was the necessary accolade for a successful married life—we shared a bottle of sparkling Burgundy.

In New York we were put up at the Hotel Astor, then relatively new—I myself had been present when the place was opened in 1904, five years earlier—one of the most fashionable hostelries in the great city. It was long before the days when the hotel owners found that the most profitable use to which the ground floor could be devoted was for shops and stores. The dining-room windows looked out over Longacre Square, not yet to be rebaptized as Times Square. We had not kept our honeymoon plans a secret. I had invited to lunch my very close friend and associate from Louisville days, Mr. Clarence Axman. He joined us with the announcement that he had three tickets to a matinee, and we walked a few blocks down the street to the theater, where we saw an uproarious farce in which a not-too-slender young female comedian was making her first hit. She was Marie Dressler. As we walked to the theater, the snow began to fall. As we came back after the matinee, the snow was already deep on the sidewalks, and not only Bess's ankles but mine were wet and cold. When later we came down to dinner, everywhere we heard from elevator boys, from waiters, and from an occasional conversation not intended for us, about the storm that was raging outside.

At that time, so far as our knowledge extended, one of the smartest dining-rooms in New York, ranking with the Waldorf and Martin's or Delmonico's, was the Orangerie in the Astor. The Messrs. Muschenheim, the hosts of the Astor, had smothered our quarters in American Beauty roses. That was Bess's color. She donned her American Beauty crepe evening dress. I, for the gala occasion which I deemed to be not too formal, put on a tuxedo and black tie. We had thought to dine at the fashionable hour of eight. Although we had heard the tales of the raging storm, we were quite unprepared for the welcome we got from the maître d'hôtel, the headwaiter, the captains, and a regiment of waiters. The room was all but deserted. We were shown a table with such attention that I am sure both Bess and I felt that we were again the victims of one of Mr. Haskin's publicity stunts. There had been entirely too much advertisement of the bride and groom, too much advance notice all down the line in all echelons of the servitors of the advent of our honeymoon. But, seated at the table, we looked around. We found only a few other tables occupied. But at one quite near us were seated a man and his wife and two teen-age children.

The maître d'hôtel, flanked by the headwaiter and two captains, came to our table. They gave us little or no chance to confer and barely gave us any opportunity to make decisions. The dinner was ordered for us with only a minimal obeisance to our desires. They served us sherry, bluepoints, a turtle soup, a filet of sole with white wine, and then, marvel of marvels, came a pressed duck à la flambeau. The wine poured was Burgundy. The maître d'hôtel, flanked by his colonels, captains, and lieutenants, exhibited the duck, put it in its execution chamber, garroted it, decanted the juices into a chafing dish, and poured into it libations from a dozen bottles of brandies and liqueurs. Then he touched off the flame, and the flame leaped to the ceiling. It overwhelmed both Bess and me, but we did not fail to catch, out of the corner of our eyes, the open-mouthed wonder and astonishment of the teen-aged boy and girl at the next table. Never did bride and groom on a honeymoon get such attention. And never did a couple on their honeymoon, dressed to go to the smart spot of the great city, encounter such a bleak white desert of snowy tablecloths. At the very last, when we were all but surfeited and were being redeemed by a crème de menthe frappé, a very hurried, a very blustery, an almost incoherent individual burst into the room. It was my brother Walter. His plans had suddenly brought him to New York. He knew we would be at the Astor. It had taken him the better part of two hours to get from the Pennsylvania Station to the Astor. It was that sort of blizzard.

The next morning at breakfast with Walter, in the main dining-room looking out over Longacre Square, not a vehicle was in sight. Nothing moved. New York was snowbound, snowbound by a storm second in recorded history only to that of 1888 and not again, at least for forty-five years thereafter, to be equaled.

Snowbound with my brother for company, with the attention of everybody in the hotel from the Messrs. Muschenheim, the proprietors, down to the lowliest page, we were happy in our familial isolation and worried by but one thing: Would we be able to get to our ship on the twenty-ninth, and would the ship be able to sail? Actually, we need not have worried. We did get to the ship. We found our stateroom and in it a bottle of Manhattans and a bottle of Martinis for me and a sheaf of a dozen of the longest-stemmed American Beauty roses we ever had seen for Bess.

That night, being the first night out, we did not dress. The next night we did. And on the night of the thirty-first of December, I made the first grave error of my married life. I declined to sit up for the festivities that at the stroke of midnight would usher in 1910. I have never been completely forgiven!

II

The storm that had paralyzed New York made rough going of the Atlantic, and days later, when the then mistress of the seas put us off at one o'clock in the morning on a lighter at Fishguard in Wales, it was dark and stormy, a not-at-all-cordial welcome to the British Isles, Fortunately we shared another thing in common. Bess had never been

seasick. Neither had I. We were both good sailors, and even that bob-
bing lighter, which rose and fell seemingly forty to fifty feet and made
nearly every other debarking passenger turn green under the flaring
lights, left us cool and calm. Then came the long train trip into
London, the arrival at five o'clock in the morning, the taking of
quarters in the railway-station hotel at Paddington, and, without too
much sleep, the next morning what was then esteemed to be an
ordinary railroad-hotel breakfast: porridge and kipper and bacon and
eggs, bread and rolls and marmalade, and then at the end, instead
of the beginning, fruit. And all of that, merely because we were recognized as Americans, washed down by a pale-brown, tasteless brew
which the waiter with elaborate ceremony and perfect manners told
us was coffee.

On board ship we had looked into some copies of the *Times* of
London. We had decided we would not go into any sort of hotel
in London where we would run into Americans. We would go
British and live English. We selected, on the basis of the charm of its
advertising, a residential hotel in Lancaster Gate. From Paddington
Hotel that morning, after a considerable ceremony and the help of a
hall porter, we had managed to telephone and engage a room in that
hotel. We set out with all of our equipage to that goal in a "growler,"
a closed two-seated carriage of the kind then known in the United
States as a coupé, with a railing on top which accommodated our
bags and gear. As we turned a corner, we saw an advertisement of
an estate agent. His name was Sims. His address was on Brownlow
Street. It seemed to us, both now Brownlows and she so lately Sims,
and myself the grandson of a Sims, that, so far as our patronymics
were concerned, in coming to England we had indeed come home.

Then came the rift in the lute. The English residential hotel was
truly English. Our Anglophilism, our sentimental attachment to our
ancestral country, had wrought in both of us an affection for the
hearths and homes of old England; but, when we found ourselves
put up in that residential hotel in Lancaster Gate, we could only
look at each other in dismay and say, "Home was never like this."
There was a hearth in our room—a hearth which was an apron to a
tiny grate, a grate the fuel supply of which, stored in a very small
scuttle, was what were called, in the plural, "coals." Coals were delivered by a houseboy and charged for at so much per coal. In the

dining-room there was a similar hearth. A few coals were heaped in it, and the fire was lighted just as the meal was served. It seemed to us that some of the other residents—all of them but us were British—got some comfort from looking at that little fire. They could not by any stretch of imagination have derived any heat from it. The weather was cold, damp; the days were dark and dismal. Not all the blankets and the feather comforters on the beds, reinforced by steamer rugs and fur coats, could keep out that penetrating chill.

We were expected to dress for dinner. We were amazed that the English women in their low-necked evening gowns could manage to keep their teeth from chattering. They most palpably did not triumph over goose pimples or sniffles. It was but a day or two until both of us were not only cold but had colds. A doctor was sent for. He most graciously agreed with us that we ought to move. He intimated that Americans were too soft for hardy English life.

Abandoning our experiment of living in England as the English lived, we betook ourselves to St. Ermin's Hotel, a hostelry off Victoria Street in the precincts of Westminster, where Bess and her sister had stayed the summer before and which establishment was graced, or disgraced, according to the point of view, by an adaptation of that American invention called "central heating." It took us three or four days to thaw out.

Ever since the summer before, Bess had had it in her mind to come back to St. Ermin's and smoke a cigarette publicly in the lounge, something that no lady would dare to do in a public place in the United States. This she did. Also she had had in mind the possibility of walking into a "pub" and publicly taking a drink of whiskey and soda, something also impossible in a stand-up barroom in America. This she did.

We found near at hand a stratified bar with one door for the common people, labeled "public"; one for the middle classes, labeled "private"; and one for the gentry, labeled "parlor." The partitions ran all the way to the ceiling, but the inner opening was on one bar, served by one barmaid, and the only differentiation in the service was a difference in price. We took the "parlor" bar. The whiskey and soda was poured. The whiskey, of course, was warm. The soda, of course, was warm. One little taste, one single little taste, and her glass was set down on top of the bar, irrevocably, never to be reclaimed. Cold as was the weather, there was no ice in England.

Knowing the town, my bride took me to see the principal sights, the historical buildings, the monuments of centuries of glory of church and state; and she tried to take me through some miles of art galleries and museums, but I was under compulsion of doing some work, so I must say, without any appreciable resistance on her part, we plunged, as long as we could go together, into the maelstrom of the most spectacular and furious political campaign either of us had ever seen or even imagined.

Two months earlier, in November, the House of Lords had rejected the annual budget which had passed the House of Commons at the instance of the chancellor of the exchequer, Mr. David Lloyd George, with the full backing of the prime minister, Mr. Herbert Henry Asquith, and his principal colleagues in the Liberal government, Mr. John Burns and Mr. Winston Churchill. That rejection led to a dissolution and the call for a general election.

While the Tory opposition disagreed with many features of the Lloyd George budget, the Lords particularly objected to the proposal to tax land values and most particularly to the proposal to levy that tax upon the owners of the land. That was a revolutionary move which the Lords could not tolerate. Here now the campaign was in full swing. There were many issues, many points of conflict, but the fiery Welshman who was chancellor of the exchequer was the leader of the Liberal battle hosts, and he was levying war particularly against the dukes and the other great landlords and was demanding that the power of the House of Lords to take negative action on a money bill passed by the House of Commons be ended.

The outcome was, of course, that in that election the Liberals won a very narrow victory, gaining but two more seats in the Commons than their Conservative opponents, and thus, perforce, had to form a government by coalition with the Irish Nationalists, whose sole concern was home rule for Ireland, and the small Labour party, which then was comprised of thirty or forty members of various schools of thought, some of them trade-unionists, a few of them socialists. That made inevitable another election within a twelve-month. It resulted, in 1910, in another victory for the Liberal-Labour coalition and in the threat of the prime minister to go to the king and demand the creation of a sufficient number of Liberal Lords to insure the adoption of the new law which would limit the House of Lords to a merely suspensive rather than an absolute veto on any legislation approved by the Commons. To this threat the Lords gave in. In other words, the campaign we were witnessing was the curtain-raiser of a grave and profound constitutional change in the polity of the United Kingdom.

I read all the papers. I talked to all sorts and conditions of persons—to cab-drivers, casual persons met in any one of the three divisions of a pub, to members of sidewalk groups who most evidently and loudly were arguing politics. I listened to scores of orators in Hyde Park. I even asked questions of silent fellow-passengers in buses and trams and found them voluble.

I sought out and talked with journalists—some American, a good many British. I tried to see as many politicians as I could, but the leaders were far too busy to pay any attention to a roving American reporter. And, indeed, reporters even on English newspapers but rarely had a chance to talk with the party leaders, for in that day the American journalistic invention, the "interview," had but barely begun to be considered quite cricket in "the right little, tight little Island."

Such crowds as I had never seen before turned out to hear the campaign orators. Bess and I went together to Battersea Park to hear the elderly, radical Liberal leader, John Burns, speak to a crowd of tens and tens of thousands in the open air. But she could not go with me to many of the meetings, or indeed to any of them that were held indoors. The reason for that was that Mrs. Pankhurst and her militant suffragettes were waging their own sort of campaign for votes for women. They were burning the letter boxes on the streets, they were throwing things, and they were cutting up in all sorts of inconvenient ways; and the Liberals and the Conservatives were agreed that they were intolerable nuisances, and therefore both parties excluded women, who of course were voteless, from their meetings.

That is, they tried to. I succeeded in getting inside a great hall in Peckham Rye to hear Lloyd George himself. It was a seething mob not more than half the members of which could get inside. In the middle of his speech, from the beams that arched over the great hall, there fell a rain of leaflets—"Votes for Women!"—and from above an unearthly feminine shrieking. The militant women had got there early, and every one of the beams was inhabited. It almost, but not quite, broke up the show.

The meetings themselves were more unruly than any I had attended —although they were not disorderly in the sense of breaking out into fistfights as I sometimes had witnessed in the United States. The unruliness consisted in what seemed to me to be a certain lack of deference to the authority of the chair, as individuals all over the hall engaged in the favorite English sport of heckling the speaker. It was a game which most certainly would have upset any American campaigner. But the British had played it so long, and from both sides, that the speaker usually was quite ready for his assailants. He had in many instances learned his debating tactics in his university. He had, in any event, experienced years of it in the House of Commons, and he knew that, if his riposte was quick, witty, and clever, he could count on the background of great applause from his own adherents. It was even whispered that some of the better campaigners were not above the sly practice of planting a heckler, ready with a planted question to enable the speaker to induce a burst of spontaneous applause.

During the election campaign I rushed back to Washington a sheaf of articles, bearing in mind that it was then only seven or eight days by post-office accounting from London to Washington and that, once in Washington, it would be seven or eight days before the machinery of the Haskin Syndicate would get the articles into print, so that I timed them to end publication on the day before the British elections began. In those articles, of course, I stressed the immediate problems and surface manifestations of the campaign, its issues, and its personages, and, by the same token, I was extremely careful not to predict its outcome.

Nevertheless, I was interested intensely in what might be the long-range results. These I discussed in a long series of articles which were published in the United States in the summer of 1910. There were sixty of them, thirty under the running title, "The British Crisis," thirty under the caption, "The German Advance." The campaign in England, which was so fast, so furious, so embittered, so fixed on the domestic issues, yet had seemed to me to display an earnest of a national unity at least so far as England, Wales, and Scotland were concerned with respect to all international affairs and especially with respect to the threat of German aggression.

Not even the wisest statesmen of Europe could see any farther than I could see into the future. Not one of them knew, any more than I realized, that an election in 1910 might be but a curtain-raiser for the debacle of 1914. Not any one of us who, calendar-minded, had thought that the nineteenth century had ended at midnight on December 31, 1900, could have the faintest notion that the nineteenth century and all that it meant really would come to its final catastrophe in the crash of August, 1914. Nor could I then have had any concept of what world affairs or world wars or the quest for world peace would mean. All but a minute minority of us naïvely believed in a system based upon nations and nationals that would forever endure.

Even at the time, however, I had a notion that my adventures in England and Germany—the things I saw, the things I heard, the things I seemed to sense in the emotions of the people—all were contributing to my political education, to the development of my own personality. In this thought, which was so deeply shared by my wife, we with our preoccupation with public affairs made the most of what then we could see.

I think the best way I can indicate to a reader of the second half of the twentieth century something of what we then thought is to quote some extracts from what I wrote as the nineteenth century—not calendar-wise but in essence—was coming close to its tragic denouement. The title of my first article of the series on "The British Crises" was "War Abroad or Revolution at Home?" The opening paragraphs read thus:

"The affairs of the British Empire approach a crisis involving the very life of the greatest and most powerful political organization which has ever existed in the history of the world. The rapid increase of the German navy threatens, for the first time since Trafalgar, the universal supremacy of British sea power. The competition of Germany and the United States in industrial production has reached the point where Great Britain no longer can claim a post of absolute pre-eminence in the manufacturing world. Although there is no quarrel between the nations, practically all Englishmen agree that a clash of arms with Germany is inevitable. Belief in the inevitability of war is a most potent cause of war, so testifies History. . . .

"Thirty per cent of the people of England are living in such dire poverty that the spectre of starvation is never out of their sight. The cold, dispassionate statistics published by the government place the percentage of the poverty-stricken at thirty percent: judged by the standards of an American onlooker the figure is all too low. An American family which can afford meat but twice a week and which never had anything for breakfast but butterless bread and tea would be rated as poverty-stricken. In England, a family so provided is often numbered with the seventy per cent of well-to-do.

"This starving people is asked to contribute millions upon millions to the desperate struggle to build Dreadnoughts more rapidly than Germany; is asked to face the immediate probability of a war with the most highly-organized military force in the world, a war in which victory would mean only to hold what they now have, in which defeat would mean the end of the glory of Britain. . . .

"But all Britons are not so pessimistic. The radicals, the socialists, the yellowest of the yellow journals and the more intemperate politicians of the so-called demagogue class unite in declaring that the gravity of the situation has been grossly exaggerated. They point out the fact that the British navy still is more than twice as strong as the German navy, and that there need be no immediate fear, although they admit that the building of Dreadnoughts and super-Dreadnoughts must be pushed forward. The radicals are forced to admit the widespread poverty and suffering, and they declare that means should be found to give work to the unemployed. They are opposed to compulsory military service and are in favor of free and compulsory trade and technical education. They agree with the other faction that the defense of the Empire must be provided at any cost. But they are rude enough and crude enough to ask that the great landowners should assist in paying a tax on land. The landowning class, which is most insistent upon huge expenditures for the Navy and Army, declares that the taxation of their land is confiscation, that its proposers are socialistic enemies of the state, that Britons never will be slaves, and that they must have 'fiscal reform.' "

In retrospect it seems odd to me, as I write this in 1954, that as the result of the failure to achieve a world order at the end of World War I, in the desolation and despond which succeeded that war, and even before the infinitely greater catastrophe of World War II enveloped all the world, not just a part of it, that an American President would assert from his high eminence that in the United States "one-third of the people were ill-fed, ill-clothed, and ill-housed."

Going on in the same article, facing up the dichotomy of the British crisis of "War Abroad or Revolution at Home?" I went on to say:

"The Conservative group, made up of the old line Tories and the modern Protectionists and Unionists, opposes all such reforms and declares that a Protective Tariff will cure all the evils of unemployment and poverty. They propose first of all to protect the British farmer by imposing a tariff duty on wheat, although England does not produce one-fourth of the bread-stuff it consumes. Thus in the next election, as in the one held in January, the question will be whether Land or Bread shall be taxed!

"But it remains a fact that Great Britain today faces a foreign war with a powerful military state and at the same time is concerned with practical social revolution at home. Not in this generation in any country has any Parliament deserved as much attention as that now sitting in Westminister."

Even then, although I scarcely had heard and certainly did not understand the terminology, I was not a determinist. Certainly I did not subscribe to the fatalistic doctrines of the economic determinists. I believed in men. I believed that man was the captain of his fate, and therefore I believed that men in their struggles between differentiated ideas were influenced by their leaders.

I was far from being a subscriber to Mr. Thomas Carlyle's theory of the hero, but, because of my very indoctrination in the events of the American Revolution, I did believe in statecraft, in political leadership, and in the effective representation of the democratic will in the voice and word of chosen leaders. Thus it was quite natural, I suppose, that, while I wrote a great deal about the clashing currents and opposing forces—economic, social, and political—I was compelled to epitomize the parties and factions in the personalities of their leaders. After forty-five years it still seems to me that the impression that these British statesmen made on me then, as I then interpreted them, has had a profound effect upon all my later life and thought.

Here are a few of the things I wrote then concerning the leaders of the Liberal party:

"Herbert Henry Asquith, Prime Minister and head of the Government of Great Britain since April, 1908, is the first middle-class, Non-Conformist, democratic Premier England has ever had. His predecessor, Campbell-Bannerman, was democratic, but his wealth and his landed estates caused him to be classed with 'the gentry.' Balfour and Salisbury were of Cecil blood, 'born with the governing instinct.' Rosebery was and is an aristocrat to the tips of his fingers, and he now appears to repent in sack-cloth and ashes the fact that once he was the leader of the democratic hosts. Gladstone, a radical democrat by conviction was yet an aristocrat in instinct and feeling. It never can be forgotten that he first entered Parliament as a Tory, the beneficiary of a corrupt nomination, and a corrupt election, under the patronage of a notoriously corrupt duke. Gladstone was like Jefferson in that the volcanic fires of his political and philosophical democracy were hot enough to set a nation ablaze but not fierce enough to destroy his personal aristocracy. And like Jefferson, Gladstone thereby earned from his enemies the dishonoring epithet 'demagogue.'

"Mr. Asquith came to his present position of supreme power from a youth of poverty. He sprang from a humble middle-class family engaged in the clothing trade, he had no money, he got his education by winning scholarships, and he made his way to prominence by hard work at the law. British prejudice against lawyers in high political place is marked, and Mr. Asquith is the first lawyer to be Prime Minister since the days of the ill-fated Spencer Perceval who held office from 1809 to 1812. Throughout his entire career Mr. Asquith has enjoyed no adventitious aids. He has risen by sheer force of his own will. He has none of the arts of the intriguing politician, Disraeli, and none of the oratorical magic of Gladstone; he has not the wit of a Rosebery, nor the icy logic of a Balfour; he never can hope to have the cavalry dash of his supporter, Churchill, nor the fiery tongue of the tempestuous Lloyd George.

"The Asquith mind is a legal mind. It deals with conditions, not theories. An Asquith policy is a case to be won in court, not a cause to be died for in battle. A democrat always, he is adamant to resist the passionate clamor of the people unless they show that they have reason as well as right, conviction as well as prejudice, upon their side. He has the hard common sense of a Grover Cleveland and the clarity of expression of a Benjamin Harrison, without Cleveland's egotism and lacking Harrison's eloquence.

"While Asquith is the leader and captain of the organized forces of the Liberal party, it cannot be said that he is the moving spirit in the present swift progress of political thought. It is Lloyd George who is leading the actual battles of democracy in Great Britain. Asquith never could have invented the radically progressive schemes proposed by his Welsh chancellor and Winston Churchill. His is not the offensive generalship of his party. But he is powerful and wise in defense, and therefore he remains the actual as well as the titular leader of Liberalism because he is recognized throughout the kingdom as the chief champion of the doctrine of Free Trade. After all, Free Trade is the citadel of the Liberal polity, and if that fortress should fall, the cause of social reform would be left hopeless for many years to come. . . .

"Arthur James Balfour, leader of the Opposition in Parliament, captain of the Conservative party, and the political head of the Cecil family, is the incarnation of all that one has been taught to believe goes to make up an English gentleman. As a matter of fact, he is not English at all, but Scotch. . . . It has been said that his birthplace, with its historic and aristocratic traditions has had much to do with shaping the intellectual personality of the great Tory statesman.

"Mr. Balfour is a strange combination of a strong man of action, positive and determined; and a dreaming philosopher, never quite sure of anything. These traits may have come to him when he breathed in the Scottish mists burdened with tales of romance and strength, stories of mysticism and fanaticism.

"But if he owes his mental makeup to his Scottish birthright, it is certain that he owes his political prominence to the fact that his mother was a Cecil, a daughter of the second Marquis of Salisbury. Mr. Balfour's mother, before her son was out of kilts, began to train him for the public service in that practical fashion practiced only by British women of the 'ruling classes.' From the time he could talk he was made to take an interest in agriculture, and his duties and responsibilities as a landlord never were forgotten. . . .

"Mr. Balfour is a Celt. He never has been anything but a Scotchman, and Scotchman will he be to the end, but his Celtic blood tells most in his love for controversial theology and a good game of golf. When

[542]

it comes to politics he is an Englishman and a Cecil, and he believes, as did his uncle, that it is the peculiar business of the Cecil family to regulate the affairs of the British Empire."

After all, it was not Mr. Asquith, the prime minister; it was not Mr. Balfour, the leader of the opposition; it was the Welshman, David Lloyd George, the chancellor of the exchequer, who had brought the simmering pot of English domestic conflict to a boil. Of him, I then wrote:

"Unlike Jefferson, unlike Gladstone, Lloyd George is like Lincoln in that he is a democrat through and through. . . . Like Lincoln he is abhorred of the classes and adored of the masses. There has been nothing like him in all the history of British politics. He is the head and front of the revolution in Britain, and as such he is the most hated and the most loved man in all the realm.

"That such a man holds the high office of Chancellor of the Exchequer, that such a man is the real leader of the party in power in Great Britain, that such a man seems destined to rule over the British Empire as the Prime Minister of the Crown, that such a man has power to sway a British Cabinet and command a British Parliament, is, in the estimation of the ruling classes who have governed England for a thousand years, an outrage and a desecration.

"That such a man has been able to reach this high position and to wield this great power, is, to the struggling and starving masses of average men and plain people, the promise of the dawning of a new and a better day—a day in which the man who works shall be equal before the law and in political power with the man who shirks."

After that youthful and no doubt naïve description of Mr. Lloyd George, I plunged in another article into a further discussion of that gentleman under the title, "Democrat or Demagogue?"

"The question is, then, is Lloyd George a democrat, as his idolizing followers do affirm, or is he a demagogue, as his abominating enemies do swear? Englishmen of the one class admire Asquith, chuckle over Churchill and love Lloyd George; while those of the other class deplore Asquith, despise Churchill and hate Lloyd George with a fanatic and zealous hatred. The late Duke of Rutland once burst into song, giving utterance to that remarkable couplet—

" 'Let wealth and commerce, laws and learning die,
But leave us still our old nobility.'

Others of the aristocratic class have been less frank, perhaps, but they are none the less earnest and sincere in upholding the peculiar privileges of the aristocracy, which they believe to be the most beneficent of all British institutions."

How clouded was my crystal ball is amusingly clear to me now that in that discussion of Lloyd George's democracy or demagoguery I ascribed without hesitation to Mr. Winston Churchill and Mr. John Burns the care and conduct of progressive social legislation and administration. The correspondence of the event with the prediction of course is inaccurate, but I wrote that a full year before the next election in England had decreed the end of the effective veto of the House of Lords, had determined the abolition of plural voting, and had opened the path which, although beset with many stones and brambles, led toward votes for women. Although Mr. Churchill again changed his party coat, I find it amusing now that then I denominated Winston Churchill as the midwife of the oncoming welfare state, a welfare state that he, as I write this, the eldest of elder statesmen, the leader of the Conservative party at home, a captain of democracy unmatched in history on the world scene, has continued to avow to and nurture, for all that he attempts, sometimes successfully, to keep the brat under control and to discipline his sometimes wayward progeny. That the progressive income tax and a managed currency would make all the fuss and fury of that debate on taxation obsolete, no one then could have dreamed.

Every day, it seemed to me, I was more amazed than on the day before by the passionate quality of the campaign. It was characterized in part by the very multiplicity of its confused issues, a complexity that, if we then had had the wit to sense it, would have indicated to us how moribund was the nineteenth century. It was true, of course, that I knew that in our young republic of the United States all had not been either white or black in politics; that conflicts of opinion in democracy were resolved to the extent that they were resolved somewhere in the middle betwixt the two extremes.

Nonetheless, I was appalled by this confusion. Over and above everything else there was the threat of war. The German aggression was feared, as the event proved, with good reason. On this the parties did not divide. They both distrusted Germany. The difference between them was on the question of how to meet that threat. But that was not the issue. The issue was one of the aspirations of the underprivileged for a greater share in the national wealth by cutting off, in one way or another, the power of the privileged.

In part the very loyalty of all men of all parties to the monarch had its influence on subordinating international and foreign affairs to the more immediate domestic difficulties so far as the campaign was concerned. . . . The threat of war was there. It was real. But it was not immediate. The next threat, as I have said, was the diminishing control of Britain over the world's commerce.

One day Bess and I, taking a walk, passed by Buckingham Palace. There was a rather smaller crowd than usual in the street looking up toward the palace window, looking across to the palace gates. The immobile scarlet-coated sentries were in their boxes. Then a carriage, a coupé, came out the gates. In it were two men. Each wore a silk hat. One man was bearded. The other was clean-shaven. The bearded man looked out toward the crowd of a dozen or more in which by sheer accident Bess and I then were numbered. He lifted his hat. It was Edward VII. It was the last time he ever left London. He was on his way to Biarritz. When he came back, he was ill and never left London again alive.

When Miss Hazlitt, the English girl who was the editorial writer for the *Colorado Springs Gazette,* had been in Washington just before our wedding, she had given me her address and had asked me to write to her as soon as my bride and I had established ourselves in London. I did so. Promptly came an invitation to luncheon. Bess and I made our way south of the river on a dark, damp, dank day into a drab quarter of Dulwich. There our cab-driver found a dismal gray-brick house, one of a long, long row of exactly the same sort of dismal gray-brick houses. Miss Hazlitt, her sister, and her mother received us with great cordiality. She, mindful of our habits, had lighted a little fire even before our arrival, and there was a suggestion of warmth in the little parlor. There was a fowl for luncheon. There was every evidence of cordiality. In their conversation the three women bore witness to their good taste, their erudition, their kinship with the great essayist of their name; but it was impossible for Bess and me to overlook the evident stigmata of poverty.

We asked them to come to lunch with us. Her mother was too frail; her sister, too occupied; but Miss Hazlitt accepted. Now it so happened that, shortly before our arrival in London, Mr. H. Gordon Selfridge, a partner of the firm of Marshall Field and Company, had set up in Oxford Street a huge establishment, the first modern (according to American notions) department store to be established in that metropolis of the world. Bess and I had been there. We knew that it had an excellent restaurant and that the conveniences of waiting-rooms and writing-rooms were available, and, quite naturally, Bess suggested that we meet in Selfridge's.

We were taken aback by Miss Hazlitt's instantly kindled anger. Miss Hazlitt said that she would rather die than set her foot in Selfridge's. It represented an invasion by a foreign competitor of the rightful province of English commerce. She said she couldn't understand why any true Briton would ever go inside the place, let alone buy anything there. She told us that the protective tariff, if the country in 1903 had only followed Mr. Chamberlain's advice, would have prevented such an outrage. And she went on to say that, if only there had been that protective tariff, which she, following her old chief, called "tariff reform," if England then had listened, there would be no poverty, there would be no threat of war from Germany, there would be only that England of the Golden Age. Recovering as best we could, we settled for a luncheon at Lyon's Corner House, an establishment as British as the lion and unicorn, as English as John Bull himself. That encounter gave us an insight into the intensity of feeling that was being manifested in this political campaign.

Selfridge's itself was quite an adventure. I had known about it and so had Bess. We went to see it. It was so much more nearly like what we thought a department store ought to be than Herod's that we felt at home there. It did have the community facilities to which we were accustomed, and it did permit, as the great English stores did not permit, a customer to wander about, eye-shopping, showcase shopping, without at the very entrance door meeting a demand of "How may I serve you, Madam?" and the instant guidance to the particular place where the particular predetermined purchase was to be found.

Then, too, Selfridge's had two other attractions for me. There one could find the *Saturday Evening Post,* and neither my bride nor I wanted to miss one single copy of that, because it was then carrying serially a semifictional book called "The Circuit Rider's Wife" written by Mrs. Corra Harris of Georgia, whose husband, a Methodist preacher, I had known in Nashville. Finding here the *Saturday Evening Post,* I also discovered a soda fountain. I went there alone one morning about eleven o'clock. I went up to the soda fountain. There was no other customer, so I, in a deliberate test of the man behind the glittering marble and metal apparatus, said, "Gimme a dope." Instantly, as his hand fell over on the Coca-Cola throttle, he responded, "Ain't this a son-of-a-bitch of a climate? Give me Atlanta every day in the week."

A week later, having made an appointment by post, I called on Mr. Selfridge. After he had told me of his plans and what already seemed to him the satisfactory working-out of his schemes and after hearing his confident predictions of his success, I told him about Miss Hazlitt. He was not at all abashed. He said that he was sure that, of the six million people in London, five millions at least felt exactly as did Miss Hazlitt. "But," he said, "the other million will welcome the experiment. They will sustain my business, and eventually all London will forgive me."

Then he went on to say that he had been extremely careful so far as personnel was concerned; that he knew there were so many unemployed persons in England and even in London that it would not do for him to bring in any Americans. "So," he said, "I am the only American in this whole store."

"All but one," I retorted.

"One?" he almost shouted. "Who other?"

"The soda-jerker," I replied.

"Oh," said Mr. Selfridge, "I had forgotten him. That was one skill I could not find in England. I had to import him. He is training two assistants. I only hope I can keep him away from his Atlanta long enough to get his training school well under way."

Two or three weeks later I wandered into that same soda fountain. Here came Mr. Selfridge. He had with him a great lady. He was showing her the store. He explained to her the soda fountain. He asked her to sample its products. The various things served there were explained. She finally settled for a raspberry soda but with the explicit instruction that it should have no ice in it. So the disgusted young man from Atlanta mixed for her a potion of raspberry syrup mixed with warm soda water out of a bottle. It was pretty and pink. The lady lifted it to her lips. She tasted it.

"Faugh! I caun't imagine how the Americans drink such disgusting slop!"

"They don't," said the delegate from Atlanta.

From day to day, as Bess and I either together or singly dropped in at that one place in the town that seemed really home to us, we ate our ice-cream sodas under the unbelieving and wondering eyes of groups of English people—principally of course, it being in a retail store—women and girls. They knew, because they had always known, that to drink ice water or anything cold was fatal. They waited expectantly to see the rash Americans fall dead. Did they not know:

> Full many a man both young and old
> Has gone to his sarcophagus
> By throwing water icy cold
> Adown his hot esophagus.

Be it understood that these little prejudices reflecting our own provinciality are recorded here merely because that was what we saw then. The decades following were to give both me and my wife a wider tolerance. As a matter of fact, the next time I was in Selfridge's, which was in 1914, the soda fountain, then a one-position job, had been extended until it took up nearly the whole length of an aisle of the store; it was ministered to by not fewer than eight evidently British soda-jerkers, and its unmistakably English patronage seemed to be limited only by its capacity to serve its eager customers.

At the evident risk of oversimplification, I shall briefly advert to the immediate issue of the campaign—that feature of Mr. Lloyd George's budget that had caused its rejection by the Lords, that instant cause of the dissolution and the general election—the land question. To be sure that I write of it now as I saw it then without many of the qualifications that now I would set down, I shall quote from what I then wrote:

"The Lloyd George Budget was the first political attempt to interfere seriously with the privileges of the landlords, and its provisions would be regarded in any other country as being mild almost to the point of futility. But the astonished landlords rose en masse and de-

clared that Lloyd George was a socialist, that his Budget was con-
fiscatory and that its operations would destroy the British Empire
and send its old nobility to the demnition bow-bows. That the owner
of land should be forced to pay a tax upon it was a notion so
novel, a proposition so preposterous, a crime so conscienceless, that it
seemed to be altogether impossible. But the Budget passed the Commons, was rejected by the Lords, was made the chief issue in a
general election, was approved at the polls, and now is the law of
England."

This business inevitably brought into the campaign as one of the
principal subjects of discussion Mr. Henry George and his book,
Progress and Poverty, and his theory of the single tax. I first had
heard of the single tax from Tom L. Johnson, an ardent advocate of
that panacea for the economic ills of America during his long career
as mayor of Cleveland. I first heard of it from his lips in Louisville,
where as a reporter on *The Courier-Journal* I had interviewed him.
He had come to Louisville as a proponent of a phase of the developing
industrial revolution. He had bought a horseless carriage. It was
painted a brilliant red. He had baptized it "The Red Cyclone." He
drove in it from Cleveland to Louisville. It took him two weeks, but
he got there. I was assigned to see him, and I not only saw him but
I saw the red monster. He gave me two long lectures. One was on the
utility of the automobile and the necessity of good roads, a good deal
of which I used in my interview; the other long lecture, none of
which, I fear, appeared in my report but which made quite an impression upon my mind, was on the single tax. Here he was, I knew,
a radical, a promoter of government ownership of streetcars, the
apostle of the three-cent fare, and, knowing that, I made a grave error.
I asked him if government ownership wouldn't be socialistic. Then
he launched into a furious attack on socialism, of which I knew very
little, and on Marx and Engels, of whom I knew nothing. He was,
he said, a Democrat. He was not a Socialist. He believed with Lincoln
that no man should be a slave, or no man a master; that the compulsory
sharing of the source of all wealth, the land, could be accomplished
by the single tax, and then all men would be free, every man would
be a master each of his own craft, and all could live together in democratic harmony.

That discussion with Tom Johnson had caused me to read *Progress and Poverty*. It had interested me a great deal. It was persuasive to a young person such as I who was inclined to thrash out against intrenched wealth or privilege. As I heard in those days so many persons say, "Accept his premises, and you cannot but admit the logical advance of his conclusions." It so happened that I never quite accepted the premises, and I never quite agreed with the conclusions, but nevertheless it had caused me to seek out in many places and get acquainted with the professors of the single-tax theory.

Here for the first time a great national campaign was being fought along those lines. I repaired to the Land Value Taxation League headquarters in Great Tothill Street. There I met the genius of the movement, a hunchback named John Paul, two or three radical members of Parliament, and one detached, perhaps, but nevertheless immemorable Welshman, Tom Jones, then a secretary to Mr. Lloyd George.

I must admit that at that time the threat of war seemed to me to be slightly unreal. Perhaps that was the reason why, on a particular morning when there was a parade of sorts celebrating a day dedicated to the navy, which, as part of the procession, swung around the crescent of that street to make its way to the rendezvous in Victoria Street for the march up Whitehall, I was utterly amazed when all my radical friends rushed to the windows to give three cheers to a passing group of naval officers and ratings. It opened my eyes. It convinced me as nothing else could have convinced me that all England, however else divided, felt its security encompassed and assured by the fleet.

Visiting central campaign headquarters, I was astonished to find how loosely organized were these parties. Neither was a well-knit establishment presided over by a national committee, as were the Republican and Democratic parties in the United States, but each was an adventitious coalition of factions, assembled, so it seemed to me then, only for the purpose of the campaign and taking direct orders from their chiefs in Westminster Palace; one from the members of the cabinet, and the other from the members of His Majesty's Loyal Opposition—the shadow cabinet.

For all that, they were busy. There were leaflets and pamphlets by the score. Already on the hoardings or, as I would have called them, the billboards, I had noted with intense interest what everyone assured me was a new feature of the campaign. It was the art work. All over the city and for that matter in other towns (since we had found time to go to Oxford, Stratford-on-Avon, Canterbury, and other near-by places) the hoardings were plastered with one-sheet posters. The Liberal posters caricatured the dukes. The Conservative posters made much of the heritage of the ages of Englishmen.

(Incidentally, I acquired from each of these two headquarters a complete set of posters. They were so numerous and so heavy that I had to buy a new steamer trunk to hold them. I believe that each party had about a hundred posters. I know that nearly every artist in England had been at work for either one or the other. I filled that steamer trunk with them, and that certainly got me into a lot of trouble later when, entering Germany, I was held up at an obscure place on the frontier while I explained, having no German, to three or four German customs officers, none of them having any English, that these things were works of art, curios only, and were not intended to be the basis of any subversive activity against His Imperial and Royal Majesty Wilhelm II. Actually, I went everywhere with the trunk, brought the posters home, and used them on an easel as material for the first public speech I had made since I left Buffalo. It was a speech at the National Press Club on the British-German crisis.)

The most valuable incident in my visit to these two headquarters was that it gave me a liberal education in the substantial difference between political parties as organized in the United States and as practiced under direct political control in Great Britain. That contribution to my education, I think, helped me a great deal in later years to understand the deeper significance of many political observations and experiences in my homeland.

The Conservative headquarters was to be found in the office of what was known as "The National Union of Conservatives and Constitutional Associations," which, for the purpose of the campaign, was being assisted by the ultra-Tory "Primrose Lee" and Mr. Chamberlain's Tariff Reform League.

The governmental party in power had its campaign activities carried on in the headquarters of what was called "The National Liberal Federation and Liberal Central Association" united for purpose of the campaign with the Free Trade Union, the Budget League, and the Irish Home Rule League.

The amusing thing was the physical arrangement in each of these establishments. The Tory headquarters in St. Stephen's Chambers was spick and span. A secretary showed me through it with great pride. It was furnished with desks imported from Grand Rapids, Michigan (how the Tariff Reform League liked that, I have no idea except that I doubt if any prominent Tory politician deigned to visit the headquarters). There were typewriters. On each desk there were fountain pens. Everything was modern. Everything was up to date, and except for a stiff climb up two pairs of stairs, it was hardly distinguishable from an American office.

Not far away on an obscure street was the headquarters of the Liberals, the Radicals. The work was being done at stand-up desks in longhand. The letters were being written with quill pens, and in lieu of paper blotters—although blotting paper seemed to be one of the most pervasive things in London at that time—the letters were being blotted with sand shaken, pepperbox fashion, from a sandbox. So the surface manifestations of the progressive Tories; so the surface manifestations of the past-worshiping Radicals!

Election day came, that is, rather, the first day of the elections, for they were stretched out over a period of nearly a fortnight in order to give a free expression to the differential desires of individuals in the several constituencies but, more importantly, so the Liberals charged, to give the Conservatives the opportunity to poll their plural votes, since the suffrage went with the land and was limited to those who owned lands and those who paid rates for the occupation of the land or the houses on the land. A landed proprietor was able to vote in as many of the constituencies as his landownership covered. Nevertheless, there had been a movement toward concentration, and most of the constituencies voted on the first day of the election. That was the big night.

Bess and I stood on the steps of the old church, St. Martin's-in-the-Fields, looking out over Trafalgar Square. It was the biggest crowd she had ever seen. It was, with the sole exception of one I had seen in India, the greatest crowd I had ever seen. There were transparent projections of the news on huge screens, and there was wild and tumultuous cheering from the completely mixed-up adherents of the two parties as one or the other forged ahead or lost ground. It was indeed a big night.

CHAPTER XXXI

THE CONTINENT

We had intended to go to Germany by way of Paris, but at that moment disastrous floods were interrupting rail traffic into that city, so that we decided to go by Brussels and thence on to Berlin, intending to come back by France. Unfortunately, the latter part of our plans had to be canceled, and I was not to see my ancestral and beloved France on that voyage or, indeed, until 1930, long after the first World War.

There was an interesting stop at Brussels to see the sights of the town and also to make a trip to the battlefield of Waterloo. This to me was a great adventure. I had seen and talked with a soldier of the Duke of Wellington. It was an adventure of itself merely to be going to Waterloo, but we made it doubly adventurous. We decided to go in an automobile. There was a way to go by way of rail and carriage, but in the Hotel Metropole the hall porter earnestly recommended a trip by motorcar. We took it. It took us all day. We were the only passengers. The chauffeur changed tires seven or eight times and stopped six or seven other times on account of engine trouble. The day of the motorcar had not yet dawned.

We took the train for Berlin, intending to stop over in Cologne. There was the embarrassing incident of my trunkful of violent English campaign posters which held me up at the border and frightened Bess almost to death because, while I was still arguing with the customs officers, the train started to pull away without me. By dint of much shouting and the shrilling of a bugle blown by a customs officer, the train was stopped, my trunk put aboard, and I went on.

It was a beautiful day, a Saturday, when we got to Cologne. Bess had been there before. We established ourselves in the Hotel Tisch, and she took me sight-seeing and, of course, first of all to the Dom,

[553]

the great cathedral. It was a thrilling and a rewarding sight. To her astonishment the great fabric was decorated with bunting and with thousands of electric lights. We inquired of a guide and found that the special decorations had been put up for the occasion of the celebration of the golden jubilee of his ordination to the priesthood of the cardinal, an event that was to be celebrated on the following morning.

At dinner at the hotel, looking out of the window at the Rhine, we selected for our *pièce de résistance,* partly at the suggestion of the headwaiter, a Rhine salmon. We were established in a bedroom of the huge dimensions then characteristic of German hostelries. It seemed to be miles and miles from one bed to the other. The room was big enough, as Mark Twain had said of a similar German bedroom, for a "protracted meeting." A little after midnight we became ill, very ill, too ill for either of us to summon help. Toward morning I, being somewhat better, managed to ring for assistance. A night hall porter came who knew no English. Our distress, however, was so apparent that he awakened someone who came to our aid. That individual, all sympathy and efficiency, said he would get a physician as soon as possible. About six or seven o'clock in the morning the doctor came. We told him that we had to go on to Berlin, that most of our baggage already had preceded us, that we had only overnight cases, and that we must go on. He looked us over, gave us a thorough examination, and said, "You cannot go. You will have to stay here for several days, perhaps a week. Mrs. Brownlow is too ill to travel."

Then he gave me a prescription which, he said, I could have filled when the drugstore opened at eight in the morning. He told me to go to a particular drugstore which happened to be directly across a narrow street from the cathedral. I found myself there at eight o'clock. The moment the doors opened I presented the prescription. With that universal solemnity which characterizes prescription clerks in all parts of the world, he told me it would be ready in thirty minutes. I thought it would be a good idea to take another look at the beautiful cathedral. Looking up toward its tall towers, hardly noticing where I was going, certainly not noticing the absence of traffic on the street, I walked across the narrow way. I saw that the great central door was open. It did not occur to me then that on the afternoon before we had gone in through one of the side doors of the three great portals of the western façade. I walked in the open door. It must have been that I chose precisely the ten seconds when such a thing could have happened, for, as I walked down the central aisle, looking up at the vaulting of the nave, I suddenly saw three bishops walking up to meet me. I looked hastily behind me. There was the cardinal, leading a great procession. I never was more terrified in my life. I looked for shelter and found it by crowding myself up against one of the great Gothic columns that supported the roof of the nave. I could sense the ire of the beholders. Frozen with terror as I was, I had gained, from what inner resource I cannot imagine, the sense to kneel. As the cardinal came slowly down the aisle toward me and as the three bishops were about to meet him just a little closer to the altar than was the column where I had taken refuge, the cardinal turned his head and gave me a beaming smile and his special blessing.

That was but the beginning of a day of adventures. I took the medicine home. Then I went in search of a hot-water bottle. There were many stores with the words "Gummi-artikel" emblazoned on the windows but none in which I could make my wishes known, until, after tramping for miles, I suddenly discovered on the other side of the very hotel in which we were established a place where an attendant spoke English, and I got a hot-water bottle. Then I started out to find a nightgown. We had been married then not quite two months. I was adept in shopping for women's gowns under the tutelage of my brother, who was in the business, but I never had bought a ladies' nightgown. Nor had I ever shopped in a language of which I was utterly ignorant. Finally I found one. It was pure linen. It was elaborately embroidered. And it had, as my wife later discovered, one great advantage. When washed and ironed, it would easily stand alone. As a matter of fact, it found good and hard usage for a full score of years before it was consigned to the rag bag.

Now the doctor spoke good English. He had taken a part of his medical education in Baltimore at Johns Hopkins University. My struggle with the food poisoning was soon over. Bess was slow recovering. He finally set the time—full seven days from the time we arrived in Cologne—when he would permit us to proceed to Berlin. One day I said, "If you think it will be all right, I believe I will take a trip to see the University of Bonn."

"It will be quite all right," he replied, "so far as your wife's health is concerned."

The doctor came in every morning. The next morning when he arrived, I already had gone. He asked where I was. Bess, somewhat astonished, said, "He has gone to Bonn as you told him he could."

"Yes," he said, "I told him he could, but I didn't think he would. I didn't think you would let him. You know, I married an American girl, a Maryland girl. I didn't think you would let him." He seemed to be better educated, in a certain sense, than most Germans.

Health recovered, the overnight cases of necessity bulging with some additional articles, we entrained for Berlin. We got there a little later, with the full knowledge that we had lost our hotel reservation. Berlin was filled to overflowing with persons who had come in from all over Germany for an agricultural convention. Thomas Cook & Son had done their best. They had found us a room, or they thought they had, in the Alexandra Hotel in Mittelstrasse, a street just off Unter den Linden. We got there about midnight. There was no room. We were put up for the night in a sample room with mattresses and bedding laid out on high tables designed and intended for the display of the samples of traveling salesmen.

But we were promised a room on the morrow. Without much sleep we went in the morning to the dining-room, where an unforgettable gnome, a veritable dwarf, came up to our table and said, "Would you like some ham and eggs?" We said we would. He said, "You should call it *Schinken mit Eier!*" and, withering us with a glance, he turned away, to come back very shortly with a delectable breakfast. And with it coffee, real coffee! Possibly we might have moved to a hotel of a higher class, but the huge front room, the commodious bath, the comfortable furniture, the solicitous and efficient maid, caused us to lose all desire to seek other quarters, and we settled down in Mittelstrasse for the rest of our visit.

There was a wide variance in my instant reactions to the things I saw and heard in Berlin which so frequently clashed with my democratic convictions and habits, a wide variance between those impressions and the conclusions to which I was driven.

So much has happened since then—the German invasion of Belgium in 1914, the German defeat of 1918, the renaissance of the German democracy under the Weimar Republic, the atavistic return to aggressive despotism under Hitler, the collapse of that system in 1945, and the uncertainty of the German future in 1955—it is better, I am per-

suaded, to set down what I then concluded about Germany in the first
of a series of thirty articles under the general title of "The German
Advance."

"The German Empire is a militant nation, ambitious and unafraid,
advancing swiftly toward its goal of world supremacy. It is the ambition of the German state, of the German Emperor, and of every German to make the German Empire what Rome was and what Britain
is. Germany is a military state, but it is even more an industrial state.
Germany is a nation of dreamers, but it is even more a nation of doers.
The Germans are philosophical, but they are even more practical. Germany is the heir of all the ages in its wealth of ancient story and
tradition, but it is foremost in the files of time as the youngest of the
great nations of the world. The German people are older than any
people of the Western world, the German Empire the youngest state
among the Occidental powers.

"Not since Waterloo have all of the nations of the world looked
upon any one power with so much suspicion. The German army, the
most powerful on earth, and the German navy, so rapidly increasing
in power, disturb the sleep of the diplomatists of all the non-German
world. And yet, since the Empire was established, the German army
has not fought a battle and the German navy has not fired a gun.

"The German advance is a deliberately planned economic campaign
in which the military forces of the Empire are used for protection
of German interests and not for threatening the safety of other nations.
Its aim is to make Germany commercially and industrially the supreme
nation of the world. Its purpose is to abolish poverty and to make the
German people the most prosperous people on earth. Its endeavor is
to claim every drop of German blood and every energy of German
body and mind for the German state, and therefore to make that state
supreme in the moral, as well as in the economic and political spheres."

But these comments, indicative as they were of my admiration for
German order, German cleanliness, German industry, and German
efficiency, could not rub out my uneasiness at what seemed to me
even on the surface the manifestation of despotism.

There was but a short step from the hotel to the great Unter den
Linden. There one morning I heard the shrill sound of a bugle, the
strange sight of every human being stopped stock still, of every horse
being pulled up sharply. The bugles continued to blow, and swiftly

down the avenue came a great motorcar, the black, white, and red flag flying from one side and the imperial standard from the other. And in the rear seat, His Majesty, the Kaiser. When he drove down the avenue from the Schloss toward the Brandenburger Tor, the world seemed to stop still.

One day we were at lunch in a great restaurant also on Unter den Linden. There were very few people in the room. Near us was a table at which were seated a man, his wife, and two small children. Three army officers came in. They indicated to the obsequious headwaiter that they wished to have that table where the family sat, only half-through their luncheon. No other table would do. They must have that one. It was exactly like a dozen other empty tables, but they were Prussian officers, and so, with a hurry and a scurry and a fluster, the family was dispossessed, banished to another table in the back part of the room, and the three swaggering swashbuckling officers took their places.

We were to hear, chiefly from English and Americans we met, journalists, businessmen, and others, that this was but typical of the incidents that were happening then all over the empire, apparently, at least so some of the English newspapermen told me, because of the concerted effort of the army to quash any general resentment that might have arisen out of an incident in Zabern. There some civilians, unmindful of their subordinate status, had vocally resented the action of an army officer who pushed a crippled cobbler off the sidewalk. But, despite all this, I found it possible, and in view of my journalistic obligations, imperative, to write thus:

"Germany possesses the imperial instinct. That is to say, the German people believe in their own greatness, and are faithfully persuaded that they will do God and man the greatest possible service by the extension of the German Empire. German political writers are fond of saying that as the Nineteenth Century witnessed the Prussianizing of Germany so will the Twentieth Century witness the Germanizing of the world. Although Germans at home may quarrel among themselves over the details of domestic political policies, all Germans, even the most radical of the Socialists, are united in support of the imperialistic ideals impressed upon every man in his everyday life."

The political phenomenon that most impressed me was the fact that numerically the largest political party, the Socialists, could not command a majority in the legislature either of the empire or of the dominant state of Prussia, which overawed the other federal units of the Reich. That was all the more amazing, since I discovered or thought I discovered in Germany two kinds of socialism. One was the monarchical, founded by Bismarck and nurtured and supported by the Kaiser and the puppet chancellors who followed in that office, if not in authority, the man who had established the new empire. Contrasted with that monarchical socialism were the democratic socialists and their demands. That contrast I set out in the following paragraphs, which, whether or not my impressions at the time were correct, certainly illustrates the fact that what I was hearing and seeing was contributing to my own learning in that it was enabling me to make distinctions between the seeming and the actual, between the theoretical and the practical, and to distrust mere labels. I wrote:

"It is a curious thing that in Germany, where the principle of state socialism is more advanced than in any other nation, the radical socialist party should be able to compress its program into ten demands, seven of which, in whole or in part, are enshrined in the Constitution of and the laws of the United States, that nation in which the propaganda of state socialism has been more unsuccessful than in any other country in the world.

"All of which illustrates the meaninglessness of words and phrases. In Germany socialism means free speech, free press and free schools; while conservatism means public ownership of railways, mines, farms, factories, breweries, and moving picture shows. In the United States it is conservatism to stand pat on the Constitution, a document guaranteeing most of the German socialists' immediate demands, while it is socialism to advocate eighty-cent gas or three-cent fares.

"As a matter of fact the intense opposition of the German Emperor and the ruling classes to the Social Democratic party is not based at all on any opposition to, or fear of, the so-called socialistic principle of collective ownership and state administration of the instruments of production. The Emperor and the conservatives are willing to meet the socialists more than half way in this regard. The bitter hatred the conservative classes in Germany manifest toward the socialists is based upon the paradoxical ground that the German socialists venture to assert the freedom of the individual. In the accepted American meaning of the words, it is the democracy and not the socialism of the German party which brings down upon it the wrath of the Kaiser and the German conservatives."

[559]

What I did find in Germany which elicited my wholehearted admiration, and which in some degree has affected my thinking ever
since, was the admirable administration of municipal government.
Of that I wrote:

"The Germans, particularly the Prussians, have more nearly approached a satisfactory solution of the problem of municipal government under modern conditions than have any other people. Their
solution is a remarkably simple one. It is that municipal government is not a political, but a business enterprise; and that as a business
enterprise in which every citizen is a partner it should be run not as
a private commercial enterprise, but as a huge industrial undertaking
to which must be applied the most modern methods of high organization and complete cooperation. To this end it is administered for the
purpose of obtaining for each citizen-partner the maximum of profit
in matters of safety, health, and convenience; mere money profits being
a negligible consideration.

"Simple as is this theory, it is much easier to put it into practice
in Germany than it would be in the United States, for the reason that
there are fundamentally different habits of thought upon governmental
problems in the two countries. The advantage is not altogether on
either side. Those Germans who are working for reform in their
federal and state government deplore the fact that the German gives
greater weight to economic and social questions, almost to the utter
neglect of political problems. In the United States the municipal government reformers have found their chief obstacle in the fact that
the American people think first of politics, and are very often entirely
unwilling to give any consideration to social and economic matters.
Great Britain, fortunately for its peace and security in its present
crisis, occupies a position midway between Germany and America,
since it gives politics the place of first importance in national matters,
but subordinates political considerations to those of sociology and
economics in local government affairs."

The very atmosphere of Berlin made Bess and me uncomfortable.
Perhaps we were not quite able to put it into words. Our admiration
was excited and compelled by many of the wonderful things we saw,
but the regimentation of the people we could not but dislike.

Our own American patriotism overflowed on February 22, 1910,
when we were invited by the United States ambassador to Germany,
Mr. David Jayne Hill, to a George Washington's Birthday Party. It

was to be held, of all places, in the clubhouse of the officers of a
Prussian army *corps d'élite*—the Death's-Head Hussars. The officers
of the club had graciously given over some assembly rooms in that
luxurious establishment, and there the celebration took the form of a
great dinner. The host was the American ambassador. The guest of
honor was a tall and somewhat ungainly gentleman whom both my
wife and I had known when he was a senator from the state of
Indiana and later when he was Vice-President of the United States in
the second term of Theodore Roosevelt. His name was Charles Warren Fairbanks. He had been on a world tour and had come back from
China and Japan over the Trans-Siberian Railway by way of Russia.
Mr. Fairbanks, by virtue of his tall and slender figure, his peculiarly
cut beard, and his rather thin face, had been a favorite subject of
cartoonists, who always had depicted him as the human icicle. As a
matter of fact, he was one of the most genial of men, always cordial,
ever ready with a pertinent witticism, and ever ready to greet a sally
of another with hearty laughter.

There were two long speeches that night. One was made by a
very able man, our ambassador. It was one of the dullest speeches I
ever heard in my life. The other was made by the former Vice-President, and of him nothing was expected. He made one of the best
speeches I ever heard. He told good stories. He kept the whole company roaring with laughter, and he did not fail in his peroration with
restraint but nonetheless with earnestness to touch the deep well-
springs of American patriotism shared by every person in the room.

At the table where Bess and I sat we fell into conversation with
two young women, both Americans, of course, one married to a Prussian army officer, the other to an Austrian army officer, an attaché of
his embassy in Berlin. I said something which might have been interpreted as poking fun at the British because of their fear of Germany.
Just at that instant came the ceremonial toast to the Kaiser; the solemn
and ceremonial toast to the President of the United States; the
celebrant toast to George Washington. And, then, a bolt from the blue,
from three officers at our table another toast: To *"Der Tag!"*

After dinner, when we were being entertained with a musical
program, each of these young women separately sought me out; each
found a way to maneuver me into a spot where we could not be overheard; each said to me the same thing, almost in the same words.
"Please, Mr. Brownlow, if you are a journalist, please do not make

fun of the British for being afraid. When these German officers drink the toast, *'Der Tag,'* they mean it. They mean war. They will have it. They have not the slightest doubt that they will win."

These two young women never had met each other before. It was a strange coincidence that one of them hailed from Athens, Georgia, and the other from Athens, Alabama. Each of them also sought out Bess separately. Each, with great care not to be overheard, told her in almost the same words the things that they had told me. From that time on, what I heard about the German officers' toast to "The Day," when their war of ultimate and final conquest would begin, I never dismissed it as I had theretofore as a mere figment of the imagination.

We stayed too long and had to give up Paris. We came home—home to America, home to Washington, and home to our home.

A little later, as the congressional campaign of 1910 waxed hot, there were a few who had questions about the peace of the world. They were very few, but, because of them, I summed up my futile endeavor to pierce the veil of the future in another article in which I said:

"Will England and Germany fight? Oceans of ink have been spilled in the last two years in attempts to answer this, the most momentous question propounded in the realm of international politics for many years. And, naturally, it is yet unanswered to the satisfaction of any-body. Curiously enough, the so-called conservative thinkers, speakers, and writers of both nations directly interested have replied in the affirmative, and the radicals have said, 'no!' The one thing certain is that both British and German governments have not scrupled to multiply burdensome taxes in order to prepare for a possible, even a probable, war.

"Imperialists, their attention directed solely to the national fortunes of the two greatest European empires, have been able to see only the growing rivalry in politics and in trade which daily increases the friction between the two countries. They do not scruple to predict an early clash of arms. They say that the continued growth of Germany's political power threatens England's diplomatic supremacy; that the increase of Germany's foreign commerce endangers the prosperity of Britain's commercial empire; and, most important of all, the avowed intention of Germany to make its navy strong enough to dispute with England the mastery of the seas—all operate together to make the war inevitable."

CHAPTER XXXII

A CONCLUSION AND A BEGINNING

Even the most fantastic of my childhood dreams in Buffalo, Missouri, could not have anticipated the world which my work with Haskin had opened up to me. By 1910 I had at least seen a large part of that world, and I had learned much from it, or so I thought. But Washington was still the center of my interests, for Washington meant politics. Since my work with Haskin was, for the most part, necessarily nonpartisan, and since it was more or less a fringe operation as far as Washington politics itself was concerned, it was natural that I seek informants and acquaintances among those I knew best—the newspapermen.

The National Press Club had been chartered in 1909 while I was in the Far East. Both Mr. Haskin and I had worked with the committee that was promoting the organization, but neither of us was in Washington when the charter was granted. When the club was set up in very modest quarters over a jewelry store on F Street, I found my way there practically every day. The talk was always charged with politics. It was there that I met Judson C. Welliver and John Snure. Both at that time were on the staff of the *Washington Times,* Welliver as editorial writer, and Snure covering the Capitol. Both had had experience in a state capitol, in a county courthouse, and in a city hall. Their interest matched mine in that our political curiosity ranged through all three levels of government.

Luncheons at the Press Club sometimes gave us too little opportunity for the private conversations that enabled us to gossip more freely and air our views at greater length and with complete freedom. So Welliver and Snure began to lunch together in the Grill Room at the Willard Hotel; and I joined them. It wasn't long until we had a recruit in the person of Fred A. Walker, managing editor, and Edgar Shaw, business manager, of the *Washington Times*. They were soon joined by Oliver Peck Newman, also from Des Moines, newly came to the *Times* as an editorial writer.

By the summer of 1910, after my wife and I had come back from Europe, the luncheon-table group in the Willard Hotel had expanded considerably. We had recruited Robert Wickliffe Woolley of the *New York World* staff and Walter J. Fahy, also of the *Times*.

Mr. Taft had succeeded Mr. Roosevelt in March, 1909, and the Colonel had betaken himself to Africa. It soon became apparent that Taft's policy would be markedly different from what "Teddy" had called his "Square Deal." Some of the Republicans at our table began to rally around Robert M. La Follette as the person to be nominated by the Republicans in 1912, a progressive who could be depended upon to redeem the party from its conservative trend and establish it firmly on the path of liberalism and progress. Welliver and Fahy were particularly interested in that endeavor, and indeed Mr. Fahy became very active in a temporary voluntary headquarters that was set up to advance the La Follette cause. Perhaps all of us at the table were interested in La Follette's presidential ambitions; but some of us who were Democrats were looking forward to a change in that party's management which would enable the Democrats once again, after long wandering in the wilderness, to come to power. The Democrats did not repudiate the leadership of Mr. Bryan, but they were sure that after three defeats he could not again be nominated. We were each equally sure that to turn to the conservative wing of the party would be only to repeat the fiasco of the Parker campaign. In the meantime, however, there was to be the congressional election of 1910.

On the night of November 8, 1910, I found myself in the editorial offices of the *Washington Times* with the consent of Mr. Shaw, the business manager, assigned by the managing editor, Mr. Walker, to work with Welliver, Snure, and Newman on compiling the election returns and writing the bulletins to be thrown on the huge screen in front of the Munsey Building before which a crowd of thousands had assembled. As the night wore on, and as the chances of Democratic victory became more and more certain, there was a great elation in that room. Only a few of us were Democrats, but nearly all of the others were anti-Taft Republicans who hoped that by means of this repudiation of Taft's policies their party would be swung back to the ideas, if not to the personal leadership, of Theodore Roosevelt. The Democrats won. The campaign had not been fought, however, on the direct issue of presidential policies. It turned rather on the conduct of affairs in the House of Representatives. There, a small group of Republicans led by George W. Norris of Nebraska, dubbed "insurgents," had joined with the Democrats in a revolt against the domination of the House of Representatives by the Speaker. Members of committees were appointed by the Speaker. The Speaker took to himself the right of recognition and refused to see any member unless that member had previously sought and arranged for recognition. The Speaker was Joseph G. ("Uncle Joe") Cannon, whose absolute tyranny over the House was second only to that of his predecessor, Thomas B. ("Czar") Reed of Maine. The rules were not then changed; but, with the Democrats in control of the House, it was certain that there would be some revision of the rules and that the Democratic leader, Champ Clark, would be elected speaker of the House of Representatives. And at that moment it became equally clear that Mr. Clark would have the very best chance for the Democratic nomination for President in 1912. Also, if Mr. Taft were to be renominated, the Democrats would have their best chance at the White House for many, many years.

The luncheon table continued to expand. Fred Walker, in particular, constituted himself a lion-hunter and occasionally would bring down to the table someone he thought would be interesting and entertaining. One such as Houdini. That master-magician was indeed entertaining and mystifying as he did for us some of his celebrated tricks right at the table. Another was David Belasco, the impresario who at that time unveiled all his theatrical performances in the Belasco Theater on Lafayette Square in Washington. Thereafter, whenever Houdini or Belasco came to town, they always came to our table. Thus, gradually, we acquired a number of nonresident members.

The editor and the assistant editor of *Collier's Weekly,* Norman Hapgood and Mark Sullivan, joined us, as did Samuel Hopkins Adams of their staff, who was then working on his great drive against patent-medicine fakery. *Collier's* at that time was liberal. Mr. Hapgood was very much so, and even Mark Sullivan considered himself a progressive. But our table was not censorious in limiting our visitors to one group. Colonel George Harvey, the ultraconservative editor of *Harper's Weekly,* also joined us.

Members of Congress rarely leave the Capitol for lunch, but occasionally we had Senator La Follette, more frequently George Norris, and once in a while William A. Jones and Carter Glass of Virginia, who were then the leaders of an anti-Martin machine movement in the Democratic party of that state.

Louis Dembitz Brandeis, the Boston lawyer who was counsel to a congressional committee investigating the administration of the Department of the Interior under Secretary Ballinger, became a regular member. I had brought him in because of my close association while in Louisville with his eccentric uncle, Louis Dembitz. Mr. Brandeis in his turn introduced Edward A. Filene, the Boston merchant and philanthropist, who came whenever he was in Washington. Thus began a series of luncheon meetings which a few years later may have merited in some degree the title that years later was given it—"The High Tide of Talk."

Mr. Welliver, who had become a regular contributor to *Hampton's Magazine,* suggested that I try my wings in the magazine field. Benjamin B. Hampton, the owner, and Ray Long, the editor of *Hampton's,* came to Washington, camped at our table for three or four days, and held conversations with me the upshot of which was that I was offered a job on the staff of *Hampton's Magazine.*

Bess and I moved to New York. We established ourselves first in the old Judson Hotel on Washington Square, soon thereafter moving to the Irving Hotel in Gramercy Park. Mr. Long was very loath to introduce new names into a big-name magazine alongside such personages as Rex Beach, Harris Merton Lyon, and Dr. Frederick A. Cook. It so happened that the first article I wrote turned out to be signed by Judson C. Welliver, because Mr. Long felt that Mr. Welliver's name should not be dropped from a single issue. In preparation for that article, I had gone down to Washington and had interviewed Champ Clark, with whom as a fellow-Missourian I had had a very pleasant acquaintanceship over many years. To my dismay I found him not entirely enthusiastic about a change in rules which would deprive the speaker of the power that had been wielded by Reed and Cannon. Mr. Clark had a choleric temper and resented my probing. He particularly resented the fact that my father-in-law, a member of

Congress from Tennessee, had conducted a similar effort to get Mr. Clark to commit himself to the Norris rules. At the time of the interview I had not known of Judge Sims's activities in this regard, but I am now convinced that Clark thought it was Sims who had egged me on.

About this time it became apparent that many of "T. R.'s" admirers, including Gilson Gardner, who was a regular member of our table, would try to get the Republican nomination for their idol. *Hampton's* came out with an article entitled "Is Roosevelt Inevitable?" by Judson C. Welliver. It was many years before I learned that that particular article, if not written in its entirety by Senator La Follette himself, was prepared under the Wisconsin leader's closest supervision.

When *Hampton's* folded (its espousal of Dr. Cook's pretended discovery of the North Pole was too much for it), I moved over to *Success Magazine,* which published a rewrite of an article of mine on China; and then it too, despite its name, collapsed. There I was, newly married, with my wife in New York, without a job and in a labor market where there was certainly a plethora of experienced magazine writers looking for a place to catch on. Through my Iowa friends at the table I had come to know the editor of the *New York Globe,* Allan Dawson, who had frequently been a guest at our table in the Willard. My wife and I had visited the Dawsons quite frequently in their beautiful house on Twelfth Street, and we had become close friends. Mr. Dawson, as soon as he found out about my condition, volunteered to give me a job. He wanted me to go back to Washington and write a daily column of political gossip for the editorial page. My very close friend, John Snure, was the regular correspondent of the *Globe.* He did not like the idea of an editorial-page columnist infringing on his field. He protested to Mr. Dawson. Mr. Dawson came down, and it was agreed that I would not write on any topic that Mr. Snure intended to handle. The consequence was that I had to find my gossip in fields far from the center of news interest. It went on for a while. Mr. Dawson was tolerant of what I considered the very poor quality of my product, perhaps because he realized that he himself by his agreement with his old Des Moines associate, John Snure, had riveted chains about me. One day Fred Haskin came to the Willard table. He was in a jovial mood. He asked me to go back with him to his office in the Metropolitan Bank Building. As a matter of fact, my own office was in that same building just one floor above the Haskin headquarters. He could have reached me at any moment, but he preferred to make this roundabout and public gesture. I went back to his office. He asked me to come back to work for him at a salary considerably larger than I ever enjoyed. I accepted at once, wrote my resignation to Mr. Dawson, and again became a cog in the machinery of Haskinitis.

In addition to the politics, however, there were other matters which drew my attention—matters which were closer to the field of public administration. One such experience involved public health and the earliest days of the Rockefeller Foundation.

I became extremely interested in matters concerning public health and sought out persons in the Marine Hospital Service, then headed by Surgeon General Walter Wyman. My acquaintanceship at the Westminster Apartment Hotel, where I lived both before and after my marriage, included Mrs. Walter Reed and her daughter, Blossom. My friendship with the Reed family served me in good stead as I began to get acquainted with the younger men on Dr. Wyman's staff —in particular, Dr. L. L. Lumsden.

Mr. John D. Rockefeller, with the advice of Dr. Frederick T. Gates, had begun his career as a philanthropist at the turn of the century in support of Baptist institutions, the University of Chicago (also Baptist at that time), and the General Education Board and was endeavoring to get a federal charter for the Rockefeller Foundation. He already had set up the Rockefeller Health Institute. The hookworm menace, first identified in Puerto Rico by Dr. Charles Wardell Stiles of the Public Health Service, interested him. He established the Rockefeller Sanitary Commission. It set up headquarters in Washington under the leadership of Dr. Wickliffe Rose.

I had known Dr. Rose in Nashville. Dr. Rose knew very few people in Washington. He sought me out; I was delighted to see him. Dr. Rose told me about the work his commission was about to undertake, a frontal assault on the hookworm and possibly other public health problems in the South. Mr. Rockefeller already had been persuaded to help finance the institution of the county agricultural agent which had been established under the aegis of Dr. Seaman A. Knapp in the Department of Agriculture.

Dr. Rose said that he felt that there must be some publicity concerning his work but that it ought to be conservative, nonsensational, and something that would not offend either the citizens or the officials of the southern states by giving the impression, through sensational articles or violent headlines, that the southerners were lazy because they were infected with the hookworm. I was so completely sympathetic with his point of view that I readily agreed to write the publicity free of charge in the service of what I thought was a worthy cause.

Having re-established our relationship, I personally invited Dr. Rose to come to our Willard table. He did come once, but he met too many newspapermen, too many magazine writers, and too many people who were eager to exploit his field. He would not come again. Instead he began to ask me to luncheon once or twice a week at the Cosmos Club, an institution that, a few years later in 1914, admitted me into its membership.

Dr. Rose's first organizational task was to recruit a corps of young medical men who would be able to assist him in the work that he planned to take to the counties of the southeastern states in such a manner as to engage the participation of the county officials, being careful not to attempt to force anything upon them unless and until he had gained their consent and their hearty co-operation. From medical schools all over the southern states, he solicited the names of young graduates who might be interested. After his preliminary screening, he asked the likely prospects to come to Washington to see him. They came one at a time. It was Dr. Rose's very careful habit to interview each prospect leisurely, perhaps two or three times over a period of two or three days. Once during each period he would ask the young medical man to lunch at the Cosmos Club and have me there. Later in the day he would consult me concerning my opinion of the candidate, what I thought in particular of his personality, especially with reference to whether or not he would have the skill to approach southern county officials tactfully and the ability to work in close co-operation with them in the field. In that manner, I was associated in the choice of a very distinguished group of young physicians who later became the leaders of their field. Among them were Allan Freeman of Virginia (a brother of Douglas Freeman, the historian), who later established the School of Public Health Administration at Johns Hopkins University; Dr. J. W. Ferrell of North Carolina, who for many years was the head of the health division of the Rockefeller

Foundation; Dr. Leathers, who did such a distinguished work in the control of malaria in Mississippi; and many others.

When the organization was set up, I decided that here would be a good story, and I later incorporated it in a series of articles for the "Haskin Letter." In pursuance of that investigation, I attached myself to Dr. Allan Freeman and with him made an extended trip of two weeks or more in the counties of Southside Virginia. Here we went literally into the cotton and peanut fields, and we covered the razorback-hog area that produced the delectable Smithfield hams. We saw in the fields both whites and blacks. We noted the utter absence of simple sanitary conveniences which made the area a happy hunting ground for the hookworm. We persuaded county officials to undertake medication and also to encourage the building of privies. We truly were the advance agents for Chick Sales, the Specialist.

When my friends in the public health service discovered that I was exploiting this field, they were quick to give me something else to do where the service would get the credit. Whereupon I wrote about the experiences of Dr. Lumsden in identifying the first water-borne epidemic of typhoid fever to be completely and scientifically established. That site was in North Yakima in the state of Washington, too far away for me to travel, but the complete records were available to me in the Surgeon General's office.

Dr. Wyman was then experimenting with the establishment of county health units. One of the first of these was to be set up in Cumberland, Maryland. I journeyed up there and spent a week with that young health officer in his laboratory, traveling with him over the county, listening in on his interviews with city and county officials and with leading citizens, including practicing physicans, and I wrote an article about the possibility of the extension of the health service by county units. Here I drew on the experiences with Dr. Knapp and the experimental establishment of county agents in the agricultural field, my experiences in the Southeast with the particular attack on the hookworm, and reports made available to me by Dr. Rose of similar attacks on the problem of malaria, as well as the Cumberland experiment.

This essay in public health had a very great influence upon me, since it modified my preoccupation with the partisan political problems so as to excite my curiosity with respect to the more intimate, even if more pedestrian, problems of the administration of any program by whomsoever undertaken in whatsoever public field.

I had not the least notion that these experiments would lead to three major developments: that the county agent system would be taken over by the federal government and extended throughout the country; that the county health unit would be established so as to cover, first of all, the southern states, and later, and gradually, a very large proportion of the other states of the country. It would have been even more preposterous to have imagined that out of these beginnings would develop the Rockefeller program for the advancement of education, science, health and the administration of government and community activities throughout not only this country but in most of the countries of the world. It would have been even more astonishing to me if someone had then told me that eventually I would come to devote a large part of my life to municipal administration and that, when I did come to that stage, I would put public health first and foremost among all the problems of local government.

One cold, drizzly, rainy Sunday morning in November, 1911, I left the Haskin office, where I had been catching up on some left-over work, and started to walk the three or four doors down Fifteenth Street to the corner of F, where it was my intention to climb the steps to the National Press Club for luncheon. At the foot of the steps I met Thomas J. Pence, the Washington correspondent of the *Raleigh News and Observer*. We stopped to chat. We regretted the cold drizzle. We drifted quite naturally into politics. He asked me if I was for Champ Clark for President. "No. Are you?" I responded.

"I am not," he declared. "Who are you for?"

"I am for Woodrow Wilson," said I.

"So am I," said he.

Mr. Wilson in 1910 had made what seemed to me a remarkable campaign which had resulted in his election as governor of New Jersey. I felt that Mr. Wilson possessed the qualifications that would make him a good candidate against Mr. Taft—at that time in November, 1911, I had no doubt that Taft would be renominated by the Republicans—and, furthermore, that he already had demonstrated in his dealings with the affairs of New Jersey that he would make a strong President.

Then and there, standing out of the drizzle on the steps of that narrow stairway, Tom Pence and I set up the preconvention publicity campaign for Wilson for President. Tom said to me, "Louis, if you will write the stuff, I will place it."

There was no money, no backing. There was nothing. We were simply volunteering our services for something that we thought would be good for the country as well as good for the Democratic party, which so long had been out of power and to which we both acknowledged allegiance. It was years afterward that I found out that Mr. Pence knew then that such an adventure would be pleasing in the sight of the editor and publisher of his paper, Mr. Josephus Daniels.

In my spare time I began to write little pieces about Governor Wilson and his "availability" for the Democratic nomination for the presidency. Tom began to place them. Tom, who spent most of his days at the Capitol as an active correspondent, soon found friendly persons with whom to consult. Among the earliest on Capitol Hill were the blind senator from Oklahoma, Thomas P. Gore; an active Democratic representative, Albert Sidney Burleson of Texas; and, among our own journalistic colleagues, Robert Wickliffe Woolley of the *New York World*.

Governor Wilson came down to Washington and met a small group of his supporters at luncheon in a private dining-room of the Willard Hotel. Mr. Daniels, Senator Gore, and Mr. Burleson were there, as well as Tom Pence and I. It was decided at that luncheon to set up headquarters in Washington to be managed by Mr. Daniels and Mr. Pence. I told the group that my situation was such that I could do nothing actively, nor could I take a position on a pay roll, but that I would continue to do what I could as a volunteer. When the luncheon broke up, Governor Wilson motioned to me to join him. We walked together away from the table. We stood at a window looking out over the intersection of Pennsylvania Avenue and Fourteenth Street. The Governor said:

"Brownlow, I think I can give you one word of advice."

"About what?"

"About a source of material that you possibly might find it convenient to use. I believe that you will find the key to my philosophy of American politics and government in just one book of mine. It is a collection of essays. It has been published under the title, *Mere Literature*. In those essays, I think, you will find some grist for your mill.

"And I would like you particularly to read one essay called 'The First American.' Already I am beginning to sense that my southern birth and origin may induce some of my opponents to resort to 'bloody-shirt' tactics and to say that my election as President would again put the 'South in the saddle.' You will find that collection of my papers has treated George Washington as a great Englishman, Andrew Jackson as a great westerner, but I have described Abraham Lincoln as the First American."

That advice from that source was not ignored. However, when the Wilson campaign for President got under a full head of steam, I withdrew from all its activities.

As the campaign of 1912 waxed warm, I greatly pleased Mr. Haskin by two series of articles I wrote. At that time he had little or no interest in politics, but of course he knew what I was doing in an extracurricular fashion. I was extremely careful never to involve him. I think he was a little bit nervous when I suggested a series of letters on the tariff and another which was to be a repetition and expansion of the series I had written four years before on presidential nominating conventions.

The Democratic majority in the House of Representatives was attacking the tariff question. Under the leadership of Oscar Underwood, chairman of the Ways and Means Committee, a new tariff bill tending away from high protection toward a tariff for revenue was in the works. The short series I wrote reviewed the history of tariff legislation during most of the nineteenth century. What pleased Mr. Haskin was that he got letters from editors of both Democratic and Republican papers each praising him for having deserted his neutrality and for his boldness in coming out on the right side. The Democratic editors thought Haskin had declared for the Underwood Bill. The Republican editors thought he had declared against it. I, under Haskin's praise, felt like going out and getting a job from Ringling Brothers and Barnum as a tightrope walker. Practically the same thing happened with respect to the series on the conventions. I prided myself on my factual and unbiased discussion of highly charged explosive material. That I was able to do only because I carefully avoided the current discussions and relied wholly on my reading in the Library of Congress of the old newspapers, old magazines, and ancient political documents.

When it became evident that the break between President Taft and his predecessor, Theodore Roosevelt, was widening, that "Teddy" intended to ask for a third cup of coffee—when the rift among the Republicans deepened—Democratic hopes rose. A very great deal depended upon the titular leader of the party, Mr. Bryan, who had been defeated by Mr. Taft in 1908 in the third presidential race that he had made as the nominee of the Democratic party. There were very few indeed who advocated a fourth nomination for Mr. Bryan, but every candidate, avowed or merely coyly expectant, was eager to have his support.

During those months Mr. Bryan came to Washington twice, and both times I managed to have a talk with him. On one occasion he and Mrs. Bryan were guests of Mr. and Mrs. Sims at dinner. Both Bess and I were there. Mr. Bryan talked quite freely to all persons who saw him, but not once did he indicate in the slightest manner, by word, deed, or change of facial expression or of emphasis on a word or phrase, any preference for or opposition to any one of the prospective candidates.

He was talking always of platforms and programs. And yet it was quite noticeable that the one vociferous Bryan-for-President man in the District of Columbia was always close to Mr. Bryan in his conferences, was always present at the lunches and dinners tendered to him by his admirers. He was Cotter T. Bride, a voteless resident of the District of Columbia, without political strength, without any appreciable following, whose sole claim to public notice was that he was first, last, and always for Bryan.

I was present at some of these lunches and dinners, and the photographic mementos I have of those occasions show always that Mr. Bryan was being entertained publicly by those who had been most active in his support in 1896, in 1900, and in 1908. So far as I was concerned, these more intimate contacts with Mr. Bryan tended to alter my opinion of him. My admiration for him as a statesman diminished, while at the same time my affection for him as a personality and my conviction of his utter sincerity increased. Nonetheless, it seemed to me that, in intellectual stature, in the understanding of the fundamental problems of the country, he did not measure up to the standard being set by Woodrow Wilson, the governor of New Jersey. Mr. Bryan seemed to me, every time I met him, to be a little bit too much influenced by his evident desire to find a panacea in one particular proposal that would encompass and expose in oratorical phraseology all the nation's ills, cure them once and for all, bring about universal peace, universal prosperity, and, in short, the millennium.

As the time for the national conventions of 1912 came on, the excitement at our lunch table at the Willard was intensified. There were a few supporters of Mr. La Follette, such particularly as Mr. Snure and Mr. Fahy. Among the La Folletteites had been Gilson Gardner of the Scripps-McRae organization. But, when "T. R." got back from Africa, Gilson went to New York to meet him. There ensued a conversation the details of which Gilson declined to report to us; but he dropped La Follette like a hot potato and began to say that only "T. R." could save the country. Soon afterward he was followed in that defection by Jud Welliver. Fred Walker, despite his lifelong and inherited Republicanism, joined Newman, Woolley, and me for Wilson.

Newman had recently lost his job as an editorial writer on the *Washington Times.* He had had a run-in with Mr. Munsey. He had just picked up a connection with the Scripps-McRae establishment. Norman Hapgood and Mark Sullivan were both for Roosevelt.

Our luncheon companion, Colonel George Harvey, the editor of *Harper's Weekly,* was one of the earliest of the Wilson adherents. He had put at the masthead of *Harper's Weekly* the slogan, "For President of the United States, Woodrow Wilson." His editorial support of Wilson was vigorous. When he came to our table, there was indeed a lively scrap between the two weeklies, *Collier's* for "T. R.," *Harper's* for Wilson.

One day I got a telegram from Colonel Harvey asking me to lunch with him at the Willard on the following day but specifying that I meet him upstairs in Peacock Alley to have lunch in the main dining-room, as he wanted to talk with Welliver and me confidentially. I called Jud. He had a similar telegram. At the appointed hour, Jud and I appeared in Peacock Alley. In a few minutes in came the tall, the imperturbable Colonel Harvey. We went in to lunch. He was in good spirits. He talked about many things. He was most entertaining. But he didn't say why he had sent us the telegrams. He didn't say anything about his proposed confidential communication. Nor would he be tempted into any discussion of current politics.

I spoke out for Wilson, Jud spoke out for Roosevelt, but the Colonel said nothing. At the very end of the meal he said, "Gentlemen, I sent you that telegram thinking at the time I would tell you something in confidence. I have decided not to do it. I have but one thing to say. Watch carefully the editorial page of the next issue of *Harper's Weekly*."

He turned and walked away. He left two newspapermen practically dying of curiosity. You may be sure that I watched for the next issue of *Harper's*. The editorial page showed only one significant change. The slogan, "For President of the United States, Woodrow Wilson," had disappeared from the masthead.

It was long after that that I learned that Colonel Harvey, the editor of *Harper's Weekly*, and Henry Watterson, of *The Courier-Journal*, had met Governor Wilson at the Manhattan Club in New York. Governor Wilson, in answer to a question, had said to Colonel Harvey that, despite his personal gratitude, in all candor, he was compelled to say that the support of *Harper's Weekly* was embarassing and unwelcome. *Harper's Weekly* was known as the organ of the House of Morgan. Mr. Watterson, to whom Bryan and Bryanism were anathema, joined in the question. Mr. Wilson indicated that Mr. Watterson's support also was embarrassing.

I never heard from any one of the three the details of that momentous conversation about which so many brilliant stories have been told, but I shall always regret that Colonel Harvey did not obey the impulse that caused him to send those telegrams to Jud Welliver and to me. We would at least have heard the Harvey side of the story.

In June the Republican party split wide open at its convention in Chicago. Mr. Taft, the beneficiary of the "steamroller," received the nomination. The Rooseveltian group withdrew and set up the Progressive Convention and nominated Theodore Roosevelt as its candidate. The former President roughly castigated his successor, who had been his own choice, and called upon his supporters to "stand at Armageddon and battle for the Lord." The presidential ambitions of Senator La Follette thus were postponed. The headlines prepared the country for a presidential campaign of almost unprecedented excitement, and it came as a matter of course to be accepted that the Democratic prospects were better than they had been at any time since before the Civil War and much brighter than they had been either in 1884 or in 1892, when that party had elected their candidate, Grover Cleveland, to the White House. The principal Democratic aspirants, so far as the newspapers were concerned, were the speaker of the House, Champ Clark, and the governor of New Jersey, Woodrow Wilson. Others, however, who looked forward to claim the prize were Judson Harmon, the governor of Ohio; Oscar Underwood, the leader of the Democratic minority in the House of Representatives; and several who hoped that, as favorite sons of their particular states, they might snatch victory from the jaws of deadlock.

As the time for the national convention in Baltimore came on, I took a leave of absence from Haskin and rejoined, for a period of two weeks, the staff of the *Nashville Banner*. Mr. Morton had asked if I would not do that so that I could send dispatches from Baltimore particularly with respect to the behavior of the Tennessee delegation and, of course, to give the added advantage of the *Banner's* having a staff correspondent at the convention. To me, it meant that I would have no difficulty with Mr. Haskin with respect to my political neutrality and that it would facilitate my being accorded the privileges of the press section of the convention.

I did not stay in Baltimore but commuted, using the interurban electric railway. Whether it was by design or chance I do not know, but, for the two or three days before the convention assembled and all during its tumultuous career, I found myself nearly always on the same car with Albert S. Burleson of Texas and very frequently with Joseph Robinson, then a representative from Arkansas. Mr. Burleson was one of the Wilson leaders. Mr. Robinson was one of the Clark leaders. You may be sure that I had lively company going to and coming from Baltimore.

Because of my earlier connection, I had no difficulty in attaching myself to the Wilson headquarters. I was welcomed there by William F. McCombs, who had become the head of the Wilson organization, and by William Gibbs McAdoo, his principal associate. And there, also, I quite naturally fell in with Mr. Daniels and my old friend, Tom Pence.

The Baltimore local arrangements' committee was headed by Robert L. Crain, a distant cousin of Champ Clark and an active Maryland Democrat. He had charge of decorating the city. He made what seemed to me then, and I have not changed my mind, a grave error, although an unwitting one. He decorated the city not only with the red, white, and blue but with the flag of Maryland bearing the arms of Lord Baltimore. The distinguishing colors in the Maryland flag are black and gold. I myself at railroad stations, meeting delegations coming in from various states as they emerged and looked out on the street, heard them say: "It's Wilson. The town's on fire for Wilson. Look at the Princeton colors!"

The Princeton men were sometimes members of delegations committed to Wilson, sometimes with delegations unpledged, sometimes infiltrated into those instructed for Clark. All saw the black and gold and thought of old Nassau, and that enkindled an enthusiasm they had not theretofore possessed. It was one of the little things that may have had a not inconsiderable influence on the decision of the convention.

First and foremost, however, was the attitude of Mr. Bryan. He was still fighting for *his* faction of the party. He was still fighting for the control of the convention. He was a delegate from the state of Nebraska and instructed for Champ Clark, but he had said little or nothing at all about his personal choice. Many persons suspected him of hoping that the lightning would strike for the fourth time in the same place.

The Democratic party had adopted the two-thirds rule requiring the concurrence of two-thirds of the delegates for a nomination from the very conception of its convention system. Once, in 1844, Martin Van Buren had won a majority of the votes of the convention but, being unable to achieve the two-thirds, lost the nomination to James K. Polk of Tennessee. Thereafter, until 1912, no candidate who had received a majority failed to reach the goal of the two-thirds.

But here in Baltimore was assembled a Democratic National Convention under circumstances which made the nomination practically equivalent to election. In Baltimore, Champ Clark did get a majority. But he failed of the nomination. A great many stories have been told about that circumstance and about that convention.

Some of these stories have been deemed to be contradictory of the others, but in my opinion all of them are substantially true. For example, Mr. McAdoo, who was to become Secretary of the Treasury, has told his tale of the happenings; Mr. Tumulty, who was to become President Wilson's secretary, has told his; Mr. McCombs, who was the Wilson campaign manager at the convention, has told his; others have told theirs; and now, if I may, I shall tell mine. The core of truth in all these accounts is simply that Wilson won first Bryan and then the convention by conspicuous courage in taking the side of the progressive wing of the party and by his dogged determination to fight the fight to a finish.

When the convention assembled, neither Clark nor Wilson had a majority, much less the two-thirds required for the nomination. The struggle between the two was, however, eclipsed at the very start by the fight between the two wings of the party precipitated by William Jennings Bryan in a telegram addressed to all the aspirants, favorite sons included, demanding that the convention choose a Progressive (with a capital *P*) and not a reactionary for its temporary chairman. To Mr. Bryan's telegram Governor Wilson replied, "You are quite right." All the others took evasive action. And that determined the lineup.

The Bryan candidate for temporary chairman was defeated, but that very defeat of other Bryan moves gave the three-time nominee again and again the opportunity to cast his oratorical spell over the convention, to rally his "progressive" following, to undermine the influence of those whom he called "the reactionaries."

On the third day, and the ninth ballot (I think it was), Clark, who had led in the voting from the first, got a majority of the votes. On the next ballot, however, the expected break in the Wilson lines failed to materialize, and Clark gained only two votes.

The Wilson campaign headquarters were in the Emerson Hotel. As the majority went to Clark for the second time, Mr. McCombs told me to hurry to the hotel and get one of the Governor's secretaries on the telephone and to keep him on the line until he, Mr. McCombs, could get there. Long-distance telephoning was not quite so easy nor so sure in those days, and such precautions were not infrequent.

There was plenty of time for Mr. McCombs to have sent a telegram from the convention hall advising Governor Wilson to withdraw, as he says he did; plenty of time for Mr. Tumulty to have torn that telegram to bits, as he says he did. There was plenty of time for Mr. McCombs to have telephoned the Governor from the convention hall and for him to have made the report of that conversation to Mr. McAdoo, as Mr. McAdoo says he did. There was plenty of time for all those things to have happened in the half-hour before Mr. McCombs got to the hotel room.

On the telephone I had reached Walter Measday, one of the Governor's secretaries at Sea Girt, the summer home of the governor of New Jersey. I told him what had happened and that McCombs was in a panic and was trying to reach the Governor to advise him to withdraw. I also told him that I thought there was no reason for the Governor to withdraw—that I doubted whether Clark ever would have got a majority had it not been for the protection of the two-thirds rule. I was sure that Mr. Bryan, who as a delegate from Nebraska instructed for Clark, still obeying his mandate, would have broken away if a majority had meant nomination—and, of course, there was more talk of the same sort all carried on in tense excitement.

Then into the hotel room came McCombs, with McAdoo almost on his heels. "Get the Governor on the wire," said McCombs, who was pale and shaky in the face of what he assumed to be defeat. "Mac," he said to McAdoo, "he must withdraw."

"He must not," shouted McAdoo, and then in came Charles W. Bryan, the brother of the Peerless Leader, Senator John W. Kern of Indiana, and Senator Luke Lea of Tennessee—all of whom were against Clark but probably hoped that the deadlock would produce a fourth nomination for Bryan, a hope I believe Bryan himself did not then share.

I heard the Governor's voice on the telephone. "Governor," I said, "this is Brownlow. Mr. McCombs wishes to speak to you."

McCombs was a very slight man, not strong at any time and now in a veritable palsy of fear. McAdoo was very tall, very strong, very sure of himself. With one sweep of his forearm McAdoo brushed McCombs to one side and seized the telephone. "Governor," he said, "McCombs is going to beg you to withdraw. I ask you not to. He is the only one of your friends who is afraid." Then he handed the telephone receiver to the agitated McCombs. We listened to McCombs plead with Mr. Wilson to recognize the fact of the majority vote for Clark, to save the party, to avoid the danger of a split, and so on. There was a brief moment of silence, and McCombs handed the phone to me. I heard a voice. It was Woodrow Wilson's. What it said was this: "May I suggest that you tell my friends of the press that I shall not withdraw."

Never have I left a place in a greater hurry. That was on Friday. Even the next day McCombs persisted in his efforts and at one time gave McAdoo the impression that the Governor had begun also to weaken. But there was no break. The roll calls went on and the shouting. It was not until the next Tuesday and on the forty-third ballot that the necessary two-thirds voted for Wilson.

It was about half-past two in the morning after Wilson had been nominated that I got the late interurban train for Washington. There were three passengers. Mr. Burleson and I, exultant, sat in the rear seat. Joe Robinson came in. He looked at us, did not speak, marched down the aisle, and sat alone in the front seat, despondent. There was little conversation in that interurban car on that last nocturnal trip from the Baltimore convention of 1912.

In 1912 it was still the assumption that the nominations of national party conventions for the positions of President and Vice-President of the United States would not be known to the candidates themselves by means of the telegraph, the United States mails, or even by grapevine. It was deemed necessary for the national convention to name a committee composed of representatives of the party from every one of the states who would, at a day fixed, proceed to the residence of the nominee and there "notify" the man that he had been named.

There is a story that, in 1848 when the Whig Convention nominated General Zachary Taylor for President, he actually was notified by mail. In those days it was not necessary to pay postage in advance. Letters were sent, and the recipient paid the postage. According to the tale, Zachary Taylor refused to pay the postage on a letter from somebody that he didn't know, and the letter was sent back, and therefore some other means had to be found of notifying General Taylor that he had been nominated for President of the United States. At any rate, in 1912 the assumption still held, and the candidates were subjected to formal "notifications." The Democrats were to notify Governor Wilson at the summer residence of the governors of New Jersey, the seaside resort of Sea Girt.

My mother was making her first visit to the East that year. She went from her home in Springfield, Missouri, to New York with my brother Walter on one of his regular visits to the metropolis to buy women's clothes. I went to New York to see them. Walter and I then took Mother to Asbury Park, where we had a week's visit. It was the first time she had ever seen the ocean. It was the first time she had been in New York. She had not theretofore seen a city larger than

St. Louis. She was keen and observant, and she enjoyed herself thoroughly. The high light of that portion of her journey came, though, when I asked her to go with me to Sea Girt on the occasion of the notification.

We came to Sea Girt early, several hours before the ceremony. The Governor and Mrs. Wilson received my mother with great courtesy, and Mother, for her part, immediately launched into a discussion of some of the political issues of the day, which seemed greatly to interest the Governor. That chat necessarily was very brief, but Mrs. Wilson called one of her daughters, Margaret, the eldest, and assigned Margaret to take special care that Mother was given a good seat. As a matter of fact, Margaret hovered about us and gave Mother very special attention. It was Mother's only adventure in personal contact with high politics.

At that time Bess and I were living in the Sims apartment in Washington—the Sims family being in Tennessee for the campaign—and Mother came to Washington and stayed with us for several weeks. Bess took her in hand, showed her all the sights, and I had the keen pleasure of seeing my mother and my wife deeply engaged in what was their common and all-prevading interest—political life in the capital of the United States.

From the very first there was little doubt about the final outcome of the presidential race in the campaign of 1912. There was some doubt about the Congress; there was some question as to whether or not the Democrats could retain their majority in the House and a great deal more as to whether or not they could achieve control of the Senate. The upshot was that the regular Republican candidate, Mr. Taft, carried only two states, got only 8 electoral votes; Mr. Roosevelt, at the head of the Bull Moose Progressive party, carried six states and got 88 votes, while Mr. Wilson carried forty states with 425 electoral votes. At the same time the Democrats carried both houses of the Congress. Thus the Democratic party came back into the control of the government for the first time in sixteen years.

I had almost no part in that campaign after the convention. Mr. McCombs was made chairman of the national committee, and I did see him frequently when he came down to Washington. Josephus Daniels became head of the publicity division for the campaign, and he chose as his assistant my friend Robert W. Woolley. I did see

Woolley frequently during the campaign. Mr. McCombs succumbed to illness, and the actual direction of the campaign was taken over by William G. McAdoo. I did not see him during that period. However, I managed to keep in touch with Mr. Wilson himself. My very closest friend, Oliver P. Newman, was assigned by the Scripps-McRae papers to accompany Mr. Wilson in the campaign. He came home to Washington whenever he could, and once or twice I saw him in New York. Personally I abstained from any political activity.

After the election, Newman was assigned to be with Governor Wilson from the day of the election until the inauguration. He stayed in Trenton until the Governor turned over the governorship to his successor and then went with the President-elect to Bermuda. That was in the days before the adoption of the Norris "Lame-Duck Amendment" to the Constitution, and consequently the President-elect had from the first week in November until the first week in March to make up his mind with respect to the organization of his new administration.

When the President-elect came back from Bermuda, Newman called me on the telephone and said that Mr. Wilson would like to have me convey one message by word of mouth to some members of the White House staff with respect to his plans. I was asked to see Rudolph Forster, the executive clerk of the White House, who had been a member of the clerical staff there since the days of Grover Cleveland, and his assistant executive clerk, Thomas W. Brahany. The suggestion was made that I not go to the White House but find an opportunity to see them somewhere else.

By good luck the very next day, walking in Fifteenth Street, I met Mr. Forster and Mr. Brahany on their way to lunch. I stopped them and told them I was authorized by the President-elect to tell them that Mr. Wilson expected them to remain on the job, that he hoped that they would make no arrangements to leave, and that it was his purpose to maintain the entire clerical and special staff at the White House without change. He would bring with him, of course, his own secretary and a few personal stenographers.

Mr. Forster had been in the White House during several administrations and at least one change of party. Mr. Brahany had not. They seemed to be glad to hear the news. As a matter of fact, Mr. Forster stayed on through both Wilson administrations and through the administrations of Harding, Coolidge, Hoover, and Franklin D. Roosevelt in the same position of executive clerk which he held under Theodore Roosevelt. He died during "F. D. R.'s" third term.

This was an act of Woodrow Wilson, a former member of the Civil Service Reform League. He was too much a politician, and he had learned too much by observation in his academic career and too much in practice during his two years as governor of New Jersey, not to know that on a change of administration there would be great pressure for jobs for Democrats, especially since that party had been so long in the minority. As the events proved, he did appoint Democrats to the key policy places and to a considerable number of positions even lower in the scale; but he also was a defender of the civil service career system and sought in many ways to extend it.

Among the other jobs that the President had to fill were the positions of the three commissioners of the District of Columbia. The law provided that two should be civilians appointed by the President for a term of three years each and that the third should be an engineer officer of the army assigned to duty by the Secretary of War with the approval of the President.

Among Mr. Wilson's academic friends was Charles Edward Merriam of the University of Chicago. Both were present in New Orleans at the time of the organization of the American Political Science Association. Mr. Wilson already had been president of that association; Mr. Merriam in time was to be. Merriam had made a spectacular race in Chicago for mayor in 1911 as a candidate of the Republican party against Carter Harrison, the Democratic candidate. Mr. Wilson from the governor's office in Trenton had carefully observed that campaign. In all probability he, as a partisan, was for Harrison; but certainly, so far as program was concerned, he was impressed by Merriam. One of the first things Mr. Wilson did after he was elected President was to ask Merriam if he would serve as a member of the Board of Commissioners of the District of Columbia. Merriam accepted with alacrity, and both the professors seemed to look forward with eagerness to trying their hand on the practical side of both the national and the local government in Washington. They got their comeuppance soon after, however, when they read the law. The law required that a District Commissioner should have had three years' residence in the District of Columbia before his nomination. That ended the Merriam matter.

A Conclusion and a Beginning

Mr. Woolley and Mr. Newman as well as several others of us who sat in the Willard Hotel luncheons were very much interested in the local government. Mr. Woolley had written some very lively magazine articles about it. My father-in-law had been the ranking minority member of the House of Representatives' Committee on the District of Columbia, and he had some very lively disputes with members of the local government. Senator La Follette had succeeded in steering through both houses of Congress a bill establishing a public utilities commission and providing for the regulation of the local public utilities. Under its provisions the members of the Board of Commissioners would serve ex officio as members of the Public Utilities Commission.

Mr. Woolley suggested to the President that a Washington lawyer, Mr. Frederick L. Siddons, be named to one of the vacant positions. The President on his own initiative invited Oliver P. Newman to become the other civilian commissioner. So, after the President was inaugurated, he sent to the Senate the names of Oliver Peck Newman and Frederick L. Siddons to become commissioners of the District of Columbia. My early interest in municipal affairs was revived and quickened by this event.

When Newman and Siddons became commissioners of the District of Columbia, something happened to our lunch table at the Willard. For years we had sat there always ordering the cheapest things on the menu and even at that sometimes feeling that we were spending too much money on lunch. We had been envious of another round-table in the same room at which sat a number of local Washingtonian lawyers and businessmen. One of them was George E. Hamilton, the president of the Capital Traction Company; another was my old friend, John W. Yerkes, once commissioner of revenue but now a law partner of Mr. Hamilton in Washington. There also was Dr. Harbin, a retired dentist who was one of the large real estate owners of Washington. They and their fellows lunched at the same time we did; and always the headwaiter, Gus Buchholz (who later was to leave the Willard to establish the Occidental Restaurant next door), would come in person and put in the center of their table a huge bowl of doughnuts. We envied those nabobs the wealth that would permit them to order and enjoy that doughnut feast.

What was our amazement, on the very first lunch after Newman and Siddons were sworn in, no sooner had we been seated than Gus

Buchholz came in person and set down in the middle of our table a big bowl of doughnuts! From that time onward until the table broke up under the stress of conditions in World War I, our table was called the "Doughnut Cabinet."

The new President called a special session of Congress to meet in April, and on the ninth day of that month Mr. Wilson went before a joint meeting of the House of Representatives and the Senate to deliver a message recommending downward revision of the tariff. No President had appeared in person before the Congress since John Adams' last speech in 1800. Mr. Wilson had shattered a precedent. He had also captured the imagination of the country. He created an atmosphere of expectation and established himself as a result of one bold stroke as the leader not only of his party but of the nation.

There followed the enactment of the Federal Reserve Act; the Smith-Lever Act for a system of agricultural extension work; the establishment of the Federal Trade Commission; and the Clayton Antitrust Act, revising, supplementing, and strengthening the Sherman Antitrust Act and also forbidding the use of injunctions in labor disputes, authorizing peaceful picketing, and providing for trial by jury in contempt cases—an act which was hailed by the leaders of organized labor as its Magna Carta.

In the winter of 1914 I put my revived interest in local government to practical use and wrote a series of ten articles on "The Federal City," in which I outlined the history of the District of Columbia, the planning of Washington, and its rebuilding after its destruction by the British just one hundred years earlier and ventured to predict something of its future. Leaving these articles to be published in the spring, I set out with my wife for a new foreign assignment.

It was planned that we go to England, France, Germany, Austria-Hungary, and Italy, the trip to consume all the spring, summer, and early autumn. Mr. Haskin's preliminary survey among his customers caused him to believe that several series of articles from England and western Europe would be timely and, more to the point, salable. The friction between the Germans and the English was continuing, and it was being aggravated by domestic difficulties in the British Isles: the flare-up of the Irish question, the increasing labor unrest, and the class tensions that had been exacerbated by the success of the

Liberal government in trimming the powers of the hereditary aristocracy as represented in the House of Lords.

In London the skies were bright, and the sun was shining. The daffodils and hyacinths were blooming. Bess and I felt quite at home as we found ourselves again in St. Ermin's Hotel, again in the now familiar precincts of Westminster, and again in the London we had come to love so much.

The political atmosphere was seething, what with the Irish trouble, the labor trouble, the votes-for-women trouble, the still-boiling controversy between the House of Lords shorn of its effective power and the House of Commons, the bitter denunciation by the hereditary aristocrats of the upstart nobodies of the Commons, and the equally bitter recriminations of some members of the Liberal and Labour parties against the aristocrats, the huge landowners, and the intrenched privileges of the Established Church. All these things seemed to be grave threats to national unity, but, on the other hand, there seemed also to be some hope of settlement. Nobody really believed, so I thought, that things would come to a violent issue. There was still the German threat, but that was now such an old story that it lacked the substance of reality.

Here now installed in the United States embassy was our ambassador, Walter Hines Page, whom I had known as the editor of *World's Work* and whose brother, Robert N. Page, a member of Congress from North Carolina, was my close friend. From him I had a cordial welcome and what seemed to be a frank and candid appraisal of the British crisis. To me, he was optimistic. Whether his dispatches to the State Department were equally so, I do not know. Certainly the great journalists I talked with—J. A. Spender, the editor of the Asquithian *Westminster Gazette;* A. G. Gardiner, the editor of the Lloyd Georgian *News Chronicle;* and Arthur Willert of the Balfourian *Times,* all three from their quite different points of view— gave me to understand that everything would be settled peaceably; that there would be no civil war; and that war with Germany seemed no longer to be an immediate danger and probably, even in the long range, not inevitable.

My wife was determined, if she could, to get into the galleries of the House of Commons. That was an easy task for me but extremely difficult for her. Because of the militant tactics of Mrs. Pankhurst's suffragettes, no woman then could be admitted to the galleries of the Commons except members of families of members of Parliament. Even when they were so admitted, they sat high behind a grill that gave but an imperfect view of the House, although the acoustics were good enough to permit those few privileged women a chance to hear. We met an elderly gentleman who was a member of the Irish Nationalist party, an ardent supporter of Prime Minister Asquith's home-rule-for-Ireland scheme, although he himself represented a constituency from the north of Ireland where armed rebellion against the ministers of the Crown was threatened by the opponents of home rule. Bess told him that one of her ancestors had emigrated to the United States from Londonderry. The old gentleman immediately said, "Then that makes you a member of my family." He escorted her to the gallery and gave her the necessary cards and documents that enabled her to visit it again and again. Both of us were enabled to go into the House of Lords and there hear the debates. We remember particularly Lord Crewe making a speech in favor of votes for women. It was a memorable occasion.

How rare was Bess's privilege to sit in the gallery of the House of Commons developed almost explosively. One day at a luncheon at the embassy, Bess mentioned quite casually something that she had heard in the debate in the Commons the night before. Ambassador Page's daughter almost jumped out of her chair. Here *she* was a daughter of an accredited ambassador of a great and friendly power, and *she* had not been able to wangle *her* way into that gallery. I am glad to say that Bess discreetly protected her friend and putative relative by a noncommital explanation that might possibly have been interpreted as an avowal of a much closer relationship than actually existed between her and Mr. McNeill.

My letters mailed from London bore the running serial title, "The British Crisis." The first article was headed, "Will There Be Civil War?" The Asquith government was proposing home rule for Ireland. The majority of the Unionist Irish of Ulster were implacable in their opposition. The Liberal and Labour parties as well as the Nationalist Irish members of the Commons were supporting home rule. The Conservatives almost unanimously were supporting the Ulstermen. I wrote at the time:

"Thousands of volunteer troops are being armed and are drilling

A Conclusion and a Beginning

daily in Ulster because responsible men of affairs had set up the provisional government in anticipation of open rebellion and because thousands of men have signed a solemn 'covenant' that they will resist Home Rule to the bitter end.

"Even if these embattled thousands should succeed in preventing the passage of Home Rule by any parliamentary trip or political coup, then the question may be asked, 'Is the danger of Civil War over?' . . .

"The real scrap over here has nothing to do with Ireland and Home Rule except in an incidental way. The real big fight is about a much more fundamental thing than whether Ireland shall have laws stamped 'Made in Dublin' or whether it shall continue to import its statutes from Westminster. The real row is between the aristocracy and the democracy. It is all about whether this government shall be run and managed by the classes or whether the masses shall take it over. More than one civil war has been fought over a question like that. The war is on here. It may be all a titanic political battle in which ballots not bullets will settle the thing, or it may take advantage of some superficial aspect of the real question such as the disaffection in Ulster and blaze forth in fire and blood."

There was, of course, a great deal more than that in the forty articles which ran to a total of eighty thousand words that I sent back to Washington from England, Ireland, and Scotland. However, that quotation from the first article struck the keynote. I followed it with articles on the discontent of labor and the increasing number of strikes, the violence induced by the militant suffragettes in their continuing campaign for votes for women, and the bitterness of the partisan strife.

My wife and I went across to Dublin and saw something of Ireland. It was inherent in our training and childhood surroundings to be sympathetic with the Irish who wished home rule. I talked with as many leaders as I could reach, with journalists and professional men; I interviewed the great agricultural planner, Sir Horace Plunkett; and I met the chief of the Irish constabulary, Sir John Ross of Bladensburg, a baronet who had got his title because his ancestor had won the Battle of Bladensburg in the District of Columbia and had burned the White House. Generally, I was as industrious as I could be in getting all the information I could find. The opinion was practically all one-sided except perhaps for a few persons who were directly connected with the British government and indirectly with the Conservative party. Dublin was for home rule. But I got more from the people in the streets. I went out at night several times to see the volunteers drilling, hundreds and hundreds of them, some with rifles but more with wooden guns.

When at last we decided to leave for Belfast, Bess went with me to the railway station. I went up to the ticket booth and asked for two tickets to Belfast. The young man at the window said, "Why do you want to go to Belfast?"

Completely astonished, I said, "Well, my business takes me there."

"Well, one thing is certain. I would never sell a ticket to Belfast," and with an expression of utter disgust he turned from me and left the window. I pounded for a little while on the counter, and finally an elderly man in the back of the ticket office came forward and sold me two tickets to Belfast. That gave me a measure of how high the feeling was running.

Then in a week in Belfast we got the other side. Here I went out at night too. Here I saw many hundreds of men drilling, and all of them were apparently well armed. Here from journalists and from businessmen whom I was able to meet I heard nothing but the resistance of the Ulsterites. There were, however, a few exceptions. There was one former member of Parliament, a Nationalist, although he sat in Westminster for an Ulster constituency. I found some Roman Catholic clergy who certainly were not on the side of the Ulster intransigents. I saw and talked with several Presbyterian ministers. They were all against home rule. The feeling here was as bitter and as strong in Belfast against Dublin as was that in Dublin against Belfast.

From Belfast we crossed in a ship to Ardrossan with a whole company of Presbyterian ministers bound for the May General Assembly in Holy Rood Palace in Edinburgh, where the King in his capacity as head of the Presbyterian Church in Scotland would be in residence and preside over the opening of the assembly.

We stopped in Glasgow. I had already met in Washington the then Lord Provost of Glasgow. When I called at the municipal headquarters, he immediately placed at our disposal a limousine with a chauffeur and a footman clad in the green livery of the ancient city of Glasgow. Here I attended meetings of the Council, I met many of the Bailies, I visited the municipal works, I looked into the operation of the municipally owned tramway system, I visited municipal housing projects, and, in general, I took a little time out from the question of whether or not there would be civil war in Great Britain to satisfy my increasing curiosity about municipal administration.

But things were not going at all well at home. We had had word that Bess's mother was very ill. That was followed by the distressing news that my mother was very ill. And all of that was on top of what I had heard in London from Mr. Haskin that the sale of the articles was not going well. The newspapers were losing interest in Europe.

The reason for that loss of interest was to be found in Mexico. The revolution in Mexico, President Wilson's firm action in refusing to recognize the Huerta government, and the incidents that were flaring up, such as those of Vera Cruz and Tampico, as well as the guerrilla clashes on the border, were causing American newspaper interest to shift from Europe to south of the border.

It was while I was in London that one morning I picked up a copy of the *Morning Telegraph,* and there, on the page devoted to foreign news, I found a dispatch which read substantially like this:

ROME. The *Osservatore Romano* this morning published a cablegram from Mexico City saying that last night under cover of darkness the Mexican Army had crossed the Rio Grande and had occupied Texas.

If that had been true, it would have represented unquestionably the greatest one night's feat in the history of military science!

While we stayed in Glasgow we also visited Edinburgh, still greatly aided by the gracious gesture of Sir Thomas Stephenson, the Provost Marshal, in furnishing us with a motorcar. One night there was a knock at the door of our room. It was a cablegram saying that Mrs. Sims was worse. A few hours later in the same night, another knock at the door, another cablegram. It said that my mother was worse and in a most critical condition.

The next day there was an exchange of cablegrams with Haskin. Then Bess and I hurried to Liverpool to board the "Lusitania" to come home. We did not get to the Continent. Had our itinerary not been interrupted, we would have been in Vienna in that fateful first week of August, 1914.

That westward crossing of the ocean was a time of grave anxiety to both of us. When we got to New York, we were happy to be greeted with the news that both of our mothers were improved. Fortunately, Bess's mother recovered entirely and lived in health and happiness for many years thereafter. My mother lived for six months longer.

I had intended going straight to Missouri, but the news from Springfield was so encouraging that I went to Washington first. Mrs. Sims was so ill that very shortly she was taken to Atlantic City, and Bess went with her to spend most of the summer months.

A few days after I got back to Washington, I went to the White House to see the President. It was on the first day of July, 1914. Mr. Wilson asked me to tell him in as great detail as possible what I thought of the situation in Europe and especially in Ireland. I told him I had had several long talks with our ambassador in London, Walter Hines Page, but that in my opinion, Mr. Page was a little too optimistic. I told him I thought there was grave danger of civil war in Britain, that the Irish situation might at any moment produce an explosion, and that I was extremely fearful from what I had gleaned in London that an outbreak in England might well be the signal for the Germans to strike. The talk lasted for nearly an hour. The President was grave and much concerned. He asked many questions. At the end of the interview he thanked me for the news I had brought and said, in substance:

"What you say happens to agree almost exactly with the letters I have been receiving from a personal friend of mine who has been traveling all over Europe. It does not quite agree with the dispatches I have been receiving through Mr. Bryan from our ambassadors and ministers. I hope and pray that the diplomats are better observers and more accurate reporters than either my traveling friend or you."

It was a long time after that before I was able to identify his traveling friend as Colonel Edward M. House.

The astonishing thing about that interview is how little emphasis was given to the assassination of the Archduke Ferdinand and his wife at Sarajevo on June 28—three days earlier. The President referred to it as a type of incident that might well be dangerous to the peace, but he, as well as I, considered civil war in Britain as a more immediate danger. Indeed, it was not until July 5—four days later—that Count Berchtold, the Austro-Hungarian minister of foreign affairs, sent an emissary to Berlin to tell the Imperial German government that Vienna was planning to send an ultimatum to Belgrade.

A Conclusion and a Beginning

Then came those intense five weeks before the German army crossed the border and invaded Belgium. World War I began; the nineteenth century died; the *Pax Brittanica* was shattered; and, while no one knew it then, the United States of America became a part of the world.

That afternoon, July 1, 1914, I bought a copy of the *Evening Star*. On the first page was a story by my old friend, Bill Price, to the effect that President Wilson intended to appoint District Commissioner Frederick L. Siddons to be a justice of the supreme court of the District of Columbia and that Louis Brownlow would be named District Commissioner to succeed Mr. Siddons. I knew that these matters were in the wind, but Mr. Wilson had not said one word to me about it, and I had no notion that the decision was so imminent.

Actually the appointments were delayed for nearly seven months, and it was on January 26, 1915, that I took the oath of office as one of the commissioners of the District of Columbia.

I was thrilled with the prospect of attempting to put into effect some of the notions about municipal administration that I had elaborated during the many years of my increasing interest in local government. The salary of the position was five thousand dollars a year. At that time my earnings were considerably larger than that. However, I accepted the reduction in income cheerfully because I was quite sure that I would serve but a single term of three years and then would go back to newspaper work.

I had not the faintest notion that the step I was taking was to turn out to be irrevocable and that on that morning I was turning my back forever on the profession of journalism and was taking up a career in the field of public administration which was to claim my thought and interest for the rest of my active life.

It was not only that I was leaving journalism for public administration—it was much more than that, although I did not realize it at the time. It was that I, who had been a looker-on, a taker of notes, an observer, was now to become a responsible actor. It was no longer for me to write about what others were doing. It was now for me to do and to be responsible to other writers and the public for what I was to do. That change marked a turning point in my thinking, in my essential interests, and opened up for me a new way of life.

[593]

INDEX

INDEX

Index

Index

Index

Index

[PRINTED IN U·S·A]

Date Due

5'55